M000210267

RELIGIONS OF INDIA IN PRACTICE

PRINCETON READINGS IN RELIGIONS

Donald S. Lopez, Jr., Editor

TITLES IN THE SERIES

Donald S. Lopez, Jr., *Religions of India in Practice*

Donald S. Lopez, Jr., *Buddhism in Practice*

RELIGIONS OF INDIA IN PRACTICE

Donald S. Lopez, Jr., Editor

PRINCETON READINGS IN RELIGIONS

PRINCETON UNIVERSITY PRESS

PRINCETON, NEW JERSEY

Published by Princeton University Press, 41 William Street,
Princeton, New Jersey 08540
In the United Kingdom: Princeton University Press, Chichester, West Sussex

Library of Congress Cataloging-in-Publication Data

Religions of India in practice / edited by Donald S. Lopez, Jr.
p. cm. — (Princeton readings in religions)
Includes index.
ISBN 0-691-04325-6. — ISBN 0-691-04324-8 (pbk.)
1. India—Religion. I. Lopez, Donald S., 1952– . II. Series.
BL2001.2.R384 1994
294—dc20 94-34695

This book has been composed in Berkeley

Princeton University Press books are printed on acid-free paper and meet the guidelines for permanence and durability of the Committee on Production Guidelines for Book Longevity of the Council on Library Resources

3 5 7 9 10 8 6 4 2

3 5 7 9 10 8 6 4 2
(pbk.)

DEDICATED TO

A. K. RAMANUJAN

1929–1993

PRINCETON READINGS IN RELIGIONS

Princeton Readings in Religions is a new series of anthologies on the religions of the world, representing the significant advances that have been made in the study of religions in the last thirty years. The sourcebooks used by the last generation of students placed a heavy emphasis on philosophy and on the religious expressions of elite groups in what were deemed the "classical" civilizations of Asia and the Middle East. Princeton Readings in Religions provides a different configuration of texts in an attempt better to represent the range of religious practices, placing particular emphasis on the ways in which texts are used in diverse contexts. The series therefore includes ritual manuals, hagiographical and autobiographical works, and folktales, as well as some ethnographic material. Many works are drawn from vernacular sources. The readings in the series are new in two senses. First, the majority of the works contained in the volumes have never have been translated into a Western language before. Second, the readings are new in the sense that each volume provides new ways to read and understand the religions of the world, breaking down the sometimes misleading stereotypes inherited from the past in an effort to provide both more expansive and more focused perspectives on the richness and diversity of religious expressions. The series is designed for use by a wide range of readers, with key terms translated and technical notes omitted. Each volume also contains a substantial introduction by a distinguished scholar in which the histories of the traditions are outlined and the significance of each of the works is explored.

Religions of India in Practice provides a particularly appropriate inaugural volume for the Princeton Readings in Religions. The thirty contributors include leading scholars of Indian religions, each of whom has provided one or more translations of key works, most of which are translated here for the first time. Each chapter in the volume begins with a substantial introduction in which the translator discusses the history and influence of the work, identifying points of particular difficulty or interest. Professor Richard Davis has provided an introduction to the entire volume, moving chronologically from the Indus Valley civilization to the modern period, identifying the place of each chapter in the currents of the religious traditions of India.

Three other volumes of the Princeton Readings in Religions are in press: *Religions of China in Practice*, *Religions of Japan in Practice*, and *Buddhism in Practice*.

Volumes currently nearing completion are devoted to: Islam in Asia, Islamic mysticism, and the religions of Tibet. Future volumes are planned for religions of Latin America, religions of Africa, as well as on Judaism and Christianity.

Donald S. Lopez, Jr.
Series Editor

NOTE ON TRANSLITERATION

The works in this volume are translated from many Indian languages. The translators have, in general, adhered to the standard transliteration system for each of the languages. Certain common place names and selected terms that have entered into English usage appear without diacritical marks.

CONTENTS

Songs of Devotion and Praise

Rites and Instructions

Remarkable Lives and Edifying Tales

Traditions in Transition and Conflict

CONTENTS BY TRADITIONS

As explained in the introduction, this volume is organized thematically, rather than by tradition, in order to suggest the interactions, intersections, and confluences in the religious practices of India. It is useful, nonetheless, to see also how the works included in this volume might be organized by tradition. Such an organization presents certain difficulties, as evidenced by the title of chapter 45, "Satya Pīr: Muslim Holy Man and Hindu God," which has been classed as "Hindu" below because Satya Pīr is more widely revered today by Hindus than by Muslims. There are three chapters, however, which are not listed below because they elude such classification: "Bāul Songs" (there are both Hindu and Muslim Bāuls), "Tamil Song to God as Child" (with songs to Muḥammad, Jesus, and Śiva's son), and "Kabīr." Kabīr (1398–1518) was an orphan raised by low-caste Hindu weavers who may have only recently converted to Islam. His guru was a devotee of Rāma. In his poetry, Kabīr criticized both Hindus and Muslims. According to a popular story, upon his death his body was claimed by both Hindus and Muslims. When they pulled back his shroud they found only petals.

Buddhist

Hindu

CONTRIBUTORS

Ali Asani teaches in the Department of Near Eastern Languages and Civilizations at Harvard University.

Guy Leon Beck teaches in the Department of Religious Studies at Louisana State University.

Douglas Renfrew Brooks teaches in the Department of Religion and Classics at University of Rochester.

John E. Cort teaches in the Department of Religion at Denison University.

Norman Cutler teaches in the Department of South Asian Languages and Civilizations at the University of Chicago.

Ronald M. Davidson teaches in the Department of Religious Studies at Fairfield University.

Richard H. Davis teaches in the Department of Religious Studies at Yale University.

Neal Delmonico teaches in the Religious Studies Program at Iowa State University.

Vinay Dharwadker teaches in the Department of English at the University of Oklahoma.

Carl Ernst teaches in the Department of Religious Studies at the University of North Carolina, Chapel Hill.

Ann Grodzins Gold teaches in the Department of Religion at Syracuse University.

Phyllis Granoff teaches in the Department of Religious Studies at McMaster University.

Lindsey Harlan teaches in the Department of Religion at Connecticut College.

Glen A. Hayes teaches in the Department of Religious Studies at Bloomfield College.

Marcia Hermansen teaches in the Department of Religious Studies at San Diego State University.

Dennis Hudson teaches in the Department of Religion at Smith College.

Rosalind Lefeber teaches in the Department of Religious Studies at McMaster University.

Todd T. Lewis teaches in the Department of Religious Studies at the College of the Holy Cross.

J. E. Llewellyn teaches in the Department of Religous Studies at Southwest Missouri State University.

Donald S. Lopez, Jr. teaches in the Department of Asian Languages and Cultures at the University of Michigan.

June McDaniel teaches in the Department of Philosophy and Religion at the College of Charleston.

Rachel Fell McDermott teaches in the Department of Asian and Middle Eastern Cultures at Barnard College.

Hew McLeod teaches in the Department of History at the University of Otago in New Zealand.

Mustansir Mir teaches Islamic Studies at International Islamic University in Malaysia.

Kirin Narayan teaches in the Department of Anthropology at the University of Wisconsin.

Patrick Olivelle teaches in the Center for Asian Studies at the University of Texas.

Michael D. Rabe teaches in the Art Department at St. Xavier's College in Chicago.

Paula Richman teaches in the Department of Religion at Oberlin College.

Carol Salomon teaches in the Department of Asian Languages and Literatures at the University of Washington.

Tony K. Stewart teaches in the Department of Philosophy and Religion at North Carolina State University.

David Gordon White teaches in the Department of Religious Studies at the University of Virginia.

RELIGIONS OF INDIA IN PRACTICE

INTRODUCTION

A Brief History of Religions in India

Richard H. Davis

Now Vidagdha, Śakala's son, asked him, "Yājñavalkya, how many gods are there?"

Following the text of the Veda, he replied, "Three hundred and three, and three thousand and three, as are mentioned in the Vedic hymn on the Viśvadevas."

"Right," replied Vidagdha, "but how many gods are there really, Yājñavalkya?"

"Thirty-three."

"Right," he assented, "but how many gods are there really, Yājñavalkya?"

"Six."

"Right," he persisted, "but how many gods are there really, Yājñavalkya?"

"Three."

"Right," he answered, "but how many gods are there really, Yājñavalkya?"

"Two."

"Right," Vidagdha replied, "but how many gods are there really, Yājñavalkya?"

"One and a half."

"Right," he agreed, "but how many gods are there really, Yājñavalkya?"

"One."

"Right," Vidagdha said. "And who are those three hundred and three, and three thousand and three gods?"

Bṛhadāraṇyaka Upaniṣad 3.9.1

In one of the world's earliest recorded philosophical dialogues, the Indian sage Yājñavalkya pointed to the multiplicity of theological views concerning the number of gods in India. He then went on to show how, following different ways of enumerating them, each of these views could make sense.

Much the same can be said about the religions of India. Some scholars and observers focus on the tremendous diversity of distinct schools of thought and religious sects that have appeared over the course of Indian history. Others prefer to specify the three or five "great" or "world" religions that have occupied the subcontinent: Hinduism, Buddhism, Islam, plus Jainism and Sikhism. And still others, of a more syncretic persuasion, maintain there is really just one religious tradition.

The readings collected in this anthology convey much of the multiplicity, and may also suggest something of the unity of intent to which the syncretists point. The selections are drawn from ancient texts, medieval manuscripts, modern pamphlets, and contemporary fieldwork in rural and urban India. They represent every region of South Asia. Some are written texts reflecting the concerns of literate political elites and religious specialists, whereas others are transcriptions of oral narratives told by nonliterate peasants. Some texts are addressed to a public and pan-Indian audience, others to a limited coterie of initiates in an esoteric sect, and still others intended for a few women gathered in the courtyard for a household ceremony.

The editor has reinforced this diversity by not arranging the selections in the two most common ways. He has not grouped together all entries affiliated with each major religious community of India, nor has he placed them in a chronological sequence. Rather, he places the readings within several overarching themes and categories of discourse (hymns, rituals, narratives, and religious interactions), and encourages us to make our own connections. There is no set order. We may rearrange them as we see fit, finding new patterns in the materials as we do so.

For all of us who want to understand Indian religions more fully, there are major virtues to this varied collection and kaleidoscopic arrangement. The selections here highlight types of discourse (especially ritual, folktales, and oral narratives) and voices (vernacular, esoteric, domestic, and female) that have not been sufficiently represented in previous anthologies and standard accounts of Indian religions. Few of the usual canonical texts are here. Moreover, the selections juxtapose materials from different religious traditions that we often regard as separate and distinct. This format has the effect of broadening the range of what we consider. More important, it should push us to find areas of shared concern and dialogue, as well as areas of contestation and conflict among the widely varied materials of different communities. If this anthology helps us to see Indian religious history less as the unfolding of distinct, self-contained formations, and more as a dynamic process of borrowing, conflict, and interaction between and within religious traditions, it will have served a valuable role.

The same multiplicity and ahistorical arrangement, however, may leave the student approaching Indian religions for the first time in a state of bafflement. In the introduction I provide a brief account of the main periods, principal schools of thought, and most significant texts in Indian religions, to enable the reader to locate the individual selections of the anthology within a larger narrative. It is a historical thread to which the readings may, when necessary, be tied. Over the course of this account, I focus on certain key issues or points of controversy that appear and reappear through Indian religious history and in the anthology selections. I focus also on a set of terms—Veda, brahman, yoga, dharma, bhakti, Tantra, and the like—that constitute a shared religious vocabulary in India. As we will see, such terms were often considered too important to be left uncontested, and so different authors or traditions would attempt to redefine the terms to suit their own purposes.[1]

The Question of Hinduism

The dominant feature of South Asian religious history is a broad group of interconnected traditions that we nowadays call "Hinduism." Although other distinct non-Hindu religious ideologies (notably Buddhism, Islam, and Christianity) have challenged its dominance, Hinduism is now and probably has been at all times the most prevalent religious persuasion of the subcontinent. According to the most recent census figures, 83 percent of India's population is classified as Hindu, a total of perhaps 700 million Hindus. This anthology reflects the dominance of Hinduism among the religions of India, devoting well over half the entries to Hindu materials, without isolating it from the other religious groups that have also made India their home.

It is important to bear in mind, however, that Hinduism does not share many of the integrating characteristics of the other religious traditions we conventionally label the "world religions." Hinduism has no founding figure such as the Buddha Śākyamuni, Jesus of Nazareth, or Muḥammad. It has no single text that can serve as a doctrinal point of reference, such as the Bibles of the Judaic and Christian traditions, the Islamic Qur'ān, or the Ādi Granth of the Sikhs. Hinduism has no single overarching institutional or ecclesiastical hierarchy capable of deciding questions of religious boundary or formulating standards of doctrine and practice.

This is not to say that Hinduism, lacking these supposedly "essential" attributes of other religions, is therefore not a religion. Rather, the historical process by which Hindus and others have come to consider Hinduism a unitary religious formation differs markedly from other traditions. In one respect, Hinduism is one of the oldest, if not the oldest continuous recorded religion, tracing itself back to a text that was already edited and put into final shape by about 1200 B.C.E. In another respect, though, it is the youngest, for it was only in the nineteenth century that the many indigenous Indian religious formations were collectively named "Hinduism." Before this, not only did these groups not have a name for themselves as a religious unity, but for the most part they did not consider that they were members of a single religious collectivity.

Since histories of names often tell us a good deal about the realities they signify, let us look more closely at the word "Hinduism." The term derives originally from the Indo-Aryan word for sea, *sindhu*, applied also to the Indus River. Persians to the west of the Indus picked up the term, modifying it phonologically to *hind*, and used it to refer also to the land of the Indus valley. From Persian it was borrowed into Greek and Latin, where *india* became the geographical designation for all the unknown territories beyond the Indus. Meanwhile, Muslims used *hindu* to refer to the native peoples of South Asia, and more specifically to those South Asians who did not convert to Islam, lending the term for the first time a reference to religious persuasion. Non-Muslim Indians did not commonly take up the terminology, however, until much later.

Only in the nineteenth century did the colonial British begin to use the word Hinduism to refer to a supposed religious system encompassing the beliefs and practices of Indian peoples not adhering to other named religions such as Islam, Christianity, or Jainism. This coinage, based very indirectly on the indigenous term *sindhu*, followed the Enlightenment reification of the concept "religion" and the scholarly attempt to define a series of distinct individual "world religions," each with its own essence and historical unfolding. "Hindu" was then incorporated into the Indian lexicon, taken up by Indians eager to construct for themselves a counterpart to the seemingly monolithic Christianity of the colonizers. As much as anything, it may have been British census taking, with its neat categories of affiliation, that spread the usage of "Hindu" as the most common pan-Indian term of religious identity. To specify the nature of this religion, Western scholars and Indians alike projected the term retrospectively, to encompass a great historical range of religious texts and practices.

Even though anachronistic, the term "Hinduism" remains useful for describing and categorizing the various schools of thought and practice that grew up within a shared Indian society and employed a common religious vocabulary. However, applying a single term to cover a wide array of Indian religious phenomena from many different periods raises some obvious questions. Where is the system? What is the center of Hinduism? What is truly essential to Hinduism? And who determines this center, if there is any? Scholars and Indians have largely adopted two contrasting views in dealing with these questions, the "centralist" and the "pluralist" views.

Centralists identify a single, pan-Indian, more or less hegemonic, orthodox tradition, transmitted primarily in Sanskrit language, chiefly by members of the brahmanic class. The tradition centers around a Vedic lineage of texts, in which are included not only the Vedas themselves, but also the Mīmaṃsā, Dharmaśāstra, and Vedānta corpuses of texts and teachings. Vedic sacrifice is the privileged mode of ritual conduct, the template for all subsequent Indian ritualism. Various groups employing vernacular languages in preference to Sanskrit, questioning the caste order, and rejecting the authority of the Vedas, may periodically rebel against this center, but the orthodox, through an adept use of inclusion and repressive tolerance, manage to hold the high ground of religious authority. Previous anthologies of Indian religious literature have generally over-represented the texts identified by the centralists as forming a Hindu "canon"; in this anthology they are largely absent.

The pluralists, by contrast, envision a decentered profusion of ideas and practices all tolerated and incorporated under the big tent of Hinduism. No more concise statement of this view can be found than that of the eminent Sanskrit scholar J. A. B. van Buitenen in the 1986 *Encyclopedia Britannica*:

> In principle, Hinduism incorporates all forms of belief and worship without necessitating the selection or elimination of any. The Hindu is inclined to revere the divinity

> in every manifestation, whatever it may be, and is doctrinally tolerant. . . . Hinduism is, then, both a civilization and a conglomeration of religions, with neither a beginning, a founder, nor a central authority, hierarchy, or organization.

Adherents of this viewpoint commonly invoke natural metaphors. Hinduism is a "sponge" for all religious practices or a "jungle" where every religious tendency may flourish freely. Within the pluralist view, the Vedic tradition figures as one form of belief and worship among many, the concern of elite brahmans somewhat out of touch with the religious multiplicity all around them.

This anthology might seem to favor a pluralist viewpoint, simply by presenting so many varieties of Hindu literature, belief, and practice side by side. Yet contrary to the pluralist notion of passive Indian "tolerance," the materials here suggest a lively religious atmosphere of interaction and criticism, of satire and polemic, existing among different Hindu groups.

In India, various contending religious groups have vied to present a view of the cosmos, divinity, human society, and human purposes more compelling and more authoritative than others. One finds such all-encompassing visions presented in many Hindu texts or groups of texts at different periods of history: the Vedas, the Epics, the puranic theologies of Viṣṇu and Śiva, the medieval texts of the bhakti movements, and the formulations of synthetic Hinduism by modern reformers. The religious historian may identify these as the paradigmatic formations of Hinduism of their respective times. Yet such visions have never held sway without challenge, both from within and from outside of Hinduism.

The most serious challenges to Hindu formations have come from outside, from the early "heterodoxies" of Buddhism and Jainism, from medieval Islam, and from the missionary Christianity and post-Enlightenment worldviews of the colonial British. These challenges have been linked to shifts in the political sphere, when ruling elites have favored non-Hindu ideologies with their patronage and prestige. In each case, such fundamental provocations have led to important changes within the most prevalent forms of Hinduism. This introduction will follow this pattern of historical challenge and transformation.

The Indo-Aryans and the Vedas

The textual history of Indian religions begins with the entry into the subcontinent of groups of nomadic pastoralists who called themselves "Āryas," the noble ones. Originally they came from the steppes of south-central Russia, part of a larger tribal community that, beginning around 4000 B.C.E., migrated outward from their homeland in several directions, some westward into Europe and others southward into the Middle East and South Asia. These nomads were the first to ride and harness horses; they also invented the chariot and the spoked wheel and fabricated weapons of copper and bronze. Such material innovations gained them obvious military advantages, and they were able to impose themselves on most of the indigenous peoples they encountered as they migrated. Wherever they went they took with them their language, and it was this language that formed the historical basis for Greek, Latin, the Romance languages, German, English, Persian, Sanskrit, and most of the modern languages of northern India. We now call these pastoral peoples the Indo-Europeans, and those who migrated south into the Iranian plateau and the Indian subcontinent we call the Indo-Aryans.

As early as about 2000 B.C.E., Indo-Aryan peoples began to move gradually into the Indus River Valley in small tribal groups. In 1200 B.C.E.. they were still located primarily in the Punjab, the fertile area drained by the five rivers of the Indus system, but by 600 B.C.E. the Indo-Aryans had gained political and social dominance over the Gangetic plain and throughout much of northern India.

The Ṛg Veda

The religious beliefs and practices of this community are contained in a corpus of texts called the Vedas. Since the term *Veda* comes up frequently in all discussions of Indian religious history, it is helpful to consider briefly some of its meanings and usages. The term derives from the verbal root *vid*, "to know," and so the broadest meaning of *Veda* is "knowledge," more specifically knowledge of the highest sort, religious knowledge. It denotes several compendia of religious knowledge composed in an early form of Sanskrit (the "perfected" language) by the Indo-Aryan community, the four Vedic "collections" (*samhitā*): the *Ṛg Veda*, *Yajur Veda*, *Sāma Veda*, and the *Atharva Veda*. Supplementary compositions were attached to each of these four Vedic collections—namely, the Brāhmaṇas, Āraṇyakas, and Upaniṣads—and these too became part of the Veda. This entire corpus of sacred literature came to be portrayed by its proponents as revelation, something that was only "heard" and not composed by human beings. Additional texts were later added to the corpus: the Vedāṅgas or "limbs" of the Veda, auxiliary works that aimed to explain and extend the significance of the Vedas. These later texts did not have the same revelatory status as the Vedas themselves, but they did belong to the Vedic corpus in an extended sense. The Vedas constitute a huge, diverse, and fascinating corpus of texts composed over many centuries.

The earliest of the Vedic collections, and one of the world's oldest intact religious texts, is the *Ṛg Veda*. It consists of 1,028 hymns, numbering around 10,000 verses, roughly equal in size to the complete works of Homer. These hymns were composed over a period of several hundred years by different lineages or families of poet-priests, and then compiled into a single large collection sometime around 1200–1000 B.C.E. This great collection was carefully memorized and transmitted orally, virtually without alterations, for almost 3,000 years by generations of religious specialists.

The hymns of the *Ṛg Veda* reflect the religious concerns and social values of the Indo-Aryan community as it settled in the Punjab. Most often the hymns address and praise a pantheon of deities, of whom the most important is undoubtedly Indra. The hymns portray Indra as an active, powerful, unpredictable, combative god who leads the other gods in a series of antagonistic encounters with a competing group of superhuman beings, the demons. The poets honor and extol Indra for his courage and strength, and also supplicate him to be generous to his votaries. Moreover, they view him as a model chieftain: as Indra leads the gods in defeating their enemies, the poets proclaim, so may our leaders guide us to victory over our enemies.

Indra's paradigmatic status reminds us that the Indo-Aryans were not simply occupying uninhabited territory as they moved into the Indian subcontinent. They encountered other peoples there whom they regarded as posing a threat to their own well-being and expansion. These others, often referred to as *dāsas*, were described in the *Ṛg Veda* as dark-skinned, flat-featured stealers of cattle, speaking a different language and living in fortified citadels.

In fact, from around 2500 to 1700 B.C.E. a complex, urbanized, centrally organized civilization flourished in the Indus River Valley, with two capital cities and a host of other towns and smaller settlements. Although archeologists have excavated a great deal of evidence from the Indus Valley civilization, including several thousand brief inscriptions, much about its religious culture remains mysterious since no one has yet convincingly deciphered the Indus Valley script. Yet most linguists believe the language of this civilization was a member of the Dravidian family, which also includes the languages of southern India where the Indo-Aryan language did not penetrate. This suggests that the Indus Valley civilization was linked, in language and presumably in culture, with pre-Aryan peoples in other parts of the subcontinent.

Many elements of Indus Valley material culture suggest religious usage, and these have led scholars to postulate Indus Valley influence on the development of later Indian religion. For example, archeologists have interpreted the numerous terra-cotta figurines of fleshy women with accentuated breasts and hips and fabulous headpieces found in the Indus Valley cities as popular representations of a "Great Mother," whose domestic and rural cult would reappear in medieval Hindu literature. While such connections remain speculative, they do point to an important problem in Indian religious history. Much that appears as innovation in recorded Indian religious traditions may have been borrowed from nonliterate or undeciphered traditions that we do not yet know.

Although the urban civilization of the Indus Valley had largely collapsed prior to the arrival of the Indo-Aryans, the dāsas of the *Ṛg Veda* were probably the descendants of that culture, and they must have posed a significant obstacle to Indo-Aryan expansion. The *Ṛg Veda* shows us an Indo-Aryan culture primed for battle. Even the poets participated in battle, apparently, as singing charioteers, invoking Indra's strength on behalf of the warriors as they drove the horses.

If Indra was for the *Ṛg Veda* poets the divine prototype of the warrior, the second most important deity in the pantheon, Agni, can be seen as the model priest. Agni is fire, in its multiple forms: the sun, the hearth fire, the fire of the sacrifice, the digestive fire in one's belly, and the fire of poetic inspiration. But Agni's primary role in the *Ṛg Veda* pertains to sacrifice (*yajña*), the central ritual practice of Vedic society. Agni is the priest of the gods and yet is also accessible to humans, so he is most fit to serve in sacrifice as the primary intermediary, bringing gods and humans together. The poets of the *Ṛg Veda* know sacrifice to be a powerful ritual, one that enables the gods to defeat the demons and that likewise can assist the Aryans to overcome their earthly enemies. It brings a host of worldly results: wealth, cattle, victory, and ultimately order. Yet in the *Ṛg Veda* sacrifice remains rather loosely organized, inchoate, experimental; only later is it systematized and elaborated into a full-fledged worldview.

One other figure in the Ṛg Vedic pantheon deserves attention: the mysterious Soma, also closely associated with sacrifice. Soma is simultaneously a plant, a liquid made by crushing the stalks of that plant, and a god personifying the effects of ingesting this concoction. The identity of the botanical soma has proved to be a major scholarly conundrum, but the effects ascribed in the *Ṛg Veda* to drinking its juice are clear enough. It is a drink of inspiration, of vision, of revelation. At their sacrificial gatherings the poets pound and imbibe the soma juice, and through it they come to mingle with the gods. They perceive the resemblances and identities between things that we normally see as different and unrelated, weaving the world together in a fabric of connectedness. The revelations inspired by soma, moreover, are not regarded as mere hallucinations or dreams, but as more real, more true than the awareness of normal consciousness. This is the first example of a recurrent theme in Indian religions: what is ontologically most real is often not accessible through ordinary human experience but must be sought through some other means—whether it be soma, yoga, meditation, devotional fervor, or ritual.

Sacrifice and Society

If the Indo-Aryans entered India as nomads over the ruins of the urban civilization of the Indus Valley, during the period from 1200 to 600 B.C.E. they reinvented urban society on a new cultural basis. The later Vedic literature reflects the social transformations of this period, particularly the growing role of sacrifice in the religious life of the Indo-Aryans and the beginnings of criticism of sacrifice. By 600 B.C.E. the Indo-Aryan community had changed from a nomadic and pastoral tribal society into a predominantly agrarian one. The introduction of iron during this period facilitated the clearing of the heavily forested Gangetic plain and the development of plough agriculture. A more stable population and greater food resources led in turn to larger settlements, and the tribal organization of the Indo-Aryan nomads began to give way to an incipient class society based on occupational specialization and status distinction. Those outside the Indo-Aryan community, rather than being treated as threatening dāsas, were increasingly incorporated into society as laborers and social inferiors, śūdras. Larger political formations, primarily kingdoms, began to form, and with these early kingdoms came the rebirth of cities as capitals and centers of trade. By 600 B.C.E. there were a dozen substantial cities in northern India.

These changes naturally had their consequences for Vedic religion. Surplus production enabled society to support a nonproducing class of religious specialists, who could devote themselves to elaborating sacrificial ritual and articulating its significance. At the same time, the new rulers found in increasingly dramatic sacrifice a means to extend and legitimate their political authority over larger, mixed populations. The interests of nascent ruling and priestly groups thus converged in sacrifice. And with the defeat of the Indo-Aryans' primary autochthonous opponents, sacrifice came to be seen less as a way of defeating enemies than as a means of creating, maintaining, and stabilizing the order of the cosmos and of society.

One can already see this in some of the later hymns of the *Ṛg Veda*, most notably the famous Puruṣasūkta (*Ṛg Veda* 10.90), where the entire cosmos as well as human society come into being out of a primordial sacrifice. The sacrificial cosmology emerges still more clearly in the later Vedic texts devoted to prescribing sacrificial procedures (the *Yajur Veda*) and the interpretive texts known as the Brāhmaṇas. These texts outline a complex system of sacrificial practice, ranging in scale from modest domestic rites around home fires to elaborate public ceremonies sponsored by the wealthiest kings. The gods who figured so importantly in the *Ṛg Veda* seem to have been demoted; what is most important in the later Vedic period is the sacrifice itself.

As the role of sacrifice grew, so did the status of the new group of religious specialists who called themselves *brāhmaṇas* (Anglicized as "brahman" or "brahmin"). Like *Veda*, this is a crucial term in the history of Indian religions. The poets of the *Ṛg Veda* employ the term *brahman* primarily to refer to the Vedic hymns themselves, understood as powerful and efficacious speech. The notion that certain kinds of liturgical speech are inherently powerful is common to many schools of Indian religious thought. The Indian term most often used for such potent verbal formulae is *mantra*. The *Ṛg Veda* poets also used *brāhmaṇa* to refer by extension to those who fashioned and recited the hymns. At that time the brahman reciters did not constitute a hereditary or endogamous social group, but in later Vedic texts *brāhmaṇa* came to be defined, at least by the brahmans themselves, as a hereditary occupational social group, specializing in ritual matters and the teaching of the Vedas.

A crucial first step in the social institutionalization of the brahman class can be found in the Puruṣasūkta hymn. According to this hymn, four social classes emerged from the Puruṣa, the original sacrificial victim: the brahmans from his mouth, the kṣatriyas (warriors) from his arms, the vaiśyas (merchants) from his loins, and the śūdras (servants) from his feet. Thus the poem portrays the brahmans and other social classes not simply as social groups, but as an order of creation. Because the brahmans emerge from the mouth of the Puruṣa, they enjoy in this order the highest status.

The Puruṣasūkta hymn is the earliest depiction of what later became known as the fourfold *varṇa* scheme, a model of society as an organic hierarchized unity of classes or castes that was to have great persistence through Indian history. The word "caste" derives from *casta*, the Portuguese word for social class. Yet historically it was a flexible and contentious model, one that was just as often questioned and opposed as it was accepted and defended. One can get a taste of the kind of criticism and satire that was recurrently directed against brahmanic claims of privilege in Kabīr's poem, "The Sapling and the Seed" (Chapter 2), while a defense of the varṇa system appears even in such an unlikely setting as the "Dog Oracles" of the *Śarṅgadhara Paddhati* (Chapter 16).

The Upaniṣads and the Renunciatory Model

Within the supplementary texts of the Vedic corpus composed around 900–600 B.C.E., one sees evidence both of a growing sophistication in reflection concerning the sacrifice and also the beginnings of an opposition to sacrifice. The texts called the Brāhmaṇas, arising from discussions and controversies that engaged the new class of brahman ritualists as they conducted the sacrifices, devote themselves particularly to explication of ritual action, providing a learned commentary on the myriad sacrifices of the Vedic system. The idea underlying these hermeneutical texts is that the most adept priest not only performs the actions of sacrifice, but also understands their inner meanings.

The Āraṇyakas (literally, "forest books") and especially the Upaniṣads ("sitting close to a teacher") took the sacrificial worldview in a different direction. As their names imply, these texts were intended for a more restricted audience, often recounting private discussions between teachers and students in the forest. The Upaniṣads pose themselves, and were later accepted by many Indians, as the "culmination of the Veda" (*vedānta*), its highest teachings. For example, in the *Bṛhadāraṇyaka Upaniṣad*, one of the earliest and most influential Upaniṣads, we learn of the brahman teacher Yājñavalkya, whom we have already met in his enumeration of the gods. At the conclusion of a royal sacrifice, Yājñavalkya claims that he is the most knowledgeable of all present in Vedic matters. A series of interlocutors—not only priests, but also a woman, a cart driver, and the king himself—question him, trying to rebuff his declaration and gain for themselves the thousand head of cattle he has claimed as his reward. Yet as Yājñavalkya substantiates his superior Vedic knowledge, he introduces several important ideas unknown to earlier Vedic tradition. So too the other Upaniṣads: together they introduce a set of new concepts that grow out of earlier Vedic thought while calling into question some of its central premises. These concepts, simultaneously old and new, proved to raise enduring issues for Indian religious and philosophical debate.

Yājñavalkya was the first recorded spokesman for the notion of transmigration, which holds that upon death a person is neither annihilated nor transported to some other world in perpetuity, but rather returns to worldly life, to live and die again in a new mortal form. This continuing succession of life, death, and rebirth is termed *saṃsāra* (circling, wandering) in the Upaniṣads. *Saṃsāra* comes to denote not just the individual wandering of a person from life to life, but also the entire world process seen as a perpetual flux. This cyclical worldview of the Upaniṣads grows out of an earlier Vedic concern with natural cycles of the moon, day and night, and the seasons, but projects it in a new direction.

Although transmigration answers the question of beginnings and ends, it also raises two new issues. What determines a person's subsequent form of rebirth? Is there anything other than eternal transmigration? To answer the first question, Yājñavalkya redefines the Vedic notion of *karman*. *Karman* (derived from the verb root *kṛ*, to do or to make, and usually Anglicized as "karma,") means action in a very broad sense; in the Vedas the term refers particularly to sacrificial actions, as the most efficacious kind of activity. In Vedic sacrifice, all ritual actions have consequences, leading to fruits (*phala*) that are often not apparent at the time but will inevitably ripen. Yājñavalkya accepts this extended notion of causality and gives it a moral dimension: the moral character of one's actions in this lifetime determines the status of one's rebirth in the next. Behave in this life as a god and you will become a god. But gods, in this view, are not immortal either, and may after a long period of heavenly hedonism be reborn as humans.

Yājñavalkya also suggests an alternative to this endless cycle of becoming. The release from the cycle of rebirth is most often called *mokṣa*, liberation or salvation. According to Yājñavalkya an individual may attain liberation through lack of desire, since desire is what engenders saṃsāra in the first place.

In postulating an alternative state superior to worldly life and attainable through individual conscious effort, mokṣa is perhaps the most consequential of all Upaniṣadic ideas for later Indian religious history. In contrast to the Vedic ideology of sacrifice, in which goals were as much social and collective as individual, the pursuit of mokṣa takes an individualist goal to be the highest attainment. If Vedic sacrifice was responsible for engendering and maintaining the world process, the search for mokṣa posed a direct abnegation of that process, an escape from saṃsāra into something transcendent. This division of aims forms a major point of contention throughout Indian religious history. "Ascetic Withdrawal or Social Engagement" (Chapter 37), a collection of passages from Vedic and other sources, engages the issue directly, and it reappears centuries later in the life stories of two modern women renouncers, Mīrāṃ (Chapter 31) and Śrī Arcanāpuri Mā (Chapter 27).

Although the Upaniṣads are not united in their views, the strategies they recommend to those seeking mokṣa most often include a regimen of renunciation and asceticism coupled with instruction in the higher forms of knowledge, namely, the world according to the Upaniṣads. If mokṣa is an escape from the world cycle, it makes sense that one would reach it through progressive abstention from worldly involvements. That is exactly what the renouncer (*sannyāsin*) does. He (or occasionally she) would leave home and family to live in relatively isolated and austere circumstances, sleeping on the ground, restricting the diet, practicing control of the breath, and bringing the senses under control—in short, withdrawing from all that might bind one to the world, with the ultimate goal of escaping from rebirth itself. Such psychophysical practices were not confined to adherents of the Upaniṣads, as we will see, but the logic of renunciatory practice was first articulated in Upaniṣadic texts such as the *Bṛhadāraṇyaka Upaniṣad*.

The Vedas, then, contained a large variety of religious ideas and practices, introducing a host of terms and questions that would recur throughout Indian religious history. In sacrifice, the Vedas provided a system of public and private rituals that engendered the order of cosmos and of society, and that was utilized by political powers to validate their own authority. The brahmans appeared as an endogamous class of religious and intellectual specialists claiming high social status, and through the articulation of the varṇa system they portrayed society as an organic unity of distinct ranked classes pursuing different occupational specialties. The renunciatory model presented by the Upaniṣads centered around the individual pursuit of liberation through austerity and knowledge.

In later times the Vedas became one gauge for Hindu "orthodoxy." Those who adhered most closely to the Vedic tradition claimed a superior status and judged others as either within or outside the Vedic fold, even though the actual language of the Vedic texts had become incomprehensible to most. Many new Hindu groups honoring new deities with new forms of worship claimed allegiance to the Vedas, or portrayed themselves as extensions of the Vedas. The epic *Mahābhārata*, for example, poses itself as the "fifth Veda," whereas the Vaiṣṇava devotional poetry of Nammāḻvār is said to constitute a "Tamil Veda." Nineteenth- and twentieth-century reformist movements like the Brāhmo Samāj and the Ārya Samāj sought to return Hinduism to what they claimed were its purer Vedic roots.

Proximity to the Vedic tradition, however, is not an altogether reliable criterion for defining Hinduism. Although non-Hindus like Buddhists and Jains define themselves by rejecting the authoritative claims of the Vedas, so too do many later religious teachers such as Kabīr and the Bengali Bāuls, whom most Hindus view as Hindu. Theistic Hindu schools often contested Vedic authority in a different manner. Rather than rejecting the Vedas outright, the Śaiva devotional poet Māṇikkavācakar, for instance, simply asserts that Śiva is "Lord over the Vedas" (Chapter 7). His strategy, typical of many, is to establish a new hierarchy of religious values, within which the Vedas are included but subsumed under the higher authority of his god, Śiva.

In the end, what is most striking about the Vedas is their longevity rather than their hegemony. In the shifting, changing, contentious discourse of Indian religious history, one hears over and over echoes of the concerns, the terms, the goals, and the practices first recorded in India in the ancient Vedas.

The New Religions of the Sixth Century B.C.E.

Upaniṣadic sages like Yājñavalkya were not the only renouncers in the seventh and sixth centuries B.C.E. From all indications, there were many peripatetic seekers wandering the fringes of Gangetic civilization during this period. The authors and teachers of the Upaniṣads allied themselves with the Vedas, recommending that renouncers continue reciting the Vedas and view their ascetic practices as "interior sacrifice." Other forest teachers of the same period, including some undoubtedly not of the Indo-Aryan community, were willing to dispense altogether with Vedic models. They developed new teachings and practices with no attempt to link them to the established ideology of sacrifice and the Vedas. A teacher named Ajita of the Hair-Blanket proclaimed a thoroughgoing materialism (later identified as the Cārvāka school), denying both ethical prescriptions and existence after death. The Ājīvika school led by Makkhali Gosāla adhered to a doctrine of fatalism, claiming that human free will was an illusion; destiny was all.

Varied as they were, most teachers accepted a common intellectual foundation, not differing greatly from that taught by Yājñavalkya. With few exceptions, they accepted the notion of cyclical transmigration (*saṃsāra*), the causal connection between act and consequence (*karman*) as the moral determinant of one's rebirth, and the possibility of escape (*mokṣa*) from this cyclical existence. Within this broad consensus, disagreement and debate continued. What is the underlying cause of saṃsāra? What kinds of activities engender karma? What are the best means of avoiding or removing the consequences of one's actions? What is the character of mokṣa? What exactly is it that attains liberation?

The seekers also generally accepted certain kinds of psychological and physical practices as particularly conducive to the religious attainments they sought. The general Indian term for such practices is *yoga*, from the verbal root *yuj*, to bind together, as one harnesses animals to a yoke. In Indian religious discourse, *yoga* refers to all sorts of disciplined practices aimed at restraining one's unruly inclinations in order to attain a higher state of concentration or "one-pointedness." In the vivid metaphor of one Upaniṣad, the senses are wild horses hitched to the chariot of the body; the mind is the charioteer who must somehow bring them under control. Yoga is what one uses to do so.

The earliest systematic exposition of yoga is found in the *Yogasūtras*, a text composed by Patañjali in about the second century B.C.E. but systematizing a much older body of practices. Patañjali describes eight "limbs" of yoga, starting with physical restraints such as limiting one's food and practicing celibacy, proceeding through a mastery of physical postures, the control of the breath, gradual withdrawal of the senses from the outer world, and culminating in fixed meditative awareness. As the practitioner masters each limb, he or she gradually detaches from the physical world, reins in the wayward senses, and achieves a reintegration or unification of self.

Patañjali himself adhered to the dualistic metaphysics of the Sāṃkhya school, but the techniques he described and systematized were practical tools for all religious seekers, adaptable to various philosophical viewpoints. Later in Indian religious history, new groups developed new forms of yogic practice as well. Medieval devotional and tantric forms of yoga emphasize such practices as meditative visualization of deities (Chapter 11), repetitive chanting of the name of God (Chapters 4, 5, 40), and ritualized sexual intercourse (Chapters 9, 20), among many others. Alchemists incorporated yoga into their transformative practices (Chapter 15), and non-Hindu religious specialists like Islamic Sufis also adapted yogic techniques to their own purposes.

Out of the questing milieu of the sixth century B.C.E. grew two new religious formations that have had a powerful and continuing impact on Indian religions—Jainism and Buddhism. Both were historically established in the Magadha region (present-day Bihar) by members of the warrior class who renounced their positions in society to find enlightenment: Vardhamāna (c. 599–527 B.C.E.) called Mahāvīra ("great hero"), and Siddhārtha Gautama (c. 566–486 B.C.E.) called the Buddha ("awakened one"). Both advocated paths of monastic austerity as the most effective means of attaining liberation, and both were critical of the Vedic formation. Adherents of the Vedas, in turn, characterized followers of Jainism and Buddhism as "outside the Veda," and accordingly modern scholars often classify the two religions as heterodoxies in contrast to Vedic orthodoxy.

Jainism

The name Jains use to designate themselves, *jaina*, derives from the verbal root *ji*, to conquer, and points to the central religious concern of the Jain community. Jaina monks must fight an ascetic battle to conquer the senses and karma, seeking to attain a purity of soul that liberates them from all bondage. Those who have succeeded in this quest are Jinas, conquerors, and their followers are Jainas.

According to Jain tradition, Vardhamāna Mahāvīra was only the most recent in a succession of twenty-four Tīrthaṅkaras, or "path-makers." His most immediate predecessor, Pārśva, may well have founded an earlier Jain community, but Mahāvīra is the first clearly attested historical Jain leader. Born of royal parents, the traditional biographies relate, Mahāvīra left his family and home at age thirty, abandoned all possessions, stripped off his clothes, and pulled out his hair by the roots. With these dramatic renunciatory acts he began twelve years of severe austerities, until finally at the age of forty-two he attained mokṣa, and so became a Jina or Tīrthaṅkara. Gradually a large group of followers grew around him. The first disciple was Indrabhūti Gautama, a proud brahman and Vedic scholar; in fact, Vardhamāna's eleven primary disciples were all converted brahmans. According to one tradition, Indrabhūti's conversion occurred when Mahāvīra delivered a sermon on the virtues of nonviolence (*ahiṃsā*) at a Vedic animal sacrifice—pointing to a major issue on which the Jains would most pointedly criticize the Vedic order.

Mahāvīra was a human being born of human parents, but he was also, as all Jain accounts make abundantly clear, something more than human. They describe his conception and birth as surrounded by auspicious omens and marvels preordaining his spiritual career. After he was liberated, the supramundane quality of Mahāvīra became still more apparent. His body, free of all impurities, was said to shine like a crystal on all sides. According to the Jain texts, the Vedic gods themselves, far from condescending to Mahāvīra as a mere mortal, recognized that his powers, knowledge, and status were superior to their own and honored him accordingly. Later Jain reformers like Ācārya Vijay Ānandsūri (Chapter 42) argue that the Jina is God.

The Jain community, male and female, divided itself into two groups: lay followers and renouncers. For lay followers, Mahāvīra and later Jain preceptors advocated self-restraints and vows. A Jain layperson should avoid meat, wine, honey, and snacking at night. One should also give up falsehood, stealing, and especially violence. Jain texts also recommend fasting and distributing one's wealth to monks, nuns, and the poor as means of strengthening the discipline of a lay adherent.

Jains soon developed forms of devotional practice directed toward the Tīrthaṅkaras and other worthy figures. Most prominent among these rituals is devapūjā, in which followers worship the Jinas physically represented by statues depicting them in poses of deepest meditation (Chapter 19). Worshipers approach and bow before the image, chant the Jina's names, circumambulate, bathe the image, make a series of physical offerings to it, and wave lamps before it. Considering the transcendent status of the liberated beings, strict-minded Jains do not regard the Jinas as actually present in their images, nor do they suppose that offerings have any effect on the Jina, but rather view devapūjā as a meditational discipline intended to remind worshipers of the ideal state achieved by the Jina and to inspire them to seek that state for themselves. However, Jain devotional hymns indicate that most Jains have looked to the Tīrthaṅkara for direct benefits, and have believed the Jina to inhabit the images they honored.

Jains also incorporated into their temple liturgy the worship of goddesses and other guardian deities, lesser beings who may intervene in worldly affairs on behalf of the votary. As the stories in "Jain Stories of Miraculous Power" (Chapter 28) indicate, Jaina goddesses like Cakrā could grant practical rewards such as wealth and release from earthly prison, as well as helping their devotees on the way to escaping the prison of karma.

The ethical and ritual disciplines of the Jain laity were regarded as preparations for the more rigorous and more efficacious life of a Jain renouncer. Indeed, Jains organized their religion largely around the necessity of renunciation for attaining true purity of soul. This central theme emerges even in the didactic stories of medieval Jain collections (Chapter 26), in which the narrator seeks to instill in his audience a feeling of revulsion toward the world and to nudge it toward renunciation through exaggeration and macabre humor.

When a lay person decides to relinquish worldly life, this is treated as a great event both in the prospective renouncer's own spiritual career and in the life of the Jain community. In the ceremony of renouncing social life and entering upon a new monastic life—a veritable death and rebirth—Jain initiates cast off all their former possessions, pull out their hair in large handfuls, and give up their own names. They are presented with the austere provisions of mendicants and with new monastic names. At this point the new monk or nun undertakes the five "great vows," abstaining from all violence, dishonesty, theft, sexual intercourse, and personal possessions, under the close supervision of monastic preceptors. Through self-restraint, careful conduct, physical austerities, and meditations, the anchorite gradually removes the karma that inhibits the soul's inherent powers and virtues, aiming always at the final victory. The Jain path of rigorous austerity may culminate most dramatically in sallekhanā, voluntary self-starvation, in which the Jain renunciant gradually abandons the body itself for the sake of the soul's ultimate purity.

One of the first major royal patrons of Jainism was the Mauryan emperor Candragupta I (r. 321–297 B.C.E.). According to Jain tradition, this ruler was also involved in the major schism of Jainism into two communities, named Śvetāmbara (white-clad) and Digambara (sky-clad—that is, naked) after the monks' characteristic robes or lack thereof. In the third century B.C.E., the Jain leader Bhadrabāhu apparently moved half the Jain community south to Karnataka in order to escape a famine in Candragupta's kingdom. Candragupta himself went along as Bhadrabāhu's disciple. Divided geographically, the two Jain communities began to diverge doctrinally, and eventually formalized those differences at the Council of Vallabhī in the fifth century C.E. The Śvetāmbaras were and continue to be based primarily in the western Indian regions of Rajasthan and Gujarat, whereas the Digambaras have always been most prominent in Karnataka, and were also influential for a time in Tamilnadu.

Throughout the early medieval period, Jain monks and advisers played prominent roles in the courts of many Indian rulers. During this period Jain authors produced a remarkable array of literary and scholarly works in virtually every field, and Jain patrons sponsored impressive Jain temples. In the later medieval period, with Islamic rulers powerful in northern India and the Hindu state of Vijayanagar dominating the south, Jains lost much of their public patronage and became a more self-sufficient, inward-looking community. They survived, however, and now number some four million adherents, mostly in India but with substantial groups of Jains in the United States, Canada, the United Kingdom, and other parts of the English-speaking world.

Buddhism

Buddhists are those who follow the way of the buddhas, beings who have fully "awakened" (from the root *budh*, to wake up) to the true nature of things. In our historical era, the Awakened One was a kṣatriya named Siddhārtha Gautama, born in the foothills of the Himalaya Mountains in about 566 B.C.E. According to traditional accounts, the future Buddha Siddhārtha spent the first twenty-nine years of his life ensconced in affluent family life before renouncing society to seek liberation as a wandering ascetic. After spending six years in austerities, study, and meditation, Siddhārtha sat down under a fig tree in the town of Bodh Gaya one night in 531 B.C.E. and vowed that he would not get up until he had gained enlightenment. That night he attained nirvāṇa and became a buddha. One may view the remainder of the Buddha's life, and indeed all of Buddhist religion, as an attempt to enable others to replicate for themselves what Siddhārtha accomplished that night under the Bodhi tree.

The Buddha delivered his first public discourse, the first "turning of the wheel of Buddhist doctrine (*dharma*)," to an audience of five ascetics outside Varanasi. As soon as he had gathered sixty disciples, he sent them out in all directions to spread his teachings. From its inception, Buddhism was a proselytizing religion, and within a few centuries it was successful not just in the Indo-Aryan society of northern India but throughout South Asia. Spreading the message still further afield, Buddhist missionaries soon traveled to Sri Lanka, Southeast Asia as far as Indonesia, China, Japan, Korea, and Tibet. From the second through the seventh centuries C.E., Buddhism was the major cosmopolitan religion throughout Asia and probably the predominant religious community in the world at that time.

As a pan-Asian religion, Buddhism receives a separate volume in this series. It would be redundant to attempt to outline the complex doctrines or practices of Buddhism here. But Buddhism was first a powerful religious movement in India, and it had a major impact on the development of other religions in India, so it is necessary to refer to a few of its salient features.

Like Mahāvīra and the early Jains, the Buddha considered that the most effective way for his disciples to work toward individual salvation was in small monastic groups. Although renunciation of society was necessary, it was desirable also to avoid the isolation of the hermit. Monastic cells would allow for instruction, support, and enforcement of moral precepts. Establishing mendicant orders, however, posed a challenge to the brahmanic religious specialists and the sacrificial order. After all, mendicants still depend on alms, and the surplus production available to support the various religious claimants was finite.

In this competitive situation the Buddha and his followers developed a penetrating critique of the Vedic religion, much as the Jains did. Not only did the Buddha denounce the public sacrifices advocated by brahman specialists as overly costly, violent, and uncertain in their results, but he also sought to undercut the brahmans' own claims to authority. Satirizing the creation myth of *Ṛg Veda* 10.90, in which the brahman class emerges from the mouth of the primordial male Puruṣa, he pointed out that anyone could see that brahmans in fact emerge from the same female bodily organ as everybody else. He questioned brahmanic claims that the Vedas were revealed texts, not human in origin, as well as their claims to a special inborn religious authority.

Even early followers in the Buddhist community, however, considered the Buddha Śākyamuni to be a superhuman figure. Buddhists preserved his bodily charisma in his ashes and relics, entombed in burial mounds called *stūpas*. Located within monastic settlements, stūpas became centers of Buddhist devotion, where votaries would circumambulate, present flower garlands, burn incense and lamps, serenade with music, and recite eulogies. By the first century C.E. if not earlier, Buddhists also began to use physical images of the Buddha and other important Buddhist figures as objects of devotion. These informal acts of homage toward the Buddha in the form of stūpa or image were later formalized as the ritual of pūjā. During this same period, bodhisattvas, those motivated by compassion to achieve enlightenment, became objects of veneration and emulation in a movement that came to be known as the Mahāyāna (great vehicle).

Buddhist monks and nuns often established their "retreats" on the outskirts of the largest cities of the time and actively sought the patronage of royalty and the wealthy urban merchant class. With the conversion of the great Mauryan ruler Aśoka in the third century B.C.E., Buddhism became the imperial religion of South Asia. Aśoka patronized Buddhist institutions lavishly and sent out missionaries to spread Buddhist teachings abroad. He also publicized his new policies with inscriptions carved on pillars or rock faces throughout the empire. In his epigraphs, Aśoka speaks of his pursuit of dharma, by which he means a common ethical code based on values of tolerance, harmony, generosity, and nonviolence. While proclaiming tolerance toward all religious seekers, he also emphasized nonviolence, thereby effectively ruling out the animal sacrifices that had been the heart of the Vedic system of sacrifice. Far better, he announced, to practice the nonviolent ceremony of dharma, by which he meant giving gifts to Buddhist monks and nuns and other worthies.

Though the Mauryan empire fell apart rather soon after Aśoka's death, he had established a model for Buddhist kingship. For several centuries, every successor dynasty seeking to claim imperial status in India would begin to patronize Buddhists as its primary, though never exclusive, religious recipients. By the time of Harṣavardhana, the seventh-century emperor of Kanyākubja, however, there were clear signs that the role of Buddhism in India was diminishing. It was at this time that the Chinese pilgrim Xuanzang toured South Asia, and he observed the dramatic ceremonies of Buddhist gift-giving that Harṣa held at his capital; but he also noticed many abandoned Buddhist monasteries and temples throughout the subcontinent. Patronage and support apparently were drying up, a trend that accelerated after Harṣa's demise. Only in eastern India, the Himalayan regions, and Sri Lanka did Buddhism continue to flourish in South Asia. By the time of the Turko-Afghan raids of the eleventh through thirteenth centuries, Buddhism in northern India was confined to a few rich monastic institutions and universities, which made ripe targets for plunder. Many of the monks fled to Tibet, and Buddhism was effectively exiled from its land of origin.

Since the 1950s, Buddhism has been revivified in India from unexpected sources. A reformer and leader in the struggle for Indian independence, B. R. Ambedkar, was a member of a Maharashtran untouchable community and spokesman for untouchables nationwide. After a lifetime fighting for social justice, Ambedkar decided that Hinduism as it existed would never allow full status to the lowest orders of society, and at a huge public ceremony in 1956 he converted to Buddhism. Many of his followers did also, and the latest census estimates nearly four million Buddhists in Maharashtra alone. During the same period, the Chinese takeover of Tibet forced many Tibetan monks and lay Buddhists to flee south. The Dalai Lama, spiritual head of the Tibetan people, established his new home in exile in India, where he leads a substantial and visible community of Buddhist refugees.

Hinduism Redefined

During the period of Buddhist initiative and imperial spread, those social and religious groups who remained loyal in some way to the Vedic tradition were not inactive. In fact, as one historian puts it, "in the face of this challenge Brahmanism girt itself up by a tremendous intellectual effort for a new lease on life."[2] This statement overstates the degree to which "Brahmanism" reacted as a cohesive entity; historical sources suggest rather a multiplicity of initiatives. Nevertheless, the intellectual and socio-political challenge posed by Buddhism, Jainism, and the other renunciatory groups did inspire many creative and fruitful responses, which collectively add up to a virtual transformation in "orthodox" circles, from the Vedic worldview to forms of classical "Hinduism" that explicitly maintained continuity with the Vedic tradition but effectively altered it into a new religious formation.

The literature of this period is extensive. There was continued production of texts within the Vedic corpus: new Upaniṣads, new auxiliary texts, and texts that styled themselves "appendices" to the Vedic corpus. During this period the formative texts of six major philosophical schools were first put together—the Mīmāṃsā, Vedānta, Sāṃkhya, Yoga, Nyāya, and Vaiśeṣika schools. Of these, the Mīmāṃsā school occupied itself primarily with the interpretation of the Vedic sacrificial texts and ritual, whereas the Advaita Vedānta reformulated some of the teachings of the Upaniṣads into a consistent monist metaphysics. Sāṃkhya developed an alternative dualist philosophy, and Yoga systematized the psychophysical practices of the ascetics in accord with Sāṃkhya teachings. Nyāya was most concerned with the logic and rhetoric of philosophical disputation and the nature of reality, and Vaiśeṣika sought to develop a realist ontology of substances.

Another major genre of religious literature was the Dharmaśāstra, whose central concern, as the name implies, was the definition and delineation of dharma. The term *dharma* comes from the root *dhṛ*, to uphold, to maintain, and dharma may well be defined as "that which upholds and supports order." Yet different parties could hold very different ideas of what constitutes "order." In the Vedas the term *dharma* referred to the sacrifice as that which maintains the order of the cosmos. In Buddhist texts it meant the teachings of the Buddha, and Jain sources spoke of a Jaina dharma. Aśoka employed the term to describe his own religio-political policies. In the Dharmaśāstra literature, dharma referred to an overarching order of the cosmos and society, and to a person's duties within the world so constituted. It determined specific duties for all groups belonging to Indo-Aryan society, varying according to sex, class, family, stage of life, and so on. The Dharmaśāstras addressed themselves especially to the male brahman householder, directing him to live a life of austerity, purity, Vedic learning, and ritual observance.

The Epics

If the early Dharmaśāstras represent the response of one important social group to the new situation, the immense epic poems formulated during this period constitute a still more significant corpus of texts explicitly meant for all Hindu society. There are two great epics: the *Mahābhārata* (at 100,000 verses, roughly six times the length of the Christian Bible) and the *Rāmāyaṇa* (a mere 25,000 verses), plus an "appendix" to the *Mahābhārata* (as if 100,000 verses weren't enough) called the *Harivaṃśa*. "Whatever is here may be found elsewhere," admits the *Mahābhārata* (1.56.34), "but what is not here is nowhere else." Not only do the epics claim to be comprehensive in depicting the world, but they also intend to be of continuing relevance. The *Rāmāyaṇa* (1.2.35) predicts, "As long as mountains and streams shall endure upon the earth, so long will the story of the *Rāmāyaṇa* be told among men." Together the epics illustrate with remarkable thoroughness and rich detail a Hindu world in transition.

Although the *Mahābhārata* was later claimed as a "fifth Veda," the Sanskrit epics developed outside the Vedic corpus. They originated as the oral literature of bards who told and retold stories of heroic battles of the past, primarily for audiences of kṣatriya chieftains and warriors. The *Mahābhārata* tells the story of a great war between two rival clans and their allies that may have taken place around 900 B.C.E. Unlike the Vedas, however, the bardic literature was never meant to be preserved and transmitted verbatim. Over the generations storytellers reworked their narratives of the great war, expanding and supplementing them with all sorts of other stories and teachings, until the tales assumed a more or less final form around the fourth century C.E.

The epics center around great battles and wars, reflecting their origins as oral literature of the warrior class. The narratives begin with family conflicts leading to disputes over royal succession. Developing this theme to an extreme, the *Mahābhārata* uses the rivalry between two related kṣatriya clans to characterize the entire warrior class as quarreling, contentious, and increasingly deviating from dharma. With the ruling classes in such disarray, disorder and violence threaten society itself. The dire situation is mirrored throughout the cosmos, where (in the *Rāmāyaṇa*) the demon Rāvaṇa has overcome Indra, the divine representative of the Vedic order, and new heroes and deities must intervene to reestablish dharma. The crises lead with tragic inevitability to great battles, involving all the warriors of India in the *Mahābhārata*—and not just humans but also demons, monkeys, bears, and vultures in the *Rāmāyaṇa*. Through war the ancient order is purged and the demonic forces are subdued. The epics conclude with victorious kings restoring the social order.

While focusing on human conflict, the epics also present a new theophany. As the Vedic gods appear unable to contend with the demons and threatening chaos of a new age, these texts introduce a deity who can overcome these threats: Viṣṇu.

Viṣṇu is not an entirely new deity. In fact, he appears even in the *Ṛg Veda*, which associates him with three steps that mysteriously stretch over the whole world; later Vedic texts relate a myth linking Viṣṇu's three steps to the sacrifice. The myth relates how the gods trick the demons, who foolishly agree to allow the gods only as much ground for their sacrificial enclosure as the dwarflike Viṣṇu can cover in three steps. The demons should have realized the danger from the name Viṣṇu, which means "the one who pervades." As the gods sacrifice at their altar, the dwarf grows to become as large as the entire world, and in three steps covers the three worlds of heaven, earth, and the netherworld. Likewise, by the time the epics were put into final shape, Viṣṇu's religious role had grown from its diminutive appearance in the *Ṛg Veda* to a position of superiority over all other gods.

The epics present Viṣṇu as a divinity with clearly heroic qualities, who takes over Indra's role as primary vanquisher of demons. Other gods have begun to recognize Viṣṇu as their superior and pay homage to him. He continues to associate himself with the sacrifice, and actively maintains the order of society. Most importantly, and paradoxically, the epics identify Viṣṇu both as the supreme deity and as an active, embodied, finite god who intervenes directly in human affairs. On the one hand, the epics assert that Viṣṇu is identical with the Puruṣa of *Ṛg Veda* 10.90, the *Brahman* of the Upaniṣads, and other previous formulations of a transcendent Absolute. Yet he also retains features of a more anthropomorphic divinity, particularly when he takes on human forms or incarnations (*avatāra*, literally a "crossing down" to human form) and intervenes directly in human society to kill demons and restore dharma.

In the *Harivaṃśa*, Viṣṇu incarnates himself as Kṛṣṇa in order to destroy the tyrannical demon Kaṃsa, who has usurped the throne of Mathura. Though born of royal parentage, Kṛṣṇa is raised among a tribe of cowherds, who only gradually become aware of his superhuman character. When Kṛṣṇa has grown to manhood, he returns to Mathura and puts an end to Kaṃsa and the other demons of his coterie. In the *Mahābhārata*, Viṣṇu appears again as Kṛṣṇa, ruler of Dwaraka and a loyal friend of the Pāṇḍava hero Arjuna. Here too the divinity of Kṛṣṇa is only occasionally revealed, though in many ways Kṛṣṇa acts as a hidden, inscrutable instigator and manipulator of events throughout the epic.

Viṣṇu takes on a different human embodiment in the *Rāmāyaṇa*, as Rāma, the young prince of Ayodhya, whose primary mission is to rid the world of Rāvaṇa and other demons. Rāvaṇa has gained a divine blessing making him invulnerable to other gods and demons, and this enables him to defeat Indra and to insinuate himself as sole recipient of sacrificial offerings. Yet he has arrogantly neglected to request invincibility from humans as well. Rāvaṇa's ruin comes about after he abducts Sītā, the beautiful and chaste wife of Rāma, and imprisons her in his palace in Lankā. With the aid of an army of monkeys and bears, the warrior-prince Rāma, divine and human, defeats Rāvaṇa's army, rescues Sītā, and finally returns to Ayodhya to rule as its king.

The concept of *avatāra*, one can imagine, offered important advantages to an expanding community of Viṣṇu worshipers. It enabled the Vaiṣṇavas to maintain their identification of Viṣṇu as the Absolute, yet also incorporate other local or regional deities and their cults as incarnations of an encompassing Viṣṇu. Historically speaking, Kṛṣṇa no doubt originated as a human hero, the warrior leader of a pastoral tribe in the Mathura region. Folkloric aggrandizement turned him into a legendary hero with godlike qualities, and finally in the *Harivaṃśa* he was revealed to be a divinity incarnate, the avatāra of Viṣṇu.

Of all portions of the Sanskrit epics, none is considered more significant to the development of Indian religions than the *Bhagavad Gītā*, the "Song of the Lord Kṛṣṇa," a part of the *Mahābhārata* composed around 200 C.E. Placed at the dramatic climax of the epic's narrative, the *Gītā* also provides the central ideological and theological vision of the epic. Just as the great battle is about to begin, with huge armies facing one another across the battlefield of Kurukṣetra, the most powerful warrior on the Pāṇḍava side, Arjuna, suffers from a paroxysm of doubt and anxiety. Why should he fight, particularly when his opponents include relatives and former teachers? Acting as Arjuna's charioteer, Kṛṣṇa responds to his doubts by offering a sustained discourse on the moral and religious propriety of war, the nature of human action, and the most effective means of attaining liberation. Kṛṣṇa argues that worldly action in support of dharma is not incompatible with mokṣa, as the various renunciatory orders had suggested. One should accept one's personal dharma as a guide to proper conduct, he avers, but without regard to the fruits of that conduct.

To clinch his argument, Kṛṣṇa also progressively reveals himself to Arjuna as a deity, indeed as the highest, supreme divinity. The teaching culminates with an overwhelming vision. Granted "divine eyes" by Kṛṣṇa, Arjuna is suddenly able to see Kṛṣṇa's complete form, the awesome, all-inclusive Viśvarūpa. Kṛṣṇa acknowledges that previous methods of self-transformation such as sacrifice and yoga may be efficacious, but in light of his self-revelation he also recommends a new and superior method of religious attainment, which he calls *bhakti* (devotion). The most efficient way to reach the highest state, he tells Arjuna, is to dedicate one's entire self to Kṛṣṇa, a personal god who is simultaneously the Absolute.

With Arjuna's vision of the embodied Absolute and Kṛṣṇa's advocacy of bhakti we are initiated into the world of Hindu theism.

The Purāṇas and Hindu Theism

Throughout the period loosely labeled as the "Gupta" and "post-Gupta" ages, 300–700 C.E., Buddhism remained a powerful religious force in India, but new groups devoted to Viṣṇu and Śiva gained in visibility and resources. The Gupta rulers themselves satisfied both sides by lavishly patronizing Buddhist institutions while also declaring themselves followers of Viṣṇu. Throughout history Indian rulers have usually diversified their religious patronage as a means of integrating multiple religious communities within their kingdoms. The earliest Hindu temples built in permanent materials appeared during this period. Images of Hindu gods increased in scale and quality of workmanship. Reflecting and consolidating this growth in the religious orders of Viṣṇu and Śiva, another genre of texts, the Purāṇas, articulated more fully the theistic worldview outlined in the epics.

The Purāṇas (literally, ancient traditions) constitute another huge corpus of texts, numbering eighteen "major" Purāṇas, eighteen "sub-major" ones, and countless others. The major Purāṇas alone run to something like 400,000 verses. Like the epics, the Purāṇas were composed orally over many centuries, so that earlier and later teachings are regularly juxtaposed in the same texts. Bards put the earliest Purāṇas into final shape by about the fifth century C.E., while other texts kept incorporating new materials. The *Bhaviṣya Purāṇa* (or "Future Purāṇa," an oxymoron), the most open-ended of the major Purāṇas, contains sections from the fifth century or earlier, yet also "predicts" such late medieval figures as Akbar, Kabīr, Caitanya, and Guru Nānak, and even foretells the coming of British rule to India.

Comprehensive and encyclopedic in scope, the Purāṇas discuss cosmology, royal genealogies, society and dharma, the sacred geography of pilgrimage sites, yogic practices, town planning, even grammar and poetics. For the religious history of South Asia, however, the most significant aspect of the Purāṇas is their presentation of the theology, mythology, and ritual of the two primary gods Viṣṇu and Śiva.

Already in the epics, proponents of Viṣṇu were advancing him as the highest lord of the cosmos. The Vaiṣṇava Purāṇas advocate this with greater confidence and fuller cosmological breadth. The cyclical epochs of creation and dissolution of the universe, we now learn, are none other than Viṣṇu's alternating periods of activity and rest. The Purāṇas flesh out the incipient notion of Viṣṇu's intervening incarnations and gradually systematize it into a list of ten embodiments, including not only Kṛṣṇa and Rāma, but also zoomorphic forms (fish, tortoise, boar, man-lion), anthropomorphic ones (the dwarf who took three steps, Paraśurāma), a future incarnation (Kalkin), and even the Buddha. As the *Viṣṇu Purāṇa* relates, once when the demons had become too powerful through sacrifice, Viṣṇu took form as the Buddha and also as a naked Jain mendicant to dissuade them from sacrificing, so that the gods could overcome them and restore the proper order of things. Generally, all his incarnations reinforce Viṣṇu's essential attributes: benevolence, a desire to preserve order in the world, and a paradoxical capacity to be simultaneously infinite and finite.

Like Viṣṇu, Śiva appears in a rather minor role in the *Ṛg Veda*, but gradually advances in status until the Śaiva Purāṇas single him out as the Absolute. In the *Ṛg Veda*, Rudra ("the howler") is a peripheral divinity. Dwelling outside society in the forests or mountains, he is associated with the destructive forces of nature and rules over undomesticated animals. Since Rudra is not numbered one of the auspicious gods, he is excluded from the soma sacrifice, and instead is offered tribute to avert his wrath. Although he is characteristically destructive in his actions, Rudra may also become beneficent if properly praised and propitiated. When Rudra shows this kinder, gentler nature he is called Śiva, the "auspicious" one.

Already in this early appearance, we can observe two traits central to Śiva's later personality. In contrast to the sociable Viṣṇu, Śiva is an outsider. Residing typically in the highest Himalayan Mountains, he is the lord and role model for yogis, less concerned with instituting dharma on earth than with leading souls toward mokṣa. Second, Śiva has a dual nature, conjoining what are to us antithetical attributes. Not only is he both malevolent and benevolent, he is also both ascetic and erotic, hermit and family man, an immobile meditator and an unruly dancer. In one iconographic form, Śiva appears simultaneously male and female, an integral hermaphrodite.

In the epics, Śiva's character remains ambiguous, capricious, fierce, and sometimes wrathful. He continues to live outside society, and if he intervenes at all it is usually to disrupt things. Though they are predominantly Vaiṣṇava in orientation, the epics nevertheless recognize Śiva's growing power and his increasing claim to certain ritual prerogatives. In one famous episode, King Dakṛa organizes a large public sacrifice but declines to invite Śiva since, after all, Śiva is rather unruly. Learning of this slight, Śiva sends a swarming horde of emanations to break up the sacrifice, and then appears in person to demand that from now on he be the primary recipient of all sacrificial offerings.

One early Upaniṣad, the *Śvetāśvatara*, had identified Rudra-Śiva as the transcendental Absolute, identical with Puruṣa and the Upaniṣadic Brahman. The Śaiva Purāṇas reassert this claim and link it with a fully developed mythology of Śiva's doings. Unlike Viṣṇu, Śiva does not incarnate himself as a human being for an entire lifetime; rather he occasionally manifests himself physically in a body to carry out his varied intentions. In the Purāṇas, Śiva's manifestations most often demonstrate his superiority over other contestants, defeat demons, and grant grace to his followers.

Viṣṇu and Śiva are not the only deities in the world of the Purāṇas. In fact, these texts present a complex, inclusive pantheon, populated with divine families, animal mounts for each deity, Vedic divinities (now cast exclusively in supporting roles), and hosts of lesser semi-divinities such as celestial dancers, musicians, titans, sages, magicians, and many more. Among them two deserve special note: Brahmā and the Goddess.

The god Brahmā, with roots in the late Vedic and Dharmaśāstra literature, appears in the Purāṇas as the god of creation and as the patron of Vedic and orthodox brahmans. Sometimes the texts portray him comically as a senile grandfather who causes trouble by indiscriminately rewarding even demons for their austerities; at other times he shows better judgment in recognizing the preeminence of Viṣṇu and Śiva. Some Purāṇas of a more integrationist tendency, however, stress the interdependence of the three principal male divinities in performing distinct cosmic functions: Brahmā creates the world, Viṣṇu protects and sustains it, and Śiva destroys it. In modern times this has become known as the "Hindu trinity."

The Goddess presents a more complex picture. In the literature of the fifth through seventh centuries, several important female deities gain a new importance. Three are consorts or wives of the principal male deities: Lakṣmī is the consort of Viṣṇu, Pārvatī of Śiva, and Sarasvatī of Brahmā. These goddesses often take on significant responsibilities in their own rights, as Lakṣmī becomes the goddess of prosperity and domestic good fortune. Some Puraṇic texts, most notably the *Devīmāhātmya* section (c. 600 C.E.) of the *Mārkaṇeya Purāṇa*, go further to present a single great Goddess not as a wife, but as the Supreme Lord, appropriating for her all the common epithets of the Absolute. In her most famous incarnation she appears as Durgā, a warrior goddess. A buffalo demon, having gained nearly invincible powers through austerities, is running rampant through the cosmos and none of the male gods can subdue it. Durgā is born from the collective anger and frustration of all the gods. She receives a weapon from each of them and then rides forth on her lion mount to confront and finally destroy the demon.

Like Viṣṇu and Śiva, this female Absolute has an absorbing personality. She incorporates many local and regional cults and manifests herself in a plethora of distinct guises and forms. Only occasionally in the major Purāṇas does she appear in full force, but these glimpses point to the existence during this period of a significant school of thought that identified the fundamental force of the cosmos as feminine in nature and devoted itself to her praise and worship. This religious sensibility reappears in new forms among the tantric schools of medieval India (Chapters 9, 20) and the Kālī bhakti of eighteenth-century Bengal (Chapter 1).

The rich and varied religious literature of the Purāṇas created a compelling portrayal of the theistic Hindu cosmos. Moreover, these narratives of divine characters and their supernatural doings became part of the cultural literacy of Indian audiences from this period on. Medieval poets composing epigraphic eulogies (Chapter 12) and devotional verses (Chapters 6, 7) could take this knowledge for granted and use it as a basis for literary allusion, exploration, and satire in their own verse. Temple sculptors rendered the puranic stories visible in their iconographic figures and narrative reliefs. Still today, hymns of praise recited in domestic and temple worship (Chapter 17) reiterate the mythic deeds and attributes of the Hindu deities much as they were first spelled out in the Purāṇas.

Temple Hinduism

By 700 C.E., the religious transformation first envisioned in the epics was complete. A new form of Hindu theism, focusing upon the gods Viṣṇu and Śiva as supreme deities but incorporating as well a host of other lesser gods and goddesses, now dominated the public sphere. Harṣavardhana was the last emperor to follow the Aśokan model by converting to Buddhism and supporting the Buddhist establishment with ostentatious gifts. No longer did sovereigns proclaim their performance of Vedic sacrifices as the principal way of asserting their authority to rule. Instead, they increasingly chose to articulate royal claims in a more concrete and lasting form, by constructing massive stone Hindu temples. These mountainlike structures, rising up to two hundred feet high and covered with sculptural representations of the Hindu pantheon, assumed a conspicuous and commanding presence in the Indian religious and political landscape during the early medieval period. During the half millennium from 700 to 1200 C.E., temple Hinduism dominated the public religious life of India.

The inscriptions of the seventh-century south Indian king Mahendravarman (Chapter 12) exemplify this shift in royal patronage. Although his Pallava predecessors had performed sacrifices as their primary ritual means of establishing royal legitimacy, Mahendravarman switched dramatically to temple sponsorship. He viewed his lordship over rival rulers as directly linked to Śiva's own cosmic overlordship. By constructing temples for Śiva, he brought God into his own territory and also proclaimed his authority over defeated rivals and their territories. Similarly, the succeeding rulers and dynasties of early medieval India sought to outbuild one another in conspicuous devotion to their chosen deity, Viṣṇu or Śiva.

A Hindu temple is primarily a home or residence for a god. Located in the main sanctum of the temple is an image or icon, a physical form that serves as a support within which Viṣṇu, Śiva, or some other principal deity may make himself physically present and accessible, enabling worshipers to enact a direct personal relationship with that divinity. At the same time, the temple offers through its physical structure a vision of the orderly cosmos presided over by that deity, with hierarchical ranks of subordinate deities, semi-divinities, devotees, and other auspicious entities all finding their proper places. Finally, in its layout the temple provides a map of the spiritual path a worshiper must follow toward participation with the deity ensconced in the "womb-room" at the center. The temple is thus a place of crossing, in which god descends from transcendence and devotee moves inward from the mundane.

Anyone may build a temple, but its size will naturally depend on the resources available to the patron. From small home shrines meant for private devotions to village temples, and on up in scale to the imposing edifices put up by Hindu kings with imperial aspirations, all serve basically the same purposes. Temple liturgy centers around physical and spiritual transactions between the incarnate deity and worshipers, mediated in the case of public temples by priests. These transactions are called *pūjā*. In this anthology, "How to Worship at the Abode of Śiva" (Chapter 17), a nineteenth-century pamphlet instructing pious Śaiva worshipers in proper temple conduct, provides a concise and reliable account of south Indian pūjā based on early medieval formulations.

The historical origins of pūjā are uncertain. In Vedic texts, the term refers to the respectful treatment of brahman guests. Jains and Buddhists, as we have seen, developed forms of pūjā to images and stūpas quite early. Small but recognizable images of the Hindu divinities, probably employed in simple household pūjā ceremonies, have been found dating back to the early centuries C.E. It is likely that all these forms of pūjā among the written traditions derive from earlier informal practices of image worship by autochthonous peoples outside the Indo-Aryan society. Hindu texts of the medieval period, however, see this new form of worship as the result of the god's own direct intervention and instruction, as in the puranic episode of the "Origin of Liṅga Worship" (Chapter 45). There, Śiva guides a group of renunciatory sages from their earlier Vedic-based rites to the new practice of worshiping Śiva's liṅga. Pūjā replaces sacrifice, but at the same time it incorporates select portions of the Vedic repertoire of mantras and ritual gestures, much as Śiva advises the sages to recite Vedic texts when offering pūjā.

In the context of large-scale royal temples, pūjā developed into an elaborate, rule-bound, priestly activity. New genres of liturgical guides were composed—Vaiṣṇava saṃhitās, Śaiva āgamas, and Śākta tantras—claiming to be the direct teachings of the deities concerning the metaphysical organization of the cosmos and how humans ought best to worship them. Pan-Indian Hindu theological orders, such as the Pāñcarātra and Vaikhānasa schools directed toward Viṣṇu and the Pāśupata and Śaiva Siddhānta schools dedicated to Śiva, employed these texts to maintain the temples as centers of community worship.

While priests and their texts emphasized proper ritual performance as a means of religious attainment, others began to assert that emotional enthusiasm, or bhakti, played a more crucial role in worshiping god. The term *bhakti* is usually translated as "devotion," but its meaning is more complex than our English equivalent would suggest. *Bhakti* comes from the verb root *bhaj*. In its earliest usage, *bhaj* means to divide or share, as one divides and partakes of the sacrificial offerings. *Bhaj* can also denote experiencing something, as one enjoys food or relishes music. It signifies waiting upon someone, as an attendant serves a king. It can mean to make love in a very corporeal sense and to adore in a more disembodied, spiritual manner. As its Indian adherents define it, *bhakti* partakes of all these shades of meaning. It is a way of participating or sharing in divine being, however that is understood, of tasting and enjoying a god's presence, of serving and worshiping him, of being as intimate as possible, of being attached to him above all else.

As a religious attitude or way of relating to a being one takes as superior, bhakti is widespread throughout Indian religions. One finds hymns of devotion throughout the Purāṇas and the liturgical texts of temple Hinduism, and similar genres of eulogistic poetry are common in Buddhist and Jain literature. Historians also use the term in a more restricted sense, however, to refer to a series of regional movements in medieval India that stressed intense personal devotion to god or goddess, the leadership of exemplary poet-saints, and the importance of a community of devotees. The earliest of these bhakti movements date from the seventh through ninth centuries, in the southern region of Tamilnadu, and are represented in this volume by the poetry of Māṇikkavācakar (Chapter 7). Later bhakti movements occurred in the Deccan and throughout northern India from the twelfth century through the seventeenth centuries; these will be discussed in the context of Hindu responses to Islam.

The groups of devotees to Śiva and to Viṣṇu of early medieval Tamilnadu were closely allied with the spread and growth of Hindu temples in the region. Itinerant poets traveled from village to village singing hymns of praise to their gods as they saw them in each new place of worship. Although they did not overtly criticize the temple priests or their ritualism, the bhakti poets of Tamilnadu proposed what they saw as a more satisfying and accessible means of reaching the divine. Whereas priests performed ritual invocations to bring Śiva or Viṣṇu into visible material supports, the bhakti saints used their poetry to evoke each deity in full and sensuous detail. Reiterating the god's activities, they often placed themselves as participants in those mythical scenes. They stressed the importance of establishing a close relationship with the god conceived in a personal and particularized manner. Using a trope that would become common among bhakti poets, Tamil devotees often spoke in the poetic voice of women infatuated with the alluring male deity, drawing on the conventions of secular love poetry and transforming the erotic into a religious allegory of soul and God. Women saints like Āṇṭāḻ did not require this metaphoric step. According to her hagiography, Āṇṭāḻ's single-minded love led her to reject all human suitors and unite with Viṣṇu himself, in the form of a temple image.

Yet at the same time, as Māṇikkavācakar's poetry shows, the poets recognized the paradox inherent in conceptualizing the divine this way. However anthropomorphically the poets might portray their god, Śiva and Viṣṇu remained ultimately beyond, and unknowable as well. The tensions between god's immanence and his transcendence (or, as Vaiṣṇava theologians phrased it, his simultaneous "easy accessibility" and his "otherness"), and between the devotee's mixed feelings of intimacy and alienation provide central themes that run throughout Indian devotional literature.

While temple Hinduism centered around Viṣṇu and Śiva held sway in the public sphere in early medieval India, many other religious formations were present, as well. As we have seen, Hindus never sought to develop a pan-Indian "church" structure nor did they establish a clear ecclesiastical hierarchy. Even the brahmans, seemingly the religious elite, formed a very diverse and permeable social group, with new priestly groups sometimes successfully claiming brahmanic status for themselves.

Vedic schools continued their intellectual activities even though sacrifice was no longer a significant public form of ritual. The Mīmāṃsā school developed elaborate means of interpreting the Vedic texts, and scholars of Dharmaśāstra applied these principles to the reading of dharma texts. Groups of brahmans loyal to the Vedic traditions often received special land grants called *agrahāras*, where they were able to maintain small-scale Vedic sacrificial programs free from economic need.

Other orthodox writers with a more philosophical bent developed and systematized the metaphysical monism implicit in some portions of the Upaniṣads, culminating in the ninth-century writings of Śaṅkara, a brilliant author and philosophical disputant of the Advaita Vedānta school. Śaṅkara's writings demoted temple image worship to the status of a useful but decidedly lower form of religious attainment, and reserved the highest place for intellectual realization of the oneness of Brahman. The other principal Vedānta school, the "qualified nondualist" system of Rāmānuja (c. 1050 C.E.) gave a more prominent role to devotion and engaged itself more directly in the doings of temple Hinduism. Rāmānuja even served as monastic superior in one of the largest south Indian Viṣṇu temples.

During this period, Buddhism was still strong in the areas of Kashmir and northeastern India, and such celebrated universities as Nālandā in Bihar served as international centers for Buddhist study. Communities of Jains were numerous in Gujarat and Karnataka, maintaining their own traditions of scholarship and asceticism, and not infrequently placing Jain ministers in the royal courts of those areas. We must assume the existence of many other forms of religious thought and practice during this period which, because they were esoteric or domestic or nonliterate, did not leave behind texts or other historical evidence.

The diversity of indigenous Indian religions was supplemented by religious and ethnic communities who migrated from elsewhere and settled in India, especially along the western coast. Jewish traders and Syrian Christians arrived in India at least as early as the fourth century, and from the seventh century Arab Muslim merchants set up a trading network around coastal India. Starting in the tenth century, the Parsees ("Persians"), who adhere to the ancient Iranian religion of Zoroastrianism, fled their homeland for the safer terrain of India. Each of these groups maintained itself as an autonomous, insular, and largely unthreatening religious minority within Hindu-dominated society.

In such a pluralistic setting, members of many religious persuasions articulated their differing positions and debated their views in public and at court. The stakes were sometimes high. Although some modern scholars and Hindus have portrayed the pre-Islamic period of Indian history as one of overriding religious tolerance, this was not entirely the case. The hymns of the south Indian poet-saints, for instance, included an often bitter polemic against Jains and Buddhists, and in the later biographies of these saints we hear of intentional destruction of Buddhist images and of a pogrom carried out against the eight thousand Jains of Madurai. Whatever the historicity of such later accounts, they clearly reflect an atmosphere in which religious concerns were taken as serious and consequential, not a matter of unobstructed personal choice.

Islam in India

Around 610 C.E. Muḥammad, a member of the Arab tribe ruling Mecca, began to receive revelations. By 622 his criticisms of Arab paganism and of the injustice of Meccan society had aroused considerable opposition. When residents of another city to the north invited him to come and act as arbiter, he led a few followers in an exodus to build in Medina a new society based on divine law. Muḥammad had embarked on his career as the Prophet of Islam. Revelations continued until his death in 632, and were later collected into the foundation text of Islam, the Qur'ān. These distant events held immense consequences for the history of Indian religions.

For the first 150 years of its existence, Islam was the most dynamic, expanding religious movement the world had ever seen. Imbued with a theological and ethical directive to transform the "house of unbelievers" into the "house of submission (*islam*)" through "righteous struggle" (*jihād*), the military forces of the early Muslim leaders conquered first the Arab peninsula, then the surrounding West Asian regions of Syria, Iraq, Iran, and Afghanistan, and the countries of North Africa. By the early part of the eighth century, Muslim armies had expanded into Spain and were pushing into the southern parts of France in the West; in the East they had reached as far as Sind, in present-day Pakistan. This success came at a price, though. The religious quest of Muḥammad's companions was stifled by disputes, and although the leaders of the Muslim community legitimated their regimes through Islamic law, they soon adopted the Roman Caesar and the Persian Shāh as their models of sovereignty, much to the disgust of Islamic religious scholars.

Over the next few centuries an Indian frontier was defined and gradually pushed back as Arab, Persian, and Turkish armies invaded and conquered Afghanistan, Kashmir, and the Punjab. Despite continued resistance by indigenous rulers, the more centralized and organized tactics of the invaders eventually proved successful. In the early eleventh century, Maḥmūd, the Turko-Afghan ruler of Ghazna (in Afghanistan), mounted eighteen campaigns into northern India. He conquered and incorporated the Punjab into the Ghaznavid empire and then enriched his state by sacking many of the Buddhist monasteries and Hindu temples of northern India, and transporting the loot back to Ghazna. Though he temporarily disrupted the existing Indian political and religious order, Maḥmūd did not seek to establish a permanent Islamic polity centered in the subcontinent. That was left to a successor dynasty also based in Afghanistan, the Ghūrids.

In 1193 Mu'izzuddīn Muḥammad of Ghūr and his general Qutb al-Dīn Aibak defeated the Cāhamāna ruler of Delhi, then the most powerful north Indian king, and in 1026 Qutb al-dīn declared himself Sultan of Delhi. The Delhi sultanate lasted some 320 years, under six different Turko-Afghan dynasties, and dominated much of north India. Other Islamic polities were established in the Deccan and southern India during this period. The sultanate was in turn supplanted by the Mughal empire, founded by the Central Asian adventurer Bābar in 1526. The Mughal empire held sway over much of India into the early part of the eighteenth century. Thus for roughly five hundred years of late medieval Indian history, from 1200 to 1700, rulers adhering to Islam prevailed in northern India. With these rulers came a conservative clerical elite who sought, with mixed success, to maintain Islamic social and legal order in the urban centers of India.

The face of the conqueror, however, was not the only visage of Islam in India, nor even the most common one. With Islamic rule in India, itinerant Muslim Sufi teachers came to till the fertile religious fields of India. *Sufism* is the generic term for Islamic mysticism. Already sharing features with some forms of Hinduism, Sufis found it relatively easy to acclimatize their messages and concerns to the Indian environment. Indeed, they came to regard themselves as a kind of spiritual government of India, responsible for the religious welfare of the people, parallel to but separate from the political government of the sultans. The Sufis taught an esoteric form of Islam aimed at an elite, and they were not consciously interested in attracting non-Muslim masses to Islam. They used their Indian mother tongues to compose mystical poetry, however, and their tombs became centers of a cult of saints that increasingly attracted both Muslims and non-Muslims.

In a history of Indian religions, it is necessary to recognize both sides of Islam in India. The conquests of the Turkic, Afghan, and Central Asian Muslim warriors and their continuing struggles for power both among themselves and with Hindu warrior elites like the Rajputs had significant repercussions not only for Indian political history but also for the development of Indian religions, continuing to the present. At the same time, the more conciliatory and assimilative activities of the Sufis played a greater role in implanting Islam as an indigenous Indian religious formation in South Asia. In this anthology most of the readings emphasize the role of Sufism in Indian Islam.

Orthodox Islam and Political Authority

Al-Bīrūnī, one of the great medieval Muslim scholars, accompanied Maḥmūd on his military forays into India in the early eleventh century, and wrote of the Indians he encountered there: "They differ from us in everything which other nations have in common. In all manners and usages they differ from us to such a degree as to frighten their children with us, our dress, and our ways and customs, and to declare us to be the devil's breed, and our doings as the very opposite of all that is good and proper." The response he observed was perhaps not surprising, considering that the Ghaznavids were plundering their way across northern India at the time. Yet al-Bīrūnī points to very real differences between the various ruling Islamic groups of late medieval India and the predominantly Hindu society they ruled.

The book of Allah's revelations to Muḥammad, the Qur'ān, specifies five basic constituents or "pillars" of the Islamic faith: the profession of faith, regular prayer, giving of alms, fasting during the month of Ramadān, and pilgrimage.

Islam is based on a simple, shared creed, in which the Muslim believer acknowledges his or her submission to a single supreme God and recognizes Muḥammad as the Prophet. Orthodox Islam is rigorously monotheistic. Allah's transcendence excludes all other claims to divinity. Medieval Hinduism, by contrast, was hierarchically pluralistic in its theological outlook, admitting a host of immanent divinities and semi-divinities who participate in every sphere of the cosmos. A Hindu might well regard one of these deities as the highest "God of gods," but this did not prevent recognition of many other divinities appropriate for other persons or purposes. To the orthodox Muslim, this divine multiplicity of the Hindus appeared as a clear case of polytheism, which would diminish the adoration due to Allah alone.

The Allah of the orthodox is all-powerful and transcendent. While acting as the creator of all things, Allah never takes on physical form in the world. Hindu deities like Viṣṇu and Śiva, we have seen, do intervene directly in the world, often in human or even animal bodies. They also enter into the physical forms of icons and images, and this makes possible the institution of temples and their liturgies of worship. For orthodox Muslims, the Qur'ān and other authoritative traditions contain strong prohibitions against any adoration of physical idols.

Relations between the Muslim faithful and Allah are best expressed in prayer, a nonreciprocal and nonmaterial communication from believer to God. All believers should pray five times daily while facing Mecca, the geographical center of the Islamic community. Early in its history, the Muslim community institutionalized public prayer as a regular collective act, and the mosque grew to accommodate this activity. The Islamic mosque provides a large, mostly open area for congregational prayer, an egalitarian space enclosed by a surrounding wall to separate believers from nonbelievers. Though there can be no central image or icon representing Allah, the mosque does provide a spatial focus in the form of a wall indicating the direction toward Mecca.

The fifth pillar, pilgrimage, indicates another important aspect of Islam. At least once in a lifetime, the Muslim believer ought to make a pilgrimage to Mecca. From its earliest decades Islam was a universalistic and international religion, spread out geographically from Spain through northern Africa, across the Middle East, and into southern Asia. In different regions Islam naturally took on various regional characters, but it always maintained the ideal of a single unified community of believers. The institution of pilgrimage brought about an annual assembly of Muslims from all over the Islamic world, and thereby strengthened this unity. Islam in India had a dual identity. While grounded in the distinctive social and cultural realities of India, it was also part of the wider world of international Islam.

As Islamic warrior elites from Turkey and Central Asia established their authority in new parts of India there was inevitably conflict. At the frontiers of contested control, the conquerors sometimes symbolized their victories through a physical metaphor: the destruction of Hindu temples (as well as Jain and Buddhist sites, equally "polytheistic"), often followed by the construction of mosques on the leveled sites (Chapter 44). Hindu chieftains, in response, might reconsecrate these same religious sites as a way of claiming independence from Delhi's political overlordship. In this way temples sometimes became indices of political control.

Within areas of settled rule, however, Muslim authorities adopted a more lenient attitude toward their Hindu subjects. Early in Islamic history, Muslims had formulated an intermediate category for those who could not be classified as either "believers" or "heathens." Christians and Jews, sharing the Abrahamic lineage with Muslims, were labeled "people of the book," and treated as tolerated religious communities within the Islamic state. The Hindus of India were idolaters and polytheists, admittedly, but brahmans could be regarded as the equivalent of Christian monks, and so could be left largely to their own religious customs. Hindu subjects might even construct temples, so long as these structures did not pose a threat to the dominating Muslim institutions. Indeed, Turkish and Mughal rulers even gave endowments of land and granted tax exemptions for certain Hindu, Jain, and Zoroastrian religious foundations. Reciprocally, Hindu rulers sometimes facilitated the construction of mosques for the benefit of their Muslim subjects.

Sufism

Sufism stresses the personal relationship between believer and Allah. The word *Sufi* (Arabic *ṣūfī*) derives from the Arabic for wool, alluding to the coarse woolen garments favored by early Muslim mystics. As with Ajita of the Hair-Blanket and countless other Indian ascetics, early Sufis chose to represent their austerity and renunciation of worldly concerns through a conspicuous rejection of comfortable clothing.

Despite its mystical and renunciatory tendencies, Sufism should not be seen as outside the mainstream of Islam. Sufis ground their teachings firmly in Muḥammad's revelation, but they draw on different portions of the Qur'ān than do more conservative exegetes. Whereas conservative Muslims focus on passages emphasizing Allah's almighty, awesome, and ineffable character, Sufi interpreters stress the sections that speak of Allah's pervasive presence in the world and in the hearts of his believers. Significantly, Sufis speak of a "jihād of the heart" as a more important religious struggle than the "jihād of the sword." In the medieval Islamic world, far from being a peripheral movement, Sufism engendered some of the most powerful and influential theological writings, such as that of Ibn al-ʻArabī, and the most moving and popular Muslim poetry, as that of the thirteenth-century Jalāl al-Dīn Rumi. To a considerable extent Islam in medieval India took on a Sufi coloring.

Sufis arrived in India early. They were already in the Punjab during the Ghaznavid period. Once the Delhi sultanate was established, Sufis of the Chishti and Suhrawardi orders began to settle throughout northern India. Two other formal Sufi orders, the Naqshbandi and Qādiri, arrived during the Mughal period and became influential within the Mughal court. At court and in the urban centers, Sufis vied with the more orthodox Islamic scholars for status and influence, and needed to maintain a degree of respectability themselves. Even so they occasionally suffered persecution for their hubris, as when the Mughal ruler Jahāngīr imprisoned Sirhindi (Chapter 34). Others held aloof as much as possible from the court and its secular ways. Certain Sufis became more involved with local culture, and adopted the local language and customs. In some cases they took on the deliberately unconventional character of the qalandar, the activist ascetic dropout who flouted the authority of respectable Muslim society.

The most basic relationship among Sufis is that of master and disciple. The master, known as a *shaykh* or *pīr*, is first and foremost a teacher, instructing his or her followers in proper ethical and spiritual conduct. As in the folk imagery of Sulṭān Bāhū's laudatory poem (Chapter 36), the master is a "washerman" for the heart, endeavoring to "shine up those begrimed with dirt, leaving them spotless." Disciples often recorded the teachings of masters as a way of perpetuating and disseminating their cleansing wisdom. "Conversations of the Sufi Saints" (Chapter 35) provides examples of this popular genre of Sufi literature.

Notable masters came sometimes to be regarded as "saints," figures possessing extraordinary capacities who could act as virtual intercessors with God on behalf of their followers. The hagiographies of these saints (such as those in Chapter 34) depict them performing a variety of miracles such as levitation, mind reading, and physical transformations. As in Indian religious discourse generally, miracles serve in these stories as visible confirmations of inner states of attainment and as criteria for determining religious powers. Tombs of Sufi saints often became pilgrimage centers, much as the stūpas and miracle sites of the Buddha had earlier. They perpetuated the charisma of the saint enshrined there and served as centers for the transmission of Sufi teachings and practices.

The saints were all subordinate to the Prophet Muḥammad. Concomitant with the rise of Sufi orders in the medieval Islamic world was an increasing veneration of the Prophet and his family expressed through ritual and song. A few puritan critics, forerunners of modern fundamentalists, objected to this reverence as idolatry, but most of the Islamic community came to see Muḥammad as a figure of loving devotion and miraculous powers. In domestic ceremonies honoring Muḥammad's birth (Chapter 22), Muslim women speak of the miracles surrounding his birth and childhood, and request his intercession in solving their everyday difficulties. In the various genres of devotional verse addressed to him (Chapter 8), Muḥammad appears as a guide, benefactor, miracle worker, and a lover, the supremely desirable bridegroom. Adapting a convention common to Hindu bhakti poetry, and employed also in Jain and Sikh poetry of the period, Indo-Muslim poets represented themselves as young women tormented by separation from their beloved, in this case the Prophet. Such mutual borrowings and recyclings of poetic themes were common in the close encounters between Sufism and Hindu devotionalism in medieval India.

Religious practice within Sufi circles centered around "recollection" (*dhikr*) and "listening" (*sama*ʿ). The Qurʾān instructs Muslims to remember Allah frequently, and Sufis developed various techniques to evoke and intensify the recollection. Most commonly, the practitioner would rhythmically chant the one hundred names of God, and often enhance the chanting through bodily postures and breath control. Much like indigenous Indian forms of yoga, these disciplines are meant to bring the body, senses, and mind under control so they would not obstruct union with the divine. Though willing to borrow useful techniques from yogic traditions, Indian Sufis were certainly not uncritical advocates or borrowers of all Hindu practices, as Chirāgh-i Dihlī shows in his vivid denunciation of image worship, reiterating a core Islamic tenet (Chapter 34).

Sufi poetry such as that of the two Punjabi poets Sulṭān Bāhū and Bulleh Shāh (Chapter 36) grows out of the musical assembly. Emphasizing their rural origins, these poets employ the vernacular language in preference to religious Arabic or courtly Persian, and draw their images from the everyday world of village Punjab. Reiterating common Sufi themes, they advocate love of Allah as the supreme virtue, and they often figure themselves as brides entreating their bridegroom Allah. From the austere and utterly transcendent God of the conservatives, these poets render him personal and accessible. They stress the importance of inner purity and criticize religious formalism, particularly ritual and intellectual approaches to the divine, in favor of an intuitive, personal approach. Again one sees here striking parallels with existing Indian traditions, in this case with the thematic repertoire of medieval Hindu bhakti poetry.

Sufism unquestionably germinated within the earliest phases of Arab Islam and flourished throughout the medieval Islamic world, but it was uniquely suited to the Indian religious setting. From the monist cosmological formulations of Ibn al-ʿArabī to the personalizing of Allah in Sufi poetry, from the familiar renunciatory appearance of Sufi masters to their use of yogalike meditative techniques, this form of mystical Islam could seem both familiar and yet new to India. Adapting to their surroundings, Sufi teachers were able to bring the message of Islam to an Indian audience that the more conservative scholars of the urban centers could never reach. In this sense, the Sufis of late medieval South Asia deserve the greatest credit in making Islam a truly indigenous Indian religion.

Although Islam did originate historically as an extraneous religious formation, it is important to bear in mind the counterargument offered in "India as a Sacred Islamic Land" (Chapter 39). Whether migrating from other parts of the Islamic world or adapting Islam through conversion, most Indian Muslims did not regard themselves as foreigners in India. Rather, from the very start they sought to integrate their homeland, India, into the larger sacred topography of the world of Islam. Indeed, in the view of Āzād, the first man—Adam—descended to earth in South Asia, and so South Asia figures as the site of the first revelation and the first mosque. For Indian Muslims no less than Hindus, Jains, or Buddhists, India is a religious terrain, a place where the divine, in whatever form, can indeed manifest itself to all.

Hinduism under Islam

Prior to the thirteenth century, as we have seen, temple Hinduism had offered a pan-Indian theory and legitimation of political authority, with royal claimants articulating their sovereignty through personal and ceremonial devotion to the Hindu deities Viṣṇu and Śiva. Subsequently, however, the most powerful rulers in Delhi and many other parts of South Asia grounded their dominion in a very different theo-political system. Hindu ruling elites were largely confined to southern India and peripheral regions. Not only was the political sphere transformed by this shift in rulership, but the growing presence in the subcontinent of new religious teachers with competing and often compelling messages, most notably the Sufis, also posed a serious challenge to the authority of existing forms of Hindu thought and practice.

Hindus responded to the presence and political sway of Islam in late medieval India in complex, diverse, and creative ways. As in any period of social change, there were many in medieval India who sought mainly to defend and hold on to what they had. Hindu warrior elites might signal their independence from Islamic overlordship by reconstructing or reconsecrating a desecrated temple. In the religious sphere this attitude manifested itself in efforts to collect, maintain, and reassert already existing aspects of Hindu traditions. By collecting and commenting on the older textual genres such as the Vedas and Dharmaśāstras, brahman scholars made a conscious attempt to recreate past formations in altered conditions. The scholarly work of orthodox brahmans at this time, aimed at conserving and reasserting what they saw as traditional Hindu values, also had a large and generally unrecognized effect. They were the first to assemble what later scholars of the nineteenth and twentieth centuries would reassemble as a Hindu canon of sacred books.

However, the eclipse of temple Hinduism as the prevailing ideological formation in northern India also set new and innovative directions in the development of Indian religions. What is most apparent in late medieval Hinduism is the vitality of forms of religion that are devotional, esoteric, or syncretic, and a corresponding deemphasis on the role of religion in constituting the political and social order.

Devotional Movements

Hindus sometimes personify bhakti as a beautiful woman, born in southern India, who grew to maturity in the Deccan. In twelfth-century Karnataka, a group of devotees called the Vīraśaivas coalesced around the Kalacuri minister Basavaṇṇa, and from the late thirteenth through seventeenth centuries, the Maharashtrian pilgrimage center Paṇḍarpur was the center of Marathi devotionalism toward the god Viṭhobā, a form of Kṛṣṇa. Tukārām, whose songs are translated in this volume (Chapter 3), was the last of the great Marathi poet-saints. Finally, according to the metaphor, the woman reached her finest flourishing in the north. Bhakti movements appeared in northern India by the fourteenth century, and from then on were a major force in north Indian Hindu life, from Kashmir and Gujarat to Bengal.

It is somewhat misleading, however, to speak of a single organic bhakti movement. Different groups used the various regional languages in their poetry, directed themselves toward different deities, and assumed distinct theological standpoints. Some poet-saints were profoundly inward and mystical in their lives and song, while others adopted a more outward, socially critical orientation to the world around them. Some north Indian poets and bhakti groups appeared oblivious to the presence of Islam, but for others this was a cardinal reality. Yet virtually all considered emotional "participation" with God as a core value. Whether devotees direct themselves toward Śiva, Kṛṣṇa, Rāma, or the goddess Kālī, they seek always to develop a personal relationship with that divine figure. For bhakti theologians mokṣa consists more in attaining or reattaining closeness to God than in gaining liberation.

The deities of medieval bhakti bring with them the mythical narratives of theistic Hinduism that had previously been set forth in the epics and Purāṇas. The Kṛṣṇa of the sixteenth-century Gauḍīya Vaiṣṇavas (Chapter 40), for instance, is the same Kṛṣṇa whose story is told in the *Harivaṃśa* and *Bhāgavata Purāṇa*. But most bhakti poets shift the cosmic scope of the Purāṇas and temple Hinduism to the background. There is less concern with God as creator and ruler of the cosmos, and more with God as humanly alive and embodied on earth. So with Kṛṣṇa, devotional poets and theologians tend to play down his earlier identity as an incarnation of Viṣṇu and instead focus on the pastoral life of his youth among the cowherds of Vraja. At the same time, they emphasize the inward presence of God in the heart and his loving regard for the faithful. Even when they do acknowledge the deity's role in creating and sustaining the world, devotionalists often portray God as playful, inscrutable, and sometimes downright devious in his or her activities. How else could one explain the bad state of things?

Not all devotionalists, however, comprehend God as an anthropomorphic form. Although most, like the Gauḍīyas, orient themselves to a God "with attributes" (*saguṇa*) like the eminently embodied Kṛṣṇa, others like Kabīr prefer to conceptualize God "without attributes" (*nirguṇa*). For the nirguṇa poets, any attempt to characterize or comprehend God is doomed ultimately to fail, and all the mythical and ritual ways we humans seek to relate to God are distractions or delusions.

According to the sixteenth-century devotional theologian Rūpa Gosvāmī, it is possible to enjoy various relationships with God. Rūpa specified five predominant ones, largely based on analogies with human relationships. One may relate to God as an insignificant human relates to the supreme deity, as a respectful servant relates to his lord and master, as a mother relates to her child, as a friend relates to his friend, or as a lover relates to her beloved. Devotional groups explore all these modes of relationship, and particularly the latter three, through their poetic and ritual practices. In the south Indian devotional genre of piḷḷaittamiḻ (Chapter 10), for example, poets address their chosen deities in the form of a child, employing a domestic idiom and redirecting parental love toward religious figures. Gauḍīya Vaiṣṇavas envision themselves as cowherd friends of Kṛṣṇa to participate in his divine sports (Chapter 13). Of all forms of association, Rūpa claims, the erotic is the highest, and much bhakti poetry explores the passionate love between the cowherd women of Vraja, who represent all human souls, and the enchanting young Kṛṣṇa. Arguing against other more conventional Hindu ways of conceptualizing one's relationship with God, Rūpa values emotional intensity over the meditative stasis of the yogis or the intellectual comprehension of the Advaitins as the highest goal.

The bhakti movements engendered various forms of devotional yoga, techniques for evoking and focusing the devotee's participation with God (Chapters 23, 30, 40). According to the Gauḍīya followers of Caitanya, the simplest technique, and therefore the one most suitable for the present age of decline, consists in repetitive chanting of God's name. Since Kṛṣṇa's name is more than just an arbitrary signifier—it is itself a portion of his reality—chanting his name as a mantra makes Kṛṣṇa himself actually present. The Gauḍīyas institutionalized chanting combined with ecstatic dancing as a collective practice, similar to the musical sessions of the Sufis. The tale of Haridāsa (Chapter 40) illustrates how these public displays of congregational revelry could provoke suspicion and suppression by civil authorities. At the same time, Haridāsa's miraculous fortitude in the face of adversity provides a metaphor for the resistant powers of inner bhakti against outward social pressure.

The practice most characteristic of medieval bhakti, though, was song and poetry. In contrast to Indian courtly traditions of poetic composition, poet-saints of north India sang in vernacular languages and drew their imagery from everyday life. They adopted highly personal poetic voices to speak of the tribulations and joys of the devotional life. The poetry of medieval bhakti in Hindi, Bengali, Marathi, and other vernacular languages of India is quite likely the richest library of devotion in world literature, distinguished not only by its religious intensity but also by the great variety of psychological states and emotional responses it explores. These medieval songs of devotion remain very much alive in contemporary India. Few of us indeed can recite as much of any author as the average Hindi speaker can reel off from Kabīr, Sūrdās, or Mīrābāī.

For devotionalists, the poetic invocation of God often supplanted ritual invocation and physical images. Although the earliest devotional movements in south India treated temples as an important locus of religiosity, some later bhakti groups dispensed with the temple as superfluous or criticized it as a place of purely formal religious observances, where priests and the dull-witted could go through the motions of worship. Bhakti poet-saints often broadened this skeptical attitude toward temple ritualism into a critique of all aspects of what they considered conventional or orthodox Hindu practice: Vedic recitation, pilgrimage, and the social hierarchy of the caste system.

The critical perspective of medieval bhakti reached its apogee in the writings of Kabīr. Raised in a poor community of Muslim weavers, Kabīr was initiated into bhakti by a Vaiṣṇava guru, and later attracted a following among both Muslims and Hindus. Throughout his poetic utterances he drew from the many religious traditions around him—Sufis, devotionalists, tantrics, Buddhists, and others. Yet, as in his poem "Simple State," Kabīr was quite happy to dish out equal scorn for the orthodoxies of Islam and Hinduism, urging instead a spiritual path of merging with an indescribable Absolute outside, or perhaps equally within, those verbose schools of thought. The historical irony is that both Hindus and Muslims later claimed this irascible skeptic and mocker of formal religions, and his verse was also incorporated into the canon of a third religion, the *Ādi Granth* of the Sikhs (Chapter 2).

Tantra

Like devotionalism, the developments we now classify as tantra originated when temple Hinduism still dominated the public sphere. It developed from older and largely unrecorded practices of yoga, medicine, folk magic, and local goddess cults. From about the seventh century, Hindu and Buddhist tantra texts begin to appear, as do descriptions, often satirical, of recognizable tantric adepts. Beginning around the time of Maḥmūd's raids into north India, Hindu tantric groups and literature began to proliferate throughout the subcontinent. Reaching its greatest influence during the period of Islamic dominance, tantra continues in varied forms in present-day India, albeit much diminished, and has made itself known and notorious in the West through such international gurus as Bhagwan Shree Rajneesh.

The word *tantra* does not admit to a single unequivocal definition. Drawn from the vocabulary of weaving, where it may refer to the threads, the warp, or the entire loom, the term *tantra* was extended to signify texts as things spun out and threaded together, both physically (since palm-leaf manuscripts require strings) and verbally. Later the word came to refer especially to one genre of texts directed to the Goddess, the Śākta tantras, and to the adherents of its teachings.

Historians of Indian religions use the word *tantra* primarily in two ways. In a broad sense they employ *tantra* to identify a whole series of ritual and yogic practices not found in the Vedic lineage of texts, such as visualization, geometrical designs, impositions of mantra powers, and Kuṇḍalinī yoga. The word *tantra* in this sense refers more to a shared repertoire of techniques than to any religious system. Many religious groups in medieval India made use of these techniques, and so there were Buddhist tantra, Jain tantra, and many "tantric elements" incorporated in the rituals of the temple Hindu schools. In a more restricted sense, tantra is taken as a system of thought and practice, based on a few shared premises and orientations. In this anthology, we use tantra primarily in this narrower definition.

Hindu tantric groups most often recognize the female goddess Śakti ("energy"), Śiva's consort, as the fundamental creative energy of the cosmos, and therefore as the Absolute. Tantrics view the human body as a microcosm of the universe, and focus on it as the only vehicle for attaining powers and liberation. Through yogic practices and ritual activities the tantric adept seeks to inculcate knowledge physically. Rather than seeking a disembodied escape from bondage or a devotional relationship with divinity, tantrics set as their highest goal the transformation of the body itself into divinity.

Tantra is often promulgated away from society, within small circles of initiates clustered around preceptors. Tantric groups often compose their texts in "intentional" or "upside-down" language, making them deliberately unintelligible to those outside the initiated group. Some tantrics intentionally transgress social proprieties and consume forbidden meat and wine, in order to escape what they consider conventional reality and proceed directly to the ultimate. Though practiced by only a few tantric circles, this antinomian tendency, combined with the esoteric and ritualistic orientation of tantra, led to its widespread condemnation as a degenerate form of Hinduism by many Western scholars and by punctilious Indians, as well.

One of the most distinctive characteristics of tantra is the role played by the Goddess. Worship of goddesses is undoubtedly very ancient in South Asia. The *Devīmāhātmya* proclaimed a single pan-Indian Goddess as the Absolute. Medieval Śaiva theologians often bifurcated the godhead into male and female. They postulated an inactive but transcendent male Śiva who carries out all his worldly activities through an immanent energetic female Śakti. From this cosmic division of labor, tantra took the next logical step: if Śakti is doing everything anyway, why not focus upon her as the real force of the universe? Tantra thereby subverted Śiva's superior role and located Śakti—identified as Pārvatī, Durgā, Kālī, and all female divinities—at the top of the divine hierarchy, indeed as the animating energy of all.

As in bhakti, tantric groups paid close attention to the erotic, but they viewed it from a different perspective. Devotional poet-saints most often directed themselves toward male divinities, figured themselves as female lovers, and used human romance and sexuality as metaphor for the complex personal relationship between soul and God. According to tantric cosmology, the world itself comes into being through the primordial, recurrent coupling of Śiva and Śakti. Since the human body in tantra is a concentrated microcosm, an embodiment of the cosmos, it makes sense to view sexual union as a way of reenacting creation, bringing the practitioner in harmony with the forces of the cosmos. Detached from the romantic narratives of bhakti and given an impersonal cosmic significance, ritualized sexual union enabled the tantric adept to transcend all dualities. Ultimately, most devotionalists did not wish to overcome duality. For them, Rāmprasād Sen's observation rang true: "I like the taste of sugar, but I have no desire to become sugar."

Tantra, like bhakti, sometimes took a skeptical view of the social categories of merit and demerit, right and wrong, promulgated by the orthodox. Followers of bhakti might be led by their passionate attachment to God to transgress normal social boundaries, much as the cowherd women of Vraja willingly left their husbands and children to rendezvous with Kṛṣṇa in the forest. Some tantric groups prescribed a more deliberate, ritualized overturning of conventional mores. For the Kaula school, five normally forbidden offerings—the famous "Five Ms" of liquor, meat, fish, parched grain, and sexual intercourse—were regularly consumed or enjoyed as part of pūjā. Here too transgression acknowledged the superior claims of religious attainment over the everyday rules of social conduct.

But by no means did all tantra groups accept this antinomian attitude. The eleventh-century tantric alchemical treatise *Rasārnava*, for instance, strongly criticized the Five-M mode of tantra (Chapter 15). As in every other religious formation we have looked at, there was always internal debate among tantric proponents over the ultimate ends and the best means to reach it.

Guru Nānak and Sikhism

When conservative proponents of two seemingly irreconcilable religious systems were struggling to gain ideological supremacy, one religious option was to declare both equally wrong. Alternatively, one could consciously adopt whatever seemed most worthwhile from both traditions. In medieval India this unitarian strategy sought a domain of spiritual peace outside the pervasive disagreement between orthodox Muslims and orthodox Hindus. The most influential of medieval Indian syncretists, Guru Nānak (1469–1539) ended up founding a new religion, Sikhism.

Born in a Hindu merchant family in the predominantly Muslim Punjab, Nānak worked as an accountant until, at age twenty-nine, he had a transformative experience. He fell into a bathing pool and disappeared from sight. Unable to find him, friends and family finally gave him up for dead. When Nānak returned to society three days later, his first utterance was, "There is no Hindu; there is no Muslim." He spent the remainder of his life traveling, teaching, singing, and gathering a band of followers. The name "Sikh" is derived from the Sanskrit word for pupil, *śiṣya*, indicating the relationship first adopted by Nānak's followers toward their guru.

In his teachings and songs, Nānak gently but firmly repudiated the external practices of the religions he saw around him—the oblations, sacrifices, ritual baths, image worshiping, austerities, and scriptures of Hindus and Muslims. For Nānak, the all-pervasive and incomprehensible God must be sought within oneself. The nirguṇa Absolute has no gender, no form, no immanent incarnations or manifestations. Despite God's infinitude and formlessness, Nānak proposed a very simple means of connecting with the divine. One must remember and repeat the divine Name. Nānak rigorously refused to specify what that Name was, though he sometimes called it "Creator of the Truth," equating truth with godliness.

During his own lifetime Nānak began to organize his followers into a community of the faithful. He set up informal procedures for congregational worship centering around collective recitation. Most important, he chose one of his disciples, Aṅgad, to follow him as preceptor and leader of the group, its guru. By choosing a single successor, Nānak established a precedent of group leadership that would last through ten gurus and nearly two hundred years. Nānak's followers collected anecdotes of his life that illustrated his central teachings and located his songs within biographical events, whether factual or imagined. Hagiography became an important genre of early Sikh literature, as it was among Sufis and devotionalists (Chapter 30).

Nānak most often identified himself as a Hindu by virtue of birth, but as his followers consolidated their own practices they gradually distinguished themselves from both Hindu and Muslim communities. The fifth guru, Arjan, collected the writings of the first five leaders and other like-minded poet-saints into the *Ādi Granth*, the foundation text of the Sikh religion (Chapter 5). In Sikh ceremonial this book came to occupy the central place on the altar, where Hindus would place an image. Guru Arjan rebuilt the temple at Amritsar and set himself up as lord of the Sikhs. With the Sikh community now a formidable social group, its Gurus began to play a more active role in north Indian political conflicts. They took sides in Mughal dynastic disputes and sometimes suffered the consequences of backing the losing side.

In the late seventeenth century, the time of the tenth and last guru, Gobind Singh, many Sikhs identified themselves still more visibly and decisively as a separate religious community. A determined opponent of Mughal rule, Gobind Singh instituted the Khālsā fellowship (the "army of the pure"), a group of Sikh initiates who accepted a code of conduct that included five insignia: uncut hair, a dagger or sword, a pair of military shorts, a comb, and a steel bangle (Chapter 18). Gobind Singh required initiates to renounce all previous religious affiliations and to repudiate all gods, goddesses, and prophets other than the one Name recognized by the Sikhs.

Under Gobind Singh, the Sikh community solidified both its socio-religious identity and its military strength. By the beginning of the nineteenth century a Sikh kingdom led by Ranjīt Singh posed the last major independent opposition to British rule in South Asia. Though finally defeated in the late 1840s, Ranjīt Singh's kingdom left a memory of a separate Sikh state, a Khalistan or "land of the pure," that would be evoked at the time of Partition, when the departing British divided India along religious lines into Muslim Pakistan and Hindu India, and again in the 1980s. Though they form a relatively small religious community of around 13 million in India, roughly 2 percent of the population, the Sikhs today constitute the most visible and in many ways one of the most prosperous communities in South Asia. Large numbers of Sikhs have emigrated to the U.K., Canada, and other parts of the Commonwealth.

The British Period

From 1757 on, British traders with the East India Company gradually increased their role in South Asia until, by the time British armies defeated the Punjabi kingdom of Ranjīt Singh in 1849, they ruled most of India. And so, from the late eighteenth century until 1947, Indians were dominated by a foreign power whose seat of authority was halfway around the world in London. These foreigners brought with them not only a new language and philosophy of rule and a different set of religious beliefs but also a worldview grounded in the secular, modernizing ideology of the Enlightenment. The encounter of existing religious formations of India with new forms of Christianity and with post-Enlightenment modes of knowledge within this colonial milieu ushered in another period of challenge, debate, and dynamism within South Asian religions.

Christianity was not completely new to the subcontinent. Syriac Christian trading communities had inhabited the Malabar coast of southern India from as early as the fourth century, and continued as autonomous groups of high status integrated within the largely Hindu society around them. The Portuguese, who established themselves on the western coast in the sixteenth century, carried out Christian missionary work with rather mixed results. Some lower-class communities realized the advantages that could result from forming religious bonds with a colonizing power and converted en masse, gradually developing their own indigenized forms of Christianity. The Portuguese were unable, however, to make much headway with the large majority of Indians they proselytized. Unlike Islamic Sufism, the Catholicism of the Counter-Reformation did not seem particularly compatible with the Indian religious environment.

British administrators took a decidedly ambivalent attitude toward missionary activity in their colonial territories, fearing it might "stir up the natives," whom they wished mainly to pacify. Under pressure from evangelicals in England, though, they eventually allowed Protestant missionaries to pursue their work on a limited scale. The missions did not achieve the conversions of great masses that they hoped for, but their incisive and often hyperbolic critiques of indigenous religion in India did have the important effect of inspiring some spirited defenses from the indigens. The Tamil Śaivite Āṟumuga Nāvalar, for instance, studied and worked for many years in a Methodist school before setting out on a personal mission to refortify the Śaiva Siddhānta religion and defend it against Christian attacks. Religious apologetics, defending one's own religion against outside attack, often has the effect of altering precisely that which one seeks to defend, giving it a definition or fixity it did not have previously, and this occurred repeatedly among Indian religions during the colonial encounter.

More challenging to the self-esteem of educated Indians were the Western scholars who for the first time began to study the religions of India as historical entities. The Western concern with delineating the various religions of the world was given tremendous impetus in India through the inspiration and organizational work of William Jones, an exemplary man of the Enlightenment. Jones was the first to publicize the linguistic connection of Sanskrit with classical Greek and Latin, enabling scholars to reconstruct the Indo-European family of languages and laying the basis for the field of historical philology, an important intellectual discipline of the nineteenth century. In Calcutta, where he served as a judge, Jones organized a small group of British civil servants who had become enamored with India's classical literature into the Asiatick Society, the first scholarly organization devoted to comprehending the religions, history, and literatures of India from a Western perspective. These officials were responsible for the earliest attempts to translate what they considered to be the most important Indian texts—all ancient and Sanskrit—into English, making them available to the West and engendering a kind of "Oriental Renaissance" among educated Europeans in the late eighteenth and early nineteenth centuries.

These classical Indiaphiles, also called "Orientalists," felt less affectionate toward the present-day Indians among whom they were living. They judged contemporary Indian religions to be debased from their lofty origins in the classical past. The Orientalists' high valuation of classical antiquity, coupled with a condescending dismissal of modern India, led to a long-standing prejudice in the Western study of India, whereby the oldest, elite Sanskrit works were valued above all others.

An alternative position, still less sympathetic to the Indians, soon took shape in England and was then exported to India. Inspired by Jeremy Bentham's utilitarian philosophy, James Mill, an official with the East India Company based in London, wrote his *History of British India* in the 1820s without needing to set foot in India. Mill's *History*, an immense and thorough indictment of the Indian peoples, tried to justify the need for British rule among a population supposedly unable to govern itself. Mill especially condemned Hinduism, blaming it for much of what was wrong with India. Hinduism is ritualistic, superstitious, irrational, and priest-ridden, Mill charged, at each step implicitly contrasting it with the deist version of Christianity that he believed to be the highest form of religion. For several decades the East India Company provided a copy of Mill's tome to new Company officials embarking for India, to sustain them in their sense of racial and cultural superiority while in the colony.

The attitudes the British held toward India had far-reaching effects on the Indians who came in contact with them. While some were satisfied to reiterate what they saw as the traditional, time-tested, and therefore superior forms of Indian religiosity, other Indians, more deeply affected by Western forms of knowledge and British criticisms of Hinduism, became highly circumspect and self-critical. From this spirit of cultural self-reproach came the widespread religious reformism of colonial India.

The prototype of the Hindu reformer was Rammohan Roy (1774–1833), a Bengali brahman who received a wide education in Persian and Arabic (languages of the Indo-Muslim court culture), Sanskrit (language of his own religious background), and then English (the emerging language of commerce and administration in colonial India). Taking advantage of new moneymaking opportunities as the British expanded their operations, Roy was able to retire young as a wealthy landlord to pursue his intellectual and religious interests. Roy valued British "progress" and Western modernity, and believed there was an urgent need to modernize Hinduism, which he had come to see as a stagnant tradition. To do this, he urged a reappraisal and selective redefinition of Hinduism. Of course, Indian religious thinkers had been doing exactly this for centuries, but never before with such a historicist self-awareness. In many cases Roy accepted British and Christian judgments as valid. He agreed, for example, that Hindu "polytheism" and "idolatry" were primitive and debased, and he joined in British efforts to outlaw and suppress satī, the practice of widow self-immolation (see Chapter 14). Concurring with the Orientalists' notion that current Hinduism had degenerated from a more glorious past, Roy recommended that Hindus return to earlier, purer beliefs and practices, and he sought to advance the ancient Upaniṣads with their idealism and monotheism as the foundation texts for a new Hinduism. In 1828 he founded the Brāhmo Samāj, a voluntary religious organization, to help put his ideas into effect.

Rammohan Roy was the first but not the only religious reformer of colonial India. Reform movements arose in every region of South Asia under British control, and while each reflected its own local culture and religious tradition, all shared the fundamentalist attitude of the Brāhmo Samāj in criticizing contemporary forms of religiosity and in seeking to return to some presumed state of purity located in the past. The Ārya Samāj, founded in 1875 by Svāmī Dayānanda Sarasvatī in western India, likewise advocated returning to the Vedic texts (Chapter 31). From the standpoint of the Vedas, Dayānanda argued, one should oppose not only religious corruption but also what he saw as the evils of contemporary Indian society, such as caste, untouchability, and the subjugation of women. Many Hindu reform movements saw their task as reforming both Hinduism and Indian society.

Among the Sikhs, the Nirankāri movement called for a rejection of existing Sikh practices and a return to the "formless" worship of the founder, Guru Nānak. The Śvetāmbara Jains had their own reform movement led by the mendicant Vijay Ānandsūri (Chapter 42), and even the Syriac Christians experienced millenarian revivalist movements during the nineteenth century.

The Muslim-controlled areas of northern India were the last to come under direct British control, and the Muslim elite, nostalgic for the lost glories of Mughal imperium, initially resisted British learning and remained aloof from British administration. Nevertheless, by the late nineteenth century colonial reformism took shape among Indian Muslims as well. Syed Ahmed Khan set out to purge contemporary Indian Islam of what he considered its extraneous and unnecessary practices and to return to a pure Islam, while at the same time he attempted to harmonize Islamic ideology with modern science. In the early twentieth century, Mohamed Ali envisioned the reestablishment of a pan-Islamic polity centered in Ottoman Turkey. By this time religious reformism had begun to take on a more overt anti-colonial dimension among Muslim and Hindu elites as well, and Ali's call for a Turkish Khilafat was simultaneously an appeal for ending British rule.

Perhaps the most renowned nineteenth-century Hindu reformer was Svāmī Vivekānanda. He was a young member of the Brāhmo Samāj when he first met Rāmakṛṣṇa, a charismatic ascetic and devotee of the goddess Kālī. Eventually Vivekānanda became Rāmakṛṣṇa's disciple, and sought to integrate within a single religious outlook the experiential devotionalism of Rāmakṛṣṇa, the social agenda of the Brāhmo Samāj, and the nondualist philosophy of Śaṅkara and the Advaita Vedānta. As a spokesman for Hinduism in 1893 at the World's Parliament of Religions in Chicago, he created a sensation. Building on this success, he toured the United States for three years, attracted many Western followers, and set up the Vedanta Society. Returning to India, Vivekānanda founded the Ramakrishna Mission, an organization dedicated to education and social service much like

Christian missions in India. Vivekānanda is still celebrated as a teacher of "practical Vedānta," which scholars sometimes label "neo-Vedānta," a significant version of modern Hindu ideology. He was also the prototype of a new breed of cosmopolitan Hindu gurus who would bring their teachings to Western audiences.

As the movement for Indian independence took shape in the late nineteenth and early twentieth centuries, activists drew upon and reworked elements from the Hindu tradition for explicitly political purposes. The Maharashtrian leader B. G. Tilak, for example, instituted a public festival to the elephant-headed god Gaṇeśa, celebrating Hindu popular culture as a means of regaining "self-rule," and not incidentally attracting large crowds for his political speeches. In Bengal the ferocious goddess Kālī lent her fierce energy to the independence struggle, and the new goddess Bhārat Māta ("Mother India") appeared, iconographically modeled on Lakṣmī, as a national focus for devotion and sacrifice. Literary and political figures alike rewrote and reinterpreted old texts like the *Bhagavadgītā* and the *Rāmāyaṇa*, making them speak to the colonial situation. Although reintroducing Hindu deities and rituals to make political statements was nothing new in India, and it certainly helped extend the politics of anticolonialism beyond the educated urban elite, in the colonial setting it also had the unfortunate effect of identifying the independence movement as a largely Hindu enterprise, alienating Muslims and other non-Hindu communities.

Throughout the colonial period, the British viewed India as a society made up of distinct, identifiable religious communities: Hindus, Muslims, Sikhs, Jains, "tribals," and so on. British administrators soon learned the advantages of "divide and rule," and often promoted religious divisions as a conscious strategy to weaken those who might oppose them. Even in seemingly nonpolitical administrative activities like census taking, the British use of unequivocal categories to classify a religious reality that was complex and mingled promoted a clarification and hardening of religious distinctions.

Indians themselves increasingly employed the same classifications, and many of the reform movements, with their weekly meetings, membership lists, and search for the essence of their traditions, also helped define and solidify community boundaries. By the early decades of the twentieth century, religious conflict increased in Indian society. The outcome of this "communalization" was that, when the English finally quit India in 1947, they felt it necessary to divide their colony along religious lines into two nation-states, Islamic Pakistan and Hindu India. This tragic decision led to terrible violence and suffering among Muslims, Hindus, and Sikhs alike during the Partition, and its consequences are still felt powerfully in the politics of modern South Asia.

Religions of Home and Village

One important dimension of Indian religions that is too often lost sight of in historical summaries like this one is the religion of the domestic sphere. Historians have frequently overlooked domestic religious traditions because the activities of the household are generally transmitted orally, from woman to woman over the generations, and do not receive the textual documentation accorded more public, male-dominated domains of religion. Only with the work of recent anthropologists and folklorists have these traditions begun to receive the attention they deserve. Several readings in this volume exemplify this new scholarly focus on the home as a locus of religiosity.

Transmitted orally, domestic religious traditions show marked local and regional diversity, but certain themes are common. Domestic forms of Indian religions directly address the concerns of women, but not only those of women. Successful marriage, healthy offspring, domestic accord, and prosperity of the home are values shared by all members of the household. Domestic rites seek to ward off the various calamities—disease, family dissension, poverty, death—that threaten the well-being of the family and lineage. Though one finds little interest here in the attainment of mokṣa that looms so large in other Indian religious traditions, these domestic concerns certainly are not trivial or parochial. Other forms of divine salvation, such as marriage or motherhood to a god, are recognized, and the world of the kitchen may even be identified with the cosmos itself, as in the Tamil poem addressed to the child-goddess Mīnāṭci, "Sway back and forth" (Chapter 10).

Female divinities figure strongly in domestic religion. Some are decidedly benign, like Mother Ten (Chapter 29) and the basil-shrub goddess Tulsī (Chapter 33), worshiped for their capacities to bring sustenance and health. But there are other goddesses of a more uneven temperament, such as Mother Ten's opposite number, "Bad Ten," or the Bengali Śītalā, goddess of smallpox (Chapter 24). Quick to take offense, Śītalā requires careful mollifying to insure that her wrath does not come down on one's own family. In Rajasthan, women sing devotional songs also to satīs, exemplary women who overcame the inauspiciousness of their husbands' deaths through extraordinary adherence to purity, and who have become protector spirits of the lineage (Chapter 14).

Although domestic religions often take a different perspective from the public traditions, they nevertheless share with them a single language of Indian religious discourse. The domestic goddess Tulsī, for instance, is linked with Kṛṣṇa, and her stories explore the jealous rivalry that may arise among co-wives attached to this famously promiscuous male god. The Rajasthani regional goddess Mother Ten, we find, is identified as Lakṣmī, the pan-Indian Sanskritic goddess of good fortune. Likewise, when Muslim women worship at moments of domestic crisis, they focus on the miraculous birth of Muḥammad, connecting their concerns about procreation and healing with the most public figure of the Islamic tradition (Chapter 21). Domestic ceremonies, too, draw upon the common Indian repertoire of ascetic and ritual practices, such as fasting, bathing, purification rites, pūjā, and the maintenance of vows (*vrata*) to bring about the desired ends (Chapter 22).

An earlier generation of anthropologists and Indianists spoke of the ongoing relationships between public, literary, pan-Indian traditions and localized, oral traditions in terms of the "great" and "little" traditions, and those terms may still be useful provided one observes some precautions. One should not imagine a single normative "great tradition," and one should not use the distinction to verify a hierarchical separation between two insular domains, such that the pan-Indian enjoys an assumed dominance over the local. Likewise, the little traditions of village and household are not unchanging. Although some of the concerns and aims of these traditions are grounded in the relatively constant struggles of rural and village populations of India, the stories, rituals, and deities may change.

In ongoing two-way cultural traffic, elements of local traditions may be selectively drawn into public, literate traditions, while other elements from those pan-Indian cultural traditions may be selectively drawn upon to enhance or reformulate religious practices at the level of village or household. We may take the Mother Ten story of the amazing cow with its magical dung (Chapter 29) as an illustration of one direction in this traffic. When the remarkable cow is brought to the royal court, the "little tradition" figure of Mother Ten receives the public recognition that incorporates her into a regional "great tradition." This kind of dynamic interchange has been going on in India for centuries.

The Contemporary Scene

A modern-day Vidagdha might ask, "What are Indian religions like now?"

In a cultural area as large and diverse as India, with its 800 million people, eighteen official languages, and strong regional traditions, it is never easy to get a fix on contemporary religion. Instead, one finds oneself returning to Yajñavālkya's Upaniṣadic perspective, from which a single question requires multiple answers.

Yes, but what do religions in India look like now?

In a trip around contemporary India, a religious sightseer will certainly encounter many characters made familiar by a study of the history of Indian religions, but they are often dressed in new clothes. One may see Buddhist monks chanting Buddha's teachings at the site of his enlightenment in Bodh Gaya, but then notice that they are political refugees dressed in the vermillion robes of Tibetan Buddhism. One will find ash-smeared yogis in their Himalayan ashrams discoursing in English to audiences of young Germans, Japanese, and Australians. In south Indian temples one can follow priests and devotees as they worship Viṣṇu and Śiva according to liturgical models set down in early medieval guidebooks, and then pause outside to purchase a brightly colored lithographic reproduction of the temple deity or to arrange an international pūjā by airmail. One may encounter street performances retelling the epic stories of Rāma, Kṛṣṇa, and the Pāṇḍavas, interspersed with Hindi film songs. Those epic narratives have also been reanimated for a nationwide television audience, the most widely followed television series ever in India. The devotional songs of Māṇikkavācakar and Tukārām are available on cassette and compact disk, and during festival seasons one cannot avoid them as they blare from loudspeakers outside seemingly every tea and coffee stall. One will read in the newspapers of "Hindutva" (Hinduness) and a new form of conservative political Hinduism, centering on a dispute over the birthplace of Rāma in Ayodhya and a mosque built by the Islamic Mughal conqueror Bābar, allegedly atop the ruins of the medieval Hindu temple.

Though historically grounded, Indian religions remain alive to their modernity—to their new political settings, the new international audiences, and the new possibilities of technology in the modern world. And in turn they are changed by them, sometimes subtly and sometimes profoundly.

Yes, but how can we best characterize the religions of India?

After this overview of Indian religions, which stresses their diversity and change throughout history, I would not attempt a definition. Any generalization I might draw would in any case be subverted by the very multiplicity of readings in this volume.

The collectivity of Indian voices represented through the translations here will bring us closer to its complex reality, no doubt. It offers a sampling of perspectives rather than any authoritative collection or canon, and in this way approximates more closely the living texture of Indian religious thought and practice. It is important when attending to these voices, however, not to hear them as isolated, self-standing statements. One should place them in conversation with one another, and listen in on their discussions of mutual religious concerns. At times they share insights while at others they disagree over fundamental premises.

If we have seen debate as a central feature in the history of Indian religions, it would be wrong to imagine that somehow those controversies have ended. Indeed, over the past decade debates about the nature and role of religion in contemporary Indian society have taken on a renewed urgency. How does one define Hinduism? Or for that matter, Islam? Sikhism? Who gets to do the defining? Should Hinduism be defined at all? What are the key texts and narratives of the Indian tradition? How relevant are the normative works of the past—Vedas, epics, Dharmaśāstras, Qur'ān, *Ādi Granth*, and the like—to present-day concerns? How should Hindus relate themselves to other religious communities in India? How clear are the boundaries between them? What are the proper roles for religious groups and institutions in the modern secular state of India? Should Indians understand their national identity in terms of a dominant Hindu heritage, or view Hinduism as one among many threads in the cultural fabric of India? And looking beyond national borders, how may Hinduism, Islam, Sikhism, and Jainism best be reformulated to meet the new social settings and needs of Indian immigrants in the United States, United Kingdom, and around the world?

These are serious discussions not likely to end any time soon. They make the study of the religions of India, that land of ancient sages and age-old scriptures, a matter of great contempory significance.

Notes

1. I would like to thank all those who offered helpful suggestions and encouragement on drafts of this essay: Pravin Bhatt, Carl Ernst, Phyllis Granoff, Valerie Hansen, Lindsey Harlan, Norvin Hein, Donald Lopez, Rita McCleary, Sandhya Purohit, Paula Richman, Phil Wagoner, and Irene Winter.

2. U. N. Ghoshal, *A History of Indian Political Ideas* (London: Oxford University Press, 1959), p. 157.

Songs of Devotion and Praise

—1—

Bengali Songs to Kālī

Rachel Fell McDermott

Kālī, the "Black Goddess," is a pan-Indian deity, known throughout the subcontinent. But it is in the northeastern regions of the country, Bengal in particular, that she is the center of an especially rich devotional (*bhakti*) tradition. Beginning in the mid-eighteenth century in Bengal with a poet named Rāmprasād Sen (c. 1718–1775), the bloodthirsty Kālī, known in Sanskrit literature since the time of the *Mahābhārata* as a battle heroine and champion of tribal and peripheral peoples, was brought within the sphere of bhakti. The fifteenth- to eighteenth-century Bengali maṅgala-kāvyas, lengthy poems glorifying particular gods and goddesses, had to some extent prepared the ground for the later bhakti poetry: the deities of the maṅgala-kāvyas were objects of propitiation, who involved themselves—often as protectors or saviors—in the lives of their worshipers, in order to spread their own cults. But it was not until the poetry of Rāmprasād Sen that Kālī's character gained a well-developed compassionate and maternal side, which made her a fitting receptacle for the heart's devotion.

Rāmprasād wrote over three hundred poems to Kālī, initiating a literary genre that has been called *śākta padāvalī*—a collection of poems to the goddess in one of her various forms. Though many questions still perplex the historian—such as, for instance, whether Rāmprasād really was the first to conceive of and write about Kālī—it is nevertheless taken for granted that his poems set the tone for Kālī's subsequent depiction and adoration in Bengal. By the beginning of the twentieth century, eighty to ninety other bhakti poets had followed suit, writing songs to and about Kālī. Even today the tradition carries on: new poets are still composing, and their work, as well as that of the more famous Rāmprasād and his followers, is heard on the radio, on cassettes, and in concerts. The greatest indicator, perhaps, of the influence of the devotional attitude towards Kālī, begun most prominently with Rāmprasād Sen, is that the modern Kālī is regarded by the majority of Bengalis today as Mother, first and foremost; her older, harsher characteristics have partially receded.

In Bengali scholarly works on the śākta padāvalī tradition, the name that almost always follows Rāmprasād's in importance is that of Kamalākānta Bhaṭṭācārya (c. 1769–1820). As might be expected of someone coming immediately after a famed innovator, many of Kamalākānta's poems incorporate themes and images used first by Rāmprasād. However, Kamalākānta was not merely an imitator; in a few areas his poetry is truly distinctive.

Kamalākānta lived his whole life in the district of Barddhamān, in south-central Bengal. He was of a poor, brahman background, with a traditional Sanskrit education. The only date connected with his life that is known for certain is 1809, the year in which Tejascānd, the "king" (actually, a rich *zamīndār*, landlord) of the Barddhamān lineage, discovered Kamalākānta in a nearby town and had him brought to Barddhamān city as court pandit, poet, and preceptor for Tejascānd's unruly son. Kamalākānta died in about 1820. It was not until 1857, however, that anyone thought to try to preserve his poems, and luckily it was still not too late. Wishing to memorialize the religious heritage of his royal line, King Māhtābcānd of Barddhamān ascertained that the wife of Kamalākānta's deceased brother still had in her possession four old, dilapidated poetry notebooks, in Kamalākānta's own hand. These he collected, edited, and published, ensuring that the 269 poems now attributed to Kamalākānta are fairly genuine reproductions of the poet's written words. For nearly seventy years thereafter, people knew of Kamalākānta only through this poetic corpus and through numerous legends that began to spread his fame.

The most famous of these legends depicts Kamalākānta as a fearless worshiper of Kālī, whose devotion is so powerful that it can even melt the most hardened hearts. In the story, Kamalākānta is traveling alone at night through a wilderness area near a village named Oṛ, when he is attacked by bandits who plan to murder him. Kamalākānta begs permission to sing one last song to Kālī before his death; upon hearing it, his captors are so overcome with remorse that they fall at his feet and become his disciples. The song traditionally associated with this story is among his most famous, and is included here as poem 20.

In 1925, a truly startling discovery was made. The librarian of a prestigious Calcutta library uncovered, in the home of the great-great-grandson of one of Kamalākānta's disciples, the manuscript of a tantric manual composed by Kamalākānta—which almost no one had previously known existed. He had it published, adding another dimension to the historical portrait of the poet. The manual, called *Sādhaka Rañjana* ("That Which Pleases the Religious Aspirant"), is written with obvious attention to meter and rhyme, unlike some of Kamalākānta's more free-flowing verses. In content, however, its style and imagery complement that of his Śakta poetry.

Like many religious poets, philosophers, and devotees throughout Indian history, Kamalākānta did not limit himself in his devotion to any one deity. Though he seems to have been particularly attracted to Kālī, 31 of his 269 poems are addressed to the Goddess in her form as Umā, the beneficent and beautiful spouse of Śiva, 24 are directed to Kṛṣṇa, and two are about Śiva. But since Kamalākānta is primarily remembered as a devotee of Kālī, the majority of the poems given below are drawn from the 212 he wrote about her. These fall into several categories: those depicting her on the cremation grounds; poems with tantric imagery and allusions; petitions to Kālī; rebukes; expressions of fulfillment; self-exhortations; and dismal portrayals of the present world. Six poems about Umā have also been included, as this is another area in which Kamalākānta developed themes beyond those undertaken by Rāmprasād.

A word about the musical aspect of these poems is necessary. Although they can stand alone as literary compositions, they are meant to be sung. Rāmprasād apparently created a single melody to fit his poems, and almost all of his over three hundred compositions can be sung to it. Kamalākānta's poems, however, were sung to individual melodies. Unfortunately, though we possess tunes traditionally associated with ten or so of Kamalākānta's most famous poems, the original melodies that he used are now lost. A modern musician trained in the performance style can approximate the way such poems might have sounded in the poet's day, through improvising a melody in the given key and rhythmic pattern. This is the way the poems are sung and heard today.

The first six poems translated below are representative of a class of poems composed for a Bengali religious festival that occurs once a year in the autumn: Durgā Pūjā. This is a ten-day festival centering on the Goddess in her form as Durgā, or Umā, the wife of Śiva, and is one of the biggest celebrations of the year. Its popularity derives from three factors, each of which is mirrored in the poetry.

First, Durgā Pūjā, perhaps in its most ancient layer, is a harvest festival of grains, and its arrival signifies the return of cool weather and the bounty of the earth. In the formal ritual worship of the pūjā, in addition to anthropomorphic images, the Goddess is depicted aniconically by a trussed-up bundle of nine plants, wrapped in a sari. The poetry reflects this emphasis on nature: Umā is frequently compared to an autumn lotus (poem 5), and her face, like the moon, cools with its soft light (poems 4 and 6). Second, this festival celebrates the victory of Durgā over the buffalo demon, Mahiṣa. Thousands of temporary shrines are erected in cities and villages all over Bengal; inside, images of Durgā slaying Mahiṣa, made from straw, clay, paint, and decorations, are worshiped ritually for several days, until the tenth day, when they are immersed in the river. For weeks before the pūjā, Durgā's face appears in advertisements, magazines, and store fronts, announcing the coming holiday. Schools close for long pūjā vacations, and families gather together, where possible.

This brings us to the third reason for the festival's popularity: the sense of longing for the return of the Goddess, conceived as a beloved daughter in Bengali religious imaginations. Unlike Kālī, whose many temples are a fixed aspect of Bengali life, Umā, or Durgā, has practically no permanent temples or cult in Bengal. Just like a real Bengali daughter who lives far away from her parents at the house of her in-laws, Umā comes only once a year to visit for a few brief days. On the first day of the festival, she sets out from her husband's home on Mount Kailāsa; from then until the sixth evening, when she finally arrives and the images of Durgā are installed in the temporary shrines, groups of musicians sing compositions known as āgamanī poems—poems in anticipation of Umā's coming. Near the end of the holiday, on the ninth evening and tenth day, before the images are submerged in the river, they turn instead to vijayā poems, which mourn her imminent departure. The musical keys for both types of song are somber and lugubrious, adding poignancy to the expectations.

Āgamanī and vijayā poems do not merely express longing and the pain of separation; they also tell a story, through which one can see Bengali attitudes towards the Goddess and Śiva, as well as Bengali experiences of the parent-daughter relationship. The cast of characters includes Umā, also called Gaurī, the "Fair One," and Bhavānī, the "Wife of Bhava," or Śiva, who is the daughter of Menakā and the Himālaya Mountain, her mother and father, respectively. The fact that Umā's father is actually a stationary mountain explains his wife's frustration at his inactivity (poem 1): he cannot move or feel, being a stone. Himālaya and Menakā are the rulers of the mountain city, Giripur, where all the inhabitants share their sorrows and joys (poem 4).

In a turn of events not uncommon for traditional Bengali households of Kamalākānta's era, the beloved daughter has been married off through the intervention of an unscrupulous rumor monger and matchmaker—here called Nārada (poem 1). Forced through their poverty or lack of connections to yield their daughter to a bridegroom they feel to be totally unsatisfactory, the parents worry constantly over her fate. In Umā's case, she has been married to Śiva, an elderly good-for-nothing, a drug-addicted, naked mendicant, who wanders around the cremation grounds with live snakes hanging on his neck, a trident in his hand, and matted hair (poems 1 and 2). To make matters worse, he is a Kulin, a brahman who takes more than one wife; Umā has to contend with a co-wife, Gaṅgā (the Ganges River). This "Celestial River," Suradhunī, dwells on Śiva's head, where she landed when she fell from heaven (poem 5).

Once a year, in autumn, Umā begs to go home to see her parents, particularly her mother, who is distraught with anxiety over her. Menakā, being a traditional Bengali woman, cannot travel alone, so she can do nothing except to beg her husband to go fetch Umā home, which he is reluctant to do for fear of Śiva's reaction. Eventually, the reunion is engineered, and for the three days that Umā spends at home, she tries to console her mother about her life with Śiva, with dubious results (poem 5). Too soon, she has to return to Mount Kailāsa, and Menakā weeps (poem 6). The visit—and Durgā Pūjā—are over.

Underlying these poems is an intentional ambiguity concerning Umā and Śiva. Who are they, really? Umā is the helpless daughter and the suffering daughter-in-law, but she is also the Mother of the World, with the ability to save her husband and her devotees. Likewise, Śiva may be the disastrous son-in-law, but at the same time he is also the Great Lord. Kamalākānta plays with these uncertain identities, maintaining Umā's status as the goddess, while continuing to humanize her. In general, such poems today in Bengal are to be found in a few cassette tapes and printed anthologies more than they are in popular devotional practice. More than the Kālī-centered poems, they are falling into disuse and neglect, particularly in cities. This can partially be accounted for by changing life styles and the increased commercialization of Durgā Pūjā itself: people live more apart from one another than they used to, and have neither the time nor the occasion to gather to listen to musicians singing of Umā's coming.

Poems addressed to or about Kālī, in contrast, are much more popular. Though especially prominent on the radio and in cassette tape stores at the time of the one-day Kālī Pūjā festival (which falls approximately three weeks after Durgā Pūjā), Śyāmā saṅgīt, or songs to Śyāmā, the "Black Goddess" Kālī, are listened to by Kālī devotees all year round. The Kālī of these poems, like her counterpart Umā, is humanized and softened. Although her gruesome iconographic features and fearsome actions are not changed, the poets tone them down. Kamalākānta, for instance, does not hesitate to paint Kālī in the traditional way: she is black and naked, with all manner of horrific ornaments, tangled hair, a sword in her hand, and her tongue lolling out. She stands on Śiva's torso, in the midst of the cremation grounds. The poet does not stop at mere description, however, and by what he adds he shows his discomfort with such a starkly portrayed goddess. He either scolds her for her indecency (poems 7 and 8), puts it in context by claiming that this naked Kālī is only one of her several manifestations (poems 9 and 10), manages to look past the dreadful attributes (poem 11), denies that such characteristics are real (poem 12), or beautifies the image, so that it is no longer frightening (poems 7 and 12). This last approach, in particular, is important: this genre is full of images and phrases that sweeten the overall picture of the goddess.

But Kālī is not only the mad dancer on top of Śiva's inert body. She is also a cosmic figure—Brahmamayī, or the "Embodiment of Brahman" (poems 10, 13, and 18). As Tripurā, the possessor of triadic attributes, she both assumes the qualities of creation and transcends them (poems 8 and 10). She is matter, spirit, and emptiness (poem 12). Everything is full of her and identified with her—even the other gods, such as Kṛṣṇa (poem 9) and Brahmā (poem 17).

Aside from her mythological and cosmic sides, Kamalākānta's Kālī has two other faces, or ways of appearing to the poet. One is her role as deluder and bewitcher: through her illusory power, she can take many forms, misleading and playing with her devotees. Sometimes, he says, even she gets caught in her own bonds (poem 9). The second, and in terms of numbers of poems written on this subject, the most prominent of Kamalākānta's portrayals of Kālī, is that of a savior. She is Tārā, the one who literally "Carries one Across" the ocean of the world to the other side (poems 10, 15, 21, and 22), and she is Cintāmaṇi, the wish-fulfilling gem that turns everything to gold at its touch (poem 19). Kālī, the supremely compassionate Mother, will rescue her worshipers in whatever way possible. This ubiquitous tendency to call Kālī, in her various manifestations, a mother, is what really gives this śākta padāvalī tradition its uniqueness.

One way of looking at the distinctive goddess-centered emphasis of this poetry is to watch what the Śakta poets, and Kamalākānta in particular, do to the characterization of Śiva, also called Hara, the "Destroyer," and Śaṅkara, the "Beneficent." According to the mainstream Hindu understanding, Śiva is the young, virile hero of the gods, whose acts of self-sacrifice such as drinking the poison churned from the ocean of milk or lying beneath Kālī to stop her world-crushing dance illustrate his personal victories over such perceived dangers. Kamalākānta's Śiva is different. In these poems, he is a disreputable old man, able to help the gods with various feats such as drinking the poison only because Umā gives him the necessary strength (poem 2). In the Kālī poems, the goddess is not Śiva's dutiful and subordinate wife, as she is in the traditional story of Satī (poem 8); Kālī is the supreme spiritual force in the universe, and it is Śiva who falls at her feet in the hopes of gaining her blessing (poems 8 and 11). He gazes up at her, bewitched; thus he is the model, par excellence, of a servant and devotee. Kamalākānta refers to him throughout his poems as his own rival; he wishes that he were lying beneath Kālī with her feet on his chest (poem 20).

Like Rāmprasād and generations of Vaiṣṇava poets before him, Kamalākānta always inserted his name in the last stanza of each poem. It is from these pithy concluding remarks, as well as from his self-descriptions in each poem, that one can glimpse at the range of attitudes and emotions he experienced in his relationship to Umā and Kālī.

In general, the point of these stanzas is to show Kamalākānta's closeness to the goddess, his involvement with her, and his desire to participate even more deeply in her activities. The concluding stanzas either continue the main speaker's thought, showing how much Kamalākānta identifies with the sentiments expressed (poems 1, 4, and 5), or depict Kamalākānta advising a character (poem 6), or actually insert the poet into the story line as an attendant (poems 2 and 3). In the Kālī poems, Kamalākānta fluctuates between emotional extremes. At times he focuses on his spiritual condition, and is dejected. The world is like an ocean which must be crossed (poem 15), or like a battleground in which the six passions (lust, anger, greed, sloth, pride, and envy) constantly assail him (poems 21 and 23). People desert him, taunt him, and lead him to fear that Kālī has forgotten him. At other times he addresses his mind, exhorting himself to the religious path. As in most Indian bhakti poetry, there is a certain anti-ritualistic tone in such compositions. Kamalākānta recommends against relying on external rituals—whether traditional (poem 18) or tantric (poem 23)—going on pilgrimage (poem 19), or using a rosary (poem 20); what is necessary is true devotion, based in the heart. The poems in which Kamalākānta addresses Kālī directly illustrate the intimacy between devotee and deity: Kamalākānta treats Kālī with a wide spectrum of human feelings. He petitions her for mercy (poem 16), rebukes her for her scandalous behavior (poems 13, 14, and 22), evinces astonishment at her divine nature (poems 11 and 12), and revels in the bliss of spiritual attainment (poems 18 and 23). In the tradition of Indian bhakti poets before him, Kamalākānta's literary creations both reflected, and inspired, his inner devotional life.

Historians of Bengali literature inevitably stress the beauty and significance of these Śākta poems on Kālī. Nevertheless, fieldwork in modern Bengal indicates that they are not very popular, and may in fact be on the decline in devotional contexts. The overwhelming popularity of Hindu film music, as well as the musical and philosophical difficulty of some of the Śākta songs, may account for this phenomenon. Another possible reason for their gradual decrease in public awareness may lie in their portrayal of Kālī. Could it be that the content of the poems no longer matches devotees' experience?

Rāmprasād and Kamalākānta berate Kālī for her appearance and her behavior—both of which are unseemly. But today's Kālī images are generally clothed, with beautiful hair and a smiling face; they are not nude, with tousled hair, and the Mother is not usually understood as sending suffering or misfortune. In other words, perhaps the modern Kālī has moved away, through the influence of the very bhakti whose introduction in the mid-eighteenth century gave Rāmprasād's and Kamalākānta's poetry such relevance and bite, towards a persona less characterized by ambiguity. Yet, how do we know that the Bengalis who heard these poets' compositions in the eighteenth and nineteenth centuries found them completely relevant? Do the literary creations of geniuses, whether religious or not, always mirror social attitudes and experiences? How much of a poet's language reflects personal eccentricity or literary convention? Perhaps these poems have never been very popular, because only a few extraordinary devotees have been willing or able to face the polarities in their once bloodthirsty goddess, now somewhat softened through bhakti. This is a problem of interpretation, and arises whenever one has little access to the historical context in which a text was written. In the case of the poems of Rāmprasād and Kamalākānta, it means that one has to be very cautious in assessing the genre's influence and internal development. What seems, in some instances, to be a strange misfit between the sentiments expressed by the poets and the opinions of today's goddess worshipers may provide clues to changes in Śākta devotionalism. Or it may simply indicate a continuity in reaction: Kālī's poets are saints because they dared express something rarely understood, then or now.

All of the translated lyrics below except one can be found in Kamalākānta Bhaṭṭcārya, *Śyāmā Saṅgīt*, collected by Nabīncandra Bandyopādhyāya (Calcutta: Barddhamān Mahārājādhirāj Māhtābcānd Bāhādur, 1857; reprint Barddhamān Mahārājādhirāj Bijaycānd Bāhādur, 1925). The one poem not in the volume sponsored by the Barddhamān king in 1857 is listed as an "unpublished" poem, and is found in the appendix to Atulcandra Mukhopādhyāya, *Sādhaka Kamalākānta* (Dhaka: Ripon Library, 1925).

POEMS TO UMĀ

1 *Yāo, Giribara he*

Go, my Lord of the Mountain,
Bring our daughter home.
After giving Gaurī away to the Naked One,

How can you sit at home
So unconcerned?
What a hard heart you have!
You know the behavior of our son-in-law—
Always acting like a lunatic,
Wearing a tiger's skin,
With matted locks on his head.
He not only roams the cremation ground himself,
But takes her, too!
Such is Umā's fate.
I heard Nārada say
He smears his body with funeral pyre ash.
The way he dresses is monstrous:
The garland around his neck is made of snakes!
And who would believe me—
He prefers poison to honey!
Tell me, what kind of a choice is that?

Kamalākānta says:
Listen, Jewel of the Mountains.
Śiva's behavior is incomprehensible.
If you can,
Fall at his feet and get permission to bring Umā home.
Then never send her back again.

Śyāmā Saṅgīt 215

2 *Bāre bāre kaho Rāṇi*

You ask me, Queen, time after time
To go get Gaurī.
But you know very well
The nature of our son-in-law.
Even a snake can survive for a while
Without its head-jewel.
But to the Trident Bearer
Umā is more than that.
If he doesn't see her even for a moment,
He dies.
He keeps her in his heart.
Why would he willingly send her to us?

Once
To win respect for the gods
Śiva drank a terrible poison.

But the pain was unbearable.
Only the shadows from Umā's limbs
Could cool Śaṅkara's burning body.
Since then
Śiva has not parted from his wife.

You're just a simple woman
You don't know how to proceed.
I will go,
But I won't say anything to the Naked Lord.
Ask Kamalākānta: see if he will go with me.
After all, she's his mother;
He may manage to bring her somehow.

Śyāmā Saṅgīt 222

3 *Ohe Hara Gaṅgādhara*

Hey, Hara, Gaṅgā-Holder,
Promise me I can go to my father's place.

What are you brooding about?
The worlds are contained in your fingernail—
But no one would know it,
Looking at your face.

My father, the Lord of the Mountain,
Has arrived to visit you
And to take me away.
It's been so many days since I went home
And saw my mother face to face.
Ceaselessly, night and day,
How she weeps for me!
Like a thirsty cātakī bird, the queen stares
At the road that will bring me home.
Can't I make you understand
My mental agony
At not seeing her face?
How can I go without your consent?

My husband, don't crack jokes
Just satisfy my desire.
Hara, let me say good-bye,
Your mind at ease.
And give me Kamalākānta as an attendant.

I assure you
I'll be back in three days.

Śyāmā Saṇgīt 225

4 *Āmār Umā elo*

"My Umā has come!" So saying,
The queen runs, her hair disheveled.

City women dash out in groups
To see Gaurī.
Some carry pitchers at the waist,
Others hold babies to their breast,
Their hair half-braided and half-curled.
They call to each other,
"Come on! Come on! Come on!
Run quickly!
Let's go see the Daughter of the Mountain!"
Rushing outside the city,
Their bodies thrill with passionate anticipation.
As soon as they glimpse that moon-face,
They kiss her lips
Hastily.

Then the Woman of the Mountain
Takes Gaurī on her lap,
Her body floating
In the bliss of love.
While instruments play sweetly,
Heavenly musicians decorate themselves,
Dancing gleefully
With the women of the mountain city.

Today Kamalākānta sees those two red feet,
And is utterly engrossed.

Śyāmā Saṅgīt 232

5 *Śarat-kamal-mukhe*

From her autumn-lotus mouth
She babbles half-formed words.
Sitting on her mother's lap,

A slight smile on her blessed face,
Bhavānī speaks of the comforts of Bhava's home.

"Mother, who says Hara is poor?
His house is built of jewels
More lustrous than hundreds of suns and moons!
Since our wedding,
Who has felt darkness?
Who knows when it's day or night?

"You hear that I'm afraid of my co-wife?
Suradhunī loves me more than you do!
From her perch in Śiva's matted hair
She sees how he holds me
In his heart.
Who else is so lucky to have such a co-wife?"

Kamalākānta says:
Listen, Queen of the Mountain.
Mount Kailāsa is the summit of the worlds.
If you ever saw it,
You wouldn't want to leave.
Forgetting everything,
You'd stay at Bhava's place,
Mountain Woman.

Śyāmā Saṅgīt 236

6 *Phire cāo go Umā*

Turn back, Umā,
And let me see your moon-face!
You are killing your unfortunate mother:
Where are you going?

Today my jeweled palace has become dark.
What will remain in my body
But a life of ashes?

Umā, stay here!
Just for once, stay, Mother!
Cool my burning body
Even for a moment.
My eyes are fixed on the road you travel.
How long must I wait
Until you come home again?

Fulfil Kamalākānta's desire,
Moon-faced One:
Call your mother,
And make her understand.

Śyāmā Saṅgīt 245

POEMS TO KĀLĪ

7 *Ke re pāgalīr beśe*

Who is this,
Dressed like a crazy woman,
Robed with the sky?
Whom does she belong to?
She has let down her hair,
Thrown off her clothes,
Strung human hands around her waist,
And taken a sword in her hand.
Her face sparkles
From the reflection of her teeth,
And her tongue lolls out.
The smile on that moon-face drips
Heaps and heaps of nectar.

Mother, are you going to rescue Kamalākānta
In *this* outfit?

Śyāmā Saṅgīt 122

8 *Kāli ki tor sakali bhrānta*

Kālī, is everything you do
Misleading?

Look, your beloved has thrown himself
Under your feet!
Mother, I beg you
With folded hands:
Don't dance on top of Śiva!
I know how Tripura's Enemy feels.
Beautiful Tripurā, kind woman,
Just this once, stop.
You're the murderer of your own husband;
You're killing your Lord!

The King of Living Beings
Is almost dead!

Once
Hearing people criticize Śiva
You got angry
And left your body
For love.
Mother! The man you're standing on
Is the same Three-Eyed One!
Calm down, and look at him;
It's the Naked Lord!

This is what Kamalākānta wants to understand:
You know everything,
So why all these deceptions?
This time, I think,
You've gone too far,
You whose seat is a corpse.

Śyāmā Saṅgīt 190

9 *Jāno nā re man*

You don't realize this, mind,
But Kālī, the Prime Cause,
Is not only female.
Sometimes
Taking the color of a cloud,
She transforms herself,
And emerges
Male.

She who terrifies demons
With her disheveled hair and brandished sword
Occasionally visits Vraja,
Captivating the cowherd women's hearts
With the sound of his flute.

Then again
Assuming the three qualities,
She creates, preserves, and destroys.
Thus bound in the illusion of her own making,
She endures, and nurses,
The pains of the world.

Whatever form you believe her to have,
She'll take that
And dwell in your mind.
In Kamalākānta's case,
She appears at the center of a lotus
In a lake,
His heart.

Śyāmā Saṅgīt 146

10 *Mā, kakhan ki raṅge thāko*

Mother,
You are always finding ways to amuse yourself.

Śyāmā, you stream of nectar,
Through your deluding power
You forge a horrible face
And adorn yourself with a necklace
Of human skulls.
The earth quakes under your leaps and bounds.
You are frightful
With that sword in your hand.
At other times
You take a flirtatious pose,
And then even the God of Love is outdone, Mother!

Your form is inconceivable and undecaying.
Nārāyaṇī, Tripurā, Tārā—
You are beyond the three qualities
And yet composed of them.
You are terrifying,
You are death,
You are a beautiful woman.

Thus assuming various forms,
You fulfil the wishes of your worshipers.
Sometimes you even dance,
Brahman, Eternal One,
In the lotus heart of Kamalākānta.

Śyāmā Saṅgīt 150

11 *Tumi kār gharer meye*

Kālī, what family are you from?
You're absorbed in your own fun and games.

Who really understands your incomparable beauty?
If I look at you
I can no longer distinguish between day and night.
I have to admit—
You're black, glossier than smeared mascara,
You don't wear saris, gold, or jewels,
Your hair's all tousled,
And you're always at the cremation grounds.
Nevertheless,
My mind forgets all this,
I don't know how.

Look! The Jewel of Men,
With masses of matted hair and snakes on his head,
Is *he* devoted to your feet?
Who are you to him? Who is he to you?
Who would ever guess
That the Crest-Jewel of the gods,
The Shelter of the shelterless,
The Entertainer of the universe,
Would cling to your feet
As the most cherished treasure?

Kamalākānta can't comprehend your endless virtues.
The earth and sky are lit by your beauty.

Śyāmā Saṅgīt 14

12 *Śyāmā Mā ki āmār kālo re*

Is my black Mother Śyāmā really black?
People say Kālī is black,
But my heart doesn't agree.
If she's black,
How can she light up the world?
Sometimes my Mother is white,
Sometimes yellow, blue, and red.
I cannot fathom her.
My whole life has passed

Trying.
She is matter,
Then spirit,
Then complete void.

It's easy to see
How Kamalākānta,
Thinking about these things,
Went crazy.

Śyāmā Saṅgīt 48

13 *Jāni jāni go Janani*

I know, I know, Mother:
You're a woman of stone.
You dwell inside me,
Yet you hide from me.

Displaying your illusory power,
You create many bodies,
With your three qualities
Limiting the limitless.

Kind to some,
Harmful to others,
You cover your own faults
By shifting the blame to others.

Mother, I don't hope for enlightenment,
Nor do I wish to live in heaven.
I just want to visualize your feet
Standing in my heart.

Brahmamayi,
This is Kamalākānta's humble appeal:
Why do you harass him unnecessarily?
What is your intention?

Śyāmā Saṅgīt 158

14 *Sadānandamayi Kāli*

Ever-blissful Kālī ,
Bewitcher of the Destructive Lord,
Mother—

For your own amusement
You dance,
Clapping your hands.

You with the moon on your forehead,
Really
You are primordial, eternal, void.
When there was no world, Mother,
Where did you get that garland of skulls?

You alone are the operator,
We your instruments
Moving as you direct.
Where you place us, we stand,
The words you give us, we speak.

Restless Kamalākānta says, rebukingly:
You grabbed your sword, All-Destroyer,
And now you've cut down evil *and* good.

Śyāmā Saṅgīt 8

15 *Śyāmā māyer bhava-taraṅga*

Who can describe the waves of Mother Śyāmā's world?
I think I will swim upstream,
But who is pulling me back?
"I want to watch something funny," says my Mother,
And throws me in.
First I sink, then I float,
Laughing inside.
The boat isn't far away
It's near—
I can easily catch hold of it.
But this is my great dilemma:
Shall I reach for it or not?
I am divided.

Kamalākānta's mind!
Your desires are useless.
Take the boat.
If it is Tārā,
She may ferry you across
Out of kindness.

Śyāmā Saṅgīt 155

16 *Śyāmā yadi hero nayane ekbār*

Tell me, Śyāmā,
How could it hurt you to look at me
Just once?
You're a mother;
If you see so much pain,
But aren't compassionate,
What kind of justice is that?
I have heard from the scriptures
That you rescue the fallen.
Well? *I* am such a person—
Wicked and fallen!

You are famed as a deliverer of the wretched.
If it pleases you,
Take Kamalākānta across.

Śyāmā Saṅgīt 43

17 *Bhairavī bhairava jay Kālī*

Unperturbed at the battle,
Frightful ghouls dance,
Saying, "Victory to Kālī! Kālī!"
Śaṅkarī, immersed in the waves of battle,
Feels the spring breezes pleasant.

That very Brahmā, Lord of the Earth,
Whose wives smear red powder on his blessed body,
When in the form of Śyāmā
Plays with blood-red colors
In the company of her female attendants.

Sweating
With the fun of reverse sexual intercourse,
Young Śyāmā's flesh thrills
On top of young Śiva,
Her boat
Amidst the deep ocean of nectar.
Her long hair reaches down to the ground.
She is naked,
Ornamented with human heads and hands.

Kamalākānta watches their beautiful bodies
And sheds tears of bliss.

Śyāmā Saṅgīt 57

18 *Yār antare jāgilo Brahmamayī*

External rituals means nothing
When Brahmamayī is aroused in your heart.
If you think on the Unthinkable,
Will anything else come to mind?
It's like unmarried girls
With their various amusements.
When they unite with their husbands,
Where are those games?
What will you worship her with?
Everything is full of her essence.

And look at degenerate Kamalākānta!
She has made even him
A storehouse of good qualities.

Śyāmā Saṅgīt 120

19 *Āpanāre āpani theko*

Stay within yourself, mind;
Don't go into anyone else's room.
You will get what you need right here.
Search in your own inner chamber.

Cintāmaṇī is like a philosopher's stone,
That greatest treasure
Able to bring countless riches:
Her front door is strewn about
With so many jewels.

Going on pilgrimage
Is a journey of sorrow,
Mind.
Don't be too eager.
Bathe in the three streams of bliss.
Why not be cooled
At their source,
Your bottom-most mystic center?

What are you looking at, Kamalākānta?
This world is full of false magic.
But you fail to recognize the magician—
And she's dwelling in your own body!

Śyāmā Saṅgīt 99

20 *Ār kicchui nei*

Other than your two red feet, Śyāmā,
Nothing else matters.
But Tripura's Enemy, I hear, has taken them.
My courage is broken.

Family, friends, sons, wives—
In good times they're all here.
But in bad times no one stays around,
And my house is deserted
Like the wilderness near Oṛ village.

If you wish to rescue me,
Then look at me with those compassionate eyes.
Otherwise
My prayers to you will have the brute force of a ghost,
Useless to win you.

Kamalākānta says:
I tell my sorrows to the Mother.
My beads, my bag, my mattress—
Let those stay hanging in the meditation room.

Śyāmā Saṅgīt 81

21 *Śuknā taru muñjare nā*

The withered tree doesn't blossom.
I'm afraid, Mother:
It may crack apart!
Up in the tree,
I feel it sway back and forth
In the strong wind.
My heart trembles.

I had great hopes:
"I'll get fruit from this tree."
But it doesn't bloom

And its branches are dry.
All because of the six hostile fires!

As far as Kamalākānta is concerned,
There is only one recourse:
The name of Tārā
Destroys birth, decay, and death.
Stamp out the flames with it,
And the tree will revive.

Śyāmā Saṅgīt 108

22 *Ekhan ār karo nā Tārā*

From now on,
Don't deprive me any more, Tārā.
Look, the danger of death is near.
What you've done to me was appropriate.
I endured, it endured.
But now I must think:
What is the recourse for a wretched man?
Death is not conquered,
But I am not afraid;
I only worry lest I forget your name
At my going.

Even though Kamalākānta is in pain,
He will smile.
Otherwise people will say
You haven't given me any happiness,
Śyāmā.

Śyāmā Saṅgīt 125

23 *Majilo āmār man bhramarā*

The bee of my mind
Is absorbed
In the blue lotus feet of Kālī.
The honey of worldly pleasures,
The flowers like lust,
All have become meaningless.
Black feet, black bee,
Black mixed with black.
Look! Happiness and suffering are now the same!

The ocean of my bliss
Is overflowing.

After so long
Kamalākānta's cherished hope has been fulfilled.
And see!
Those who get intoxicated by the Five Ms,
Seeing the fun,
Have beat a retreat.

Śyāmā Saṅgīt 165

—2—

Kabīr

Vinay Dharwadker

Kabīr's name is of Arabic origin and is derived from *al-Kabīr*, meaning "great," one of the ninety-nine titles of God in the Qur'ān. Kabīr probably lived in or around the holy city of Varanasi, or elsewhere in what is now eastern Uttar Pradesh (he is also frequently associated with the town of Maghar), at some time between the late fourteenth and early sixteenth centuries (traditionally, 1398–1518). He was orphaned or abandoned at birth, and apparently was brought up by a poor Muslim family belonging to the community of julāhās (weavers). In the fifteenth century the julāhās were relatively recent converts to Islam, having previously been low-caste Śaivas. As a boy Kabīr learned the craft of weaving, but at some point in his adolescence he probably found a guru who initiated him into bhakti. This guru may have been Rāmānanda, a famous Vaiṣṇava master of the late fourteenth or early fifteenth century who preached Rāma-bhakti, devotion to Lord Rāma.

After his initiation into bhakti, Kabīr appears to have become famous as a sant (good or holy man, saint), a bhakta (devotionalist), or a vairāgī (a Vaiṣṇava renouncer or ascetic). He also seems to have been popular as an iconoclast, a social satirist, and an uncompromising poet-singer unaffiliated with any particular school, sect, or religion. He criticized Hindus and Muslims alike for their beliefs and practices, and hence may have been persecuted by orthodox pandits and mullas, and even by a prominent local or regional ruler, identified most often as Sikandar Lodī, the sultan of Delhi between 1488 and 1512. Nevertheless, Kabīr acquired a large number of followers from both religions: a popular story tells us that, when he died, the Hindus wanted to cremate him while the Muslims wished to bury him, but when the two quarreling factions lifted up his shroud they discovered only a heap of petals.

Kabīr's poems and the poems ascribed to him come down to us in a large heterogeneous body that can be divided into four distinct but overlapping traditions. Three of these traditions are based on written works canonized by specific religious institutions. The "northern tradition" consists of the Kabīr poems included in the *Guru Granth Sāhib*, the holy book of the Sikh community in the Punjab, which was given its basic form at (or just after) the end of the sixteenth century. The "eastern tradition" centers around the *Bījak*, a substantial collection of Kabīr poems preserved by the Kabīr Panth (the path or sect of Kabīr) and other orders in Varanasi and elsewhere in Uttar Pradesh and Bihar, probably since the mid-seventeenth century. The "western tradition" is located around Jaipur, Rajasthan, and contains what is now called the *Kabīr Granthāvalī*, derived from the manuscripts of the sect of Dādu Dayāl, a late sixteenth-century follower of Kabīr, as well as the *Sarbāngī*, compiled by Rajjab Dās, believed to be a seventeenth-century follower of Dādu Dayāl. In most cases, the surviving manuscripts in the eastern and western traditions date back only to the eighteenth and nineteenth centuries. The three textual traditions, together with various related sources, attribute more than six thousand poems to Kabīr, only a few dozen of which, at most, are common to all the traditions.

The fourth tradition surrounds the other three on all sides, as it were. It is a mixture of thousands of oral folk versions of Kabīr's poems and sayings, hundreds of songs set and performed in a variety of musical styles, and anywhere between forty and eighty full-length written works associated unverifiably with his name. This amorphous tradition is still alive in many different parts of the subcontinent, from Bengal and Bihar in the east to Rajasthan and Gujarat in the west, and from the Punjab in the north to Maharashtra in central and western India. In colonial India, the fourth tradition played an important role in nationalist politics, for Rabindranath Tagore and Mahatma Gandhi invoked Kabīr's poetry, in various ways, as an ideal or model of folk spirituality, social criticism, and secularism. In postcolonial India it has continued to provide writers and theorists, as well as Hindustani classical musicians (especially singers like Kumar Gandharva and Kishori Amonkar), with material for important interventions and innovations.

The heterogeneity of the traditions directly affects the process of reading and interpreting the Kabīr texts at two distinct levels. First, Kabīr's poems (whichever particular poems we consider his authentic works) do not come to us in a uniform literary language. Different poems may be composed in different languages and dialects, and a single poem may contain more than one dialect or language, or may be composed in a hybrid medium called *sant bhāṣā*, the specialized and often technical language shared by the nirguṇa saint-poets of north India. In addition, a special group of Kabīr's poems, called ulaṭabāṃsīs (upsidedown sayings), are written in sandhyā bhāṣā, an "intentional language" in which common words become uncommon symbols, everyday meanings are inverted, and commonsensical "logic" is displaced by paradox, irony, and apparent absurdity. This linguistic diversity prevents us from construing Kabīr's discourse as a cohesive or homogeneous one.

Second, the heterogeneity of the language and the text goes hand in hand with the heterogeneity of the religious and philosophical content of the Kabīr poems. Whichever tradition we follow, we find a mixture of positions and beliefs, none of which seems to be privileged or immune to criticism from within the text itself. Some poems, for example, draw on Islamic ideas: they may use Qur'ānic monotheism and iconoclasm to attack Hindu "polytheism" and "idol-worship," or utilize Sufi concepts of dhikr (invocation of God's name) and 'ishq (intense personal love for God) to develop the "Hindu" concern with nām-simaran (remembrance of God's name) and viraha-bhāvanā (the tormented feeling of separation from God as lover). Other poems turn to Buddhism, especially to Buddhist tantrism, emphasizing the notions of "ultimate reality" as emptiness and nirvāṇa as a sahaj stithī (the simple, easy state). A large number of poems also use the technical vocabulary and concepts of tantric yoga, particularly the variety called *haṭha yoga*, referring frequently to tantric constructions of the human body and yogic exercises designed to achieve bodily immortality and spiritual freedom. The Buddhist, tantric, and yogic references in general help the poet to dismantle the edifice of what is broadly called Hinduism, with many of its long-standing components. Among other things, Kabīr thus unstitches Vedic ritual, brahmanical learning and authority, the logic of the caste system, social and religious conventions based on the Dharmaśāstras (the code books of Hindu ethics and praxis), religious practice based on the *Rāmāyaṇa* and the *Mahābhārata*, the ritual and devotional Hinduism of the various Purāṇas, and the Vaiṣṇava theory of the incarnations of Viṣṇu, which are supposed to number ten.

At the same time, even though many poems in the Kabīr traditions attack Hindu institutions on the basis of Islamic, Buddhist, and even tantric and yogic theories and practices, many more accept (with important modifications) the two major forms of Hinduism, Śaivism and Vaiṣṇavism. Thus, a substantial portion of the poetry emphasizes ascetic practice and the concept of God as the satguru or "true master" which seem to echo the Śaiva notion of Śiva as the foremost ascetic and as the ādi-guru or "first master." A similar proportion of the poetry also stresses the idea that the Godhead which is the object of devotion is King Rāma. This idea conforms to and yet substantially modifies Vaiṣṇava doctrine, because it turns Rāma, an anthropomorphic form of Viṣṇu with attributes, into a deity without attributes (*nirguṇa*). Because of this vacillation from one system of beliefs and religious context to another, the Kabīr text as a whole seems to maintain a systematic ambiguity or doubt with respect to all the established religious systems of premodern India, using each to question the others in remarkable ways.

The following selection includes six poems from the so-called eastern and western textual traditions, and one complete account of Kabīr's life, taken from an important eighteenth-century Vaiṣṇava hagiographic work, Priyadās's *Bhaktirasabodhinī*. The first poem, "The Simple State," is clearly a satire on religion as it is practiced in Kabīr's time by pious brahmans, Hindu ritualists and idol-worshipers, Muslim scholars and teachers, and a variety of ascetics, meditators, pilgrims, and so on, all of whom value outward appearance above anything else. "The Sapling and the Seed" is also a satire, but it is aimed specifically at brahmans, Hindu priests and priestly scholars. If the first poem claims that the purpose of spiritual effort is to attain the sahaj stithī (the simple, easy state), then the second suggests that the goal is nirvāṇa, or the situation of stasis that is both disembodied and everlasting.

The next two poems are more technical. "The Doer and His Deeds" argues from a dualistic viewpoint that an individual's true self is his or her ultimate principle of identity as an agent of action. However, the true self is essentially different in nature from the actions the individual performs, as also from the fruits, consequences, or products of those actions. As a result, creator and creation are different in kind from each other, as are sky and earth, parent and child, husband and wife, or bindu (point, drop, concentration of energy) and nāda (loud sound, resonance, reverberation). An individual's "phenomenal self" may be a slave to his or her deeds, but his or her true self is not. Kabīr's dualistic argument about agent and action in this poem is a variation on that found, for example, in the *Bhagavad Gīta.*

The fourth poem, "The Warrior," uses more obscure concepts from the tantra and yoga traditions, in which the process of controlling the mind is sometimes called "killing the mind," and the yogi's final victory over his principal "enemy," the mind, coincides with his achievement of the sahaj stithī. Kabīr thus personifies the self as a warrior who has to kill the mind (together with the five capacities of sense perception and the five motor organs), in order to achieve final liberation from the otherwise endless sequence of birth, death, and rebirth.

In the poem here entitled "Māyā," Kabīr returns to somewhat more familiar and accessible ideas. In abstract terms, māyā is the pervasive phenomenon of observable "facts" created playfully (and perhaps even perversely) by God. At the level of ordinary human experience, the universe is nothing but appearances which create the illusion that they constitute reality. Kabīr personifies Māyā as a woman who deceives human beings by seeming real or by simulating reality. In effect, he argues in this poem that if a person realizes that what he or she has been dealing with in the world is merely illusory, mere māyā, then he or she has already broken through the layer of appearances to the truth and to reality.

The final poem in the selection, "The Love of Rāma," then attempts to define who the true seer of reality is. For Kabīr the true seer is neither a person who obeys brahmanical authority and follows the ritual texts of Hinduism in normal society, nor someone who renounces the everyday world and becomes an ascetic in the forest. Instead, the true seer is a devotee or lover of King Rāma, in this case perhaps simply the well-known incarnation of Viṣṇu.

The selection of translations ends with Priyadās's eighteenth-century Vaiṣṇava sectarian account of Kabīr. The account is highly archetyped (and stereotyped), and gives Kabīr's life a pattern we also find in the lives of many other bhakti saints. The bhakta is initially an outcaste or a person of low social origins. He hears a "voice in the sky" and finds a Vaiṣṇava guru or spiritual master by stratagem, and hence starts out on a path of devotion. His devotion is simple (even simplistic) and pleases Viṣṇu, who helps him with divine grace, but also tests him repeatedly and in stages. The devotee persists against social and political opposition, overcomes various obstacles with his goodness and with miraculous deeds, wins over the most powerful worldly antagonists, and resists the most tempting of temptations. He then sees God in his most magnificent form and, with his grace and reciprocal love, "becomes one with him."

The poems below are translated from originals in P. N. Tiwari, ed., *Kabīr granthāvalī*, 2 vols. (Allahabad: Hindi Parishad, 1961), and Shukdev Singh, ed., *Kabīr Bījak* (Allahabad: Nilabh Prakashan, 1972). The biography of Kabir is from Priyadās, *Bhaktirasabodhinī*, verses 268–81.

Further Reading

For extensive translations, commentaries, and background information on the "eastern" and "western" Kabīr traditions, see Linda Hess and Shukdev Singh, trans., *The Bījak of Kabīr* (San Francisco: North Point Press, 1983); and Charlotte Vaudeville, *Kabīr*, vol. 1 (Oxford: Clarendon Press, 1974). For an alternative general discussion, see William J. Dwyer, *Bhakti in Kabīr* (Patna: Associated Book Agency, 1981).

The Simple State
Santo dekhata jaga baurānā

Listen,
you saints—
I see that the world
is crazy.

When I tell the truth,
people run
to beat me up—
when I tell lies,
they believe me.

I've seen
the pious ones,
the ritual-mongers—
they bathe at dawn.

They kill the true self
and worship rocks—
they know nothing.

I've seen
many masters and teachers—
they read their books,
their Qur'āns.

They teach many students
their business tricks—
that's all they know.

They sit at home
in pretentious poses—
their minds are full
of vanity.

They begin to worship
brass and stone—
they're so proud
of their pilgrimages,
they forget the real thing.

They wear caps and beads,
they paint their brows
with the cosmetics
of holiness.

They forget the true words
and the songs of witness
the moment they've sung them—
they haven't heard
the news of the self.

The Hindu says
Rāma's dear to him,
the Muslim says it's Rahīm.

They go to war
and kill each other—
no one knows
the secret of things.

They do their rounds
from door to door,
selling their magic formulas—
they're vain
about their reputations.

All the students
will drown with their teachers—
at the last moment
they'll repent.

Kabīr says,
listen,

you saintly men,
forget all this vanity.

I've said it so many times
but no one listens—
you must merge into
the simple state
simply.

Bījak, śabda 4; p. 111

The Sapling and the Seed
Paṇḍita bhūle paḍhe guni bedā

When learned priests
forget their stuff,
they read the good old Vedas—
without their books,
they don't know
the secret of things.

When they see
someone's suffering
they pounce on it
with words like "karma,"
they apply their theories
about the stages of life.

They've taught the Four Ages
the gāyatrī mantra—
go ask them
whom it has set free.

Whenever they touch someone
they bathe
to purify themselves—
tell them who's really
the inferior one.

They take great pride
in their many good qualities,
but so much vanity
doesn't make them any good.

Only the One
who's the Destroyer of Pride
can deal with their arrogance.

Give up the thought
of being proud of your birth,
look for the text
of nirvāṇa.

You'll find
the eternal bodiless
resting place
only when the sapling
has spoiled the seed.

Granthāvalī, ramainī 7; vol. 2, pp. 120–21

The Doer and His Deeds

Sādho kartā karam te nyāro

O saints,
the doer is different
from his deeds.

He doesn't come and go,
he doesn't die,
he isn't born—
think this over
with a cool mind.

Just as sky and earth
are two,
so do creator and creation
stand apart.

Just as the point of energy
is held back
from the reverberation,
so is my lord and lover
from me.

Who was the real wife
of the man named Daśaratha,
father of Rāma?
And where did Daśaratha's father,
Rāma's grandfather,
come from?

Rādhā and Rukmiṇī
were Kṛṣṇa's queens,
and Kṛṣṇa was the master

and husband of both,
but he also tasted the love
of sixteen thousand lovers—
who was the one
who did all that?

Vasudeva was Kṛṣṇa's father,
and Devakī his mother,
but Kṛṣṇa appeared
in the good Nanda's home.

Kabīr says,
the doer isn't the one
who has gone and sold himself
as a slave
to his deeds.

Granthāvalī, pada 158; vol. 2, p. 92

The Warrior
Khatrī karai khatriyā dharmā

The warrior does
the warrior's duty.

His stock of good deeds,
like money lent to others,
truly increases
by one-fourth.

He kills the living
to preserve the living—
he gives up his life,
yet stays alive
and watches all this happen.

The true warrior
is the one
who goes down fighting
to keep his promise
to protect his clan.

He kills the five
enemy-senses
because he knows
the one true self within.

The hermit who has learned
this lesson from his master
overthrows his mind
right then and there.

Drunk on the senses,
his mind falls fighting
the moment he wounds his target.

Only the mind,
that self-crowned king,
dies in the battle—
and not the true self,
which never perishes.

Love is a void without Rāma,
it goes about
lost in itself.

Bījak, ramainī 83; p. 108

Māyā
Māyā mahā ṭhaginī ham jānī

We know
what Māyā is—
the great con-woman,
a companion to con-men.

She wanders all over the world
with her threefold noose,
she sits rocking in each place,
using a sweet tongue.

At Keśava's place
she masquerades as Kamalā,
in Śiva's mansion
she's Bhavānī.

She has settled down
at the priest's
as an idol,
she has become the holy water
at the pilgrim's destination.

She has planted herself
at the ascetic's

as an ascetic woman,
in the king's palace
she sits on the throne
as a queen.

In some homes
she's diamond and pearl,
in some she has become
a worthless cowrie shell.

She has moved in
with the common devotee
and become a devotee herself,
she lives with the Muslim man
as his Muslim woman.

Kabīr says, listen,
O holy men—
this is the whole
untold story.

Granthāvali, pada 163; vol. 2, pp. 95–96; *Bījak*, śabda 59; p. 131

The Love of King Rāma
Mana re sarayau

Dear heart,
don't do a thing
if you haven't worshiped
King Rāma.

People hear the words
of the Vedas and the Purāṇas
and begin to nurse
their hopes
for the fruits of action.

All these enlightened people
are engrossed by the moment,
but they blame
the learned priests
for their disappointments.

The ascetic withdraws
into the forest
to master his senses,
and feeds on roots and stems.

So do all those shamans,
singers, scholars, and saints
whose lives are written down
on plaque and parchment—
but it doesn't make
a jot of difference.

This one is thin and penniless,
he wraps his loins
in a loincloth—
but the love of God
that Nārada had
hasn't touched his heart or mind.

That one sits
singing holy songs
with great self-satisfaction—
but what God has he seen
or recognized?

Time and death
hack away at the world,
yet everyone describes himself
as a true seer within.

Kabīr says
the only man
who serves a single master
is the one who knows
the love of Rāma.

Granthāvali, pada 86; vol. 2, pp. 50–51

Kabīr

268. Kabīr's mind was very deep and intense; he was steeped in pure emotion. He seized the feeling of devotion, he gave up caste and sect. A voice in the sky said to him, "Mark your brow with the holy symbol of Rāma, make Rāmānanda your master, wear a string of beads in your neck." Kabīr said, "Rāmānanda won't even look at me, he thinks I'm an outcaste." The voice said, "He goes to bathe in the Gaṅgā. Put yourself in his way." Rāmānanda came out in the darkness before dawn and was walking along when his foot struck Kabīr. Rāmānanda cried "Rāma!" and Kabīr took up this word as his secret spiritual formula.

269. Kabīr did what the voice had told him to do. He wore the beads and the mark on his brow and sang and prayed. When his mother saw this she was outraged and made a big noise about it. The outcry reached Rāmānanda. Someone came and said to him, "When anyone asks Kabīr who his master is, he mentions your name." "Get hold of him and bring him here," Rāmānanda said. When Kabīr was brought there, Rāmānanda sat behind a curtain and asked him, "When did I make you my disciple?" Kabīr said, "The name of Rāma is the secret formula. This is written in all the manuals of spiritual practice." Rāmānanda drew aside the curtain. "That's the true faith," he said and embraced Kabīr.

270. Kabīr wove cloth on a loom for a living but his heart and mind were set on Rāma. How shall I say it, what can I say, his ways were so different. He remembered nothing else, devotion was so dear to him. Once he stood in the marketplace selling his cloth when a man came up to him and said, "Give it to me, I have nothing to cover my body." Kabīr began to tear the cloth in half, when the man said, "Half won't do, give me the whole." Kabīr replied, "If you've set your heart on the whole piece, take it."

271. Meanwhile, Kabīr's children, mother, and wife sat watching the path to their home. They were hungry; they wondered, "When will he come home?" He hid himself in the marketplace, wondering, "What will I take home?" When Lord Viṣṇu, who is so quick, who understands everything, and who is the storehouse of grace, realized that Kabīr had the true feeling of devotion, even he fell to wondering. Three days passed like this. Then a man arrived at Kabīr's house loaded with goods. He left everything there and said, "I'm giving you this for your comfort." Kabīr's mother kicked up a fuss, saying, "This is a rich man's trick. He'll have us arrested for robbing him. My son never takes anything without first finding out the price."

272. Two or three men went out in search of Kabīr and brought him back. When Kabīr came home and heard about what had happened, he knew that it was the Lord's doing. Kabīr had found prosperity and happiness but he thought, "Lord Viṣṇu has been kind to me." He immediately called in a crowd of [poor, low-caste] devotees and told them to take away everything. He stopped working his loom; he was immersed in great happiness. When the brahmans who were his enemies heard about it, they were agitated and angry and came running. "Why, you weaver," they said, "you got hold of wealth but you didn't call us. You gave it all to those low-caste men. You'll have to leave this place."

273. "Why should I go away?" asked Kabīr. "Should I steal someone's wealth and give it to you? I sing about Lord Viṣṇu's goodness. I haven't gone and killed someone on the highway." The brahmans said, "You honored the low-caste devotees. That's an insult to us. Give us what you have. Or else you can't live in the same town as us." "There's nothing at home," said Kabīr, "I'll go to

the market. Stay here while I'm gone." So Kabīr got away from the priests with great difficulty. He went and hid in the marketplace to keep out of trouble. The Lord himself came and brought good things with him. He satisfied the brahmans, who took the things and were happy. Thus Kabīr's fame went on shining brightly.

274. Then the Lord came in the guise of a brahman to the place where Kabīr was hiding and said to him, "Why are you starving yourself to death? Go to Kabīr's house. Kabīr gives three pounds of food to anyone who comes to his door. Go there quickly and get some food." Kabīr came home and saw everything. He immediately became engrossed in the Lord. But with all these new miracles, how could Kabīr remain wise and firm? One auspicious day he went out with a whore. It seemed that he was totally absorbed in her. But you should know that he did this because he was afraid of the huge crowd of followers [that is, Kabīr felt that if his followers saw him with a prostitute they would disavow him].

275. When the saints saw this they were afraid for Kabīr, but the evil men were pleased. Then Kabīr was struck by a different idea. He went with the whore to the place where the king was holding court. The king did not extend Kabīr any courtesy. Then Kabīr did something amazing. He scooped up some holy water in his hand and poured it on the ground. The king wondered about it, then asked him, "Why did you do that?" Kabīr said, "I saved a priest in Jagannath Puri from burning his leg." The king was incredulous. He sent a man to the city of Jagannath Puri. The man came back with the news and said, "He told the truth."

276. The king said to the queen, "What Kabīr said turned out to be true. There was a fire. Now tell me what we should do." The queen said, "The only way out is to submit to him." The king and queen went to seek Kabīr's protection. The king carried a big heavy load of grass on his head and tied an axe around his neck. They passed through the marketplace and lost all honor and respect. The king kept cringing all the while at the thought, "I did an evil thing [in not being respectful to Kabīr]." Kabīr saw the king in the distance coming and got very upset. He rose and came up to the king and said, "Put down your burden. I'm not angry with you."

277. When the brahmans became aware of Kabīr's influence, they were filled with envy and hatred. They went and complained to the emperor Sikandar Lodī. Kabīr's enemies went in a large group with his mother, who had joined them. They shouted loudly, "This man has made the whole town unhappy." The emperor said, "Arrest him and bring him here. I want to see what kind of a trickster he is. I'll wipe out his self-esteem. I'm a tough ruler, I'll have him put in tight chains." Kabīr was brought in and made to stand before the emperor. The emperor's [Muslim] judge said, "Sạlaam to the emperor." Kabīr

replied, "I don't know how to salaam. All I know is Rāma. His feet [*pada*, also songs, texts] are my support in moments of danger."

278. Kabīr was put in chains and thrown into the Gaṅgā. But he came out and stood on the bank. The people said, "He knows some magic formula." Then wood was heaped on him and set on fire. But another miracle took place. Kabīr's body glowed so much it even put gold to shame. These methods were unsuccessful, and yet those people did not submit to Kabīr. They brought a mad elephant to overwhelm him. But the elephant would not even come close to him. It bellowed and gave up and ran away. This happened because the Lord sat before Kabīr in the form of a lion and drove away the elephant.

279. When the emperor saw this he jumped up and fell at Kabīr's feet, and the people lost their fight when they saw these miracles. "Save me from God's anger," cried the emperor, "don't perform any more miracles. Take what you want: villages, towns, the whole land. You can have many pleasurable things." Kabīr said, "I only want Rāma, who is one and whom I worship all day long. I want and value nothing else, since everything else is full of millions of defects and diseases." Kabīr thus won and came home. All the holy men met him and expressed their love for him. Only men who love the Lord like this are worth singing about.

280. The brahmans were embarrassed and furious. Then they chose four brahmans, painted their faces, and put beautiful clothes on them. These four men went even to the remotest towns and villages. They asked about all the holy men who lived there. They falsely used Kabīr's name and invited everyone to a feast. All the holy men turned up [at Kabīr's home] when they heard about it. When this happened, Kabīr went away. But the Lord came running, since he travels in the four directions for the sake of his saints and devotees. He put on the guise of Kabīr and sat in different places at the feast. Kabīr himself came back and mingled with the crowd. The Lord fed them all and brought them great happiness.

281. A beautifully dressed celestial woman once came down to lure Kabīr. But when she saw how engrossed he was in God, she went back to heaven. Her tricks did not work. Lord Viṣṇu then came and manifested his four-armed form before Kabīr. Kabīr thus found the fulfillment his eyes had sought. He was truly fortunate. The Lord placed his hand on Kabīr's head and said, "Come to my home, bring your body with you. Sing of my goodness. Live as you wish, take what you want. Your mind is steeped in the true emotion [of bhakti]." Kabīr then went to Maghar. He showed the people there what true devotion is. In the end he asked for huge quantities of flowers. He lay down on them and became one with God. That was what his love was like.

—3—

Poems of Tukārām

Vinay Dharwadker

Tukārām probably lived in the first half of the seventeenth century, most likely between 1608 and 1649, near what is now the city of Pune. He composed a large body of short lyric poems called abhangs, which are mainly in the Vaiṣṇava tradition of devotional poetry, but also carry traces of the Śaiva tradition, among others. He is one of the four most important bhakti poets or sants canonized by the Vārkarī sect in premodern and modern Maharashtra.

Tukārām's poems and the hagiographic tradition surrounding him portray him as the second son in a low-caste Hindu family of Dehu, a small village on the Indrayāṇī River. The family probably belonged to the *kunbī* caste, which in Maharashtra consists primarily of agricultural laborers, sharecroppers, and poor farmers. Tukārām's family appears to have been relatively secure at the time of his birth, since it cultivated about fifteen acres of land, managed a grocery shop on weekly market days, and engaged in some local moneylending. Tukārām's elder brother lost his wife prematurely and, in response to the tragedy, became a wandering ascetic or renouncer of the world associated with the Gosavīs, an order of spiritual practitioners of the Nāth sect in premodern Maharashtra. As a consequence, Tukārām had to play an active role in the family occupations at an early age. At thirteen he was married to Rukmābāī, but since she turned out to be severely asthmatic, a second marriage was arranged for him, this time to a shrewish woman named Jījābāī. When Tukārām's parents died in his seventeenth year, he became the sole support of two wives, some children, and younger brothers and sisters. In the terrible famine that overran the Deccan between 1629 and 1631, Tukārām lost his livelihood, and his first wife and eldest son died of starvation.

In or around 1630, apparently in the midst of this turmoil, Tukārām became a devotee of Viṭṭhala, the god of the Vārkarī sect. Viṭṭhala (also known as Viṭhobā and Pāṇḍurang) was the famous god of the holy town of Paṇḍharpur in southern Maharashtra, who had been assimilated into the Vaiṣṇava pantheon as an avatar of Kṛṣṇa several centuries earlier, but had nevertheless remained a common folk deity in the Maharashtrian countryside. During the next fifteen years or so, Tukārām became famous throughout the western Deccan region as a devotee, and drew a large number of followers to Dehu. However, reports of his simple but strong poetry, his numerous miracles, his criticism of some Hindu rituals and social conventions, and his advocacy of devotion to Viṭṭhala apparently angered a number of powerful priests and landowners in the region. Rāmeśvar Bhaṭṭ, a well-known brahman and perhaps Tukārām's most formidable antagonist, secured an administrative order to have the poet's notebooks thrown into the Indrayāṇī River. But the notebooks containing the text of numerous abhangs surfaced thirteen days later, unharmed by the water, and with the help of this miracle Tukārām overcame his persecutors. Sometime in the year 1649 he disappeared mysteriously, without leaving behind the kind of monument associated with the other major Marathi saints of the premodern period. One popular account of Tukārām's life suggests that he "flew up to heaven" on the eagle Garuḍa, Lord Viṣṇu's vehicle.

The text of Tukārām's poems, preserved and transmitted by the poets, commentators, and priests of the Vārkarī sect, was closed only in the nineteenth century. It contains more than 4,600 abhangs (most of them in Marathi, but also several dozen in Hindi), of which about 1,300 can be traced back to the seventeenth century and probably constitute the authentic core of the poet's work. The poems vary in length, mostly from five stanzas to about fifteen, and are at once literary and folk compositions, written and oral, fixed and fluid, verbal and musical, textual and preformative. Tukārām's phrases and lines are frequently quoted in modern Marathi discourse. The poems are still recited, chanted, sung, and danced to regularly during the monthly, seasonal, and annual pilgrimages to Paṇḍharpur organized by the Vārkarī sect, and they often serve as models and reference points in modern Marathi literature, especially poetry.

A Tukārām abhang usually has a simple poetic structure and makes a commonplace religious or social argument. Its devotion is frequently directed toward Viṭṭhala, a small dark god with large eyes who stands akimbo on a brick in his temple in Paṇḍharpur. The speaker of an abhang often portrays himself as a poor, low-caste man who has faced much misfortune, humiliation, and torment. He frequently addresses God directly, calling him interchangeably Viṭṭhala and Pāṇḍurang, Hari and Nārāyaṇa (the last two being among Viṣṇu's older, more general names), and sometimes going so far as actually to quarrel with him face to face. The imagery and symbolism of an abhang most often relates directly to the Maharashtrian countryside, its system of villages and small towns, its basically Hindu organization, and especially its agricultural economy.

The following selection of twelve abhangs draws on several distinct types of poems in the Tukārām tradition, and can be divided into three sets, each containing four interrelated poems. The first set is broadly social in its orientation. Of these four poems, "The Rich Farmer," "The Harvest," and "The Waterwheel" are situated explicitly in the farming community of rural Maharashtra. "The Rich Farmer" is a criticism of a representative of a locally powerful group of farmers, from the double viewpoint of a poor farmer and a Vaiṣṇava householder. Unlike the rich farmer, a good Vaiṣṇava (like Tukārām in this poem) would consider the recitation of a sacred text, the domestic cultivation of basil, charity to poor brahmans, and courtesy to guests very meaningful rituals in Hindu society. "The Harvest" figuratively uses the familiar activities on a farm (guarding the crop near harvest time, working on the threshing floor, distributing fair shares of the grain to the farm hands) to establish social, economic, and ethical ideals, and even to describe the process of working out one's salvation. Similarly, "The Waterwheel" uses the Persian wheel, commonly employed for drawing irrigation water from wells, to explain the notion of rebirth in poetic terms. In Indian theories of karma and saṃsāra, a "living thing" is born 8,400,000 times on earth during the existence of a particular universe. Tukārām compares this succession of lives to the series of clay pots strung onto a waterwheel, which seems endless when the wheel rotates in the mouth of the well. The fourth poem in this set, "The Jangamas" is similar to "The Rich Farmer" in that it criticizes a particular social type in Tukārām's immediate world. The target in this case, however, is not a social class but a religious group or subsect, the Jangamas, who are Vīraśaiva devotees of Śiva, and originate in the Kannada-speaking area (now the state of Karnataka) just south of Maharashtra.

The second set of four poems is concerned more directly with the devotee, his chosen god, and their mutual relationship. "The Divine Play" portrays the ignorant and symbolically blind devotee in search of the one who will grant him final liberation from suffering and rebirth. The poem also portrays the one as a two-faced god. On the one hand, he is the compassionate "driver" of the universe (here conceived of as something of a machine or vehicle), who responds favorably to his devotees' cries for help. On the other hand, he is a cruelly playful master who unleashes "the dogs of desire upon us." The next poem, "The Prisoner," depicts the devotee as someone trapped helplessly in the world by action and suffering from the fruits of action, and identifies his god as the only one capable of freeing him permanently from that situation. "God as a Thief" and "Quarreling with God," however, dramatize the elusive, perplexing, and contradictory nature of that god. In one perspective, he is like a thief who raids his own house (the devotee's embodied self) and then cunningly, even deviously, eludes his would-be captors (the "posse" of devotees on a godhunt that is similar to a manhunt). In another perspective, God is like a bully in the marketplace, inclined to obscene self-display and to picking on innocent passers-by.

The last set of four poems uses this general social and religious context to deepen the expression of the devotee's predicament and anguish. These abhangs are composed in the personal confessional mode, and are addressed directly to God or are meant to be overheard by him. "Begging for God's Compassion" is a typical supplication, in which Tukārām narrates his entrapment in action and rebirth, denigrates himself for being a victim of worldly and spiritual impoverishment, and begs God to free him forever. In "Viṭṭhala," Tukārām uses the invocation of God's name and form to praise both Viṭṭhala and the practice of devotion itself, and to contrast divinity and divine things with the created world, which possesses serpentlike "sharp and hostile stratagems." In contrast, "The Resting Place" stays within the confessional mode, but moves beyond self-abasement to arrive at a sense of fulfillment in oneness with God. At this stage of Tukārām's spiritual evolution as a bhakta, Viṭṭhala is initially a generalized male god (Nārāyaṇa) but then changes into a very maternal goddess figure (Pāṇḍurangā). Finally, "The Flood" articulates the state of perpetual joy, happiness, or bliss, which the devotee enters when he has broken through to God with his many good deeds of devotion.

The translations below are based on the Marathi text and numbering in *Śrītukārāmmahārājgāthābhāṣya,* with a commentary by Shankar Mahārāj Khandārkar, 2 vols. (Ambarkheḍ, District Yavatmāḷ: Śrīsādhumahārāj Sansthān, [1965?]).

Further Reading

J. Nelson Fraser and K. B. Marathe, trans., *The Poems of Tukārām,* 3 vols. (1909; reprint Delhi: Motilal Banarsidass, 1981), contains prose translations of all the abhangs. For background, interpretations, and some translations, see G. A. Deleury, *The Cult of Viṭhobā* (Poona: Deccan College, 1960); Arun Kolatkar, "Translations from Tukārām and Other Saint-Poets," *Journal of South Asian Literature,* 17:1 (Winter-Spring 1982), 111–14; R. D. Ranade, *Mysticism in India: The Poet-Saints of Maharashtra* (Albany: SUNY Press, 1983 reprint of *Indian Mysticism: Mysticism in Maharashtra* [Poona: Aryabhushan Press Office, 1933]); S. G. Tulpule, *Classical Marathi Literature from the Beginning to A.D. 1818,* vol. 9, fasc. 4 of *A History of Indian Literature,* edited by Jan Gonda (Wiesbaden: Otto Harrassowitz, 1979); and Eleanor Zelliot, "The Medieval Bhakti Movement in History: An Essay on the Literature in English," in *Hinduism: New Essays in the History of Religions,* edited by Bardwell L. Smith (Leiden: E. J. Brill, 1976).

The Rich Farmer
Dagaḍācyā devā

He has vowed undying devotion
to a god of stone,
but he won't let his wife go
listen to a holy recitation.

He has built a crematorium
with his hoarded wealth,
but he thinks it wrong to grow
holy basil at his door.

Thieves plunder his home
and bring him much grief,
but he won't give a coin
to a poor brahman.

He treats his son-in-law
like a guest of honor,
but he turns his back upon
his real guests.

Tukā says, curse him,
may he burn.
He's only a burden
and drains the earth.

Abhang 2,712; vol. 2, p. 1,060

The Harvest
Seta āle sugi

The field has ripened:
watch its four corners.
The grain is ready for harvest,
but you mustn't stop working.

Guard it, guard it!
Don't fall asleep,
don't take it easy:
the crop's still standing on the ground.

Put a stone in your sling:
the force of your shot,
your shouting and shooing
will scatter all the flocks of birds.

Light a fire, keep awake,
keep changing places:
when your head rolls,
you won't have your strength, your wits.

Give generously from the threshing floor,
make the world happy.
When the grain's piled up,
pay your taxes, give everyone his share.

Tukā says that's the moment
when there's nothing left to be done.

What's ours is in our hands,
and the chaff and husks have been thrown away.

Abhang 813; vol. 1, p. 322

The Waterwheel
Kiti yā kāḷācā

How long must you endure
the whirlwind of death, of time?
It's at your back
all the while.

Free yourself
from your eighty-four hundred thousand births:
enter the shelter
of Pāṇḍurang.

The seed that sprouts to life
brings death with it,
and when it dies
it's quickly born again.

Tukā says one's lives
are strung like pots on a waterwheel:
a pot frees itself
only when the cord is broken.

Abhang 939; vol. 1, p. 376

The Jangamas
Houni jangama

They've become Jangamas
and put on the sacred ash:
they go from house to house
blowing their conches.

They don't serve Śiva's shrine,
where the offerings have gone stale:
they ring their bells
only for their own bellies.

Tukā says they don't have
the true devotion to Śiva:

they merely carry on
the commerce of this world.

Abhang 3,061; vol. 2, p. 1,190

The Divine Play
Bahuta sosile

I suffered a lot in the past
because I was ignorant.
Now I should be blind
to what lies ahead.

I should put this in the hands
of the one who's one.
I shouldn't grope about
for the other gods, who're many.

Whoever he may be
who drives the universe,
he'll call out to us
if we call out to him.

Tukā says he has set
the dogs of desire upon us.
Without this divine play
there would be no torment.

Abhang 889; vol. 1, p. 357

The Prisoner
Suṭāyācā kāhi

I find ways and means
to set myself free:
but, look, they only
entangle my feet.

I'm caught like a prisoner
under this sorrow's warrant:
I've lost my strength,
my wits.

All my past deeds
and present actions,

gathered in one place,
come dragging after me.

I'm trapped in the snare
of do's and don'ts:
I cut them one by one
but they can't be sorted out,

I collect them, but they grow back
like each other's limbs.
In desire's company
I've found unhappiness.

Tukā says, Lord,
now you must set me free:
I've become
completely powerless.

Abhang 676; vol. 1, p. 264

God as a Thief
Devācyā ghari

God was the thief
who raided God's home.
God plundered God
and left him begging.

Run a posse! Run a posse!
He wasn't in the villages
we left behind.
Where shall we hunt him now?

The thief chose
to stay put in the house.
At the first opportunity
he wrecked everything.

Tukā says
there's no one here at all.
Who plundered
whose what?

Abhang 1,844; vol. 1, p. 730

Quarreling with God
Lāja na vicāra

You're shameless,
and you don't think.
You quarrel with us
like a man in the marketplace.

And then you're delighted
whenever you meet
someone who has become
just like you.

You're itching to take off
your loincloth.
And in the end
you'll strip us all naked.

Tukā says, you heartless man,
you don't give a damn
about yourself
or anyone else.

Abhang 1,817; vol. 1, p. 719

Begging for God's Compassion
Bahuta jācalo sansārī

The world has bothered me no end.
I've lain in the womb in my mother's belly.
I've become the beggar who begs at the doors
of eighty-four hundred thousand yonis.

I live like a slave in someone else's hands.
I'm caught and whirled in the powerful snare
of all my deeds, done now and in earlier births,
whose fruits stick to me, to ripen now and later.

My belly's empty and there's no rest.
No destination, no resting place, no home town.
Lord, don't spin me like this, I've lost my strength.
My soul sputters in torment, like a rice grain on a hot griddle.

So many times have gone by like this,
and I don't know how many more lie ahead of me.
They come around again and again without a break.
Maybe the string will snap only when the world ends.

Who will take away such anguish from me?
On whom can I press my burden?
Your name ferries us across the world's ocean,
but you hide in a hole, waiting in ambush.

Strike me now, run me over, O Nārāyaṇa.
Do this for me, impoverished wretch that I am.
Don't ask a man without goodness for good things.
Tukā begs for your compassion.

Abhang 4,029; vol. 2, p. 1,700

Viṭṭhala

Cāngale nāma

His name is good, his form lovely.
They cool my eye and drive away my fever.
Viṭṭhala, Viṭṭhala is my rosary.
So short and sweet, so easy, and always there.

This name is a weapon, the arrow of nirvāṇa,
a means for the moment when death is near.
What's the use of preparing for a funeral?
Nārāyaṇa breaks up your pain if you fix your sights on him.

This is the very best of all that's known.
Because it frees you from the world, and frees you forever,
you must go and seek out the Lord's protection.
It's all you need to do, and it's enough.

That's why I'm angry with the world,
this gleaming, poisonous serpent.
It keeps us apart, me and you, my giver,
with its sharp and hostile stratagems.

It has made me taste the fruit of this world,
it has fixed the wrong verses in my mind.
I've grown fat and heavy with my many sojourns,
I've grown bald with the mockery heaped on me.

I've had the punishment for what I've done,
I've eaten what's eaten in many castes and births.
I must break it up now, put an end to it.
Lord, Tūka lays himself down at your feet.

Abhang 4,031; vol. 2, p. 1,702

The Resting Place
Barave jhāle

It's good that I was born this time,
that I fastened my link with a human body.
I got the best lot, which brought me great gain,
I've become the vessel of every happiness.

You've given me the organs of sense and action,
hands, feet, ears, and eyes, and a mouth to speak with.
Thus you've connected me with you, O Nārāyaṇa,
and the world's sickness of living rots away.

Goodness accumulates grain by grain,
and yet it links up so many births,
letting your name surface in our speech,
letting the communion of saints take place.

So I've found my resting place.
How shall I give you thanks and praise?
I'll leave this piece of life at your feet,
for you're my mother, O Pāṇḍurange.

You've wiped out the longing locked in my eye,
you've washed away my dirt of good and bad.
You've cooled me by placing me at your breast,
you've put me to sleep like a child in its resting place.

There's nothing to pair with this joy,
I taste its sweetness even as I tell my story.
Tukā says you even found your form and shape
because of our love, which must be encountered face to face.

Abhang 4,012; vol. 2, p. 1,986

The Flood
Pūra ālā ānandācā

This is a flood
of sheer bliss:
love's waves splash,
fly up in a spray.

Let's tie ourselves
to Viṭṭhala's float:
we'll swim across
to the other shore.

Everyone's a servant
of the lord:
dear brothers,
take the plunge.

This doesn't happen
all the time:
the waters of bliss
can't be measured.

Tukā says
our merits are great:
this water flows down
the path they've made.

Abhang 339; vol. 1, p. 138

—4—

The Litany of Names of Mañjuśrī

Ronald M. Davidson

The Litany of Names of Mañjuśrī is an evocative text from the final phase of Buddhism in India. It proclaims itself to be the recitation of the various epithets of the bodhisattva of intellectual and gnostic excellence, Mañjuśrī, "Gentle Glory." Because Buddhism defined the problem of the human condition in terms of ignorance or perverted understanding, it frequently extolled intelligence as the liberating virtue. We should not, therefore, be surprised that the Great Vehicle (Mahāyāna) figure closely associated with intelligence, Mañjuśrī, should become the focus of a cult employed by intellectual Buddhists. But this is a text growing out of tantric Buddhism, called the Vehicle of the Thunderbolt (*Vajrayāna*) or the Vehicle of Secret Spells (*Mantrayāna*) which set forth a wide range of ritual and meditative practices aimed toward the goal of attaining both mundane and supramundane powers—including, of course, the attainment of buddhahood. *The Litany of the Names of Mañjuśrī* became one of the most popular liturgical works of later Indian Buddhism, and was recited daily by monks and laymen in India.

Buddhism has traditionally defined reality in terms of multiplicity and its resolution into nonduality, rather than the model of a transcendent divine creator wholly independent and separate from phenomenal existence. Because the Buddha represented the embodiment of the resolution into nonduality, his supermundane virtue and omniscience was the subject of verses of praise right from the beginning of Buddhist literature, in which statements concerning the ultimate reality of the Buddha's cognition were seen as one means of expressing a fraction of his nature. The development of verses of praise was both an indication of devotion to the Buddha and an expression of the desire to recreate in an imperfect medium the limitless ramifications of the Buddha's cognition for the benefit of those who sought to produce in their own minds a mythic reenactment of his awakening.

The Litany of Names of Mañjuśrī belongs to the late seventh or early eighth centuries C.E. This text consists in its present form of 167 verses and a lengthy prose section. It begins, like so many other Buddhist texts, with a request from a disciple on behalf of the assembled audience that the Buddha provide a certain teaching. In this case, however, the one who makes the request is the heroic tantric deity (whether he is himself a buddha or a bodhisattva is not clear here) named Vajradhara ("Bearer of the Thunderbolt," also known here as Vajrapāṇi). Śākyamuni Buddha accedes to the request to set forth *The Litany of Names of Mañjuśrī*, offering effusive praise to Mañjuśrī in the form of multiple epithets and identifications. In the course of the verses, Mañjuśrī comes to be identified with all that is auspicious and worthy of honor. Special attention, however, is paid to his identity with the myriad categories of Buddhist wisdom.

The core of the work, verses 26–162, sets forth the use of syllables as a precursor to the actual visualization of many divinities, all of whom are considered forms of Mañjuśrī. It is here that the Buddha also elaborates the meditative environment of the circle of divinity (*maṇḍala*, mandala) in the Path of Secret Spells. A mandala in tantric Buddhism is a perfected environment, often depicted as a buddha's palace. Ritual entry into this environment is the central event in tantric Buddhist initiation, and the manifestation of oneself as a buddha and one's environment as a perfect mandala is one of the prime goals of tantric Buddhist practice. The initial verse concerning Mañjuśrī (v. 28) identifies him with the letter *a*, the first syllable of the Sanskrit alphabet. Each name in the *Litany*, then, is conceptualized as a reflection of the initial syllable *a* in the same way that each divinity is a reflection of Mañjuśrī. Thus the esoteric system preserves the paradigm of one reality reflected in multiple realities—Mañjuśrī is observed in the pronouncement of each name, and each of his reflections takes its place in the drama of crystalizing the universal diagram (*maṇḍala*).

The second part of the text, the prose section, extols the virtues of its own recitation. This kind of self-reflective advertisement is a common component of Buddhist literature of the Great Vehicle, providing a self-contained claim to efficacy and authority for works composed long after the Buddha's death which nonetheless claim to be the word of the Buddha. Here it is explained that those who recite the *Litany* three times daily will not only gain all manner of transcendent benefits but will also be protected wherever they may travel by the gods of the Hindu pantheon, including Viṣṇu (Nārāyaṇa) and Śiva (Maheśvara).

Unlike most earlier works in praise of the Buddha or the great bodhisattvas, the *Litany of Names of Mañjuśrī* was evidently written for an esoteric audience, one that would have had the mandala revealed to them in the ritual of consecration by a master of the Path of Secret Spells. Perhaps the most curious aspect of the *Litany of Names* is its unusual ability to have crossed over into a popular cultus of the bodhisattva of intelligence while retaining its function as the evocation of various esoteric diagrams. That one text could speak simultaneously to multiple communities seems to indicate that it directly addressed an important facet of both popular and monastic Buddhism in India.

For an edition of the Sanskrit text and further discussion of the text and its commentaries, see Ronald M. Davidson, "*The Litany of Names of Mañjuśrī*—Text and Translation of the *Mañjuśrīnāmasaṃgīti*," in Michel Strickmann, ed., *Tantric and Taoist Studies in Honour of R. A. Stein, Mélanges Chinois et Bouddhiques*, Vol. 20 (Brussels: Institute Belge des Hautes Études Chinoises, 1981), pp. 1–69.

The Litany of Names of Mañjuśrī

HOMAGE TO MAÑJUŚRĪ WHO IS A TRUE PRINCE

Sixteen Verses on Requesting Instruction

1. Now the glorious Vajradhara, superb in taming those difficult to tame, being victorious over the triple world [the underworld, the surface of the earth, and the sky], a hero, an esoteric ruler, a lord with his weapon,

2. his eyes as opened white lotuses and face like a pale red lotus in bloom, in his hand waving now and again the best of vajras [a ritual scepter],

3. with endless Vajrapāṇis showing billows of angry brows, heroes in taming those difficult to tame, their forms heroic and fearsome,

4. their hands waving the flashing-tipped vajras, excellent agents for the benefit of the world by their great compassion and insight and means,

5. by disposition happy and joyful, delighted, but with forms of wrath and hostility, protectors in doing the duty of buddhas, altogether they stood bent down in homage.

6. Bowing to the protector, the completely awakened, the blessed one, the tathāgata [Vajradhara] stood in front, his hands folded in homage, and spoke these words:

7. "For my sake, my benefit, O Overlord, through compassion toward me, may I be an obtainer of the realization process of illusion's net.

8. "For the sake of all beings sunk in unknowing, their minds confused in defilement, that they may obtain the highest fruit,

9. "may the completely awakened, the blessed one, the teacher, the guide of the world, knowing the reality of the great vow, highest in knowing the faculties and dispositions, may he reveal

10. "[*The Litany of Names*] *of Mañjuśrī*, the gnostic entity, who is self-produced, embodied gnosis, the blessed one's gnostic body, vocal lord, the great coronal dome.

11. "This excellent *Litany of Names* with depth of meaning and lofty meaning, with great meaning, unequaled and blessed, wholesome in beginning, middle, and end.

12. "That which was spoken by previous buddhas, will be spoken by the future ones, and that which the completely awakened in the present recite again and again.

13. "[That *Litany of Names*] extolled in the *Great Scripture of Illusion's Net* by unlimited delighted Mahāvajradharas, bearers of mantras,

14. "until deliverance I will preserve it with steadfast intention, since I am, O Protector, the esoteric bearer for all the completely awakened.

15. "For the destruction of their every defilement and elimination of all their unknowing, I will reveal this [*Litany*] to beings, each according to his own disposition."

16. Having beseeched the Tathāgata thus for instruction, Vajrapāṇi, the esoteric leader, his body bent, his hands folded in homage, stood in the fore [of the assembly].

Six Verses in Reply

17. Then Śākyamuni, the blessed one, the completely awakened, the best of men, having thrust from his mouth his beautiful, long, wide tongue,

18. displayed a smile cleansing the three evil states [of existence as animals, ghosts, and beings of hell] throughout the worlds, illuminating the triple world and chastening the enemies, the four Māras [of the aggregates, defilement, death, and the deity Māra];

19. flooding the triple world with this divine sweet praise, he replied to Vajrapāṇi, the esoteric leader of great power.

20. "Well done, O glorious Vajradhara; it is proper of you, Vajrapāṇi, that, prompted by great compassion for the world's benefit,

21. "you are eager to hear from me the *Litany of Names* of the gnostic body of Mañjuśrī, having great meaning, purifying and clarifying transgression.

22. "That is well done, and I will teach it to you, O esoteric ruler. Listen with your mind one-pointed, O blessed one; that is well done."

Two Verses Reflecting on the Six Families

23. Then Śākyamuni, the blessed one, reflected on the three families, the entire great-mantra family, the mantra-knowledge-holder family,

24. the worldly and superworldly family, the grand world-illuminating family, the foremost family, the *Mahāmudrā*, and the great family, the exalted coronal dome.

Three Verses on the Steps in the Realization Process of Illusion's Net

25. [Śākyamuni] pronounced this mystic verse, having six kinds of mantra and possessing unarisen characteristics, being nondual in arising and joined with the vocal lord [Mañjuśrī]:

26. "[The letters] *a ā i ī u ū e ai o au aṃ aḥ* stand in the heart. I am Buddha, the embodied knowledge of the buddhas occurring in the three times.

27. "Oṃ homage to you, Embodied Knowledge of Insight, Cutter of Suffering, Sharp as a Vajra. Homage to you, Lord of Speech, Gnostic Body, Arapacana!

Fourteen Verses on the Vajradhātu Mahāmaṇḍala

28. "And in this way the blessed one, the Buddha [Mañjuśrī], the completely awakened, born from the syllable *a*, is the syllable *a*, the foremost of all phonemes, of great meaning, the supreme syllable.

29. "Aspirated, unoriginated, without uttering a sound, he is the foremost cause of all expression, shining forth within all speech.

30. "His great desire is an exalted festival, securing the happiness of all beings; his great anger is an exalted festival, being the great enemy of all defilements.

31. "His great delusion is an exalted festival, subduing the delusion in those with dull wit; his great wrath is an exalted festival, the great enemy of great wrath.

32. "His great avarice is an exalted festival, subduing all avarice; his great desire is the great delight, grand happiness, and great pleasure.

33. "Of great form and great body, with great color and grand physique, with exalted name he is very noble, having a grand expansive maṇḍala.

34. "Bearing the great sword of insight, with a great elephant goad for defilements, he is foremost, greatly famous, very renowned, with great light and exalted splendor.

35. "Bearing the grand illusion, he is wise, accomplishing the object [of beings in] the grand illusion. Delighted with the pleasure of the grand illusion, he is a conjuror of grand illusions.

36. "Highest in being a lord of great giving, foremost in exalted morality, firm through embracing great forebearance, he is zealous with great heroism.

37. "Present in exalted meditation and concentration, bearing the body of great insight, he is great strength, great means; his is aspiration and the gnostic ocean.

38. "Unlimited in loving kindness, greatly compassionate and most intelligent, with great insight and grand intellect, he is great in means with profound performance.

39. "Arrived at great strength and psychic power, very intense and very fast, employing great psychic power and bearing the name 'Great Lord,' his zeal is in great strength.

40. "Splitter of the vast mountain of existence, being Mahāvajradhara, he is indestructible. Being very fierce and very terrible, he creates fear in the very ferocious.

41. "Being highest with great incantations, he is the protector; being highest with great mantras, he is the guide. Having mounted to the practice of the Great Vehicle, he is highest in the practice of the Great Vehicle.

***Twenty-five Verses, Less a Quarter, on the Very Pure Gnosis of the Sphere of All Phenomena* (dharmadhātu)**

42. "Being Mahāvairocana, he is buddha; he is a great sage with profound sapience, and as he is produced by the great practice of mantras, by nature he is the great practice of mantras.

43. "Having obtained the ten perfections, he is the basis for the ten perfections [giving, virtue, patience, effort, meditation, insight, means, aspiration, power, and gnosis]. Being the purity of the ten perfections, he is the practice of the ten perfections.

44. "Being the lord of the ten stages, he is the protector established on ten stages. Himself pure with the ten knowledges [of phenomena, successive knowledge, knowledge of worldly usage, of others' minds, of suffering, of its arising, of its extinction, of the path, of final destruction, and of no future arising], he is the pure bearer of the ten knowledges.

45. "Having ten aspects, his purpose being the ten referents, he is the leader of sages, a ten-powered one, an overlord.[1] Performing all and every sort of purpose, he is great, with control in ten aspects [over life, over mind, necessities, activity, birth, interest, aspiration, psychic power, dharma, and control of knowledge].

46. "Beginningless and by nature without diffusion, naturally pure and in nature suchness, exclaiming just how it is, and, as he says, he does so without any other speech.

47. "Nondual and proclaiming nonduality, he stands just at the limit of actuality. With his lion's roar of egolessness, he frightens the deer that is the evil heretic.

48. "Penetrating everywhere, his path is fruitful; with a speed like the Tathāgata's thought, he is a victor whose enemies are conquered, and a conqueror, a universal ruler with great strength.

49. "At the head of hosts, a preceptor of hosts, a lord of hosts, and a commander of hosts with power, he is foremost through great sustaining power and with an excellent practice, not to be guided by others.

50. "As the lord of speech, the commander of speech possessed of eloquence, he is the master of speech unending in fluency, and with true speech he speaks the truth, teaching the four truths [of distress, its origin, its extinction, and the path].

51. "Not turning back and not seeking rebirth, he is like a rhinocerous, a leader of the self-enlightened; having been delivered by various kinds of deliverance, he is the unique cause of the great elements [earth, water, fire, air].

52. "An arhat, a bhikṣu with his impurities exhausted, he is separated from passion, his senses subdued. He has obtained ease and fearlessness, becoming cool and limpid.

53. "Completed in wisdom and good conduct, he is well-gone, the best as knower of the world. Without a sense of an 'I' and 'mine,' he is established in the practice of the two truths [the absolute truth and the relative truth].

54. "Standing at the uttermost limit of existence, he rests on this terrace, his duty done. Having rejected isolating knowledge, he is the cleaving sword of insight.

55. "With true dharma, a king of dharma, shining, he is supreme as luminary of the world. A lord of dharma, a king of dharma, he is the instructor in the path toward well-being.

56. "His aim accomplished and thought accomplished, he has abandoned thought. Devoid of mentation, his sphere is indestructible, the dharmadhātu, supreme, imperishable.

57. "Possessed of merit, with accumulated merit, he is knowledge and the great source of knowledge. Possessed of knowledge in knowing the real and unreal, he has accumulated the two accumulations.

58. "Eternal, a universal ruler, a yogin [yogi], he is meditation and to be reflected upon, the lord of the intelligent. He is to be personally realized, truly unshakable, primeval, bearing the triple body [of a buddha].

59. "A buddha in his nature of five bodies, an overlord by his nature of five types of gnosis, wearing a diadem whose nature is five buddhas, having five eyes, he maintains dissociation.[2]

60. "The progenitor of all buddhas, he is the Buddha's son, supreme, the best. Arisen from existence in insight, he is sourceless; his source is the dharma while he puts an end to existence.

61. "His unique essence impenetrable, himself a vajra, immediately arisen he is the lord of the world; arisen from the sky and self-arisen, he is the exalted fire of insightful gnosis.

62. "Vairocana, the great lumen, the light of gnosis, he is the illuminator; the lamp of the world, the torch of gnosis, with great splendor he is radiant light.

63. "Vidyārāja, the lord of excellent mantras, he is mantrarāja performing the great goal. As the exalted coronal dome, the marvellous coronal dome, he teaches in every sort of way, the lord of space.

64. "Foremost, as he is the physical presence of all buddhas, with his eyes bringing happiness to the world; with manifold form he is the creator, a great sage to be worshiped and honored.

65. "Bearing the three families, he is a possessor of mantras, bearing up mantras and the great vow; he is best in bearing up the triple gem and the highest teacher of the triple vehicle.[3]

66. "Being Amoghapāśa, he is victorious; as Vajrapāśa he is a great grabber; he is Vajrāṅkuśa with a great noose.

Ten Verses, Plus a Quarter, on the Mirrorlike Gnosis

"The great terror-bearing Vajrabhairava,

67. "King of furies, six-headed and terrible, six-eyed and six-armed and strong; he is a skeleton baring its fangs, hundred-headed Halāhala.

68. "Yamāntaka, the king of obstructions, with the force of a vajra, the creator of fear, his is the famous vajra, with a vajra in his heart, having the illusory vajra and a great belly.

69. "A lord with his weapon, whose source is vajra, with the essence of vajra he is like the sky, and having a unique, unmoving multitude of tufts of hair, he is wet in bearing the elephant-skin garment.

70. "With great terror, saying Hā Hā, and creating fear saying Hī Hī, with a terrible laugh, a great laugh, he is Vajrahāsa, the great clamor.

71. "He is Vajrasattva, the great being, and Vajrarāja with great bliss. Indestructibly violent with great delight, he performs the Hūṃ of the Vajrahūmkāra.

72. "Taking as a weapon the arrow of vajra, with the sword of vajra he slashes. Holding the crossed vajra, a possessor of vajra, with the unique vajra he is victorious in battle.

73. "Having terrible eyes blazing like a vajra and with hair blazing like a vajra, he is Vajrāveśa, in exalted possession, with a hundred eyes, eyes of vajra.

74. "His body hairs bristling like vajras, a unique body with vajra-hairs, the origin of his nails in the tips of vajras, he has skin which is impenetrable and in essence vajra.

75. "Glorious in bearing a rosary of vajras and ornamented by ornaments of vajra, his is the great noise and the terrible laugh Hā Hā, and the six syllables [the first five letters of the esoteric alphabet and the "etc." sign, arapacanādi] with noise like a vajra.

76. "Gentle-voiced, with a great roar, he is great with the sound unique in the world. He is sonance as far as the end of the sphere of space and the best of those possessed of sound.

Forty-two Verses on the Gnosis of Individual Inspection

77. "Being suchness, actual egolessness, the limit of actuality, and devoid of syllables, he is a bull among the speakers of emptiness with a roar both deep and high.

78. "As the conch of the dharma he has great sound, and as the gong of the dharma he has great noise; by his nonlocalized nirvāṇa he is the drum of the dharma in the ten directions.

79. "Without form and with form he is the foremost, with various forms made from thought. Being the majesty in the shining of all form, he bears the reflected images in their totality.

80. "Invincible, distinguished, the lord over the triple sphere, being well advanced on the noble path he is the crest ornament of the dharma with great sovereignty.

81. "His body uniquely youthful in the triple world, he is an elder, old, the lord of creatures. Bearing the thirty-two marks [of the Mahāpuruṣa], he is charming and handsome in the triple world.

82. "A preceptor of the qualities and knowledge of the world, with confidence he is the preceptor to the world. He is protector, preserver, trustworthy in the triple world, a refuge and the highest defender.

83. "His active experience the extension of space, he is the ocean of the Omniscient's gnosis. He splits the shell around the egg of ignorance and tears the net of existence.

84. "With the general defilements totally pacified, he has gone to the far shore of the ocean of existence. Wearing the diadem of the gnostic consecration, he has for his ornament the perfectly awakened.

85. "Easing the distress of the three kinds of suffering [of pain, change, and conditioned existence] and bringing the three to an end, he is endless, passed to the triple liberation [of the disciple, private buddha, and buddha]; released from all veils he has passed to the state of equality, like space.

86. "Beyond the filth of all defilements, he thoroughly comprehends the three times [past, present, future] and timelessness; he is the great snake for all beings, the crown of those crowned with qualities.

87. "Released from all residues he is well established in the track of space; bearing the great wish-fulfilling gem, he is the highest of all jewels, the overlord.

88. "He is the wide wishing tree and the best of great good vases; an agent acting for the sake of beings, he desires their benefit, with affection toward beings.

89. "Knowing the skillful and the destructive and aware of timing, he understands the occasion and, possessing his vow, is the overlord. Knowing the faculties of beings and the correct opportunity, he is skilled in the triple release.

90. "Possessed of qualities, knowing qualities and knowing dharma, he is auspicious, arisen from the auspicious. The auspiciousness of all that is auspicious, he is fame and fortune, renown and goodness.

91. "Being the great festival, the great respite, the grand happiness, and the great pleasure, he is a considerate reception, hospitality, prosperity, real joy, glory, and the lord of renown.

92. "Possessed of excellence, the best benefactor, giving refuge he is the highest refuge. Best among the enemies of great fear, he destroys without exception all fear.

93. "With a tuft of hair, with a crest of hair, an ascetic with braided hair and twisted locks, he has a shaven head and diadem. Having five faces and five hair knots, his flowered crown is of five knots of hair.

94. "Holding on to the great vow of austerity, he wears the ascetic's grass girdle, his practice pure and highest in his austere vow. Having great penance and having gone to the fulfillment of asceticism, he has taken his ritual bath to be the foremost Gautama.

95. "A divine brahman, knower of Brahman, he is Brahmā having obtained brahmanirvāṇa. He is release, liberation, his body true liberation; he is true release, peacefulness, and final blessedness.

96. "He is nirvāṇa, cessation, peace, well-being, deliverance, and termination. Ending pleasure and pain, he is the utter conclusion, renunciation, with residues destroyed.

97. "Unconquered, incomparable, indistinct, invisible, and spotless, he is partless, with total access, all-pervading, yet subtle, a seed without impurities.

98. "Without dirt, dustless, stainless, with faults expelled, and free from disease, he is wide awake, himself awakened, omniscient, universally knowing and supreme.

99. "Gone beyond the conditionality of consciousness, he is gnosis, bearing the form of nonduality. Devoid of mentation, spontaneous, he performs the duty of the buddhas of the three times.

100. "Without beginning or end, he is Buddha, Ādibuddha without causal connection. Stainless with his unique eye of gnosis, he is embodied gnosis, the Tathāgata.

101. "Lord of speech, the great expounder, the king of speakers, the chief of speakers, he is supreme in being the most excellent among those speaking, the invincible lion of elucidators.

102. "Seen in all directions, elation itself, with a garland of splendor, handsome, the beloved of Śrī, radiant, illuminating, he is light, with the splendor of the illuminator.

103. "Being the best of great physicians, he is superb, and as a surgeon, the finest. As the tree of every sort of medicine, he is the great enemy of the sickness of defilement.

104. "In being the tilaka mark of the triple world, he is pleasing and glorious, with a mystic circle of the lunar mansions. Extending as far as the sky in the ten directions, he raises high the banner of the dharma.

105. "Being the unique vast umbrella for the world, his is the mystic circle of loving kindness and compassion. As Padmanarteśvara he is glorious, variegated like a jewel, the great overlord.

106. "Being an exalted king among all buddhas, he bears the body of all buddhas; as the mahāyoga of all buddhas, he is the unique teaching of all buddhas.

107. "Glorious with the consecration of Vajraratna, he is lord among all jewel monarchs. Being lord over all Lokeśvaras, he is the monarch over all Vajradharas.

108. "As the great mind of all buddhas, he is present in the mind of all buddhas. Having the exalted body of all buddhas, he is the Sārasvatī of all buddhas.

109. "The vajra-like sun, the great light, with the stainless brilliance of the vajra-like moon, and having the great desire of renunciation and so forth, he is the blazing light in every sort of color.

110. "Maintaining the cross-legged position of the completely awakened, he preserves the dharma discussed by the buddhas. Arisen from the lotus of the Buddha, he is glorious, wearing the treasury of the Omniscient's gnosis.

111. "Bearing every sort of illusion, he is king, and as the holder of the incantations of the buddhas, he is exalted. Vajratīkṣṇa with a great sword, he is pure with the highest syllable.

112. "Whose great weapon is the Vajradharma of the Great Vehicle which cuts off suffering, he conquers the victors and, deep as a vajra, with vajra-like intellect, knows objects just as they are.

113. "Fulfilling all the perfections, he wears as ornaments all the levels; as the egolessness of the pure dharma, his light in his heart is from the moon of perfect gnosis.

114. "With the great perservance of the net of illusion, becoming the monarch of all the tantras, he is supreme. Maintaining every cross-legged position, he bears every gnostic body.

115. "As Samantabhadra the very intelligent, being Kṣitigarbha supporting the world, as the great womb of all buddhas, he bears the wheel of every sort of transformation.

116. "Foremost as the proper nature of all existents, he maintains the proper nature of all existents. By nature unarisen, yet with every sort of referent, he bears the proper nature of all phenomena.

117. "Having great insight in one instant, he maintains the internal comprehension of all phenomena. With his realization toward all phenomena, and as the sage at the end of actuality, he is very sharp.

118. "Motionless, himself very clear, he bears the enlightenment of the perfect completely awakened, face-to-face with all buddhas, having fire-tongues of gnosis and radiant light.

Twenty-four Verses on the Gnosis of Equality

119. "As the accomplisher of the desired object, supreme, purifying all evil existences, being the highest of beings, he is the protector, the liberator of all beings.

120. "Alone the hero in the battle with defilements, he kills the pride of the enemy 'unknowing.' He is intelligence and glorious, maintaining an amorous manner, yet he bears a form heroic and fearsome.

121. "Shaking a hundred hand-held clubs, dancing with the placing of the feet, with the extension of a hundred glorious arms, he dances the full expanse of space.

122. "Standing on the surface at the summit of the earth which is being overcome by the bottom of one foot, he stands on the nail of the foot's big toe, overcoming the peak of the egg of Brahmā.

123. "Being the one goal in the ultimate sense of the nondual dharma, he is absolute truth, imperishable. While his sense objects are in the forms of various representations, he is uninterrupted in mind and consciousness.

124. "With pleasure toward every existential object and with pleasure in emptiness, he has the foremost intellect. Having gone beyond desire and so forth within existence, his great pleasure is toward the three kinds of existence.

125. "White like a pure, radiant cloud and shining like the beams of the autumn moon, with the beauty of the mystic circle of the newly risen sun, the light from his nails is intensely red.

126. "His fine hair locks with points of sapphire and in his hair crest bearing a great sapphire, glorious with the luster of great jewels, his ornaments are transformations of the Buddha.

127. "Shaking hundreds of world spheres, he strides wide with the 'feet of psychic power'. Bearing the great recollection, he is reality, the king over the concentration of the four recollections [on the body, on feelings, on thought, and on phenomena].

128. "Fragrant from the blossoms of the limbs of enlightenment, being the ocean of qualities of the Tathāgata, in knowing the practice of the eight-limbed path [correct view, correct intention, correct speech, correct conduct, correct livelihood, correct effort, correct recollection, and correct concentration], he knows the path of the perfect completely awakened.

129. "Greatly adhering to all beings, he adheres to nothing, like the sky; arisen from the mind of all beings, he has the speed of the minds of all beings.

130. "Knowing the value of the faculties of all beings, he captures the hearts of all beings; knowing the reality of the meaning in the five aggregates, he is the pure bearer of the five aggregates [the constituents of the person: form, feeling, ideation, mental and emotional formations, and consciousness].

131. "Established at the limit of all modes of deliverance, he is skilled in all modes of deliverance; established on the path of all modes of deliverance, he is the teacher of all modes of deliverance.

132. "Rooting out existence in its twelve limbs, he is the pure bearer of twelve aspects; with the aspect of the practice of the four truths, he maintains the realization of the eight knowledges.[4]

133. "His referent truth in twelve aspects, knowing the sixteen aspects of reality, he is totally enlightened to the twenty aspects, awakened, omniscient, and supreme.[5]

134. "Sending forth tens of millions of emanating bodies of uncountable buddhas, his complete realization is in every moment, knowing the objects of every instant of the mind.

135. "Considering the purpose of the world by the means of practicing the various vehicles, while delivered by the triple vehicle, he is established in the fruit of the unique vehicle.

136. "Himself purified from defiled elements, he subdues the elements of karma; having crossed over the ocean of the floods, he has departed the wilderness of the adhesions.

137. "Along with the perfuming elements he casts off the defilements, the associate defilements, and the general defilements. Being compassion and insight and means, he acts successfully for the sake of the world.

138. "His purpose the casting off of all conceptions, toward the objects of consciousness he maintains suppression. His referent the mind of all beings, he is present in the minds of all beings.

139. "Established within the minds of all beings, he enters into equality with their minds; satisfying the minds of all beings, he is the pleasure of all beings' minds.

140. "Being the final statement, free from bewilderment, he is exempt from all error; having three referents [acceptance, rejection, and equanimity], his mind is free of doubt, and having all objects, his nature is of three qualities [emptiness, signlessness, and wishlessness].

141. "His referents the five aggregates and the three times, he considers every instant; obtaining total awakening in one instant, he is the bearer of the proper nature of all buddhas.

142. "Having a bodiless body, the foremost of bodies, he sends forth tens of millions of bodies; displaying forms without exception, he is Ratnaketu, the great gem.

Fifteen Verses on the Situationally Effective Gnosis

143. "To be realized by all buddhas, as the enlightenment of the Buddha, he is supreme; devoid of syllables, his source is in mantra; he is the triad of the great mantra families.

144. "The progenitor of the significance of all mantras, he is the great orb, devoid of syllables; with five syllables and greatly void, he is voidness in the orb, with one hundred syllables.

145. "Having all aspects, having no aspects, he bears four orbs, partless, beyond enumeration, he sustains the limit at the level of the fourth meditation.

146. "Directly knowing all the branches of meditation, knowing the lineages and families of concentration, with a body of concentration, the foremost of bodies, he is the king of all enjoyment bodies.

147. "With an emanating body, the foremost of bodies, bearing the lineage of the Buddha's emanations, he emanates forth in every one of the ten directions, acting for the needs of the world just as they are.

148. "The deity beyond gods, the leader of gods, the leader of heavenly beings, he is the lord of demigods, leader of immortals, the guide of heavenly beings, a churner and the lord of churners.

149. "Having crossed over the wilderness of existence, he is unique, the teacher, the guide of the world; celebrated, and being the donor of dharma to the world in its ten directions, he is great.

150. "Dressed in the mail of loving kindness, equipped with the armor of compassion, with a volume of insight scripture, a sword, a bow and an arrow, he is victorious in the battle against defilements and unknowing.

151. "Having Māra as an enemy, he conquers Māra, a hero putting an end to the terror of the four Māras; the conqueror of the army of all Māras, he is the completely awakened, the leader of the world.

152. "Praiseworthy, honorable, laudable, continually worthy of respect, he is the best of those to be worshiped, venerable, to be given homage, the supreme guide.

153. "His gait being one step through the triple world, his course as far as the end of space, triple-scienced, learned in śrūti and pure, his are the six sublime perceptions and the six recollections.[6]

154. "A bodhisattva, a great being, beyond the world, with great spiritual power, completed in the perfection of insight, he has realized reality through insight.

155. "Knowing himself and knowing others, being all for all, indeed he is the highest type of person; completely beyond all comparisons, he has to be known, the supreme monarch of gnosis.

156. "Being the donor of the dharma, he is best, the teacher of the meaning of the four seals; he is the best of the venerable ones of the world who travel by the triple deliverance.[7]

157. "Glorious and purified through absolute truth, great with the fortune in the triple world, glorious in making all success, Mañjuśrī is supreme among those possessed of glory.

Five Verses on the Gnosis of the Five Tathāgatas

158. "Reverence to you, the giver of the best, the foremost vajra.
Homage to you, the limit of actuality.
Reverence to you, whose womb is emptiness.
Homage to you, the enlightenment of the Buddha.

159. "Reverence to you, the desire of the Buddha.
Homage to you, the passion of the Buddha.
Reverence to you, the joy of the Buddha.
Homage to you, the delight of the Buddha.

160. "Reverence to you, the Buddha's smile.
Homage to you, the Buddha's laugh.
Reverence to you, the Buddha's speech.
Homage to you, the Buddha's internal reality.

161. "Reverence to you, arisen from nonexistence.
Homage to you, the arising of Buddhas.
Reverence to you, arisen from the sky.
Homage to you, the arising of gnosis.

162. "Reverence to you, illusion's net.
Homage to you, the Buddha's dancer.
Reverence to you, the all for all.
Homage to you, the gnostic body.

Eleven Observations in the First Round of [Discussion on] Benefits

"This, then, O Vajrapāṇi, Vajradhara, is that *Litany of Names* which is pure and unique to the gnostic entity Mañjuśrī, the blessed one, embodied gnosis, the gnostic body of all tathāgatas. For the sake of producing in you the highest pleasure, certainty, and great rapture, for the sake of the esoteric purity of your body, speech, and mind, for the purity and completion of those stages, perfections, and accumulations, both of knowledge and merit, which may yet be impure and incomplete, for the realization of the yet unrealized highest goal, for the obtaining of what is yet unobtained, and moreover for the sake of preserving the practice of the true dharma of all tathāgatas, this *Litany of Names* was taught, brought to light, uncovered, detailed, proclaimed, and then established in your mental stream, O Vajrapāṇi, Vajradhara, by me through the transforming influence natural to all mantras.

Fifty-two Observations in the Second Round of [Discussion on] Benefits

"Moreover, O Vajrapāṇi, Vajradhara, this *Litany of Names* is the real secret of the gnosis, body, speech, and mind of the very clean and perfectly purified omniscient. It is the awakened enlightenment of all tathāgatas and the method of realization of the complete and perfect buddhas. It is that which is highest in all tathāgatas and the realization of the dharmadhātu for all the sugatas. It is the overcoming of the strength of all Māras for all the victors and contains the power in the ten powers of the ten-powered. It is the omniscience for every kind of gnosis of the omniscient. It is the traditional scripture for the dharma of all buddhas and the attainment of all buddhas. It is the completion of the stainless and pure collections of knowledge and merit for all great bodhisattvas, and is the birthplace of all disciples and private buddhas. It is the field of excellence for all gods and men and the abode of the Mahāyana. It is the source of the bodhisattva's activity and the culminating point of the perfect noble path. It is the touchstone of liberation and the arising of the path of deliverance. It is the continuity of the Tathāgata's lineage and the growth of the family and lineage of the great bodhisattvas. It is the suppression of disputants of all rival doctrines and the ruin of all heretics. It is the overcoming of the forces and army and power of the four Māras and the attracting to the dharma of all beings. It is the maturation on the noble path for all those traveling to deliverance, and concentration for those dwelling in the four divine states [of loving kindness, compassion, sympathetic joy, and equanimity]. It is the meditation of those with one-pointed minds, and the yoga of those intent on body, speech, and mind. It is the dissociation of all fetters and the removal of all defilements and associate defilements. It is the stilling of all veils and the liberation of all bondage. It is freedom from all residues and peace for all mental afflictions. It is the rich source of all wealth and the loss of all misfortune. It is the closing of the doors to all evil existences, the true path to the city of liberation. It is the disengagement of the wheel of existence and the turning of the wheel of the dharma. It is upraised parasols, banners of victory, and flags of the Tathāgata's doctrine, and the transforming power of instruction on all phenomena. It is the quick success of those bodhisattvas implementing their practice by means of mantras, and the realization in contemplation for those intent on the perfection of insight. It is the penetration into emptiness for those intent on the contemplation of nondual penetration. It is accomplishment in the accumulation of all perfections, and purity in completion of all stages and perfections. It is the penetration of the perfect four noble truths and the penetration into all teachings with one-pointed mind in the four applications of mindfulness. This *Litany of Names* is even as much as final completion of the qualities of all buddhas.

Fifty-two Observations in the Third Round of [Discussion on] Benefits

"Moreover, O Vajrapāṇi, Vajradhara, this *Litany of Names* quiets every sort of evil in the physical, vocal, and mental conduct of all beings. It purifies all the evil existences for all beings and prevents all lower births. Cutting through the veils of all karma, it suppresses the arising of all the eight untimely existences [that is, circumstances such as birth as an animal or with a physical condition that prevents practice of the dharma]. Pacifying the eight great terrors [lions, tigers, rutting elephants, snakes, punishments by kings, fire, water, and demons], it eliminates all evil dreams. Removing all evil omens, it pacifies all bad signs and obstacles. Quelling all the activities of the enemy Māras, it causes increase in all roots of goodness and merit. Fashioning the nonorigination of mental fixation on the inessential, it strikes down mental inflation, arrogance, conceit, and self-importance. Causing the nonorigination of all suffering and depression, it is the real heart of all tathāgatas. The real mystery of all bodhisattvas, it is the true secret of all disciples and private buddhas. It is all the seals and all mantras. It is the producer of recollection and clarity for those asserting the inexpressible character of all phenomena. Creating the highest insight and mental vigor, it produces health and strength, dominion and wealth. Producing an increase in glory, virtue, peace, and wholesomeness, it brings to light fame, renown, celebrity, and praise while quelling all disease and the great terrors. It is the purest of the purest, the very best method of purification among the best methods of purification, the best fortune of best fortunes, and the very best auspiciousness of all that is auspicious. It is a refuge for those desiring a refuge, a place of rest for those desiring a place of rest, a haven for those wishing a haven, and final relief for those without final relief. It is the true island of those needing an island, the highest resource of those who are resourceless, and the true ship of those traveling to the other shore of existence. It is the true great king of medicines for the elimination of all disease, real insight for the discrimination of elements to be abandoned and accepted, and the very light of gnosis for the dispelling of all darkness, obscurity, and unwholesome views. It is the real wish-granting gem for the fulfilling of the aims of all beings just as they each intend. It is the omniscient ones' true gnosis for obtaining the gnostic body of Mañjuśrī and the real vision of pure gnosis for obtaining the five eyes. It is the true completing of the six perfections through the giving of possessions, of fearlessness, and the gift of the dharma. It is true attainment of the ten stages through the completion of concentration and the accumulations of knowledge and merit. It is nondual natural reality since it is separated from all characteristics of duality. It is the actual fact of suchness and not other than natural reality since it is separated from all false assertions. It is the actual fact of the limit of actuality by being the proper nature of the pure Tathāgata's gnostic body. It is in every respect the actual fact of the great emptiness through destroying without the slightest residue the path through the dense forest of unwholesome views. This *Litany of Names*, with the inexpressible form of all teachings, may be said to be thus since it brings to light the preservation of [Mañjuśrī's] names for the sake of entrance into nondual natural reality.

Nineteen Observations in the Fourth Round of [Discussion on] Benefits

"Moreover, O Vajrapāṇi, Vajradhara, whatever son or daughter of good family implementing his practice by means of mantras will—without interruption three times every day, with just these verses, words, and syllables—support, proclaim, master, and apply his mind to the essentials of this nondual crest jewel of names possessed of absolute truth, this totally complete, neither fragmentary nor deficient *Litany of Names* of the blessed one, the gnostic entity Mañjuśrī, who is embodied gnosis, the gnostic body of all tathāgatas, and [whatever son or daughter of good family] will teach [the text] in full suitably to others, or even one or another of the many names individually, [that son or daughter] making the gnostic body of Mañjuśrī his object of meditation will become mentally one-pointed. Dwelling in the state of "facing everywhere" through intense interest and the application of his mind on reality, he will be endowed with supreme clear faith, pierced through with insight and intent on all teachings. To him all the buddhas and bodhisattvas from all the three times and timelessness, having approached and assembled, will display all the means of the dharma. In addition, they will demonstrate their physical presence. Moreover, the great wrathful kings, beginning with Mahāvajradhara, the tamers of those who are difficult to tame and who are the very preservation of the world, will demonstrate the strength of vitality, splendor, inviolability, and all seals, mantras, and mandalas of the various methods of realization through their visible forms performing every sort of transformation. So too, the Mantravidyārājñīs without exception and all the destroyers of obstacles, the enemies of Māra, Mahāpratyaṅgirā and Mahāparājitā will every instant, day and night, guard, protect, and defend [that son or daughter] in all the four sorts of circumspect behavior [going, standing, lying down, and sitting]. They will produce the transforming influence of all the buddhas and bodhisattvas and, with all their bodies, voices, and minds, will perfectly establish it in his mental stream. They will confer kindness through the kindness of all buddhas and bodhisattvas. They will also induce in him toward all teachings fearlessness and its eloquence. They will demonstrate to him a physical presence with the affectionate intentionality in the noble dharma, even from all arhats, disciples, and private buddhas. Moreover, Brahmā, Indra, Upendra, Rudra, Nārāyaṇa, Sanatkumāra, Maheśvara, Kārttikeya, Mahākāla, Maṇḍikeśvara, Yama, Varuṇā, Kuvera, Hārītī, and the guardians of the world in its ten directions will supremely guard, protect, and defend him continually day and night, whether going or standing, lying or sitting, dreaming or waking, in peak experience or not, in solitude or in a crowd of people, even through town and city, in metropolis and district, through kingdom and citadel, on the threshold to the capital or the open highway, on the main street or at the city gate, on a lane or crossroads, at an intersection or strange city, in the common market or private shop, even as far as in fast solitude and the mountain cave. Whether he is approaching a river or wood or dense forest, whether personally defiled or not, whether insane or heedless, [they will protect him] always, in every way, with every means. Day and night they will confer on him supreme success. Still other gods and nāgas, yakṣas and gaṇḍārvas, demigods and garuḍas, kiṃnaras and mahoragas, humans and nonhumans, and other planets and lunar mansions, divine mothers and lords of hosts, as well as the seven divine mothers, yakṣinīs, rākṣasīs, and piśācīs, all united and harmonious, with armies and attendants, will guard, protect, and defend him. Still more they will infuse in his body vitality and strength, and they will induce in him the strength of health and the extension of life.

Fifty-one Observations of the Fifth Round [of Discussion on] Benefits

"Moreover, O Vajrapāṇi, Vajradhara, [whatever son or daughter of good family], out of this unbroken undertaking, will recite thrice daily this crest jewel of names, this *Litany of Names*, or will set about reciting it inscribed in a book—and in making his object of meditation the form of the blessed one, the gnostic entity Mañjuśrī, while reflecting and meditating on that form, and employing the discipline of the dharma—even before very long [that son or daughter] will see [Mañjuśrī's] form in its visible manifestation. Further he will see accompanying it all the buddhas and bodhisattvas with visible forms performing every sort of transformation in the vault of space. Never will that great being at any time or in any way fall into an evil existence or lower birth. Neither will he be born into a low family, nor in a border country. Neither will he take birth in a family holding false views, nor will he be born in buddha-fields devoid of buddhas. Never for him will there be the invisibility [of a path due to the] lack of the arising of a buddha and the dharma taught by such a one. Never will he be born among the gods fond of long life. Neither will he take birth in intermediate aeons characterized by famine, disease, and weapons, nor will he be born in times of the five degradations [at the end of an aeon—the degradation of life, aeon, defilement, view, and beings.]. Neither for him will there be fear of kings, enemies, and thieves, nor fear of any kind of deficiency or poverty. Never will he fear ill repute, slander, censure, or disgrace. He will be of fine class, family, and lineage. Always having a form and color attractive in every way, he will be beloved, charming, pleasant to be with, and pleasing to the sight of the world. He will be splendid, with good fortune, and felicitous in speech. In whichever places he will take birth, in each of them he will remember his previous births. With great enjoyment and vast retinue, he will remain undiminished in both enjoyment and retinue. Foremost among all beings, he will be accompanied with the highest qualities. Naturally he will be accomplanied with the qualities of the six perfections while dwelling in the four divine states. Accompanied by recollection, clarity, means, strength, aspiration, and gnosis, he will be eloquent with fearlessness toward all scholastic works. With clear speech, not foolish, he will be clever, sagacious, energetic, satisfied, with an exalted goal, free from grasping. He will have the supreme trust of all beings and the respect of preceptors, masters, and guides. Scholastic works of gnosis, sublime perception, and the arts and crafts, though not previously heard by him, will all be realized according to the words and meaning, as if clear reflected images. He will act with very pure discipline, livelihood, and manner of conduct; he will be well gone forth and well ordained. He will remain undistracted in omniscience with the exalted mind of enlightenment, while never passing through the entrance to the certain fixation of the disciples, arhats, and private buddhas.

Unlimited Observations in the Sixth Round of [Discussion on] Benefits

"Thus, O Vajrapāṇi, Vajradhara, that [son or daughter of good family] in implementing his practice by means of mantras will be accompanied by other innumerable masses of qualities of the same kind and with the same nature [as those enumerated above]. Just before very long, O Vajrapāṇi, Vajradhara, that bull among men, the preserver of this *Litany of Names* which has absolute truth, having well collected the collections of merit and knowledge, and having gathered to perfection the qualities of the Buddha, will most quickly and thoroughly awaken to utter complete perfect enlightenment. The highest teacher of dharma to all beings, his dharma the vast wholesome final nirvāṇa, he is empowered as dharmarāja, his drum of the true dharma sounding in the ten directions.

The Arrangement of the Mantra

"Oṃ, O pure vajra whose proper nature is the nonexistence of all phenomena, *a ā aṃ aḥ*—that is to say, employing the purity of Mañjuśrī, the gnostic body of all tathāgatas, *a aḥ*, bear up, bear up the heart of all tathāgatas—Oṃ Hūṃ Hrīḥ. O blessed one, O Lord of Speech who is embodied gnosis, with great speech, O embryo of the gnosis of the dharmadhātu, being very pure and stainless like the spatial field of all phenomena—*aḥ*."

Five Verses as an Epilogue

163. Then the glorious Vajradhara, joyful and glad, with his hands folded in homage, bowed to the protector, the completely awakened, the blessed one, the Tathāgata.

164. And with many other kinds of Vajrapāṇis, all of them esoteric leaders, protectors, and kings of wrath, he loudly replied,

165. "We rejoice, O protector, it is good, it is fine, it is well said. Great benefit is done for us in causing us to obtain perfect enlightenment.

166. "And also for this unprotected world desiring the fruit of liberation, this purified path to well-being is proclaimed as the practice of illusion's net.

167. "It is deep, lofty, and extensive, with great meaning, performing the aims of the world; indeed, this object of knowledge of the buddhas has been taught by the perfect completely awakened."

Proclaimed by the blessed one, the Tathāgata Śākyamuni in the "Net of Concentration" chapter occurring in the *Mahāyogatantra*, the *Noble Illusion's Net* in sixteen thousand lines, this *Litany of Names* of the blessed one, the gnostic entity Mañjuśrī, possessing absolute validity is hereby complete.

Notes

1. The ten aspects and the ten referents are differently defined in the commentaries, but one opinion is that the former represent a list of ten truths: provisional truth, absolute truth, truth of characteristics, of distinction, of certain identification and realization, of existents, of renunciation, of the knowledge of extinction and no further arising, of knowledge of entrance into the path and the truth of the perfect arising of the gnosis of the Tathāgata. The ten referents, according to this opinion, are the these same ten as purposes for teaching. "Ten-powered one" is a standard epithet of the Buddha and indicates ten powers of knowledge: of the possible and impossible, of the fruition of action, of the meditations, emancipations, concentrations, and meditative attainments, of the degree of faculties of other beings, of the diverse interests of beings, of the diverse dispositions of beings, of the ways passing into every sort of circumstance, of previous lives, of the deaths and rebirths of beings, and the power consisting in the knowledge of the final destruction of the impurities.

2. The five bodies of the Buddha are the emanation body, the enjoyment body, the body of dharma, the essential body, and the gnostic body. The five forms of gnosis are those indicated by the division titles here and for the following four divisions. The five buddhas are Vairocana, Akṣobhya, Ratnasaṃbhava, Amitābha, and Amoghasiddhi—together forming the fundamental maṇḍala arrangement. The five eyes are the corporeal eye, the heavenly eye, the eye of insight, the eye of the dharma, and the eye of the Buddha.

3. The three families are those represented by the images of the wheel, the vajra, and the lotus, representing the transformation of ignorance, anger, and desire. The triple gem are the Buddha, the reality taught by him (dharma), and the clerical community (*saṅgha*). The triple vehicle indicates the vehicle of the disciples, the Mahāyāna, and the Mantrayāna.

4. The twelve limbs are the twelve phases of dependent origination, beginning with ignorance and ending with old age and death. The twelve aspects are the purified senses and sense fields.

5. The twelve aspects are as in v. 132, whereas the sixteen aspects are the sixteen varieties of emptiness; the twenty are the sixteen forms of emptiness and the four kinds of gnosis from the mirrorlike to the situationally effective.

6. The six sublime perceptions: the realization of the knowledge of the object of concentration, of divine hearing, of the gradations of others' minds, of the memory of previous existences, of the arising and passing away of beings, and of the utter destruction of impurities. One interpretation of the three sciences indicate that they are the final three of these six sublime perceptions. The other interpretation is that they are śrūti, that is, the first three of the Vedas known to the early Buddhists. The six recollections are practices recollecting the Buddha, the dharma, the saṅgha, one's own discipline, one's renunciation, and one's protective divinity.

7. The four seals are categories of embodiment in the esoteric system: the great seal, the seal of the vow, the dharma seal, and the action seal. While multiple interpretations exist, one standard explanation identifies three of the seals as equivalent to the three bodies of the Buddha—the great seal being the enjoyment body, the vow seal being the dharma body, and the action seal being the emanation body. The dharma seal, according to this idea, is then speech itself.

—5—

Sikh Hymns to the Divine Name

Hew McLeod

The fifth guru of the Sikhs, Arjan (who occupied the position from 1581 until his death in 1606) was responsible for compiling the first sacred scripture of the Sikhs, the *Ādi Granth.* This is by far the most significant scripture that the Sikhs possess, and is universely known among them as the *Guru Granth Sāhib,* the "Revered Granth (or volume) which is Guru." It is believed that the tenth guru, Gobind Singh, shortly before he died in 1708, announced that the line of personal gurus was at an end. Thereafter the Sikhs should look to the scripture (the *Guru Granth*) and the community (the Guru Panth) as the joint embodiment of the eternal Guru.

In the scripture that he compiled, Guru Arjan brought together the works of the first five gurus, together with those of a number of other hymn writers of like views. He was himself the largest contributor, and of his numerous hymns one stands out for the beauty of its expression and for the profoundity of its thought. This is the lengthy hymn called *Sukhmanī,* to which the respectful *Sāhib* is normally added.

The theme of Guru Arjan's *Sukhmanī* is the grandeur of the divine Name. In lyrical poetry of sustained quality it extols the beauty of the Name, repeatedly declaring its crucial importance in a person's quest for liberation. The title of the work incorporates a pun, in that *manī* can mean either "pearl" or "mind." It can thus be translated either as "The Pearl of Peace" or as "Peace of Mind."

The complete poem, which runs to almost 2,000 lines, is divided into twenty-four parts. Each part comprises an introductory couplet and a sequence of eight stanzas. The only variation to this pattern occurs in the first section, which is preceded by a four-line superscription in place of the usual couplet, and which includes an additional couplet between the first and second stanzas. This inserted couplet is regarded as an epitome of the entire poem:

> The Name of God is sweet ambrosia, source of all inner peace and joy.
> The Name of God brings blissful peace to the hearts of the truly devout.

According to tradition the poem was composed by Guru Arjan beside the sacred pool of Rāmsar in Amritsar. The date of its composition is not known, but it must have been before 1604 (the date when the compilation of the *Ādi Granth* was begun). A date shortly before 1604 seems likely, for *Sukhmanī* is obviously a work of great maturity. It is also a work that inevitably suffers serious injury in translation. No rendering in English can hope to capture the skill of Guru Arjan's epigrammatic style or the beauty of his language.

Sukhmanī commands a notable popularity. Although it is not a part of the regular *Nitnem* (the "Daily Rule," portions of scripture appointed for daily recitation), many Sikhs include it in their early-morning devotions. Many Punjabi Hindus also recite it regularly. Following an invocation to the eternal Guru, the poem states its theme in the opening stanza. The first octave proceeds to develop the theme of nām simaran or remembering the divine Name, listing the many blessings that accrue to those who devote themselves to regular remembrance of it. The second octave and its introductory couplet raise the problem of suffering and announces its remedy. The sure and certain panacea is the divine Name. Octave 3 contrasts the liberating power of the divine Name with the inadequacy of the ancient scriptures and the futility of conventional religious practices. Alms and oblations, sacrifice and renunciation, ritual bathing and austerities—all are useless. Only the Name can bring a person to deliverance.

In octaves 4–6 Guru Arjan contrasts God's greatness with man's infirmity. Apart from God and the guru's guidance, man is a creature of vicious desires. To outward appearances he may appear to be a person of great piety. Inwardly, however, he nurtures falsehood, lust, greed, deceit, and a host of other sins. Seduced by the attractions of the ephemeral world, he ignores the divine Name, spurning thereby the peace and joy that God proffers to all. Let him turn again to God, for only thus can he achieve the bliss of deliverance.

This insistent claim raises the question of how one is to find God. The introduction to octave 7 acknowledges the problem and enunciates an essential part of the answer. All who seek deliverance must seek it in the company of others dedicated to the same objective. The concept is fundamental to the teaching of the gurus, and nowhere does it receive a more insistent emphasis than in the seventh octave of *Sukhmanī*. The terms normally used for this feature of the gurus' teaching are *saṅgat* (assembly), *satsaṅg* (the assembly of those who have found the truth), and *sādhsaṅg* (the assembly of those who have brought their minds and instincts under control). All three, together with other variant forms, express the same basic features of the gurus' message.

Subsequent stanzas expand this definition of the guru's fellowship, stressing the qualities bestowed on all who join it. Octaves 8 and 9 shift the focus, directing attention instead to a definition of the braham-giānī. The braham-giānī is he who possesses an understanding of God's wisdom, the person who has found enlightenment in the company of the devout. Such a person acquires thereby an impressive range of virtues, some involving his relationship with men and others his relationship with God. The former include such qualities as purity, humility, patience, kindness, and detachment. The latter preeminently requires remembrance of the divine Name. He who devotes himself to the discharge of these obligations attains deliverance for himself and the power to confer it on others by means of word and example. Men teach and observe various beliefs concerning the means of deliverance. All should realize that there is but one way. Evil is universally proscribed and the Name is accessible to all.

Octaves 10 and 11 bring us back to the infinite greatness of God and the absolute nature of his power. The infinity of the creation bears witness to its maker and over its boundless span countless creatures join to honor him in their various ways. He who brought this creation into being reigns supreme, determining by his unfettered will all that takes place. Man, in contrast, is powerless except for the strength conferred by grace. His birth and status, his understanding and actions, his hope of deliverance—all are dependent on the absolute will of God.

Foolish men fail to recognize God's authority, and the next two octaves describe the fate that awaits them. The perverse will be punished, the proud brought low. They who put their trust in riches, worldly power, or outward piety will all be disappointed. He who denigrates the truly pious will suffer all manner of retribution and by his churlish behavior will bind himself more firmly to the round of transmigration. Octave 14 follows this catalogue of sinful deeds with an appeal to all who so foolishly commit them. All men should abandon worldly concerns and turn to God. Trust in him; remember the Name; walk in his way. Octaves 15–17 continue the theme of God's greatness and of the rewards to be secured by those who put their trust in him.

The presence of God is signified by the divine Name and man's duty is devout contemplation of the Name. There remains, however, the problem of how man can recognize the Name and follow the contemplative discipline which will enable him to appropriate its benefits. The answer is the guru, God's mediator here on earth. The remaining octaves return again to the Name, the source of true bliss and the essential means of deliverance. Octave 24 summarizes the message of *Sukhmanī.*

Guru Arjan concludes the entire *Ādi Granth* with two more works of his own, *Mundāvaṇī* and *Shalok.* Like *Sukhmanī Sāhib,* these brief compositions testify both to the beauty of his expression and to the nature of his thought, at once simple and profound.

Further Reading

See Hew McLeod, *Textual Sources for the Study of Sikhism* (Chicago: University of Chicago Press, 1990), from which much of this selection is drawn (pp. 110–14). Reprinted by permission.

Selections from *Sukhmanī*

Turn to the Lord in contemplation; in his remembrance find peace.
Thus is our inner turmoil stilled, all anguish driven away.
Behold the glory of the earth's Sustainer, numberless those who repeat his Name.
The hallowed pages of sacred scripture are but a fragment of all it contains.
He who receives a glimpse of its meaning will earn a glory that none may describe.
With those who seek that glimpse, O God, your servant Nānak finds release. (1.1)

Through remembrance of the Lord one is freed from rebirth.
Through remembrance of the Lord death's messenger flees.
Through remembrance of the Lord death itself succumbs.
Through remembrance of the Lord all enemies are scattered.
Through remembrance of the Lord all barriers fall.
Through remembrance of the Lord one remains alert.
Through remembrance of the Lord our fears are dispelled.
Through remembrance of the Lord all pain is relieved.
Through remembrance of the Lord one is numbered with the devout.
Steeped in remembrance of God's divine Name,
we gather all the treasures which His grace supplies. (2.1)

Solace of all in need or anguish, Help of the helpless, dwelling within.
Remain with me forever, O Lord, for I cast myself on your grace.

When the time comes to leave this life, bereft of parents, sons and friends,
The Name of God goes with us, our comfort and support.
When Death's dread messengers hover near, seeking to capture and destroy,
The Name alone stays by our side, our only sure protection.
When grievous problems weigh us down, the Name of God brings instant help.
Futile our acts of expiation; only the Name can cancel sin.
Repeat the Name as the guru directs, for this is the means to abundant joy. (1.2)

So many scriptures, I have searched them all.
None can compare to the priceless Name of God.
Better by far than any other way[1] is the act of repeating the perfect Name of God.

Better by far than any other rite is the cleansing of one's heart in the company of the devout.
Better by far than any other skill is endlessly to utter the wondrous Name of God.
Better by far than any sacred text is hearing and repeating the praises of the Lord.
Better by far than any other place is the heart wherein
God is infinite, beyond all comprehending,
Yet he who repeats the Name will find himself set free.
Hear me, my friend, for I long to hear
The tale which is told in the company of the free.

Faces shine in the company of the faithful;
There, in their midst, sin's filth is washed away.
Pride is conquered in the company of the faithful;
There in their midst, God's wisdom stands revealed.
God dwells near in the company of the faithful;
In the calmness of their presence all doubt is laid to rest.
There one obtains that precious jewel, the Name,
And striving by their aid one finds that blissful peace with God.
Who can hope to utter the wonder of their glory,
The glory of the pure and true in union with the Lord. (1.7)

Man has no power to work his will, for power resides in God alone.
Helpless he follows as God directs; what pleases God must come to pass.
At times exalted, at times abased; now plunged in sorrow, then raised to joy.
Sometimes led to slander and blame; lifted to heaven and then cast down.
Sometimes blessed with wisdom divine, man comes to God in God's own time. (5.11)

By the guru's grace he perceives his nature, and in that knowledge sheds all desire.
He praises God in the company of the faithful and sets himself free from the body's ills.
Singing God's praises by day and by night,
He keeps himself pure though he lives with his family.[2]
He who puts trust in God alone shall tear the net which death has laid;
And he who craves the presence of God shall find all suffering stilled. (4.14)

Tell of his glory day and night, for the power to praise is the gift of God.

They who love Him with ardent devotion dwell rapt in the mystic presence divine.
Putting behind them all that is past they strive in the present to honor his will.
Who can hope to recount his glory? The least of his wonders must shame our art!
Fulfilled are they who day and night eternally dwell in the presence of the Lord. (7.17)

The guru leads and instructs his disciple, freely bestowing his grace;
Cleansing his mind of the refuse of falsehood, teaching him how to repeat the Name.
By the guru's grace his bonds are severed; set free he renounces all that defiles.
The wealth of the Name is the gift of the guru, and he who receives it is wondrously blessed.
Saved by the guru both here and hereafter, he dwells with his Guide and Protector forever. (1.18)

Give heed to the words of the perfect Guru; see God ever present and near at hand.
Repeat God's Name with every breath, for thus shall your cares depart.
Turn from the world of transient desire, seek the blessing the faithful bestow.
Abandon pride, put your trust in God; find the peace which their company brings.
Gather the treasures which God bestows and honor the perfect Guru. (1.24)

He who nurtures the Name within will find the Lord ever present there.
Gone forever the pain of rebirth, his precious soul in an instant freed.
Noble his actions, gracious his speech; his spirit merged in the blessed Name.
All suffering ended, all doubts, all fears; renowned for his faith and his virtuous deeds.
Raised to honor, wondrous his fame! Priceless the pearl, God's glorious Name! (8.24)

Mundāvaṇī

In this dish three things are mingled—truth, contentment, deep reflection.[3]
With them mixed the Master's Name, its nectar sweet sustaining all.

He who eats with lingering joy shall know the truth, his soul set free;
He who tastes will make this food his constant fare for evermore.
Darkness reigns, yet they who trust the all-fulfilling grace of God
Find beyond this sunless world God's all-pervading light.

Shalok

Blind am I to all your deeds, my worth sustained by grace alone.
Base am I, devoid of virtue; grant your pitying mercy, Lord.
Grace, O Lord, and tender mercy brought me to the guru's feet.
Finding there the blessed Name, my spirit blooms in joyous bliss.

Notes

1. Way-*dharam* (*dharma*): religious obligation, pattern of religious observance determined by one's caste.
2. Traditional Hindu piety assumes that purity requires the renunciation of family ties. The Sikh view is that purity can be attained within the context of the family.
3. The "dish" is variously interpreted as the heart of the believer and the sacred scripture.

—6—

Devotional Hymns from the Sanskrit

Guy Leon Beck

In India, hymns in the Sanskrit language are read, recited, and memorized by thousands of pious Hindus in their daily devotions at home or in temples. The popular appeal of these hymns indicate a ready accessibility of the Sanskrit language to social classes other than the traditional priestly brahman caste. As they are not officially related to orthodox Vedic or brahmanical rituals, and are quite freely—and inexpensively—available through printed media, the hymns are often the sole connection between written Sanskrit and the Indian people.

In this section, eleven hymns have been chosen for translation from a popular anthology known as *Bṛhat-Stotra-Ratnākara* ("The Great Collection of Jewel-like Hymns"), a volume of 464 hymns compiled and edited by Ram Tej Pandey (Benares: Pandit Pustakalaya, 1976). Each one of the eleven hymns selected contains eight verses, and is thus referred to as an "eight-stanza hymn" (*aṣṭakam*). Exhibiting characteristic features of the genre, and representing a cross section of current lay practice in Hindu India, these hymns address an assortment of gods and goddesses in the Hindu pantheon—Gaṇeśa, Śiva, Viśvanātha, Paśupati, Śiva-Liṅga, Tripurasundarī, Viṣṇu, Lakṣmī, Rāma, Kṛṣṇa, and Sūrya. Other hymns in this anthology, though not included here, address other types of icons such as holy places, rivers, or saints. Some of our hymns are said to be authored—though this is by no means certain—by celebrated saints such as Śaṅkara, Vedavyasa, Bṛhaspati, and so on. Yet the actual source for a large percentage of the hymns remains virtually unknown. In content they portray in a concise fashion the most essential mythological and iconographic features of their subjects. And as they also contain many sacred names and epithets of the gods and goddesses, Sanskrit hymns prove to be an effective aid to meditation and the development of devotional sentiments.

When recited according to their specified Sanskrit poetic meters, the following hymns display charming and creative sequences of rhythm and balance, often resonating in new and unusual patterns of rhyme and alliteration. The meter of each hymn is determined by the number of Sanskrit syllables per line. Divided into a series of eight four-line verses, many of the hymns contain a refrain that is repeated in some or all of the verses.

GAṆEŚA-AṢṬAKAM

This is an eight-verse hymn to Lord Gaṇeśa, the elephant-headed god. Pious Hindus begin any auspicious activity with an obeisance to Lord Gaṇeśa in order to remove all obstacles. It is said that persons who recite these auspicious prayers composed by the sage Vedavyasa experience the removal of all suffering and enjoy untold knowledge and prosperity.

1. I salute Lord Gaṇeśa with the crooked trunk, who removes the fear of the material world and the misery of poverty. As Lord of the family of Gaṇas, he wears a charming pearl necklace and armlet. And wandering among the circles of women practicing yoga, he is the essence of men of strength.

2. I adore Lord Gaṇeśa who, appearing like a pink flamingo, personally destroys all impurities by his hand-noose. He appears as a multitude of suns in the shape of a golden mountain. O worship him who resides near white jasmine flowers and destroys the mountain of material existence.

3. I admire Lord Gaṇeśa with the crooked trunk, who is resplendent with the glow of various gems such as lapis lazuli. He whose neck is embellished with beautiful golden ornaments and a spotless pearl necklace is always the epitome of will power.

4. I praise Lord Gaṇeśa, who is always filled with bliss. He appears to be sluggish and dull due to intoxication, yet is truly knowledgeable in the Vedas as he dances blissfully to the tune of the universe. In this way he is especially charming with his moonlike tusk and elephant goad.

5. I salute Lord Gaṇeśa, whose palm always displays a wheel diagram, whose large forehead is beautified by three eyes, and whose rounded head is decorated with a garland of white flowers and a jeweled crown containing multitudes of pearls.

6. I respect Lord Gaṇeśa, who resides among wish-fulfilling trees. He sits above a triangle that rests upon a radiant throne within an eight-petaled lotus flower.

7. I salute Lord Gaṇeśa, whose trunk is always crooked, and whose hand cleverly bestows purity and kindness. His mind is fixed in intelligence as he also bestows mercy and fearlessness. His variously curved trunk is flanked by only one tusk.

8. He who worships Lord Gaṇeśa with the crooked trunk, and is enamored of his wonderful form situated among the cows of plenty, gems, and desire trees, attains all perfection.

ŚIVA-AṢṬAKAM

This is an eight-verse hymn to Lord Śiva. It is said that anyone who continually recites this prayer with attachment to Śiva, having attained sons, wealth, good friendships, and beautiful wife, enters into the state of liberation.

1. I praise Lord Śiva who is known as Śaṅkara, Śambhu, and Iśana. While also known as Master, Lord of Life, Great Lord of the Universe, Lord of the Universal Lord, Master of the Movement of Present and Future, and Lord of Ghosts, he is worshiped with bliss by the righteous.

2. I respect Lord Śiva who is known as Śaṅkara, Śambhu, and Iśana. He is also the ruler of Gaṇeśa the elephant god, and the movement of all-devouring time. His greatness is augmented by the rolling waves of his matted hair. On his body he wears a multitude of snakes, and around his neck a garland of mutilated bodies.

3. I emulate Lord Śiva who is known as Śaṅkara, Śambhu, and Iśana. He is without beginning, transcendental, and destroys the great illusion of material existence. In his joyous form he is decorated with ashes and adorned with ornaments such as the great mandala [circle].

4. I praise Lord Śiva who is known as Śaṅkara, Śambhu, and Iśana. He is the Great Lord, Lord of Mountains, Lord of Gaṇas, Lord of Demigods. Always visible residing on the lower slope of a mountain, Śiva emits a very loud laugh, yet destroys the great sins of the world.

5. I adore Lord Śiva who is known as Śaṅkara, Śambhu, and Iśana. Residing on a mountain, he is always sitting as if homeless. Being the supreme Brahman himself, he is saluted by the demigods headed by Brahmā. One-half of his body is possessed by his wife Pārvatī, the daughter of the Himalayas.

6. I praise Lord Śiva who is known as Śaṅkara, Śambhu, and Iśana. Being chief of the demigods, he associates with Nandi, his bull companion, and radiates pleasure from his lotus feet. In his hands, he holds a begging bowl and trident.

7. I glorify Lord Śiva who is known as Śaṅkara, Śambhu, and Iśana. He whose body is both an autumnal moon and a reservoir of bliss, and whose three eyes are spotless, is the friend of Kubera the Lord of Wealth, and performs marvelous pastimes with his wife Durgā.

8. I praise Lord Śiva who is known as Śaṅkara, Śambhu, and Iśana. Wearing a snake for a necklace, always unchanged, and being produced from the essence of the Vedas, the mind-born Śiva revels as he resides in the burning cremation ground.

VIŚVANĀTHA-AṢṬAKAM

This is an eight-verse hymn to Lord Viśvanātha, the form of Lord Śiva who resides in Varanasi. It is said that whoever recites this hymn describing the glories of Śiva as the Lord of Varanasi, having already attained vast knowledge, wealth, and unlimited fame, attains, at the demise of the body, final release. One who recites this pious hymn composed by the sage Vedavyasa also achieves the abode of Lord Śiva and enjoys in his company.

1. Please worship Viśvanātha, the Lord of Varanasi. Being constantly accompanied on his left side by his consort Gaurī, he is very dear to Lord Nārāyaṇa and steals the madness of the God of Love. His matted hair is enjoyed by the rolling waves of the Gaṅgā River.

2. Please worship Viśvanātha, the Lord of Varanasi, who is ineffable and contains unlimited qualities. Accompanied by his wife on his left side, he stands on a throne served by all the gods including Brahmā and Viṣṇu.

3. Please worship Viśvanātha, the Lord of Varanasi, who is also the Lord of Ghosts with three eyes, matted hair, and a body decorated with snakes. Wearing a tiger skin as a garment and holding a trident, noose, and goad in his hands, he bestows fearlessness.

4. Please worship Viśvanātha, the Lord of Varanasi, whose shining crown is adorned with the beautiful moon. He also wears a radiant earring made by the Lord of the Nāga snakes. The mere glance of his eyes dries up the fire of passion of the God of Love.

5. Please worship Viśvanātha, the Lord of Varanasi with five faces. Being free from death, lamentation, and old age, he is the lion who destroys the wandering elephants of sin and intoxication, he is the great snake Seśa who kills the evil serpents, and he is the great forest fire that burns up the material world.

6. Please worship Viśvanātha, the Lord of Varanasi, who is effulgent, both with and without qualities, without a second, full of bliss, unconquered, and immeasurable. As the cosmic destroyer, he is garlanded with snakes.

7. Please worship Viśvanātha, the Lord of Varanasi. Having given up desires, finding fault with others, and attraction to sin, place your mind in deep meditation and worship Śiva within the lotus of the heart.

8. Please worship Viśvanātha, the Lord of Varanasi, who is without faults such as attachment, anger, and greed. He is the abode of peace, renunciation, and worldly attraction for his followers. Accompanied by his consort Pārvatī, he takes pleasure in drinking poison yet possesses qualities like good fortune, sweetness, and sobriety.

PAŚUPATI-AṢṬAKAM

This hymn is to Lord Śiva as Paśupati, the Lord of Beasts. It is said that one who recites and hears this wonderful prayer written by the sage Bṛhaspati will attain joy in the residence of Lord Śiva.

1. O descendants of Manu, the first man: please worship Lord Śiva, the husband of Pārvatī, the daughter of the Himalayas. He is also known as Indupati, the Lord of the Moon; Paśupati, the Lord of Beasts; the Lord of the Earth; the Lord of the Snake Region; and the husband of Satī. He removes all the afflictions of his devoted followers.

2. No one escapes the control of all-devouring time, not father, mother, brother, or son. O descendants of Manu, please worship Lord Śiva, the husband of the daughter of the Himalayas.

3. O descendants of Manu, please worship Lord Śiva, the husband of the daughter of the Himalayas. He is served by ghosts and other attendants, is skilled in the five kinds of sweet musical sounds, and brandishes musical instruments such as the muraja and dindima drums.

4. O descendants of Manu, please worship Lord Śiva, the husband of the daughter of the Himalayas. As an ocean of compassion and protection, he bestows fearlessness, shelter, and happiness upon people who bow down, chanting Śiva! Śiva! Śiva!

5. O descendants of Manu, please worship Lord Śiva, the husband of the daughter of the Himalayas, whose form is whitened with dust from the funeral pyre. He who wears a jeweled earring made with human heads and a serpent necklace carries the flag of Nandi, the bull that carries him.

6. O descendants of Manu, please worship Lord Śiva, the husband of the daughter of the Himalayas, who supports a moon on his crown. Though destroying sacrifices, he bestows the fruits of all sacrifices, and consumes all gods and demons in the cosmic conflagration.

7. O descendants of Manu, please worship Lord Śiva, the husband of the daughter of the Himalayas. Having discarded the passion of intoxication and seen the universe afflicted with the fears of birth, death, and old age, he is forever situated in the heart.

8. O descendants of Manu, please worship Lord Śiva, the husband of the daughter of the Himalayas. Being worshiped by Lord Hari, Lord Brahmā, and all the demigods, he is also saluted by the attendants of Yama, the Lord of Death, and Kubera, the Lord of Wealth. Having three eyes, he is Lord of the Three Worlds—heaven, earth, and the underworld.

LIṄGA-AṢṬAKAM

This is a hymn in eight verses to the Śiva-liṅga, the phallic form of Lord Śiva worshiped and revered virtually all over India. Though appearing as a male phallus, the liṅga is actually situated in union with the symbol of the sacred female organ known as the yoni, and represents the cosmic force of reproduction. It is said that whoever recites this pious prayer to the Śiva-liṅga quickly achieves the association of Lord Śiva on his planet.

1. I always offer obeisance to the Śiva-liṅga, the spotless and radiant form of Lord Śiva that is worshiped by Lord Brahmā, Lord Kṛṣṇa, and the demigods, and which destroys the sufferings of human life.

2. I always offer homage to the Śiva-liṅga. Adored by the best of the gods and sages, this compassionate liṅga removes all traces of lust, and even destroys the pride of demons like Rāvaṇa.

3. I always offer obeisance to the Śiva-liṅga. Praised by perfected beings, gods, and demons, and besmeared with sweet-smelling oils, this liṅga increases our intelligence.

4. I always offer homage to the Śiva-liṅga. Decorated with precious gems and gold, and surrounded by the King of Snakes, the liṅga has destroyed the sacrifice of Dakṣa, Śiva's father-in-law.

5. I always offer obeisance to the Śiva-liṅga. Smeared with saffron powder and sandalwood paste, and decorated with a garland of lotus flowers, the liṅga removes heaps of sins.

6. I always offer respect to the Śiva-liṅga. Served and worshiped with intense devotion by gods and divine beings known as Gaṇas, the liṅga appears radiant like a thousand suns.

7. I always offer obeisance to the Śiva-liṅga. Resting within an eight-petaled lotus flower, the liṅga is the primal cause of the universe and removes all kinds of misery and poverty.

8. I always offer salutations to the Śiva-liṅga. Constantly worshiped by the best of the gods and teachers with special flowers from the heavenly forest, the liṅga is the greatest of the great.

BHAVĀNI-AṢṬAKAM

This is an eight-verse hymn to the goddess Tripurasundarī, also known as Bhavāni, one of the forms of the spouse of Lord Śiva who is especially worshiped in south India.

1. O Mother of the Universe! Please come to me always. You give pleasure to the minds of all who serve you. You remove all the dangers of those who worship you. Yet you frolic and enjoy in the forest of sandalwood trees.

2. You are worshiped by Śiva and the demigods. You are saluted by great sages and other exalted beings. O Goddess Tripurasundarī! Many divine beings worship your lotus feet.

3. O Goddess! Your lotus feet are constantly worshiped by exalted beings. Since many days have passed for me in such worship, your otherwise unyielding and ruthless nature has bestowed compassion upon me.

4. O Goddess! As I am weak and lying in discomfort, kindly remove my scarcity of fresh food, grains, land, and proper residence by granting me a fresh glance of your mercy.

5. If you do not take pity on my miserable condition, who will free me from material attachments? You who are wearing a garland of human heads, please relieve me of this suffering condition.

6. Please uplift your fallen servant. Even the most degraded sinners who have plunged into the terrible ocean of rebirth and suffer the threefold miseries are completely saved by your grace.

7. Nowadays many people all over India suffer hunger and the scarcity of proper food. O Mother of the Universe! Please bestow happiness on them by just one swift glance of your mercy.

8. O Goddess! When Lord Śiva himself cannot adequately describe your unlimited glories, how can I, a mere human with little understanding or belief?

KAMALĀPATI-AṢṬAKAM

This is an eight-verse hymn to Lord Viṣṇu as Kamalāpati, the husband of Kamalā or Lakṣmī, the Goddess of Fortune. Viṣṇu is widely revered and has thousands of different names, yet is most popularly worshiped in the form of Rāma or Kṛṣṇa. It is said that the person who recites with dedicated mind this magnificent prayer, which is constantly uttered by great sages, goes to the feet of Lord Viṣṇu.

1. O descendants of Manu the first man, please worship Lord Viṣṇu as Kamalāpati. Reclining with lotuslike eyes on a couch of snakes, accompanied by Garuḍa the eagle who carries him, and holding a lotus flower, wheel, and club in hand, he appears unchanging and full of beauty.

2. O descendants of Manu, please worship Lord Kamalāpati. Wearing a charming spotless yellow garment, with hair as soft and pleasing as black bumble bees, he is accompanied on his left side by the goddess Lakṣmī, the daughter of the ocean.

3. O descendants of Manu, please worship Lord Kamalāpati. Whether by chanting on rosary beads, by strict penances, by sacrifices, by meditation in holy places of pilgrimage, or by careful study of all the scriptures, worship Lord Kamalāpati.

4. O descendants of Manu, please worship Lord Kamalāpati. This human form of life on earth is very difficult to achieve and is even desired by the demigods. Therefore, avoiding unnecessary greed and attachment to material objects, take to the worship of Lord Kamalāpati.

5. O descendants of Manu, please worship Lord Kamalāpati. Neither wife, son, brother, father, mother, nor friend will accompany you beyond this lifetime. Therefore, worship Kamalāpati.

6. O descendants of Manu, please worship Lord Kamalāpati. Everything in this universe is perishable, including progeny, youth, and wealth. Quickly recognizing this condition with discriminating vision, take to the worship of Kamalāpati.

7. O descendants of Manu, please worship Lord Kamalāpati. Our own bodies are extremely fragile, always under others' control, subject to various diseases, and beset with innumerable other afflictions. Considering all this, immediately worship Lord Kamalāpati.

8. O descendants of Manu, please worship Lord Viṣṇu as Kamalāpati. He is always saluted by Lord Śiva, Lord Brahmā, and all the demigods, and constantly meditated on in the heart by the best of sages. Moreover, he frees us from the fears of death, rebirth, and old age.

MAHĀLAKṢMĪ-AṢṬAKAM

This is an eight-verse hymn to the spouse of Lord Viṣṇu, known as the goddess Lakṣmī or Mahālakṣmī. It is said that anyone who recites this prayer to Mahālakṣmī with devotion attains all perfection and reaches the divine kingdom. Someone who recites it once will destroy all kinds of sins. One who recites it twice achieves untold wealth, and one who recites it three times is able to slay the greatest enemy and enjoys the supreme blessing of the goddess.

1. O Mahālakṣmī! Let there be salutations unto you. While seated on the opulent throne of the Goddess of Fortune, you are worshiped by all the demigods. You are the custodian of the supreme creative energy of Māyā, and hold within your hands the conch shell, wheel, and club.

2. O Mahālakṣmī! Let there be obeisance unto you who ride the eagle carrier Garuḍa. O Goddess, while removing all sins you appear frightening to the barbarians and demons.

3. O Mahālakṣmī! Let there be salutations unto you who are all-knowing and all-giving. O Goddess, by frightening away all villains you remove everyone's unhappiness.

4. O Mahālakṣmī! Let there be respect unto you who are the giver of both worldly enjoyment and liberation. O Goddess! You are composed of holy sounds and bestow yoga perfection and intelligence on the deserving.

5. O Mahālakṣmī! Let there be salutations unto you who are without beginning or end. O Great Goddess! You are born from yoga and are known as Ādi-Śakti, the original energy.

6. O Mahālakṣmī! Let there be homage unto you. O Goddess! Appearing very terrible in your gross and subtle forms, you are the great energy and womb of the universe that removes all sins.

7. O Mahālakṣmī! Let there be praise unto you. O Goddess! You are known as the Great Goddess and the Mother of the Universe. Placed on a lotus seat, you embody the supreme spirit of Brahman.

8. O Mahālakṣmī! Let there be obeisance unto you. O Goddess! Wearing your white gown and decorated with various ornaments, you establish the universe as its Divine Mother.

RĀMA-AṢṬAKAM

One of the most popular gods in Hinduism is the form of Lord Viṣṇu known as Rāma.

1. I always worship Lord Rāma, who is unique, and especially beautiful as he removes all types of sins and delights his devotees.

2. I always worship Lord Rāma, who is unequaled. Decorated with a beautiful waist ornament and matted hair, he removes the fears of his devotees and destroys all kinds of sins.

3. I always worship Lord Rāma, who is special, full of mercy, equal to all, auspicious, spotless, self-aware, and who removes the pains of material existence.

4. I always worship Lord Rāma, who is unparalleled. Though manifesting in the material world, he is also viewed as nameless, formless, and without material contamination.

5. I always worship Lord Rāma, who is without a second. While his own nature is pure, spotless, unmanifest, and inconceivable, his creations appear with distinctly intelligible forms.

6. I always worship Lord Rāma, who is exceptional, full of qualities and mercy. He is viewed both as having an unlimited body and as being a vessel to cross over the ocean of material existence.

7. I always worship Lord Rāma, who is extraordinary. He manifests the Supreme Spirit through his illuminating and intelligent speech.

8. I always worship Lord Rāma, who is unique. He is a splendid teacher, giver of blessings and happiness, and remover of material pains and errors.

KṚṢṆA-AṢṬAKAM

It is said that anyone who recites this special hymn will become a great devotee and experience deeper and deeper rapture with Lord Kṛṣṇa.

1. I worship the clever Kṛṣṇa, the special jewel of Vraja who removes all sins, delights the minds of his devotees, and gives pleasure to his father Nanda. While his head has a large topknot, his hand holds a beautifully sounding flute. He is an ocean of love.

2. I worship the Lotus-eyed One, whose rolling eyes cause trees to tremble and remove the vanity of the God of Love. I bow to Lord Kṛṣṇa, who knocks down the pride of Indra, the King of Heaven, yet appears beautiful, smiling as he holds a flute with his lotus hands.

3. I worship my beloved Lord Kṛṣṇa, the darling of the women of Vraja, who wears saffron earrings made of kadamba flowers and has pleasing designs on his cheeks. I bow to the leader of the cowherd boys, the source of pleasure and happiness for his mother Yaśoda and all the residents [of Vraja].

4. I worship Lord Kṛṣṇa, the child of Nanda, who always brings pleasure to the choicest young girls with his dazzling charm and his lotus feet. I praise my beloved Kṛṣṇa, the soul of the cowherd girls, who also dries up all personal transgressions and nourishes the entire universe.

5. I worship Lord Kṛṣṇa the Butter Thief, the darling of his mother Yaśoda, who is also the helmsman for traversing the material ocean of existence and the incarnation that supports the cosmic space. I bow to the son of Nanda, who is always in the company of his friend Subala, and reveals newer and newer dimensions every day.

6. I worship Lord Kṛṣṇa, the beloved of the cowherd men. Full of all qualities like compassion and bliss, he brings devastation to both the gods and the demons. He appears like a beautiful cloud with the glow of lightning flashing through it, yet continues to engage in his clever and erotic pastimes among the cowherd folk.

7. I worship Lord Kṛṣṇa, who is a leader in the forest grove by dint of the sweet sounds emanating from his flute. With his charming glance he reduces the lust of the God of Love. Entering into the forest grove with his beautiful shining limbs, he bewilders the hearts of all the residents of Vraja.

8. I worship Lord Kṛṣṇa who charms all the cowherd women by his clever manner of sleeping, yet consumes all the offerings made into the sacred fire in the forest. Whoever sings and recites this hymn at any time will receive infinite mercy.

SŪRYA-AṢṬAKAM

It is said that many benefits await anyone who recites this prayer to Sūrya, the sun god, who removes the harmful effects of a solar eclipse: a sonless person will obtain a son, and a poor person will obtain wealth. However, dangers await those who commit certain transgressions: one who eats meat and drinks liquor on sunny days will be diseased for seven lifetimes. But if one is able to give up sex, bodily perfumes, wine, and meat eating on sunny days, that person, being relieved of disease, grief, and poverty, will reach the planet of Lord Sūrya.

1. I offer respect to Lord Sūrya the Sun God, the original god. Please overwhelm me with your radiance and brilliance.

2. I offer obeisance to Lord Sūrya, who is riding a chariot drawn by seven horses. Born of the sage Kaśyapa, he looks magnificent holding a white lotus flower in his hand.

3. I offer praise to Lord Sūrya, who is riding a chariot made from reddish iron. As grandfather to the universe, he removes all sins.

4. I offer homage to Lord Sūrya, who destroys all sins. As a great hero, he contains all qualities plus the gods Brahmā, Viṣṇu, and Śiva in his being.

5. I offer respect to Lord Sūrya, who is Lord of All the Planets. His radiant effulgence has covered the entire sky and atmosphere.

6. I offer salutations to Lord Sūrya. Holding a special wheel in his hand, he looks radiant as he wears beautiful earrings and necklace, appearing like a bandhuka flower.

7. I offer obeisance to Lord Sūrya, who destroys all sins and cuts away material existence. His glowing effulgence lights up the entire universe.

8. I offer respect to Lord Sūrya, the Lord of the Universe who destroys all sins and gives knowledge of the science of salvation.

—7—

Tamil Game Songs to Śiva

Norman Cutler

The poet and saint Māṇikkavācakar, who lived in south India (most likely in the ninth century C.E.) composed two poetic works, *Tirukkōvaiyār* ("Glorious Garland of Verses"; *tiru* is equivalent to *śrī*, "glorious," in Sanskrit) and *Tiruvācakam* ("Glorious Composition"), both of which are included in the *Tirumuṟai*, the canon of Tamil Śaivism. To this day verses from Māṇikkavācakar's works are chanted in Śiva temples in Tamilnadu during pūjā, and they are often set to music and sung at gatherings in temples and in people's homes. *Tirukkōvaiyār* is a work obviously intended for an audience with specialized literary training, and draws liberally on the conventions of classical Tamil love poetry. In the Śaiva Siddhānta sectarian tradition this poem is frequently interpreted as an allegory of love between the life-breath or soul (*uyir*) and god (*civam*). The fifty-one poems included in *Tiruvācakam* (from which selections appear here) are, in contrast, far more accessible and far better known by Tamil Śaivites, and they are highly valued for their "heart-melting" emotional power.

Many of the poems included in *Tiruvācakam* are narrated by a first-person voice that Tamil Śaivites hear as the voice of the historical poet. Thus for Tamil Śaivites the subject of *Tiruvācakam* is the joys and sorrows Māṇikkavācakar experienced in his quest to establish a lasting union with Śiva. However, several poems included in *Tiruvācakam* break the pattern. Among these poems are several that are narrated by a collective female voice. According to legend, during the course of his pilgrimage to various sacred sites located in the Tamil country, Māṇikkavācakar encountered groups of girls engaged in playing various games and in other activities appropriate to their age and gender, such as pounding scented bath powder and picking flowers. It is said that the songs these girls sang while they played inspired Māṇikkavācakar to compose devotional poems that appropriate certain characteristic features of game songs.

Selected stanzas from several of Māṇikkavācakar's devotional "game songs" included in *Tiruvācakam* are translated here. The refrain in the stanzas of *Tiruvammāṉai* (Selections 1–3) allude to songs associated with a game in which players throw small objects such as pebbles, cowrie shells, or dried beans into the air and catch them on the back of their hands. In *Tiruccāḻal* (4–11) we hear two voices, one that disparages Śiva and another that defends him. Commentators have identified two, not necessarily mutually exclusive, sources of inspiration for the poem's format. Some commentators have proposed that a debating game, in which the players express their arguments in song, is the model for *Tiruccāḻal*. The poem has also been read as an allusion to an event in Māṇikkavācakar's legendary biography. The saint, we are told, debated Buddhist monks from Sri Lanka and scored a decisive victory for the Śaiva cause. The refrain of *Tiruppūvalli* ("Song of the Flowering Creeper"; 12–16) refers to the act of picking flowers, and in the context of this poem the association with flowers offered in worship is self-evident. Most commentators on *Tiruvācakam* accept the premise that the stanzas of *Tiruvuntiyār* (17–23) are modeled after a type of game song, but they are less certain about how this game would have been played. The word *paṟa* (fly) that occurs in the refrain implies that it involves some kind of airborne object such as a shuttlecock. Commentators are equally uncertain about the nature of the game alluded to in *Tiruttōṇōkkam* (24–27); the title literally means "gazing [or aiming] at the shoulders." The stanzas of *Tiruppoṉṉūcal* (song of the golden swing; 28–32) clearly invoke songs that girls would sing while riding a swing.

Although the poems translated here are atypical of most Tamil bhakti poetry by virtue of their formal association with game songs, the religious themes and sentiments they express provide a profile of the ethos of Tamil Śaiva bhakti which, if not comprehensive, is in harmony with a core of central themes in the literature of Tamil Śaivism. For example, there is the notion that Śiva enters into a relationship of great intimacy with his devotees even though he is remote and unattainable for everyone else, even for the gods in heaven (1, 2, 16, 29). Śiva is frequently called Lord of the Vedas. A number of possible interpretations of this epithet come to mind—Śiva is the ultimate source of the Vedas; Śiva embodies the essence of the Vedas; Śiva, as divine teacher, instructs the world in the meaning of the Vedas (1, 2, 5, 32). Śiva is considered the source or the essence of the entire cosmos and of all living things (1, 3, 4, 25); Śiva and his devotee relate to one another as master and servant or as ruler and subject, and sometimes Śiva is said to enslave his devotee (12, 13, 14, 27, 31, 32). Śiva is said to eradicate his devotee's karma and thus save his devotee from rebirth (12, 20, 21, 23, 30, 31, 32).

In addition to these theological themes, there are several others for which no pattern of replication can be found in this limited sample, but which nonetheless may be numbered among the central themes of Tamil Śaiva bhakti poetry. Paradox is at the heart of Śiva's identity (2); there is a communal bond among Śiva's devotees (13); and the devotee's bodily drives (especially the sexual appetite) are obstacles that can be overcome only by surrendering oneself to Śiva (15). Similarly, the devotee can overcome the obstacle of egoism only through total surrender (27).

A common iconographic representation of Śiva is Ardhanarīśvara ("Lord who is Half Woman"). The right side of this image of Śiva is male and the left side is female, both in bodily contours and in ornamentation. This image underscores the belief that Śiva and his consort are ultimately one, and that the god's identity encompasses the duality of gender (1, 3, 30, 31). As Lord of Destruction, Śiva is associated with the cremation ground and is frequently depicted covered with ash; worshipers at temples of Śiva typically receive a pinch of ash as a tangible gift of grace from the god (2, 4, 6). Śiva is often depicted wearing a snake around his waist or in his hair. According to Śaiva mythology, a group of forest sages became furious with Śiva when the god disrupted their sacrificial rites with his dancing. They conjured a deadly snake in the sacrificial fire and turned it against the god, but Śiva effortlessly subdued the snake and wrapped it around his waist. When the sages then conjured a tiger in the fire, the god killed it and wore its skin as a garment (4, 6, 9, 11, 16). As Kāpālī ("One with a Skull"), Śiva wanders from place to place holding a skull in his hand. On one level, this image of the god underscores his importance as the prototype for ascetics, the skull serving Śiva as his begging bowl (9, 15). (The Sanskrit word *kapāla,* from which the name Kāpālī is derived, can denote both "skull" and "a mendicant's begging bowl.") The image also alludes to a myth: Śiva and the five-headed god Brahmā became embroiled in an argument. When one of Brahmā's heads hurled a particularly galling insult at Śiva, Śiva cut off the offending head with a flick of his fingernail, and thus Brahmā became the four-headed god. By this act Śiva became tainted by the sin of brahmanicide, and Brahmā's severed head stuck to Śiva's hand, as if to mark Śiva indelibly as perpetrator of this crime. Eventually Śiva rid himself of his burden of sin at Varanasi. In another myth, Śiva swallowed the poison called halāhala which appeared when the gods and anti-gods churned the primeval ocean of milk in hope of obtaining the nectar of immortality, and thus he saved the world from calamity (7, 11, 15, 30).

When the fierce goddess Kālī killed the demon Dāruka, she worked herself into such a frenzy her destructive power became a threat to the very world she had rescued from the demon's assault. Śiva averted this second threat to the world's well-being by attracting the goddess's attention and defeating her in a dance contest (10). On another occasion, Śiva came to the rescue of the gods when the residents of Tripura (Triple Fortress) were causing the gods great pain. The story begins when the anti-gods secured a boon from the creator god Brahmā as a reward for performing rigorous penance. Brahmā allowed the anti-gods to build three great cities, one in heaven, one in the air, and one on earth. Brahmā also stipulated that the only way these cities could be destroyed would be for them to be somehow consolidated, and then destroyed by a single arrow. The anti-gods flourished in their cities, and in the course of time they became arrogant and began to behave in a manner offensive to justice and morality. The gods, whom they oppressed, eventually turned to Śiva for help. Drawing together the combined energies of the many gods and constructing a chariot from various elements of the cosmos, Śiva demolished the anti-gods' cities with a single fiery arrow (15, 17).

Many of the twenty verses of *Tiruvuntiyār* allude to the myth of Dakṣa's sacrifice. Dakṣa, the father of Śiva's consort Umā, held a great Vedic sacrifice but failed to invite his daughter and son-in-law, against whom he bore a grudge. The goddess implored Śiva to punish her father for the insult, and Śiva complied with her request. He emitted the fierce Vīrabhadra from himself, and Vīrabhadra laid waste to the sacrifice and punished all the gods who were present. According to some versions of the myth, Dakṣa was beheaded and was given a goat's head in exchange for his own (18, 19, 20, 21, 22).

Unlike the other mythological allusions found in these verses, which can be traced to Sanskrit sources and are well known throughout India, the story of the hunter-devotee Kaṇṇappar, alluded to in *Tiruttōṇōkkam* 3 (Selection 24), belongs exclusively to the lore of south Indian Śaivism. Kaṇṇappar's manner of worshiping Śiva, detailed in the verse, violates the most fundamental canons of "proper" worship. Nevertheless, he proved himself willing to forfeit even his own eyes for Śiva's benefit, and thus he is viewed as a paragon of unselfish devotion.

Some of the names of Hindu gods that occur in these verses may be opaque to readers who are unfamiliar with the Tamil language, even if they would easily recognize the gods signified by these names. In Tamil bhakti poems Viṣṇu frequently bears the name Māl or its variant Tirumāl (7, 9, 16), which may be translated either as "Great One" or "Black One." Ayaṉ (7, 9, 16) is a Tamil adaptation of Sanskrit Aja ("Unborn One"), an epithet of Brahmā. Purantaraṉ (19) means "destroyer of fortresses" and is an epithet of Indra.

It is well known that sacred places play a central role in Tamil bhakti; and pilgrimage to these sacred places is an important element in the legendary biographies of the Tamil bhakti poets, Māṇikkavācakar being no exception. The emphasis on sacred places in the biographies of the Tamil saints and in their poems underscores the saints' role in the Tamilization of puranic Hinduism.

For the Tamil devotees of Viṣṇu and Śiva, these gods are the protagonists not only of myths set in remote mythological space and time, but also of stories that are played out in the Tamil country. Not only is Śiva the Lord of the Universe, in a very specific sense he is a member of the ruling dynasty of the Pāṇṭiya kingdom, a historical kingdom located in the southern part of the Tamil country (3). The verses translated here mention several places, all sites of Śiva temples, that are located in the Tamil country: Aiyāṟu (2), Āṉaikkā (3), Iṭaimarutu (28), Northern Kōcamaṅkai (28–32), Peruntuṟai (1, 3, 15), and Tillai (8, 10, 13). The last two of these are of special importance in Māṇikkavācakar's biography. It was at Peruntuṟai that Māṇikkavācakar is said to have had his first direct encounter with Śiva and to have undergone a conversion experience. Tillai, known nowadays as Chidambaram, was the final destination in Māṇikkavācakar's journey which took him to many places in the Tamil country, and it was there that, according to legend, he merged with the god's image in the temple. Śiva is enshrined at Chidambaram as Naṭarāja, "lord of the dance," and the sanctum of this temple is known as Ciṟṟampalam, the "Little Hall" (8, 10, 13). It is here that Śiva is said to perform the dance that sustains the universe.

The poems translated here are published in G. Varadarajan, ed., *Tiruvācakam-Virivurai* (Madras: Palaniyappa Brothers, 1971).

FROM *TIRUVAMMĀ<u>N</u>AI*

1

Let's sing of the Lord
who dwells in the hearts of people
who keep him fixed in their thoughts
without a moment's lapse.

He's the remote Lord,
the hero who favors the southern town, Peruntu<u>r</u>ai,
the Lord of the Vedas
who keeps the goddess as half of his body,
the master who took me, a lowly dog, for his slave.

He's the embodiment of truth, our mother,
our ruler who became all the seven worlds.

Let's sing an ammā<u>n</u>ai

Tiruvammā<u>n</u>ai 7

2

Bangles jangle on our wrists,
earrings dance on our ears,
bees clamor for honey that clings to our black curls,
and we sing of the red Lord who wears white ash,
the Lord who fills every space
and yet can never be found,
Lord of the Vedas
who appears as truth for his friends
and stays remote from the loveless,
the Lord who dwells at Aiyā<u>r</u>u.

Let's sing an ammā<u>n</u>ai

Tiruvammā<u>n</u>ai 13

3

Let's sing about the Lord, older than the three great gods,
who became the whole world
and will remain when the world ends,
the Lord with ornamented hair
who made his home in Perunturai, the town we hold dear,
Lord of the Sky who keeps the Goddess as half of his body,
our Uncle who stays in the south at Āṉaikkā
and in the Pāṇṭiya land,
the Lord who is sweet as nectar
for people who call him Father.

Let's sing an ammāṉai

Tiruvammāṉai 19

FROM *TIRUCCĀḺAL*

4

He smears his body with white ash,
and he wears a hissing snake.
The words he speaks are obscure like the Vedas,
See, my dear!
  What he smears, what he wears, what he speaks—
  what of them?
  Lord Śiva is the essence of every living thing.
  Cāḻalō

Tiruccāḻal 1

5

My dear, you call him—my father, our Lord, everyone's God
but why does he wrap a tattered rag around his loins?
  The string he ties around his waist
  is the essence of the arts
  and that rag is the four Vedas
  Don't you see?
  Cāḻalō

Tiruccāḻal 2

6

His temple is the cremation ground
and his best cloak is a deadly tiger's skin,
with no mother and no father he lives all alone.
See, my dear!
  He may have no mother or father and live all alone,
  but if he loses his temper
  the whole world will turn to dust.
  Don't you see?
  Cāḻalō

Tiruccāḻal 3

7

My dear, if he's so smart,
why did he swallow deadly poison
that rose from the roaring sea?
  If he hadn't swallowed poison that day
  Ayaṉ, Māl, and all the gods above would have perished.
  Don't you see?
  Cāḻalō

Tiruccāḻal 8

8

The Lord who dances facing south
at Tillai's Little Hall
takes delight in women.
He's a madman, my dear.
  Stupid girl,
  if he didn't take delight in women,
  all who live on this great earth
  would aspire to the yoga of heaven
  and leave this world behind.
  Don't you see?
  Cāḻalō

Tiruccāḻal 9

9

He wears the skin of a wild tiger,
he eats from a skull, and the jungle is his home,
so who would want to be his slave, my dear?
  What you say may be, but listen—
  Ayaṉ, Tirumāl, and the king of all the gods in heaven
  serve him generation after generation.
  Cāḻalō

Tiruccāḻal 12

10

The Lord of the Little Hall at Tillai
where cool fields flow with honey,
this Lord performed a dance.
Why is that, my dear?
  If he didn't dance
  this whole world would become a meal for Kālī
  who wields a bloody spear.
  Don't you see?
  Cāḻalō

Tiruccāḻal 14

11

If he's so clever, why does he wear a spotted hide
and why did he drink deadly poison
as if it were precious nectar?
Tell me, my dear!
  No matter what he wears, no matter what he eats,
  our Lord is greater than he himself knows.
  Don't you see?
  Cāḻalō

Tiruccāḻal 19

FROM *TIRUPPŪVALLI*

12

Even a mother's love can't compare with the mercy of the Lord
who paid attention to me though I am lower than a dog.

We'll pick flowers for my ruler
who slashed away birth's illusion
and threw dust in the mouth of my stubborn deeds.

Tiruppūvalli 3

13

My Lord gave me a head to bow before his long feet,
he gave me a mouth to sing of his glory,
and he assembled his servants so I could join them.
We'll pick flowers and tell all about the Lord
who dances with the Goddess
at the Hall of beautiful Tillai.

Tiruppūvalli 7

14

I praise the Lord who showed me the way of virtue,
led me to the golden feet of his devotees
and took me for his slave.
We'll pick flowers and tell how he made us his bondsmen
and cheated the old deeds that brought us pain.

Tiruppūvalli 8

15

When the master, Lord of Peruntuṟai,
placed his blessed feet on our heads
we were freed from our bodies, seat of desires.
We'll pick flowers and sing of the Lord
who holds a skull in his hand,
who waged war on the three cities
and joyfully swallowed the poison
that rose from the murky sea.

Tiruppūvalli 10

16

He is praised by eminent Māl, by Ayaṉ,
by all the gods and demons
who will never know the glory of his golden feet,

yet he entered my mind and became my ruler.
We'll pick flowers and sing of the cobras
he wears like sparkling jewels.

Tiruppūvalli 17

FROM *TIRUVUNTIYĀR*

17

He drew his bow, the war began
then the three forts fell
fly unti, fly
All at once they burned to the ground
fly unti, fly

Tiruvuntiyār 1

18

When greedy Fire reached for food
he cut off his hand
fly unti, fly
The sacrifice turned into a rout
fly unti, fly

Tiruvuntiyār 7

19

Purantaraṉ became a koil bird, bright as a flower
then he fled to a tree
fly unti, fly
And yet they call him King of the Gods
fly unti, fly

Tiruvuntiyār 9

20

Tell how that rite raised his ire
and how he lopped off the priest's head
fly unti, fly

That's how the chain of births is destroyed
fly unti, fly

Tiruvuntiyār 10

21

When the sun came to eat he trapped him
and plucked out his eyes
fly unti, fly
That's the way he helps us conquer rebirth
fly unti, fly

Tiruvuntiyār 12

22

The Goddess of Speech lost her nose,
Lord Brahmā lost his head,
and the moon's face got smashed
fly unti, fly
That's the way he destroys our old deeds
fly unti, fly

Tiruvuntiyār 13

23

He gives shelter to robed sages
and he watches over the sky
fly unti, fly
He guards the realms beyond the sky's limit
fly unti, fly

Tiruvuntiyār 20

FROM *TIRUTTŌṆŌKKAM*

24

Play tōṇōkkam so the world may know the glory of the hunter
who cooled the Lord's body and received his grace.
Though his feet were shod,
his mouth carried the Lord's water

and his offering was flesh,
his worship shone as if he knew the learned books.

Tiruttōṇōkkam 3

25

Play tōṇōkkam and tell how
one became many:
how he became the seven worlds and the ten directions,
and how he's wedded to the eight elements
as earth, water, fire, wind, sky, moon and sun,
and as the Lord who rules the senses.

Tiruttōṇōkkam 5

26

While Buddhists and followers of other trifling creeds
flounder in error,
the Lord, our father, transforms intellect into enlightenment
and deeds into penance.
We'll play tōṇōkkam and sing of his compassion.

Tiruttōṇōkkam 6

27

We quelled our pride and surrendered our minds,
so play tōṇōkkam, good ladies.
As servants of the Southerner, the Lord worshiped in heaven,
we'll turn our thoughts to his long feet.
We'll receive the joyful Dancer's grace
and enjoy supreme bliss.

Tiruttōṇōkkam 8

FROM *TIRRUPPONNŪCAL*

28

Sing of Iṭaimarutu,
the abode of Northern Kōcamaṅkai's king,
the Lord sweet as honey, with three shining eyes,

who floods us with nectar,
who clears my mind and melts my flesh.
Even ever-youthful gods in heaven
can't see his feet, bright as flowers.

O girls beautiful as noble peacocks, graceful as swans,
Let's ride the golden swing

Tirupponnūcal 2

29

Sing of the palace so tall
lightning plays around its towers
at Northern Kōcamaṅkai, town splendid as a jewel,
home of the Lord who has no beginning or end.
While councils of wise men and countless gods
stand in attendance,
he blesses me with sacred ash
and drowns me in his mercy.

O girls whose breasts are adorned with gold,
Let's ride the golden swing

Tirupponnūcal 3

30

O girls wearing stacks of glittering bangles,
sing about the Lord of stainless reputation,
the compassionate Lord who frees us from birth and death.
United with the Goddess who speaks gentle words,
he enters the hearts of his servants
and bathes them in nectar.
The Lord, leader of gods, whose throat holds deadly poison,
dwells in Northern Kōcamaṅkai, the town brilliant as a jewel
with towers that touch the clouds.

Let's ride the golden swing

Tirupponnūcal 4

31

O girls whose breasts are adorned with buds,
melt with love and sing about the dangling earrings

that adorn the Lord, half woman,
who wears cassia blossoms in his hair.
The Lord of Northern Kōcamaṅkai
chose me over all his other servants
to be his own slave
though I am just a lowly dog.
He sheltered me from my old sins
and freed me from rebirth.

Let's ride the golden swing

Tiruppoṉṉūcal 6

32

O girls beautiful as sleek, dancing peacocks
with jeweled breasts bright as gold,
When you soar high on the swing, like swans in flight,
sing about the glory of the Lord, my father,
the master who took me for his slave,
the radiant Lord of the Vedas,
Lord who dwells in Northern Kōcamaṅkai
who eludes the mind's powers.
If we chant his praise and bow our heads in worship,
he'll burst the chains of our sins.

Let's ride the golden swing

Tiruppoṉṉūcal 7

—8—

In Praise of Muḥammad: Sindhi and Urdu Poems

Ali Asani

Every day, millions of Muslims, following the injunctions of the Qur'ān, recite the ṣalawāt, a formula invoking blessing on the Prophet Muḥammad whom they affectionately call ḥabīb Allāh, God's beloved. They also recite, in virtually every language of the Islamic world, devotional verses praising the virtues of their beloved Prophet. Out of love for him, every year, since at least the thirteenth century, they have celebrated the maulid, the Prophet's birthday, with great pomp and rejoicing.

Although Islam is a monotheistic faith, professing total submission to the one almighty God, yet veneration of Muḥammad, God's last messenger to humanity, has become an important aspect of Islamic religious life. Muslims see in him the model or paradigm for all human conduct, the perfect man whose lifestyle is most worthy of imitation. In the words of the Qur'ān, he is "a beautiful model" (*uswa ḥasana*) whose example is to be followed by the faithful. Throughout Islamic history, members of the Muslim religious intelligentsia have collected and commented on accounts of Muḥammad's actions and sayings (ḥadīth), establishing legal codes for Islamic societies and pietistic norms for individual believers. Many of them have written elaborate theological and historical treatises on the nature of the Prophet's mission. Those with more mystical dispositions have indulged in high-flown abstract speculation concerning his spiritual and mystical status. At a more popular level, veneration of the Prophet has become so widespread that in many regions of the Islamic world it is one of the cornerstones of Islamic religious practice and, indeed, the mark of its uniqueness.

Muslims have expressed their devotion to the Prophet Muḥammad in many different ways. Among the Muslims of South Asia poetry provides an extremely popular and effective means of expression, so that in every major language of the subcontinent there are many touching verses extolling the virtues of Muḥammad, a small sampling of which is translated here. All classes of Muslims, from the educated elite of the major urban centers to the illiterate peasants in the fields, could and did engage in the pious acts of composing and reciting these poems.

Naturally, the literary quality varies greatly from the refined and well-rhymed compositions of accomplished poets to the comparatively unsophisticated and repetitive lyrics sung by village women. Furthermore, the ideas they express about Muḥammad, as we shall see, do not agree with the "official" doctrinal conceptions of Islamic prophetology espoused by theologians. They are simply utterances of pious souls expressing through language and imagery the devotion they feel in their hearts for their beloved Prophet.

Further Reading

See Ali Asani et al., *Celebrating Muhammad: Images of the Prophet in Popular Muslim Poetry* (Columbia: University of South Carolina Press, forthcoming), and Constance Padwick, *Muslim Devotions* (London: SPCK, 1960). Perhaps the greatest Western interpreter of Islamic mystical poetry is Annemarie Schimmel; see her *And Muhammad is His Messenger: The Veneration of the Prophet in Islamic Piety* (Chapel Hill: University of North Carolina Press, 1982). Also relevant is her article, "The Veneration of the Prophet Muhammad, as Reflected in Sindhi Poetry," in *The Saviour God: Comparative Studies in the Concept of Salvation,* edited by S. G. F. Brandon (Manchester: Manchester University, 1963), pp. 129–43.

Sindhi Poems

The region of Sind, currently a province in southern Pakistan, was among the earliest areas of South Asia to come under Islamic rule. In the year 711 C.E., a small military force in the command of a remarkable seventeen-year-old Arab general, Muḥammad ibn al-Qāsim, set out from Iraq to avenge the capture of some Arab Muslim women by local pirates. This small Arab force conquered Sind and created a state along the Indus Valley, establishing the first modest foothold for Islam in the area. In subsequent centuries, the presence of Islam grew stronger as Sind received many Muslim immigrants from Central Asia, Iran, and Afghanistan, including a large number of Sufis or Muslim mystics who made it their home. Thanks to the activities of these saintly men, a significant portion of the local population came into contact with the Islamic mystical tradition and gradually became Muslim.

The people of Sind developed several distinctive poetic genres for eulogizing the Prophet. The most important of these is the maulūd. The word maulūd means the "newborn child." Since the birth of Muḥammad was a significant event in the history of humanity, songs composed in his honor came to be called maulūd, emphasizing the greatness of the newborn child. In contrast to the maulūd in other Islamic languages, the Sindhi maulūd is a short lyrical poem of five to ten verses on subjects that include not only the Prophet's birth but also various aspects of his life and character. Sindhi poets often express in the maulūd their love and affection for Muḥammad as well as their yearning for his city, Medina. Patterned after the indigenous poetic forms of the wāī and kāfī, Sindhi maulūds always possess a thal, a beginning verse that is repeated as a refrain. The last verse often contains the name of the poet, who usually takes the opportunity to offer a supplication to the Prophet. According to one Sindhi manual, maulūds are meant to be recited in "a sweet and harmonious voice," either by an individual or a chorus, so that the listener's heart is "correctly guided." To this day, maulūds are popularly recited throughout the villages and towns of Sind, not only at religious assemblies and gatherings but during weddings and general occasions of rejoicing, as well as at times of mourning; a few examples are translated in the first section below.

Several other literary genres are also used to pay tribute to the Prophet. Of these, the madāḥ and the munājāt are closely related in substance and style, being strongly influenced in their meter and rhyme schemes by the Arabic panegyric form of the qaṣīdah. Both are laudatory poems usually comprising fifty verses or more; in the madāḥ, the laudatory element predominates whereas in the munājāt, the supplications of the singer are paramount. Similar to the madāḥ and munājāt are the manāqibā, whose distinguishing feature is that they are simultaneously narrative and didactic, employing stories of an historical nature from Muḥammad's life to illustrate superior qualities of his character and achievement. For recounting the miraculous or supernatural incidents in the Prophet's life, a Sindhi poet may compose a mu'jazo (pl. mu'jazā) in which the miracle becomes the central theme. Examples of each of these forms are included here.

Sindhi poetry in praise of Muḥammad is remarkable for its attempt to assimilate the figure of the Prophet to the local Sindhi milieu. Typically, he is represented in symbols and idioms that are familiar to a Sindhi audience. For this purpose, many Sindhi poets adopt into their eulogies the symbol of the virahinī, a loving and yearning young woman, usually a young bride or bride-to-be, who is tormented by the absence of her husband or beloved. Most likely originating in the plaintive songs sung by village women in periods of separation from their husbands, this symbol and the associated concept of *viraha*, "longing in separation," occurs in almost all the vernacular literatures of South Asia.

The virahinī has enjoyed widespread popularity in a variety of South Asian religious contexts, where she is identified as a symbol for the human soul, in relation to a deity who is male. The most renowned use of the virahinī in Indian literature occurs, of course, in poetry dedicated to the Hindu god Kṛṣṇa. Jain, Sant, and Sikh religious poetry, too, have their virahinīs. Within an Islamic context, the virahinī appears in many genres of vernacular Sufi poetry, ranging from the romantic epics of Avadh to the folk songs of the Punjab and Bengal.

In keeping with the literary conventions of the woman-soul symbol, the Sindhi poet represents himself as a virahinī who can no longer bear the agonies of being separated from her beloved, in this case, the Prophet, Muṣṭafā ("The Chosen One"). Love for the Prophet afflicts the virahinī like a sickness for which he is the only cure. Out of intense desire for him, for being in his presence, the Prophet's faithful virahinī is so anxious to visit his mausoleum at Medina that the very "love for Medina" is difficult to bear. She undertakes the grueling journey, traversing difficult, desolate distances to prove her love. As she approaches her destination, she sees the minarets of the Prophet's mausoleum—a sight that acts as a soothing balm for her tired and burning eyes.

But the most dramatic aspect of the virahinī symbol recalls the image of the young bride-to-be and her impending marriage with Muḥammad. The representation of the Prophet as a bridegroom, the bridegroom prince of Medina, is a distinctive feature of many Sindhi panegyrics. Particularly in the maulūds, we find condensed references to a host of terms and images pertaining to weddings in Sindhi society: the henna night, when the bride's hands and feet are stained with henna; the noisy processions of rejoicers; the bridal party anxiously awaiting the arrival of the turbaned bridegroom mounted on a horse or a camel; the showers of flower petals; the expensive gifts; the fragrant wedding bed on which have been strewn pearls and roses. The poet employs this imagery to allude to the true nature of the woman-soul's devotion to the Prophet in a form that arouses immediate associations and emotions among his listeners.

In addition to the symbol of the Prophet-bridegroom, Sindhi poets utilized another literary device, equally fashionable in Sindhi poetry, namely, the use of references to popular Sindhi folk romances and their heroes and heroines. The poet does not narrate these tales, for he assumes his audience is well aware of the details. Merely by using significant words and phrases, he judiciously refers to those tales that feature a virahinī and a prospective bridegroom. In this way he continues to preserve a consistency in the overall symbolism.

A tale particularly favored in many maulūds is the Sassui-Puṅhuṅ romance. Sassui, the adopted daughter of a washerman, is the greatest beauty of the town of Bhambhore, and a considerable sensation in society. Puṅhuṅ, a handsome Baluchi prince, much to the distress of his noble father and brothers, not only falls in love with her but stays with her family as a lowly washerman until he finally is able to marry her. Outraged by his behavior, Puṅhuṅ's brothers, through force and stratagem, manage to kidnap a very drunk Puṅhuṅ from Sassui as she lies peacefully asleep. Upon awakening, the deserted bride is heartbroken and desolate. She sets out, alone, in pursuit of her beloved on a fatal two-hundred-mile march across a dreadful desert and still more dreadful hills. For the Prophet's panegyrist, the heroine Sassui is the virahinī, separated from her beloved Puṅhuṅ. She represents the soul who longs to meet the beloved Prophet, ready to undergo all trials and afflictions in the process. The poet assumes the persona of Sassui and addresses the Prophet as Puṅhal, an affectionate form of Puṅhuṅ:

> Dear sweetheart, I will not forget my beloved, the Prophet.
> For you, I spread my hair as a mat, O Puṅhal, my prince!
> Beloved, more fragrant than musk and ambergris is your sweat;
> On account of your beauty, the moon sacrifices itself.
>
> *Maulūd 5*

Though the Puṅhuṅ of folklore was a Baluchi, the Puṅhuṅ of the maulūds is, of course, the Prophet. Hence, he may alternatively be addressed as the Hashimite, that is, coming from the Banu Hāshim, the Arabian clan of the Prophet. The poet may allude to Sassui's arduous journeys in quest of her beloved; or he may capture Sassui's agony and pain as she awakens from her sleep to find that Puṅhuṅ has disappeared. She is distraught; there is no reason for staying any longer in the town of Bhambhore. She is determined to set out in pursuit of him, even if it means being ground by the "fist of death" (see *Maulūd* 71).

Selections from the major genres of Sindhi poetry in praise of the Prophet are presented here. The translations are based on texts edited by Nabibakhsh Baloch and published by the Sindhi Adabi Board in Karachi and Hyderabad, Pakistan, as part of an extensive project documenting the folklore and literature of Sind: *Maulūd* (Hyderabad, 1961), 5–33; *Madāhūṅ ain munājātūṅ* (Karachi, 1959); *Manāqibā* (Hyderabad, 1960); and *Mu'jazā* (Hyderabad, 1960). The texts themselves represent material collected and compiled from the oral tradition of village folk as well as the written record.

SELECTIONS FROM THE MAULŪDS: POEMS BY 'ABD UR-RA'ŪF BHAṬṬĪ

'Abd ur-Ra'ūf Bhaṭṭī (d. 1752) or 'Āṣī "the rebel/sinner," as he calls himself, was among the first poets to compose maulūds in Sindhi. Over time his compositions became so popular that they were learned by heart from generation to generation, and are being sung to this day. He exercised great influence on his successors in the maulūd tradition in both form and expression. The first line (in italics) is also the refrain.

My moist [tearful] eyes remember the lord [Muḥammad]

The sweetest of relationships is that with the Prophet;
all the rest are meaningless!
The Creator created you [Muḥammad] in the highest rank.
My moist eyes. . . .
The Lady Amina gave birth to the Lord smilingly.
My moist eyes. . . .
O Muḥammad, the Arab, I, "the rebel," am afraid
My moist eyes. . . .

Maulūd 1

The chief of princes was born; the prince of apostles has come!

The Lord [Muḥammad] is my beloved, adorn him with wondrous color.

Gently rub my beloved with perfumed oil [*cūhā*], sandalwood, and sweet-smelling fragrance [*kevṛā*].
Around the neck of that dear Puṅhuṅ place a necklace of diamonds.
Lord, fulfill all the hopes of ʿAbd ur-Raʾūf.

Maulūd 2

Long may he live, the bridegroom, Muḥammad the Arab;
seek mercy from him who is filled with mercy

Beauteous guidance came into existence when the prince Prophet was born
As the chief of the Lords grew up, the world was fragrant with perfumes and ambergris.
This grieved one has come to your door; hearing his grievances, console him!
The "rebel" ʿAbd ur-Raʾūf has come to you. [O Prophet], accept his pleas.

Maulūd 3

I will marry you [Muḥammad] to a rich princess

I will spend my entire life as your slave;
Goods, wealth and household items, the Lord will provide as dowry.
For the bridegroom Prophet I will sacrifice ten million rubies.
All ornaments will be of gold, and clothes embroidered with silver.
The "rebel" ʿAbd ur-Raʾūf says, "I have met the beloved, the consoler!"

Maulūd 7

Welcome to that bridegroom Muḥammad, the Hashimi

He comes, the master for whom the fragrant bed has been spread.
He comes with ten million angels as his attendants.
Prince Aḥmad's [Muḥammad's] attendants have seated their hero in their midst.
The beloved came and strolled around ʿAbd ur-Raʾūf's courtyard.

Maulūd 9

Weddings! What enjoyment, what fun!
On the Prophet's wedding night, the ḥūrīs *[paradisical virgins] make joyful noises*

The parrots in the meadows, the nightingales in the gardens;
The bridegroom mounted the horse, [seated] on a gold saddlecloth.
The Lord sat on the bed; roses strewn on the cushions!
Come Muḥammad, come and meet the "rebel" ʿAbd ur-Raʾūf.

Maulūd 10

O bridegroom, support of the world; O handsome leader!

The Lord tied on you the turban of honor, the turban of faith.
On the Prophet's wedding night, the ḥūrīs tied garlands.
On the Prophet's henna night, ten million angels were present.
The "rebel" ʿAbd ur-Raʾūf says, "Grant us good fortune, master."

Maulūd 16

Muḥammad, you went on the miʿraj [journey to heaven]; the angels said: "Welcome!"
The inhabitants of the heavens said: "Welcome, a hundred welcomes!"

[The angel] Gabriel aroused him [Muḥammad] from his pure sleep;
The Lord sent for him: "Let's go, beloved of the Lord."
Accompanying the Prophet's mount were angels in close proximity.
How many thousands there were, standing respectfully!
The ḥūrīs adorned themselves with garlands, on account of the master;
"You are most welcome, virtuous beloved; sweetheart, the heart longs for you!"
There is no one indigent and sinful like me [the poet].
ʿAbd ur-Raʾūf will be saved, along with the ummah [the Muslim community] in the next world.

Maulūd 18

Remembering, my little heart longs for the beloved [Puṅhuṅ]

Difficult desolate distances, dear Puṅhuṅ makes me travel.
Remembering, my little heart longs for the beloved.
O Generous One, show me the tomb of the Prophet.
Remembering, my little heart longs for the beloved.
Woe on my condition that I forgot his abode.

Remembering, my little heart longs for the beloved.
Love for Medina kills the "rebel" ʿAbd ur-Raʾūf.
Remembering, my little heart longs for the beloved.

Maulūd 45

O love-intoxicated Muḥammad, meet your yearning lovers.
Countless beings have sacrificed themselves, Muḥammad, meet your yearning lovers

For the youthful beloved, the Sassuis have been pining.
When it [love] took firm hold, I listened to no one and nothing!
Those who leave their homeland, they smile in the middle of the battlefield [of love].
The moths of the beloved Prophet burn while they circle.
I, the slaughtered lover, sacrifice myself for Prince Aḥmad.
The lover, ʿAbd ur-Raʾūf says, "Honor is appropriate to [his] status."

Maulūd 48

No sickness afflicts me; I am afflicted by love for you

I am love-sick, beloved, may you be my health!
If the beloved comes to my house, then all pains and afflictions will be cured.
If he [the beloved] curtails the pain, the soul gets peace;
My master, come to me, come to me! An end to this separation!
O sweetheart, if I were to meet you, then so quickly would all afflictions depart!
O Meccan sir, as dowry, cover the vessel of pains.
Kissing you on the head, I say, I will be entrusted to you.
The "rebel" ʿAbd ur-Raʾūf says, "Grant me a place in paradise."

Maulūd 49

I pass time till the day of resurrection; to whom shall I tell,
would that I meet him! O intercessor, O Arab, I still yearn for you

Would that I would give up my life crawling along the road to Medina!
Except for you, guardian, to whom should I talk about my state?
I look with my eyes raised in the direction of the Arab.
The "rebel" ʿAbd ur-Raʾūf says, I fall down in front of the beloved.

Maulūd 52

Return with news of [our] meeting, why not, O my beloved,
return with news of [our] meeting

The love of the prince Muḥammad in the heart and the refuge of the [Qur'ān] recitation in the body.
O Lord, show me one whose body contains the fire of viraha.
May the King Aḥmad come to the courtyard, may the soul that wanders with secrets of love encounter the Lord Muḥammad, may it meet that sweet, comforting beloved!
Deep passion for the beloved entered my heart; immediately there followed pain.
O compassionate one, save me now; remove the burdens of viraha.
The darling heart moves toward the beloved, disclosing all its pains to the master;
The dear little soul burns for the beloved, cure this sickness of love.
'Abd ur-Ra'ūf is a petitioner at your door; Lord do not make him return empty-handed.
You are the ruler of the whole world, O dear one, fulfill your promises.

Maulūd 65

O girlfriends! How can I bear this?
I, who am walking toward the beloved Puṅhuṅ

While awake, I weep; while sleeping, I have no peace;
Thoughts of the Hashimite friend overcome me!
Sisters, staying in this Bhambhore is poison to me!
The fist of death grinds me along the road;
Seizing me by the roots, love has carried me away!
The grasped hem no longer remains [in my hand];
I live but my life has gone.
The "rebel" 'Abd ur-Ra'ūf says, "Treat me kindly:
I am going to the Prince of Medina and I will return."

Maulūd 71

SELECTIONS FROM MADĀḤ AND MUNĀJĀT

Faqīr Ghulām Ḥaidar

For God's sake, pay heed to my complaint, O Muḥammad, the chosen one;
But for you I have no other support, pay heed, O Prophet the guide.

You are the true chief of all the prophets and messengers; the breath of life of the pīrs [holy men];
O perfect leader, for you they recite thousands of ṣalawāt and kalmah [the profession of faith];
They have all been freed by your hand, you are the master of all leaders;
My champion hero, means of my protection, pay heed to my complaint, O Aḥmad [Muḥammad].

At every moment, O leader, humans and angels recite blessings on you;
Be it the heavens or the earth, the tablet or the pen, they all recite happily;
O Aḥmad, remedy my faults; dispel this pain and misery;
O Aḥmad, listen to my sighs, O lord, listen to my cry!

You are God's pure light, the master of the universe, the prince,
[Yours] is the rule of the two worlds, the luminous heart of the morning sun;
You are the refuge of sinners; the minister of the One and Only;
Be mindful of me, efface this sorrow; listen to my supplication, O Aḥmad!

O master, I remember you! Guardian, I long for you!
In trouble and distress I think of no one else but you;
O perfect one! My eyes look toward you, with clasped hands I lament;
O master, listen to my urgent cry; pay heed, O Prophet, the guide.

O Prophet! You are light, pure and holy; the master of the apostles;
Be mindful of me, dispel this sorrow; I desire mercy, O compassionate one!
O intercessor for sinners, you are for everyone in the universe;
I need help, O Muṣṭafā [Chosen One]! O resplendent one!
I am a [rebellious] sinner.

Your devoted lovers perpetually weep for you, O prince;
For your intercession, they recite thousands of blessings and greetings on you;
Ghulām Ḥaidar, the slave, sings your praise day and night;
O believers, recite always the kalmah for the prince messenger:

There is no god but God and Muḥammad is the messenger of God.

Madāhūṅ ain Munājātūṅ, pp. 137–38.

Ḥasan

By the divine name, the Omnipotent, the Concealer [of Faults], O Prophet!
Help me, my master, my leader, O Prophet!

Whatever pleases you is pleasing to God as well,
You are the ruler of God's kingdom, O Prophet!

Without doubt you are the cause of the creation of possibilities,
For you God created the entire universe, O Prophet!

To be a slave at your door is the glory of kings,
You are the commander of all [God's] messengers, O Prophet!

God made your religion victorious over the religions of the world,
See now the strength of the infidels, O Prophet!

"After God you are the greatest, let's cut the story short!"
You are the most special of God's pious, O Prophet!

Make me perform the ḥajj; call me to your door;
Oh that I may be a pilgrim and your visitor, O Prophet!

Everything has a limit except for my sins!
I am sinner beyond all limits, O Prophet!

I am very weak, confused, and anxious;
Except for you there is no one to help, O Prophet!

Do not look at my sins; forgive my trespasses,
I am very weak and destitute, O Prophet!

But for you no one can intercede for me,
I am a member of the [Muslim] community, you are the community's support, O Prophet!

During the agony of death, in the grave, and at resurrection, help me,
O support and refuge of [rebellious] sinners, O Prophet!

If you so desire, God will forgive the sins of creation,
Ḥasan is one among the sinners, O Prophet!

Madāhūṅ ain Munājātūṅ, p. 231

SELECTION FROM MANĀQIBĀ: POEM BY FAQĪR MUḤAMMAD MĀCHĪ

A Manāqibo of the Prophet (Peace be upon Him) Concerning the Perpetually Hungry Person

Ibn Abbas, the narrator, relates
That a person joined the Prophet's companions.
He was a merchant with limitless wealth.
Coming in front of Prince Aḥmad [Muḥammad], he made a request:
"O true Messenger of God, beloved apostle!
The guarantor for the weak on the day of judgment!

Apostle! Please be so kind as to come to my house;
Accept my invitation, out of your benevolence,
So that my wealth may become lawful;
It will not be right and proper without my feeding the intercessor."
Having extended the invitation, he returned home.
That gentleman had prepared every variety of food;
Earthen jars of Egyptian honey were made into sweet sherbet;
A thousand places were adorned with cloth and ornaments;
In four directions were erected colorful fountains with shade;
Everywhere there was the fragrance of musk.
A crowd of people arrived and the bridegroom [the Prophet] entered the house;
With a special welcome, he came and sat on a couch.
The people who were in the house all became humble,
And came forward into his presence with clasped hands and in awe;
To that sweet bridegroom, they offered innumerable gifts and offerings.
Then that gentleman served the Prophet food:
A tray of pulāo [rice mixture] with a special meal.
There came to that place a person,
A pagan who was extremely hungry.
Coming before Aḥmad, he began to plead:
"O true Prophet of God, the beloved of Medina!
I am ill, O apostle, sick!
My stomach is never full no matter how much food I eat;
My hunger never subsides; the entire day I eat!
Give me a remedy for this affliction, O Aḥmad, a cure!
Medicine has made no difference; I just keep eating lots of food;
Give me a remedy for this affliction, my beloved!
So that I can have faith in you and be free from this malady."
Then God's beloved said to that sick man:
"Take a bath, for you are dirty;
Wear clean clothes and make yourself pure;
Then come and eat with me this delicious food."
Obeying Muḥammad's command, he took a bath,
Cleaned his body and the clothes on his limbs,
And came respectfully before Prince Aḥmad.
Saying, "In the name of God the most benificient, the most merciful," he broke bread;
Together with the beloved, he began eating food;
He had eaten only half a plate of rakībī from all this food,
When he suddenly withdrew his hands from the food and said before the beloved:
"I was satiated with merely the millet cake and my body feels constricted;

I recite the profession of faith on the Prophet, the intercessor, and the
proper ṣalawāt;
Remove infidelity from my heart and corrupt thoughts;
Keep in my heart always friendship with certainty."
The Apostle's Māchī says, "Enter the divine way."
Māchī says, "See what an astonishing thing, the noble one, the
Messenger did;
Aḥmad always does well by those under his protection:
He surmounts difficulties; satiates the hungry; and has bad deeds
forgiven by God."
Faqīr [fakir] Muḥammad says, "Obey the Prophet, the sweet
Muḥammad, the chosen one;
Never forget him, because he is God's special friend;
He is the provision for salvation; there is absolutely no other support.
Always recite ṣalawāt on the noble Prophet as well as blessings:
Those who recite the kalmah will depart [this world] with faith."
There is no god but God and Muḥammad is His messenger.

Manāqibā, pp. 149–51

SELECTION FROM MU'JAZĀ: POEM BY VALAṆ VALHĀRĪ

The Miracle Story of the Prophet (Peace be upon Him) and the Doe

God Almighty with His power created the world,
And from His light the Lord produced the Prophet—
The chief of all the prophets.
Now, the miracles of Aḥmad [Muḥammad] are famous in many
nations.
Here I relate the story of the doe; listen, believers, to what has been
narrated:
A hunter, having set a noose-trap, lay in wait at a certain place.
A doe, venturing to this spot, suddenly was ensnared.
Unable to think of any other means of escape, she called out to the
Prophet.
Hearing her cries, Muḥammad came and inquired:
"Why do you call for help, doe? Why do you grieve?"
She replied, "Master, I have left my two dear little children hungry in
the desert.
O Muḥammad, will you stand as guarantor for this weak one?
I will go and return as soon as I have fed them some milk."
The noble Prophet, with his noble hands, undid the snare and released
her.

The doe ran swiftly away in the direction where her children were.
Just then, the foolish hunter returned and, approaching the Prophet, he said:
"Out of love of hunting, I torment lives.
There was a trapped doe at this place; where did you let her go?
Who are you? where are you going? what is your name?
Either produce the doe or give me a quick reply."
The Messenger [of God] told the hunter, "Patience, my dear sir.
My name is Muḥammad, the trustworthy one.
The doe has given me a promise that she will return;
I stand as a visible guarantor for her.
As long as the doe does not return, I will remain at this spot."
The hunter was not at all convinced; he immediately
Flew into a rage, became abusive, and threw a tantrum.
"I have been patient for an hour; God knows another hour and quarter may pass!
Neither gold nor money will buy the exact same doe!"
[Meanwhile] she [the doe] resembled a whirlwind in great speed,
For the fawns were nearby in a delicate sleep.
She began calling softly in the shrubs for her young ones.
Hearing their mother's calls, the little fawns awoke:
"Dear mother, we have been here for several days.
Never have so many cries for help been made from such longing.
Today your body quivers; tells us the news candidly."
She said: "I was grazing on a pasture eating grass for my food,
When I was ensnared in a noose-trap so that I was in great pain.
I pushed hard, I exerted great effort,
But with the pushing the ropes tightened around my head and neck.
My strength was exhausted: how would they [the ropes] ever break or loosen?
Finally, with longing, I called out for the Prince Messenger [Muḥammad]
And that Arab, the refuge and the protector, came.
I have left behind the Prophet, the guide, as my guarantor;
So dear children, take heed, I have to suckle you hastily.
I have to return so that I am not late;
I cannot break the promise I gave to the generous one.
My body trembles out of fear for the knife."
At once, from the teats, they said:
"We, too, are coming to the place where the Prophet of God is.
Let's go, lead us speedily to the master
Lest the hunter be angry with the true messenger."
So they, too, departed from that place, taking the road.
They entered the court and the presence of the Prophet.

The fawns, coming and falling on their knees, began
To kiss with their lips the feet of that noble one.
The hunter, upon seeing this miracle, attained faith [in Islam], saying:
"I truly acknowledge you, the giver of light to the community.
Now, revered sir, give the good deer permission to leave."
On account of kind compassion, she [the doe] merrily skipped away
with her fawns.
Whoever seeks refuge in the master [Muḥammad] escapes harm.
Those who recite the kalmah, they are the people of paradise.
There is no god but God and Muḥammad is the messenger of God.

Mu'jazā, pp. 130–32

Urdu Poems to the Prophet

In Urdu, generally regarded as the language of Islamic civilization in the subcontinent, poems and songs in praise of the Prophet Muḥammad are called na't. They constitute such a significant literary genre that every Urdu poet, no matter how minor he or she may be, has composed at least one na't. Na't is a general term referring to any poetic composition that glorifies Muḥammad, and thus could be written in any of several forms: the qaṣīdah, a panegyric of twenty to one hundred verses, with a monorhyme consisting of one letter or word employed at the end of every line; the rubā'ī or quatrain, with the rhyme scheme a, a, b, a; the masnawī or long poem of rhyming couplets; the musaddas, a poem of six-line stanzas; the sīḥarfī, an "alphabet" poem in which each line or stanza begins with a different letter of the alphabet; the bārahmāsa, a "twelve-month" poem or "lover's calendar" in which the poet assumes the role of a young lady, expressing her longing for the beloved (in this case, Muḥammad) with the changing seasons of the year. Frequently, Urdu na'ts employ more popular forms associated with public musical performances such as the qawwālī, a folk song with a rhythm steadily increasing in its tempo, in which certain phrases are constantly repeated as they are sung by a chorus; or the ghazal, a love poem with a monorhyme, five to twelve verses in length, generally sung by a solo singer. By poetic convention, the last verse of each na't, whatever its form, contains the poet's "pen name" (*takhalluṣ*). Over the course of time, the composition of poetry in praise of Muḥammad has become such a significant literary activity that even Hindu poets writing in Urdu, influenced by the Islamic environment in which they lived, have been inspired to write na'ts. Some of these are so fervent in their expression of devotion that one cannot tell that they were written by non-Muslims. At a broader level, na'ts have so pervaded popular South Asian culture that several contemporary Hindi/Urdu motion pictures feature, as part of their musical repetoire, songs sung in Muḥammad's honor.

In our selections, the poets fervently express their powerful, all-consuming love and devotion, using a range of symbols and ideas. Many have been influenced in their expression by a popular ḥādith (saying of the Prophet) that the relation of the faithful to the Prophet is like that of children to a father. Just as one would turn to a dear relative or a friend for assistance, it is customary for many Muslims to beseech the kind Prophet for his guidance in solving every problem, no matter how mundane. So common is this tendency that it manifests itself in popular Hindi/Urdu films. For example, the song we have included below is from *Mughal-e-Azam*, a film set in the court of the sixteenth-century Muslim Emperor Akbar, during which the wrongly imprisoned heroine Anarkali sings to the Prophet of her tragic plight: *be kas pe karam kījie, shāh-i madīnah* ("Be kind to this destitute one, O Lord of Medina!").

The symbol of the Prophet's shelter and protection, as our qawwālī selection illustrates, is his cloak or shawl (*burdā* in Arabic, *kamlī* in Urdu). It was an Egyptian poet, al-Būṣīrī (d. 1298), who first honored this cloak by composing a moving eulogy of the Prophet and naming it the Burdā. Legend has it that al-Būṣīrī was inspired to compose this poem, later translated into many different Islamic languages, when, in a dream, the Prophet cured him of an illness by throwing his mantle on his shoulders.

Many poets clothe their feelings and emotions for the Prophet with language borrowed from the profane realm of human romance, while avoiding any explicit eroticism. They see themselves as intoxicated with love; they yearn to be with their beloved just as earthly lovers long for their mortal sweethearts. It is in this context that they express their longing for the Arabian city of Medina, the site of the Prophet's last resting place and tomb. Poets elaborating on this theme, a standard topos in na't poetry, might express their desire to undertake the ardous journey from the subcontinent to Arabia or, if unable to go in person, they request the wind or a bird such as the crow to deliver a message of love. Significantly, even Hindu poets of na'ts talk about going to Medina and fulfilling their love for Muḥammad. As one of them puts it: "Love of the Prophet is not conditional on being Muslim; Kauṣarī is Hindu and yet he seeks Muḥammad." In fact, many na't poets claim that love for Muḥammad is universal. Since he is God's beloved, all of God's creatures, from the angels and the animals to the birds and trees, are engaged in expressing their love for him, each species in its own way.

In addition to Muḥammad's role as a friend, helper, and beloved, his followers frequently conceive of him as a guide and leader to the truth. He is a shining lamp that illumines the road of faith through the darkness of infidelity. Alternatively, Muḥammad is the pilot who can navigate the fragile boat of human existence through the whirlpools and sandbanks of this world to the heavenly shore. But far more central to the conception of the Prophet is his role as intercessor for the entire Muslim community. Na'ts, in not only Urdu but every Islamic language, are filled with warm verses asking the Prophet for his mediation at the Day of Reckoning, when every soul has to account for its actions before the Creator. Relying on traditions that highlight Muḥammad's kindness and generosity, and Qur'ānic statements that have been interpreted to mean that he has been granted a special status by God (17:79) or that he was sent as a "mercy to the worlds"

(21:107), many Muslims have come to hold that a believer who trusted and loved the Prophet would be protected in the hereafter by him. The notion that even a sinner who sincerely attests to the existence of one God will be saved by Muḥammad's intercession has led many Muslim poets to utter countless prayers and verses with moving words to implore the Prophet not to withhold his intercession from them. There is one sure way of ensuring this: the recitation of the ṣalawāt, imploring God to bless the Prophet and his family. According to the Qur'an (33:56), God and his angels "pray upon" or bless the Prophet; can humans do any better than follow the divine example? According to popular belief, for every blessing on the Prophet, the reciter is elevated by ten degrees and is credited with ten good actions. Since the recitation of the ṣalawāt brings so much benefit to the reciter, it is hardly surprising that poets frequently call for a blessing on Muḥammad.

Finally, the naʿts also reveal a mystical dimension to the veneration of the Prophet. The main impulse that gave rise to speculation about Muḥammad's spiritual status was the story of his mysterious night journey and ascension to heaven (the *miʿrāj*). The climax of the Prophet's travels through the spheres was a face-to-face meeting with God. This journey, often interpreted metaphorically, provides for mystically minded Muslims the prototype for the ascent of their own souls to higher spiritual realms. The mystical aspects of Muḥammad's prophethood were further elaborated by the concept of the Light of Muḥammad, conceived as a metaphysical principle in pre-eternity out of which God created the entire universe. This light was the fountainhead of all prophetic activity, first manifesting itself in Adam, then in all other prophets, until it found its full expression in the historical Muḥammad. Indeed, some of the Prophet's devotees went as far as to claim that Muḥammad was in fact the ultimate cause of creation. As proof, they cited an extra-Qur'ānic revelation in which God says to the Prophet "*laulāka ma khalaqtuʾl-aflāka*" ("but for your sake, I would not have created the spheres"). Speculation on the spiritual and mystical status of the Prophet even centered on one of his popular names, Aḥmad. There is an extra-Qur'ānic saying, according to which God declares "*Anā Aḥmad bilā mīm*," "I am Aḥmad without the letter *m*, that is Aḥad, One." This proved to many, especially in the eastern Islamic lands, that Aḥmad-Muḥammad is separated from God only by a single letter!

Not all Muslims have been comfortable with the intense veneration accorded to the Prophet, as illustrated in these poems. The elevation of his status beyond that of an ordinary human being, they feel, compromises the basic Islamic principle of tawhīd or the oneness of God who has no partners or associates. For them, the axis of Islam is not Muḥammad but God and His Word as revealed in the Qur'ān. Muḥammad served simply as God's chosen messenger and faithful servant. There is a story that a Muslim claimed that his soul was so filled with love of God that there was no room left for the love of the Prophet. The Prophet, tradition alleges, replied, "He who loves God must have loved me." This story underscores a concept with which all Muslims would agree—the Prophet's special relationship to God, his special status as God's last Prophet, as God's beloved, as

God's chosen one. Notwithstanding his rank, Muḥammad has remained for centuries a person to whom Muslims from diverse social and cultural backgrounds could turn and express their love, their admiration, their sorrows, their joys, and their hopes. As Shakīl Badāyūnī, a prominent contemporary Urdu poet, puts it:

> My wish is this that when I die, I still may smile
> And while I go, Muḥammad's name be on my tongue.

The selections below, culled from the enormous na't corpus in Urdu, come from the following sources: poems from a published collection entitled *Armaghān-i na't* ("A Gift of Na'ts"), compiled by Shafīq Brelvi (Karachi: Maktaba-i khatūn-i Pakistan, 1975); a sound recording of a qawwālī by Akbar Mīraṭhī, recited by Khursheed Aḥmad, from a cassette entitled *Gulhā-yi 'aqīdat,* produced by EMI (Pakistan) Ltd, serial #TC CEMCP 5356; a song from the motion picture "Mughal-e-Azam," lyrics by Shakeel Badayuni, music by Naushad, sung by Lata Mangeshkar, and recorded by the Gramaphone Company Ltd., India, under the Odeon label; a qawwālī by Sabri Brothers from a cassette recording by Ghulam Farid Sabri and Maqbool Ahmad Sabri Qawwal and party, produced by the Shalimar Recording Company, Islamabad, Pakistan, under the Maria label, serial #M-634 vol. 17; a na't recited by Qārī Wāḥid Zafar Qasmī from a cassette entitled *Jashn-e-Milad-un-Nabi,* produced by the Audio Visual Department, His Highness Prince Karim Aga Khan Shia Imami Ismailia Association for Pakistan; and poems by Hindus from Fānī Murādābādī, *Hindū shu'arā kā nā'tiyyah kalām* (Lyallpur: Arif Publishing House, 1962).

PUBLISHED NA'TS

Khalīl

Morning breeze, what good news do you bear that every bud is blossoming?
Here the tulip flutters, there the basil quivers;
From somewhere rises the exclamation, "Glory be to our Lord," and elsewhere there is the roar,
"Blessings be upon him!"
Everywhere the birds chirp in praise of God; the nightingale sings;
Now the peacock cries, then the pigeons coo;
Here the parrots with their elaborate melodies, there the young, tender rose full of fragrance!
The king of the two worlds is born; today is the birthday of the chosen one [Muḥammad].
The entire universe shines from the radiance of Muḥammad's light;

God created him unique, for nowhere has such a handsome being been seen
Even the angels and the virgins of paradise are dazzled by his sparkling beauty.

Whether through Ṭāhā, Yāsīn, Mūzammil, or Mudaththir[1]
Aḥmad's [Muḥammad's] name shines in the entire Qur'ān like a sun.
He has secured the great creation and all prophets yearn for him.
He went on the mi'raj, to which the heavens are witness;
He will have his community forgiven, for he is the intercessor of the day of reckoning.

If there is the hope of "do not despair" [Qur. 39. 53],
then why does this sinful heart palpitate so?
He is the final Prophet of time; he will give us the water of kauṣar [a fountain and river in paradise] to drink.
I am a victim of the pain of separation, I no longer have the strength to wait.
Grant me just a glance of you in my dream, for the strength of my eyes is faltering.
May God grant that the soul leave the body reciting the durūd [blessings on the Prophet];
He who is absorbed in the love of Aḥmad soars like a bird.
[O Prophet,] your kindness to me will be complete when you summon me to Medina,
For on account of separation from you, the afflicted Khalīl yearns eagerly day and night.

Armaghān-i na't, p. 292

Saif

Arise! arise! for the famous king comes,
God's specially chosen one comes.
Even the highest heaven bows to the ground,
As angels descend one after another.
All this is good fortune for the community of sinners,
For today its consoler comes.
Let us enhance our vision and see the manifestation of his beauty,
For that high exalted king comes into the world.
Creation has been blessed with a brilliant dignity,
For he is one who conceals and veils all blemishes.
Saif, for all sinners there will be mercy without exception,
For the special intercessor of the day of reckoning comes.

Armaghān-i na't, p. 171

Dāgh

Free me from sorrow, O Muṣṭafā [God's Chosen One],
To you I plead, O Muṣṭafā.

May destiny not trample me,
May I not be disgraced, O Chosen One.

May my tongue constantly utter your name,
May my heart remember you always, O Chosen One.

May I never abandon the way of virtue,
May it never become one of tyranny and injustice, O Chosen One.

May God bestow on me the courage
That I may fulfill his commands, O Chosen One.

May I remain, on the day of judgment, [nothing but]
A seeker of assistance from your essence, O Chosen One.

May a glance of your favor fall on him,
So that Dāgh may remain happy, O Chosen One.

Armaghān-i naʿt, p. 125

Nashtar

Day and night, I am occupied with praying for God's blessing on the Prophet,
For I am servant of the seal of prophets.
Do not withhold from me the glance of generosity,
I am yours whether I am good or bad.
I, too, should have a miʿrāj, O master of the miʿrāj,
For I am intoxicated by the night of the miʿrāj.
The Prophet David is envious of my melodies,
For I am the singer of the streets of Medina.
Why should I not be proud of my love?
For as a lover of the Prophet, I am a rival of God.
Nashtar, I am free from both worlds,
Even though I am a prisoner of the tresses of God's Prophet.

Armaghān-i naʿt, p. 180

Qamar

Whoever has longing for Muḥammad in his heart,
Wherever he be, he is in Medina.

Even the roses do not possess such a fragrance
As there is in your sweat, kind sir!
Noble sir, the wealth [resulting] from obedience to you
Remains in the treasuries of Muslim hearts.
Thinking of you is a part of faith;
Pleasure lies in drinking from the goblet of [your] love.
Qamar, whoever does not possess love of Muḥammad,
He is among neither the dead nor the living!

Armaghān-i na'‘t, p. 282

Sā'il

For how long will longing remain in my heart for Medina?
For how long can my restless heart sigh: ah! Medina!

May I die in Medina and let my grave be in Medina;
Carry me to my grave, for I am desirous of Medina!

Come, sit yourself in my heart, for it is the sublime heavenly throne;
But if you wish, my bosom could become Medina!

O Lord, my heart craves for Yathrib, Yathrib [the pre-Islamic name for Medina].
O Lord, my mind is melancholic for Medina.

O eye of imagination! it is enough for you that,
Seated at home, in my sight appears Medina!

O God! Sā'il's yearnings are constant day and night;
At every moment, my heart contains passion for Medina!

Armaghān-i na‘t, p. 163

Firāqī

If I were to be born in Medina, how great would that be!
If I were to die while on Muḥammad's street, how great would that be!

O heart, do not waste your life frivolously in the streets of the [earthly] beauties,
If you were to visit Medina, how great would that be!

O Majnūn, you became infamous for giving your heart to Lailī,
If you were to give your heart to the Prophet, how great would that be!

On the last day, O Lord, if I am to be an indigent beggar,
If I were [instead] a supplicant at the Prophet's threshold, how great would that be!

Firāqī has set his sight on the science of logic and eloquent expression;
If it were the science of the Prophet's ḥadīth, how great would that be!

Armaghān-i na't, p. 74

Khalīl

O God, give me love for him who is the ruler of Medina.
Muḥammad is his name, the crown of the prophets, the king of the virtuous;
Muḥammad the qiblah [the direction of prayer] of the two worlds; the Ka'bah [the site of the annual pilgrimage] of the soul;

The friend of the destitute; the one who cures the afflicted!
What good fortune for the [Muslim] community that it found the beloved Prophet.
The guardian of the orphans; the asylum for the poor.
Even in the face of countless misfortunes what do [Muḥammad's] passionate lovers have to fear?
Whoever is a martyr for the Prophet is protected by God.
I proceed to the day of resurrection with only the thought of Muḥammad,
For this is the only means of forgiveness; not obedience, not piety.
The shadow of the Exalted has made a wonderous impression on the name of Muḥammad,
For he is the nourishment of human souls, the medicine for the afflicted.
Seeing this king's mount, even the angels say:

He is truly the pride of the two worlds, the beloved of the Divine.
What rank do I possess to proclaim this love for whom
God himself is the praiser, to whom divinity itself is devoted.
The rank of prophethood has been given to those dear to God:
They are all brothers of Muḥammad, indeed Muḥammad is the pride of his brothers.
My desire is to visit your tomb—fulfill it if you desire:
For me it is most difficult [to accomplish], for you most easy.
None can go astray while following you,
Because those footsteps are the lamps on the road of faith.

O Creator, for the sake of Aḥmad [Muḥammad] and his family, forgive me;
The heartbroken Khalīl seeks absolution from You.

Armaghān-i naʿt, p. 67

Salīm Aḥmad

My state was very precarious;
Nothing appealed to me;
I was extremely tormented, besides myself;
It had been ages since I last celebrated;
Sorrowful emotions wandered freely through my heart;
Dust had settled on the mirror of my soul;
I was suffering from an affliction;
My very inner being was sick;
In this way life flowed by.
Then, suddenly, one day I received the good news of a cure:
The greeting of life came to me,
For my tongue uttered the name of Muḥammad.
Muḥammad, the repose of the hearts of the destitute,
Muḥammad's name is comfort for the soul,
The rose of God's garden,
Muḥammad is eternity without beginning, Muḥammad is eternity without end,
Muḥammad, who praises [God] and is praised,
Muḥammad, who bears witness and is also attested,
Muḥammad the lamp, Muḥammad the illuminating,
Muḥammad the bearer of good news, Muḥammad the warner,
Muḥammad the sage, Muḥammad the word,
Muḥammad on whom be thousands of salutations and greetings.

Armaghān-i naʿt, p. 266

SELECTIONS FROM SOUND RECORDINGS OF NAʿTS

A Naʿt by Akbar Mīraṭhī

The wearer of the crown of mercies, the ruler of the two worlds
The one who ascended the highest heaven, the protector of the reputation of sinners:

Chorus [in Arabic]:
O Prophet, peace be upon you; O Apostle, peace be upon you.
O Beloved, peace be upon you; blessings of God be upon you.

I have this yearning to go to his door so that rivers of tears may flow
That I may reveal the wounds in my breast and, facing him, proclaim:
O Prophet, peace be upon you. . . .
O God, fulfill this prayer: that I may go to the door of the master;
After having sung some naʿt, I may bow my head and recite:
O Prophet, peace be upon you. . . .

Afflicted with pain and sorrow, I have come from afar
Taking great pride in you, [I recite] with outstretched arms:
O Prophet, peace be upon you. . . .

Knowing you to be an effective refuge, I have come to your door
Protector of God's creation, please accept my greetings:
O Prophet, peace be upon you. . . .

Yes, may this wish be fulfilled, that when I am in God's presence
You be clearly present on the side, so that from here the cry rises:
O Prophet, peace be upon you. . . .

The shore of sorrow is distant, O leader of God's universe!
Grant us protection quickly so that our boat crosses [the ocean of existence]:
O Prophet, peace be upon you. . . .

Listen to this addicted lover, listen to the sponsor of this gathering
Listen to the hearts of the audience, listen to Akbar, the sacrificed:
O Prophet, peace be upon you. . . .

From a cassette entitled *Gulhā-yi ʿaqīdat*

Song from Motion Picture "Mughal-e-Azam"

O solver of difficulties! I have a complaint, I have a complaint:
Even though I am devoted to you, yet my world is destroyed.
Be kind to this destitute one, O Lord of Medina.
My destiny adverse, my boat has run into a powerful eddy,
Be kind to this destitute one, O Lord of Medina.
Now is the time for your assistance to counteract the danger,
The stories of my heart are not hidden from you,
This helpless, trapped one is fraught with wounds.
Be kind to this destitute one, O Lord of Medina.
O you with the tresses, the armies of affliction have come;
For God's sake, save my sinking boat;
As a result of these storms, living is so difficult,
Be kind to this destitute one, O Lord of Medina.

A Qawwālī by the Sabri Brothers

We, too, know that there is a retribution for sins;
But the concealer of our sins is God Himself.
If it is appropriate for an ascetic to have pleasure in the enjoyment of worship,
Then, on our part, we may engage in praise for Muḥammad.
O God, I do not ask for the wealth of this world or the next;
I do not ask for a crown, a throne, or worldly rule;
O God, nor do I ask for paradise.
In my petition to you, O God, I ask that you fulfill only this:
That whenever my heart craves for him, Muḥammad should know.
Qais selected a Lailī of passionate blandishment;
Farhād selected a queen of elegant charms;
Handsome Yūsuf [Joseph] selected a Zulaikhā [his lover] of splendor;
In this manner, everyone selected their own sweethearts;
But we, the poor, selected Muḥammad, the chosen one!
But we, the poor, selected Muḥammad, the chosen one!
But we, the poor, selected Muḥammad, the chosen one!
Abū Bakr accumulated sincerity;
ʿUmar accumulated the wealth of justice;
ʿUṣmān accumulated the grandeur of generosity;
ʿAlī accumulated, in the field of battle, bravery;
But he with the cloak [Muḥammad] gathered under it the community of Muslims!
But he with the cloak [Muḥammad] gathered under it the community of Muslims!
But he with the cloak [Muḥammad] gathered under it the community of Muslims!
I sacrifice myself completely for Muḥammad's elegance and charm;
From the beginning of time to the time of prophethood, my heart is consecrated to you;
Every human, out of affection for him with the cloak, declares:
I have abandoned the pleasures and delights of both worlds,
Instead I have procured intimacy with the holy Prophet.
Maqbūl and Farīd, in the Qur'ān is found this truth:
None is higher than the Prophet in this world.
God be my witness, the breath of life has entered my soul,
For merely by sitting and reciting naʿt in honour of the Prophet
We have attained paradise! We have attained paradise!

From a cassette recording

A Naʿt Recited by Qārī Wāḥid Zafar Qasmī

The light of dawn radiates from your face and the luster of the evening glows from your tresses!

Chorus: *Allāh Hū Allāh Hū Allah Hū Allah Hū; there is no god but God!*

My dear sir, as Prophet you are exalted; your grandeur is preeminent in its perfection.
With proof and evidence, he brings the astray to the [true] path.

My master is a treasury of blessings, my lord is a storehouse of mercy;
A guide for the entire community; a leader to the divine law.

Holy is his lineage, exalted is his pedigree; before him the entire Arab religion is respectful.

With a sign from his finger, trees moved; with his permission, stones began to talk;
And the moon split into two pieces when he pointed his forefinger!

The trusted [angel] Gabriel came to him on the eve of the night journey, bearing God's message;
God summoned him to the throne and granted him the honor of [divine] proximity.

All the sins of the community have been forgiven;
All previous registers [of sins] have been cleared;

For Muḥammad is our lord, indeed on his name rests our glory and endurance.

From a cassette entitled "*Jashn-e-Milad-un-Nabi*"

SELECTIONS FROM NAʿTS COMPOSED BY HINDU POETS

Kauṣarī—1

Call me to Medina, O Muḥammad!
Show me your street, O Muḥammad!
Don't make me cry from separation, O Muḥammad!
Don't torment your lover, O Muḥammad!
People say that my love for you is insane;
What else can I say, O Muḥammad?
So radiant is the brilliance of your manifestation that I cannot open my eyes,
[Nevertheless] your image is eternally present, O Muḥammad!
God is your lover and you are God's;

I sacrifice myself for you both, O Muḥammad!
In God's creation, none is like you,
For next to God, you are unique, O Muḥammad!
I care not at all for kings,
For I am a supplicant at your door, O Muḥammad!
I do not associate with drunkards nor am I inclined to ascetics,
What is this state of mine, O Muḥammad?
May God forgive me on account of you,
May my prayers be granted, O Muḥammad!
[Even though] your Kauṣarī lives among Hindus,
Yet in darkness is found the water of immortality, O Muḥammad!

Hindu shu'arā, p. 64

Kauṣarī—2

I loved Muḥammad even when this universe did not exist,
There was only void, nothingness; neither Eve nor Adam was there,
Nor the moon, the sun, the sky, the stars, the earth, the ocean;
Neither the rose nor the rose garden; even the dew-drops were not there!

The [governing] principle for the revolution of time was the word *annihilation;*
Happiness was totally nonexistent and sorrow uncreated;
The register of births and deaths was still closed;
Neither were there parties of happiness nor the houses of mourning!

A confused picture album was this worthless world,
No one was yet king and there were no coins or dirhams.
Water and fire were dissolved in the art of dissolution;
Neither was there humility in the dust nor any life in the wind!

The secret of love between lover and beloved was concealed;
Neither were there friends, intimates, and confidants.
Kauṣarī, then too, I loved the chosen one:
Just as much as I do now, not any less.

Hindu shu'arā, p. 46

Shād

My heart is madly in love with Muḥammad!
The star of good fortune shines [on me].
Only he enjoys the love of the Prophet,

In whose eyes he [Muḥammad] is contained.
There is no rival for you, nor will there ever be;
This much has been seen, this much has been understood.
Just as the Lord of the Universe is only one,
So God's beloved, too, is unique.
Between Aḥad (the One) and Aḥmad (Muḥammad) there is only this difference:
One became the servant while the other is the Lord.
Some call me an infidel, others, a Muslim,
Let them say whatever comes to mind.
I am a monotheist, a gnostic, a mystic true,
On my situation has been the grace of the Lord.
O Shād, only by reciting naʿt
Have you attained this honor, acquired this dignity.

Hindu shuʿarā, p. 32

Fānī

I am in love with Muḥammad, what should I do?
What should I do to meet him, what should I do?

The streets of Medina are paradise for me;
I desire the garden of paradise, what should I do?

If I were to obtain my heart's desire,
How thankful I would be for the blessing, for the mercy!

O Fānī, I am a supplicant of the chosen one;
What other expression of belief can I make?

Hindu shuʿarā, p. 157

Note

1. Some of the names or epithets for the Prophet that Muslims claim to have discovered in the Quʾrān.

—9—

Bāul Songs

Carol Salomon

The Bāuls of Bengal belong to a heterodox devotional (*bhakti*) tradition which was influenced by all three major religions of the Indian subcontinent—Hinduism, Buddhism, and Islam—and yet is distinctly different from each of them. They come primarily from economically and socially marginal groups, and live on the fringes of both Hindu and Muslim society, with the majority of Hindu Bāuls residing in the state of West Bengal in northeastern India, and most Muslim Bāuls (generally called by the generic term "fakir") in Bangladesh.

Bāuls travel from place to place, singing their mystic folk songs to the accompaniment of an ektārā, a one-stringed drone instrument held in one hand, and a ḍugi, a small drum hung on the shoulder and played with the other hand. It is mainly through these songs that they give literary expression to their beliefs and practices; only rarely do they compose any treatises. Bāul songs are short compositions consisting of a refrain and three or four verses ending in a signature line (*bhaṇitā*) in which the name of the poet, and often that of his guru, are given. They are composed in colloquial Bengali, using imagery from daily life—activities such as fishing, farming, sailing, trade and even robbery, foreclosure, and litigation—as spiritual metaphors.

The Bāuls and their songs are an important component of Bengali cultural identity. Yet middle-class urban Bengalis have ambivalent feelings toward the tradition. On the one hand, they often idealize the Bāuls, regarding them as almost saintly figures who are free of social conventions, inhibitions, and prejudices. They also highly value their songs for their musical and literary qualities, and consider them one of the main types of Bengali folk songs. But on the other hand, they often condemn or deny their tantric sexual rituals.

The Nobel laureate Rabindranath Tagore, whose thought and writing were substantially influenced by the Bāuls, is credited with bringing Bāul songs to the attention of middle-class Bengali society. In 1915–1916 he published twenty songs of the great Bāul poet Lālan Fakir in the literary journal *Prabāsī*. He also had in his private collection two notebooks containing a total of 298 songs by

Lālan that are among the oldest and most authoritative sources of Lālan's songs. It was largely Tagore and his associate Kṣitimohan Sen who elevated the Bāuls to the status of a cultural symbol. This idealization took place at the expense of the Bāuls' esoteric aspect, and had a deleterious effect on scholarship, leading scholars to eschew field work and focus exclusively on their humanistic beliefs. As a result, Bāul sādhanā (religious practice) was given short shrift. Scholars mistakenly characterized the Bāuls as practicing different sādhanās, united only by a common spirit of extreme unconventionalism. In 1968, Upendranāth Bhaṭṭācārya published his ground-breaking study *The Bauls of Bengal and Baul Songs (Bāṅglār Bāul O Bāul Gān),* based on many years of field work. In this book he proved that Bāuls, whether Hindu or Muslim, practice more or less the same sexual rites, and that these rites are central to Bāul religion and to an understanding of their songs. Though subsequent field work done by scholars has corroborated his findings, the old romantic image of the Bāuls continues to hold sway today.

Although there are many outstanding Bāul poets, Lālan Fakir, also known as Lālan Shāh, is considered to be the greatest of them all. He lived in the village of Cheuriya, in present-day Kushtia District, Bangladesh (formerly part of Nadíya District, India) where he died in 1890, purportedly at the age of 116. No Bāul poet has had such widespread popularity in both West Bengal and Bangladesh and as great an impact on Bengali literature as Lālan.

Not much is known for certain about Lālan's early life, but both Hindus and Muslims lay claim to him. It is clear from several of his songs in which Lālan complains at the outset that people always ask him about his religious affiliation that even his contemporaries were puzzled about it. For example, one such song, "*Sab loke kay lālan ki jāt saṃsāre,*" opens with the following verse:

> Everyone asks: "Lālan, what's your religion in this world?"
> Lālan answers: "How does religion look?"
> I've never laid eyes on it.
> Some wear mālās [Hindu rosaries] around their necks,
> some tasbis [Muslim rosaries], and so people say
> they've got different religions.
> But do you bear the sign of your religion
> when you come or when you go?

Lālan maintained silence concerning his birth religion for two reasons: first, as is the Bāul custom, he had renounced the world and severed family ties when he became a Bāul; second, he was strictly nonsectarian, believing that there is only one true religion—the "religion of man," in Tagore's words. According to the earliest biographical accounts of Lālan, the first of which was published in an obituary in the journal *Hitakari* on October 31, 1890, just two weeks after his death, he was born to Hindu parents, contracted smallpox while on a pilgrimage, and was left for dead. He was found by a Muslim, some say by his guru Sirāj Sā̃i, who nursed him back to health. The story of Lālan's Hindu birth cannot be uncritically accepted, since the anonymous author of the obituary, which is the oldest and most reliable account of Lālan's life, states that he was unable to verify it. There can be no doubt, however, that more recent legends ascribing to Lālan a Muslim birth are apocryphal, as they have an obvious ulterior motive; they did not surface until the 1960's when Bengali Muslims, searching for an identity rooted in the culture of Bengal rather than deriving from Islam as practiced in the Middle East, began to raise Lālan to the status of a cultural hero.

The Roots of the Bāul Tradition

Scholars have placed the origin of the Bāul sect anywhere from the fifteenth to the seventeenth century. Bāul songs provide no clues as to how far back the tradition goes. They are primarily transmitted orally from guru to disciple and from singer to singer, although they may also occasionally be written down in notebooks. As they are passed down, the language tends to be modernized, thus giving no indication of the date of composition. To my knowledge, the oldest songs that can be dated are those of Lālan Fakir. Notebooks of his songs are also the earliest manuscript evidence of Bāul songs that have been discovered. Nor is it possible to date the tradition by tracing the occurrences of the word *bāul* in medieval Bengali literature. The word, derived either from Sanskrit *vyākula,* "confused," or *vātula,* "mad," is found in Bengali texts dating back to the fifteenth century, where it generally has its literal meaning "mad" (cf. Hindi *bāur*).

The Bāuls have presumably been so named because, to the average Bengali, they do indeed seem mad in their extreme unconventionality. They reject commonly accepted beliefs and practices such as the caste system and worship in mosques or temples. Their lifestyle is also unusual. In theory, at least, Bāuls are supposed to subsist on alms from begging (*mādhukari*), although in practice many earn their living by singing professionally or by engaging in other occupations. Moreover, their appearance often differs from that of the general population; Hindu Bāul men in particular dress distinctively, with their long hair twisted into a topknot, long loose white or saffron-colored upper garments, and patchwork coats made of rags. To the Bāuls, however, "mad" does not have a pejorative connotation; rather it has the positive sense of "mad with love for God." In fact, *pāgol* and *kṣepā* are two Bengali words for "mad" that Bāuls often proudly affix to their names.

Not until 1870, with the publication of *Bhārat Barṣīya Upāsak Sampradāy* ("Indian Devotional Traditions") by Aksay Kumar Datta did the Bāuls appear in the pages of history. Whatever the date of its origin, there can be no doubt that the heyday of the Bāul tradition was in the last century and early part of the present one; it was during this period that the thousands of Bāul songs that comprise the present-day corpus were composed.

The Bāuls as a Tantric Tradition

The Bāuls' tradition is eclectic, drawing from tantric (Sahajiyā) Buddhism and tantric Hinduism (primarily Vaiṣṇava Sahajiyā, but also Śaiva-Śākta), Bengali

(Gauḍiya) Vaiṣṇavism, and Sufi Islam. They are essentially a tantric yogic sect, and as such share common ground with other tantric yogic traditions. For example, like other tantrics, they believe that women embody the mystery of the universe and hold the key to liberation, since every woman is an incarnation of the śakti (female power), the manifestation of the Supreme's creative energy. Also like other tantrics, they hold that the body is a microcosm of the universe in which the Supreme resides, and that it is the only instrument for gaining liberation and conquering death. Moreover, as is true of many tantric traditions, the Bāuls do not believe in going against man's nature by suppressing sexual instincts; rather, through sexual union involving yogic practices of breath control, they seek to regain the state of cosmic unity that existed before the creation of the universe. Furthermore, in the manner of all tantrics, they place great importance in the guru who gives the adept indispensable guidance and instruction that cannot be found in any written text. Finally, Bāul songs are composed in an ambiguous style that resembles the sandhā bhāṣā ("intentional language") of the Buddhist tantric *Caryāgīti* or *Caryāpad* (Caryā songs; about tenth to twelfth centuries C.E.), the oldest extant texts in Bengali, as well as the enigmatic language of many other esoteric Indian traditions with a tantric background, such as the Sants, Nāths, and Vaiṣṇava Sahajiyās.

Sufism and tantrism, both being mystic traditions, have several essential features in common that facilitated their synthesis in Bāul ideology. For example, both Sufis and tantrics are opposed to discursive learning and knowledge. The goal of both is to return to the original nondual state before creation. Sufis strive to experience the "Day of Alast," the day of the primordial covenant referred to in the Qur'ān (7:172) when God, who was the only being in existence, asked mankind, who had not yet been created, "Am I not your Lord?" (*alastu bi-rabbikum*). Sahajiyās endeavor to reach the state of sahaja; the word *sahaja,* from which the Sahajiyā tantrics take their name, literally means "easy," "natural," "innate," and the sahaja state refers to the innate state of absolute unity that existed in the time before the creation of the cosmos. Both Sufis and tantrics believe that the body is a microcosm of the universe, that God is within the body, and that the creator and the created are one and the same. Both identify the divine with light, although light-theology generally plays a more central role in Sufism than in tantrism. Both revere the spiritual guide, the guru or murshid on whom all spiritual progress depends. Finally, the Sufi practice of dhikr (remembrance of God by repeating his name) involves breathing techniques that resemble those used by tantric and yogic traditions.

Where the Bāuls depart from the majority of tantric traditions and most closely resemble the Sufis and the Vaiṣṇavas, both orthodox and Sahajiyā, is in the importance they attach to love in the realization of the divine. Like Sufis and orthodox Vaiṣṇavas, the Bāuls conceive of love as the yearning of the individual for the divine. Bāul songs about love are often expressed in terms of viraha, love in separation. The Bāuls are continually searching for the ever-elusive God within, the Man of the Heart (*moner mānuṣ*). Perhaps no Bāul has used more evocative imagery to describe this frustrating search than Lālan Fakir: "The Lord is near, but seems far away. Don't you see? He's hidden from you like a mountain by the hair in front of your eyes" ("*Āmār āpan khabar āpnār hay nā*" ["I'm Out of Touch with Myself"]). Like the tantrics, however, the Bāuls believe that the means to experience divine love is through human love; through the union of the physical forms (*rūp*) of man and woman, their divine nature (*svarūp*) can be obtained.

Bāul Religion

As is true of mystics in general, the Bāuls believe that the truth cannot be found in books and that external rituals are empty, futile acts. They reject the authority of Hindu scriptures such as the Vedas and Purāṇas as obscuring the way to the divine: "Vedic clouds darken the sky. The jewel of day doesn't rise" (Lālan Fakir, poem 10). Similarly, they reject the authority of the Qur'ān as interpreted by orthodox Muslims. The Bāuls, like the Sufis, assert that the Prophet taught two types of doctrines, one exoteric (*zāhir*), recorded in the Qur'ān and meant for the general public, and the other esoteric (*bātin*), only hinted at in the Qur'ān and aimed at the select few who are able to grasp its meaning and who pass it down from heart to heart. Sharī'at, Islamic law, is for followers of the exoteric path, while Ma'rifat, mystic knowledge, is for followers of the esoteric path. The Bāuls regard Ma'rifat as superior to Sharī'at; whereas Sharī'at requires blind faith and devotion, Ma'rifat leads to a vision of the divine (see poem 4).

Since, as will be discussed in some detail below, everything is contained within the microcosmic body, all worship not centered on the body is useless. Pilgrimage, whether it is the Muslim's ḥajj to Mecca or the Hindu's pilgrimage to Varanasi, is merely a waste of time and effort: "Pilgrimage is just walking for nothing until you're ready to drop. You can take care of your business in Peṛo [Pandua, considered an efficacious pilgrimage place for exorcising ghosts] from your very own porch" (Lālan Fakir, "*Calo dekhi mon*" ["Come On, My Mind"]). The merit gained from such ritualistic acts may secure for the worshiper a place in heaven, but it will be of no help in escaping from the cycle of birth and death. Worship in mosques and temples and at the tombs of saints is likewise of no value: "Temples and mosques block the path to you. . . . There are many locks on the door of love. The Purāṇas, the Qur'an, tasbi and mālā—O guru, what torture, sobs Madan, dying of grief" ("*Tomār path ḍhekyāche mandire masjide*"). Asceticism and celibacy are also ridiculed, since lust cannot be conquered just by withdrawing from the world: "Some men swear off women and retreat to the jungle. But do you think they don't have wet dreams?" (Lālan Fakir, poem 9).

The Bāuls not only reject external rituals, but also, as mentioned previously, strongly condemn caste. In this, they resemble the Buddhist and Vaiṣṇava Sahajiyās, the Gauḍiya (Bengali) Vaiṣṇavas, the Sants, and other bhakti (devotional) traditions. To the Bāuls, caste is an artificial distinction created by man and hypocritically transgressed by him when it suits his purpose. "Does a man lose caste if he eats the rice a whore serves him, in secret?" asks Lālan ("*Jāt gelo jāt gelo*" ["Outcaste! Outcaste!"]). The Bāuls are likewise fiercely opposed to sectarianism. In words remarkably similar to those of the Sant poet Kabīr (śabda 84), Lālan sings in his famous song "*Sab loke kay lālan ki jāt saṃsāre*" ["Everyone asks . . ."]: "Circumcising a man makes him a Muslim. But what's the rule for a woman? I recognize a brahman man by his sacred thread. But how can I recognize his woman?"

In religions that reject scriptural authority, the guide who teaches the adept the practices of the tradition is all-important. The Bāuls believe that God is within every human being, but he is more fully manifest in the guru or murshid who has attained liberation and is a perfected man (*siddhapuruṣ, insān-i-kāmil*). The guru or the murshid is regarded as an intermediary (*barzakh*) between man and God. The Prophet Muḥammad (see poem 15) and Caitanya (often referred to in songs by his sobriquet Gaur "fair-complexioned" [see poem 14]) represent the fullest manifestations of God on earth.

The Bāuls call the divinity by a number of names, reflecting their eclecticism, such as Allah and Ahad ("the One"), Kṛṣṇa, Man of the Heart, Uncatchable Moon, Unknown Man, Natural Man (*sahaj mānuṣ*), Uncatchable Man, Golden Man, Unknown Bird, or simply Lord (*sā̃i*). But no matter what they call the divine, the underlying conception is the same. The Bāuls, like all tantrics, hold that the godhead is androgynous. At the same time, however, they identify it with semen and the male. In addition, the supreme is equated with light, breath, and the self. Although the tantric conception of the deity is at core of their belief, the Bāuls' intense feeling of pain at being separated from the divine, so poignantly expressed in song after song (see, for example, poems 1–3 and 5), reflects the influence of Vaiṣṇava and Sufi traditions.

The Gross and Subtle Bodies

The Bāuls, like other tantric yogic practitioners, conceive of the body as having two forms. There is a material or gross body (*sthūla śarīra*) made up of the skeleton, muscles, organs, etc., and having nine or ten openings or "doors." (The ears, nostrils, eyes, mouth, anus, and sexual organ constitute the nine openings; in the Bāul tradition, the tenth door may refer to the female sexual organ or to the two-petaled lotus located between the eyebrows.) But there is also an invisible subtle body (*sūkṣma śarīra*). The Bāul conception of the subtle body for the most part resembles that of the Hindu tantras and of other yogic texts, but also reflects the influence of Bengali Sufism and has some idiosyncracies of its own as well.

The Bāuls adopted from the Hindu tantras the system of cakras (centers) arranged along the spinal column from the perineum to the top of the head. These cakras are visualized as lotuses of varying number of petals and are often referred to in Bāul songs by the number of petals rather than by name. The seven principal cakras in ascending order are as follows: the mūlādhār cakra at the base of the spinal column, with four petals; the svādhiṣṭhān cakra in the region of the genitals, with six petals; the maṇipur cakra at the level of the navel, with ten petals; the anāhata cakra at the level of the heart, with twelve petals; the viśuddha cakra in the region of the throat, with sixteen petals; the ājñā cakra between the eyebrows, with two petals; and the sahasrār cakra at the top of the head or above the head, with a thousand petals. Sometimes, however, the Baul conception of the cakras differs somewhat from the usual Hindu tantric view, reflecting Buddhist tantric and Vaiṣṇava Sahajiyā influences. For example, the hundred-petaled lotus seems to have been taken from the Vaiṣṇava Sahajiyā system. But as in Vaiṣṇava Sahajiyā texts, it is variously described; sometimes Bāul poets seem to locate it in the heart and other times, in or near the sahasrār.

Muslim Bāuls also describe the body in terms of mokāms (Arabic *maqāmat*), "stations" or "stages." In Indian Sufism there are generally four stations on the path to God: nāsūt (human nature), malakūt (the nature of angels), jabarūt (divine power), and lāhūt (divine nature). Sometimes a fifth, hāhūt (divine essence) is added. The Sufis of Bengal equate the first four mokāms with the mūlādhār, maṇipur, ājñā, and anāhata cakras, respectively. In addition, the Bāuls include another mokām, the lā mokām, equivalent to the sahasrār or ājñā cakra, giving a total of five or six stations, depending on whether hāhūt is included. Lā mokām, literally "no place," is so called because it represents transcendent space where all dualities are reintegrated into the Supreme.

The subtle body contains a network of numerous channels or nāṛīs that serve as conduits for breath. As in Hindu and Buddhist tantrism, three nāṛīs are of prime importance in sādhanā. The Bāuls refer to them by the Hindu tantric terms *iṛā, piṅgalā,* and *suṣumnā:* The iṛā is to the left of the spinal column, the piṅgalā to the right, and the suṣumnā is in the middle. These nāṛīs are identified with the holy rivers Gaṅgā, Yamunā, and Sarasvatī. The place where they come together in the mūlādhār cakra is named the Triveṇī (see poem 12) after the confluence of these rivers in Prayāg (Allahabad), which is a famous Hindu pilgrimage place. The Triveṇī is an important locus in sādhanā.

The Microcosmic Body

The Bāuls give no credence to heaven or hell, or to liberation after death. For them it is only possible to escape from the cycle of death and rebirth and gain liberation while one is still alive and has a human body. They seek to reach a state called "dead while alive" (*jyānte marā*), a state in which the adept is dead to the phenomenal world and all consciousness is drawn inward. By experiencing his own death, the Bāul defeats Yama, the god of death, who has no power over those already dead.

The Bāul saying, "Whatever is in the universe is in the receptacle [that is, the body]," sums up the doctrine of *dehatattva,* "the truth in the body." The Bāuls, like other tantrics, take this saying literally and locate cities, mountains, rivers, pilgrimage places—virtually everything on the map—in the human body. Lālan Fakir sings ("*Kibā rūper jhalak dicche dvidale*" ["What Beauty Flashes on the Two-petaled Lotus"]): "He has no other worship. The worship of the body is the essential thing. Pilgrimage places and vows—in this body you'll find it all." And in another song, using Islamic imagery, he sings ("*Āche ādi makkā ei mānab dehe*"): "The original Mecca is in this human body."

Most important of all, the Supreme resides in the human body and can only be reached through it. As Jādubindu puts it in his song "*Khūjle tāy mele āpan deho mandire*": "Search and you'll find him in the temple of your own body. The father of the world speaks in a sweet, melodious voice." The Bāuls reject worship of a transcendent God because the existence of such a divinity is only a conjecture (*anumān*); it cannot be proven. In contrast, the Supreme who is imminent (*bartomān*) can be directly experienced, or as the Bāuls say, "caught."

Male and female principles (*puruṣa* and *prakṛti* or *śakti*) are contained within the microcosmic body of each person, mirroring the macrocosm. The male principle, equated with semen, resides at the top of the head in the highest cakra, the sahasrār. Here the Supreme exists in a state of perfect unity without any qualities or form; here he is the aṭal īśvar, "motionless Lord." Since in the sahasrār everything is integrated into the motionless Lord, there is no duality between enjoyer and enjoyed, between God and the devotee, and the Bāul is unable to feel the bliss of the Lord's presence. The Supreme takes on an effulgent form and sports in the two-petaled lotus, the ājñā cakra in the middle of the forehead, where semen is believed to be stored. (Both the sahasrār and the ājñācakra are associated with the storage of semen, but the Bāuls place more emphasis on the latter.) It is here that he can be directly experienced by the devotee. A Bāul who succeeds in sādhanā (religious practice) sees multi-colored lights filling this cakra.

Other parts of the body such as the eye, are also associated with the manifestation of the Supreme. Lālan, using the symbol of the bird for the Supreme identified with the soul (see poems 4, 5, and 8) sings in "*Dekh nā ebār āpanār ghar ṭhāoriye*" ("This Time Search your Own House"): "The bird's nest is in the corner of your eye." As the name Man of the Heart (*moner mānuṣ*) implies, the heart is another abode of God. "Diving into the Ocean of the Heart" (*del dariyā*) to learn the ultimate truth is a recurrent image in Lālan's songs (see poem 12). In addition, as noted previously, the hundred-petaled lotus is mentioned by Bāul poets as a place where the Supreme dwells: "The Dark Lord sits on the throne of the void in the hundred-petaled lotus" (Lālan Fakir, "*Paṛ gā nāmāj* . . ." ["Pray to Allah . . ."]). Finally, the active form of the Supreme, called the sahaj mānuṣ, "Natural" or "Innate Man," or adhar mānuṣ, "Uncatchable Man," becomes manifest in the lowest cakra, the mūlādhār, during a woman's menstrual period. It is at this time that the Bāuls perform their sādhanā to "catch" him.

The female principle, the śakti or prakṛti, is located at the base of the trunk in the lowest cakra, the mūlādhār, and is conceived of as a coiled serpent called *kuṇḍalinī*. The śakti is also identified with menstrual (uterine) blood which the Bāuls believe to contain the female agent of procreation analogous to the male agent in semen, and which is thought to result in conception when combined with semen. Its appearance in the mūlādhār is often described as a flower without roots (see poem 4). Although man and woman each contains both male and female principles, the woman is considered to be superior to the man, at least for the purpose of sādhanā, since it is in her body that the sahaj mānuṣ (Natural Man) becomes fully manifest. The male practitioner's success in sādhanā is dependent on her help. As the Bāul Haure Gosāi puts it in his song "*Keno pārbi jete premer pathe*" ("How Will You Be Able to Go on the Path of Love?"): "In that land woman is king." But although women are esteemed for their ritual importance, the sādhanā is largely male-oriented; it is described from the male point of view and done mainly for the benefit of the male practitioner.

The body in its unrefined "raw" state is not fit to withstand the rigors of sādhanā. For sādhanā to be successful it is necessary to bring under control the six enemies (lust, anger, greed, infatuation, vanity, and envy) and the ten sense organs (the five organs of perception and the five organs of action). Unbridled lust (*kāma*) personified by the god Kāma (also called Madan) is man's worst enemy. Lālan, using the stock metaphor of a house for the body, sings (poem 7): "The thief who drove me into exile—I see he's come along. Madan's drum is irresistible. Flames of lust burn the inner rooms of my house." And yet, true love is not possible unless lust is there first. The two are inextricably linked. In order to effect the transformation of lust, kāma, into true love, prema, the male practitioner imagines himself as a woman. By "becoming a woman," it is felt, his union with a woman will no longer be motivated by desire for physical pleasure. As a result, he will be able to conquer his lust, thereby preventing the ejaculation of semen.

Sādhanā

Bāul sexual rituals closely resemble those of the Vaiṣṇava Sahajiyās and the earlier Buddhist Sahajiyās. The Bāuls practice sexual intercourse with seminal retention during a woman's menstrual period. The aim of these rituals is to reunite the dual principles that were separated when the world was created. The Bāuls seek to reverse the cosmic process that leads to death and rebirth, proceeding "upstream" (*ujān*), against the natural current, back to the sahaj state, the original state of nonduality that existed before creation. The return to origins, or to the "homeland" (*svadeś*), as the Bāuls sometimes call it, is achieved within the microcosmic body on several planes.

First, the adept makes his semen flow upward back to the sahasrār through the middle of the three nāṛīs, the suṣumnā. Semen is equated with life itself. Its preservation results in a long life span and its loss, in early death. For this reason, it is of vital importance that sādhanā not end in ejaculation. Once a Bāul has taken initiation (*bhek* or *khilāfat*), he is not supposed to father any children. Second, the Bāul practitioner returns the sahaj mānuṣ to the sahasrār. This retrieval of the sahaj mānuṣ is the main focus of sādhanā and the act on which its success hinges. The Bāuls believe that on the third day of a woman's menstrual period the sahaj manuṣ, who feels an irresistible attraction to the śakti in menstrual blood, descends from the woman's sahasrār to her Triveṇī (the place in the mūlādhār where the three nāṛīs meet). Through coitus the sahaj mānuṣ is separated out of menstrual blood, attracted into the male practitioner's penis, and brought back to the sahasrār. The resulting feeling of bliss that the adept experiences is called "catching the Uncatchable," "catching the thief" (see poem 6) or "being dead while alive." This is also what is known as the sahaj state. Third, the adept awakens the kuṇḍalinī śakti (serpent power) within his or her own body by means of yogic practices of breath control and sexual intercourse and likewise draws her up to the sahasrār through the suṣumnā where she is reintegrated into the Supreme. In his song "*Harike dharbi jadi āge śākti sahāy karo*" ["If You Want to Catch Hari, First Get the Śakti's Help"], the Bāul Gosāi Caṇḍī sings: "In the mūlādhār is the mother of the world, and in the sahasrār is the father. If you unite the two, you won't die or be born again." And finally, the Bāuls ritually ingest semen, menstrual blood, feces, and urine. According to Bāul belief these bodily excretions are homologous with the elements and their consumption effects reabsorption of the elements into the Supreme, while at the same time replenishing the body with substances considered vital to one's existence.

Bāul Songs

Bāul songs are often composed in an ambiguous style characterized by technical terminology, code words that may have several meanings, obscure imagery, erotic symbolism, paradoxical statements, and enigmas. Although this style is typical of songs on esoteric subjects, it can be found to some extent in those on other themes, too. The language of the songs is intended to veil their ritual significance from the uninitiated who would find these esoteric practices objectionable, and at the same time to reveal to the initiated the ineffable truth which defies logic and cannot be communicated directly through ordinary discourse.

At the most basic level of the ambiguous style are code words or phrases that are the building blocks of the esoteric songs. Some metaphors are common to the language of tantric texts, such as "sky" for the sahasrār cakra and "moon" for semen and the Supreme. Others are peculiar to the Bāuls; for instance, "new moon night" to signify menstruation, or "full moon on the new moon night" to indicate the appearance of the sahaj mānuṣ in menstrual blood. Poets freely invent code words, so that many of them are idiosyncratic, such as Lālan's "city of mirrors" (poem 2) symbolizing the ājñā cakra. Moreover, the same symbol may have several meanings depending on the context, further complicating the task of interpreting the songs. Thus "moon," in addition to semen and the Supreme, can also designate the female, as in "the moon's new moon night" (that is a woman's menstrual period). Numbers are often used as ciphers. For example, the number sixteen, whether it modifies "guards" (poem 6), "enemies" (poem 9), or "rich men," refers to the ten senses and the six enemies (see above). Sometimes more than one number can indicate the same concept; nine or ten modifying doors (poem 5) stand for the nine or ten openings of the body. In one song Lālan even mentions "nine and a half doors" (poem 11).

Sometimes an entire song is an extended metaphor. This is often the case with dehatattva songs. The body may be depicted as a house (poem 11) with two pillars (legs), nine rooms (the cakras; although the standard Hindu tantric system lists seven, they can vary in number depending on the tradition), a basement (*mūlādhār*), and an attic (*sahasrār*) in which a madman who is the Lord sits; or a bird cage (poem 5) with nine doors, housing an unknown bird (the soul); or a broken-down boat (poem 10) constantly leaking water (semen); or a tree of beauty (poem 13) that produces moon fruit (offspring). Everything from a watch to the city Mecca has been used in Bāul songs to symbolize the body.

Occasionally, an allegory is composed around a central metaphor, as in Lālan's song, "A Thief Keeps Breaking into the Palace" (poem 6). Here the "thief" symbolizes the sahaj mānuṣ and the "palace" (*raṅgmahal*) is probably here the two-petaled lotus where semen is believed to be stored. The "lion-gate" also seems to be located in this cakra. The "watchman" stands for breath. "Patrimony" is a code word for semen (also in poem 10) and "the swiping of a loincloth" (like "the looting of a storeroom" in poem 7) signifies the spilling of semen. The meaning of the allegory is as follows: control of semen is dependent on control of breath. If during ritual intercourse the mind is distracted and the adept fails to control his breath, then the thief—the sahaj mānuṣ—will rob him of his patrimony—semen.

Parodoxes in Bāul songs are of two types: those that do not seem to have any esoteric significance other than hinting at the ineffable and paradoxical nature of the nondual sahaj state, and those that when decoded yield a hidden meaning alluding to secret doctrines. Lālan's "Just Dive into the Ocean of the Heart and You'll See" ("*Del dariyāy ḍube dekho nā*"; poem 12) is one example of a song with self-contradictory, "upside down" (*ulṭa*) expressions. Some statements such as "the dumb speak" and "the deaf hear" do not seem to have any specific symbolic significance. Others, like "waves surge without wind," have sexual import; the "waves" refer to the menstrual flow that "surge without wind" because they are enclosed in the vagina. The enigmas in the last verse of this song can similarly be interpreted in terms of dehatattva. Taken together they describe the mystery of conception and birth. The "mother of the world" who "floats in the sea" is the śakti, the female agent of procreation in menstrual blood. The "father" who is in the belly of the śakti (here, referring to the woman herself) is semen. Lālan says "when he is born he drinks his wife's milk" because semen is equated with the child produced from semen as well as with the father who engenders the child.

Enigmas are occasionally created by using letters of the Perso-Arabic alphabet. In Lālan's song "An Unknown Man Roams the Land" ("*Ek ajān mānuṣ phirche deśe*"; poem 4), the "unknown man" who signifies the sahaj mānuṣ is described as: "zer on aliph, zabar on mim." "Zer" is the vowel marker *i*, and "aliph" stands for Allah, while "zabar" is the vowel marker *a*, and "mim" symbolizes Muḥammad. The solution to the enigma lies not in the phonetic values of "zer" and "zabar," as one would expect, but in their positions and literal meanings. "Zer" is placed below a letter and means "inferior," whereas "zabar" is placed above a letter and means "superior." Thus by referring to the "unknown man" as "zer on aliph, zabar on mim" Lalan is saying that this figure is "inferior" to or beneath Allah and "superior" to or above the Prophet. Often enigmatic imagery paints a surreal picture, as in the third verse of the song about the unknown man: "The strange flower without roots" is the śakti, and the "river of love" is the menstrual flow. The "passionate nightingale" signifies the sahaj mānuṣ (also often symbolized by a bee or fish) who is attracted to the śakti in menstrual blood.

Though the meaning of the songs may sometimes be obscure, their simplicity, vigor, and felicity of expression, their humor and dazzling imagery, and their aphoristic statements that apply to a specific religious context as well as to everyday life make them some of the best poetry in the Bengali language.

There is no standard, authoritative edition of Lālan's songs. Since published editions are full of errors, I have based my translations on manuscripts transcribed by Lālan panthi fakirs and on oral versions of the songs. These texts may differ substantially in some places from those in printed collections.

Further Reading

See Charles Capwell, "The Esoteric Beliefs of the Bāuls of Bengal," *Journal of Asian Studies* 33:2 (1974), 255–64; and *The Music of the Bāuls of Bengal* (Kent, Ohio: Kent State University Press, 1986). Also useful is Shashi Bhusan Das Gupta, *Obscure Religious Cults,* 3rd ed. (Calcutta: Firma K. L. Mukhopadhyay, [1946], 1969). Edward C., Dimock, Jr.'s seminal work is *The Place of the Hidden Moon: Erotic Mysticism in the Vaiṣṇava-sahajiyā Cult of Bengal* (Chicago and London: University of Chicago Press, 1966), Chap. 8 on the Bāuls. His more recent work on the subject is "The Bāuls and the Islamic Tradition," in *The Sants: Studies in a Devotional Tradition of India,* edited by Karine Schomer and W. H. McLeod (Delhi: Motilal Banarsidass, 1987), pp. 375–88. See also Carol Salomon, "A Contemporary Sahajiyā Interpretation of the Bilvamaṅgal-Cintamaṇi Legend, as Sung by Sanātan Das Bāul," in *Patterns of Change in Modern Bengal,* edited by Richard L. Park (East Lansing: Asian Studies Center, 1979), pp. 97–110; and "The Cosmogonic Riddles of Lalan Fakir," in *Gender, Genre and Power in South Asian Expressive Traditions,* edited by Arjun Appadurai, Frank J. Korom, and Margaret Mills, (Philadelphia: University of Pennsylvania Press, 1991), pp. 267–304.

Translations of Bāul songs may be found in Deben Bhattacharya, *Songs of the Bards of Bengal* (New York: Grove Press, 1969); Brother James, *Songs of Lalon* (London: Unwin Ltd., 1969, reprint Dhaka: University Press Limited, 1987), and Abu Rushd, *Songs of Lalon Shah* (Dhaka: Bangla Academy, 1991 [1964]). See also Alokranjan Dasgupta and Mary Ann Dasgupta, 1977 *Roots in the Void* (Calcutta: K. P. Bagchi and Co., 1977).

SONGS OF LĀLAN FAKIR

The title of each song, which is the same as the first line of the song, is given in Bengali after the number.

1 *Amār moner mānuṣeri sane*

When will I be united
with the Man of my Heart?

Day and night
like a rainbird
I long for the Dark Moon,
hoping to become his maidservant.
But this is not my fate.

I caught a glimpse
of my Dark Lord in a dream,
and then he was gone
like a flash of lightening
vanishing into the cloud it came from,
leaving no trace.

Meditating on his image,
I lose all fear of disgrace.
Poor Lālan says,
He who always loves,
knows.

2 *Āmi ekdino nā dekhilām tāre*

I have not seen him even once—
my neighbor
who lives in a city of mirrors
near my house.

His village is surrounded
by deep boundless waters,
and I have no boat
to cross over.
I long to see him,
but how can I reach
his village?

What can I say
about my neighbor?
He has no hands, no feet,
no shoulders, no head.
Sometimes he floats high up in the sky,
sometimes in the water.

If my neighbor just touched me,
I wouldn't feel the pain of death.
He and Lālan are in the same place,
yet five hundred thousand miles apart.

3 *Sādhya ki re āmār se rūp cinite*

Will I ever be able to recognize him?
Night and day, blinders of delusion
cover my eyes.

Someone keeps stirring
in the northeast corner of my room.
Am I moving or is he?
Groping, I search myself.
I just can't see.

The two of us,
this stranger and I,
live in the same place.
But when I try to catch him,
he's five hundred thousand miles away.

I got tired of searching.
Now I just sit and shoo flies.
Lālan says, What's the trick
of being dead while alive?

4 *Ek ajān mānuṣ phirche deśe*

An unknown man
roams the land.
You have to know him.
You have to know him
and honor him too.

Rely on Sharīʿat
and finding him
is out of the question.
You can reach him
only through Maʿrifat,
if you get over
your state of delusion.

A strange flower
without roots
blooms on the banks
of the river of love.
From time immemorial
a passionate nightingale
has been drinking the flower's nectar.

I've heard tell of a man:
zer on alif, zabar on mim.
Lālan says,
Don't get lost in confusion.
Turn to a murshid
and you'll learn the solution.

5 *Hāy cirodin puṣlām ek acin pākhi*

What a pity!
I spent my whole life
raising an unknown bird.
Yet I never learned the secret
of his identity.
The anguish of it
brings tears to my eyes.

I can hear the bird's chatter, brother,
but I can't see how he looks.
I see only this thick darkness.
If I could find someone
to reveal his identity,
I'd get to know him.
Then my heart would stop throbbing.

But I don't know my pet bird.
There's no end to the shame I feel.
What am I to do? Any day now

that bird's going to throw dust in my eyes
and fly away.

The bird's cage has nine doors.
Through which one
does he come and go,
playing tricks on my eyes?
Sirāj Sā̃i says, Lālan,
lay a trap in his path
and stay there.

6 *Raṅ mahale sĩd kāṭe sadāy*

A thief keeps breaking
into the palace.
Where does this thief come from?
If I could catch him,
I'd imprison him,
shackling his feet
with the chains of my heart.

At the lion-gate
is a watchman,
vigilant day and night.
What spell does the thief
cast over him?
At what hour
does he break in?

Sixteen guards surround the building,
men of unlimited powers.
Even they can't detect him.
Whose hands should they bind
with rope?

Today the thief stole all my patrimony.
He even swiped my loincloth.
Lālan says, What a grudge
this thief suddenly holds
against me!

7 *Bhulbo nā bhulbo na bali*

I won't forget.
I won't forget, I say.

But when it's time for action,
my resolve wavers.

I won't forget, I say.
But my nature doesn't change.
Seductive glances
from the corners of her eyes
drive me crazy and wipe out
divine wisdom.

A man's character is colored
by the qualities of his friends;
so I learned from experience.
When I took up with bad companions,
my good intentions vanished.
I landed in trouble. Now I'm at my last gasp.
My shame can't be washed away.

The thief who drove me into exile—
I see he's come along.
Madan's drum is irresistible.
Flames of lust burn
the inner rooms of my house.
I've forgotten the pilot of my mind.
What more will the sinners do?

Stagestruck,
I put on a clown's costume
and got lost in my act.
If I had kept company with good men,
if I had known good companions, says Lālan,
would that robber have looted my storeroom?

8 *Rāt pohāle pākhiṭe bale de re khāi*

When dawn breaks,
my bird anounces:
"I'll eat now."
I resolved to follow
my guru's orders,
so what can I do?
How can I leave?

I answer: "My soul,
say Kṛṣṇa's name

and set me free."
But he doesn't care for the name.
He just keeps screeching,
"I want to eat."

Who can raise such a bird?
He'd like to suck the ocean dry.
How to satisfy him?
I've lost my senses,
been sapped of my strength,
turned into a total glutton.

I'm Lālan, the drooler.
My bird got sick of his perch.
Lālan says, What's a guru to you, anyway,
on a full stomach?

9 *Kon deśe jābi mon calo dekhi jāi*

What land
will you go to, my mind?
Come on, let's see
where you become a saint.
So you want to go on a pilgrimage?
No sinners there, you say?

Some men swear off women
and go off to the jungle.
But do you think
they don't have wet dreams?
When the tiger
of your own mind
is devouring you,
who can stop him?

Your adversaries
are all inside you.
They make trouble
night and day,
drive you crazy
wherever you go.

Traveling or staying put—
it's six of one,
half dozen of the other.

This you've heard over and over.
Sirāj Sāi says, Lālan,
you're such an idiot!

10 *E deśete ei sukh holo*

So this is the happiness I find here,
and yet I don't know where else to go.
I got a broken-down boat
and spent my life bailing water.

Who is mine and whose am I?
I set no store by my patrimony.
Vedic clouds blacken the sky.
The jewel of day doesn't rise.

Will this sinner be so lucky?
Will the merciful moon have mercy on me?
How much longer must I go on this way,
rowing my boat of sin?

Who in the world can I blame?
My worship fell far short.
Lālan says. How long before
I get to the feet of my Lord?

11 *Dhanya dhanya boli tāre*

I've got to hand it to the fellow
who built a house like this,
with its foundation up in the sky!

The house has just two pillars, no more,
and their bases aren't attached to the floor.
How will this house stay in one piece,
when it's battered by a raging storm?

It has a basement and nine rooms,
even an attic at the very top.
There a madman sits,
in solitude, the sole Lord.

Upstairs and downstairs,
one after the other,
are nine and a half doors.

Lālan asks, So which one
do I open to get in?

12 *Del-dariyāy ḍube dekho nā*

Just dive
into the Ocean of the Heart and you'll see.
You can learn the deepest secrets.

The city on the ridge
is an extraordinary place,
built with astounding skill.
There's no water in the lakes,
but the land is flooded.
Would you believe such strange business
if you just heard about it?

At the slippery quay of the Triveṇī
waves surge without wind.
The dumb speak, the deaf hear,
and a halfpenny tests as gold.

This story is not fit to be told.
The mother of the world floats on the sea.
Lālan says, The father
is in her belly,
and when he is born,
he drinks his wife's milk.

13 *Cā̃d āche cā̃ de gherā*

The moon is surrounded by moons.
So how do you intend to catch
that moon today?

The radiant beauty of millions of moons
and in the middle, the Uncatchable Moon's
brilliant light—
Just glance at that mass of moons
and they start to spin.
Be careful! Be careful!
Make sure you don't black out!

Moon fruit grow
on the tree of beauty.
Every now and then
you can see them flashing.
I try to take a look,
but my eyes fail me.
The rays of beauty are dazzling.

This city called "invisible"
is built with strange skill.
At night the sun rises,
by day lamps burn.
Those who know
what's on the ridge
have eyes that see.
Lālan says, They have seen the moon.

14 *Jānbo he ei pāpī haite*

Hey Gaur,
I'll find out from this sinner
if you really came to save mankind.

You gave out the treasure of love
to everyone in the city of Nadīya.
Well I'm a rotten fellow
and don't know what love's all about.
Hey Gaur, you didn't even glance at me.

The touch of your pure love
can make a wooden puppet come alive.
But I'm worthless and wretched
and never worship God.
I just keep sitting on the wrong side
of a bad road.

Nearly all the trees
on the Malaya Mountains
have heartwood.
Everyone knows only bamboo trees
are hollow.
Lālan has a heart like bamboo—
empty of love.

15 *Tomār mato dayāl bondhu ār pābo nā*

We'll never get another friend
as compassionate as you again.
You revealed yourself, O Prophet.
Don't desert us now.

You are God's companion,
the true pilot to the other shore.
Without you we will never see
our destination.

We people of Medina
were like wildmen in the forest.
You made us wise.
We are content.

You gave us the divine law
and brought us to the path.
Don't sneak out on us today.

Who but you
can govern this way,
oh herald of religion?
Lālan says, A light like this
will never shine again.

—10—

Tamil Songs to God as Child

Paula Richman

In Hindu tradition adherents can relate to their deity in a number of different ways—as an abstract entity, as the lord of the universe, or a lover, or a friend, or a child, for example. Building on this last alternative, the Hindu Tamil poetic tradition developed a genre of poetry called piḷḷaittamiḻ, in which the poet envisions, addresses himself to, and praises a god or goddess conceived of in the form of a baby. These verses became a way of expressing closeness and love toward the chosen deity, who is thought of as accessible and responsive to devotion. Until quite recently all the authors of this poetry were males, and even in the last decade few women have chosen to write in the piḷḷaittamiḻ genre. The question of the extent to which this genre represents women's voices and concerns remains a vexed issue. On the one hand, we are dealing here with male constructions of the domestic sphere. On the other hand, similarities between some of the poetry and traditional lullabies that mothers have sung to their children suggest that women's literary traditions have influenced the forms of the piḷḷaittamiḻ.

Although the vast majority of piḷḷaittamiḻs were written to Hindu deities, and Śaivite goddesses in particular, over the centuries other religious groups took up the genre. Muslim poets wrote a number of piḷḷaittamiḻs to Muḥammad and a few to selected female members of the Prophet's family (one of his wives and his daughter), and to local Tamil Muslim holy men. Christian poets wrote several piḷḷaittamiḻs to Jesus and Mary. Within Hindu tradition there have also been piḷḷaittamiḻs written not just to deities but to saints, heads of monasteries, religious preceptors, and even Mohandas Gandhi. The meaning of the genre's name, literally "Tamil [poetry] for a child (*piḷḷai*)," indicates that, despite the genre's diversity in subject matter, one of its two distinguishing features remains portraying the subject of the poem as a child.

The other distinguishing feature is its highly conventionalized poetic structure. Piḷḷaittamiḻs are composed of ten sections or paruvams, and each paruvam usually consists of ten verses. Poetic tradition prescribes the subject matter for each paruvam; the first seven are always concerned with the following specific activities:

1. invoking protection from the gods for the baby; 2. encouraging the baby to sway gently back and forth; 3. encouraging the baby to prattle, moving its tongue (*tala*); 4. asking the infant to clap its hands; 5. requesting a kiss; 6. telling the child to come near; and 7. asking the moon to come and be a playmate for the child.

After the seventh paruvam, the conventions differ by gender. If the poem is addressed to a male, the last three paruvams ask the boy to beat on his little drum, beseech him not to knock down the little playhouses of the girls, and request that he pull his toy chariot. If the poet writes to a female, in contrast, the little girl is asked to play jacks, bathe in the river, and ride on a swing. Although the writer must work within the confines of this ten-paruvam system in order to produce a poem clearly recognizable as a piḷḷaittamiḻ, individual verses demonstrate how much opportunity exists for religious and poetic creativity.

The scope for creativity helps to explain the long, rich, and diverse history of the genre. The first extant piḷḷaittamiḻ written in a predominantly religious milieu, *Tiruccentūr Piḷḷaittamiḻ* [henceforth TCPT] by Pakaḻikkūttaṉ, appeared in about the early fifteenth century and is widely recognized as one of the greatest examples of the genre. In praise of Śiva's son Murukaṉ, who is known, appropriately enough, for his youth, this poem celebrates him as manifested in the seaside shrine of Tiruccentūr. By the seventeenth and eighteenth centuries, the piḷḷaittamiḻ had become a mainstay of Śaivite devotional writing. Tamil tradition recognizes two piḷḷaittamiḻ poems from this period addressed to Śaivite goddesses as particularly sophisticated in their use of literary ornamentation and poetic conceits: *Maturaimīṉāṭciyammai Piḷḷaittamiḻ* [henceforth MMPT] by Kumarakuruparar, written to Śiva's wife in the form of the fish-eyed goddess with the parrot perched on her shoulder, whom devotees worship at the large temple in the center of Madurai; and *Kuḷattūr Amutāmpikai Piḷḷaittamiḻ* [henceforth AAPT] by Civañāṉa Cuvāmikaḷ, addressed to Śiva's consort the goddess Amutam, whose temple is located outside of Madras. From among more than 350 Hindu piḷḷaittamiḻs, sections of these three texts have been chosen for translation here.

Excerpts from Muslim and Christian piḷḷaittamiḻs demonstrate the continuities and changes in nuance that occur when poets from other religious traditions appropriate the genre. Evidence suggests that more than twenty-five Muslim piḷḷaittamiḻs have been written. Presented here are selections from *Napikaḷ Nāyakam Piḷḷaittamiḻ* [henceforth NNPT], a poem in praise of the prophet Muḥammad. Seyyitu Anapiyyā Pulavar, who flourished in a literary milieu that valued both the popular veneration of the prophet and the love of Tamil literary forms, composed this poem, first published in 1833. Also included is a selection from a very recent (1985) Christian piḷḷaittamiḻ to Jesus titled *Iyēcupirāṉ Piḷḷaittamiḻ* [henceforth IPPT] written by Arul Chelladurai, an engineer and poet whose aim was to express adoration for baby Jesus and admiration for modern science.

The reader encountering the piḷḷaittamiḻ genre for the first time needs to be aware of some of its characteristic topics and rhetorical strategies. (In this discussion, texts are referred to by both their poem number in the translations below and the abbreviated title and verse number in the original Tamil text.) A frequent subject of the piḷḷaittamiḻ is a description of a woman taking care of a baby. In Poem 1 (TCPT 28), for example, the mother lovingly tries a number of strategies to make baby Murukaṉ rest. She recites a head-to-foot litany of his glittering ornaments in an attempt to lull him to sleep, beginning with praise of the two kinds of earrings he wears, and working down to his jeweled anklets. Trying another tack, she asks him to consider his poor devotees, who are exhausted by trying to keep up with him. Next, she threatens him with the evil eye. When that does not work, she tempts him to slumber by describing the rich gems that adorn his cradle. In resignation, she asks the baby to lie and suck his finger, hoping that he will eventually fall asleep. This choice of subject matter enables the poet to suggest the love, commitment, and occasional disappointment that a devotee can feel toward a deity.

One of the most intriguing rhetorical techniques found in piḷḷaittamiḻ poetry involves juxtaposing stanzas that present the deity as a tiny baby with lines that present the deity as an adult capable of performing salvific deeds. Consider, as an example, poem 3 (TCPT 54). The body of this section emphasizes baby Murukaṉ's smallness and vulnerability: he takes such tiny steps, needs his mother to keep him clean, and depends upon her for nourishment. But the refrain at the end abruptly reverses the reader's perceptions of the deity, describing the baby as powerful and located in his own shrine. The poet specifically praises Murukaṉ's sharp spear, reminding his audience of the deity's salvific deeds as killer of demons. He praises the god's power to bring wealth by describing his shrine, using imagery that shows how his divine presence there has enriched the surrounding land and brought prosperity to its owners. The comfortable mother-son domesticity of the main part of the poem thus contrasts with the message of the refrain. By juxtaposing the two, the poet reminds us that the deity is both as accessible as a tiny baby and as powerful as a salvific adult deity.

Because piḷḷaittamiḻ poetry deals with household life, one tends to find poets appropriating, highlighting, and investing with religious meaning incidents in the domestic sphere, as can be seen in poem 5 (MMPT 15). The poem begins by describing the construction of an unusual dwelling, whose identity is unlocked through the key of Hindu cosmological symbolism. Its walls support the Cakravāla Range, that set of mountains believed to surround the cosmos. Mount Meru, the column that Hindu myths describe as linking heaven and earth, serves as its central pillar. The vast sky, illuminated by the sun and the moon, functions as a roof for the house. Thus when the goddess builds her home, she performs a cosmogonic act, establishing the world. Not only does she create, she must save the world from her husband Śiva. In this poem, the soiling of dishes stands for Śiva's repeated destruction of the universe. Despite his mad acts of destruction, the goddess never becomes angry. Instead, she simply begins her task of washing the dishes anew, recreating the universe. Here baby Mīṉāṭci's playing house becomes a metaphor for ensuring the continued welfare of the universe.

If these three examples have shown how the child motif shapes the subject matter and religious import of piḷḷaittamiḻ poetry, the other distinguishing feature, its paruvam structure, also significantly influences poetic form and religious meaning. An examination of sections from the same paruvam in different poems will suggest some of the diverse aesthetic and rhetorical effects of the structure. Poems 6, 7, and 8 come from the paruvam in which the speaker asks the moon to come down and play with the baby. Tamil tradition considers this paruvam to be both the most difficult and the most challenging to poets, and commentators have identified four commonly used rhetorical strategies: in some cases the mother tries to convince the moon that he and the baby share so many similarities that they would make excellent companions; in others, the mother proves to the moon that the baby is so superior that the moon, as an inferior, must come to be the baby's playmate; the mother may also offer the moon gifts in exchange for coming; and finally she may threaten the moon with punishment if he does not come.

In poem 6 (TCPT 68), a carefully detailed threat lies beneath a seemingly polite invitation to the moon. According to Hindu tradition, a miraculous ambrosia that, if swallowed, would enable one to live forever, lay at the bottom of the sea. In order to bring this liquid to the surface, the gods determined to churn the ocean. Using Mount Mandara turned upside down as the churn and a snake wrapped around it as a churning rope, the gods raised the ambrosia to the surface. As a by-product of the churning, they also produced the moon. The speaker inquires, in a way that implies that she already knows the answer, whether all of the principal items and actors in the famous churning event are still available. Then she conveys how much little Murukaṉ wants the moon to be his playmate, noting that the deity always gets what he wants. The implication is that if this moon refuses her request, the gods can surely churn out another one that will be more cooperative.

Poem 7 (IPPT 61), in contrast, adopts the strategy of noting similarities between the moon and baby Jesus. In a feat of poetic virtuosity, as well as astronomical observation, the poet manages to fit eight similarities between Jesus and the moon into the body of this short section. By punning or using phrases that can be interpreted in two ways, the poet creates a series of descriptions that can apply to either the moon or Jesus. For example, the first line suggests both that the moon receives light from another source, the sun, and that Jesus receives his light from the Father. Just as the moon rises while people watch from below, Jesus ascended to heaven. Similarly, just as we know that the moon is in fact very large, though we see it as a small white disk in the sky, Lord Jesus conceals his large form in a small white wafer. Each of the eight comparisons demonstrates how similar baby Jesus and the moon are. The end of the poem draws the logical conclusion from this evidence—namely, that the two would be perfect companions.

Poems 9, 10, and 11 provide contrasting examples of the paruvam in which the poet takes on the voice of a group of young girls and asks the young boy not to knock over their little houses made of sand. One is by a Hindu poet and the other two by a Muslim. In Poem 9 (TCPT 84) the poet plays with the notion of domesticity, creating a charming verse about the clever ways that girls fabricate the elements of nurturing. In this verse the girls build their house and then stock it with the equipment and ingredients for cooking. Conches function as pots, honey as cooking liquid, pearls as grains of rice, and flower petals as vegetables and spices. Because the girls fear that Murukan̲ might destroy their carefully created home, the paruvam culminates with their poignant plea to be saved from such destruction. "See how eagerly we cook our precious rice. Don't destroy our little houses," shows their desire to please and their fear of his tremendous power; their words have the tone of supplication to a deity. The refrain of this verse serves to remind the hearer of Murukan̲'s power; his feet are redolent from the head of Indra, king of the gods, because the latter has bowed in submission to him. The verse suggests that without the divine compassion of Murukan̲, the domestic existence of everyday life would be endangered. Thus this "play" domesticity becomes the occasion for seeking protection from god.

In contrast, poems 10 (NNPT 85) and 11 (NNPT 91) take the basic premises of this paruvam and turn the focus from domestic concerns to martial ones. Focus shifts from the little girls' playhouses to the military threat of the situation. The girls question why baby Muḥammad considers attacking their little houses, when it would be more appropriate for him to attack the houses where sinners live. In the process of making their argument, the girls also provide religious instruction to their audience, identifying those thought to lack virtue in Islam—people who ignore the learned, those who are miserly, or unjust, the denigrators, and the wicked. This comparison between Hindu and Muslim poems indicates the range of sentiments that can be expressed within a given paruvam.

Piḷḷaittamil̲ paruvams can also provide a structure with which to explicate the nature of complex theological systems. Poem 12 (AAPT 102), for example, belongs in the paruvam in which the poet urges the little girl to play on a swing. The poet uses parts of the swing as components of an elaborate religious allegory based on the theology of Śaiva Siddhānta, one of the major schools of thought in south Indian Śaivite tradition. The activity of swinging stands for living a deluded life. The parts of the swing—illusion, egotism, the karmic consequences of actions, the grossness of matter—all function to keep the individual self in a state of ignorance. The truth is veiled by the deity; most people do not realize the nature of reality. Although the verse indicates that the goddess has created this entrapment for people, it reveals the grace of the goddess as well. She will protect them from destruction at the end of the aeon and help them to attain religious liberation. At that point, like a true mother, she will feed her children, but in this case she will feed them a particularly satisfying meal—the sweet nectar of eternal bliss.

The piḷḷaittamil̲ genre reveals how poets have appropriated the language of domesticity, traditionally identified with the women's sphere, into religious poetry. Although many religious poets use the language of lover and beloved to describe the relationship between devotee and deity (as other translations in this volumes demonstrate), the piḷḷaittamil̲ provides an alternative mode of devotional expression. Until quite recently in the West, assumptions about the nature of literary masterpieces have resulted in the exclusion from the canon many works of literature whose contents were considered domestic and therefore, minor or secondary. In piḷḷaittamiḻ poetry, images of domesticity are used in the service of praising and expressing devotion to one's chosen deity, an act considered not at all minor in South Asian culture. Rather than being denigrated, the domestic has been elevated as a means of expressing the highest kind of sentiment—love for a god or goddess.

This genre also demonstrates how dramatically poetic structures shape the expression of religious devotion. Because the piḷḷaittamiḻ is defined by the presence of the ten paruvams, we find poets shaping their expressions of praise within the framework of a particular set of activities, no matter what the individual deity's corpus of mythology. Religious sentiments take form through the prescriptions of the genre.

Finally, it is notable that a number of different religious traditions express feelings of devotion by adopting the same Tamil literary genre. Despite the variation in nuance among different religious traditions, the fact that Hindus, Muslims, and Christians—with very different concepts of divinity, notions of virtuous behavior, and ideas of community—adopt the same literary form suggests that the form possesses adaptability and scope despite its seemingly highly structured format. Viewing the piḷḷaittamiḻ as a multireligious genre also moves us away from exclusive categories like "Hindu" or "Muslim" or "Christian" toward a notion of Indian religion that encompasses many different strands, which share and exchange certain literary characteristics and modes of expression.

TCPT, MMPT, and AAPT are found in *Piḷḷaittamiḻkkottu,* 2 vols. (Tinnevelly: South India Saiva Siddhanta Works Publishing Society, 1970 and 1979). NNP is found in Seyyitu Anapiyyā Pulavar, *Napikaḷ Nāyakam Piḷḷaittamiḻ* (Colombo: Publication Committee of the Sea Street Meelaad, 1975). IIPT is found in Aruḷ Cellatturai, *Iyēcupirāṉ Piḷḷaittamiḻ* (Tirucchirappalli: Aruḷ Vākku Maṉram, 1985).

1 [To Murukaṉ]: Prattle

Who hasn't seen the beauty of
your earring studs
your dangling earrings
your twelve arms, heavy with garlands
your six faces, radiant in unchanging kingly splendor
your waist-string
your leglet
your loin-gem like lightning
your ankle bells and other jewels?

Look at those who fall at your feet:
dust has fallen on their soft fragrant hair,
their limbs grow weak,
and their bellies are shrunken.

If you crawl all over,
the evil eye may harm you
and bad things will happen.
Nothing good will come of it.

Come to sleep on the grand bed
inlaid with gold and gems from mountains.

Child who is my life,
you smile beautifully
but you don't go to sleep.

Won't you just lie and enjoy
the ambrosia of your finger?
Won't you speak sweetly?

Skanda, who makes prosperous
the rich city of southern Centūr,
where the waves dash,
O little one begotten by Śiva,
tāla, tālelō.

Son of the supreme goddess,
boy worshiped by Brahmā and Pārvatī,
tāla, tālelō.

TCPT 28

2 [To Muḥammad]: Prattle

Your cradle's wheel
resembles the rich golden wheel of the sun,
so bright it blinds the eye.

Your cradle
is like the sky chariot,
that the lord of the star-filled sky
joyously rides.

Its frame is inlaid
with gems so full of color
that they radiate sunlight,
as if lightning were stolen from the sky.

The tips of the cradle's legs
are like pots
made of shining green emeralds.

It has chains
made of pure gold.

Celestial women sing you lullabies
while eminent celestial men praise you.

Prophet Qāsim [Muḥammad],
who sits rocking back and forth so wonderfully
that it overwhelms the eye, *tālelō*.

Ocean of mercy, *tālelō*.
Friend full of wisdom, *tālelō*.

NNPT 24

3 [To Murukaṉ]: Come

Come so I can fasten your waist-string, adorned with rare jewels.
Come so I can slip a ring 'round your finger.
Come so I can place a tilak on your forehead.
Come and play in the lane.

Come let me take you to my lap and hug you.
Come so I can bathe you in fresh rose water.
Come drink ambrosia from my full breasts.
Come so you can get kisses.

Come let me wipe the dust from your body.
Come and speak a few words.
Come so I can watch your tiny steps.

Come, Murukaṉ with the sharp spear,
of Tiruccentūr,
where towering houses abound
with lustrous gems.

Come, husband of Vaḷḷi,
the woman whose budding breasts,
adorned with sandalpaste,
are like tender coconuts.

TCPT 54

4 [To Muḥammad]: Come

Come so I can bedeck, with anklets and bells,
your feet like day-blooming lotuses.
Come so I can put on, with delight,
your warrior's anklets that confound the enemies
who battle you, as the ocean wars against the land.

Come so I can adorn you with tinkling jewels.

Come so I can anoint with attar, rose water,
the four perfumes, and excellent sandalpaste
your shoulders and chest like tall mountains
and lovingly clothe you.

So I can place you in the cradle
and rock you with delight,
come joyously.

Muḥammad, who has the truth,
come joyously, come.

NNPT 57

5 [To Mīṉāṭci]: Sway Back and Forth

You prop up the eight mountains
to support the high encircling Cakravāla Range.
You plant Mount Meru in the middle
as a pillar.
You cover the top of the sky,
then you hang the sun and moon as lamps.

In the dashing waters
you wash the old cooking vessels—
all the worlds—
and stack them up.
Then you cook sweet ambrosia
from fresh food.

Mother, you've done this many times.

While you do this
the great madman with the umattai flower
wanders through the courtyard of space
destroying your work again and again,

and then comes before you
dancing.

You never get angry.
Every day,
you just pick up the vessels.

Tender young girl
who plays house
with the ancient universe,
sway back and forth.

Only daughter of the southern king
and the king of the Himalayas,
sway back and forth.

MMPT 15

6 [To Murukaṉ]: Moon

The ancient Mandara Mountains still exist
so we can churn sweet ambrosia like in the old days,
can't we?

The wide ocean—that deep moat—didn't turn to mud
and dry up into a bed of sand,
did it?

Did Indra and his gods in the sky die?
Did a huge darkness settle in?
Did the seven outer worlds become empty?

The huge snake Vasuki,
his long teeth flowing with poison,
didn't split into pieces,
did he?

Incomparable Vāli still has a tail,
doesn't he?

Foolish moon,
what isn't possible
if this boy wants it?

So moon,
come and play with the Lord of the gods—
the one from Tiruccentūr
with the sharp spear.

Moon, come and play with Murukan
who rides a peacock,
making the steep mountains tremble.

TCPT 68

7 [To Jesus]: Moon

Since you receive light from another source

Since you rise into the high skies,
while many people watch

Since you receive life again,
even though your body dies

Since you remove the darkness of the world
by your light

Since you conceal your large form
in a round white disk

Since you carry a blemish

Since those who look at stars [the wise men]
sought you

Since you give light for everyone,
being appropriate for supplicants

Since the hero of my poem, the Lord who was born of a virgin girl
who conceived through the Holy Spirit
is like you,
moon of the beautiful sky,
it is right that you immediately agree
to rejoice and happily play.

With him who is united with Tamil
that flows like a waterfall,
O moon, come to play.

With the son of God seated
on the right side of gracious God,
O moon, come to play.

IPPT 61

8 [To Amutāmpikai]: Moon

All of these—
the Gaṅgā River
snakes
the tumpai flower
a thickly-woven garland of pure, golden cassia flowers
a skull
the feather of a crane
fragrant umattam flowers, from which fragrant honey drips,
Agni
the erukku plant
cool aruku grass
the celestial mantaram flowers,
showered from above by the gods,
and flowers picked and strewn by the sages—

they stay [as does the moon]
in the Lord's forest of matted hair.

Therefore,
you have nothing but a tiny claim
on that place,
do you?

But the goddess lives, taking as her own
exactly one half of all
of the flawless thirty-two parts
of Śiva's body.

So, she is greater than you.
Of that there is no doubt.

Come, then, moon, to play with her.
Come to play with Amutavaḷḷi from Kuḷattūr,
whose beauty ever increases.

AAPT 65

9 [To Murukaṉ]: Little Houses

We little girls
make the outer walls
of our playhouse
with pearls from golden conches
that surround the fragrant golden water.

We make our cooking pots
from right-whirling conches.

We fill the pots with rich honey,
produced when buds break
in the seed pods of red lotuses
growing in newly planted fields.

We cook our rice,
made of pearls found in bamboo.

We make our curry
from freshly picked bunches of flowers
grown in a grove
as fragrant as rose water.

See how eagerly we cook
our precious rice.

Don't destroy our little house,
with your fair young feet,
redolent from the head of Indra.

Don't destroy our little house,
rich one of Tiruccentūr,
where waves wash up pearls.

TCPT 84

10 [To Muḥammad]: Little Houses

Don't you know the homes
of fools who ignore learned scholars' words
that elucidate the ocean of knowledge?

Don't you recognize the houses
of embittered men who refuse to give alms
for the sake of our precious God?

Don't you see the abodes
of treacherous people who plead legal suits
that violate justice?

Haven't you noticed the dwellings
of those who despise scholars
of the revealed books of God?

This is not the house of wicked people
who cause hardship and destruction,
is it?

Don't destroy the little houses
made by us little ones who play in the sand
with our little friends.
Noble Messenger Muḥammad,
don't destroy our little houses.

NNPT 85

11 [To Muḥammad]: Little Houses

Thinking that there is one God who created
all the worlds filled with entities,
you confronted the sinful infidels,
who lacked devotion.

You defeated and drove away those infidels,
who came to raze beautiful houses
surrounded by pools and walls.

King who protected us by destroying
their houses like mountain fortresses,
if you have destruction on your mind,
to whom will we confide our misery?

Therefore, precious gem
who is light from the Great One,
don't destroy the little houses
of your servants and believers.

Muḥammad, prophet for the world,
don't destroy the little houses
of your servants.

NNPT 91

12 [To Amutāmpikai]: Swing

With cruel illusion, both pure and impure,
as pillars,

dark egotism
as the long beam that joins the pillars,

huge accumulations of karma
as the hanging ropes,

matter as the seat,

the endless sky and million of worlds
as the space where souls joyfully play,

you place the children—
those precious souls—
on the jeweled swings,
that are death, birth, and disease.

Then you swing them.

And at the end of the yuga
you pick them up and hug them so that
they will not be destroyed.

You grant them great knowledge
and drive them on to exalted supreme mokṣa.
Then you feed them the ambrosia
of endless bliss.

You, who have raised them
as a true mother,
play on the golden swing.

Play on the swing,
one seated on the lotus,
who granted grace to the full moon.

AAPT 102

13 [To Muḥammad]: Beat Your Little Drum

The entire celestial world
totters [on Judgment Day].

The seven clouds
turn frenzied with terror.

Meru and the eight mountains
that touch the skies
tremble.

The oceans
shake.

The whole earth
quakes.

The celestial serpent
reels.

The elephants of the eight directions
spill out rut, stunned.

The sky,
so vast it overwhelms the eye,
is startled.

The moon and sun
feel disturbed,
cannot maintain their positions,
and disperse, along with their horses.

With your true, strong, shapely hands,
beat your little drum.

Muḥammad with the shade-giving parasol
of thick clouds,
beat your little drum.

NNPT 79

Rites and Instructions

—11—

The Power of Mantra: A Story of the Five Protectors

Todd T. Lewis

Good health, provident weather, the birth of children, protection from property loss, and just plain luck have remained central concerns in all cultures, including that of India. Buddhist texts prescribed ways of achieving the good life, and traditionally they included instruction on how to make good karma and project auspicious powers. The "Five Protectors" (*Pañcarakṣā*) provides a striking example of how the Mahāyāna monastic community extended its service beyond instruction in soteriological belief and practice to the performance of rituals for pragmatic ends.

Early texts highlighted certain of the Buddha's words that, when carefully recited, were thought to have extraordinary effects. In Pali literature, short recitations called *paritta* were presented as efficacious for alleviating suffering from a variety of causes and for creating a sort of radiant auspiciousness. These texts recognized that all not events were caused by karmic retribution, and they sought to harness the powers of the Buddha and his teachings to affect such nonkarmic chains of events. This was no doubt a precedent for the later elaboration of Buddhist ritual.

In Mahāyāna Vajrayāna Buddhism, precisely worded Sanskrit verses (shorter formulas are usually called *mantras;* longer ones, *dhāraṇī,* although no exact definition separates them) occupy a prominent place in meditation and in the rituals of the saṅgha (community of monks). As is the case in all Indic religions, formula verses composed by enlightened Buddhist saints were regarded as concentrated expressions of truth that commanded power over the unseen forces; if spoken correctly and by appropriate individuals, their recitation could affect the world—and the mind of the reciter—in highly beneficial ways.

Mahāyāna Vajrayāna theory in this field evolved elaborately, and the entire celestial pantheon of buddhas and bodhisattvas were "garlanded" with heart mantras as the tradition highlighted specific verses essential for their worship. As part of this development, certain mantras and dhāraṇīs became popular for specific sacred and mundane purposes. The later Mahāyāna schools and their texts assured the devout that mantra recitations could even alter karmic destiny itself. The most dramatic of these were elaborate death-ritual traditions designed to influence rebirth. How might such practices be reconciled with the doctrine of karmic retribution and Buddhist moralism expressed in more philosophical tracts?

The *Pañcarakṣā* text was the most popular text used across the Mahāyāna world to confer upon laymen and their settlements protection from evil. The work has been edited into many short and long versions in the course of its translation into Chinese, Tibetan, Mongolian, and Japanese. The oldest individual manuscripts have each dhāraṇī printed separately, so it appears that the five protective formulae were probably developed in separate traditions, and that this five-part text was a later consolidation. As was the case in the evolution of other Mahāyāna textual lineages, each dhāraṇī tradition came to have a deity embody its respective protective power. The Newar recension translated in part below includes a mantra for each of the five deities, along with an exact iconographic description necessary for visualization meditation; by placing the image of the deity in the mind's eye, the practitioner enhances the effect of each formula.

The story translated here is an explanation of the powers underlying the *Mahāpratisarā* mantra, as well as dramatic testimonials to its effectiveness. Śākyamuni states that the mantra is "enshrined in the hearts of buddhas" and was derived from fundamental doctrinal ideas and meditation practices known from the earliest eras of the tradition.

In the Newar Buddhist community of Kathmandu, Nepal, the text's very presence in the household is thought to be beneficial, and many families call upon members of the local saṅgha to read their hand-copied manuscripts for a variety of reasons, especially during the holy month of Guṃlā. Amulets derived from the *Pañcarakṣā* and the system of medicine described in the text have also been popular in traditional local medicine. There is even a piece of jewelry commonly worn by laymen that is fashioned of five metals (iron, copper, brass, silver, gold), which represent the five goddesses of the *Pañcarakṣā* text.

What follows is a translation of the text connected with the first of the five protective goddesses, who is called Mahāpratisarā. It is translated from *Pañca Rakṣā Kathāsāra* (Kathmandu: Jana Kalyana Press, 1980).

Further Reading

See B. Bhattacharyya, *Indian Buddhist Iconography* (Calcutta: Firma K. L. Mukhopadhyay, 1968), as well as D. C. Bhattacharyya, "The Five Protective Goddesses of Buddhism," in P. Pal, ed., *Aspects of Indian Art* (Leiden: E. J. Brill, 1972), pp. 85–92, and idem, "Iconography of the Pancaraksa" in his *Studies in Buddhist Iconography* (New Delhi: Manohar, 1978), pp. 78–100. Also see Tadeuz Skorupski,

The Sarvadurgatipariśodhana Tantra (Delhi: Motilal Banarsidass, 1983), and Michel Strickmann, "The Consecration Sūtra: A Buddhist Book of Spells," in Robert Buswell, Jr., ed. *Chinese Buddhist Apocrypha* (Honolulu: University of Hawaii Press, 1990), pp. 75–118. An informative recent article is Peter Skilling, "The Rakṣā Literature of the Śrāvakayāna," *Journal of the Pali Text Society* 16 (1992), 109–82.

Mantra: *Oṃ maṇi dharī vajriṇī mahāprati sare rakṣa rakṣa māṃ sarvasa tvānāñca hūṃ hūṃ hūṃ phaṭ phaṭ phaṭ svāhā*

MAHĀPRATISARĀ MEDITATION

Emanated from the germ syllable *pra,* seated in the lotus position; four-faced: the left one black, the back one yellow, the right one green, the middle one white; eight-armed, holding (on the left) the eight-spoked wheel, vajra [thunderbolt], arrow, and sword; on the right side, an axe, trident, bow, and noose held by the index finger; each head has three eyes and a shrine on the crown.

Mantra: *Oṃ namo bhagavatyai āryamahāpratisarāyai*

The Story of the Mahāpratisarā Mahāyāna Sūtra

Once the Lord Buddha was dwelling in a monastery atop Mount Sumeru. It was a delightful place, covered with fruit-laden trees and dotted with ponds full of lotus blossoms. A splendid palace of Indra also stood there. The whole estate was surrounded by a footpath covered with raw gold dust. A large number of superhuman beings were there, such as the bodhisattvas, the perfect ones; arhats, including Śāriputra; Maheśvara [Śiva], accompanied by a host of gods including Brahmā and Indra; and countless demons, spirits, and nāga [serpent deity] kings. All assembled there calmly turned to the Buddha, ready to listen to his sermon. At that time the Buddha, in simple and intelligible language, gave a sermon on celibate discipline, the renunciation of sensual pleasure which applies to all epochs—past, present and future—and which is full of knowledge that can lead one to the blissful state of nirvāṇa.

At that time there shone forth miraculously from the Buddha's brow a radiant light known as "a vision of all buddhas." Immediately after the radiant light shone forth, the whole world was illuminated and everything, including the incarnate buddhas giving sermons to their disciples, was visible. Then Lord Buddha paid his respects to all of the buddhas dwelling in all the worlds, and said "*Oṃ nāma: sarva tathāgatebhyo arhadabhya: samyak sambuddhebhya.*" He turned to those assembled there and said, "Listen! I tell you that the Mahāpratisarā dhāraṇī is for the welfare and happiness of humanity. Hearing this dhāraṇī, one can destroy the cause of whatever distress one is suffering. One who recites this Mahāpratisarā dhāraṇī will be free from harm by demons, monsters, spirits, hungry ghosts, astral divinities, Śiva-demons (*kuṣmāṇḍas*), madness, epilepsy, and dangers from all beings, human and nonhuman. All one's sworn enemies will be reconciled. One will be immune from the dangers posed by poison, fire, weapons, water, wind, and so on, and will be immune from contagious diseases. If one wears around the neck or wrist an amulet containing the mantric phrase of the Mahāpratisarā dhāraṇī, one will succeed in all endeavors, besides being free from all dangers. This places one under the protection of the goddess Māmakī. A woman wanting to be blessed with a son will have a son if she wears such an amulet. And she will conceive and deliver the baby with ease. A person, male or female, who follows the teaching of the Mahāpratisarā and observes the moral precepts solemnly will live in plenty. He or she will earn honor. Misfortune from certain evil omens or bad dreams will disappear. A large store of religious merit will also be accumulated. There will be prosperity all around. I will now reveal this Mahāpratisarā dhāraṇī, so listen to me."

When the Buddha was preaching the discourse, among his audience was the great Brahmā. Addressing Brahmā, the Lord said, "Hearing this dhāraṇī, one can be free from danger of all sorts. One who learns it by heart will have an adamantine body, strong like a thunderbolt.

[He continued:] "Once in the city of Kapilavastu, [a woman] Gopā was made to leap into a blazing furnace. At that time Rāhula Bhadra Kumāra, the unborn offspring in her womb, who remembered the Mahāpratisarā dhāraṇī since the time when Siddhārtha Kumāra touched his navel with his big toe, called to mind this dhāraṇī. As a result of his recollecting this holy dhāraṇī, the flame died in the furnace. And Gopā was found in the embers as if she were seated in the middle of a lotus blossom.

"Not only this, O Brahmā! In the great city of Surpāraka there once dwelled the merchant's son Kauśāmbika, who was skillful in catching nāgas. The son compelled Takṣaka, the nāga king, to come to him, but locked him by mistake in a closet. The serpent king struck Kauśāmbika before it could be brought under his magical control. The bite became unbearable and he lost consciousness.

"A number of healers came to cure him, but they could not do anything. In the city of Surpāraka, there was an upāsaka [devout householder] named Bimala Biśuddhi who had committed the Mahāpratisarā dhāraṇī to memory. Taking pity upon him [Kauśāmbika], Bimala Biśuddhi went to recite the dhāraṇī for him. Immediately after the recitation of the dhāraṇī, the merchant's son regained his consciousness. After this he was also made to repeat and recite the dhāraṇī and was thus saved from danger.

"Not only this, O Brahmā! In the remote past there ruled in the city of Varanasi a king named Brahmadatta. Once his neighboring enemy kings used their military power to seize the city, and came to attack him. When the ministers went to the king, they said, 'Your Majesty! We have been surrounded by enemies on all sides. Command what we should do to defend ourselves and safeguard our country.' The king replied, 'My dear subjects! It is my duty to safeguard the country and the people. You need not be afraid of anything. I will do all that is needed.'

"After saying this, King Brahmadatta bathed and cleansed himself with many different kinds of sweet-smelling waters. Purified in body, mind, and speech, the king put amulets of the Mahāpratisarā dhāraṇī into his crown and armor, then went alone to meet the enemy. The army of the enemy kings retreated and ran away in a panic, believing that the king must have a large number of soldiers coming after him, for he would not have dared to come alone onto the battlefield. O great Brahmā! The Mahāpratisarā dhāraṇī should be considered fruitful in this sense. It should be treated as something enshrined in the hearts of the buddhas. Those born to die young will have their life span expanded. Those born not fortunate or lacking religious merit can have their happiness ensured.

"Not only this O Brahmā! There was once a greedy monk. He was not living up to the teachings of the Buddha: he went so far as to take something not given to him by its owner; he always asked persons for one thing or another shamelessly; he coveted the saṅgha's possessions and other things belonging to many monks; he even treated the offerings left on the surrounding area of stūpas as his own personal belongings. After a certain time, this ill-natured monk became afflicted with a very terrible disease and had to spend his time in painful lament. There lived in the same country a brahman. He could not bear the sight of the monk's misery and kindly placed round his neck an amulet with the Mahāpratisarā dhāraṇī in it. Immediately after this, the monk became relieved of all pain and regained his consciousness.

"Full of remorse for all the evil deeds he had committed before, the monk's mind was enlightened, but he passed away the same night and was consigned to the Avīci hell. Through the effect of the Mahāpratisarā dhāraṇī amulet placed round the neck of his dead body, those suffering in the Avīci hell were relieved of their sufferings. The blazing fire burning bright within the radius of several miles also died out. Those suffering for their evil deeds also were relieved of their sufferings. Aware of all this, the messengers of death greeted King Yama and said, 'O King Yama! Although we have tried to drive the wedge into wicked transgressors, we have not been able to make any cuts on their bodies. Although they have been led to walk on the blades of swords or laid on beds of needles, they have been found as if they were treading on velvet beds. Iron maces with spikes and hot balls of fire have broken and cooled by themselves. A huge cooking pot—with a vast holding capacity—was filled with hot molten iron but cooled by itself. Further, none of the transgressors suffered any injury, although they were led into the Asipatra Forest where trees have grown with swords as their leaves. What has caused these miracles?'

"King Yama replied to them, 'O messengers of death! Things such as these are not unusual when bodhisattvas are condemned to hell for their evil deeds. If you do not believe this, you may go to the city called Puṣkarāvatī and see with your own eyes the mortal body of the bodhisattva. An amulet of Mahāpratisarā dhāraṇī can be found on his body and a large number of gods must be there protecting it.' After hearing this, the guards of hell went to the place in question, and they indeed saw gods and demigods all around the dead body, preparing the Mahāpratisarā diagram (*yantra*) and paying last respects with sweet-smelling flowers, smoking incense, and camphor. When the guards went back to King Yama to make a report, they noticed that the monk who had been there previously was no more to be found, because he had already left for the Heaven of the Thirty-Three, where he was celebrated as 'a Mahāpratisarā god.'

"Therefore, O great Brahmā! Let it be known that it is a righteous act to learn by heart and recite this dhāraṇī or to wear an amulet of this dhāraṇī. Not only this, O Great Brahmā! In the great city called Hiṅga Mardana there once dwelled a well-known merchant named Vimala Śaṃkha, who had great wealth, gold, silver, and supplies of food. He had hundreds of assistants at work in his business firm. In the course of his overseas trade in jewelery, one day he set out for Jewel Island with his assistants in a ship loaded with merchandise. In the middle of the sea, a huge long sea monster called Timiṅgala kept in check the motion of the ship in which he was traveling. At that time the angry nāga kings also caused heavy rainfall interspersed with thunder and lightning. Those on board were panic-stricken for fear of being drowned. At that time the merchant Vimala Śaṃkha comforted them and hoisted a flag in which was written the Mahāpratisarā dhāraṇī. He also started reciting the dhāraṇī. Immediately after this, the nāga kings became pacified and went away calmly, according respect to the Mahāpratisarā. The sea monster Timiṅgala also ran away, mistaking the ship for a huge ball of fire. Then the ship reached Jewel Island safely. O Brahmā! Know that hoisting a flag with the Mahāpratisarā dhāraṇī written on it helps safeguard one's country.

"And further, O great Brahmā! In Magadha there was once a famous king named Prasāritapāṇi. He was given this name of Prasāritapāṇi because he was born with his arms outstretched. When someone came to him begging for something, he turned to the sky with his hands outstretched, and the gods put in his hands valuables like gold, silver, jewelry, and so on, which he in turn gave generously to the beggars who approached him. (For this reason also he became known by this name.)

"The king had been born in Kuśinagara in his previous life. At that time the incarnate Buddha was Prabhūta Ratna. The essentials of Mahāpratisarā were preached even then by Prabhūta Ratna Buddha. A merchant, Dharmamati by name, used to invite this Buddha and his fellow monks to give religious discourses in his house. A poor person came to know this, and approached the merchant Dharmamati with the double purpose of working in his household to earn a living and also to have the privilege of listening to the religious discourses of the Buddha. Very much pleased with the service of the poor fellow, the merchant one day gave him a gold coin as a bonus. The poor fellow spent the coin to organize a religious discourse on the Mahāpratisarā. In organizing this discourse, he wished for the poverty of the poor to be ended and for progress and prosperity all around, with the religious merit gained therefrom.

"It was because of this meritorious deed in his past life that King Prasāritapāṇi could miraculously get the things he wanted merely by raising his outstretched hands aloft in the sky, and could generously give them in charity to the poor.

"Sometime later, King Prasāritapāṇi was still issueless: he could not beget a son despite his meritorious deeds, and so he had no peace of mind. One night, a celestial deity appeared to him in a dream and said, 'O King Prasāritapāṇi! With the meritorious deeds of upholding the Mahāpratisarā in your previous life, you have now been able to give generously to all beings! If you place an amulet of Mahāpratisarā around your wife's neck, you will beget a son.' The king did as instructed in the dream, constructed a Mahāpratisarā mandala, made an amulet, and placed it around his wife's neck. As a result, he begot a son showing auspicious signs." Thus the Tathāgata extolled the significance of Mahāpratisarā.

[The Tathāgata continued:] "Not only have I expounded the truth of this Mahāpratisarā: it has been expounded by previous buddhas as well. In the remotest antiquity there was a tathāgata called Vipulaprahasitavadanamaṇikanakaratnojvala Raśmiprabhāpratyugdatarāja. Ready to preach a religious discourse, he was surrounded by fierce-looking yakṣas [demons] holding dangerous weapons. They caused strong winds to blow and heavy rains of fire to fall. Then the Tathāgata recited the great secret knowledge of Mahāpratisarā. Immediately after this, within the sight of all the yakṣas, there came out from each of his pores beings holding weapons in their hands and shouting, 'Hold fast the yakṣas and knock them down.' Then the yakṣas lost their powers and ran helter-skelter in panic. Some of them sought their refuge in the Buddha and thereafter remained calm and quiet.

"O great Brahmā! Those upholding the Mahāpratisarā are immune to premature death. In the remote past, there lived in Ujjayanī city a king named Brahmadatta. In that city once a person committed a capital crime and the king sentenced him to death. The king's executioners took him to a mountain cave and unsheathed their swords to behead him. At that time the criminal was chanting the Mahāpratisarā dhāraṇī with his eyes fixed on an amulet of Mahāpratisarā tied around his right wrist. As a result of this, although the executioners wielded their swords over him, he did not suffer any injury; on the contrary, the swords were smashed to pieces. This news reached the king and irritated him. Then the king wanted him to be eaten up by monsters. So his men took him to a cave where monsters dwelled and left him there. The monsters also came running in great delight to eat him up, but they could not cause him any harm because of the effect of Mahāpratisarā. The monsters found his body ablaze with flames, and they retreated in fear.

"When this news reached the king, he became more irritated than before. In a fit of anger, he told his men that the criminal should be thrown into a river with his hands and feet bound. Accordingly, the criminal was thrown into the river with his hands and feet bound. But as soon as he reached the river bed, the water in the river dried up by itself and the ropes by which he was bound also fell away.

"When this news reached the king, he became very much surprised and sent for the criminal. The king asked him the reason why he could not be put to death in these three consecutive attempts. When the king insisted on a reply, the criminal told him all about his knowledge of Mahāpratisarā, and showed him the amulet worn on his right wrist. Highly pleased with this man, the king then decorated him with the title 'Honored Citizen' and gave him shawl as a token of respect.

"O great Brahmā! Due to the effect of the Mahāpratisarā, premature death is thus avoided." The Buddha then proceeded to describe the correct procedures for constructing and worshiping the Pañcarakṣā mandala, with Mahāpratisarā at the center.

—12—

Royal Temple Dedications

Michael D. Rabe

One of the vexing ambiguities of Indian epigraphy concerns the relationship between the royal patron and the patron deity, when their names are linked in the foundation inscriptions of certain ancient Hindu temples. Does the name Rājarājeśvara, for example, as the great temple at Tanjavur was officially designated, mean that it was dedicated to Īśvara (Lord Śiva), by Rājarāja I (985–1015 C.E.), the Cōḻa "king of kings"? Is the king merely being identified as chief votary, the major beneficiary of merit accrued for pious acts of religious endowment? Or is the name also intended to qualify the king and the deity in some way, or even to fuse the royal and divine identities? What might it mean, in other words, to characterize Lord Śiva as the "Rājarāja" god? Were temples like the Rājarājeśvara, at least from their patron's perspective, conceived to be instruments of apotheosis? Were their construction and ceremonial life means whereby kings themselves might be venerated or even deified? Alternatively, if only divine sanction for earthly sovereignty was being sought (not to mention an afterlife in paradise), the question still remains: how was the conjoining of a king's name with god's perceived to be efficacious?

Vital access to these questions, if not definitive answers, may be gained by careful reading of early dedicatory inscriptions in which this royal-god designation occurs. With the exception of a few parallel epigraphs in Southeast Asia, the first inscriptions of this type are attributed to a remarkable and long-lived king of the Pallava dynasty, Mahendravarman I (c. 571–630).

When Mahendravarman came to the throne, first as a co-regent with his father, Siṃhaviṣṇu (c. 550–c. 585), the Pallavas had already enjoyed three centuries as the predominant ruling house of south India. Consistently since the late third century, they claimed Kanchipuram, in northern Tamilnadu, as their capital, a city of even greater antiquity—and distinction—as one of India's seven most sacred centers of religious authority.

Like several of his successors who followed suit, the Pallava king Mahendra had emblazoned on several temples that he commissioned a long series of honorific titles. Beginning as they do in two instances with his official regnal name, Śrī Mahendravikrama ("Illustrious Mahendra [Great Indra, king of the gods], Valorous"), they are unmistakably intended to herald his presence, to magnify his names literally, rather than that of any deity—unless, of course, a comingling is to be understood, which is the question at hand. It should be noted that several of Mahendra's honorifics occur in Telugu. Though the Pallava kingdom was centered in Tamilnadu, one assumes that the king spent a considerable part of his life in Andhra, perhaps when serving under his father, Siṃhaviṣṇu, as crown prince.

The question of when the royal patronage of temples may have begun is complicated by several factors. Stray archaeological finds confirm literary references to temples built of ephemeral brick and wood many centuries before the oldest surviving monuments of stone. Throughout India, many early temples preserve no trace of their donors' identities, whether royal or otherwise. Others are ascribed to lesser court officials or the patronage of queens. But the most significant explanation for the apparent dearth of direct royal involvement in the construction of the earliest Hindu temples is that kings were otherwise preoccupied, with the patronage of Vedic rites. Starting with the Śunga king Puṣyamitra, who overthrew the predominantely Buddhist Mauryas in the second century B.C.E., many historical rulers declared territorial hegemony by sponsoring year-long horse sacrifices (*aśvamedha*), the preeminent brahmanical rite of kingship since prehistoric times. The early Pallavas were no exception, and several kings are credited in dynastic records with the successful performance of the aśvamedha and other Vedic rites intended to infuse the king with divine efficacy, and even to deify him by an unction-induced rebirth.

Certainly the transition must have been a gradual one, from reliance on Vedic performances (out of doors), to the endowment of permanent temples as the preferred means of legitimating kings. To the extent that devotional, or bhakti, Hinduism arose as a sort of brahmanical counter-reformation to caste-rejecting Buddhists and Jains, the increasing interest of kings in temple patronage was but part of a larger pattern that encompassed other segments of society. Nevertheless, for Tamilnadu at least, this much is clear: the first temple patron identifiable by name is the Pallava king Mahendra I (c. 571–630). However many predecessors may have constructed temples of ephemeral materials before him, he was certainly among the first to commission immutable cave-temples in rock, several of which bear his highly idiosyncratic verses.

Before turning to the inscriptions themselves, a few prefatory words about Mahendra's temperament and remarkable erudition are in order. With a characteristic presumption that anticipates the Renaissance *l'uomo universale,* he styled himself the *Vicitracitta,* literally, the "Multifarious Mind." The title gains credence from a lengthy, though now abraded, résumé of achievements that appears in a cave at Māmaṇḍūr. Line six secures its attribution to Mahendra, for it names a pair of one-act comedies that he authored, both of which survive in the repertoire of Kathakali troupes in Kerala. In the better known of these, the *Mattavilāsapra-*

hasana, loosely translated as, "Farce of the Drunken Scamps," the peccadillos of Hindu and Buddhist monks alike are lampooned. In the other, *Bhagavadajjuka-prahasana,* "Farce of the Ascetic Whore," a yogi demonstrates the existence of souls by astrally projecting himself into the body of a snake-bit prostitute, but then cannot return to his own body when she is mistakenly revived in his. The litany at Māmaṇḍūr of Mahendra's accomplishments also includes the following: treatises on music and painting; commentaries or original compositions inspired by the *Rāmāyaṇa* and *Mahābhārata;* a new system of notation for music, and modification of an instrument to better evoke qualities of the human voice; distillation of a "fourth color" in an uncertain context, possibly musical; possibly the distillation of perfumes as well. The chief relevance of this impressive vita to our reading of Mahendra's dedicatory verses is that it alerts us to their wide-ranging semantic fields. As is known from Sanskrit treatises on poetics, the literati of classical India exercised a heightened appreciation for nuance, even at the risk of sanctimony. Palindromes, like crossword puzzles, could be read in all directions, and the ultimate tour de force was the dvisaṃdhāna-kāvya, an extended double-entendre poem in which two or more simultaneous narratives were carried forward with each verse. Little wonder, therefore, that ambiguities of reference to god and king might arise in temple inscriptions.

The first epigraph presented here, the single-quatrain dedication of the rock-cut cave temple at Maṇḍagappaṭṭu, is customarily cited as evidence that Mahendravarman inaugurated the practice of rock-cut architecture in Tamilnadu. The opening circumlocution, "without brick or timber, metal or mortar," expresses a consciousness of novelty, it is said, despite the history of rock-cut architecture elsewhere in the country over many centuries. However, the relative maturity of sculptural style that is evidenced by the cave façade's flanking guardians suggests a somewhat later date than may be assigned to several more archaic-appearing caves in the region. The expression, therefore, together with the royal title, "(His) Multifarious Mind" (which appears elsewhere together with Mahendra's proper name), must both be seen as evidence primarily of verbal artistry, rather than a false, or naive, claim to have (re-)invented the rock-cut technique.

A second of Mahendra's titles is hidden in the final, name-giving line of the inscription. The cave is "distinguished," by virtue of having three sanctuaries rather than the more usual one, and they are clearly designated for the Hindu trinity, namely, Brahmā, Śiva (at the hieratic center), and Viṣṇu. But elsewhere the word for "distinguished," lakṣita, appears among the honorifics of Mahendra himself. Knowing his multifarious tendencies, we may infer that he appreciated the stark, almost-stigmatizing sense of *lakṣita* when taken literally—"marked." By extension, from usage in reference to a word's sometimes indecent, figurative sense, it also may be translated "suggestive." Unavoidably, this train of thought brings us around to recalling that Śiva's "mark," or "sign" (the literal translation of *liṅga)* is the phallus, or male attribute. The metaphoric aptness is extended by the notion that a temple's sanctuary, where a liṅga may be placed, is called the garbhagṛha ("fetus-chamber" or womb). Thus, contemplation of *Lakṣita* as a royal honorific, leads to realization that he too is "distinguished" by the phallus, and further, by force of many other occurrences of the linkage-by-naming formula, that the liṅga once consecrated in this cave's central shrine was also his, in some more profound sense than sponsorship.

Mahendra's implicit self-identification with deity was not exclusively Śaiva in affiliation. A second of his cave sanctuaries, scooped from the core of a single boulder at Mahendravāḍi, is dedicated to Kṛṣṇa, a major incarnation of Viṣṇu. Scooped from the core of a single boulder, measuring scarcely eight meters across and four high, the shrine was dedicated to Viṣṇu's most beloved incarnation, Kṛṣṇa. It is difficult to say whether or not this choice was favored by reason of the eroticism associated with this lover of others' wives (especially Rādhā) and 16,008 of his own! Perhaps a clue awaits discovery in the mythic reference to Kṛṣṇa as Murāri, "Enemy of (the demon) Mura." In any event, this temple, called in the final line of the quatrain, Mahendra Viṣṇu House, is the only one that bears the king's actual regnal name instead of a secondary epithet. With measured deliberation, the name was also placed in the first and third lines, with reference to a major irrigation lake (that survives nearby), and the local township. Perhaps all three—reservoir, town, and temple—were established on the occasion of Mahendra's investiture as king.

Ironically, however, it is not this name by which the king identifies himself: that would have been far too straightforward. Rather, in the second line, he is called Guṇabhara, the "Virtue-Burdened One." This title must have borne special significance for the king, as it recurs four times in his great panegyric at Tiruchirapalli, with which this chapter closes. As we shall see, the title Guṇabhara is pivotal to recovery of an important historical reference to Mahendra in a twelfth-century hagiography. The term is also glossed in the prologue of the king's *Mattavilāsa* farce. There it appears to be derived, together with the play's title, from a longer compound meaning "he who performs wild or intoxicated sports in the fullness of the qualities of youth." The English idiom that best captures this nuance for Guṇabhara when standing alone is "well-endowed." If one could rank words according to their potential to exude rasa ("flavor": in Indian aesthetics, the sentiment-evoking power of art), Guṇabhara would certainly be a superlative. Here, it encompasses four of the eight quintessential rasas, namely: love, valor, humor, and astonishment.

The temple dedication at Śīyamaṅgalam is prototypical of the naming formula that became most common in subsequent centuries, wherein the consecrated Śiva liṅga is personalized. This cave temple is named with a conjunction that fuses the final vowel of a royal name or title with the initial *i* of Īśvara, for Lord. By the precedents of widespread usage, this name is known to designate the liṅga consecrated in the inner sanctum, and only in a secondary sense does it identify the temple as well. What must be understood implicitly here is that a king's divine essence was regarded to be a "portion" (*aṃśa*) of Lord Śiva. Described as the king's "subtle inner self" (*sūkṣmāntarātman*), this portion of Śiva, partially incarnate as king, was invoked to reside in the royal liṅga.

No ambiguity whatsoever surrounds Mahendravarman's personal authorship of the magnificent upper cave at Tiruchirappalli. It is by every measure his greatest surviving achievement, just as its dedicatory panegyric declares it to be. Excavated with supreme mastery of the medium, near the summit of an imposing precipice at the heart of recently conquered Cōḻa territory, Trichy's upper cave (so called to distinguish it from a later cave at the rock fort's base) is the largest and most richly embellished of the eight cave temples that may be attributed to him. Again, in conformity with Mahendra's express wishes, the rock temple's crowning glory is a wall-filling relief sculpture, the "inimitable image" of Lord Śiva that doubles as a deifying portrait icon of the king himself. One of the great and unduly neglected masterpieces of Indian art, this depiction of Śiva as Lord of the Gaṅgā is indeed so unprecedented that its multireferential nature remains a matter of controversy. Yet in anticipation of resistance to his broad conceits from less "multifarious minds," Mahendra, the Vicitracitta, literally framed the sculpture panel with a poetic gloss. An uncharacteristic first-person voice, presumably none other than Mahendra's, ventures to guess (see inscription L.I.) that Lord Śiva's wife Pārvatī may be present. Still jealous of his role in catching and taming the goddess Gaṅgā when she fell from heaven (as the accompanying sculpture shows), the Mountain's Daughter (Pārvatī) wishes to remind her river-loving husband that the Kaveri River, flowing near the foot of *this* mountain, belongs to the Pallava king! Even without the vaguely scandalous innuendo that arises from secondary connotations when Kaveri ("Courtesan") and Pallava ("Amorous") are juxtaposed, the equation between god and king could hardly be more pronounced. Anyone reading the inscription in the presence of the relief would inevitably realize that it represents the former and was commissioned by the latter, and must therefore be a visualization of the analogies raised. As the third verse on both sides reiterate, the Pallava king, like Śiva as Lord of the Gaṅgā, now controls the prestigious Cōḻa heartland of Tamilnadu, enriched and beautified by the River Kaveri.

A parallel though somewhat more arcane conceit conflates Śiva and the king as mountain lords. Not only does Mahendra invite the Himalayan god to reside on this southern mountain, but the epithet "Mountain Lord" pertains also to him insofar as a secondary reference in his name is to a mythical Mount Mahendra. Then, in verses three on the left and four on the right, the name of the mountain upon which the cave is excavated comes into play. The modern name Tiruchirappalli has been formed by accretion to a word for "head": freely translated it means the "Venerable Mount Head with (Jain) Retreats." Never one to spurn the convoluted, Mahendra claims that by successfully creating here a stone likeness of the god who defies representation, he who always keeps Śiva in mind (literally in his head), has made the mountain worthy of its lofty designation as Mount Head. Only if the paradoxical "image of the unimaginable" is also a royal portrait does the phrase about keeping Śiva in mind become integral with the rest of the statement. So construed, the notion of Śiva's presence in the head becomes triply meaningful with reference to the mountain, Mahendra's consciousness, and his deifying portrait. The king's avowed piety, in other words, further guarantees Śiva's presence also in the portrait-icon.

Second on the left, the most controversial verse in the Trichy inscription speaks of the liṅga by which the king should long be known as *liṅgin,* denoting the one who possesses it, or who is otherwise modified in some way by Śiva's phallic icon. Again as at Mahendravāḍi, but here in proximity to a massive stone liṅga (now missing from its rock-cut floor socket), the king styles himself as Guṇabhara, the Virtue-Burdened, or, more aptly for a liṅgin of such substantial proportions, the Well-Endowed! Read as an argument (loaded with additional double-entendre references), the verse becomes a bold challenge to any that might accuse liṅga worshipers of obscenity, or apostasy. According to the twelfth-century Śaiva hagiography, the *Periyapurāṇam,* a king named Guṇadhara (virtually synonymous with Guṇabhara) had once been a practicing Jain but was converted by Appar, one of the founding patriarchs of devotional Śaivism. Other evidence supports this synchronism sufficiently to construe in this verse at Trichy (second on the left), an allusion to former hostility toward liṅga-worshipers. Whether or not Mahendra was ever a Jain, his ridicule of Śaivas (among others) in the farces cited earlier certainly give credence to the idea that some kind of former disparagement is being alluded to and that there is, by contrast, an almost defiant (convert's?) zeal for liṅga worship now. That being the case, we can rest assured that by calling himself a *liṅgin,* in the context of multiple equations between god and king, Mahendra is claiming not just ownership of the temple, but an identity melded with Siva's.

This reconstruction of the text is further corroborated by meaning inherent in the epithet chosen for Śiva in the top right verse (R.I.). Sthāṇu, cognate with "standing," pertains to Śiva rather than any other immortal, because of his aniconic attribute, the stationary pillar, or liṅga. Accordingly, reasoning proceeds, the stone icon(s)—whether figural, as is the adjacent Lord of Gaṅgā panel, or aniconic, like the cylinder originally fixed within the sanctum at the opposite end of the cave—are equally instruments of royal apotheosis. Both serve to make the king also Sthāṇu—his glory immortalized on earth so long as the mountain cave survives, but also deified in spiritual terms, by invoking in them a portion of Śiva as the king's subtle inner spirit.

Further Readings

See J. Gonda, *Ancient Indian Kingship from the Religious Point of View* (Leiden: E. J. Brill, 1966), reprinted from NUMEN 3 and 4, with addenda and an index; Johannes Cornelis Heesterman, *The Ancient Indian Royal Consecration: The Rājasūya Described According to the Yajus Texts and Annotated* ('s-Gravenhage: Mouton & Co., 1957); Michael Lockwood and A. Vishnu Bhat, "The Philosophy of Mahendavarman's Tiruchirapalli Epigraph," *Studies in Indian Epigraphy* 3 (1977), 91–102; K. R. Srinivasan, *Cave-Temples of the Pallavas,* Vol. 1, Architectural Survey of Temples (New Delhi: Archaeological Survey of India, 1964); and V. Venkatasubba Ayyar, *South Indian Inscriptions,* vol. 12, *The Pallavas* (Madras: Government Press, 1943). For Mahendravikramavarman's works, see "Matta-vilasa: a Farce," translated by L. D. Barnett, *Bulletin of the School of Oriental Studies* (University of London) 5 (1930), 697–717; and *Bhagavadajjuka Prahasana: a Philosophical Farce by King Mahendravikramavarma Pallava,* translated by Michael Lockwood and A. Vishnu Bhat (Madras: Christian Literature Society, 1978).

Maṇḍagappaṭṭu: The Distinguished Abode

Without brick or timber, metal or mortar,
By the king, His Multifarious Mind,
This was created, the Distinguished
Abode for Brahmā, the Lord [Śiva], and Viṣṇu.

Mahendravāḍi: Mahendra Viṣṇu House

This temple for Mura's Enemy [Kṛṣṇa], near the Mahendra Reservoir,
Celebrated by the righteous, immutable and spacious,
Which [the king named] Well-Endowed [or Virtue-Burdened One, Guṇabhara] made by fracturing the rock,
In the great city of Mahendrapura, this attractive resort of virtue is named Mahendra Viṣṇu House.

Śīyamaṅgalam: The Avanibhājana-Pallaveśvara

By Amorous Sprout (Lalitāṅkura), the King,
This temple (for the Śiva liṅga) named
The Earth-possessing Pallava's Lord,
Was made, by his wish,
Like a reliquary for jewels of merit.

Tiruchirāpaḷḷi: The Lalitāṅikura Pallaveśvara House

Selected Honorifics Engraved on Pillars

Mahendravikrama [namesake of the "Great Indra, Valorous"],
Hedonist [Mattavilāsa, lit., "Drunken Dilettante"]
Great-cloud [raining benefactions]
Intellectual
Improbably fortunate [in gambling]
Great shrine builder
Captivating intelligence

Unstiffled passion
Virtue-burdened, Well-endowed (Guṇabhara)

All-guiding
Auspicious sceptor, Superpower (Tirudaṇda)
Ever decorous
Unbeholden
Neither here nor there [neither worldly nor other-worldly]
Mixed breed [composer of the Saṃkīrnajāti "medley," a rhythmic progression in music]
Ascetic aesthete [Virasa; tasteless, or with varied tastes]
Steadfast
Resolute, Enterprising
Inconstant passion, Enthusiast (Anityarāga)
Logical
Earth-possessor (Avanibhājana)
Tiger among painters
Guarantor of truth, Faithful (Satyasaṃdha)
Forthright, Foreseeing, Progressive (Abhimukha)
Merciless
Amorous sprout [Lalitāṇkura, compounded homonyms of Pallava]
Severe
Distinguished, Marked (Lakṣita)

Engraved around the Śivagaṅgādhara Panel

R.1. When king Virtue-Burdened (Guṇabhara) installed a rock icon in this beautiful cave temple, on the regal mountain's brow,
He gave new meaning to Śiva's epithet Sthāṇu [stationary, pillarlike, everlasting],
and [by the same token] became Sthāṇu [or, immortalized] himself in the world with Him.

R.2. By making a temple on this mountain for the husband
of the Himalaya's daughter [Pārvatī], Enemy wrestler, the king, also confirmed the meaning of Śiva's epithet,
the Mountain Lord.

R.3. After Śiva graciously enquired, "How can I, from an earthly shrine,
observe the splendors of Cōḻa country or the broad River Kaveri?"
The Virtue-Burdened king, like the primodial Manu,
generously bestowed on Him this cloud-scraping mountain temple.

R.4. By satisfactorily capturing Śiva's inimitable likeness in rock,
that Supreme Person [the godlike king], who always bore Śiva in his head,
gave significance to the Head Mountain's loftiness.

L.1. Fearing that her husband Śiva, the god who is fond of rivers,
might become enamored with the lovely charms of Kaveri,
The ["courtesan"] River, whose eye-pleasing waves are garlanded with gardens,
The Mountain's Daughter has, I suspect, left her Himalayan home and stays permanently here,
Referring pointedly to this river as the one cherished by the Pallava ["Playboy," king].

L.2. By this sign [the liṅga installed in the sanctum] may the knowledge
long be spread in the world that the king called Well-Endowed is the signified (*liṅgin*),
Having converted from the opposition [or from hostility to the practices
of phallic worship and dedicating royal liṅgas].

L.3. This mountain, like the Head of Cōḻa province, bears the Śiva temple as its crown jewel,
Whose luster is the luster of the Auspicious One [Śiva] himself.

L.4. By the stone chisel which gave physical form to the Faithful One
[Satyasaṃdha, "Guarantor of Truth," a divine epithet assumed by the king],
A body of eternal glory also was produced.

L.5. By Amorous Sprout (Lalitāṅkura), world-renowned as the Lovely One (Lalitam),
by the accomplished Pallava king,
Was this temple made, the Lalitāṅkura Pallaveśvara House.

—13—

How to Partake in the Love of Kṛṣṇa

Neal Delmonico

The text that is translated here, the *Ambrosia of the Sport of Govinda (Govinda-līlāmṛta)* by Kṛṣṇadāsa Kavirāja (sixteenth century C.E.), is the basis of a meditational practice involving visualization that is practiced by members of the Caitanya Vaiṣṇava tradition. The practice is called *līlā-smaraṇa,* or remembering the sport of one's chosen deities. Sport (*līlā*) here means all of the activities of the divine couple, none of which can be, almost by definition, anything other than sport or play. In India the play of a deity is both the proof and the symbol of its divinity. Deities, resting on inexhaustible cushions of power, play; humans work. Of course, humans, too, emulating deity, play in their own limited ways, but only after accumulating a cushion, however meager, of surplus (that is, power) through their work. So it is with Rādhā and Kṛṣṇa (Govinda), the principal deities of the Caitanya tradition, whose whole existence centers around the play of repeatedly finding love in each others' arms.

According to the Caitanya tradition, this creation of ours, full of renegade souls, all seeking with their minuscule powers to enjoy the pleasures of their own sport, may be said to be an insignificant and disturbing side-effect of the eternal sport of the divine lovers, Rādhā and Kṛṣṇa. The real raison d'être of existence is to nourish and in some way participate in the lovemaking of that divine couple, a fact which we the inmates of this turbulent, changing corner of existence have wanted to forget, and apparently with great success; and for our forgetfulness we suffer here, separated from them. This, in a nutshell, is the theology behind the Caitanya tradition's cultivation of passionate devotional attachment to Rādhā and Kṛṣṇa. The essential aim of religious practice, therefore, is to undo the forgetfulness that has enshrouded the living beings of this world through various techniques of remembering. The direct recollection of the sport of Rādhā and Kṛṣṇa is the final stage in the process of returning to one's own true state of being.

Religious practice in the Caitanya tradition seeks to change the desire to forget into a desire to remember. It begins with a recognition of the impossibility of any enduring enjoyment, apart from the divine lovers. This is a recognition that usually has the form of an alienation founded on a sense of frustrated acquisitiveness, a feeling that one is somehow out of place, and is both incomplete and unable to do anything about it. The early stages of practice center around listening to readings of sacred scripture, usually the *Bhāgavata Purāṇa,* cultivating habits of cleanliness and good conduct, and reciting the holy names of Kṛṣṇa under the guidance of a teacher. This recitation takes the form of private recitation called *japa* or congregational singing called *kīrtana.* After years of such practice, one learns the basic elements of Vaiṣṇava theology and frees oneself from bad habits and the kinds of desire that prolong one's forgetfulness. Finally, when a rudimentary desire to regain the association of the divine couple develops, a disciple is given mantra initiation. During mantra initiation, technically called *dīkṣā,* the disciple is given a set of esoteric incantations (*mantra*) to be used in the worship of Rādhā and Kṛṣṇa. Without these sacred formulas, received from an empowered teacher, the ritual worship of the images of Rādhā and Kṛṣṇa and the forms of mental worship, including this practice of remembering their sport, cannot be performed. The teacher (*guru*) whispers the incantations into the right ear of the disciple, the most essential of which are the kāma-gāyatrī and the Gopāla-mantra. With the bestowal of these sacred chants the doorway to the eternal sport of the divine lovers is opened.

The doorway may be open, but in order to enter into that mode of existence one is in need of an appropriate form and identity. In many forms of Indic religion, the highest state of existence is thought of as a formless one, full of consciousness unrelated to any object, but not so in Vaiṣṇavism. In Vaiṣṇavism, the highest state of existence is one formed and embodied with indestructible, unchanging bodies of consciousness. Thus, in order to enter into the sport of Rādhā and Kṛṣṇa, one needs an eternal body of consciousness. Even if our present bodies have been transformed by the techniques of alchemy, or "baked" in the fires of sexual passion in the sexual rites of tantra, into bodies of adamantine hardness and durability, our entry into the divine sport of Rādhā and Kṛṣṇa is still inappropriate. One needs, along with that body of consciousness, an identity or "role" that fits into the eternal narrative that informs the unending sport of Rādhā and Kṛṣṇa. The cultivation of these bodies of consciousness with their appropriate identities forms the substance of the final level of religious practice in Caitanya Vaiṣṇavism, and it is to this level of practice that Kṛṣṇadāsa's text pertains.

Perhaps the earliest discussion of practice involving a separate body and identity suitable for participation in the sport of Rādhā and Kṛṣṇa in the Caitanya tradition is found in a work by Rūpa (sixteenth century), the *Ocean of the Ambrosia of the Rapture of Devotion (Bhakti-rasāmṛta-sindhu).* Rūpa was one of the leading poet-theologians of the Caitanya tradition and a direct student of Caitanya. In an important passage of his work (1.2.294–5), in which he teaches the practice of devotion in pursuit of passionate devotion, he says:

> Remembering his dearest one, Kṛṣṇa, and an associate of his [Kṛṣṇa's] who appeals to him, he [an aspiring practitioner], engaged by story about them, should always

> live in Vraja. In this practice, one who desires that [special associate's] feeling should serve with his practitioner's body and his perfected body, following the people of Vraja.

Rūpa's nephew, Jīva, commenting on this passage, explains that the "practitioner's body" means the body one happens to be situated in and the "perfected body" is an internally imagined body suitable for the kind of service to Kṛṣṇa that one wants to perform. Thus, Rūpa is recommending two sets of practice, one to be performed by our ordinary bodies and another to be performed by another body, our mentally conceived or imagined one. Essential to this practice is the "remembering" of Kṛṣṇa and an associate of his who is already in the eternal sport and whose relationship to Kṛṣṇa one finds appealing. In addition, Rūpa stresses the importance of stories describing that associate and Kṛṣṇa. One fashions in one's imagination, then, on the basis of this remembering and hearing, a body and identity similar to that of one's favorite associate of Kṛṣṇa. Kṛṣṇadāsa Kavirāja's work, the *Ambrosia of the Sport of Govinda,* is a text for use in the practice that Rūpa has outlined here, in which the sport of Rādhā and Kṛṣṇa is described in detail throughout an entire day and night.

Although Rūpa suggests that an attraction to a relationship that exists between Kṛṣṇa and one of his associates develops gradually and organically to form the basis for fashioning one's own perfected body, in practice as we find it today, a practitioner who has arrived at this level generally will learn of his perfected body from his or her teacher. This takes place in yet another initiation in which the disciple not only learns about his or her own "perfected" or "accomplished" form but also learns about that of his teacher and of all of the members of his initiating lineage of teachers going back to Caitanya or one of his close associates. At this time the disciple receives his "perfected" name, age, type of service, body color, customary dress, and so forth. On the basis of this kind of information the disciple is expected to engage in the visualization practice that Kṛṣṇadāsa's text and others like it foster.

In his description of this practice, Rūpa suggests that any of Kṛṣṇa's eternal associates might act as models for a "perfected" body and that thereby one can cultivate the feelings of that associate in the exercise of his or her relationship with Kṛṣṇa. As the Caitanya tradition has developed, however, only two of the five possible relationships (the peaceful and remote meditator, the servant, the friend, the parent, and the lover) have been cultivated with any degree of sophistication, and one of them vastly overshadows the other. It is uncertain why this is so. One possible explanation is that they are connected with the two most powerful personalities of the early Caitanya movement, Caitanya and Nityānanda. The most common relationship to Rādhā and Kṛṣṇa is that represented by the mañjarī, which literally means "flowering bud." A mañjarī in the sport of Rādhā and Kṛṣṇa is a younger girlfriend of Rādhā who is in part a friend (an equal) and in part a servant (a subordinate). As a girlfriend she is included among Rādhā's confidantes when the latter goes to meet and enjoy Kṛṣṇa. As a servant she is given certain intimate services to perform that make her a witness to and participant in the most private aspects of the sport of Rādhā and Kṛṣṇa. The members of the tradition regard this intimate access as a special grace bestowed upon them by the loving couple through Caitanya. This identity probably grows out of Caitanya's experience of the sport of Kṛṣṇa. An important part of the tradition views Caitanya as being overwhelmed with the feelings of Rādhā. Caitanya's followers would view themselves, therefore, as servant-friends of Rādhā. The other identity that has been cultivated in the Caitanya tradition is that of the male cowherd friend of Kṛṣṇa. Some texts have survived describing that relationship. Members of the tradition identify Caitanya's associate Nityānanda with Balarāma, Kṛṣṇa's older brother, who is associated with the male cowherder friends of Kṛṣṇa. He may thus have been the inspiration for the second relationship cultivated by the tradition.

The Ambrosia of the Sport of Govinda is one of the longest poems ever written about Kṛṣṇa. It consists of twenty-three chapters, each of which contains at least a hundred verses. Yet Kṛṣṇadāsa describes only one day in the sport of Rādhā and Kṛṣṇa, elaborating their daily activities in the spiritual paradise called Vṛndāvana on the highest plane of existence. The day of Rādhā and Kṛṣṇa is divided into eight periods that act as divisions of their sport, and these periods correspond to eight divisions of roughly three hours each in the day of the practitioner, and thus can be given exact times in the earthly day of twenty-four hours. This allows a practitioner to visualize what Rādhā and Kṛṣṇa are doing at any time during the day. The practitioner is expected to fill his or her day with the visualization or "remembering" of the sport of Rādhā and Kṛṣṇa as Kṛṣṇadāsa has described it, using his or her perfected body and identity as the perspective from which the sport is viewed. Eventually, the sport comes alive and the practitioner becomes a spontaneous participant in the sport, gradually shifting his or her identity from the "practitioner's" body to the "perfected" body. When the practitioner's material body dies, as it must in time, the erstwhile practitioner's consciousness moves permanently to the perfected body and lives on in the eternal sport of Rādhā and Kṛṣṇa in its new form and identity as an eternal associate.

It is not certain what the source of the events of the eternal day in the life of Rādhā and Kṛṣṇa is. The commentator on Kṛṣṇadāsa's text, Vṛndāvana Cakravartin, says in his commentary on verse three of the first chapter that Rūpa gave an outline of the story in an eleven-verse hymn called the *Auspicious Hymn of Remembrance (Smaraṇa-maṅgala-stotra)*. The eleven verses look suspiciously unlike Rūpa's work, however, which is usually quite elegant and finely fashioned, and since all of the verses are found in the *Ambrosia of the Sport of Govinda*, where they introduce each new division in the sport, they are probably the work of Kṛṣṇadāsa Kṛṣṇavirāja who, though an accomplished poet, was not a master poet like Rūpa. There is another point to be considered here, however. The entire cycle of events appears in one of the chapters of the *Padma Purāṇa*. That account is almost certainly earlier than both Rūpa and Kṛṣṇadāsa, for, although it is not impossible that the *Padma Purāṇa* was still being added to in the sixteenth century, it is highly unlikely. Thus, the story of Kṛṣṇa's eternal daily sport and the practice of contemplating or remembering it were around before Rūpa and Kṛṣṇadāsa, and one of them, probably Kṛṣṇadāsa at Rūpa's suggestion, wrote the hymn briefly outlining it. Later Kṛṣṇadāsa elaborated it into the *Ambrosia of the Sport of Govinda.* Since only the first and part of the second chapters of Kṛṣṇadāsa's work is translated here, and since the short hymn is available in translation elsewhere and is otherwise quite terse, I have included the moderately elaborate description found in the *Padma Purāṇa.* This will provide a useful overview of the events in the entire story.

The portion of the *Ambrosia of the Sport of Govinda* that is translated here describes the sport of Rādhā and Kṛṣṇa during the first period of the day, which begins about an hour and a half before sunrise. It is called the "night's end sport," and depicts the divine lovers waking up in each other's arms after a night of enjoyment in the forests outside of their cowherd village. A small portion of the next period, called the "morning sport," has also been included.

Two editions of the *Śrī-Śrī-Govinda-līlāmṛtam* by Kṛṣṇadāsa Kavirāja were used for the translation: one edited by Haridāsa Dāsa (Navadvīpa: Haribola Kuṭīra, Caitanyābda 463 [1949 C.E.]); the other, with the commentary of Vṛndāvana Cakravartin and a Hindi translation, vol 1., edited and translated by Haridāsa Śāstrī (Vṛndāvana: Śrī Gadādhara Gaurahari Press, 1977). The final selection is from chapter eighty-three of the *Pātāla-khaṇḍa* of the *Padma Purāṇa* by Krishna Dwaipayan Vedauyas, part 3, Patal Khand, Gurumandal Series no. 18 (Calcutta: Manasukharāya Morā, 1958), which describes briefly the entire cycle of sport.

May Gaura and Gadādhara be glorified!
Glory be to Rādhā and Kṛṣṇa!

The Ambrosia of the Sport of Govinda (Govinda-līlāmṛta)

CHAPTER ONE

1. I pay homage to Śrī Govinda, the great abode of all the joys of Vraja ["the pasture lands"], the joy of the forest of Vṛndāvana, who himself is pleased by the association of Śrī Rādhā.

2. I surrender in astonishment to Śrī Kṛṣṇa Caitanya, the compassionate one who has cured the world of the madness of ignorance and then maddened it again with the nectar of the treasure of sacred love for himself.

3. The ultimate goal of spiritual development, the loving service of the lotus-like feet of the friend of the heart of Rādhā, though unattainable by Brahmā, Ananta, and others, is achieved only through intense longing by those absorbed in his activities in Vraja. In order now to reveal the Lord's meditative service,

by which his [direct] loving service is attained and which is to be contemplated by those travelers on the path of passion, I praise the Lord's daily activities in Vraja.

4. At night's end he returns from the forest bowers into the cow settlement. In the morning and evening he performs such sports as milking the cows, eating, and so forth. In the forenoon he plays with his friends and tends the cows. In the midday and also at night he sports with Rādhā in the forest. In the afternoon he returns to the settlement and in the late evening pleases his well-wishers. May this Kṛṣṇa protect us.

5. Let this nectar of the eternal sports of Govinda which squashes the desire for the nectar of the gods (*soma*) be glorified! Though it is constantly drunk by the speech and the mind, it astonishingly makes one thirsty, and though it is the cure for the disease of material existence, it brings on the madness, blindness, and delusion born of love. Moreover, though it is constantly chewed, it provides an undiminishing flavor (*rasa*) and nourishes the body, mind, and heart.

6. How shall I not be a tremendous cause of laughter for Vaiṣṇavas who constantly play in the ocean of the nectar of Kṛṣṇa's sports, for though I am incompetent, extremely mediocre, of small intelligence, and unqualified, I desire to taste the full flavor (*rasa*) of that ocean?

7. Let the speech of such a fool as me, like that of a clown, cause laughter and mirth among the Vaiṣṇavas of Vraja whose minds are absorbed in the nectar of the love-dancelike sports of Kṛṣṇa revealed by other, real dramatists like Śrī Rūpa.

8. Encouraged by statements of the saints such as: "That verbal creation which in each verse [contains the name of the Lord] destroys the sins of the community (*Bhāgavata Purāṇa,* 1.5.11)," even though I am dull I shall make my words respected by the saintly through description of the sports of Govinda.

9. May those saintly souls who are moistened by proximity to the reservoir nourish this cow [text] of mine which is headed toward Gokula but afflicted by wandering across the desert of my lips.

10. At the end of night I remember Rādhā and Kṛṣṇa awakened by many noises instigated by anxious Vṛndā and made to rise from their bed of joy by the charming and pithy songs of the parrots and sārīs [a type of bird]. They, tremulous from the erotic passion that is aroused at that time, are gazed upon and pleased by their girlfriends. Then, frightened by the report of the old monkey Kakkhaṭī, even though they thirst for each other, they return to their own beds in their homes.

11. Seeing that night was ending, Vṛndā enlisted a flock of birds under her control to awaken Madhusūdana [Kṛṣṇa] and Rādhā.

12. Having obtained the order of Vṛndā, the birds, who until then because of her order had remained silent though their hearts longed for service, began to sing in joy surrounding the bower of love-play.

13. On the grapevines sang the sārīs, the parrots in the pomegranates, and the cuckoos with their mates in the mango trees; the pigeons sang in the pīlu tree, the peacocks in the nīpa tree, the bees on the vines, and on the ground, the roosters.

14. Then a swarm of black bees desirous of honey began to hum like the conch shell of the Lord of eros in the charming bower made of blossoming vines and containing a bed made of lotus flowers.

15. A swarm of joyous female honey bees, intoxicated with honey, hummed like the auspicious cymbals of the god of love in order to awaken Govinda.

16. A flock of parrots repeatedly sang forth a loud "kuhu-u" on the fifth note of the scale like the vīṇā [the stringed instrument] of the mind-born one [eros].

17. In the mango tree, the flock of cuckoos seated by the sides of their lovers who were cooing in the intoxication of amorous love made a soft, seductive tone, their voices sharpened by tasting the flamelike, soft buds [of the mango tree], giving the impression of the sound of the sweet sitar of the lord of eros.

18. I suspect that the hyena of desire became angry at the wolves of love-pique and growled in the disguise of the warbling of pigeons, causing the forest animals of the bashfulness, morality, and fortitude of the cowherd girls to run away.

19. The peacocks, while awakening those two in the morning, cried out "kekā" as though asking who (*ke*) besides Kṛṣṇa can uproot that mountain of Rādhā's composure and what (*kā*) other fetters [women] besides the fortunate Rādhā, though they be highly praised for their beauty, can control the maddened elephant Kṛṣṇa.

20. The rooster, too, like a brahman reciting the Veda in the morning, called forth the sounds: 'ku ku-u ku-u-u ku-u-u-u,' with short, long, and prolonged vowels.

21. Then, though awakened by the sounds of the birds, these two [Rādhā and Kṛṣṇa], each unaware that the other was awake, and disturbed at the prospect of breaking their intense embrace, craftily remained still with their eyes closed.

22. A learned pet sārikā [a type of bird] named Mañjubhāṣiṇī in a shiny golden cage, who was dear to the daughter of Vṛṣabhānu [Rādhā] and who had witnessed all of the love sports of the night, then addressed the couple in the early dawn.

23. "Victory, friend of Gokula! O, ocean of rapture, wake up! Leave your moonlike bed and awaken your beloved resting in your arms, who favors you with her love and is fatigued by excessive erotic play.

24. "This faint reddish glow, by nature cruel to young women, is speeding toward sunrise. Stealthily return home in haste, Lord of Vraja, from the bank of the daughter of Kalinda [the Yamunā River].

25. "O, lotus-face [Rādhā]! That you are sleeping at the end of the night is not your fault since your body is extremely languid from the exertion of love play. But look, virtuous lady, this eastern horizon, being unable to tolerate your happiness, has become reddened like [your rival] Candrāvalī.

26. "O, lotus-eyed! Night has gone; morning has appeared. The globe of the sun is on the rise! Now, friend, put away your attraction for that bed of cool blossoms."

27. Then an excited parrot named Vicakṣaṇa, full of love for Kṛṣṇa and most proficient at eloquent speech, slowly recited a series of verses made charming by a combination of clear and sweet syllables, and effective at waking Mādhava [Kṛṣṇa].

28. "Victory, victory [to you], O source of the auspicity of Gokula, lotus of the honey bee young ladies of Vraja, O joy of Nanda increasing at every moment, Govinda, Acyuta, bestower of happiness on the surrendered!

29. "Dawn has come, O lotus of the thirsty, beelike eyes of unlimited herdsmen. Return to your distant and dear village, the home of the most distinguished of all elders.

30. "O lotus-eyed one [Kṛṣṇa]! See how this eastern horizon, seeing the reddish sun desirous of rising, has become crimson like the crimson cloth, deeply dyed with saffron, worn by a wife [on the return of her traveling husband]. Therefore, Kṛṣṇa, give up your sleep in your hidden bower.

31. "Lady night, frightened by the sun, has hastily gone away along with the moon. Therefore, [you, too] quickly go from the bank of the river along with your beloved, who is like her [the night].

32. "The female goose has cast one eye toward the east, which is reddened by the rays of dawn, and the other quickly toward her departing lover. The fearful owls in their tree hollows have become silent. I fear the sun has arisen, O Kṛṣṇa! Give up your sleep."

33–34. Then a soft-spoken sārī named Sūkṣmadhī, who was trained by Vṛndā, who had memorized many verses and who, drunk with the honey of great affection for Rādhā, was intent on chasing away her sleep, horripilating out of love, made speech dance on the stage of her tongue.

35. "As long as the people are not all traveling on the path to the pasture you can easily go to your home, sweetheart of the son of Nanda.

36. "O pretty one, therefore quickly get out of bed and go home. The lord of day whose pace is swift is moving toward Mount Sunrise.

37. "Give up your sleep and leave your bower bed. Return home, friend, and don't be languid. Awaken your lover, but don't awaken shame before your people. Those who are clever know which action is proper to the moment."

38. Neither Kṛṣṇa, embraced by his beloved, nor his beloved, embraced by him, is asleep. Though this couple is troubled by the coming dawn they are not able easily to rise from their delicious bed.

39. With her buttocks bound by Kṛṣṇa's knees, her breasts pressed against his chest, her face placed on his face, her arms resting around his neck and his arm as her pillow, though she is awake, the beloved [Rādhā] does not show it even slightly.

40. Her lover, too, is aware that he should quickly return to the village and is anxious to get up from bed. Yet, with his mind freed from such obligations by the fear of ending the pleasure of the tight embrace of Rādhā's body, he does not move even one limb the slightest bit.

41. Then a parrot named Dakṣa, who was an expert at arranging the sports of Śrī Kṛṣṇa and who had trained thousands of other parrots, spread his wings out of a joy produced of love for him [Kṛṣṇa], and spoke from within the inner chamber of the bower:

42. "While your mother has yet to arise and say: 'My child is still sleeping, fatigued by wandering around the forests. Therefore, the churning of curds should not be done loudly,' you should quickly return unnoticed to your bedroom, Kṛṣṇa!

43. "You know for certain that your cows, Kālindī and the others, with unmoving ears and raised faces, their eyes turned toward your path out of enthusiasm to see you, are calling their thirsty calves with their 'moos' and are sinking down because of the pain produced by the weight of their udders.

44. "Quickly return before that anxious Paurṇamāsī, having finished her morning duties, enters your bedroom with your mother to see you."

45. Then Hari, because of the words of the parrot, became anxious to return quickly to the cowherd village and, quietly withdrawing his limbs from the body of his beloved, sat up.

46. Now their previously awakened girlfriends were watching, along with Vṛndā, with their faces pressed to the openings of the lattices of the bower, the tender actions of the couple in the early morning.

47. A peahen named Sundarī, excited by great love for Rādhā, left her lover and came from the kadamba tree to the courtyard of the love cottage.

48. Then a peacock called Tāṇḍavika quickly descended from the kadamba tree and, spreading his tail, danced joyfully, filled with Hari.

49. After that a doe called Raṅgiṇi suddenly left her lover and with a joyful heart came quickly from the base of the mango tree to the door of the bower, fixing her eyes, which were quivering with love, on the lotus faces of the lords of her life [Rādhā and Kṛṣṇa].

50. At that time, a deer of Hari named Suraṅga, who gave him [Hari] great pleasure, arrived at the bower from the mango tree and fixed his eyes on Kṛṣṇa's face, his body free of languor.

51. When the Lord rose up and sat on the bed, he drew his slim lover, whose eyes were closed in pretended sleep, to his lap with his arms and observed her sweetness carefully.

52. Acyuta [Kṛṣṇa] with a faint smile drank in with his eyes the face of his dear one, which was like a morning lotus. Her rolling eyes were like wag-tails [a bird], and the flowing locks of her hair surrounding her forehead were like a network of black bees.

53. Watching his lover moving all her clasped fingers and her two arms and stretching her body, and seeing the splendor of her teeth appear through her waking yawns, Mukunda felt joy.

54. Seeing his love-exhausted lover in the early morning light resting face up on his lap, her face faintly smiling through a soft, feigned weeping, the end of her braid half undone, wearing a crushed flower garland and a torn necklace, opening again and again her languid, rolling eyes, which were anxious to look upon his face, the Lord of Vraja [Kṛṣṇa] experienced unequaled joy.

55. If torpid lightning were to achieve permanence in the midst of a new rain cloud, then it would have been exactly like the image of Śrī Rādhā, whose body, like a golden lotus, being languid because of the exertion of intense love making, rested in the lap of her lover whose color is that of a shining tamāla tree [greyish blue].

56. Seeing the face of Hari with his glistening crocodile earrings, his sweet, gentle, broadening smile, his eyes dull with intoxication, his small curls of hair having the fragrance of lotuses, and lips with cuts made by her own teeth and blackened with the coryllium of her eyes, the lotus-eyed one [Rādhā] desired to make love again.

57. Then Kṛṣṇa also, seeing the faintly smiling face of his lover with her eyes slightly closed, their flirtatious movements inhibited by the shyness caused by seeing one another, again became intensely aroused.

58. Raising the back of her head with his left hand and her chin with his right, he repeatedly kissed his beloved's face whose cheeks were brightened by a smile and whose throat was curved.

59. She, though immersed in an ocean of happiness at the touch of her lover's lips, by resisting his hands, wincing slightly and saying softly: "don't, don't," with a choked voice increased the delight of the watching eyes of her girlfriends.

60. Then, apprehensive because of the imminent, unavoidable dawn, her friends, smiling with joy, entered the bower, which was filled with the sounds of buzzing bees, teasing their friend [Rādhā] and encouraging one another.

61. She, seeing that her friends, with smiling faces and roving eyes, had come near, got up from the lap of her lover, doubling his pleasure.

62. Having gotten up quickly, she hurriedly took the yellow upper cloth [of Kṛṣṇa] and covered her body. Then Rādhā, looking into her girlfriends' embarrassed faces, sat down by her lover's side.

63. Observing their two dear friends before them, they repeatedly felt pleasure. The couple's lips bore cuts from biting each other; they were languid from making love; their bodies were marked with scratches; the lines of their makeup had run; their clothes were unfastened; their hair was disheveled; and their necklaces and garlands were torn.

64. Their bed told them of the nature of the lovers' sports. In the middle it was soiled with the unguent and saffron from Acyuta's body. Its two sides were adorned with the red lac of Rādhā's feet and it was spotted with drops of coryllium and particles of sandal and vermilion.

65. Her friends saw that the bed, which was the site of a collection of crushed flowers and spotted with betal, red lac, and coryllium, and bore the clear signs of the lovers' sports, was in the same condition as the body of their friend [Rādhā].

66. They savored with their eyes the restless lips of Hari, about to speak a few words of wit, and the lotuslike face of the beautiful one [Rādhā], which was lowered out of bashfulness.

67. Showing them his chest, Hari said with a wink, hoping to see the sweetness of a medley of emotions on his beloved's face:

68. "Ladies, look how Rādhā [the asterism of that name], seeing that her lover the moon will depart at dawn and becoming fearful of separation from him, has drawn hundreds of moon lines on the canvas of the sky as if out of a desire to see him."

69. When Kṛṣṇa said this, she saw her friends in front of her laughing, and, wincing her trembling eyes, wrinkling raised eyebrows, and expanding spotless cheeks, she looked at her lover as though striking him with her crooked, sidelong glances.

70. Rādhā's gaze was full of the joy of wanton sport, her eyes slightly closed and, around the edges, tearful and reddish. Possessing a somewhat startled and tremulous quality from shyness and doubt, and bent from the weight of her jealousy, that intensely smiling gaze in which the pupils of her eyes blossomed on seeing the face of her lover increased the pleasure of her beloved's eyes.

71. Their friends thus tasted the sweetness of the early morning amorous agitation of those two, who were in this way submerged in an ocean of the happiness of sacred love for each other, and, becoming intoxicated with joy, forgot the duties that were appropriate for that time.

72. Seeing the couple absorbed in an ocean of the ambrosia of play and their friends, too, blinded by the intoxication of affection, Vṛndā, fearing the coming of morning, signaled a sārī who knew the meaning of her sign language.

73. The sārikā named Śubhā, who helps awaken Rādhikā and who prevents [Rādhā's] shame before her elders, fear of her husband, and ridicule from society, said:

74. "Your husband's mother will get up from her bed and harangue you with: 'Oh Rādhā, your husband will return now from the cowshed with loads of milk. Get up, get up and perform the auspicious household rites in the house.' Before that you must most secretly return to your bedroom from this bower, my lotus-eyed friend.

75. "Friend, the stars who have variously sported the entire night with their husband [the moon] have dissolved into the veil of the sky. You too, sincere one, must return from the bower to your house.

76. "The path of the moon is reddened by the rays of the sun; the roads of the king are now occupied by crowds of people. Give up your fascination with the path to the bower. The path to the village is the auspicious one now.

77. "Kṛṣṇa, her husband's mother, whose heart is soiled by the mud of suspicion, mistrusts her. Her fault-finding husband is very caustic and lives up to his name Abhimanyu ["the Angry One"]. Her rotten sister-in-law, too, is hot-tempered and speaks abusively to her. What's more, dawn is here and still you haven't released this unassuming woman."

78. Rādhā's heart was like the milk-ocean disturbed by the churning of Mount Mandara at the words of the sārī. With her eyes wandering about like baby fish and saddened by her immanent separation [from Kṛṣṇa], she then got up from the bed.

79. Kṛṣṇa also, seeing that the eyes in the beautiful face of the daughter of Vṛṣabhānu were agitated with fear, took his lover's fine, blue cloth and quickly got up from the bed.

80. With their clothes thus switched with one another, these two, full of anxiety, came out of the bower holding each other's hands.

81. Holding Rādhā's hand in his left hand and his flute in his right, Kṛṣṇa left the bower shining like a cloud embraced by a bolt of lightning.

82. One girlfriend brought the golden pitcher, another the fan with the golden handle. Someone picked up the beautiful mirror, another the pretty jar of saffron and sandal. Someone else carried the jewel-inlaid vessel of betel nut and another the parrot in the cage. In this way some of the girlfriends left the bower cottage with joyful hearts.

83. Another girlfriend collected the ivory and gold box of cinnabar with the sapphire lid which was shaped like the dark-nippled breast of a pregnant woman and, softly smiling, left the bower.

84. Someone else joyfully gathered together the shining pearls that had fallen from the necklace broken during the embraces of the lovers and, tightly tying them up in the border of her cloth, left the bower cottage.

85. Ratimañjarī quickly picked up from the bed the earrings that fell off during the love sports and, leaving the bower, put them back in the ears of her mistress [Rādhā].

86. The dear playmate, Rūpamañjarī, collected Rādhā's blouse from the edge of the bed and, after leaving the bower, secretly returned it to her girlfriend.

87. The female servant, Guṇamañjarī, took the spittoon and, dividing the chewed betel nut from it among the girlfriends, left the bower.

88. Mañjulālī gathered from the bed the garlands and sandal which fell from the couple's bodies and, distributing some to all the girlfriends, also left.

89. Then, noticing in front of them that the dearest one [Kṛṣṇa] was wearing on his body [Rādhā's] cloud-colored cloth and that their joyful girlfriend was wearing [Kṛṣṇa's] yellow cloth on hers, the girlfriends began to giggle, covering their faces with their hands, and, glancing all around and at each other, they were filled with delight.

90. Seeing indications of the laughter of their friends, those two, their blossoming eyes fixed on each other's faces, absorbed in a boiling ocean of the joy of sacred love, became like figures drawn in a picture.

91. The lovely lady was unable to recognize her own dark blue silk cloth clinging to the dark-complexioned body of her dear one, and, Hari, too, did

not recognize his large yellow silk cloth covering his dearest's body, [which looked] like milk in a golden conch shell.

92. Then Lalitā, angry at the obstacle to the lovers' tasting of the nectar of their sports, censuring the coming dawn, said to her friend:

93. "You see this dawn, Rādhā! Because of breaking up the sport and love making of the best of women at daybreak, his two legs have been lost through leprosy; yet he still does not quit. The saying that one's own nature is difficult to change is certainly true."

94. At that, casting her eyes, which were reddened out of anger at the interruption of her love games, at the sky ruddy with dawn, the daughter of Vṛṣabhānu, who speaks softly and sweetly, said, smiling at the sarcasm of Lalitā:

95. "This one [the sun] sets and, crossing, even without legs, the entire sky in half an instant, rises again. If fate had given him legs there would be no question of night at all!"

96. Seeing the charming daybreak and enjoying the ambrosia of her words, Mukunda, intoxicated with joy and forgetful of returning to the village, said to the queen of his heart:

97. "See how this eastern direction, seeing the sun approaching at dawn, his body reddened by association with the other directions, has become crimson out of envy like a woman in love who sees her lover arrive at dawn after having been enjoyed by another woman.

98. " 'Look, intoxicated one [a nearby lily], your beloved, the lord of the twice-born [the moon], who though peaceful is a destroyer of the darknesses of all people, has gone to the west [or, by double entendre, has drunk wine] and has suddenly and completely fallen down.' For this reason, I'm afraid, the lily covers her face with her closing petals, embarrassed by the laughing of the lotus, who is now exultant because of association with her own lover [the sun].

99. "Seeing the destruction of darkness at night by the moon, these dark cuckoos are frightened [for their own safety] and call out at dawn 'kuhū,' for Kuhū, the moonless night that occurs when the sun has been devoured by eclipse because it is a supporter of the moon.

100. "The forest is filled with joy because of uniting with her lover, Spring, and it is as though the female pigeon, maddened by love, shrieks in ecstasy on the pretext of hooting.

101. "Look over there, moon-faced! A wandering bumble bee, his coat turned tawny from playing among the white water lilies, is following a female bee who spent the night in the whorl of a lotus and who is now curtsying to him.

102. "A female ruddy goose, thinking that her lover has arrived, kisses with her beak a red lotus made twice as red by the rays of dawn.

103. "Sweet-voiced one, this goose named Kalasvana, noticing us, has left his mate, though she wants to make love, and has come to the bank of the river before us, his wings spread in pleasure.

104. "Look, lotus-faced! His mate, moaning sweetly in passion, picks up with her beak a lotus stalk, half-eaten and left behind by her husband. She is a goose named Tuṇḍikerī, and follows her lover with her eyes fixed on your lotus face.

105. "Moving through the tops of sandal trees, bearing the fragrance of lotuses and teaching the dance of love to the dancing-girl-like vines, the wind, who sports around water, destroys fatigue, and carries away the net of perspiration from the best of women and their lovers, is blowing."

106. Seeing that the Lord and his lady, who were engrossed in the sport of fine speech, had forgotten about returning to their homes and also that their girlfriends, brightened by smiles, were intoxicated with joy, the mistress of the forest (Vṛndā) became troubled by fear of the daybreak.

107. Then, in a tree, an aged monkey matron named Kakkhaṭī, who was versed in the sign language of Vṛndā and who knew the time of day, recited a verse:

108. "Daybreak, a female ascetic, clothed in red with matted locks (*jaṭila*) and praised by the good, has arrived, spreading above the rays of the sun." [Or, by double entendre: Jaṭilā (the mother-in-law of Rādhā) clothed in red, who is praised by the quarrelsome and performs austerity (early bath) at daybreak, has arrived, spreading her cloth in the sun (to dry).]

109. Thus the two best of the village of cowherds, Kṛṣṇa and the girl with the choicest body, becoming filled with dread on hearing of the crooked Jaṭilā, became fearful and, though they felt a strong desire for making love, departed [from the bower].

110. Their girlfriends then, seeing the frightened couple moving off down their respective forest paths, pulling up their falling garments, locks of hair, and garlands, and trembling because of the name "Jaṭilā," became startled and scattered in different directions.

111. Kṛṣṇa, thinking that the friends of Candrāvalī [Rādhā's rival] were on his left, that the cowherds were in front of him, and that the crooked Jaṭilā was coming up behind him, and being anxious to watch his fearful lover moving off to his right, returned to the village, his neck turning every which way as he cast his eyes in one direction and then another.

112. His mistress [Rādhā], fearing Jaṭilā's pursuit and yet afflicted by carrying the weight of her buttocks and breasts, returned to the village, charmingly

alternating between quickness and slowness, holding on to her clothes and flowing hair with her hands.

113. Rūpamañjarī, desiring to bring her [Rādhā] safely to her house, seated her in the chariot of her own [Rūpamañjarī's] mind and then followed her, covering the path with a curtain of her eyes, which were dark and restless because of fear and love.

114. Ratimañjarī, too, followed her [Rādhā], warding off intruders with the arrows of her darting glances, shot in all directions, and with the palpitations of her heart, troubled by fear, which lead the way like an advance guard of soldiers.

115. Though not afraid, [Rādhā and Kṛṣṇa] stepped very timidly across their own courtyards, their delicate eyes fixed on the doors of their elders, very stealthily entered their own rooms and fell asleep in their own beds, their minds filled with exhaustion.

116. Like the Vedas who, at each cosmic dissolution, return to the Lord when Acyuta, having completed his amusement, goes to sleep in his own abode, the highly qualified girlfriends, who are expert at expanding the Lord's sports and whose movements cannot be traced, returned to their own homes.

117. Thus ends the first chapter, entitled: "A Sketch of the Love Sport in the Forest Bowers at the End of Night," in the poem, *The Ambrosia of the Sport of Govinda,* which is born out of the boon of Raghunātha Bhaṭṭa, inspired in the association of Śrī Jīva, encouraged by the capable Raghunāthadāsa, and a result of service to that honeybee at the lotuslike feet of Caitanya, Śrī Rūpa.

CHAPTER TWO

1. I seek shelter in Rādhā, for whom, having been bathed and adorned, the matron of Vraja [Yaśodā] sends in the morning and who, at Yaśodā's house, cooks the morning meal along with her friends and then tastes Kṛṣṇa's remnants. I also seek shelter in Kṛṣṇa who, awakened by his mother, milks the cows in the barn and then, after bathing, eats breakfast with his friends.

2. Thus, in the early morning, Paurṇamāsī, radiant with the moon of sacred love, finished her morning rites and arrived early at the compound of Nanda, her heart agitated with love for Acyuta [Kṛṣṇa].

3. The house of the lord of Vraja [Nanda] has a beautiful courtyard sprinkled with drops of milk scattered from the churning of butter and adorned by people filled with sacred love. Its interiors are decorated with many types of jewels, and overflow with waves of milk. In a shining, serpentlike bed, sleeping happily, lies Acyuta. Seeing this dwelling so much like the fabled White Isle of Viṣṇu, she [Paurṇamāsī] became filled with joy.

4. Noticing her arrival like the radiance of austerity itself, the exalted queen of Vraja [Yaśodā], who was experienced and knew etiquette, rose up in joy.

5. "Come in, venerable lady, praised by all of Vraja. You are welcome. I offer obeisance to you." Saying this, Yaśodā bowed down near her, and Paurṇamāsī, in response, embraced the mother of Mukunda.

6. After pleasing Yaśodā with blessings, she [Paurṇamāsī], anxious to see Govinda, inquired about the well-being of her husband, sons, and herds.

7. The queen of Vraja wished her well also and, full of longing, entered the bedroom of her son along with the excited lady.

8. Meanwhile Gobhaṭa, Bhadrasena, Subala, Śrīstokakṛṣṇa, Arjuna, Śrīdāma, Ujjvala, Dāma, Kiṅkiṇī, Sudāma, and the other friends of Kṛṣṇa came hurriedly from their homes and, joining joyfully with Baladeva in the courtyard, began to call, "Kṛṣṇa, get up! Come to your favorite cowpen."

9. Madhumaṅgala, too, exclaimed, "Hee, hee, why it's dawn! How can our buddy still be sleeping, friends? I shall wake him," and got up from his own bed.

10. Madhumaṅgala chattered, "Get up, friend, get up," and entered the bedroom of Hari, wobbling from his own drowsiness.

11. Though the Lord wanted to get up, and his sleep had been driven away by Madhumaṅgala's words, with his eyes rolling about, he was unable to rise for a moment.

12. In the midst of a room like an ocean of pure milk, on a bed shining with countless jewels, is it Hari's mother trying to awaken him or is it the Veda at the end of the universal dissolution?

13. His mother placed her left hand on the bed and, bending over slightly, placing her weight on it, touched Kṛṣṇa's body with her lotuslike right hand. Then, sprinkling his bed with tears of joy and a flow of milk from her breasts, she said, "Wake up, dear, get up quickly. Give up your sleepiness and show us your lotuslike face.

14. "Though the cows have been with their calves for a while now, without seeing you they will not give their milk. Even so, your father, afraid of disturbing the happiness of your sleep, has gone alone to the cowpen without calling you, dear."

15. She said, "Get up! Let me wash your face. Is this Balarāma's cloth here on your body?" She removed the blue cloth from his body and then said to the elder woman:

16. "Ooh, holy mother, look at my son's body, which is as soft as a lotus! It has been wounded by the sharp fingernails of his restless and over-excited

playmates in their wrestling matches and colored by minerals from the ground. I'm so distressed. What can I do?"

17. When he heard those words of his mother, which were heavy with affection, Murāri's eyes began to quiver because of his shame.

18. Then the brahman boy, Madhumaṅgala, who was skillful at causing laughter, suspecting Kṛṣṇa's discomfort, said to Kṛṣṇa's mother, whose heart was moved by affection:

19. "It's true, mother! Even though I forbade them, his friends [by double entendre: girlfriends] who are anxious for play [erotic sport], have constantly enjoyed [themselves] with this very greedy [lusty] boy in the forest bowers."

20. Then Kṛṣṇa, displaying his boyish charm, repeatedly opened his eyes with effort and, seeing his mother in front of him, closed them again with a smile on his lotuslike face.

21. Hearing the words of the queen of Vraja and seeing Kṛṣṇa's boyish behavior, which concealed a mood different from his mother's, Paurṇamāsī smilingly said to him:

22. "Since you are tired from endless, magnificent sports with your numerous friends [and girlfriends], it is fitting, my good boy, that you should be sleeping now. But the calves, even though they are thirsty, will not drink their milk without seeing you, lord of the clans of Vraja. Therefore, wake up!

23. "Get up, quickly, son of the lord of the cowherd settlement! See how your elder brother along with your friends, though wanting to go to the cowpen, is waiting for you in the courtyard with the calves."

24. Extending his hands tightened into fists and stretching out his body which was languid from rapture and as blue as a tamāla tree, he sat up, creating a web of flashes from his teeth as he yawned.

25. Seated on edge of the cot with his feet placed on the ground, he said, stammering with a coming yawn, "My venerable mother, obeisance to you."

26. Then his mother, who was overwhelmed with immense, mature affection for him, straightened out and tied into a topknot his soft, disheveled hair, more beautiful than a mass of black collyrium, in which the flowers had slipped down.

27. From a nearby golden pot his mother brought some water in her hands, gaily washed her son's face, in which his eyes still rolled with drowsiness, and dried it with the end of her cloth.

28. Then, holding Madhumaṅgala's hand in his right hand and his flute in the other, Kṛṣṇa, followed by his mother and the elderly woman, came out of his bedroom into the courtyard.

29. His wide-eyed friends, excited by love, surrounded him at once, some taking hold of his hands, others his clothes, and still others his arms.

30. His mother said to him: "Now, dear, go to the cowpen and after feeding the calves and milking the cows, come home quickly for breakfast."

31. Thus, being sent off by her, he started immediately, along with his friends, toward the shed of his cows. On the way the jocular brahman boy [Madhumaṅgala] said, gazing up at the sky.

32. "Look, my friend. Seeing the sun spreading the nets of his rays in the lake of the sky like a fisherman, the small, glittering fishlike stars, becoming frightened, have disappeared in all directions.

33. "And the deer-marked moon, seeing the sun, an eater of game with an enormous appetite, rising, has entered a cave in the mountain of the horizon to save its deer.

34. "Look there. It is as if the sky is a woman, shorn of her starry ornaments, whose fetus, the moon, having reached its full term, is dropping out and whose cries in labor are disguised as the hooting of pigeons in the dawn.

35. "Hey, look over there! This lotus flower seems to be smiling now, after seeing the ocean-born [moon], which, despite being its sibling, is unfriendly, moving out of the sky after being defeated by its friend, your visage, moon-faced one."

36. Thus, hearing the funny words of Madhumaṅgala, the boys of the herdsmen, themselves protected by the cowherd men, each entered his own barn, laughing.

37. Gopāla, too, with Balarāma and Madhumaṅgala, entered his barn like the moon entering the night sky along with Venus and Jupiter.

38. Balarāma, surrounded by the cows, appeared to the gods like the mythical elephant, Airāvata, surrounded by the massive boulders of Mount Kailāśa.

39. Acyuta, moving amidst the cows, which were scattered about with their faces turned up, appeared to the people like a bumblebee moving among a cluster of blooming lotuses.

40. "Hee hee, Gaṅgā, Godāvarī, Śavalī, Kālindī, Dhavalā! Hee hee, Dhūmrā, Tuṅgī, Bhramarī, Yamunā, Haṃsī, Kamalā! Hee hee, Rambhā, Campā, Kariṇī, Hariṇī!" The moon of Vraja [Kṛṣṇa] repeatedly called the cows by their names.

41. Squatting down and placing the milk pail between his knees, he milked some cows himself, others by means of his helpers, and yet others he let feed their calves, pleasing them with scratching. Thus, the son of Nanda enjoys giving pleasure to his cows in the morning.

Pātālakhaṇḍa of the Padma Purāṇa

CHAPTER 83. DESCRIPTION OF THE DAILY SPORT OF KṚṢṆA IN VṚNDĀVANA

Nārada said: "You have told me, guru, everything I wanted to know relating to the Lord. Now I want to hear about the unsurpassed path of contemplation." (1)

Śiva replied: "You question me well, O sage, desiring the best for the whole world. I will tell you about it even though it is a secret; therefore, listen [to what] I say. The servants, friends, parents, and lovers of Hari [Kṛṣṇa], all eternal and full of good qualities, live here [in Vṛndāvana], best of sages. Just as they are described in the Purāṇas in their revealed sport, so do they exist in the land of Vṛndāvana in their eternal sport. He comes and goes between forest and cowherder village eternally, and herds cows with his friends without the killing of demons. Also his lovers, thinking themselves his paramours, please their dearest in secret. (2–6)

"One should think of oneself there among them in the form of an enchanting woman, possessed of youth and beauty, just past puberty, conversant with the many arts and crafts suitable for Kṛṣṇa's enjoyment, but who, though requested by Kṛṣṇa, is opposed to enjoyment with him, a follower of Rādhā intent upon her service, loving Rādhā even more than Kṛṣṇa, bringing about, out of love and with great care, the meetings of those two each day, and overwhelmed with the joys of their service. Visualizing oneself in this way, one should perform service there beginning from the period of Brahmā [one-and-a-half hours before sunrise] until late at night." (7–11)

Nārada said: "I want to hear of Hari's daily sport as it really is. Without knowing that sport how, indeed, can Hari be served in one's mind?" (12)

Śiva said: "I do not know that sport of Hari as it really is, Nārada. Go from here to see Vṛndādevī; she will describe the sport to you. Not far from here, near Keśītīrtha, lives that servant of Govinda [Kṛṣṇa] surrounded by her friends." (13–14)

Sūta [the bard] said: "Being advised thus, Nārada circumambulated Śiva and, overjoyed, bowed repeatedly to him. Then that truest of sages went to Vṛndā's residence. Vṛndā too, seeing Nārada, bowed repeatedly and said: "Best of sages, how is it that you have come here?' " (15–16)

Nārada said: "I want to know from you of the daily deeds of Hari. Describe them for me from the beginning, if I am fit [to hear them], beautiful one!" (17)

Vṛndā said: "Even though it is secret I will tell you, Nārada, [for] you are a devotee of Kṛṣṇa. You, however, should not reveal it; this is the greatest of mystery of mysteries. (18)

"In the midst of beautiful Vṛndāvana, which is adorned with fifty bowers, in a bower of desire-trees, in a cottage of divine jewels they [the couple, Rādhā and Kṛṣṇa] are asleep on a bed, intensely embracing each other. Though they are awakened after a while by birds, who follow my orders, they feel such joy in their intense embrace and such distress at [the thought of] breaking it, that they do not want to get up from bed even a little. Then, being repeatedly awakened from all sides by groups of sārikās and parrots with various speeches, they rise from bed. Seeing the couple sitting up, their joyful girlfriends then enter and serve them as is suitable for that time. Once again, at the words of the sārikās, the couple get up from their bed and return to their homes, filled with fear and anxiety. (19–24)

"Being awakened at daybreak by his mother, Kṛṣṇa, along with [his brother] Baladeva, rises from bed and after brushing his teeth goes, with his mother's permission, to the cowshed surrounded by his friends. Rādhā, too, is awakened by her friends, O sage, and rises from her bed. After brushing her teeth, she rubs oil into her body. Then going to the bathing platform, she is bathed by her servants. She [next] goes to her dressing room where her friends decorate her with various shining ornaments, fragrances, garlands, and unguents. Then she, after carefully begging permission from her mother-in-law, is called, along with her friends, by Yaśodā [Kṛṣṇa's mother] to cook fine food [at Kṛṣṇa's house]." (25–29)

Nārada said: "Why does Yaśodā call the lady [Rādhā] to cook, when there are good ladies, headed by Rohiṇī, [at Kṛṣṇa's house] who are cooks?" (30)

Vṛdnā said: "Great sage, previously a boon was given to her by Durvāsas; so have I heard before from the mouth of Kātyāyanī. 'Whatever you cook, lady, shall be, by my grace, as sweet as nectar and shall increase the duration of life of its eater.' Thus the good lady Yaśodā, fond of her son, daily calls her [thinking], 'In this way may my son be long-lived through his desire for tasty foods.' Hearing that she [Rādhā] should go to the house of Nanda, and being permitted [to go], she too is pleased, and she goes there along with her friends, and cooks. (31–34)

"Kṛṣṇa also, having milked some cows and had others milked by his people, returns at the request of his father to his house, surrounded by friends. Having rubbed his body with oil, he is bathed happily by his servants. Wearing clean clothes, garlanded, his body anointed with sandalwood, appearing with his hair parted in two above his neck and forehead, beautified by the curls and a sandalwood mark on his forehead shaped like the moon, his arms and hands shining with bracelets, armlets, and jeweled rings, with a pearl necklace shining on his chest and alligator-shaped earrings, he, being repeatedly called by his mother, takes the hand of a friend and enters the dining room, following [his brother] Baladeva. He then, along with his brother and friends, enjoys different kinds of foods, making his friends laugh with a variety of jokes and laughing along with them. After eating and rinsing his mouth, he rests for a while on a shining cot, dividing up and chewing the betel nut given him by his servants. (35–41)

"Kṛṣṇa, dressed as a cowherder, with the herd before him, is followed down the path [to the pastures] affectionately by all the residents of Vraja. Bowing to his father and mother and with glances at [the rest of] the gathering, he turns them back as is proper, and heads toward the forest. After entering the forest, he plays with his friends for a while. He happily amuses himself with various games in that forest. Then, tricking all of them, he goes joyfully, accompanied by only two or three dear friends, to the tryst eager to meet his dear one. (42–45)

"She [Rādhā], too, after watching Kṛṣṇa go to the forest, returns home and out of a desire to be with her dear one, she, on the pretext of worshiping the sun, fools her elders and goes to the forest in order to gather flowers. Thus, the two with great effort meet in the forest and spend the day there happily in various games. Sometimes they are seated on a swing together and are pushed by their friends. Sometimes Hari [Kṛṣṇa], his flute having dropped from his hand and being hidden by his lover, is scolded by his "insulted" girlfriends as he searches for it. They keep him laughing with many jokes there. Sometimes happily entering a forested stretch that is blown by a spring breeze, they sprinkle each other with sandal and flowered waters, using sprinklers, and smear each other with ointments. The girlfriends, too, sprinkle them and are sprinkled in return by the couple throughout those groves filled with spring breezes. (46–52)

"O twice-born, sometimes the couple along with their friends become tired from the many games suited to those various moments and, finding the base of a tree, most true of sages, they sit on shining seats and drink honey wine. Then, becoming intoxicated by that honey wine, their eyes drooping with sleep, they take hold of each others' hands and fall to the arrows of desire. Desiring to make love they enter a bower along the path, their words and minds faltering, and they enjoy themselves there like leaders of elephants. The friends too, being intoxicated with honey, their eyes laden with sleep, all lie down in pretty bowers all around, and Kṛṣṇa too, the powerful, visits all of them simultaneously with separate bodies, being repeatedly urged on by his dearest. After giving them pleasure as the king of elephants does his female elephants, he goes with his dearest and them to a pond in order to play. The couple with their friends enjoy themselves splashing water on each other. They then are adorned with clothes, garlands, sandal paste, and shining ornaments right there on the shore of that pond in a shining, bejeweled house. (53–60)

"I arrange fruit and roots in advance, sage, and Hari eats first, served by his beloved. He then goes, accompanied by two or three ladies, to a bed made of flowers. Being served with betel nut, a yak-tail fan, foot massages, and so forth, he, smiling and thinking of his dear one, is pleased by them. Rādhikā, too, when Hari is asleep, though her very life is with him, eats his remnants, among her friends, her heart pleased. Then after eating a little, she goes to the bedroom to gaze on the lotuslike face of her lover like a cakora bird gazing on the moon, and the ladies there offer her his chewed betel. She eats the betel, dividing it among her friends. Kṛṣṇa, covered with a cloth, wanting to hear their uninhibited conversation with each other, though not asleep pretends to be and they, [learning the truth] somehow from inference, make faces, bite their tongues with their teeth, and look at each others' faces. As though dissolved in an ocean of embarrassment, they do not say anything for a while. Then after a moment they pull the cloth from his body and say, 'A fine sleep you've gone to,' making him laugh and laughing themselves. (61–69)

"Thus, the two, enjoying themselves with their friends with various humorous remarks, taste the happiness of sleep for a while, truest of sages. They then sit happily among their friends on a broad, shining seat and, wagering each other's garlands, kisses, embraces, and clothes, play dice with love amidst the banter of merriment. His dear one scolds him when, though beaten, he says, 'I have won,' and begins to take her garlands and things. And after being scolded, Kṛṣṇa with his hand on his lotus-face becomes despondent and makes up his mind to go, saying: 'If you have defeated me, lady, let what I wagered, kisses and so forth, be taken.' She does just that. [He behaves like that] to see the furrowing of her brow and to hear her scolding speech. (70–75)

"Then, hearing both the words and calls of the parrots and sārīs, they, desiring to return home, leave that place. Kṛṣṇa, taking leave of his lover, heads toward the cows, and she goes to the temple of the sun along with her circle of friends. Going off a little ways, Hari turns back and, putting on the disguise of a brahman, goes to the temple of the sun. There he is invited by the girlfriends and helps them worship the sun with fabricated Vedic hymns pregnant with humor. Then the clever girls, recognizing him as their lover, become absorbed in an ocean of joy and lose all track of self and other. In this way they spend two and a half periods [seven and a half hours], sage, and then they [the cowherder girls] go to their houses and Kṛṣṇa goes to the cows. (76–81)

"Kṛṣṇa joins with all his friends and, collecting together the cows from all over, returns to the village joyfully playing his flute, sage. Then Nanda and all the other cowherders, including the women and children, hearing the sound of Hari's flute and seeing the surface of the sky spread with a veil of cow dust, give up all their activities and go toward Kṛṣṇa, anxious to see him. On the main road, at the gate of the village, where all the residents of the village [wait], Kṛṣṇa too approaches them [and greets them] properly in succession: with looks, touches, words, smiling glances, [he greets] the cowherder elders; with verbal and physical obeisance and prostrations, [he greets] his parents and Rohinī, O Nārada; and with decorum through the indications of his side-long glances, [he greets] his beloved. Thus, after being suitably greeted by those residents of Vraja and after taking the cows into the cowshed, at the request of his parents, he goes home along with his brother. (82–89)

"After bathing and having something to eat and drink there, he, with the permission of his mother, goes again to the cowshed, desiring to milk the cows, and after milking some, having some milked, and having some watered, he who pursues hundreds of feelings returns home with his father. There along with his father, his uncles, their sons, and Balarāma, he eats varieties of foods, some chewed, some sucked, and so forth. Thinking of him, Rādhikā then, even before being asked, sends cooked foods to his house through her friends, and Hari, praising those dishes, enjoys them along with his father and the others. He then goes with them to the assembly hall, which is replete with bards and other performers. (90–93)

"The girlfriends who previously brought the food return with many of those dishes and some of Kṛṣṇa's leftovers, sent by Yaśodā. Bringing it with them, they offer all to Rādhikā and she, then having eaten along with her friends, in proper order, waits surrounded by them, ready to meet her lover. I then send some friend from here who guides her to a house made of shining jewels in this bower of desire-trees near the Yamunā. Dressed in attire suitable for either a light or dark night, she departs surrounded by friends. (94–99)

"After watching various wondrous performances there [in the assembly hall], listening to beautiful songs of Kātyāyanī, and then pleasing them [the performers] with [gifts of] money, grains, and other things according to custom, Kṛṣṇa, honored by the people there, returns home with his mother and friends. When after feeding him his mother leaves, he comes here unnoticed, to the house appointed by his lover. Joining each other, those two sport here among the forests. For two and a half periods of the night [seven and a half hours] they enjoy various amusements headed by the circle dance (*rāsa*), the dance of love, and much laughter. The sleepy lovers enter the bower unnoticed by the birds, and alone fall asleep on an enchanting love-bed made of flowers, being served there by their personal servants. Thus, the entire daily activity of Hari has been told to you. Even sinners are liberated by hearing this, Nārada." (100–105)

Nārada said: "Lady, there can be no doubt that I am fortunate to have been blessed by you, for, Hari's daily sport has been revealed to me now." (106)

Sūta said: "This said, after circumambulating her and being worshiped by her, Nārada, the best of sages, disappeared, brahman. I too, have made all this known in proper order. One should forever utter with care the unsurpassed pair of mantras.

"This was attained previously by Rudra from the lips of Kṛṣṇa. By him it was told to Nārada and Nārada told me. Now after performing purification I have told this to you. You, too, should keep this most amazing secret confidential." (107–110)

Śaunaka said: "I have achieved my goal by your direct grace, guru, since you have revealed the secret of secrets to me." (111)

Sūta said: "Devoting yourself to these truths and reciting the mantras day and night, no doubt you will attain to servitude of him without delay. I, too, brahman, go to the eternal abode of the Supreme in the company of the Guru of gurus, the daughter of Bhānu [Rādhā], and of the Lord of the cowherder girls.

"This most purifying account, great in might, was told by Maheśa [Śiva]. Those devoted human beings who hear it will go to the eternal realm of Acyuta. [This account] bestows fortune, fame, long life, health, desired objectives, success; causes the attainment of heaven and liberation, and destroys sin. Those human beings, intent on Viṣṇu, who read this regularly with devotion will not in any way return again from Viṣṇu's realm." (112–116)

So ends the glorification of Vṛndāvana, the eighty-third chapter in the *Pātālakhaṇḍa,* the fifth section of the great *Purāṇa,* the *Padma.*

—14—

Women's Songs for Auspicious Occasions

Lindsey Harlan

The following songs are sung by Rajasthani women at rātijagās (literally "night wakes"), which are held in conjunction with auspicious occasions such as births, weddings, and home consecrations. Women gather together with female relatives, friends, and perhaps servants to spend an entire night singing praises to their ancestors and to the various deities who protect their families. If women neglect to perform these wakes, ancestors and deities may retaliate by making mischief; they may cause sickness, poverty, and discord.

Included in this collection of songs are various ancestral songs that introduce the reader to well-known categories of ancestral spirits and fundamental Hindu conceptions of the afterlife, salvation, fertility, prosperity, and devotion. The first few songs are dedicated to satīs or satīmātās, women who immolated themselves on their husbands' funeral pyres and so became divinities. Following these are songs devoted to jhūṇjhārs, divine heroes who once died in battle. Like satīs, jhūṇjhārs are powerful protectors of descendants. The next two songs are dedicated to ancestors, (pūrbajs) particularly those who, like heroes, died suddenly or unexpectedly. The final song is about the rātijagā itself and is included here to provide ritual context.

Further Reading

See Stuart H. Blackburn, "Death and Deification: Folk Cults in Hinduism," *History of Religions* 24:3 (1985), 255–74; Peter J. Claus, "Medical Anthropology and the Ethnography of Spirit Possession," *Contributions to Asian Studies* 18 (1983), 60–72; Diane M. Coccari, "The Bir Babas of Banaras and the Deified Dead," in *Criminal Gods and Demon Devotees,* edited by Alf Hiltebeitel (Albany: State University of New York Press, 1989), pp. 259–69; Paul Courtright, *The Goddess and the Dreadful Practice* (New York: Oxford University Press, forthcoming); Ann Grodzins Gold, *Fruitful Journeys: The Ways of Rajasthani Pilgrims* (Berkeley and Los Angeles: University of California Press, 1988); Lindsey Harlan, *Religion and Rajput Women: The Ethic of Protection in Contemporary Narratives* (Berkeley and Los Angeles: University of California Press, 1991); and Sudhir Kakar, *Shamans, Mystics, and Doctors: A Psychological Inquiry into India and Its Healing Traditions* (Delhi: Oxford University Press, 1982).

Satī

The first song relates a conversation between a satī and her devar or husband's younger brother. In Indian folklore and popular imagination, the relationship between a wife and her devar is a close one; the rule of avoidance that applies to a woman's older male in-laws does not pertain to younger ones. Here the wife enlists her devar to help her get ready to follow her husband's body to the pyre so she can become a satī (literally, a "good woman"). She asks her devar to fetch or buy jewelry so she can proceed to the pyre adorned with all the marks of an auspiciously married woman—earrings, a nose ring, bangles, and so on. Devoid of these, she would appear as a widow, an inauspicious woman, and not a satī, a woman who retains her auspiciousness despite her husband's death.

The ornaments are listed in head-to-toe order, as is typical of devotional songs of this nature in Rajasthan and elsewhere in India. The sari for which she asks is saffron (*kesar*), the color associated with renunciation of desire and with sacrifice of life. The saffron sari is usually draped over a red skirt and blouse. Connoting auspiciousness, red is the color worn by brides. Together the saffron and red convey the auspiciousness of the satī's self-sacrifice.

The song employs a dialogue between two people, which is a common convention in rātijagā songs. The dialogue is punctuated with a refrain that continually reestablishes the presence of the singers. Their command, "cool the satī under a shady banyan tree" suggests that the satī becomes especially warm as she prepares to join her husband in the afterlife. A satī is believed to possess great stores of *sat,* a moral fuel that heats up at the time a woman decides to become a satī, and it can spontaneously ignite. The singers want the satī to be comforted, perhaps with sprinkles of water—the Rajasthani word they use, sīlāo, means both "cool" and "dampen." Banyan trees are often located near village wells or tanks. Here the water with which they cool the satī may be coming from such a source. Support for this reading comes from the variant "lead the satī to the shady banyan tree" and from the line in a jhūṇjhār song (below), which has a jhūṇjhār adorning himself by a tank under a banyan tree. In this context, the satī's cooling could be associated with the ritual bathing that a satī does before ascending a pyre. An alternate reading of the line has the singers asking that the satī's memorial stone be cooled or dampened, as the monuments marking a satī's presence are frequently located under such trees and near water. Memorial stones receive lustrations as part of ritual devotion. The problem with this reading is that it seems inconsistent with the "lead the satī" variant, unless the leading of the satī refers to establishing her presence in a memorial stone for the very first time. Native exegesis favors the first reading.

The second song is sung by someone, presumably a female relative or maidservant, who is helping a satī dress for the procession to the pyre. Here the satī is not instructing but being instructed; she is encouraged to hurry as her husband's body and entourage are waiting for her. Her husband rests under a balcony, an oriel of sorts, adorned with a screen of tiny windows through which women, who keep seclusion (*parda*), can observe the outside world without being observed. The satī's companion looks out through a screen to the screened oriel she is describing. The architectural references suggest that the scene is an estate or palace. The husband who awaits her is a young man, which makes the satī an especially poignant paradigm of self-sacrifice. This song employs the head-to-toe convention found in the first one. In such songs many different ornaments could be listed by the singers. Any list of this sort reflects caste or family convention, the taste of the singers, and the amount of time singers feel motivated to devote to detail.

The final song portrays a visit by a woman who has already died a satī to a household she protects by exercising her supernatural powers. The satī's footprints are of two colors, saffron (from saffron itself and from turmeric) and red (from kaṅkū—turmeric and lime—and meṇhdi-myrtle stain), which again connote sacrifice and auspiciousness. The head-to-toe description includes jingling anklets, which indicate the satī's motion as she moves through the household. The description not only conveys an image of what a satī looks like, but also constitutes a list of decorations with which devotees would typically adorn a satī stone. It is thus a useful detailing of both iconography and ritual veneration. The song concludes with a petition for the satī's presence during this degenerate age, the Kaliyuga or "dark age" of humanity, a time in which it is particularly difficult for human beings to live according to dharma or righteousness.

Satī—1

"Buy me a forehead ornament—do it quickly little brother-in-law.
I will follow my husband (as a satī).
Dear younger brother-in-law—yes, O dear little brother-in-law."
Cool the satī under a shady banyan tree.

"Bring me earrings—do it quickly, little brother-in-law.
Buy my earrings—do it quickly, little brother-in-law.
I will follow my husband. O dear little brother-in-law—yes, O dear little brother-in-law."
Cool the satī under the shady banyan tree.

"Bring me a nose ring—do it quickly, little brother-in-law.
I will follow my husband.

O dear little brother-in-law—yes, dear little brother-in-law."
Lead the satī to the shady banyan tree.

"Buy a necklace—do it quickly, little brother-in-law.
I will follow my husband.
Dear little brother-in-law—yes, O dear little brother-in-law."
Cool the satī under the shady banyan tree.

"Buy me bangles—do it quickly, little brother-in-law.
Buy me bangles—do it quickly, little brother-in-law.
I will follow my husband.
Dear little brother-in-law—yes, O dear little brother-in-law."
Cool the satī under the shady banyan tree.

"Buy a saffron-colored sari—do it quickly, little brother-in-law.
Buy a blouse piece quickly, little brother-in-law.
I will follow my husband.
Dear little brother-in-law—yes, O dear little brother-in-law."
Cool the satī under the shady banyan tree.

"Buy toe rings—do it quickly, little brother-in-law.
Buy ankle bracelets—do it quickly, little brother-in-law.
Dear little brother-in-law—yes, O dear little brother-in-law."
Cool the satī under the shady banyan tree.

Satī—2

Satīmātā, take a forehead ornament and wear it.
O take a forehead ornament and wear it.
Why the delay for the forehead ornament [hurry up!], Satīmātā?
Your husband's litter is waiting under the balcony.
Your young man's litter is waiting under the balcony.
Waiting under the balcony, waiting under the balcony windows.

O Satīmātā, take your earrings and wear them.
O Satīmātā, take your earrings and wear them.
Why the delay for the earrings, Satīmātā?
Your husband's litter. . . .

O Satīmātā, take your nose ring and wear it.
O Satīmātā, take your nose ring and wear it.
Why the delay for the nose ring, Satīmātā?
Your husband's litter. . . .

The song continues with other auspicious signs of a married woman—a forehead dot, necklace, bangles, saffron sari, and toe rings.

Satī—3

Why are there saffron footprints in my courtyard?
Why are there turmeric footprints in my courtyard?
Why are there kaṅkū footprints in my courtyard?
Why are there meṇhdi footprints in my courtyard?
Come sit on this throne, Mother.
Sit on this platform (*bājoṭ*).
With your loose hair, O Mother,
On your forehead a line of saffron,
On your eyes a line of lamp black,
Your teeth are decorated with gold.
Your lips are reddened with pān [betel].
On your hands meṇhdi.
On your feet, pungent perfume.
You are covered with a deep red sari,
and the bells on your ankle bracelets are jingling.
In this degenerate age [Kaliyuga], O Satīmātā, come and be my guest!

Jhūṇjhār

There are many different kinds of heroes venerated in Rajasthan. All have in common the fact that they died in combat. The most championed hero is the jhūṇjhār, who continues to fight even after his head has been severed. The word derives from the verb to fight (jhūṇjhno or jūṇjhno), but the nominal form indicates a person who struggles on in battle to avenge his own death. Whereas the term satī has no good English equivalent ("good woman" is misleadingly broad) the term jhūṇjhār can be loosely glossed as "struggler," as this captures the spirit of the warrior's miraculous efforts to recover his dignity and spill enemy blood.

The first song invites the struggler to accept pān, a concoction of spices and tobacco wrapped in betel leaf. Jhūṇjhārs are fond of the same treats and vices they enjoyed while living, and this particular jhūṇjhār has retained a liking for pān. The singers inform him of the devotion to him shared by all the members of their royal family. They also seek blessings from him: they want indestructible wedding saris and bangles, that is, longevity for their husbands; they want marriage and longevity for male offspring; and they want long-lasting eyes and knees for themselves as they approach old age. Having died violent deaths and struggled on despite their deaths, the jhūṇjhārs have great powers over life—the power to extend life and the power to produce it by granting children.

At one point the singers point out that the jhūṇjhār died alone while fighting in a forest. Many jhūṇjhārs die while attempting to retrieve cows single-handedly from a band of cattle thieves. Dying alone, they have no one to perform proper cremation rites, but these are unnecessary because the hero's death has assured him a place in warrior heaven or vīrgati (literally, "goal of heroes"—the destiny of Hindu warriors since Vedic times). Ascent to warrior heaven is a permanent achievement; it brings liberation from karmic reincarnation.

The jhūṇjhār is called by the epithet "saffron" or "kesariyā," a designation used to refer to all heroes and, by extension, to all husbands, who are heroes to their wives. I have glossed the epithet as "saffron-donning" because jhūṇjhārs and other heroes wear turbans or clothing of this sacrificial hue as they give up their lives in battle. The hero here is also characterized as "merry" (*rangraliyā*) and "ruddy" (*rangbhariyā*), both terms indicating that he is excited and flush with red color due to intoxicants taken before battle, to the intoxication of battle itself, or probably both. The saffron and red colors convey the same connotations as they do in the satī songs.

The second song is a dialogue between a woman and a jhūṇjhār, which is interrupted by the singers' refrain. It begins with the struggler bathing and adorning himself with appropriate oils, clothing, ornaments, and so on (doing his sṛngār), then going to his fields, where he enjoys a cucumber, a favorite cool snack during the heat of the Indian summer. Throwing seeds into planting rows, he becomes responsible for the future fertility of the fields. From the fields he goes to his house, where he passes through the major rooms as he visits his wife and children.

Like many rātijagā songs, this song reads both as a scenario leading to death—Lord Rāma's (God's) invitation is an invitation to die—and as depiction of a visit after death, one like that described in the last satī song. According to the first reading, the hero tours his property and says a final good-bye to his family before facing death. His actions are described through his conversation with the unidentified woman. The dialogue exemplifies a motif common to many jhūṇjhār stories: the hero encounters a woman either on his way to battle, in which case the woman (generally a female relative) tries to stop him, or after his head has been severed but his body has not fallen, in which case the woman (usually a stranger) serves as a witness to the miracle of his headless struggle. According to the second reading, the heroic spirit blesses his house with his presence and is observed by a woman who converses with him. In this case the jhūṇjhār does his toiletry by the tank under a banyan tree where his memorial stone is established. That this reading is also intended is suggested by the verse describing the struggler as having played (*khelgyo*) in the field. The word "playing" is often used to depict visits by spirits, who enjoy themselves as they visit their properties and families.

The final verse expresses the widely cherished belief that no true warrior can turn his back on his duty to fight. To shrink from a challenge would reflect badly on all relatives with whom the warrior shares blood (*kul* members). It would especially shame his mother, as mother's milk is thought to endow sons with strength and courage.

The final song gives a head-to-toe depiction of a jhūṇjhār. It works as a description of the struggler going into battle, a depiction of the spirit appearing in a vision, and as an enumeration of iconographic detail on a memorial stone. The vast majority of strugglers are depicted both in song and in stone as equestrians. Of particular note is the "lovely watch" the struggler wears over his traditional warrior-bracelet. This anachronism reflects the rage for fashionable watches that has swept India, among other countries, in recent years, and illustrates the way rātijagā songs are evolving to accommodate contemporary taste.

Jhūṇjhār—1

My merry struggler—take pān.
My saffron-donning struggler—take pān.
The king worships you—take pān.
Lord, my sons' wives and grandson's wives grasp your feet—take pān.
My ruddy struggler—take pān.
The king's son worships you—take pān.
Lord, make our bangles and red saris indestructible.
My saffron-donning struggler—take pān.
My ruddy struggler—take pān.
Lord, in the forest you fought alone—take pān.
Lord, the king worships you—take pān.
Lord, to the brothers give long life.
Lord, make our bangles and saris indestructible—take pān.
My saffron-donning struggler—take pān.
The grandsons worship you—take pān.
Lord, give the children and adolescents long life—take pān.
Lord, make sure they get married—take pān.
Lord, we singers grasp your feet—take pān.
Lord, give all sons and grandsons long life—take pān.
Lord, make our eyes and knees long-lasting—take pān.

Jhūṇjhār—2

"O struggler, you bathed and washed your dhoti.
O struggler, you bathed and washed it and adorned yourself."
Lord Rāma's invitation came to you.

"O lovely lady, I washed my dhoti at the tank.
Lovely lady, under the banyan tree, I adorned myself."
Lord Rāma's invitation came to you.

"O struggler, you ate a cucumber in the field and dropped its seeds in the planting row.
O struggler, you dropped seeds in the planting rows."
Lord Rāma's invitation came to you.

"Lovely lady, I ate the cucumber at the row.
Lovely lady, I threw the seeds on the ground."
Lord Rāma's invitation came to you.

"O struggler, you left the row and went to your chambers.
O struggler, you left the row for your parlor."
Lord Rāma's invitation came to you.

"Lovely lady, laughing I went to the chambers.
Lovely lady, smiling I went to the parlor."
Lord Rāma's invitation came to you.

"O struggler, you left the planting row, having played there.
O struggler, you left the planting row to see your wife."
Lord Rāma's invitation came to you.

"Lovely lady, laughing and laughing I left my playing children.
Lovely lady, smiling I left my wife."
Lord Rāma's invitation came to you.

"Lovely lady, if one turns back, the family (*kul*) is shamed.
Lovely lady, one shames his mother's breast."
Lord Rāma's invitation came to you.

Jhūṇjhār—3

Struggler, you wear a very fine turban.
On the turban a lovely ornament is attached.

You wear a very fine pearl ornament.
Over the pearl lovely clusters of glass pendants are attached.

You wear a very fine necklace.
Struggler, over the necklace a fine neck ornament is attached.

Struggler, you wear a very fine bracelet
Over the bracelet a lovely watch is attached.

Struggler, you sit on a very fine horse
Struggler, on the horse is seated a very fine rider [that is, you].

Struggler, you wear fine shoes,
And your feet are stained with myrtle.

Pūrbaj

The next two songs are dedicated to pūrbajs, ancestors who did not die in battle. Although all ancestors are regularly venerated by descendants, certain ones receive special attention because they refuse to leave their families and become reincarnated. The vast majority of these are male. In general, they are ancestors who died unexpectedly, and usually violently. They are apt to possess family members and indicate how they want to be worshiped. If properly venerated, these special ancestors bless their descendants. Like their heroic relatives, they have the power to grant offspring and to promote prosperity. In fact, such ancestors are often implicitly compared to heroes. The iconography of hero stones and ancestor stones is often identical. Moreover, hero songs and ancestor songs are often very similar; sometimes they are identical except for the fact that words "hero" and "ancestor" are substituted for one another. The implicit comparison flatters the ancestors.

The first song, which is an extremely popular one, repeatedly states that an ancestor was welcomed wherever he visited family members, and that he therefore blessed them with children and wealth. A single exception to this pattern provides a brief comic interlude. When the pūrbaj visits the narrator's infant son, the frightened little one begins to cry, an understandable and endearing response to seeing a disembodied spirit. The narrator then asks the ancestor if he had unfulfilled desires or if he died alone in the forest. In the first question she asks whether he is particularly disenchanted with his premature demise, and in the second whether he died alone (and therefore failed to have the funeral rites that would have allowed reincarnation). The answer to both questions is negative. Although the ancestor has died in such a way that he has been motivated to stay with his family, he is not especially ill-natured or jealous. When he is properly welcomed as a family member, he brings good fortune.

The second ancestor song is set on the banks of Lake Pichola, which is located in the heart of Udaipur, a major city in Rajasthan. Some ancestors are invited to partake of a feast prepared for them and for all the members of their spiritual lineage (*gotra,* an exogamous kinship unit) by auspicious married women. The ancestors are initially designated by the term *pūrbaj*. As the song progresses, they are referred to as *pitṛ,* which means "father" and by extension "forefather," and also as *putra* and *kanvar,* both meaning "son." Addressing the ancestors as sons both identifies them as sons of the lineage (*gotra*) and expresses a certain feeling (*bhāva*) of devotion. The women who serve the ancestors treat them with the same tender affection they give their own children.

Pūrbaj—1

My ancestor came to the gullies near my house.
I spread flowers—campā flower buds.
My ancestor was welcomed.

My ancestor came to my cow pen.
The cows gave birth to a white bullock and a she-calf.
My ancestor was welcomed

My ancestor came to my buffalo pen.
One of the buffaloes gave birth to a brown she-calf.
My ancestor was welcomed.

My ancestor came to my horse stable
One of the horses gave birth to a sweet little colt.
My ancestor was welcomed.

My ancestor came to my elephant stable
The elephant gave birth to a virile (*mast*) calf.
My ancestor was welcomed.

My ancestor came to my daughters' houses.
A daughter gave birth to a dutiful [dharmic] grandson.
My ancestor was welcomed.

My ancestor came to my daughter-in-laws' quarters.
A daughter-in-law gave birth to a beloved grandson.
My ancestor was welcomed.

My ancestor came to my home's storage room.
He brought crops, wealth, and good fortune [Lakṣmī].
My ancestor was welcomed.

My ancestor came to my stove and water-storage area.
The boiled milk overflowed [there was so much of it].
My ancestor was welcomed.

My ancestor came to my son's cradle.
My son was playing and he started to cry.
My ancestor was welcomed.

"My ancestor, do you have unfulfilled desires?
Or did you fight alone in the forest?"
My ancestor was welcomed.

"My sisters, I did not fight in the forest.
And I am not one with unfulfilled desires."
The ancestor was welcomed.

Pūrbaj—2

Under a mango branch, beside Lake Pichola,
My ancestors enjoy themselves.
Come for your night wake.
For your night wake we feed our lineage (gotra) members cold and warm [food].

Relatives come and wait for you.
Come, sons, for your night wake.

Under a mango branch, beside Lake Pichola,
My ancestors enjoy themselves.
Come, sons, for your night wake.
For your night wake we feed our lineage members cool and warm [food].
Married women come and wait on you.
Come, sons, for your night wake.

Under a mango branch, beside Lake Pichola,
The satīmātās enjoy themselves.

The song continues as above, according to the needs of the singers. Although this song is sung as a pūrbaj song, it also invokes other ancestral spirits and deities according to the design and needs of the singers. As one singer remarked, "this song is long and wide."

Rātijagā

The final song reveals the ritual context in which the preceding songs are sung. The singers sing about the wake they are undertaking. Throughout the night they light tiny clay lamps to welcome their supernatural guests. While the men of the household sleep, their wives and daughters stay awake to welcome all the supernatural beings who protect the household. As the women light the lamps, they name all the female relatives participating in the rātijagā and all the men who have extended their household and lineage through marriage. Through all four watches of the night, the women make sure that the lamps are lit, that their companions' attention is unflagging, and that all supernatural guests are treated hospitably.

Rātijagā

Who put the wick in the lamp?
Whose wife filled it with clarified butter (*ghi*)?
Light the lamp for the four watches of the night.

Bagvat Kumvar put the wick in the lamp.
Mahavir Singh's wife filled it with ghi.
Light the lamp for the four watches of the night.

Vishnu Kumvar put the wick in the lamp.
Bhanu Singh's wife filled it with ghi.
Light the lamp for the four watches of the night.

Nand Kumvar put the wick in the lamp.
Virendra Singh's wife filled it with clarified butter.
Light the lamp for the four watches of the night.

(The song continues to include all the female relatives participating in the rātijagā.)

—15—

The Ocean of Mercury: An Eleventh-Century Alchemical Text

David Gordon White

Alchemy, the "way of mercury" (*rasāyana*), was essentially a Hindu enterprise in India; there are no extant Buddhist texts devoted to the subject. Within the Hindu sphere, the roughly eleventh-century *Rasārṇava* or "Ocean of Mercury" is the most important textual source for what is known as tantric alchemy. In contrast to earlier (third to tenth centuries C.E.) "gold-making" alchemy and later (fourteenth to twentieth centuries) therapeutic uses of mercurial and mineral medicines, tantric alchemy, which saw its heyday in the tenth to thirteenth centuries, was most concerned with the alchemical production of an elixir of immortal life with which to realize the supreme goals of bodily immortality (*jīvanmukti*), supernatural powers (*siddhi*) and a state of being identical to that of the supreme god Śiva.

Tantric alchemy is so called because these goals were identical with those of the broad-based medieval Indian body of religious practice and doctrine known as tantra. What made tantric alchemy unique was its emphasis on the use of mineral, mainly mercurial, preparations (but also botanicals, as well as a number of animal substances) as the means toward its tantric end. The theory behind this practice was the identification alchemists made between mercury (*rasa*), the fluid metal, and the semen (also called *rasa*) of Śiva, the great Hindu god whose millenarian icon has been a phallus (*liṅga*). Mercury was, for them, the seminal essence of a god who (pro-)creates the universe sexually; indeed, the origin myth of mercury tells us that quicksilver first arose when Śiva spilled his seed at the end of a long bout of lovemaking with his consort, the goddess Pārvatī. This seed, once spilled, became polluted through its contact with the earth. The alchemist's craft therefore consists of returning mercury, through a series of chemical reactions of incredible complexity, to its original pristine state. Once he has perfected it in the laboratory, the alchemist may then ingest this mercury, which then transforms him into an immortal superman, a "second Śiva."

Tantric alchemy was tantric in more than its goals: in addition to their emphasis on manipulating mercury and other mineral substances, its principal texts also prescribed the use of geometric diagrams (*yantras*), powerful formulas (*mantras*), and forms of worship (*pūjā*) proper to the broader tantric tradition. It was also tantric in its worldview, which held that the manifest universe (identified with the Goddess under one of her many names) was the self-realization of an absolute, unmanifest source (often identified with the god Śiva), the dynamics of this process of self-realization often being portrayed as the sexual union of the two divinities. Tantric alchemy also considered itself Hindu, and as such located itself within the broader Hindu tradition. It is in this context that chapter one of the *Rasārṇava,* translated here, must be read: it is an attempt to situate the way of mercury or the mercurial science (*rasavidyā*) within the broader contexts of tantric and Hindu doctrine and practice. What makes the *Rasārṇava* special in the annals of tantric literature (apart from its subject matter) is its anonymous author's rhetorical flair, which makes for livelier reading than the usual tantric fare.

The *Rasārṇava* is, like most "revealed" tantric texts (called tantras), cast in the form of a dialogue in which the Goddess (here called by the names Pārvatī, Devī or Bhairavī) asks the questions and Śiva (also called Bhairava here) answers them. Verses 1–6 set the scene and introduce one of the main themes of the chapter, the gaining of bodily liberation through alchemical practice. Bhairava begins his answer by stressing the concrete nature of the alchemical path: in contradistinction to the teachings of more conventional Hinduism (the six schools of Indian philosophy), which maintain that liberation occurs after the shedding of one's mortal body, here it is this body of flesh and blood that is transformed and rendered immortal (verses 8–9, 12–17).

The author reserves his greatest scorn and rhetorical ammunition for the practices of other tantric sects which, he clearly feels, are on the wrong track. These he condemns for their antinomian practices, which he groups under the common heading of the five makāras, the "Five Ms": the consumption of flesh (*māṁsa*), fish (*matsya*), alcohol (*madhu*), and parched grain (*mudrā*), and the practice of sexual intercourse (*maithuna*) as means to realizing tantric goals (verses 10–11, 24, 29–30). He does, however, seek to defend himself vis-à-vis the tantric sects in an obscure verse (verse 27), in which he maintains that the Alchemical school or order (*sampradāya*) is a "womb," because mercury is a "womb." Here, he is referring to the tantric notion that each sectarian order was a household (which was part of a broader clan, that is, the confederation of tantric sects) into which one is born as a son or daughter of the Goddess, upon initiation. The biological nature of the tantric lineage is emphasized in the old tantric initiation rituals, in which the initiate ingests "lineage-nectar"—in the form of sexual fluids—which originally arises from the Goddess's own womb. It is in this context that the *Rasārṇava* states that mercury itself is the Alchemical school's "womb."

In verse 26, the author appears to contradict himself regarding his anti-makāra position of prior verses, when Bhairava praises the eating of "cow meat" and the drinking of "liquor." This, however, is a mystic reference to a technique, known as *khecarī mudrā* ("the seal of moving in the ether"), which was a commonplace of the body of breathing techniques, bodily postures, and so on, grouped under the heading of haṭha yoga, the "yoga of violent exertion." The internal practice of haṭha yoga was in fact the necessary complement to alchemical practice: without a body "primed" by yoga, the high-energy mercury ingested by the alchemist would destroy him. Moreover, perfected mercury served as a catalyst for the internal transformation of the gross mortal body into a perfected and immortal one (verses 18–22). Alchemical and yogic works alone were not sufficient, however; without the grace and teachings of a spiritual preceptor (*guru*), the alchemist would fail in his quest for power, pleasure, and immortality (verses 54–57).

Much of this chapter is devoted to the greatness of mercury itself. It is the seed of Śiva (verse 36), or the product of the sexual union of Śiva and the Goddess (verse 34), whose own sexual emission takes the form of mica (mentioned in verse 44) in the mineral world: the goddess also can take the mineral forms of red arsenic or sulphur, both identified with her uterine blood. Itself possessed of wonderful powers, mercury affords the same powers to alchemists who eat it (verses 22, 27–28, 31, 53, 57). Because it gives (*da*) the highest end (*pāra*), it is called *pārada* (*pārada* is a synonym for *rasa,* mercury: verse 35).

Beyond being identified with Śiva's semen, mercury is identified with Śiva's phallic emblem, the liṅga from which it arose in the beginning. Therefore, the construction and worship of mercurial phalluses (*rasaliṅgas*) are central to alchemical practice, just as liṅga-worship is central to devotional cults of Śiva, for which such liṅgas as Kedārnāth in the Himalayas are important pilgrimage sites (verses 37–43). Abuse of or lack of faith in mercury is, in this context, a sacrilege, the punishments for which are detailed in verses 45 and 47 through 52. The chapter ends (verse 59) with a reference to a ritual form of tantric worship called *nyāsa,* in which mantras of the god and goddess of alchemy are superimposed upon one's own body, as a preparation for self-divinization. The final verse (verse 60) opens the way to the remaining seventeen chapters of the *Rasārṇava,* devoted in the main to alchemical "recipes" and descriptions of the wondrous powers to be gained through the use of perfected mercury.

Chapter 1 of the *Rasārṇava* is found in *Rasārṇava Nāma Rasatantra,* 2d ed., edited with a Hindi commentary by Indradeo Tripathi, Haridas Sanskrit Granthamala, no. 88 (Benares: Chaukhamba Sanskrit Series Office, 1978), pp. 1–14.

The Ocean of Mercury: Chapter One

1. He in whom everything is, from whom everything will be, who is everything and everywhere, who is all-encompassing and eternal, salutations to that universal soul!

2–3. While on Kailāsa's delightful peak, a peak adorned with a multitude of jewels and strewn with myriad trunks and vines, the goddess Pārvatī, bowing her head before the blue-throated, three-eyed God of gods who was comfortably seated there, asked with circumspection:

4. "O God among gods, O great God, O incinerator of Time and Love, O preceptor of the Kaula, Mahākaula, Siddhakaula, etc. lineages!

5–6. "By your grace, all of revelation has been made known to the world in its entirety. If I am worthy of your favor, if I am your beloved, then tell me this: there are things that have been told in all of the tantras; yet there are things that have not been brought to light. O Lord! What is this liberation in the body? You alone are capable of describing that."

7. "Well said, well spoken, O fortunate Goddess! Well spoken, O Daughter of the Mountain! The question you have asked is a matter that concerns the welfare of our devotees.

8–9. "Eternal youth, immortality of the body, and the attainment of an identity of nature with Śiva—that is, liberation in the body (*jīvanmukti*)—is difficult even for the gods to attain. The liberation that occurs when one drops dead, that liberation is worthless. For in that case, a donkey would also be liberated when he dropped dead.

10. "If liberation is to be identified with the excitation of the female genitilia, whom could donkeys not liberate? Indeed, what ram or bull would not be liberating?

11–13. "Therefore, one should safeguard one's body with mercury and mercurial elixirs. If liberation came from utilizing one's semen, urine, and excrements, which of the races of dogs and swine would not be liberated? Liberation is indeed viewed in the six schools as occurring when one drops dead, but that kind of liberation is not directly perceivable, in the manner of a myrobalan fruit in the hand. Ineffable reality, even that shall I tell you, O Goddess!

14–17. "In no wise can he who is merely without sin or who offers mantras maintain his body. If the maintenance of the body is difficult even for the gods, O great Goddess, then how much more difficult it must be for men living on the face of this earth! When righteousness is destroyed, how can there be righteousness? When righteousness is destroyed, how can there be practice? When practice is destroyed, how can there be yoga? When yoga is destroyed, how can there be a way to liberation? When the way is destroyed, how can there be liberation? When liberation is destroyed, there is nothing at all. Therefore, O fortunate Goddess, the body is to be vigorously preserved.

18. "The maintenance of the body is realized through the practice of yoga. Mercury and breath control are known as the twofold practice of yoga.

19. "When swooning, mercury, like the breath, carries off disease; when killed, it raises from the dead; when bound, it affords the power of flight.

20–22. "Liberation arises from insight, insight arises from the maintenance of the vital breaths. Therefore, where there is stability, mercury is powerful and the body is stable. Through the use of mercury one quickly obtains a body that is unaging and immortal, with a mind absorbed in meditation. He who eats calcinated mercury truly obtains insight as well as worldly knowledge, and his mantras succeed.

23. "So long as the Goddess does not descend, and so long as one's fetters to this world remain uncut, there is no way that true discrimination can arise in the use of calcinated mercury.

24. "For those people who have lost their powers of reason through indulgence in liquor, flesh, sexual intercourse, and the male and female organs, the mercurial science is exceedingly difficult to realize.

25. "He who is without instruction in the alchemical tradition and who does not strive after the true religion, for him the mercurial science does not succeed. He drinks the water of mirages.

26. "He who eats cow meat and drinks the liquor of immortality, I consider to be one of the lineage and a connoisseur in the science of mercury. Other experts in the science of mercury are inferior.

27. "To those who say that this [alchemical] order (*sampradāya*) is not a 'womb': it is maintained that mercury is a 'womb.' It is by means of it that the siddhi is obtained. No siddhi without mercury.

28. "Until such time as one eats Śiva's seed—that is, mercury, rasa—where shall he seek his liberation, where shall he seek the maintenance of his body?

29–30. "There are those ignorant ones who, wholly besotted with liquor and flesh and deluded by Śiva's illusion, prattle that 'we are liberated, we have gone to the world of Śiva.' Then there are those dim-witted ones who are dissatisfied with the yogic preservation of the body. The universe, O Goddess, is enamoured with partial knowledge!

31. "Let him who has realized the power of flight and Śiva-hood in his own body, and who has knowledge of mercury always practice the mercurial science, my darling."

32. The Goddess said: "I wish to hear of the worldly descent and greatness of mercury, O Lord of the gods! You can tell me that in its essentials."

33. Lord Bhairava said: "Well asked, O fortunate Goddess! That which you contemplate is highly esoteric, a matter for the support and welfare of the worlds.

34. "You, O Goddess, are the mother of all beings and I am their eternal father. That which was generated from our great sexual union, that is rasa.

35. "Because it arose of its own volition, that great one [mercury] is praised as pārada, and because the greatest of practitioners use it to the highest ends it is also called pārada.

36. Mercury is identical to me, O Goddess. It arises from my each and every limb. It is my own vital fluid. It is for this reason that it is called *rasa.*

37–42. "From viewing, touching, eating, indeed merely recalling, worshiping, and offering mercury, six types of fruits are realized. The merit one gains from viewing all of the liṅgas in the world—of Kedārnāth, and so on—as well as all others that may exist is gained from the mere viewing of mercury. By worshiping Śiva in the form of calcinated mercury, with sandal, camphor, and saffron, one attains the world of Śiva. Eating mercury destroys the triad of sins (in word, deed, and thought), afflictions, and morbid states. The highest station, difficult even for fully realized brahmans to reach, is attained. By recalling mercury in the center of the lotus in the space within one's heart, O Goddess, one is immediately freed from the sins accumulated in past lives.

43. "The combined fruits that one might gain from worshiping one thousand of Śiva's self-generated (*svayambhū*) liṅgas, are reaped a hundred thousandfold by worshiping Śiva's mercurial liṅga.

44. "The 'doctrine of mica' is the lowest alchemical doctrine; the 'doctrine of mineral salt' is a middling doctrine; the 'doctrine of mantra' is highest; and the 'doctrine of mercury' is the very highest.

45. They who, possessed of a consummate knowledge of mantra and tantra, put mercury to an evil use, annihilate their accumulated good acts, and go to hell.

46. The mercurial science is a transcendent form of knowledge, difficult to gain in the three worlds. It affords worldly enjoyment and liberation. For this reason, it should be promulgated by persons eminent in the field.

47–48. "Some say 'it exists'; some say 'it does not exist.' He who believes it exists gains siddhis and realizes his goals on this earth. Those who, out of unbelief, say, 'it is not, it does not exist,' their goals are not realized, my darling, even in a billion rebirths.

49–52. "The sinner who, considering himself to be liberated through his knowledge of the absolute, disparages mercury, loses my protection even for a billion rebirths. He is born as a dog, O Goddess, for as many as a thousand births; by offending mercury, he is born as a cat for 30 million births, a donkey for a hundred thousand births, a crow for a hundred thousand births, a worm for a hundred thousand births, a wild cock for a hundred thousand births, and a vulture for a hundred thousand births. He who talks to or has bodily contact with those who are revilers of mercury, he too becomes afflicted with sorrows for as many as a thousand rebirths.

53. "Mercury is, in its fluidity, potency, and fullness of development, the equivalent of ambrosia (*amṛta*). By virtue of this, mercury carries off death and rebirth, disease and injury.

54. "First, one should, with a purified inner soul, propitiate one's guru. Once the guru is satisfied, the rays of light emanating from his teachings bestow upon one the secret doctrine.

55. "The slow-minded person who performs alchemical practice without taking a guru meets with no success. His acts are like the money one makes in dreams.

56. "He who performs acts that have been taught by the guru meets with success at every step. Therefore, my dear, one should put into practice the alchemical doctrine imparted by a satisfied guru.

57–58. "This teaching that is a path to realization affords both enjoyment and liberation. This great tantra called the *Ocean of Mercury,* exceedingly difficult of access and esoteric, may be accessed, for the realization of alchemical goals, through the grace of the guru. Once one has gained access to the alchemical practice, one should not then become egotistical.

59. "Then, having received the mantra called the 'elephant goad of mercury,' one should, with the guru's permission, superimpose the goddess Bhairavī upon one's own body, and carry out the worship of the mercurial Bhairava.

60. "O Goddess! The origin and greatness of mercury has now been told. What other matters you would like to hear me tell about?"

—16—

Predicting the Future with Dogs

David Gordon White

The fourteenth-century *Śārṅgadhara Paddhati* ("Śārṅgadhara's Guidebook") is one of a number of encyclopedic anthologies of medieval India written by brahman ministers for the edification of their royal patrons. Drawing material from a wide array of treatises on every imaginable subject, compendia of this sort were intended to provide the king with all he needed to know to insure the well-being not only of his kingdom but also of his own royal person. So it is that the *Śārṅgadhara Paddhati* (1363 C.E.) follows the lead of countless earlier encyclopedias by providing a great wealth of practical information on the nature and worship of the major Hindu gods, human virtues and vices, metaphysics, ornithology, botany, theories of kingship and royal polity, the raising and training of war horses and elephants, military strategy, human physiology, medicine, yoga, and so on, and so forth.

About halfway through this rambling work, wedged between discussions of tree medicine and veterinary medicine, chapter 83, 494 verses in length, is devoted to the "science of omens." The Sanskrit term for this science is *śakuna,* a term which also means "vulture" or "kite." On the basis of terminology alone, one might deduce from this that the Indian science of omens, not unlike that of the augurers of ancient Rome, was one that predicted future events by observing the flight patterns of birds. Yet one finds in this chapter, as well as in a number of other Indian sources, that birds shared the field of potential omen creatures with jackals, owls, deer, serpents, small lizards, scorpions, mongeese—and, most importantly, dogs.

The Indian science of omens was, moreover, not limited to the interpretation of animal behavior. Already in the first (if not the second) millennium C.E., sortition or oracular gambling was a means for divining future events through random dice throws. The distribution of arrows shot by a bow could also serve an oracular purpose. Palmistry and the reading of marks on the soles of a newborn infant's feet were also current in ancient and classical India, as were astrology, numerology, and the interpretation of dreams. Birthmarks and throbbing sensations in various parts of the body (the arm, eye, and so on) could also be interpreted to predict the future. So, for example, Sītā, the kidnapped heroine of the great epic *Rāmāyaṇa,* sensed that help was on the way when her eye, right arm, and thighs begin to throb. Unusual phenomena and calamities—atmospheric (great storms, meteors, etc.) and terrestrial (earthquakes, floods, and plagues)—were also viewed as precursors of future events.

Systematized discussions of divination on the basis of animal behavior first began to appear in the early centuries of the common era, in such works as the sixth-century *Bṛhat Saṁhitā* ("Great Compendium") of Varāhamihira. Although it was mainly devoted to astrology, this work devoted a number of chapters (especially chapter 89) to the oracular interpretation of animal behavior, and particularly to the prediction of future events in the light of the random behavior of urinating dogs. Varāhamihira's observations would be duly reproduced, nearly verbatim, in at least two later sources. These were the twelfth-century *Mānasollāsa* ("Splendor of the Mental Faculties"), an encyclopedic work attributed to king Bhūlokamalla Someśvara—which devotes portions of the thirteenth chapter of its second volume to urinating dogs—and a portion of chapter 83 (verses 275–312) of the *Śārṅgadhara Paddhati* entitled "Traveller's Omens Deriving from the Auspicious Movements of Dogs." (These verses, not reproduced here, are an expansion on a passage from the *Bṛhat Saṁhitā.* A partial translation of this original source may be found in chapter five of my book, *Myths of the Dog-Man*).

Because the medieval encyclopedists generally satisfied themselves (and their royal patrons) with merely re-editing—or even simply plagiarizing—earlier works, it is only rarely that one chances upon examples of truly original or creative writing in their compendia. A striking exception, in the work of Śārṅgadhara, are the opening 120 verses of chapter 83, which begin with the statement that this chapter is based not only on previously existing treatises on the subject of omens, but also on the author's own great practical experience. With these words, he launches nearly directly into what may well be the most meticulously detailed study of canine oracular behavior in all of Indian literature.

Śārṅgadhara almost immediately singles out the dog as the most eminent of all omen creatures. He clearly states his reasons for his choice: the dog's wide variety of behavior patterns, as well as its bark, are easy to understand. Dogs are, moreover, easy to come by and easier to approach and observe than are wild animals or birds (verses 7–9). There are also, however, a number of implicit grounds for Śārṅgadhara's choice that merit discussion here. These concern the particular socio-religious role the dog has played in India—if not in all of human culture—since the dawn of human society. One of the first creatures to be domesticated by humans, the dog, "man's best friend," has also often been his "best enemy." Perhaps as a result of the familiarity that has obtained between the human and canine species, the dog is, in its behavior, more like man than are any other creatures. Dogs do what people do, only differently and, it must be allowed, with much less refinement. Dogs talk (bark), cry, show joy, yawn, scratch themselves, hiccup, cough, urinate, defecate, have sex, eat, drink, sleep, and so on, in ways that are quite human. Yet, at the same time, they are indiscriminate about when they sleep (often remaining awake and vigilant at night), what they eat (a common Indian term for them being "vomit-eater"), with whom they have sex (members of their immediate family, females in menses: verse 24), and so on. As such, they can be "little loved" (verse 25) by humans.

The contempt in which humans often hold dogs in India runs much deeper, however, than mere disgust they may feel at the incongruousness or crudeness of canine behavior. Dogs have always been, by their very place in the domesticated human world, marginal or liminal creatures. The watchdog who stands guard on its master's porch at night is neither in the house nor outside of the house. It protects its human family, yet can, when rabid, turn on them and even kill them. When it is a shepherd's dog, it protects the herd from rustlers as well as from its wild "cousin," the wolf; yet, dogs can also run in packs, killing livestock and threatening human life. In both herding and hunting, the dog constitutes a moving boundary between the human world (of the herd or the hunter) and the savage world (of predators or of wild game) from which it originally came.

It is this marginality that renders the dog indispensible, yet at the same time dangerous to its human master. This marginality, combined with the dog's indiscriminate sexual and eating habits, also forms the basis for an important classificatory model in traditional Indian society. In the Indian system of castes (*varṇas*, literally "colors"), the "good society" of the upper castes (brahmans, kṣatriyas, and vaiśyas) is counterbalanced by the dregs of society, the low-born śūdras and untouchables or "outcastes." These latter groups, defined by their indiscriminate eating habits (the dietary prohibitions that apply to the higher castes do not apply to them) and sexual practices (they are said to be the product of miscegenation, the unnatural mixing of castes), have been identified, throughout India's history, with dogs. It is this ideology that underlies verses 13 and 14 of our text, in which it is said that black, the color of śūdras, is the dog's true color.

Scavenging their food like dogs, living like dogs, even eating dogs ("dog-cooker" being a common term for "outcaste" in ancient and medieval India), low-caste and "outcaste" Indians are marginal, dangerous, and polluting to the persons belonging to the upper levels of society. Yet, at the same time, they are indispensible to good society, for none but a low-caste or "outcaste" can dispose of the refuse that even a brahman cannot help but produce: garbage, excrement, and, most importantly, dead bodies.

Since the time of the Vedas, the Indian cremation ground, tended by "outcastes" and haunted by carrion-feeding dogs, has constituted the dangerous yet unescapable pivot between two worlds, the world of the living and the world of the dead. It is only by passing through the cremation fire that the soul of the deceased can be released from the corpse in which it is trapped and enter a new life on another plane. And what creatures do we find at this, the most liminal and marginal locus in the Indian world? Hellhounds. No sooner has the soul of the deceased passed through the cremation fire than does it find itself moving along the path of the dead, a path that leads to the world of the dead, lorded over by Yama, the god of the dead. Standing guard along this path between this world and the next are two dogs, the dogs of Yama, who can just as easily guide the soul of the deceased along the path as wolf it down when it strays from that path. These two dogs are called the "sons of Saramā" (*sārameyau*)—Saramā being the name of the divine bitch who, in a myth from book ten of the ancient *Ṛg Veda,* blazed a trail across unknown regions to find the cows of the gods that had been rustled by thieves working in the service of the antigods. As a synonym for "dog," "son of Saramā" (verse 12) refers directly to the marginal place of the dog as guardian, herder, and hunter along the paths of the dead.

It is undoubtedly its close association with death that also contributes to rendering the dog an omen creature of choice. The dog, vigilant by night, haunting the paths that lead from the domesticated world of the village to the uncharted wilderness of the surrounding forest, knows both the day side and the night side of existence. It can predict the future because it has, in a sense, already been there, crossing over the threshold between the world of the living and the world of the dead while his human master sleeps, seeing what humans cannot see, and carrying out the bidding of its other master, Death himself.

This threshold is further represented in the preparatory nocturnal ritual (verse 17) that Śārṅgadhara presents at the beginning of this chapter. Since the time of the Vedas, every ritual sacrifice in India has symbolically constituted a sacrifice of the very human who is offering the sacrifice. The animal victim of the Vedic sacrifice was, in fact, nothing other than a surrogate, a stand-in, for the sacrificer himself. As such, the sacrificer was able symbolically to sacrifice his own body—and thereby gain, as his reward, access to the elevated world of the gods—without ever having to leave this world, the world of humans. He could die and enjoy the rewards of self-sacrifice, without dying.

The same symbolism appears to be operative in the ritual described by Śārṅgadhara. The dog is placed in the middle of a ritual diagram, on a symbolic altar upon which it is itself worshiped like a god, with flowers, incense, and so on—but upon which it is also symbolically sacrificed in the form of the baked flour-cake shaped like a brace of dogs (two dogs, like the Sārameyau: verses 22–23). Like the human sacrificer in ancient India, the dog is both the victim and the enjoyer of the (fruits of the) sacrifice. The dog "dies" ritually, yet at the same time lives to enjoy the sacrifice and—more importantly for the omen-master who is performing this ritual—lives to communicate future events, that is, what it has "seen" while passing beyond this world, through the world of the dead, and thereby into the future—to people trapped in the present. Oracular rituals of this sort continue to be performed, albeit in simplified form, in modern-day India, using rams and mares.

The ritual that Śārṅgadhara describes has the same basic form and dynamic as do many Hindu rituals of the medieval and modern period. The diagram (*maṇḍala*) upon which it is performed is a symbolic representation of the entire universe, ordered into the eight cardinal directions, with a divine guardian at each of its cardinal points. The directions are, in fact, designated in Śārṅgadhara's description by the names of these gods: the eastern direction is called Indra (king of the gods), the southeast Agni (the god of fire), the south Yama (god of death), the southwest Kravyāda (the devourer of flesh), the west Varuṇa (god of the waters), the northwest Vāyu (the god of wind), the north Kubera (the god of wealth), and the northeast Śambhu (the supreme god Śiva in his benevolent form).

Each of these gods is worshiped with both offerings of food, flowers, and so on, and ritual formulas (*mantras*), after which the dog itself is worshiped with offerings of food and, once again, mantras (verses 24–26). The person performing the ritual is, moreover, instructed to superimpose (*nyās*) the ritual upon his own mind and body (verse 25), and thereby identify himself with the dog that is at once the sacrificial victim and the divine object of the ritual. This too, is a common feature of Hindu—and especially tantric—worship, in which the devotee identifies himself with the divinity to whom he offers his devotion. (An allusion is made to tantrism in verse 90, with the mention of the siddhas, the "accomplished ones" of a number of medieval esoteric traditions.) It is through just this sort of ritual reordering of the entire universe that one can secure one's own place in the universe and in the world beyond (verse 26).

Following his description of this ritual, Śārṅgadhara enters into the heart of the matter, that is, the interpretation of canine behavior as a means of predicting future events. Here, he lays out the basic principles of the science of omens, albeit in a loosely connected way. The augurer is able to predict the future by observing five canine phenomena (verse 42). These are: the dog's orientation (the direction in which it is facing); movement (the movements and gestures it makes with its legs, mouth, etc.); location (the place in which it is found); motion (the direction in which it displaces itself), and utterances (barking, howling, crying, etc.).

The first four of these phenomena are categorized along a certain number of axes or vectors. Generally speaking, all that concerns the right side of an omen dog's body portends favorable events, while all that has to do with the left side is inauspicious (verses 38–40, 46, 92). This division, into dexter and sinister, is so common to Indo-European culture, if not humanity, as to require no comment. The fact that left-sided canine behavior is often auspicious for women (verse 48)–the opposite of the male case—derives from the place of women vis-à-vis their husbands in Indian society. A man's wife, his "distaff side," is always symbolically located to his left in religious representations. Furthermore, woman is, in more than one sense, the opposite of man, and it follows that a reversal of directions should be operative as concerns omens. Thus a dog's right-sided movements will portend the birth of a son, and its left-sided movements that of a daughter (verse 77).

East and west are also of major importance in the interpretation of canine omens. The former direction is called *śānta,* "extinguished," "peaceful," "auspicious," while the latter, *dīpta,* is "ignited," "blazing," and "inauspicious" (verses 41–42). The point of reference here is the sun, in the context of the extreme climate of India. The morning sun, pleasant and relatively unoppressive, is associated with the birth of the day and new life. The afternoon sun, however, blazes down, draining the strength and life out of creatures. The sun at the close of the day is associated with death, the funeral pyre, and the great conflagration that will burn up the entire universe at the end of a cosmic cycle. In this context, the distinction between east and west, "away from the sun" and "into the sun," becomes comprehensible in the context of omens. Whereas a dog's easterly orientation, location, movements, and motion, tending toward life, are auspicious, these same attitudes and behaviors, when they are westerly, tend toward death, and are inauspicious (verses 66, 71, 72). The time of day or night in which the omen dog moves, barks, or displaces itself also play a determining role in the future events it portends (verses 98–99, 102).

Combinations of right with east and left with west produce the expected results (verse 51), whereas more complex or contradictory movements require more complex interpretations (verses 43, 70). Certain special cases nonetheless run counter to these general rules (verses 67, 73, 83). Another variable is introduced by whether the inquiry is being made about something auspicious or inauspicious (verses 41, 79). An important distinction is further made between the oracular behavior of dogs from one's own household (*kṣaitrika-śakunam:* verses 4, 10–83), dogs from other people's households (*āgantu-śakunam:* verses 5, 84–120), and stray dogs from no apparent household (*jāṅghika-śakunam:* verses 6, 275–312 [not translated here]).

The systematic elements laid out by Śārṅgadhara in his discussion of the science of canine oracles are, however, far outweighed by the unsystematic. Beyond the apparently contradictory interpretations with which the text is riddled, there is either no visible correlation whatsoever between what the dog does—yawning, urinating, eating, etc.—and what its actions mean (verses 81, 98, 115, etc.); or, conversely, the correlation is so obvious as not to require a "science" to explain it (verses 53–54, 58–64, 93, etc.).

What is the point of so much sound and fury? Is it possible to believe that there actually were people who planned their lives according to random canine behavior? Or—to paraphrase Cato's description of the Etruscan augurers who predicted the future by looking at the livers of sacrificial animals—might we not imagine that one Indian omen-master could not look at another omen-master without laughing?

Here, it is appropriate that we frame our answer to these questions in terms of the socio-political context in which chapter 83 of the *Śārṅgadhara Paddhati* was written. In this society, members of the (generally brahman) intelligentsia served as advisors to (generally kṣatriya) kings, in return for which they received royal patronage and support. This advisory role pertained primarily to the king and his kingdom's religious life, in which brahman priests, through their performance of the great and complex rituals of state, insured the harmonious continuation of the king's realm. This role also extended into affairs of state, the waging of war, public works, and all manner of other vital matters, including divination. No royal court worth its salt was without a full complement of astrologers, palm-readers, soothsayers—and omen-readers.

There can be no doubt, in the case of Śārṅgadhara, that the science of omens was intended for the edification of his king—in his particular case, King Hamir

(*Śārṅgadhara Paddhati* 1.2), founder of the kingdom of Mewar, in present-day Rajasthan. Over one-fourth of the omens he interprets directly concern royal welfare or warfare (verses 28–37, 56–73, etc.), and most of the remaining omens may be seen as concerning the king indirectly. In this light, we can read this portion of his text as the work of a royal employee who, not unlike the meddlesome lawmakers and bureaucrats of the modern state, claimed that there was a method to his madness, but that the method was so complex as to require his own indispensible expertise. This is an attitude that Jonathan Z. Smith has termed "scribalism," according to which a given intelligentsia insures its monopoly on certain forms of power and authority, and defends its own vested interests, by generating data that it alone is capable of interpreting.

Śarṅgadhara Paddhati 83.1–120 is found in *The Paddhati of Śarṅgadhara, A Sanskrit Anthology,* edited by Peter Peterson (Bombay: Government Book Depot, 1888), pp. 340–360.

Further Reading

David Gordon White, *Myths of the Dog-Man* (Chicago: University of Chicago Press, 1991).

Śārṅgadhara Paddhati 83.1–120

1. Having consulted a multitude of texts and having gained much practical experience in these matters, I now begin an exposition of the science of omens, for the benefit of men and women alike. 2. These are omens that reveal both the good and evil fortune that will befall a person, from his birth until his death, and predict the life expectancies of living beings. The entire universe, composed of earth, heaven, and midspace, indeed falls within their purview. Without them, nothing concerning the past, present, or future can be clearly known. Omens open one's eyes to the entire universe. A constant shining light, they overcome all adversity.

3. An omen makes it possible to tell what will be one's lot—loss or gain; joy, sorrow, or unalloyed misfortune; long life or death; and the realization of one's wishes and endeavors. When two armies are locked in battle, it can tell which will win the undisputed victory, which will deal the crushing blow. In answer to the question "What is happening in the world?" a mortal may place his entire trust in the omen creatures.

EXPANDED DISCUSSION OF OMEN CREATURES

4. There are three kinds of omens in the present system: there are those which are "indwelling," those which are "arriving," and those which are "pertaining

to the hindquarters." That which originates within a given household is called "indwelling." 5. But if the omen creature is from the outside world, from any direction whatsoever, its omen—like a bud whose two halves are "good fortune" and "bad fortune," when it opens to reveal a fruit, is called "arriving." 6. An omen that manifests itself through the utterances, motion, movements, or presence of an omen animal one may encounter along a path, from either the right or left side, from in front or behind, and whether the animal be domesticated or wild, is called "pertaining to the hindquarters."

7. The fawn, the spotted owl, the crow, the she-jackal, and the dog—the greatest sages have declared these to be the five optimal omen creatures. 8. The first four of these creatures are, by their nature, barely intelligible. The dog is easier to understand than these creatures. Therefore, our discussion begins with it. 9. As concerns omen animals, I say that no other living creature is so observable and accessible as the dog. Nowhere is there any creature like it whatsoever.

"INDWELLING" OMENS

10. Now the meaning of the dog's bark will be discussed. It is a meaning that applies, most assuredly, to every kind of omen—that is, those pertaining to outward behavior, good qualities, and the consequences of acts committed in previous births, both auspicious and inauspicious. 11. One who has a probing mind, who is well versed in the omen texts, of pure intellect, diligent, truthful, virtuous, and skilled in the interpretation of animal movements may qualify as a master in the present system.

12. The dog is called "dog," the "auspicious one," the "talker," "of good pedigree," the "tawny-colored one," the "wakeful one," the "curled up one," "bow-wow," the "swift one," "puppy," and "son of Saramā." 13. White is the color associated with brahmans; red with kṣatriyas; yellow with vaiśyas; and black with śūdras. So it is, in this regard, that dogs (being of many colors) belong to a mixed race and have a wide variety of names. 14. But someone will say, "The question one should be asking here concerns what is natural to each respective species." It is the stated opinion of the sages that "concerning the dog, black is the only natural color."

15. The ritual of bringing the dog before the omen-master should be performed on an auspicious day. A brace of dogs made of pure flour, having been worshiped, should then be offered together with milk, for the dog's pleasure, to its male and female pups and other kin. 16. The dog should be black all over, without bodily defects, even-tempered, healthy, young, and strong. His tail should not bend toward the left; he should be balanced in his movements; and have a total of twenty claws.

17. A man who has domesticated the dog, won its confidence, and taken care of it, should bathe it at sundown. The ritual should be performed that night under a clear sky. One should perform the ritual in its entirety, with the

greatest of care, to the accompaniment of the following mantra. 18. Placing his own hand on the dog's head, the man should consecrate it with these words. "Oṃ, O finest of dogs, you who have been raised in my house. Speak the truth, svāhā!" Then, at daybreak, he should, using fresh cow dung, trace a square diagram measuring three cubits on each side, on a cleared, pleasant, isolated, and purified piece of ground. 19. The eastern quarter of the ritual diagram should be painted yellowish white; the southeast red; the southwest blue; the south black; the west silvery white; the northwest ochre; the north variegated; and the northeast white. 20. These are the pigments, made of perfumed powder, that one should use in painting an eight-petaled lotus, upon which each of the gods should be placed at its corresponding cardinal direction.

21. Having consulted with the omen-master, one should perform the worship ceremony, with flowers, and so on, using a series of mantras, composed of the names of the gods, and beginning with the word "Oṃ" and ending with the word "namo." 22. The dog to be worshiped with the rite is accordingly placed in the middle of the ritual diagram. A flour cake in the shape of a brace of dogs should be offered by the daughter, together with an oblation that has been cooked inside a sacrificial vessel and covered with clarified butter, to the honored gods. 23. Once the gods' oblation has been taken out of the sacrificial vessel, one should make another ball-shaped oblation for the dog itself. Thereafter one should prepare for the worship of the dog [which is placed in the middle of the ritual diagram] with all of the following mantras: 24. With the words "Oṃ, the curled up one, svāhā!" one offers sandalwood. With the words "Oṃ, the auspicious one, svāhā!" one offers flowers. With the words "Oṃ, O tawny one, svāhā!" one offers unhusked barley corns. With the words "Oṃ, O wakeful one, svāhā!" one burns incense before it. With the words "Oṃ, O stooping one, svāhā!" one holds a burning lamp before it. With the words "Oṃ, you who have sexual intercourse with one in her menses, svāhā!" one offers fruit. With the words "Oṃ, O eater of sacrificial offerings, svāhā!" one offers food. With the words "Oṃ, you who are faithful to your master, svāhā!" one offers honey. This is how one should worship the dog at the center of the ritual diagram. Then, having led the dog away from the ritual diagram, and having purified it, one should place one's hand on the dog's forehead and pronounce the following mantras: 25. "Oṃ, O knower of acts, come, come; Oṃ, you who are awake by night, come, come; Oṃ, knower of the supernatural, come, come; Oṃ, you who speak clearly, come, come; Oṃ, O snake-tongued one, come, come; Oṃ, O little-loved one, come, come. Taking this offering, speak the truth, truly speak, svāhā." This is how one should consecrate the dog. Then the man, having fully internalized the ritual in his own mind, should mold together a ball-shaped oblation and throw it into the ritual fire while pronouncing the following mantra: 26. "Oṃ, salutations to you, O blessed one, O finest of the canine race, O most excellent omen creature, you of the deep voice, O lord of creatures, O you who have sexual intercourse during menses, come quickly, taking the offering and carry out my wish; speak, speak truly,

Oṃ, Hūṃ, Phaṭ, Svāhā!" With these words one makes the offering. One should perform the proper rites at the end of the year, at the solstices, the end of each season, month, fortnight, and day. He who fails to observe all of these periodic rites, his every omen is proven false in this world.

27. Having recalled the ritual, and thinking "the future will or will not be such," he should release the dog. Once the dog has eaten the ball-shaped offering, its behavior, even when it is not moving, is worthy of investigation.

BEHAVIOR CONCERNING THE FATE OF THE KING

28. A dog scratching its brow with its right forepaw indeed portends that a prince whose royal chariot wheel has humbled the mighty will be crowned with the royal tiara in the ceremony of royal consecration. 29. A dog that scratches its left paw with its right paw portends that a king, having assembled a great troop of war elephants, will rise to dominion over the entire earth. 30. A dog that rubs its right eye gently with its right paw portends that a king who has celebrated his royal consecration will beget, together with his wife, a son who will rule over hundreds of thousands of subjects and the entire earth. 31. A dog that scratches the region of its right ear with its right paw and makes sounds of pleasure during the playing of vocal and instrumental music portends dominion over the entire earth. 32. A dog that scratches its muzzle with its right forepaw portends that the king, together with his subjects, warriors, and nobles, will enjoy a constant supply of provisions and foodstuffs.

33. A dog that scratches its chest with its right forepaw portends a reign endowed with herds of horses, elephants, she-buffalos, and so on, troops of musicians, and great wealth. 34. A she-dog that scratches her belly with the claws of her right paw portends a great conquest. 35. If a dog looks, sniffs, claws, scratches, furrows, washes, or licks its right side after having turned toward the right, this is an auspicious omen. 36. A dog that lies on its right flank, or that urinates with its right hind leg raised and then lies down on its right side is a favorable portent. 37. A dog urinating in an agreeable place is an auspicious portent for that place and the entire region; climbing up on a bed, seat, altar, or terrace is an auspicious portent for the royal household.

38–40. All movements of the dog's nose toward the right are known to portend happiness, but movements and motion toward the left side all portend misfortune, as for example when a dog yawns, vomits, runs away, behaves anxiously, contracts its limbs or trembles while asleep, agitates its forehead and ears, chews on some body part, hiccups, coughs, covers itself with ashes, wags its head, digs, cries, hides its food, howls, shuts its eyes, lays hold of a rock, or looks into the sun. 41. The "ignited" (western) direction is closely connected with danger, cessation, lawsuit, and so on. When one's inquiry concerns some favorable matter, the western direction portends disgrace; when one's inquiry concerns some inauspicious matter, it portends fearsome events. 42. Orientation, movement, location, motion, and utterances—these five may be "ignited" [westerly] just as they may be "extinguished" [easterly]. It is my feeling that all grounds for prognostication, apart from these ten, are generally worthy of the contempt they receive from omen-masters.

43. Compound movements made with the left half of his body and which also tend in a left-to-right direction, neither multiply nor diminish the result. The portents to which the dog's complex movements give rise will be discussed presently. 44. With its five auspicious types of behavior, the dog assuredly grants men sovereignty and great fortune; likewise, with its five inauspicious forms, it necessarily takes these away.

INQUIRIES BY A SUITOR CONCERNING A BRIDE

45. The successive movements of a dog are enumerated here for the mutual inquiries made by a suitor in the process of choosing bride, and by maidens in search of a husband.

46. When the dog's movements tend toward the right, the maiden is marriagable; when they tend toward the left, she is not. If the dog couples felicitously with a bitch, then the man will marry and pass his days together with the maiden. 47. When the dog has intercourse while facing the suitor, then the maiden is surely not fit for marriage. A dog that sniffs the genitals of a bitch indicates that the girl has been deflowered.

INQUIRIES BY A MAIDEN CONCERNING A HUSBAND

48. When a maiden makes inquiries concerning the choice of a husband, a dog's left-sided movements are auspicious, and not the opposite. When a dog urinates on a she-dog, this means that her marriage is imminent. 49. When a dog licks its own urine and then walks to the left, the man she loves will be hers. When it strokes its tongue with its right forepaw, this means she will enjoy the love and sexual pleasure of the young man.

INQUIRIES CONCERNING THE RAINS

50. Omens concerning the rains, which take the form of a particular group of movements on the part of an excellent dog, have been duly expounded by experts in the science of omens. All should hear the supreme knowledge of these omens in its entirety. 51. Omens concerning the rains are assuredly propitious when the movements of the excellent dog are right-sided and easterly. Indeed, those of the dog's movements that are left-sided and westerly are highly inauspicious. 52. When a dog rubs its right eye and then either licks its own navel or climbs up on a bed located on the roof of a house, this means that the clouds will pour down a great volume of rain. 53. When a yawning dog, having looked at the sky, sheds copious tears, he portends a rainy season in which the swollen clouds, pouring down torrents of rain, will produce an abundant grain

harvest. 54. When a dog, having come out of a body of water, shakes the water off its body at the water's edge, this assuredly portends the satisfaction of cultivators in the rainy season. 55. When a dog that has climbed up to a high place barks repeatedly while looking at the sun, this means that rain will be fall from the clouds in great profusion.

INQUIRIES CONCERNING ROYAL VICTORY INVOLVING A PAIR OF DOGS

56. The experts say that inquiries concerning the victory or defeat of two kings preparing for war may be carried out by observing the movements of a pair of dogs.

57. The two kings who are seeking war are indeed represented by the pair of dogs. Having determined which dog represents which of the two king's armies, one should then drop an offering of food on the ground. When one of the two dogs, gaining the upper hand, eats the food, victory will be on the side of his king. 58. If it happens that the two dogs lay hold of the offering and eat it together with great affection, this means that a pact of friendship will be effected between the two warring kings. 59. According to persons conversant in the interpretation of manifest canine behavior, if a renowned dog is quickly put to flight, such is surely worthy of investigation. If that dog should then overcome its fear and return, this means that the king has nothing to dread. 60. When the two dogs let out a growling sound, and in no way wish to eat the offering, and then return to their own respective dwellings, then there will be no war, in spite of any quarrel the kings may have.

61. But when a third dog, manifestly superior to these two dogs, forcefully takes and eats their food offering, then one may be sure that a third king, of unsurpassing might, will quickly advance to conquer the two kings. 62. When an offering of food lying between the two dogs has been taken by one of them, and then a third dog, by virtue of its superior strength, tears it away and eats it—this means that adversity will befall the previously unrivaled king. 63. As in the aforementioned case, one of the two dogs has taken the offering of food and is eating it. A third dog unexpectedly comes along, and behaves in a friendly manner. This means that friendship will develop out of a hostile relationship. 64. If the two dogs who are eating food together affectionately share that food together with a third dog who has come along, this assuredly portends reconciliation and friendship between the two kings.

INQUIRIES CONCERNING ROYAL BATTLE INVOLVING A SINGLE DOG

65. "Is victory certain?" Indeed, when this question is duly posed by a wise man, regarding two kings, and the dog's movements are easterly, then war will certainly occur between the two kings. 66. Orientation, location, movements, and utterances made in regular succession in an easterly direction portend a fruitful reconciliation. If these four attitudes [orientation, etc.] are made in

both a westerly and an easterly direction, this means that will be neither reconciliation nor war.

67. When the dog turns, such that its left side rather than its right side is facing the questioner, this means that war will lead directly into peaceful reconciliation. If the dog gradually becomes pleased (and turns back the other way), then alliance will be followed by war. 68. When the dog pricks up its ears while barking at the sky, leaps up while running, or moves off to its left, this portends the cessation of hostilities between two kings.

INQUIRIES CONCERNING IMPENDING WAR

69. If, in answer to the question "Will there be war or not between the two kings?" all of a dog's movements are inauspicious, this means a terrible war will follow. 70. Should two canine omens indicate contradictory—that is, both auspicious and inauspicious—results, tradition holds that the former of the two will bear no fruit while the latter will be brought to fulfillment.

INQUIRIES CONCERNING ROYAL VICTORY INVOLVING A SINGLE DOG

71. A dog may encourage a king—whose kingdom, together with its war animals and chariots, ministers, and footsoldiers, is the pivot of the universe—to go into battle. Easterly movements stand for victory; while westerly movements signify defeat.

INQUIRIES CONCERNING RECONCILIATION

72. A dog's easterly movements being considered auspicious, such indicate that reconciliation will occur, even if preparations for war are underway. If, however, it faces directly into the sun or runs away, this means a breach will occur and that there will be no reconciliation.

INQUIRIES CONCERNING BATTLE

73. Westerly orientation, location, movements, and utterances systematically stand for a warrior's victory in battle. But if the dog behaves similarly in an easterly direction, this portends that the warrior will be taken captive, slain, or defeated in the war.

MISCELLANEOUS OMENS

74. A dog that makes auspicious utterances and movements, and that urinates in an auspicious location indicates the realization, in the form of great wealth and gain, of an endeavor on which one has set one's heart.

75. A dog has drawn near or is already in the vicinity for the purpose of

eating raw, holy, or cooked food. When it either touches its head with its right forepaw or makes right-sided movements, it insures prosperity in the region.

76. If during a game of dice, a dog looks through half-opened eyes and makes left-sided movements while breathing deeply, hiccupping, lying down, contracting its limbs, defecating, urinating, panting, or yawning, these activities are prophetic.

77. A dog who urinates abundantly while sporting in a delightful place with right-sided movements will have as its consequence the birth of a son to a pregnant woman. Left-sided movements portend the birth of a daughter to the woman. 78. If a dog defecates, urinates, pants, yawns, or coughs in its sleep in the presence of a pregnant woman, or breaks a leg while running toward her, she will surely miscarry.

79. A dog, by its easterly orientation, location, movements, and utterances, portends favorable events when the inquiries one makes concern some auspicious matter. When the inquiries one makes concern an inauspicious matter and the dog is westerly in these four attitudes (orientation, etc.), it portends favorable events.

INQUIRIES CONCERNING DISEASE

80. When, upon hearing the omen-question, the dog first shakes and contracts its entire body before lying down, this portends the imminent death of a member of the household. 81. A dog that, having curled itself to the right, refrains from scratching its hindquarters, portends that a person suffering from disease will surely enter, on that very day, into the house of death. 82. A dog repeatedly licking the right side of its body portends death within five days. A dog licking its belly assuredly casts one directly into the abode of death.

83. The two left limbs and left-sided movements produce favorable results when one is inquiring about a sick person. Bristling body hairs and urination while in a high place are considered to be auspicious omens.

"ARRIVING" OMENS, IN WHICH THE MOVEMENTS OF THE AFOREMENTIONED DOG ARE AUSPICIOUS

84. A dog that sniffs at its body while standing in a high place portends gain. When a dog urinates on one's merchandise, this portends commercial profits.

85. A dog scratching its ear with its right rear paw indicates that one will live to an old age. A dog scratching its eye means union with one's beloved. 86. If a dog steps on a pillow and then lies down, this portends the imminent coming of one's beloved to one's house.

87. A dog rubbing its hindquarters against a doorway portends the coming of a traveller whom one should treat with honor; when it lies down there, it portends a meeting between men who are dear to one another.

88. A dog whose four limbs are completely covered with distinctive markings

and which is leading a pack of dogs bestows overwhelming success. That same dog, by digging up the ground, gives rise to misfortune.

89. A dog picks up a broom, a piece of cotton, an arrow, or a winnowing basket in its mouth. The house into which it enters will become filled with wealth in the form of grain. 90. "If, indeed, a dog, having touched a particular spot on the ground with its forehead, looks fixedly at that place, then a great treasure lies there." This is a secret shared by the siddhas.

91. When a she-dog urinates, this is auspicious with regard to marriage. It means that the maiden, having made a favorable marriage, will enjoy happiness and wealth. 92. Many are those who consider that when a dog touches its right rear paw with its right forepaw, such means fortune in marriage. 93. When a woman who is about to be married beholds a dog whose face is full of joy as it plays with its beloved, this means that she will enjoy great happiness.

94. If, during the rainy season, a dog, beholding the sun and moon, howls with upturned face, this means that a stream of water will fall from the sky in seven nights' time. 95. If a dog, standing on the shore of a sacred bathing place, causes its body to tremble, this portends an amassing of clouds and rainfall in that country.

"ARRIVING" OMENS, IN WHICH THE MOVEMENTS OF THE AFOREMENTIONED DOG ARE INAUSPICIOUS

96. If a dog should be to the right of plowmen who are going out of the fields and to the left of those who are entering the fields, it declares "Do not farm today."

97. A dog that barks while facing into the sun at the end of the day portends danger for the plowman; but a dog facing northwest at nightfall portends danger from wind and thieves. 98. A dog that barks while facing north in the middle of the night portends injury to twice-born persons and the death of cows. At the end of the night, this means the defilement of a virgin and miscarriage. At dawn, it means good fortune. 99. A dog that barks while facing the east at daybreak portends danger from thieves and fire; at noon, fire and death; at the end of the day, bloody strife.

100. A dog barking in the center of a town while facing the sun at dawn portends the fall of the king. If a dog is seen defecating there, this portends a national calamity, even when the situation has apparently been brought under control. 101. A dog that howls with its face turned upward toward the sun portends great peril. If, indeed, it does so at dawn or dusk on a given day, the people of that city will be slaughtered.

102. When several mad dogs howl by night during the autumn season, then nothing evil will come of it. But if they do so at some other time, then nothing good will come of it. 103. A pack of scraggly dogs howling together at night portend that a village will become deserted. When dogs, after howling in the village, go and howl on a cremation ground, this portends the death of the

village headman. 104. A dog portends death when it runs away or howls for no reason, or else descends into a body of water and then, afflicted with pain, enters into a house with a bloody bone from a dead body in its mouth.

105. When a dog digs up the wall of a house, there will be a break-in. When it digs around a cowpen, there will be cow-thieving. If it digs in a grain field, this means there will be a wealth of grain.

106. If a dog licks its own penis during a marriage ceremony, this means that the bride, even if she be the equal of the goddess Gaurī, will bring disgrace upon her family.

107. A dog lies with its head in a doorway and its body outside, and howls at great length while looking at the mistress of the house. This portends disease. Lying with its body inside and its head outside means that the mistress of the house is unchaste. 108. If a dog defecates after digging on the upper side of a house, this means that the mistress of the house's paramour is on his way. If it does so after digging on the lateral side of the house, it means her husband is coming. 109. A dog that enters a house and scatters food all around indicates to the mistress of the house that her paramour is having doubts about her at that very moment. 110. If a dog remains constantly curled up on a cotton pillow, this always means that the paramour will enter that house at nightfall. 111. When a dog places a mortar and pestle, a winnowing basket, an arrow, or a sword on a pillow, the dog's master is given to understand that a paramour is in his house.

112. A dog, after having yawned and looked up at the sky, either sheds tears or howls. One should thus know that lightning will strike in that place.

113. If a dog, taking a piece of meat in its mouth, plunges into a body of water, this means that a war will erupt in which all will be consumed by fire. 114. A dog, laying hold of a piece of cow manure and entering into a house, portends the rustling of cows. By biting itself with its teeth, it means that place will become deserted.

115. A dog howling on the roof of a house at sunrise is a fearsome portent. When it defecates on a chair, etc., this portends a legal dispute. 116. When a dog sniffs at both of its forelegs, this means a man will encounter enemies and thieves. A dog hiding meat, bones, and food in ashes portends the danger of a raging fire. 117. If a dog should at some time bark while looking toward an enclosure surrounding a number of houses, then one should know that a fearsome situation will surely arise in that group of buildings.

118. A man whose well-fed and well-housed dogs, two or several in number, fight at dawn to the northeast of his house will himself fight with enemies.

119. A she-dog who attempts to have sexual intercourse with a calf at a crossroad with the King's Road portends danger from the king's enemies in the course of that very month.

120. A dog entering a house with a bone in its mouth portends the deaths of the master, son, and other members of the household. Playing on a bed together with its mate portends happiness.

—17—

How to Worship at Śiva's Temple

D. Dennis Hudson

Āṟumuga Nāvalar (1822–1879) wrote his composition, "The Proper Way to Worship at Śiva's Temple" (*Śivālaya Darśana Vidhi*) in 1851 and published it on the Tamil press he had established two years earlier on the Jaffna peninsula of Sri Lanka. He addressed it to the Tamil-speaking men and women of India and Sri Lanka who had been formally initiated into the Śaiva religion, but who were either indifferent to its way of life or ignorant of it. Such Śaivas, he believed, were prey to the criticisms and arguments against Śaivism promulgated by Christian missionaries, especially the Protestants. Ignorance of their own way of life, he believed, explained the conversion of Śaivas to Christianity, a conversion that inevitably led them to painful future births. He was a devout adherent of Śiva and spent his life educating the Śaiva population in order to regenerate the Śaiva religion so that people fortunate enough, he believed, to be born as Śaivas could receive its benefits, the greatest of which is complete emancipation from birth and death.

Since Āṟumuga Nāvalar was learned in Śaivism and in Tamil literature and was exacting in his representation of the tradition, his works are reliable expositions of the Śaiva religion as it is found among the Tamils. It is known theologically as "Śaiva Orthodoxy" (*Śaiva Siddhānta*) and is found today in India, Sri Lanka, Singapore, Malaysia, and North America. The religion, however, is not essentially theology, but an observance (*samayam*) that mixes practice and doctrine so that practice leads the initiate gradually toward a greater vision of God, the soul, and the world.

Practice begins with the worship of God in one of the "palaces" or temples where he resides in the form of icons, primarily as a pillar (*liṅga*) embedded in a pedestal (*yoni*). Śiva with his Śakti or energy indwells the liṅga and yoni, the liṅga signifying Śiva and the yoni signifying his Śakti, the Goddess. God and Goddess took up residence in that double icon through elaborate liturgies conducted by priests who followed rites believed to have been revealed by Śiva himself. Āṟumuga Nāvalar explains in detail what people are obligated to do when they visit the temple in order to obtain the vision (*darśana*) of Śiva. Following convention, he uses the male worshiper to represent practices obligatory for both men and women, making a distinction between them only when the rites require it. In Śaiva Orthodoxy women and men may receive the same initiations for worship and yogic practice, and both may attain the ultimate goal of emancipation. Nāvalar explains the ideal practice, knowing that approximation of the ideal depends on individual motivation. Yet, as is customary in Hindu instruction in rites, he does not explain what those actions mean. One reason is that some meanings are embedded in traditional Tamil culture and do not have to be explained to traditional Tamil Hindus. Another is that an explicit interpretation of the rites will be given to initiates later, only after they have first mastered them.

Notably, correct performance is crucial whether or not one understands the meaning of the rite. Unintended faulty performance will generate negative karmic fruits that nevertheless may be removed through rites of purification, whereas intended faulty performance may not be purified at all. The concepts of rebirth and multiple hells explain how acts are punished after death. The intention of one's actions is crucial to Hindu thought, and Nāvalar was concerned about the matter, believing that intention is shaped by education. Among his many Tamil works, for example, is an extensive Śaiva catechism.

In order to make sense of the rites that Āṟumuga Nāvalar describes in the composition, let me indicate some of the patterns of thought implicit to Hindu temple architecture and liturgy as Śaivas developed them. Those developments are believed to express the instructions revealed by Śiva in the treatises known as the Vedas that he made relevant to the present degenerate age through treatises known as the Āgamas.

Worship in the temple is the beginning stage of the Śaiva way of life, and is an instrument designed to meet the normal human limitations of our "demonic age," the Kaliyuga. It engages the mind, voice, and body of the worshiper by focusing them on material images, built structures, and bodily rites that are apprehended through the senses in thinking, seeing, hearing, speaking, touching, and tasting. By yoking those modes of apprehension in one-pointed focus on Śiva, it is believed, Śiva's energy-that-is-grace (*arul-śakti*) will lead the devotee to eventual apprehension of God directly. Obtaining an audience with the Lord Śiva residing in the throne room—actually seeing the liṅga that is his material body and being seen by him gazing through that liṅga—is the primary way to begin a path that will lead to the direct vision of that embodied Śiva at the center of one's own soul.

Various tropes inform the concept of Śiva's dwelling place, not all of them literally consistent with one another. Central among them is that of a palace where subjects may obtain an audience with their enthroned king and queen, which we may understand this way: subjects carrying gifts walk into the outer court of the palace and walk through a series of enclosures toward the throne room, expressing servitude to the sovereign through physical gestures and prostrations along the way. They ask permission to enter from the officer in charge of the guards at the doors (Nandi) and enlist the help of a minister to remove any obstacles to a successful audience (Vighneśa). Once granted entrance to the throne room, they give gifts and praise to the sovereign (Śiva) and then humbly ask for a favor. They then venerate the sovereign's various expressions of himself on behalf of the kingdom (Dakṣiṇamūrti, Somaskanda, Candraśekhara, Subrahmaṇya, and the four ācāryas), venerate the queen on her own throne (Pārvatī), and then visit the official who administers the granted favor (Candeśvara) and leave.

Modifying the figure of the palace is that of human body. As understood by yoga, the body consists of a visible physical sheath that subsists on food, an invisible sheath inside it that subsists on breath, and inside that a sheath of mind that envelopes a sheath of insight that envelopes a sheath of joy. All those sheaths, even those of mind, insight, and joy, are composed of obscuring matter (*pāśa*) and constitute the body. Accordingly, the closer a person's thoughts move from the experiences of the physical body dependent on food to the inmost center of the body, the more insightful and joyous that person becomes.

Enveloped by the body is the soul (*paśu*), which in part shares in nonobscuring matter while at the same time it shares in Śiva, who is not matter but pure consciousness. The soul is both the same as Śiva and different from him. Śiva dwells in the soul through grace (*arul-śakti*); one might say that the soul is the "place" where God and matter meet. According to Śaiva Orthodoxy, the final purpose of human birth is to let Śiva's grace extricate the soul from the body so that it may dwell eternally emancipated from obscuring matter and united with Śiva in love.

The palace of the first trope, then, is built on the body of the second trope. The body is of a man entranced through yoga who lies on the ground, face up. His body in turn signifies the "body of God," which is the universe in its visible and invisible modes. The palace's entire outer wall is God's visible physical sheath. The tall entrance gateway is God's feet. Worshipers venerate that gateway as they approach, just as they venerate the feet of Śiva, on whom all things depend for their existence.

Passing through the "feet" of God, worshipers enter the invisible sheath of God's body inside the outer wall. There they encounter a flagstaff, an altar of sacrifice, and a reclining bull. The erect flagstaff signifies consciousness in that sheath of breath that the yogi has raised up to his head and brought to a standstill through the yogic control of breathing. His mind, insight, and joy are entranced in the vision of Śiva transcendent to the material world. The one, three, or five temple walls enclosing the liṅga's inner sanctum signify the sheaths of the yogi's body that his consciousness had moved through when it made its upward journey to rest in a region corresponding to the place above his nose and between his eyes. That entranced consciousness in the yogi's forehead corresponds to the temple's inner sanctum or "womb," and the Lord Śiva dwells inside both.

The "womb" brings us to the One before anything existed. The trope explaining the One is a king whose queen gives birth to his realm and sovereignty by gestating a son that is a "rebirth" of both the father and the mother. In his formless essence,

God the One is thought of as androgynous, like a king and queen enthroned as a unified pair. As that formless One, he is pure consciousness, she is primordial matter; he is intention, she is enactment; he is resolve, she is victory. The Goddess is Śiva's energy-that-is-grace (*arul-śakti*), the Śakti who, when he wills it, transforms the androgynous One into a mode that is both with and without form, represented by the liṅga standing in the yoni. The androgynous liṅga-yoni inside the temple's "womb," resembling a fetus inside the uterus, is a transformation of both king and queen. That square and dark inner sanctum called the "house of the embryo" (*garbhagṛha*) or "womb" is liturgically infused with Śiva's Śakti, which is why only the pure may enter it.

Once the One has been transformed into the primordial parents, they interact to give birth to themselves over and over in multiple forms, becoming in the process time and space and all the worlds. That is the "emission" or "creation" of the universe. Architecturally, the temple represents that process by the way manifold icons and walls appear to unfold from the "womb" outward to the outer wall and the gateway, like an artist sketching the yogi's body by beginning from his head and measuring down to his feet.

Returning to the trope of the palace, when worshipers have had their audience and walk away from the throne room and pass out through the palace gateway, they walk through the emanation of the universe. Likewise, when they walk into the palace toward the throne room, they symbolically walk through the reabsorption of the universe into the primordial parents residing in the throne room. Their walking inward and outward, moreover, corresponds to the movement of the yogi from waking consciousness into entranced consciousness and then out of it again.

The temple also illustrates the doctrine of emancipation taught by the dominant tradition of Śaiva Orthodoxy as formulated by Meykaṇṭadevar in the thirteenth century. Śiva, the infinite number of souls, and the matter that obscures those souls remain eternally distinct, even when souls unite with Śiva in emancipating love. Using ancient agricultural symbols, they denote Śiva as the master (*pati*), the soul as a beast that may be sacrificed (*paśu*), and obscuring matter as the cord that ties up the beast for sacrifice (*pāśa*). In the temple, the liṅga in the inner sanctum signifies the master, the recumbant bull Nandi who always faces the liṅga signifies the soul, and the altar of sacrifice behind Nandi signifies the binding cords of matter. The position of the altar of sacrifice behind the bull and the bull's continous gaze on the liṅga suggest the condition of the emancipated soul: It has been freed from obscuring matter and exists in a pacified state continuously exchanging gazes with its master in whose service it finds its true life. For reason of that symbolism, it appears, worshipers are forbidden to break the gaze between Nandi and Śiva by walking between them.

There is also the trope of the human body as a complex set of parts with varying qualities. Among them, the head has the highest status and the feet the lowest, with the navel as the dividing line. To venerate another person or a god or an object, one places the head at that person's feet or at the equivalent of the feet.

The region below the navel is impure compared with the region above the navel, and therefore worshipers must carry their gifts to Śiva above the waist. The right side has a higher and more auspicious status than the left side, so worshipers and priests will always give and receive with the right hand, and will generally circumbulate with the right side toward the object they are venerating.

Among the genders, men and women have different bodies and thus different rules for behavior. There is a distinction between an eight-part prostration for males and a five-part prostration for females. Whereas females are required to be covered above the waist, males should be uncovered above the waist in the presence of Lord Śiva. Relations between the genders in the temple are to be completely nonsensual, not because sensuality is evil, but because desire is to be focussed only on the king one has come to see. The proper setting for sensual pleasure is in the household between husband and wife, where desire can be kept in check while being satisfied.

Anything that moves from inside the body to the outside like saliva and urine, or comes off the body like hair and nails, or that dies becomes a pollutant to ritual purity. Worshipers are therefore prohibited from eating and drinking, shaving, combing the hair, spitting, blowing the nose, passing gas, urinating, defecating, emitting sexual fluids, and menstruating in the temple. They also may not enter when polluted by the birth or a death of a relative, because birth and death pollutions automatically travel along kinship relations whether actual physical contact with the pollutant (birth fluids or corpse) has been made or not. The bodies of kin are assumed to interpenetrate. If the temple does not sustain its ritual purity, it is believed, the daily rites conducted by the priests will be faulty and the government and the realm will suffer. The liturgical service of Śiva thus has direct bearing on social well-being.

The exception to the rule of pollution are cattle. Since the cow gives birth and then the milk essential to Śiva's rites, she represents female transformative power and gracious self-giving; since the powerful bull fertilizes the cow so that she gives birth and the milk, he represents male potency controlled in obedient service to Śiva. Cattle therefore top the animal hierarchy. Their bodily effusions (milk, urine, and dung) are not polluting but purifying. Cattle dung mixed with water is a purifying agent used domestically and liturgically by Hindus; cattle dung has none of the unclean connotations found in modern urban cultures, though Hindus share those feelings with regard to the dung of other animals.

Similar to the figure of the human body is the figure of the universe, which is thought of as being like a human body turned inside out: The visible bodily sheath exists at the center and the invisible material sheaths exist at its outer boundary. The world we inhabit and see through our senses is that visible bodily sheath of God's body. Like our own, it goes through stages of purity and pollution, which are measured by the sun, the moon, and the stars. Humans must adjust their actions to those cosmic rhythms of purity and pollution. Sunset, for example, is the time when demons emerge from the west to rule the night; sunrise is the time when sun emerges from the east to rule the day.

The Śaiva's personal rites should begin before sunrise to harmonize with increasing purity. Bathing removes the pollutions brought about by sleep and the night. Worship in the temple around sunset purifies one against demons during the dangerous transition to night. Similar patterns emerge in the distinctions between the "dark half" of the waning moon and the "light half" of the waxing moon; between the "dark half" of the year beginning from the summer solstice and the "light half" beginning from the winter solstice; and between the days of the week and periods of the day ruled over by the seven "graspers of human destiny" (Sun, Moon, Mars, Mercury, Jupiter, Venus, Saturn), Saturn being especially dangerous.

Not only time but also directional space has differing qualities. In the cultures of Bhārata (the region extending from the southern end of Sri Lanka to the Himalayas in the north), the meanings of the cardinal and intermediary directions always have had a determining influence on the way people build structures and lead their lives. Without explaining why, Āṟumuga Nāvalar gives precise instructions on where to place the head when prostrating, where not to place the feet, and where the priest is to stand when conducting the worship of the liṅga. It depends on the direction in which the Lord Śiva faces in a particular temple, usually east, but sometimes west, south, or north. Temples are almost always built aligned to the cardinal directions and their rites must be adjusted to the distinctive qualities of those directions.

The east is an auspicious direction because the sun rises and purity begins there, while the west is an inauspicious direction because the sun disappears there as demons arise and pollution begins. The north is auspicious because the gods dwell in the Himalayas (such as Śiva on Kailāsa), which lie south of the mountain at the center of earth called Meru. The south, however, is inauspicious because Yama, the god of the dead, dwells there overseeing a variety of purgatorial hells, and from the south he sends servants north to fetch those on Bhārata whose time it is to die and face rebirth or purgation.

Consequently, during temple worship one may point the feet (the low-status part of the body) toward the west or south (the inauspicious directions), but not toward the east or north (and not toward the west whenever the sun is undergoing a crucial transition). Similarly, when conducting rites the priest serving the liṅga must stand to the side of Śiva that will allow him to face north or east with his back to the south or west: When Śiva is facing east, for example, he stands at Śiva's right side, facing north with his back to the south while worshipers stand at Śiva's right side facing northwest toward him.

The circumambulation of Śiva's "womb" clockwise (from east to south to west to north back to east) is believed to follow the direction in which the sun circumambulates the central mountain, Meru; it signifies the auspicious emanation of the universe, of daylight, and of life. Worshipers move in that direction when desiring well-being. The counterclockwise direction signifies the inauspicious resorption of the universe, the emergence of night, and of death. Ascetics who have renounced the well-being of the householder life in favor of emancipation circumambulate in that direction, as do those householders who want emancipation along with worldly well-being.

Finally, we may note the social distinctions made explicit by the temple liturgy. Following ancient thought, Śaivism recognizes the four-class division of society that is believed to be built into the hierarchical structure of the universe. In any ritual context, brahmans take precedence over kṣatriyas, who take precedence over vaiśyas, who take precedence over śūdras, who take precedence over "the fifth class," the untouchables. Yet the Āgama tradition modifies that classification when it comes to the worship of Śiva and the relations among Śaivas. Men and women of the first four classes may receive the same initiations and worship in the temple. Śūdras who have been initiated have the same status as vaiśyas and need not recognize the authority of brahmans who have not been initiated. Untouchables may receive other initiations and worship Śiva outside the gateway.

The Tamil social context modifies the practice even further, because the society has long been composed primarily of castes classified as śūdra and untouchable with a minority of brahmans. There have been few kṣatriyas and vaiśyas. The social, cultural, and intellectual leadership of the society and of Śaivism has been in the hands of śūdras and brahmans for centuries, and Āṟumuga Nāvalar was himself from a caste classified as śūdra. Belief in the power of initiations and mantras taught in Śiva's Āgamas to purify anyone for the worship of God that leads to emancipation from birth and death has made Śaivism the dominant religion by far among the Tamils for centuries.

The following translation is of the fifth edition of *Civalayataricanaviti* (The Proper Way to Worship in Śiva's Temple), published in Madras by the Vittiyanupalana Yantiracalai in 1882, with Āṟumuga Nāvalar's proof texts from Tamil scriptures omitted. As customary, Nāvalar began his composition by invoking the Goddess, Śiva's Śakti, with a symbol and by appealing to Gaṇapati, the Lord of Obstacles (Vighneśa), to remove obstacles to its successful completion. He ended it by invoking Śiva residing at Cidambaram, the cultic heart of Śaiva Orthodoxy, and by blessing the feet of the thirteenth-century theologian, Meykaṇṭādevar, whose authoritative interpretations Āṟumuga Nāvalar intended to articulate.

Further Reading

Other texts by N. Āṟumuga Nāvalar include the *Caiva Vinavitai* (Śaiva Catechism), Book One, 30th printing (Madras: Arumuganavalar Vittiyanupalana Accakam, 1980); and *Caiva Vinavitai* (Śaiva Catechism), Book Two, 16th printing (Madras: Vittiyanupalana Yantiracalai, 1953).

For further information on Āṟumuga Nāvalar, see the following articles by D. Dennis Hudson: "Āṟumuga Nāvalar and Hindu Renaissance among the Tamils," in *Religious Controversy in British India: Dialogues in South Asian Languages*, edited by Kenneth W. Jones (Albany: State University of New York Press, 1992), pp. 27–51; "Winning Souls for Śiva: Āṟunuga Nāvalar's Transmission of the Śaiva Religion," in *Modern Transmission of Hindu Traditions in India and Abroad,* edited by Raymond Brady Williams (Chambersburg, Pa.: Anima Publications, 1992), pp. 23–51; and "Tamil Hindu Responses to Protestants: Among Nineteenth-Century Literati in Jaffna and Tinnevelly," in *Indigenous Responses to Western Christianity,* edited by Steven Kaplan (Albany: State University of New York Press, forthcoming).

More generally, see Mariasusai Dhavamony, *Love of God According to Śaiva Siddhanta: A Study in the Mysticism and Theology of Śaivism* (Oxford: Clarendon Press, 1971), and E. V. Singhan, *Temple Worship: Tirukkovil Valipatu* (Singapore: EVS Enterprises, 1986).

Śiva's Śakti
With the help of Ganapati

The Proper Way to Worship at Śiva's Temple
Written for the easy use of all Śaiva initiates
by Āṟumuga Nāvalar of Nallur in Jaffna

1. Śaiva initiates are those people who have determined that the primordial God, who is without beginning and whose form is joy and consciousness, is the Lord Śiva himself. With true love, they follow him as appropriate to their respective classes and stages of life according to the rules of the Vedas and Āgamas that he has graciously created.

2. The Lord Śiva, the repository of compassion, graciously receives adherence from those who live in this world by dwelling externally in the Śiva liṅga and in other auspicious forms within auspicious temples and in the auspicious guise of his true slaves, and by dwelling internally within the soul. These are therefore places to adhere to him.

3. This adhering to Śiva is a body whose limbs are virtues such as desiring few possessions, not killing, not eating meat, not stealing, not drinking liquor, not desiring another's wife, not hankering for prostitutes, mercy, truth, patience, self-control, liberal giving, and adhering to one's mother and father and other elderly people. The conclusion, therefore, is that adherence to Śiva without these virtues will produce not the slightest benefit.

4. The insignia of Śiva worn as protection by Śaiva initiates who follow this adherence are ash and the "eyes of Rudra" beads. It is certain that meritorious

deeds performed for Śiva without wearing them will produce not the slightest benefit. . . .

5. The Śiva liṅga inside the auspicious temple is called "the liṅga for the sake of others." It has five types: the self-generated liṅga, the liṅga of Śiva's companions, the liṅga of gods, the liṅga of seers, and the liṅga of humans. Among them, the self-generated liṅga appeared on its own. The liṅga of Śiva's companions was established by Vināyaka, Subrahmaṇya, and other companions. The liṅga of gods was established by Viṣṇu and other gods. The liṅga of seers was established by the ṛṣis and also by the anti-gods and the demons. The liṅga of humans was established by humans. Of higher status than the liṅga of humans is the liṅga of the seers, higher than that is the liṅga of the gods, higher than that is the liṅga of the companions, and higher than that is the self-generated liṅga. . . .

6. The Lord who is the Śiva liṅga is inside the "womb" [inner sanctum] within the auspicious temple, and the place surrounding it is the first enclosure. Beyond it is the second enclosure, beyond it the third enclosure, beyond it the fourth enclosure, and beyond it the fifth enclosure. Beyond it is the realm of the village, which is the sixth enclosure. The benefits of circumambulating the Śiva liṅga in the "womb" are greater for walking around the second enclosure than around the first, for walking around the third enclosure than around the second, for walking around the fourth enclosure than around the third, for walking around the fifth enclosure than around the fourth, and for walking around the sixth enclosure [the village] than around the fifth. . . .

7. Those who are qualified to perform the worship of "the liṅga for the sake of others" are Śiva's ācāryas. They are Śiva brahmans known as "the original Śaivas" because they were born in lineages of the five seers beginning with Kāśyapa that appeared from the five faces of the form of the eternal Śiva at the time of emanation. They should have have no mental or physical defects, have received the four initiations (samaya-dīkṣā, viṣeśa-dīkṣā, nirvāṇa-dīkṣā, ācārya-dīkṣā), and know how to recite the Vedas and Āgamas. They should be adept in performing the six types of liturgies (the daily liturgies and their subsidiaries, the periodical liturgies and their subsidiaries, the liturgies performed to fulfill specific desires and their subsidiaries) and the three elements of mantra, visualization, and rite faultlessly, with faith, and according to the rules. If anyone other than these people even touches "the liṅga for the sake of others," ruin will arise for king and society. . . .

8. The Śiva ācāryas who conduct worship should conduct it standing on the right side of the iconic Presence of God if it faces east or south and on the left side if the Presence faces west or north. . . .

9. The Śaivas qualified to administer an auspicious temple are those who have no mental or physical defect, have received all three initiations (samaya-dīkṣā,

viṣeśa-dīkṣā, nirvāṇa-dīkṣā), know the Śaiva Āgamas and the Śiva Purāṇas, and are devoted to Śiva. Those who administer an auspicious temple with faith and according to the rules, without designs on the property and other things that bring worldly profit, receive Śiva's glory in this life and then attain Śiva's realm. But those who conduct their administration with the purpose of worldly profit and steal Śiva's property curtail the ancient regulations and will be punished. . . .

10. Worship and other things must be conducted within an auspicious temple every day without fail and according to the rules. If there is a lapse, evil will arise for the king and the world. . . .

11. Śaiva initiates should go to an auspicious temple each day, obtain the sight of Śiva with faith and according to the rules, and then return home.

12. Those who want to obtain the vision of Śiva ought to go to an auspicious temple once they have bathed according to the rules in the Śiva bathing place near Śiva's abode and, standing on its bank, dry themselves with a dry cloth, place ash on the forehead, tie the hair into a knot, remove the wet loincloth and replace it with a dry one, purify both hands, tie two pieces of clean cloth that are untorn and have been washed and dried around the waist, and complete the rites and prayers. Those who go to an auspicious temple without the bath and other disciplines are like those who sneer at Śiva. . . .

13. When going to the auspicious temple, they ought to go with a plate held up in the hands so that it does not fall below the waist, on which they have placed such things as a coconut, fruit, and areca nut and betel leaves. When going to serve the Lord Śiva, the mandate of Śiva, or the ācārya, it is proper not to go empty-handed but to place the things to be given in his Presence and then venerate. He who possesses nothing should give beautiful flowers and then venerate. He who cannot do even that should remove such things as dry leaves that are in the Presence and then venerate. . . .

14. When they approach the auspicious temple they ought to venerate the gateway, which is the "massive liṅga," enter inside with both hands piled on the head, and then prostrate on this side of the altar of sacrifice, which is the "beautiful liṅga." . . .

15. Men should perform the prostration with eight parts of the body, women with five parts. Prostration with three parts of the body is common to both. . . .

16. The eight-part prostration is to venerate by touching eight bodily parts to the ground: the head, both hands, both ears, the chin, and both arms, with the legs stretched out their full length. The five-part prostration is to venerate by touching five bodily parts to the ground: the head, both hands, and both knees, with only the legs below the knee stretched out. The three-part prostration is pressing both hands together on the head. . . .

17. Prostrations should be done three times or five times or seven times or nine times or twelve times. Doing it only once or twice is a mistake.

18. When prostrating, the legs should stretch to the west or south, not to the east or north. . . .

19. They ought to perform prostration by placing the head at the Agni corner [SE] of an altar of sacrifice when the Presence faces east, at the Nirṛti corner [SW] of an altar of sacrifice when the Presence faces south or west, and at the Vāyu corner [NW] when the Presence faces north; by stretching the right hand straight ahead and the left hand straight behind in order to span the ground and then reversing the order; by stretching the hands at the waist in order to rub the right arm and left arm in the dust; and by first rubbing the right ear in the dust and afterwards the left ear. . . .

20. If they go to obtain the vision of Śiva in the late afternoon of a dangerous eclipse or of the beginning of the sun's northward course, they may not stretch their feet toward the west where the sun is beginning to set; therefore they should not perform the eight-part or five-part prostration at the Presence that faces south or north, but only the three-part prostration. . . .

21. Having venerated in the above manner, they ought to arise and join the hands in worship and conduct a circumambulation [of the inner sanctum] while thinking steadily of the Lord Śiva, holding prayer beads in the hand and uttering the five-syllable mantra (*namaḥ śivāya*) or folding both hands together at the region of the heart; and, walking like a woman in an advanced state of pregnancy who places a pot full of oil on her head and puts one foot carefully in front of the other, they ought to watch the ground while absorbed in thinking, "Will I injure any creature?" and place their feet carefully. . . .

22. They should perform the circumambulation of the Lord Śiva three times or five times or seven times or nine times or fifteen times or twenty-one times. . . .

23. They should perform circumambulation of Vinayaka one time, of Sūrya two times, and of the goddess Pārvatī and of Viṣṇu four at a time. . . .

24. If a shadow falls within the enclosure for circumambulation from the tower above the inner sanctum or from the flagstaff, they ought to avoid the shadow by three-fifths and walk in the remaining two-fifths. If there is a shadow when walking during a festival of God, however, it need not be avoided. . . .

25. At the time of the unction rites for the gods, acts such as circumambulation and veneration are not to be performed inside the inner wall. . . .

26. Students before marriage ought to circumambulate with the right side toward the inner sanctum or "womb," clockwise. Householders and forest-dwellers ought to walk both clockwise with the right side toward the "womb" and

counter-clockwise with the left side toward the "womb." Renunciant ascetics ought to walk counterclockwise. Worldly enjoyment arises from walking clockwise; emancipation arises from walking counterclockwise; and both worldly enjoyment and emancipation arise from walking both clockwise and counterclockwise. . . .

27. The *Svāyambhuva Āgama* speaks of walking clockwise and counterclockwise inside the "womb." It enjoins that only the Śiva brahman who conducts the worship may circumambulate inside the "womb." Circumambulating clockwise and counterclockwise inside the "womb" should be done if one does not walk across the shadow of the Śiva liṅga or unremoved offerings or the drain for the liṅga's unction. The *Kalottara Āgama* enjoins that circumambulation clockwise and counterclockwise should be done inside the "womb" and circumambulation clockwise inside the outer walls.

28. They ought to walk around [the inner sanctum] until they reach the altar of sacrifice and the bull within the enclosure in which they are circumambulating. If there is no altar of sacrifice within that enclosure, they ought to circumambulate up to the altar of sacrifice and bull inside the next outer wall. According to the *Kalottara Āgama,* they should not go in the middle between the Śiva liṅga and the altar of sacrifice and the bull, in whichever enclosure they are located.

29. Once they have circumambulated and have performed veneration in the manner stated above they ought to arise and join the hands in worship, venerate the door guardians, and then venerate and praise the auspicious god Nandi, who is master of the companions, and beseech him, "O Bhagavān, graciously grant permission for me your slave who has attained your auspicious feet to enter in so I may receive the fruit of having seen the Lord Śiva," and go inside.

30. First they ought to reach the iconic Presence of Vighneśa, the Lord of Obstacles, press both hands together, gaze at him and visualize him mentally, make fists with both hands and hit their forehead three times, seize their right ear with their left hand and their left ear with their right hand, pull down three times, and praise him.

31. Then, with both hands piled on the head, they ought to reach the Presence of Lord Śiva, gaze at him and visualize him mentally, join the hands at the head and the heart, and while the mind dissolves, body hair stands on end, and joy wells up and overflows, sing hymns of praise to him with one out of the thirty-two ragas that is appropriate to that time of day.

32. The most elevated of the hymns of praise are certainly from the five Tamil poems inspired by divine grace, which are the *Tēvāram,* the *Tiruvācakam,* the *Tiruvicaippā,* the *Tiruppallāṇṭu,* and the *Periyapurāṇam.*

33. Once they have had the priest make the bael leaf offering to the Lord Śiva, feed him the fruits and other items purified according to the rules, and perform the service of waving burning camphor, they ought to give him the appropriate ritual gift that makes those acts theirs rather than his.

34. In order to perform the offering of flowers with Śiva's primordial mantra (*namaḥ śivāya*), Śiva's brahmans ought to enter into the "womb," other brahmans into the entrance hall to the "womb," and kṣatriyas into the great hall before the entrance hall. Vaiśyas ought to move to the front of the bull and śūdras ought to move to the rear of the bull, make a four-cornered figure on the ground with cowdung, and worship with Śiva's primordial mantra. That is prescribed in the *Aṁcumān Āgama*

35. They then ought to gaze at images of deities such as Dakṣiṇamūrti, Somaskanda, Candraśekhara, and Subrahmaṇya and of all four of the ācāryas of the religion, and venerate and praise them.

36. Afterward they ought to approach the Presence of the goddess Pārvatī, fold their hands at their head and heart, gaze at her, visualize her mentally, perform offerings and other rites, and praise her.

37. Finally they ought to receive ash and apply it, circumambulate, approach the iconic Presence of Candeśvara, venerate and praise him, and clapping three times beseech him to give them the fruit of having obtained the vision of Śiva.

38. They ought then to return to the god Nandi and venerate and praise him, come to this side of the altar of sacrifice, prostrate three times, arise, sit down facing north and while visualizing the Lord Śiva mentally utter the five-syllable mantra a suitable number of times, and then arise and go home.

39. When returning from the vision of Śiva they should leave without showing their backside either to their Lord Śiva or to Nandi, the god who is a bull.

40. If the vision of Śiva is obtained at daybreak, sin committed during the night disappears; if obtained at midday, sin committed from the day of birth disappears; if obtained in the evening sin committed during seven births disappears. Therefore all Śaiva initiates every day, at all times without fail, ought to obtain the vision of Śiva with true love according to the rules.

41. Obtaining the vision of Śiva on Monday, on the eighth lunar day, on the evening of the thirteenth lunar day of the waxing moon and of the waning moon, on the full moon, on the new moon, on the auspicious day of the Ārdrā constellation, on the first day of the sun's northward course after the winter solstice, on the first day of the sun's southward course after the summer solstice, on the spring equinox, on the autumn equinox, on the day beginning a month, on the eclipse of the sun, on the eclipse of the moon, on the Night of Śiva, and on other such meritorious times is deemed meritorious action of the highest order for Śiva.

42. Those who, while visualizing the Lord Śiva mentally and reciting the five-syllable mantra verbally, perform bodily prostration from the beginning of sunrise until sunset or for a period of three hours will become free of all evil deeds, and attain emancipation. . . .

43. The "drain circumambulation" is done this way. Gaze at Nandi, the god who is a bull, and walk to his left [around the inner sanctum] and gaze at Candeśvara; returning the same way, gaze again at the bull and proceed to his right to the north, but do not cross the cow gargoyle whose mouth is the mouth of the drain from the liṅga inside the "womb"; return the same way, gaze at the bull, and walk to his left [around the inner sanctum] to gaze at Candeśvara; return again but without gazing at the bull pass to his right, to the north, and to the mouth of the drain; return again without gazing at the bull and pass to his left to gaze at Candeśvara; return and gaze at the bull and then gaze at the Lord who is Śiva's liṅga and worship. When leaving the temple, a "circumambulation of one's own soul" should be performed. A single circumambulation performed in this manner produces an endless quantity of fruit. It is especially excellent if this circumambulation occurs within the "evil period.". . .

44. The "evil period" is the name for the ninety minutes before and the ninety minutes after sunset on the thirteenth lunar day that comes in each of the two halves of the month, the "light half" of the waxing moon and the "dark half" of the waning moon. When Viṣṇu and the other gods were churning their Ocean of Milk for the elixir of "deathlessness," they saw the Halāhala poison arise first, and were racked by fear. When it closed in on them from the right and left they fled to the auspicious mountain Kailāsa and hid in the testicle of Nandi, the god who is a bull. The Halāhala poison followed them there, and to protect them the Lord Śiva sat down between the bull's horns, picked up the poison in his auspicious hand, and ate it. Then he stood between the horns and graciously danced. That happened during the crescent moon in the evening of the thirteenth lunar day, a Saturday. A different version of this story of the "evil period" is also told. According to it, the Lord Śiva ate the Halāhala poison and protected the gods in the evening of the eleventh day. When the elixir of "deathlessness" appeared from the Ocean of Milk on the twelfth day the gods ate it, and on the evening of the thirteenth day the gods venerated the Lord Śiva by worshiping him. The Lord Śiva then graciously stood on the bull. During the "evil period" one should touch the testicle of the god who is a bull and utter "Hara, Hara" with the mantra Oṃ while gazing between his two horns at the Lord who is Śiva's liṅga.

45. If, with true love, one obtains the vision of Śiva during the "evil period," debt, poverty, sickness, anxiety, distress, untimely death, the pangs of death, and sin disappear and emancipation will be realized. . . .

46. Meritorious acts to perform for Śiva inside a temple are these: Arising every day before sunrise, bathing, and when the daily rites are completed, sweeping

up the insects in the temple with a soft broom without killing them; collecting dung emerging from a cow that has not recently calved and is not sick on a leaf before the dung falls on the ground, or, if that is not possible, turning upside down dung that has fallen on a clean place and, picking up the middle portion, mixing it with water selected from such places as a reservoir or river and smearing it on the temple floor to clean it; picking flowers from an auspicious garden according to the rules, removing the ruined parts, tying them into a garland, and adorning the Lord Śiva with it; singing the Tamil Veda with rāgas in Śiva's Presence; playing it on the sāraṅgi; singing hymns to Śiva while clapping the hands and dancing joyously; burning fragrant incense; lighting auspicious lamps; reading Śiva Purāṇas aloud and explaining their meanings; listening to them; sponsoring temple service and acts of worship according to one's own means; etc. . . .

47. Mistakes not to be made inside an auspicious temple are these: Going to the temple without the proper conduct; going without washing the feet; going while polluted because of a birth or a death; spitting; excreting and urinating; blowing fluid from the nose onto the ground; passing intestinal gas; chewing areca nut and betel leaves; spitting chewed betel; eating and drinking; sleeping; having oneself shaved; taking an oil bath; examining the hair; combing and tying the hair; playing dice; tying a cloth around the head; wearing the upper cloth over the shoulders; covering oneself up; wearing a jacket; riding in a vehicle; carrying an umbrella over oneself; carrying a torch for oneself; sitting on a high place; sitting on a throne; treading on shadows cast by the tower, the flagstaff, the altar of sacrifice, the bull, and the images; touching the images and offerings already made; placing one's own shadow in the shadow of the auspicious lamp and in the shadow of the Śiva liṅga; flattering women; touching women; looking at women covetously; copulating with women; performing prostration and uttering prayer on the left side of the Presence that faces south and of the Presence that faces east; prostrating only once or twice; performing circumambulation only once or twice; circumambulating at a run; going between the Lord Śiva and Nandi, the god who is a bull; showing one's backside to them; crowding together in a bunch; obtaining the vision of Śiva at an inauspicious time; prostrating between the Lord Śiva and the altar of sacrifice; talking idly; talking indecently; listening to indecency; laughing; singing idle songs; listening to idle songs; hankering for the gods' wealth; flattering the vulgar; disparaging the esteemed; following malignant gods; worshiping while standing directly in front of the Lord Śiva or behind him or to his left; not trimming an auspicious lamp although one sees that it has gone out; worshiping when there is not an auspicious lamp; entering inside to worship instead of worshiping at the place where a festival is graciously taking place; worshiping gurus and others; and so on. Impure acts such as excreting and urinating, spitting, blowing the nose, and copulating are also not to be performed in Śiva's bathing place, in an auspicious garden, or in an auspicious hall. If any one

makes one of these mistakes out of ignorance and utters the Rudra mantra, that mistake disappears. If a person not qualified for the Rudra mantra utters the Aghora mantra one thousand times, that mistake disappears. People who make these mistakes knowingly will fall into hell and suffer and there is no purification for them. . . .

48. Those who want to make a pilgrimage to a distant place of Śiva ought to bathe on an auspicious day, complete their daily rites, place a ring of darbha grass on the fourth finger of the right hand in front of a true brahman outstanding in culture, knowledge, and conduct, and make the solemn vow, "I am obliged to make a pilgrimage to the place of Śiva," and perform the auspicious feeding of the ascetic slaves of Śiva. They then ought to take in hand the goods pertaining to one on the path of the good and right and set out from the house. Having discarded completely all evil qualities like desire and anger, they ought to travel without eating the food of strangers or buying the handgoods of others, and each day do such things as utter the five-syllable mantra, worship Śiva, recite the *Tēvāram* [Tamil Veda], obtain the vision of Śiva, hear the Śiva Purāṇas, and worship the gods by worshiping the devotees of Śiva. Traveling in this manner, when they reach the intended place of Śiva, they ought to prostrate to the gateway from a distance and then rise up and proceed, forsaking food for that day. They then ought to have themselves shaved, bathe according to the rules, offer balls of cooked rice to their ancestors, give the required ritual gift to a brahman of the highest worthiness that is appropriate to him, and then enter the auspicious temple and obtain the vision of Śiva according to the rules, give the Lord Śiva substances befitting him, and worship. . . .

49. Those of highest worthiness qualified to receive the required ritual gift are brahmans who recite and understand the Vedas and Āgamas and the Śiva Purāṇas, who have completely discarded sins, who perform the morning twilight worship, the worship of Śiva and other such rites without fail, according to the rules, and with faith, who live according to the duties of householders, and who are learned. They who give the ritual gift to anyone else will be born for ten births as a lizard, three births as a donkey, two births as a frog, one birth as an untouchable, and then as a śūdra, a vaiśya, a kṣatriya, and a brahman, and will whirl around suffering from poverty and disease. They therefore should give the ritual gift only to brahmans of highest worthiness. If there is no such person of high status in that place, they should resolve formally to give generously to a high-status person in another place and take property worthy of him and give it to him. If he has died, they should give it to his son. If he also has died, they should give it to the Lord Śiva. . . .

50. They ought to bathe in Śiva's bathing place there each day for three days, or five days, or fifteen days, or a month, or a year, and dwell there worshiping Śiva, obtaining the vision of Śiva in his abode, worshiping the gods by wor-

shiping Śiva's devotees when appropriate, and studying texts about Śaivism. Those who have no wealth ought to give the ascetic slaves of Śiva just a single handful of food before they eat. Once they have stayed their allotted time, they ought to worship the Lord Śiva and take leave of him, come to the outer limit of the temple and go to the gateway and prostrate, and then prostrate at the auspicious boundary of the realm. When, by following the discipline described earlier, they have reached their own village they ought to perform the feeding of brahmans and the worship of the gods by worshiping Śiva's devotees. . . .

51. Even though they possess human birth that is difficult to obtain and were born in Bhārata, which is the land of meritorious action where the true treatises that are the Vedas and Āgamas flourish, and in a Śaiva lineage of a caste that performs the rites of devotion, many people nevertheless pay no attention at all to the great value of these things. And even though they have studied and heard about the greatness of the Lord Śiva who is the repository of compassion and about meritorious deeds and sins and about their fruits, they remain ignorant, do not renounce sins and perform meritorious deeds, but spend the days of their lives idly and become prey for burning hells. A few people, even though they try in some way or another to begin to perform a few meritorious deeds, have no knowledge at all about the proper way to do them and they cover themselves only in sin, like one who spreads mud over himself when he has gone to bathe. Yet those Śaiva initiates who do not destroy themselves in this way but consider instead that this human birth is rare to obtain and the boundary that transcends it is rare know, who read and understand this composition, and who renounce sins and adhere to the Lord Śiva's feet with mind, speech, and body according to the rules and with love, ought to receive the transcendent joy that is eternal and be freed. . . .

Auspicious Cidambaram

May the auspicious feet of Meykaṇṭadesikan flourish.

—18—

The Order for Khālsā Initiation

Hew McLeod

Since the time of Guru Gobind Singh, the tenth and last personal guru, Sikhs have been divided into two categories, with one of the divisions further subdivided. At the end of the seventeenth century (probably in 1699) Guru Gobind Singh summoned a large gathering to his center at Anandpur and there established the Khālsā. All Sikhs who volunteered to enter this disciplined fellowship took initiation and promised that thereafter they would abide by a certain set of rules. These were the Amritdhari Sikhs (those who have taken amrit or the water of baptism). The set of rules that they were obliged to follow was the Rahit (the Khālsā code of belief and behavior).

Other Sikhs who did not choose to enter the Khālsā were known as Sahajdhari Sikhs. This distinction continues today, and so too do the various kinds of non-Khālsā Sikhs. Of the Sikhs who have chosen not to enter the Khālsā in any formal sense, many are clean-shaven. Many more, however, have elected to obey the principle rules of the Khālsā, notably the compulsion to keep the hair uncut. These Sikhs are known as Keśdhari Sikhs (Sikhs who, in the case of men, retain their beards—all beard-wearing male Sikhs are known as Keśdhari Sikhs). Of these Keśdharis some are also Amritdhari (initiated members of the Khālsā).

It is impossible to estimate the number of initiated members of the Khālsā (the Amritdhari Sikhs), but within the total Panth (the Sikh community) they would be only a small minority. In fact it matters little, for the Keśdhari Sikhs serve the same purpose as the Amritdharis. Both keep the traditions of the Khālsā vigorously alive, and the division that has meaning is between those Sikhs who cut their hair and those who do not.

During the eighteenth century, rahit-nāmas or written versions of the Khālsā Rahit were prepared, thus serving to record its injunctions. None of these, however, proved to be satisfactory, as was also true of attempts made during the nineteenth century. It was not until 1950 that a manual appeared that has, in succeeding years, won widespread acceptance. This was the *Sikh Rahit Maryādā,* "The Sikh Code of Conduct," published by the Shiromani Gurdwara Parbandhak

Committee in Amritsar. The rite of Khālsā initiation translated here is from this manual.

Further Reading

Hew McLeod, *Textual Sources for the Study of Sikhism* (Chicago: University of Chicago Press, 1990), from which much of this section is drawn (pp. 83–86.). Reprinted by permission.

The Rite of Khālsā Initiation

An open copy of the *Guru Granth Sāhib* is required at the place of initiation, together with at least six baptized Sikhs, each of them bearing all five of the Khālsā symbols. One of the Sikhs will sit with the *Guru Granth Sāhib* while the remaining five will administer the actual initiation. Either men or women may serve in both capacities. Prior to the ceremony they should bathe and wash their hair.

Any man or woman who affirms belief in the Sikh faith and vows to live according to its principles may receive initiation, regardless of nationality, [previous] creed, or caste. Those who are to receive initiation should be old enough to understand the meaning of the ceremony. They should bathe and wash their hair, and should present themselves wearing all five Khālsā symbols. These are uncut hair (*keś*), a sword or dagger (*kirpān*) suspended from the shoulder, a pair of shorts (*kach* or *kachahirā*), a comb (*kaṅghā*), and a steel bangle (*kaṛā*). [These are the "Five Ks." The kaṅghā is a wooden comb used to hold the topknot of the keś in place.] No symbols associated with other faiths may be worn. The head must be covered, but not with a hat or cap. Earrings and nose ornaments must not be worn. Prior to receiving initiation, the candidate should stand reverently before the *Guru Granth Sāhib* with palms together.

One of the five officiants should then address those who are seeking initiation, explaining to them the principles of the Sikh faith in the following terms: "The Sikh faith requires you to abandon the worship of man-made objects. Instead you should direct your love and devotion to the one supreme Creator. This obligation is discharged by attending to the words of sacred scripture; by serving the congregation and the Panth; by acting benevolently toward others; by maintaining love for the divine Name; and after receiving initiation by living in accordance with the Rahit. Do you gladly accept this faith?"

When an affirmative answer has been given one of the officiants should offer an appropriate prayer and take a hukam [opening the *Guru Granth Sāhib* at random and reading the portion which appears at the top of the left-hand page]. The five officiants should then take their places beside the large bowl [which is to be used for the baptism]. The bowl should be made of iron and should be set on something clean and appropriate, such as a gilded stool. Fresh water should be poured into the bowl and soluble sweets added. Having done this, the five officiants should sit around the bowl in the "heroic posture." [The right knee is laid on the ground with the body's weight on the right foot. The left knee is held.] The following passages from scripture should be recited: *Japjī, Jāp,* the *Ten Savayyās, Benatī Chaupaī,* and the six prescribed stanzas of *Ānand Sāhib.*

The officiant who performs this recitation should do so with his left hand placed on the rim of the bowl. With his right hand he should stir the water with a two-edged sword (*khaṇḍā*), keeping his attention intently focused on the task he is performing. The other officiants should gaze intently into the water with both hands resting on the rim of the bowl. After the appointed passages have been completed, one of the officiants should recite *Ardās.* [The "Sikh Prayer." For a translation see *Textual Sources for the Study of Sikhism,* pp. 104–5].

The candidates should now be instructed to adopt the "heroic posture," turning their thoughts to the tenth guru as they do so. Each should cup his hands, placing the right hand over the left. Five times the sanctified water (*amrit*) is poured into the candidate's cupped hands. As he does this the officiant shall say to him, "Say '*vāhigurū jī kā khālsā, vāhigurū jī kī fateh*' [Hail to the guru's Khālsā! Hail to the victory of the guru!]." After drinking each portion, the recipient shall repeat, "*vāhigurū jī kā khālsā, vāhigurū jī kī fateh.*" Amrit is then sprinkled onto his eyes five times, and five times it is sprinkled over his hair. After each sprinkling the officiant shall cry "*vāhigurū jī kā khālsā, vāhigurū jī kī fateh*" and the recipient shall repeat the words after him. The amrit which still remains is then consumed by the initiates [both men and women], all drinking from the same vessel.

Next the five officiants should impart the Name of God to the initiates by reciting the basic credal statement (*mūl mantra*) in unison and by having the initiates repeat it after them. . . .

One of the five officiants should then expound the Rahit as follows: "As from today you are 'born to the guru and freed from rebirth.' You are now a member of the Khālsā. Guru Gobind Singh is your spiritual father and Sāhib Kaur [the third of Guru Gobind Singh's three wives] your spiritual mother. Your birthplace is Keśgarh Sāhib [the gurdwārā at Ānandpur Sāhib that commemorates the founding of the Khālsā] and your home is Ānandpur Sāhib. Because you are all the children of the same father you are spiritual brothers, one with another and with all others who have received the amrit initiation. You must renounce your former lineage, occupation, and religious affiliation. This means that you should put aside all concern for caste status, birth, country, and religion, for you are now exclusively a member of the sublime Khālsā. You must worship God alone, spurning all other gods, goddesses, incarnations, and prophets. You must accept the ten gurus and their teachings as your only means of deliverance.

"You can already read the Gurmukhi script (if not you must learn how to do so) and at least once a day you must read or hear the following works which together constitute the daily rule: *Japjī, Jāp,* the *Ten Savayyās, Sodar Rahirās,* and *Sohilā.* You should also read or hear some additional passage from the *Guru Granth Sāhib* at least once a day, and you must always wear the Five Ks. These are uncut hair (*keś*), a sword or dagger (*kirpān*), a pair of shorts (*kach*), a comb (*kaṅghā*), and a steel bangle (*kaṛā*).

"There are four sins which are particularly serious and which must be scrupulously avoided: 1. cutting one's hair; 2. eating meat which has been slaughtered according to the Muslim rite; 3. sexual intercourse with any person other than one's spouse; and 4. using tobacco. Anyone who commits any of these cardinal sins must be reinitiated, unless the act has been unintentional, in which case no punishment should be administered.

"Have no dealings with initiated Sikhs who cut their hair, nor with Sikhs who smoke.

"Always be prepared to support the Panth and to provide whatever assistance may be required in a gurdwārā. Set aside a tenth part of whatever you earn and dedicate it to the guru. Let all that you do be done in accordance with the principles of *gurmat.*

"Observe at all times the discipline required of those who belong to the Khālsā. If you violate the Rahit in any respect you should present yourself before a congregation of the Khālsā and request a penance. . . . The following offences warrant a penance:

"**1.** Associating with Mīṇās, Masands, Dhīr-malīās, Rām-rāīās [the Mīṇās, Dhīr-malīās, and Rām-rāīās were schismatic groups which emerged during the late sixteenth and seventeenth centuries. The Masands were territorial supervisors who had provided faithful service under earlier gurus, but who had become arrogantly independent by the time of the tenth guru], and other enemies of the Panth; or with smokers, those who murder baby daughters, or initiated Sikhs who cut their hair.

"**2.** Eating from the same dish as a person who has not received the Khālsā initiation or an apostate Sikh (*patit*).

"**3.** Dyeing one's beard.

"**4.** Giving or receiving a cash dowry in return for a son's or a daughter's hand in marriage.

"**5.** Consuming any drug or intoxicant [cannabis, opium, alcohol, cocaine, etc.].

"**6.** Performing any rite or ceremony that conflicts with Sikh belief, or commissioning anyone else to do so.

"**7.** Neglecting to fulfil any part of the Rahit."

At the conclusion of this homily one of the five officiants should recite *Ardās*. The person sitting in attendance on the *Guru Granth Sāhib* should then take a hukam. If any of the newly initiated bears a name that was not selected from the *Guru Granth Sāhib* he should now receive a new name [chosen in the approved manner]. ["A passage (from the *Guru Granth Sāhib*) should be chosen at random and the officiating granthī (the gurdwārā custodian conducting the ceremony) should propose a name beginning with the same word as the randomly chosen hymn. If the suggested name meets with the congregation's approval, it shall be the name bestowed on the child. To a boy's name 'Singh' should be added, and to a girl's name 'Kaur.' " *Sikh Rahit Maryādā*, p. 18.] Finally kaṛāh praśād [sacramental food dispensed in gurdwārās] should be distributed. All who have enlisted in the guru's service, both men and women, should take kaṛāh praśād from the same dish. [This ensures that caste is necessarily broken in a religious sense. Other features of Sikh ceremony also ensure that caste can have no bearing on a person's access to liberation. All drink from the same vessel during the Khālsā initiation; all sit without concern for status in the gurdwārā; and in the free kitchen attached to every gurdwārā all must occupy status-free rows where they eat the same food.]

—19—

The Rite of Veneration of Jina Images

John E. Cort

The Jain community is divided into two broad traditions, the Digambaras ("sky-clad") and Śvetāmbaras ("white-robed"), named after the most distinguishing features of their respective mendicant practice. The Śvetāmbaras are further divided into three traditions, the Mūrtipūjakas, who worship images of the Jinas in temples, and the Sthānakavāsīs and Terāpanthīs, who do not worship such images. The Jinas ("conquerors"), also known as Arhats ("worthy ones") and Tīrthaṅkaras ("congregation founders"), are the twenty-four enlightened beings of this time period who taught the Jain tradition and established the fourfold congregation of monks, nuns, laymen, and laywomen. The last of these was Vardhamāna Mahāvīra, a slightly elder contemporary of the Buddha. Scholars also accept the historicity of the twenty-third Jina, Pārśva, but the other twenty-two recede into an area of Jain universal history that has not been confirmed by scholarship.

The Rite of Veneration of the Jina Images (*Caitya Vandana*) is performed daily in the temple by many Śvetāmbara Mūrtipūjaka Jain laity and mendicants, and the texts involved are known by heart by many thousands of Jains. The rite, translated here from a recent ritual manual, has its roots in the ancient six obligatory rites (*āvaśyaka*) of all Jain mendicants. The second of these rites is the Hymn to the Twenty-four Jinas (*caturviṃśati stava*), which is incorporated into the rite as step 3b. This hymn is also found at the earliest level of the Digambara tradition, and is still recited by Digambara mendicants today. The Rite of Veneration also incorporates elements of the fourth obligatory rite, Absolution of Faults (*pratikramaṇa*), which is performed in an abbreviated form at the outset of the rite (step 2), and the sixth obligatory rite, Abandonment of the Body (*kāyotsarga*), which is performed at both the beginning and the end of the rite (steps 3a and 13). The Rite of Veneration is also closely modeled on the third obligatory rite, Veneration of the Guru.

The Rite of Veneration has grown in elaboration over the centuries, as is seen in the linguistic layerings of material in the Prakrit, Sanskrit, and vernacular languages. The oldest layers are in the Jain ritual language of Prakrit. To these were added several Sanskrit verses, and the latest layers incorporate several hymns in the vernacular, in this case Gujarati. At several places the worshiper can sing a vernacular hymn of his or her own choosing: one that is appropriate to the identity of the Jina image in the temple, or to the day if it is a special holy day, or else a personal favorite. The linguistic layerings are lost when all three languages are translated into English. To best approximate the layerings, the rite should be translated into Greek or Hebrew, Latin, and English—and the English of eighteenth-century church hymnody, at that! I have indicated the linguistic shifts by P (Prakrit), S (Sanskrit), or G (Gujarati) after the relevant passages; the instructions themselves are in Hindi. The growth of the rite through incorporating parts of the different obligatory rites is also seen in the repetition of various parts of the rite. Repetition, of course, is an integral part of most ritual idioms.

The concept of veneration is found at the earliest levels of the Jain tradition, and the Jain practice of veneration may well be an important, but hitherto unstudied and unacknowledged, source for the later concept of bhakti (devotion) in all the Indian religious traditions. Veneration involves the praise and adoration of a superior being, whether a departed, enlightened, and liberated Jina or a living, unliberated mendicant. In the Jain case it also plays an integral part in the process of liberation, which is attained by the removal of all karmic attachments and stains. By venerating the superior qualities of a being who is more advanced along the path to liberation, one absorbs some of those qualities into one's being, and thereby both eradicates previously accrued karma and prevents the accrual of more karma. These are integral elements in the Jain process of liberation.

The description and texts here are taken from one contemporary manual from among the dozens of essentially identical ones available to all Jains: Muni Ratnasenvijay, *Caityavandan Sūtra Vivecanā,* (Fālnā, Rajasthan: Śārdā Prakāśan, 1983), part 2, pp. 30–39. This description has also been informed by fieldwork observation of the rite.

The Rite of Veneration of the Jina Images

1. The worshiper enters the temple wearing pure clothes. Using the end of the upper-body cloth, s/he carefully sweeps the floor immediately in front of her/himself three times in order to remove any insects or other living creatures.

a. S/he stands facing the image of the Jina, and says:

> I wish, O forbearing mendicant, to praise with strong
> concentration and with renunciation; [P]

b. Doing the five-limbed prostration [kneeling with hands folded before the chest, then touching the floor with two hands, two knees, and forehead], s/he says:

I praise with my forehead. [P]

2. Standing, s/he says:

a. Instruct me, O Lord, according to my desire. Should I do the absolution of faults (*pratikramaṇa*) committed in the course of walking? It is desired, I desire to do the absolution of faults. For injury in the course of walking, in going and coming, in treading on living things, in treading on seeds, in treading on green plants, in treading on dew, insects, mold, mud, clay, spiders, and cobwebs, whatever living beings have been injured by me—one-sensed, two-sensed, three-sensed, four-sensed, five-sensed, have been hurt, knocked down, squashed, struck, collided with, oppressed, fatigued, frightened, displaced from one spot to another, deprived of life—for all those, may the wrong action be of no karmic consequence. [P]

b. For those, as an additional effort, as penance, as purification, in order to be without the thorns of sinful karmas, for the destruction of sinful karmas, I stand in the body-renouncing posture (*kāyotsarga*). [P]

c. Except for inhaling, exhaling, coughing, sneezing, yawning, hiccuping, passing wind, dizziness, fainting, very slight movements of the limbs, very slight movements of mucus, very slight movements of the eyes, and other such faults, may my body-renouncing posture be unbroken and unhindered. As long as I have not completed the homage to the blessed Arhats, I shall abandon my body in this place, in silence, and in meditation. [P]

3. a. S/he stands in the body-renouncing posture [hands held downward at the side of the body, palms facing inward and slightly removed from the legs, feet slightly apart, and eyes focused on the tip of the nose], also known as the Jina posture, and silently recites once the Hymn to the Twenty-four Jinas (3b) or else four times the Namaskāra Mantra:

Praise to the Arhats
Praise to the Perfected Ones
Praise to the mendicant leaders
Praise to the mendicant preceptors
Praise to all mendicants in the world
This fivefold praise
destroys all sinful karmas
and of all holies
is the foremost holy. [P]

b. Then s/he recites aloud the Hymn to the Twenty-four Jinas:

I will glorify the illuminators of the world, the creators of the ford of dharma,
the Jinas, the Arhats, the twenty-four Omniscient Ones. (1)

I venerate Ṛṣabha and Ajita, Saṃbhava and Abhinandana and Sumati,
I venerate Padmaprabha, Supārśva Jina, and Candraprabha. (2)

Suvidhi and Puṣpadanta, Śītala, Śreyāṃsa, and Vāsupūjya,
I venerate Vimala and Ananta, the Jina Dharma and Śānti. (3)

I venerate Kunthu, Ara, and Malli, Minisuvrata, and the Jina Nami,
I venerate Ariṣṭanemi, and Pārśva and Vardhamāna. (4)

Thus I have praised those who are freed from the dirt of karma,
and who have destroyed illness and death.
May the twenty-four excellent Jinas, the Tīrthaṅkaras, be gracious to me. (5)

Thus glorified, venerated, and honored, supreme in the world,
Perfected Ones,
May they grant the benefits of health (that is, liberation) and
knowledge, and the best, highest enlightenment. (6)

Purer than the moon, much more radiant than the sun,
Deeper than the ocean—may those Perfected Ones give me perfection. (7) [P]

4. Bowing three times in the five-limbed prostration, s/he says each time:

I wish, O forbearing mendicant, to praise with strong concentration
and with renunciation;
I praise with my forehead. [P]

5. Seated in the yoga posture [right leg tucked under the right buttock, left knee raised, and hands folded before the mouth] s/he says:

Instruct me, O Lord, at my wish, to do praise.
Should I perform image-veneration? It is wished. [P]

6. a. S/he recites:

Like a vine of all that is good, or a blue-lotus cloud,
the sun that drives away darkness, or the wish-granting tree;
a raft on the ocean of rebirth, the cause of all success;
may he be forever beneficent to us, Śāntinatha (or Pārśvanātha). [S]

b. S/he sings or recites a hymn in the vernacular. The choice of this hymn is up to the worshiper, and may be one that is appropriate to the day if it is a special holiday, or one that is addressed to the main image of the temple. For example:

Hail wish-fulfilling Pārśvanātha! Hail Lord of the three worlds!
Victor over the eight karma enemies, attainer of the fifth realm
[liberation].

The root of joy is found in the name of the Lord, obtain happiness and success.
Fear of rebirth is removed by the name of the Lord, burn off all sins.

Recite the couplet "Oṃ Hrīṃ," repeat the name of Pārśva.
Poison is transformed into nectar, attain the immovable state. [G]

c. S/he recites:

Whatever is called a shrine in the celestial, infernal, or human realm:
however many Jina images are there, I praise them all. [P]

d. S/he recites the Indra Hymn, so called because it is said to have been recited by Indra, the king of the celestial beings, to Mahāvīra at the time of his conception:

Praise to the Arhats, the Lords, who cause the beginnings, the Tīrthaṅkaras, who by themselves have attained enlightenment, the best of men, lions among men, excellent lotuses among men, excellent perfumed elephants among men, the best in the world, lords of the world, benefactors of the world, lights of the world, illuminators of the world, givers of freedom from fear, givers of insight, givers of the path, givers of refuge, givers of enlightenment, givers of dharma, expounders of dharma, leaders of dharma, guides of dharma, the best world emperors of dharma, possessors of the irrefutable best knowledge and faith, freed from bondage, the victors, the conquerors, who have crossed over, who bring others across, wise, enlightened, liberated, who liberate others, omniscient, all-seeing, who have attained the place called Abode of Perfection which is beneficent, firm, inviolable, eternal, imperishable, undisturbed, and from which there is no return; praise to the Jinas who have conquered fear. In this threefold manner I praise all the Perfected Ones, those who have been, those who will be in a future time, and those who are in the present. [P]

e. S/he recites:

As many Jina images there are in the upper, lower, and middle worlds,
I residing here praise them all residing there. [P]

7. S/he again does the five-limbed prostration and says:

I wish, O forbearing mendicant, to praise
with strong concentration and with renunciation;
I praise with my forehead. [P]

8. Seated in the yoga posture, s/he recites:

a. As many mendicants there are in Bhārata, Airāvata, and Mahāvideha [the continents where liberation is possible] who maintain the three disciplines of mind, speech, and body—to them all I bow down. [P]

b. Praise to the Arhats, the Perfected Ones, the mendicant leaders, the mendicant preceptors, and all mendicants. [S]

9. S/he sings another hymn in the vernacular. If one does not come to mind, s/he should sing the "Obstacle Remover Hymn":

> I praise Pārśva the Obstacle Remover, Pārśva who is freed from clinging karma,
> the destroyer of the venom of the poisonous serpent,
> who is an abode of holiness and goodness. (1)
>
> The man who always holds in his throat this serpent–slayer spell
> is freed from evil planets, disease, pestilence, troubles, and senility. (2)
>
> Should this spell remain out of reach, just bowing to you gives great rewards.
> Souls in men and even animals are saved from sorrow and bad rebirth. (3)
>
> Attaining right faith in you, greater than a wish-granting gem or a wish-granting tree,
> souls easily attain that state free from old age and death. (4)
>
> Singing this hymn, O Greatly Glorious! full of devotion in my heart,
> O God! grant me wisdom in birth after birth, O Pārśva Jinacandra! (5) [P]

10. Seated in the pearl oyster posture [identical to the yoga posture, except the hands are folded in front of the forehead and nose instead of the chest], s/he recites the Hymn to the Dispassionate One:

> Victory to the Dispassionate One, Guru of the world;
> through your splendor may these be mine, O Lord:
> detachment from the world, following of the path, attainment of desired results, (1) [P]
>
> renunciation of what is censured in the world,
> worship of the gurus and parents, and practice of aid to others,
> attachment to a good guru, and service of his words, in full in this world. (2) [P]
>
> Even though I have renounced and stopped worldly aims,
> O Dispassionate One, according to your teachings,
> nonetheless I want to serve your feet in birth after birth. (3) [P]
>
> May suffering be destroyed, may karma be destroyed,
> may death in absorption and the reward of enlightenment
> be granted to me, O Lord, by my bowing to you. (4) [P]

The holiness of all holies, the cause of all beneficence,
the chief of all dharmas: the Jain teaching is victorious. (5) [S]

11. S/he stands and recites:

a. I do the body-renouncing posture to the images of the Arhats. For the sake of praising, for the sake of worshiping, for the sake of gifting, for the sake of honoring, for the sake of the reward of enlightenment, for the sake of liberation, I stand in the body-renouncing posture with faith, with intelligence, with steadfastness, with mindfulness, and with increasing absorption. [P]

b. Except for inhaling, exhaling, coughing, sneezing, yawning, hiccuping, passing wind, dizziness, fainting, very slight movements of the limbs, very slight movements of mucus, very slight movements of the eyes, and other such faults, may my body-renouncing posture be unbroken and unhindered. As long as I have not completed the homage to the blessed Arhats, I shall abandon my body in this place, in silence, and in meditation. [P]

13. a. S/he then remains in the body-renouncing posture while silently reciting once the Namaskāra mantra:

Praise to the Arhats
Praise to the Perfected Ones
Praise to the mendicant leaders
Praise to the mendicant preceptors
Praise to all mendicants in the world
This fivefold praise
destroys all sinful karmas
and of all holies
is the foremost holy. [P]

b. At the conclusion of the silent recitation, s/he says:

Praise to the Arhats. [P]

14. S/he recites another vernacular hymn, such as:

Worship Śaṅkheśvara Pārśvajī [the image at a popular pilgrimage site], take the benefit of a human birth.
The wishing-tree of all the heart's desires, hail the most beautiful human-born. [G]

15. S/he concludes by again doing the five-limbed prostration and saying:

I wish, O forbearing mendicant, to praise with strong
concentration and with renunciation;
I praise with my forehead. [P]

—20—

The Vaiṣṇava Sahajiyā Traditions of Medieval Bengal

Glen A. Hayes

How can men and women get to heaven, given the demands of a body of flesh and blood? As sexual beings, how should we relate to those of the other gender? What does it mean to be a man? A woman? How was the universe created? Can we use our emotions to reach ultimate reality? Can we really become like the gods? Can mastery of the human body lead to cosmic consciousness and to freedom from the painful cycle of reincarnation? These and other questions were major concerns for an important medieval Hindu tantric movement called the Vaiṣṇava Sahajiyā tradition. The term "tantric" is explained elsewhere in this volume, but essentially refers to a range of Asian religious movements using different yogic techniques, emphasizing the correspondence between the human body and the universe, and using an equilibrium between male and female energies to reach ultimate reality or liberation. They also generally regard the world as "real," in contrast to other Asian traditions that treat the world as basically "unreal" or "illusory." The term *Sahajiyā* is derived from the Sanskrit and Bengali word *sahaja,* which means "together-born"; this refers to the belief that all differences and dualities are unified—"together-born"—in an elevated state of consciousness. Thus, Vaiṣṇava Sahajiyā means "those who seek the together-born state by following the god Viṣṇu." Although called a Vaiṣṇava tradition (those who follow Viṣṇu, the "All-pervading" god), the Sahajiyās actually dealt more specifically with the playful and erotic god Kṛṣṇa (the "Dark Lord"). For the Sahajiyās, Kṛṣṇa functions on two levels: as the popular mythological god of Hinduism and as an abstract cosmic principle, with greater emphasis given to the abstract form. Although mainstream Hinduism regards Kṛṣṇa as an incarnation of Viṣṇu, the Sahajiyās reverse this and view Kṛṣṇa as the supreme power of the universe. Viṣṇu, when he does appear, generally functions as a less-powerful celestial being. However, since scholars have traditionally called them "Vaiṣṇava" Sahajiyās, we will use that term for reasons of consistency.

Found primarily in northeastern India during the sixteenth through nineteenth centuries, especially in greater Bengal (Bengal, Bihar, Orissa, Assam), their leaders blended together a curious range of beliefs and practices from several Hindu, Buddhist, and possibly even Islamic sources. Because some of their most important religious practices required having ritual sexual intercourse, they were regarded as rather scandalous and controversial by many people in the community. This unsavory reputation was magnified during the British period, and continues to this day. As a result, the Vaiṣṇava Sahajiyās tried to keep their practices hidden from the larger community, imposing a veil of secrecy upon both teachers and disciples. However, the Vaiṣṇava Sahajiyās, like other tantric groups, had definite religious reasons and explanations for their practices.

Followers of Vaiṣṇava Sahajiyā traditions consisted of both men and women; in contrast to most other South Asian religious traditions, women often served as masters (*guru*). Furthermore, it was believed that a man could not realize ultimate reality without the cooperation of a woman, and likewise a woman's realization depended upon the companionship of a man. The reasons for this cooperative nature of Sahajiyā belief and practice comes from their blending of earlier tantric traditions with contemporary devotional practices directed to the god Kṛṣṇa and his consort Rādhā ("Prosperity"). These influences will be explained shortly.

There were many reasons for the Vaiṣṇava Sahajiyās to keep their practices hidden from the community at large. Most of the people in Bengali Hindu society were fairly conservative when it came to issues of sexuality, and the Sahajiyā practices frequently involved violations of caste, as well. As with many other tantric traditions, the Sahajiyās disregarded the prevailing norms and attitudes, but since their members may have held responsible positions in society, they typically preferred to keep their status as Sahajiyās a secret. They lived in constant danger of social condemnation by the Hindus and harassment by the Muslim authorities who controlled much of medieval Bengal. They also wanted to keep the true meanings of their teachings within a closed circle of masters and disciples, and so virtually all Sahajiyā texts were composed in Bengali and Sanskrit using a special esoteric (hidden) code language called "intentional language" (*sandhyā-bhāṣā*). Since they felt that their practices conferred the power to shape reality and travel to inner heavens, they did not want the teachings falling into the hands of the uninitiated. They warned that unprepared people would suffer the pains of hell if they tried to use Sahajiyā techniques without being properly initiated by a qualified master. Those attracted simply to the sexuality and sensuality of Sahajiyā practices would instead be eternally tormented, never reaching the blissful heavens beyond this material world.

Unfortunately for modern scholars, this evasiveness has made the study of the Vaiṣṇava Sahajiyās difficult at best. Exactly when and where they originated is unknown. Many scholars believe that they appeared in Bengal soon after the time of the great Vaiṣṇava religious leader Kṛṣṇa-Caitanya ("He Who Makes the World Conscious of the Dark Lord"; c. 1486–1533), who popularized the worship of the god Kṛṣṇa and his divine consort Rādhā. But others argue that the Vaiṣṇava

Sahajiyās are direct descendants of an earlier (eighth to thirteenth century) form of tantric Buddhism that made use of the concept of *sahaja*. Another problem involves the authorship of the songs and texts that have come down to us. Far too many have the signature line (*bhaṇitā*) of a famous person of the past, like Caṇḍīdāsa ("Servant of the Furious Goddess") or Kṛṣṇadāsa ("Servant of the Dark Lord"). Why? Because the authors felt that more people would respect their composition if it was thought to be by a legitimate authority from the past. Some medieval teachers, as noted below, did give their own names, but typically their disciples went back to using fictive names. They were concerned not about claiming personal pride of authorship, but rather with conveying powerful liberating knowledge. The overall message, not the individual messenger, was what mattered most. So we know very little about the people themselves apart from what we can infer from the texts.

Another major problem in understanding the Vaiṣṇava Sahajiyās is the esoteric code language they use. Since they are dealing with controversial issues like sexuality, including the use in religious rituals of penises, vaginas, semen, and uterine blood, they generally use other words to indicate these concepts. Semen, for example, can be indicated by using the word *rasa,* which basically means "juice" from a sugarcane, or some sweet fluid. However, in other places in Sahajiyā compositions *rasa* can mean an elevated mystical experience according to the Caitanyaite tradition. So the word *rasa* in the text might mean semen or it might mean the mystical state—or both. A variety of metaphors are also used to refer to the sexual process and to genitalia; for example, the woman's pubic hair might be referred to as a garden with rows of vines, the vagina is a whirlpool, and the action of coitus is called "churning." In the translations that follow, I have tried to use the context to determine which meanings are implied. This uncertainty about the secret code in other tantric traditions is usually clarified by later commentators, who laboriously comment on important words, phrases, and images and explain what they "really" represent. Unfortunately, the Vaiṣṇava Sahajiyā tradition is the only major tantric movement for which we lack such later commentaries. It seems that the gurus themselves provided a living commentary, transmitted orally from master to student, thus maintaining the veil of secrecy concerning Sahajiyā traditions and practices. Faced with these difficulties, I have tried to break the code using information from context, other parts of the text, other texts, and interviews with modern tantrics who follow similar beliefs and practices.

It is likely that we will never fully understand the Sahajiyā code, since most research and fieldwork suggests that the traditional teaching lineages disappeared during the late nineteenth century. One Bengali scholar with extensive contacts in the villages and among many religious communities has never been able to locate a genuine Sahajiyā whose master continues the old lines of instruction. Some modern tantrics claim to be Sahajiyās, but they have not demonstrated proof of an unbroken connection to the medieval schools; in fact, these modern Sahajiyās may have been inspired by the publication of some Bengali Sahajiyā texts by Indian scholars in the 1930s and more recently by some popular presses in Calcutta. Certainly, groups like the Bāuls ("divinely mad ones"; see Chapter 9 above) help shed light on some of the Sahajiyā beliefs and practices, but only to a degree.

Given their obscure origins and development, it is also difficult to trace the influences on the Vaiṣṇava Sahajiyās beyond certain general trends. First, they were influenced by earlier schools of tantra and yoga, which emphasized the need to use a variety of psychological, physical, and sexual techniques in order to realize the highest states of consciousness and ultimate reality. From these traditions came ideas about the correspondence between the human body as a microcosm (miniature universe) and the universe as a macrocosm (large universe). This is based on their belief that the human body is mysteriously connected to the larger universe outside of the body and vice versa. The body is also connected to a hidden inner universe. Like a vast mystical network, all of the bodily parts and processes are linked to cosmic forces and substances. By manipulating that part of the network which one should be able to control (the body), one may then be able to interact with the overall network that one needs to control (the universe). An uncontrolled universe leads to suffering, confusion, death, and endless rebirths according to the laws of karma. By mastering the body—especially the breath, the mind, and the sexual energies—one could control the entire universe and be liberated from subsequent rebirths and deaths. For tantrics, the human body is a vital means for attaining the highest levels of reality.

A critical concept from tantric yoga involved sexuality and gender: since the created universe emerges from the interaction between cosmic male and female principles, the way to return to cosmic unity is to stimulate those principles using special rituals and statements. Although nontantric yoga traditions viewed this as the interaction between the male consciousness of the cosmic man (*puruṣa*) and the female matter (*prakṛti*), tantrics grounded this interaction in the bodies and sexuality of ordinary men and women. The problem, from the tantric point of view, is that we are separated from a state of divine cosmic bliss and unity due to the process of creation and existence as men and women. The solution, therefore, is to perform the practice of reversal (*ulṭā sādhanā*), in which the man identifies himself with a divine masculine being like Śiva (the "Auspicious One") or Kṛṣṇa, and the woman with their respective female consorts Śakti ("Power") or Rādhā. In the case of the Vaiṣṇava Sahajiyās, the man regards himself as Kṛṣṇa and the woman as Rādhā. Although in physical form (*rūpa*) they may seem like an ordinary man and woman, their essential form (*svarūpa*) is that of powerful cosmic principles—the very principles that create the universe. The overall process is difficult and usually requires years of preliminary practices, beginning with basic meditations, breathing exercises, and chanting, and culminating in the advanced stages of ritual sexual intercourse and powerful visions. By engaging in ritual coitus (*sambhoga*), the couple seeks to return to the unity of the together-born state of sahaja—the absolute state prior to and beyond creation. Most importantly, the man is not supposed to ejaculate during this ritual; in fact he is to use his control over his physical body to draw into his own body the fluids from the woman. As impossible as this may seem, the goal is to direct the mixed sexual fluids inside the man's body along a mystical channel (*nāḍī*) or river (*nadī*) into an interior universe—complete with ponds, villages, gardens, and various beings. Of note is the fact that the essence of the woman is brought into the man's body—certainly a clear reversal of the ordinary sexual process. Both the woman and the man are believed to attain the mystical state of sahaja; although the divine body seems to be located within the man's body, the "together-born inner person" (*sahaja mānuṣa*) consists of both the male and the female principles in a perfect state of equilibrium. Thus, the final goal is experienced only when the couple share their bodies, minds, and emotions in the state of divine love (*prema*). It is worth noting that this hydraulic or liquid system contrasts with that of other tantric traditions, which conceive of a powerful type of fiery cosmic energy, the serpent power (*kuṇḍalinī śakti*) that moves upward along a mystical yogic artery (*suṣumnā*) through several circles (*cakra*) that make up the inner body.

This concern with the transformation of physical bodies into internal spiritual bodies is termed "the principles of the body" (*deha-tattva*), and is a vital component of all Sahajiyā belief and practice. As with nontantric yoga, Sahajiyās believe that somewhere within, distinguishable from the body of flesh, blood, bones, and nerves is another body, a divine body (*deva deha*) which must be ritually constructed and used to reach the highest heavens. As tantrics, however, they use potent ritual techniques that involve sexuality to reach their goal. Another esoteric dimension that they have taken from earlier schools is that of alchemy (*rasāyana*), which, on the surface seems to involve the transformation of base metals like iron and lead into gold. Behind this process, however, is a spiritual process: that of transforming the physical body (likened to base metal) into the divine body (likened to gold). To this end they prepared ritual substances for consumption, the ingredients for which may have included camphor, mercury, and even sexual fluids. Through the use of ritual intercourse, ingestion of the alchemical preparations, and the utterance of powerful words and phrases (*mantra*), the Sahajiyā couple hoped to experience the together-born state, realizing their true inner nature as the inner person (*mānuṣa*). Several of the following translations deal with this type of sexual alchemy.

The other broad area of influence, apart from that of tantric yoga and alchemy, is that of the devotional system of Bengali Vaiṣṇavism popularized by Caitanya. The key elements taken from this dynamic tradition are that of divine love (prema), devotion (bhakti), and the state of pure appreciation (rasa). Regarding Kṛṣṇa as the supreme manifestation of the sacred, Bengali Vaiṣṇavas sought to identify themselves with one of the numerous characters in the mythic drama concerning the cowherd Kṛṣṇa and his adventures in pastoral locales as described in the classic Hindu devotional text, the *Bhāgavata Purāṇa* ("Ancient Tales of God"). The favorite role for both male and female devotees was that of one of the comely cowherd girls (*gopīs*), the most beautiful and pure of whom was Rādhā. Based partly upon earlier concepts of Sanskrit drama and aesthetics, these Vaiṣṇavas held that Kṛṣṇa represented the divine and the cowherd girls the human soul. Thus, in the longing of the cowherd girls for Kṛṣṇa, we have a representation of the human search for the sacred. Of critical importance is the role of emotions and eroticism to stimulate this passionate love for god. Using techniques such as chanting the names of Kṛṣṇa and singing his songs (*nāma-saṃkīrtana*), the Bengali Vaiṣṇavas tried to intensify their love and devotion in order to experience the reified essence of love, its rasa, in which one is completely absorbed in the love of Kṛṣṇa—as he in turn showers divine love on the devotee.

The Sahajiyās made some radical changes in the system popularized by Caitanya and his followers. The Caitanya movement is first of all theistic, as its members believe in Kṛṣṇa as a supreme divinity. They are also basically dualistic: humans are of an order of existence different from the divine and can never become fully divine, nor could the cowherd girls (the human soul) ever merge with Kṛṣṇa as one entity. In terms of ritual activity, Caitanyaites engage only in the symbolic lovemaking between Kṛṣṇa and the cowherd girls. Only Lord Kṛṣṇa could dare to make love to the wife of another man, as only the gopīs would dare to leave their husbands for another man. Much to the chagrin and outrage of orthodox Vaiṣṇavas, the medieval Sahajiyās transformed all of this into a basically humanistic system, in which Kṛṣṇa was simply the masculine "true form" (*svarūpa*) latent in all ordinary men, and Rādhā the corresponding feminine "true form" in all women. For most Sahajiyās, the two figures metaphorically embody the abstract cosmic principles of the masculine and the feminine, not the mythological characters of orthodox Vaiṣṇavism. They represent cosmic forces rather than the supreme God and his favorite devotee. In contrast to the orthodox dualists, the Sahajiyās were monistic; that is, they believed that humans are divine—that they are in essence divine being itself. This monism also includes the belief that the male and female powers would ultimately unify in the together-born state. The Vaiṣṇava Sahajiyās thus blended the mechanics of tantric yoga (including alchemy) with the emotional devotionalism of Bengali Vaiṣṇavism. This makes it a truly fascinating subject to study, but raises many challenges for the scholar and student. At the very least, the Vaiṣṇava Sahajiyās illustrate distinctive perspectives on human nature and reality, some of which are conveyed in the following translations.

During the seventeenth and eighteenth centuries, the Sahajiyās composed extremely esoteric works consisting of several hundred to a few thousand couplets, yet the most numerous type of composition is the pada, a short lyrical Bengali poem of usually four to eight couplets in length. Most of these poems deal with subjects like ritual practices, meditation, sacred love, devotion to the guru, and the need to realize the "inner body" of advanced yogic practice. The selections chosen for translation here consist of four short poems, one excerpt from a longer allegorical text, and two excerpts from a lengthy Sahajiyā "response" to a famous Bengali Vaiṣṇava biography of the religious leader Kṛṣṇa-Caitanya. The four poems are but a few of the hundreds that have come down to us. It is extremely difficult to date them precisely; although the manuscripts generally come from the nineteenth century, the language suggests earlier composition, probably from as early as the sixteenth century. Indeed, some of the themes and concepts clearly derive from much older tantric traditions. Most have been circulated due to their popularity and ability to convey the depth of the Sahajiyā mystical experience. These poems would often be sung to a musical rhythm which unfortunately is not indicated on the manuscript versions that have survived. Additionally, they are composed using several different poetic meters and rhyming patterns. In the day-to-day life of a Sahajiyā student, such short poems perhaps played a greater role than longer works of several hundred couplets, complementing the frequent guidance of the master. Since none of the poems have definite titles, I have used the first line or a phrase therein as the title. Introducing each selection are some brief comments intended to clarify the main points of interest in the composition.

Further Reading

For additional information on the Vaiṣṇava Sahajiyās, the following works may be consulted. For a detailed analysis of the beliefs, practices, and history of the medieval tradition, see Glen A. Hayes, *Shapes for the Soul: Cosmic Bodies and Transformation in Vaiṣṇava Sahajiyā Tantric Tradition,* SUNY Series in Tantric Studies, edited by Paul Muller-Ortega (Albany: State University of New York Press, forthcoming). This includes the complete Bengali text and English translation of an important medieval treatise on the divine body and the sexual alchemy. The relationship between the Sahajiyās and the Bengali Vaiṣṇava tradition is treated in Edward C. Dimock, Jr., *The Place of the Hidden Moon: Erotic Mysticism in the Vaiṣṇava-Sahajiyā Cult of Bengal* (Chicago: University of Chicago Press, 1966; Phoenix Books, 1989). Earlier useful works now available in reprinted editions are: Manindra Mohan Bose, *The Post-Caitanya Sahajiā Cult of Bengal* (reprint, Delhi: Gian Publishing House, 1986) and Shashibhusan Dasgupta, *Obscure Religious Cults* (reprint of third edition, Calcutta: Firma KLM, 1976). Bose tends to focus on the Sahajiyā connections to Bengal Vaiṣṇavism, whereas Dasgupta deals more with the earlier tantric influences and other contemporary tantric traditions.

Lyrical Poems

This first poem deals with the nature of the "inner person" (*mānuṣa*) with which the Vaiṣṇava Sahajiyās seek to identify. Reminiscent of classical Upaniṣadic concepts of the "cosmic man" (*puruṣa*), the mānuṣa is a mysterious being, paradoxically close-yet-distant to the physical world, and beyond all things. Among Sahajiyās, this "inner person" is also identified with Kṛṣṇa, reinforcing their belief in a form of ultimate humanism: the fully realized human being possesses divine qualities and powers, and knowledge can lead to this divine fullness of human existence. Those who realize this inner being will have disposed of their earthly connections, gained the liberation of ultimate reality, and will have essentially "died" to the ordinary world. This is called being "dead-while-alive" (*jiyante mara*), a concept found in other yogic traditions.

Although the author gives the name Caṇḍīdāsa, a title used by at least one famous earlier poet, this is clearly a pen name taken to lend legitimacy to the composition. This poem is written using the tripadī (three-footed) meter, in which each half of the couplet consists of three sections. This poem and the next three are translated from Maṇīndramohan Basu, ed., *Sahajiyā sāhitya* (Calcutta: University of Calcutta, 1932). The poem numbers appear in parentheses.

Mānuṣa mānuṣa sabāi balaye (21)

Everyone is talking about the inner person (*mānuṣa*), the inner person;
But what kind of being *is* the inner person?

The inner person is a jewel. The inner person is life itself.
The inner person is the treasure of the vital breaths (*prāṇa*).

All the world's people are deluded by errors and confusion.
They do not understand the true inner meaning (*marma*) of life.

The divine love (*prema*) of the inner person does not usually appear in the earthly realm,
but only through the inner person can people experience divine love.

Those people who experience the inner person *are* the inner person,
because the inner person recognizes the inner person.

These people and the inner person seem to exist separately,
yet it is the inner person who realizes the inner person.

Those who experience the inner person are dead-yet-alive (*jīyante marā*).
They have become the very essence of that inner person.

Initial experiences of the inner person are signs of great good fortune.
The inner person is on the far shores of experience.

Chanting the name of the inner person leads to a separate mystical place.
Distinct from this world, it has its own customs.

Caṇḍīdāsa says: Everything about it is distinct.
Who can fathom its customs?

Even beyond its role as the inner being, the inner person is also said to be a type of androgyne, together-born (*sahaja*) as a result of uniting the male and female powers through the use of the secret sexual rituals. During these rituals the uncontrolled lusts are transformed into a state of being called *rāga*, "controlled passion." The result is not a fetus but rather a special kind of consciousness and inner being. From the point of view of the ordinary world, therefore, the inner person cannot exist; upon leaving this world in order to reach the inner person, the Sahajiyā couple realizes that the ordinary world is just a lower level of reality. As in the previous poem, the next one describes the state in which one has seemingly "died" to the ordinary world and has, by dwelling in the inner universe, established relationships with "the dead." This transformation leads to a secondary birth, into a divine body born of the state of controlled passion and substances produced during the rituals. Once this divine body is obtained, the physical body is regarded as a mere shell, effectively cast away.

This poem is composed in the basic couplet style, and is signed by "Caṇḍīdāsa."

Sahaja mānuṣa kothāo nāi (23)

The together-born inner person (*sahaja mānuṣa*) is nowhere,
but if you search you will find it nearby.

It is not born from the womb,
but gains its birth through controlled passion (*rāga*).

Such birth through controlled passion is most extraordinary;
through the pursuit of such controlled passion, all is made firm.

Establishing a relationship with the dead,
one then maintains that relationship with the dead.

Dwelling forever among the dead,
one's hope is to transform the physical body.

If this physical body is lifted away,
then one has truly been touched by divine love (*prema*).

The great people say: "Dwelling in the nectar of immortality,
let my mind enter and remain in the together-born state."

Caṇḍīdāsa says: This is profoundly esoteric.
The mystic understands, the ignorant do not.

The concept of *rasa*, which has been translated as "divine juice," is complicated and important to the Vaiṣṇava Sahajiyās. On the one hand, the influence from the Bengali Vaiṣṇava tradition gives it one level of meaning as an elevated state of religious rapture in which the practitioner identifies with one of the characters in the mythical adventures of Kṛṣṇa. However, the tantric influence gives it the additional, and more fundamental, meaning of sexual fluid—especially, but not always, male semen. The goal of the sexual ritual is to reverse the sexual fluids during intercourse and elevate them to a mystical place somewhere within the man's body. This reservoir, within the physical body, is regarded as a part of the divine body. It is compared to an ocean of the elixir of immortality (*amṛta* or *amiyā*, the poetic form). The three streams of juice refer to the male, female, and mingled streams of fluid. Once the "divine juice" (understood as both substance and state of consciousness) has been brought into the divine body, the realization of the inner person can take place. The imagery of the ocean of nectar, churned by the gods in a contest with the demons, is an important part of classical Hindu mythology. In a typically oblique Sahajiyā adaptation of this metaphor, the poem refers to the "churning" that takes place in the vagina during intercourse and mentions the preferred partner for the ritual, literally a woman "belonging to another" (*parakīyā*). Following the adventures of Kṛṣṇa, the Sahajiyās literally sought to practice a form of sacred illicit sex, feeling that the risk and danger only heightened the state of passionate rapture. This practice probably led to their marginal position in Bengali Hindu society and to their apparent demise.

Like the first poem, this is signed by "Caṇḍīdāsa" and is composed in "triple-footed" meter.

Rasera sāyare rasika janamila (31)

The mystic was born in the sea of divine juice (*rasa*).
To whom will I speak about that divine juice?

By whom and where was it cultivated? Who tasted it?
Who is able to speak about it?

The essence of the nectar of immortality (*amiyā*) is named "divine juice."
The divine juice flows in three streams.

The experience of divine juice is eternally renewed.
Who has the power to understand this?

The treasure trove of nectar is churned without stopping.
Divine juice is produced by that churning.

That woman who is called "faithful to her husband" (*pativratā*) is devoted to the nectar.
Through the motions of her husband, divine juice is made.

The sweetness of divine juice overwhelms everything.
Who has the power to understand this?

This divine juice is very rare, the most extraordinary thing of all.
Within it is the inner person (*mānuṣa*) who controls reality.

Caṇḍīdāsa says: Most difficult to obtain
indeed is the divine juice of the inner person.

In mere conversation about it, suffering and fear are destroyed.
Among everything, it is the juiciest of all.

The divine body that the Vaiṣṇava Sahajiyās seek is said to be made out of the substances of the physical body (semen and uterine blood). When transformed through their "reversal" in ritual and through the state of selfless divine love (*prema*), they become very different substances. This is what their alchemy consists of: changing the base substances of the body into the golden radiance of the divine form. Through the power of the ritual, the sexual fluids are changed into a "cosmic substance" (*vastu*) which is then used to create and build the parts of the divine body (the rivers, ponds, flowers, and villages). Although other tantric traditions envision the divine body as made out of different cosmic energies, the Sahajiyās prefer the more substantive and hydraulic approach. The divine body is thus made out of the yogically reversed and alchemically transformed sexual substances that are prevented from flowing outward into the world to create an ordinary body. This is somewhat reminiscent of the image of the inner man (*homunculus*) of Western alchemical traditions.

This next poem is written using the basic couplet meter, and is signed with the name of another famous early poet, Kṛṣṇadāsa.

Vastutattva jāne yei pāya vastudhana (59)

One who understands the principles of cosmic substance (*vastu*)
will receive the treasure of that cosmic substance.
Without the cosmic substance, you'll never reach the Dark Lord
in his pastoral heaven.

No one understands that the principles of the cosmic substance
are found within the divine juice (*rasa*).
Without the divine juice, there can be no cosmic substance
in the three regions of the universe.

Within the glowing divine juice, there is a singular cosmic substance.
If you do not experience that cosmic substance, you will never reach
the Dark Lord.

The delectable experience of the erotic state is the embodiment of
divine juice.

While in that erotic state, the Dark Lord has command of that cosmic
substance.

Extract of extracts, the cosmic substance is profoundly esoteric.
Only the foremost of practitioners is able to taste that cosmic
substance.

That person who is the guru can taste that cosmic substance.
There is nothing to talk about—nothing to say.

When Caitanya came, he made the devoted followers eat that cosmic
substance.
Through the grace of Caitanya, the devotees tasted it.

Kṛṣṇadāsa says: Listen, my fellow practitioners!
Worship the together-born inner person (*sahaja mānuṣa*),
for it is the refuge of the highest devotees.

Esoteric Manuals

In addition to the numerous short poems produced over the centuries by the Vaiṣṇava Sahajiyās, certain influential gurus and their students produced longer works focusing on ritual practices and meditations. As with the poems, they are composed in a special esoteric code language intended to conceal the details from the uninitiated. The best known of these manuals were produced by the medieval guru Siddha Mukundadeva ("The Perfected Divine One Who Gives Liberation") and the various teaching lineages begun by his students. Mukunda lived approximately 1600–1650 C.E. and seems to have been responsible for synthesizing many of the diverse concepts and practices that are found in the manuals: Bengali Vaiṣṇava religious devotionalism and aesthetics, Hindu tantrism, alchemy, and classical yoga cosmology and symbolism. His major work was called "The Collection of Liberating Statements of Mukunda" (*Mukunda-muktāvalī*), which consisted of six related works composed in Sanskrit. The Bengali translations were probably prepared by his disciples during the seventeenth and eighteenth centuries. The Bengali translation of one of these works, "The Collection of Immortal Divine Juice" (*Amṛtarasāvalī,* c. 1650 C.E.), has been attributed to either Mukundadāsa or to Mathurādāsa ("Servant of the Pilgrimage Place of Kṛṣṇa"), although the specific manuscript used for this printed version does not provide a name.

This excerpt discusses the inner yogic body and how it is created during ritual sexual intercourse. This mystical cosmography of ponds and flowers is made through experiencing the divine juice (*rasa*)—here both an elevated religio-aesthetic state and the human sexual fluids—which must be directed along the yogic channel or "river" (*nadī*) that runs from the penis upward into the yogic body. The text warns of those unprepared and impure people who, like thieves, would try to enter the yogic body to improperly experience the rasa. The leader is Everyman, and his nine fellow thieves represent the several organs of perception and activity known to classical yoga tradition. The distance of "eight measures" traversed by the river refers to the eight constituents of the body, such as bone, ligament, sweat, semen, blood, and so forth. Their five weapons stand for the five cosmic elements: earth, air, water, fire, and space. Of interest are the references to the three colors of the river water (red, white, and mixed: representing uterine blood, semen, and the mingled fluids, respectively), to the cosmic mountain Sumeru, and to the potent alchemical substances (*dravya*) to be extracted from the whirlpool running down the body into the river. Reflecting the daily scenes of the riverine life of deltaic Bengal, passage along the mystical river is likened to the movement of merchant vessels, whose lights represent the yogic vision of the practitioner as the inner vision unfolds. This excerpt clearly illustrates the Vaiṣṇava Sahajiyā tendency to employ allegory and natural symbolism to convey the dynamics of the divine yogic body. It is written using both the basic and "triple-footed" couplet meters. The Bengali text is found in Basu, *Sahajiyā sāhitya*, pp. 163–66.

Selection from *Amṛtarasāvalī* of Siddha Mukundadeva

There is a lotus pond (*sarovara*) within the inner world,
and in this pond the lotus flowers grow.

The divine juice (*rasa*) of the flowers fills the lotus pond
and flows outward in two streams.

That person who is able to prevent ignorance and confusion
is the grandchild of the inner person.

He drinks just a little of that divine juice, letting the rest flow on,
as the mythical swan extracts only the milk from the mixture of water
and milk.

In all humility I ask you once again
to understand that there is an inner world.

All of the deities themselves hope to experience
those flowers, the divine juice, and that lotus pond.

The mystical lotus flowers grow only in that lotus pond.
All of the deities enjoy the divine juice of those flowers.

Around the lotus pond are posted five guardians.
"Carefully guard this place where the juices are united (*yoga*)!"

Saying this to the guardians, the gods returned to their abode.
As they were leaving, they reminded the guardians to be watchful.

Now, it happened that there was a thief who wanted to steal the divine juice, and his name was Everyman (*sabā*).
He was the leader of nine other thieves.

Terrifying indeed was the sight of their five hand-weapons.
These thieves usually roamed around the city doing nasty things.

One day the gang set out to steal the divine juice.
They crept along the riverbank, within sight of the river (*nadī*).

[The narrator interjects:]
Once again I humbly ask you to pay attention.
Eight measures (*krośa*) away from the river is a special place.

In that place there is a lotus pond.
A blue-colored flower blooms upon its waters.

From that flower the divine juice flows a distance of eight measures.
Emerging from the pond, the divine juice mixes with the waters of the river.

In that place which I call "Eye of the Great Lord" (*maheśa locana*) there is a corner, and in that corner is a garden.
That garden has been beautifully constructed

With so many of the finest trees and so many plants and creeping vines,
in delicate lines like rows of ants.

The river surges through the garden, as so much water flows and flows—
but water that I cannot write about.

That water which flows in the cool season is white in color,
while the water of the hot season is colored red.

During the rainy season the water is colored much like ordinary water.
In these three colors it flows during the twelve months.

Above the river there is an encircling mountain.
In front of the mountain there is a whirlpool.

Within this whirlpool are substances (*dravya*) of tremendous value.
By diving into the whirlpool, one will certainly obtain such substances.

In this river there is no sand—everywhere there is mud.
But along the two banks the sand is piled up like mountains.

How many hundreds of merchant vessels have plied those waters?
The river is illuminated by the equipment aboard the vessels.

What kind of landings (*ghāṭa*) are along the river and how does one dock there?
Looking in all directions, one is dazzled by all the sights.

How many hundreds of noble women have bathed in its waters?
At the touch of the river, their beautiful forms (*rūpa*) flourish.

It is most difficult to explain the characteristics of these beautiful forms.
Great effort is required in making such beauty permanent (*sthāyī*).

Vaiṣṇava Sahajiyā Responses to Bengali Vaiṣṇavism

Approximately two or three generations after Siddha Mukundadeva composed his works, some of his followers issued texts arguing that the most famous personalities of Bengali Vaiṣṇavism had in fact secretly been Sahajiyās—that is, practiced the secret sexual rituals. Their argument was simple: due to public pressure, these early Vaiṣṇava notables had to make themselves seem to be only symbolically involved in the erotic devotions of Kṛṣṇa and the cowherd girls in Vṛndāvana—so the Sahajiyās claimed, much to the outrage of orthodox Vaiṣṇavas. The major text making these controversial claims is "The Erotic Sport of Transformation" (*Vivarta-vilāsa*) by Ākiñcanadāsa ("Servant of the Lowly Ones"), dating from around 1700 C.E. In this very extensive treatise of several thousand couplets, the author uses numerous quotations from a famous sixteenth-century hagiography of the religious leader Kṛṣṇa-Caitanya, "The Immortal Acts of Caitanya" (*Caitanya-caritāmṛta*) to show how Caitanya and most of his important followers—including the author of the hagiography, Kṛṣṇadāsa Kavirāja ("King of the Poets, Who Serves the Dark Lord," although *kavirāja* also means "physician")—were actually Vaiṣṇava Sahajiyās.

The first excerpt presented here comments on the necessity for the assistance of experienced Sahajiyās in the preparation of the "alchemical candy" (*bhiyāna*) that is made from the sexual fluids during ritual love making, and uses one quote from "The Immortal Acts of Caitanya" to argue that these powerful yogic substances are the final products of a series of processes that refine worldly things into divine experiences. It is probable that an actual mixture was made out of the sexual substances and other additives such as camphor and mercury in order to make the alchemical pill used to create the divine body. The details are unclear—probably for reasons of secrecy. This passage is composed in the basic couplet meter.

I have used the seventh printed edition of the *Vivarta-vilāsa*, edited by Kṛṣṇa Bhaṭṭācārya (Calcutta: Tārācāṅd Dāsa and Sons, n.d.). The first excerpt comes from pp. 92–93. All quotations from the *Caitanya-caritāmṛta* refer to the edition edited by Rādhāgovinda Nāth, *Śrīśrīcaitanyacaritāmṛta*, 6 vols. (Calcutta: Sādhanā Prakāśanī, B.S. 1392/C.E. 1986).

The Erotic Sport of Transformation

Without the help of experienced devotees, devotion to the divine juice (*rasa*)
cannot be understood.
The alchemical candy (*bhiyāna*) is ritually prepared using the instrument of divine love.

The alchemical candy was made by seizing the divine juice,
and blending into that precious treasure the female and the male principles.

As many sugar-drops and candy pieces that can be made from the juice of the sugarcane,
in direct proportion, that much cosmic substance (*vastu*) and power (*śakti*)
are to be gained in the great mystical condition (*mahābhāva*).

In *The Immortal Acts of Caitanya* (2.23.23) it is said:

From the sugarcane plant come seeds, stalks, juice, and molasses, but they share the same basic essence.
Sugar candy is really just the finest white sugar mixed with spices.

Just as these products introduced into the sugarcane gradually increase the flavor,
so do controlled passion and divine love incrementally increase religious experience.

The juice and cosmic substance are always present in a special place.
If they remain, what happens? You must understand all of this.

Take the juice in that place and mix spices with it.
You must fashion the confection by transforming that juice.

The second excerpt begins with an unattributed poem concerning the use of alchemy in transforming the human body. Just as the proverbial alchemist used the magical touchstone to turn iron into gold, the Sahajiyā uses the sexual substances collected in ritual to transform the physical body into a divine or spiritual body. Throughout India one finds notions of the conservation of semen by the male; in some versions it is kept in a reservoir within the body—likened to a pitcher or, more elegantly, to a lotus pond (*sarovara*). Much attention is directed, as a result, to the sexual ritual, sexual fluids, and sexual organs. With the Sahajiyās, however, both the female and male contributions are valued. Of interest is the distinctive correspondence between the different aspects of the secret initiation and the act of coitus. The praises to Kṛṣṇa and the seed-syllable (*bīja*) are identified with the female and male fluids, respectively, while the tongue of the master and the initiate's ear are likened to the penis and the vagina. While the physical form of such intercourse leads to the birth of the body of flesh and blood, the Sahajiyā initiation leads to the birth of the divine body. Attainment of this divine body means that the couple has realized the all-powerful inner person (*mānuṣa*), who is at the heart of reality.

This selection is composed using the basic couplet meter. It comes from the *Vivarta-vilāsa* of Ākiñcandāsa, edited by Bhaṭṭācārya, pp. 113–15.

In a lyrical poem [anonymous] it is said:

Upon the touch of the alchemist's touchstone (*sparśamaṇi*) iron is turned into gold.
Iron becomes gold—this happens very often.

If you take some secret cosmic substance (vastu), and touch iron with it,
time and again the iron will become gold—know how to distinguish them!

Use judgment to behold that which seems not to exist.
Keep the company of practitioners, hold them close to your heart.

The crest-jewel and the touchstone are Lord Caitanya.
Without him the touchstone cannot be found anywhere.

He is the touchstone which makes the river Jambu into gold
as it flows down from the heavens.
That same divine love touched his disciples Rūpa ("Form") and Sanātana ("Eternal One").

Some souls have the good fortune to associate with practitioners.
Seeing the cosmic substance that has been obtained, they become very powerful.

Day and night they focus their minds on that form,
beholding with the eyes that which is eternally radiant.

That same form has no similarity to physical beauty,
seeing that the two—the moon and the sun—are within a single body.

The mind is continually focused on that same form.
At the feet of the Dark Lord, I ask for a vision.

[The narrator resumes:]
Those rituals which deserve the highest praise involve childless asceticism.
Please, I implore you, behold and understand the secret meanings!

On his head there is a pitcher (*kumbha*) to be filled.
When the pitcher is filled, the practitioner becomes very powerful.

Then divine love appears in his body.
Thus everyone says: "That inner country is a remarkable place."

Hear about the different kinds of birth from the manuals of the practitioners and from the mouths of practitioners.
It is not even worth considering other viewpoints concerning the nature of devotion.

The grace of the guru and the grace of practitioners come after the grace of mother and father.
This tells you that there are two separate and distinct births.

There is no birth at all without uterine blood, semen, vagina, and penis.
How can that be? I will discuss its significance.

At first there was a birth due to the bonding between mother and father.
But behold how just a little grace from the guru can cause a rebirth (*punarjanma*).

That also involves uterine blood, semen, vagina, and penis.
Clear your mind and listen, for I speak the essence of this.

The praises for the Dark Lord are like the uterine blood,
while the seed syllable is like the semen.
The tongue of the master (*guru*) is like the penis,
while the ear of the disciple is like the vagina.

So, your birth should come about from these things.
You should really try to understand how you can be born through the grace of practitioners.

The eye and ear are some of the five organs of knowledge (*jñāna-indriya*).
In the beginning and intermediate stages of practice, you must make them compassionate.

Use the organ of knowledge that is the ear to hear about birth.
Use the eye to see the grace of the practitioners and the eternal order (*nitya dharma*).

You will then progress gradually through the three stages of practice: beginner, intermediate, and perfected.
Hear with the ear and see with the eye how these are all really one process.

You must realize, brother, that everything has its uterine blood and semen.
Semen and uterine blood will develop when one assumes the condition of Rādhā.

The condition of being Rādhā I call the "law of loving one who belongs to another" (*parakīyādharma*).
All of the principles of greed and devotion can be found in that condition.

Thus it is said [in an anonymous Sanskrit couplet]:
One should act according to Vaiṣṇava conduct.
Such a devout condition is hindered by greedy impulses.

Realize that there are many viewpoints and teachings in the world.
No one can understand their duty (*dharma*) with such confusion.

How will you know the nature of the self (*ātma*), the soul (*jīva*), and passionate love (*rati*)?
I say that the inner person will appear—yet nothing is known about it.

In its control are the god Brahmā and the souls, in birth and in death.
Time and time again it does nothing, simply reflecting on eternity.

Purity, activity, and inertia are the three qualities (*guṇa*) of the one who has been born.
By the hand of the physician a single vessel of wind, bile, and phlegm is delivered.

In *The Immortal Acts of Caitanya* (2.20.258) it is said:
Brahmā, Viṣṇu, and Śiva are the incarnations of the three qualities.
Fulfilling the promise of the three qualities is the process of creation.

[In 2.20.264:]
Just as milk becomes yogurt when mixed with a sour substance,
The active substance is not milk itself, so yogurt is not the same as milk.

[In 1.5.57:]
From far away, the cosmic man (*puruṣa*) is placed in a state of illusion (*māyā*).

—21—

The Goddess Ṣaṣṭhī Protects Children

Tony K. Stewart

Vrata in Bengali literally means "vow," but it serves as a shorthand to signify an array of closely related Hindu religious practices carried out primarily by the women of the traditional household. Vratas are undertaken to attain certain specific goals, usually related to generating wealth, protecting and maintaining the health of the family, and ensuring a general prosperity for all. The vratas are timed to the lunar calendar, with an appropriate worship set aside for nearly every day. But no household follows every vrata. In practice we find a wide combination of vows, although a handful of these seem to provide a core around which each household will construct its significant set. Part of this variety is simply the result of local custom, part of it depends on the number and ages of the women in the household, and part of it reflects the economics of each family, although few ritual vows are expensive to undertake. Among the most popular gods and goddesses to receive homage and promises of future fidelity, worship, and respect, are Lakṣmī, the goddess who provides wealth, prosperity, and fertility, and Ṣaṣṭhī, giver and especially protector of children. In this section we will focus on Ṣaṣṭhī, whose name literally means the "sixth" and whose worship occurs on the sixth day of the bright half of each lunar month.

It is virtually impossible to trace the origins of the vrata ritual vow, but suggestive analogs are found in the Brāhmaṇa ritual compilations of the late Veda. Later Purāṇas contain detailed instructions for ritual vows. Most of these require male participation and supervision, generally through the offices of the brahman priest. The modern household vrata ritual, however, is predominately a woman's affair in preparation and execution, although men often figure prominently in the story explaining the vow. Modern priestly handbooks, which compile puranic and popular religious ritual, tend to articulate two compelling reasons for undertaking a vow: liberation from the rounds of existence (*mukti;* cf. Sanskrit *mokṣa*) and enjoyment of the material benefits of this world (*bhukti*). Although generalizations for the whole of India are difficult, in Bengal, the former type tend to find expression most frequently in the vratas of older women, especially widows, whereas the latter dominate most other exercises of vows. Bhukti, material gain in this world, is primarily the concern of unmarried girls within the household, who undertake vratas for quality marriages and for guarantees of fertility. Married women likewise pursue worldly benefits by invoking the deities to protect their children and to enable them to provide well for their families. The stories of Ṣaṣṭhī, while of interest to the unmarried, receive strongest support among younger married women, for these young mothers are the direct focus—both as recipients and nurturers—of Ṣaṣṭhī's activities.

The ritual vow in its generic form consists of four basic parts, each of which can be abbreviated or embellished in actual practice. The first part is the preparation (*āharaṇa*), in which the necessary items to be used in the ritual are gathered. Substitutions are allowed for items that cannot be procured or prove too expensive for the participants, as long as the reasons for these substitutions are honest; penurious preparation will adversely affect the ritual's outcome. The second part of the vow requires the participants to explain the action of the vrata, the reasons for undertaking the vow, and the procedures for executing it. The participants initiate this action by demarcating a sacred space and decorating it with auspicious designs commonly drawn with rice flour or paste, called *ālpanā*. These designs are highly stylized and, through a complex geometry and direct representation, they depict the god or goddess who is being invoked and the story associated with that divinity; in the case of Ṣaṣṭhī one occasionally sees her cat drawn in the elaborate pattern. A clay pot is frequently used to represent the goddess herself. Three-dimensional representations can also be used to relive the action or represent the hoped-for result; for example, in the vow of Ṣaṣṭhī of the Rice Cake (Cāpaḍā Ṣaṣṭhī) the action revolves around a tank or pond, which is replicated in miniature, dug in the ground, and filled with water to complete the ritual. The following instruction for preparation of the vow of Ṣaṣṭhī of the Golden Hairclip (Luṇṭhana Ṣaṣṭhī) is translated from *Bāramāsera Meyedera Vratakathā*, edited by Pavara Gopālacandra Bhaṭṭācārya, revised with notes by Ramā Devi (Calcutta: Nirmmala Buka Ejensi, n.d.), pp. 80, 83. It illustrates this preparatory stage.

UNDERTAKING THE VOW OF ṢAṢṬHĪ OF THE GOLDEN HAIRCLIP

This vow is to be performed on the sixth day of the light half of the month of Śrāvaṇa (July-August). It is designated for those women who are pregnant. This vow must never be undertaken by barren or sterile women or by widows. The worship is not performed when the sixth falls on Monday, Tuesday, Friday, or Saturday. This vow will be effective only when the ritual prescriptions are scrupulously followed.

DIRECTIONS FOR THE VOW

Draw the ālpanā figures with rice powder. Fix into the earth a branch from a banyan tree and place in front of it a fired, unglazed earthen pot [representing

Ṣaṣṭhī]. Mix mustard oil, turmeric, and yogurt into a paste. Using only leftover cream, fashion seven pieces of thickened milk fat into the shape of hair clasps and place them next to Ṣaṣṭhī's pot. At the end of the ritual, make obeisance to Mother Ṣaṣṭhī and listen attentively to her story.

THE FRUIT OF THE VOW

The children of the woman who observes this ritual will never suffer an untimely or inauspicious death.

Note the brevity of instruction; this is basically an oral tradition for which the text serves merely as a reminder, rather than a detailed guide; the older women see to it that the younger women and girls perform the ritual properly.

The third constituent of the ritual vow is the uttered verse, a mantra, which is in Bengali or, less frequently, Sanskrit. In its most streamlined form this utterance, known as *chaḍā,* will be a single line of verse, functioning as an incantation to activitate the vow. In their more elaborate forms, these utterances punctuate and precipitate the action; the sounds propel the action of the ritual with their aural power. Other utterances become objects of meditation to help the participant adopt the proper attitude and to ensure that the sincerity of the vow is registered by the goddess. In the story of the Forest or Araṇya Ṣaṣṭhī, the participants are urged to reflect on this image of the goddess, the chaḍā being a multi-line Sanskrit strophe. It is translated from *Bāramāsera Meyedera Vratakathā,* p. 58.

> She whose golden limbs, draped with jewels, glisten like mountain snow,
> whose hands proffer boons and dispel fear,
>   whose visage eclipses yellow harvest moons,
> whose swollen milk-engorged breasts strain the shimmering silk of her blouse,
> in whose belly rests the male child, the primordial unborn man—
> this goddess Ṣaṣṭhī, the Sixth, may you fix clearly in your mind!

Prepared through meditation and ritual action, the participants then come to the heart of the vow, the recitation of the goddess' story (*kathā*).

The story attached to a vrata tends to explain the circumstances leading to the creation of that particular vow or to teach and illustrate basic ethical principles. The latter prove vital for the harmony of the household by instilling a strong sense of morality in the participants. The etiology of the vow and its moral frequently intertwine, as we find in the example of Forest Ṣaṣṭhī translated below. The story tends to follow relatively predictable plot lines: the goddess is displeased by the failure of an individual to conduct him- or herself properly, so she inflicts great suffering on that person. The increasing trauma finally brings the protagonist to the point of recognition, where he or she can understand the root cause of the problem, this realization being an act that connects the character to the goddess and places this newly found relationship on a firm moral ground. The prior ill-treatment is then rectified and the protagonist regains his or her former position, often much enhanced. The story generally ends with a paean to the goddess, describing her wondrous traits and the benefits of observing her vow.

Several medieval texts of the maṅgala kāvya genre extol the feats of the goddess Ṣaṣṭhī, but these tales bear only slight resemblance to the modern popular stories of the Ṣaṣṭhī vows. These vows number twelve, one for each month of the year and the stories appear in inexpensive booklets, generally called *Meyeder Vratakathā* ("The Stories of Women's Vows"), each containing a wide mix of monthly observances. The language tends to be very colloquial and modern, although one occasionally finds more formal productions, including Sanskrit translations of the stories. Frequently, as is the case here, the booklet shows no author or editor or publisher. As noted in our examples above, the articles required for worship and the requisite chaḍā utterances are generally listed briefly prior to the story. The tale itself can be printed in skeletal outline, to be embellished by the raconteur in the course of the ritual, or in more developed form. The five stories translated and retold here suggest the breadth of this elaborate tradition dedicated to the responsibilities of child bearing and rearing in a perfect family life.

The translations are from an old text that has neither title page nor printing information. The style of printing and formating suggests that the edition I used was issued by a popular press, possibly Tārācānda Dāsa, about thirty or forty years ago.

Further Reading

On vratas, see Sudhir Ranjan Das, *Folk Religion in Bengal: A Study of Vrata Rites* (Calcutta: S. C. Kar, 1953) On Ṣaṣṭhī, see Edward C. Dimock, Jr., "Manasa, Goddess of Snakes: The Ṣaṣṭhī Myth," in *Myths and Symbols: Studies in Honor of Mircea Eliade,* edited by Joseph M. Kitagawa and Charles H. Long (Chicago: University of Chicago Press, 1969), pp. 217–26.

ṢAṢṬHĪ OF THE FOREST

Once there was a brahman woman. She had three sons and those three sons had wives. The youngest of the three wives in the extended family was terribly greedy. Whenever she had the chance, she would steal fish and milk and eat it, and then place the blame on a certain black cat. After a time, the youngest wife had a child and it was a boy, beautiful as the moon is brilliant. That first night, taking the child in her lap, she lay down. In the morning she arose and saw the child was missing. The young wife searched here and there, but could not find her child.

The youngest wife had seven more boys and one girl. Yet in exactly the same fashion, the boys and the girl were stolen one by one from her arms. The rumors began to circulate: "The youngest wife is a demon. She herself has eaten her own children!"

Broken-hearted, the youngest wife escaped to the forest and sat down, crying bitterly. When Mother Ṣaṣṭhī saw her weep like this, she took pity. Dressed like an old brahman woman, she came and asked the youngest wife why she was crying. The youngest wife related her long tale of woe.

Mother Ṣaṣṭhī said, "There is no one in your household as awful as you, stealing all those things, eating them, and then lying and unfairly blaming my black cat. That is why my cat has spirited away your children and brought them all to me. Now that you understand the reason for your plight, you need only perform a single difficult but sincere penance for your wrongdoings and I will return your children."

Sobbing, the youngest wife said, "Whatever harsh penances you prescribe, I shall readily consent to do."

Testing her, Mother Ṣaṣṭhī replied, "Look over by the tree. There lies a dead cat, its body decomposing, liquid with putrefaction. First, you must bring a bowl of curds and smear those curds over that cat's body. Then you must lap up all of the curds into the bowl and bring that concoction back to me."

Without hesitation, in her desperation and remorse, the youngest wife did exactly as the old woman directed. As soon as she did, she beheld all of her children—her eight boys and her girl—standing beside her. Then Mother Ṣaṣṭhī lectured her, "Mark their foreheads with these curds. Never be guilty again of stealing food and eating it yourself, and then shifting the blame onto the cat or anything else. Never kick a cat, for that is my companion and vehicle. Likewise, never strike your children with your left hand, nor refer to their mortality lest it become true. Never, never verbally abuse them!" Then Mother Ṣaṣṭhī instructed her to observe ritual vows of Ṣaṣṭhī of the Forest or Araṇya Ṣaṣṭhī on the sixth day of the light half of the moon of the month of Jyeṣṭha [May-June]. After imparting to her these rules and regulations, Mother Ṣaṣṭhī left.

Soon thereafter, the youngest wife gathered her children and took them home. She told everyone her strange and marvelous tale. And from the youngest wife, all of the other wives quickly learned the rules and regulations of this particular Ṣaṣṭhī worship. They began to perform regularly and with devotion the proper Ṣaṣṭhī worship for the month of Jyeṣṭha.

The youngest wife was able to see all her children provided with extravagant weddings. Her daughter and son-in-law returned to the house on the sixth day of Jyeṣṭha. She marked the son-in-law's forehead with curds and served him dishes of succulent mango and delicious jackfruit. In turn the other wives, too, successfully gave their children in marriage and brought their daughters' husbands home. For this reason this sixth day of Jyeṣṭha became known as "the son-in-law's sixth" or the day of offering ritual vows to Ṣaṣṭhī.

ṢAṢṬHĪ OF THE GOLDEN HAIRCLIP

There once was a brahman who had six sons, all of whom had wives, and who also had a single daughter. All of his sons had children and his daughter had two children, as well. At the beginning of the month of Śrāvaṇa [July-August] the daughter came to her father's house with her children. Staying for a few days of Śrāvaṇa, she would then return to her in-laws' house.

The brahman was happy with his family life. His home resounded with the sounds of his grandsons and granddaughters. Witness to this, all of the neighbors were jealous, while others would say, "Aha! It's as if Mother Ṣaṣṭhī has borne fruit on every branch!" All of the sons adored their parents like deities, and the wives their in-laws. The sons earned their own living and there was paddy in every field and fish in every pond. [In short, they were prosperous.]

Meanwhile the sixth day of the light half of the moon in the month of Śrāvaṇa came. The brahman's wife took her six daughters-in-law and her own daughter and sat down to perform the worship of Ṣaṣṭhī. They prepared all kinds of offerings, the appropriate metal trays and ten different fruits. When the brahman woman lifted the lid of the wicker basket in order to take out some golden hairclips, which are special decorative ornaments, she saw that three of the four ornaments which had been kept there were missing. When she saw this, the brahman woman flew into a rage and interrogated everyone. Hearing this outburst, the eldest daughter-in-law was surprised and commented, "What are you saying, Mother? For days on end they have remained in place, but now, suddenly, they are gone." Then, in an effort to establish her innocence, she placed her hand on the forehead of her son and swore, "If I took the hairclips I will eat the heads of my children."

The brahman's daughter said, "I am in my parents' house only for a few days. I do not know where things are kept. So, how could I have known where they were? In two days I will go back to my in-laws' house. My eldest sister-in-law is the only one who knows what goes on in your home."

The brahman woman fashioned some new ornaments out of dried milk to replace the missing ones and then she performed the worship. The eldest daughter-in-law revealed everything within her heart to Mother Ṣaṣṭhī and pleaded, "Mother Ṣaṣṭhī, my dear Mother, you heard everything. My sister-in-law has slandered me. Please adjudicate this matter!"

When all the brahman woman's sons returned to the house and heard what had transpired, they got exceedingly angry. Without stopping to think, the eldest blurted out the first things that came to mind, compounding the problem immensely. When she listened to all of the ravings, the eldest daughter-in-law—because of her embarrassment and shame—refused to eat anything at all that night. Gathering her children, she shut the door to their room and lay down in her own.

In the morning, when the eldest daughter-in-law awoke she opened the door and saw that all seven children were still—they were dead! She burst into tears. Hearing her weep, the brahman woman, the other daughters-in-law, and the daughter came running. All were stunned at the sight before them. Immediately the daughter screamed, "Now you have seen! My eldest sister-in-law herself stole the hairclips. She played the pious part, trying to hoodwink Mother Ṣaṣṭhī! She took an oath with her hand on the heads of her seven children and the fruit of that heinous act has quickly ripened!"

At her sister-in-law's condemnation, the eldest daughter-in-law, crying openly, touched the feet of her mother-in-law, the brahman's wife, and took another oath. The daughter of that brahman woman pulled away the hands of the eldest daughter-in-law and pressed further her accusations, "And now do you want to eat me, too?" At this remark the eldest daughter-in-law's heart ached with shame and misery. She ran into her room and bolted the door, sobbing. Then she started praying for Mother Ṣaṣṭhī, summoning the goddess to her aid. The goddess appeared to her in the form of an old brahman woman.

The eldest daughter-in-law cried bitterly. Because of the sharp words of the brahman's daughter, she found herself crying out, "Oh Mother, my sister-in-law has accused me falsely! No one believed what I said, but I did not steal the hair ornaments!"

Hearing her plea, the old woman replied, "Dear, you are the mother of several children, yet don't you understand that if you take an oath with your hand on the head of your child you shorten its life? Whether your statement be true or false, never swear with your hand on your child's head! Calm down and have no fear. Go to the place of worship, and you will find some bamboo leaves lying there. Take those leaves, dip them in the waters of the landing ghat, and, while chanting the name of Mother Ṣaṣṭhī, sprinkle that water from the leaves over the bodies of your seven children. Then each will be brought back to life."

As soon as the old brahman woman finished talking, she vanished; the eldest daughter-in-law could not see her anywhere. Without hesitating, she quickly came out from her room, took the leaves designated for worship, dipped them in the water and, while repeating the name of Mother Ṣaṣṭhī, poured the water over the bodies of her seven dead children. The instant she did, the children came back to life and cried out, "Ma! Ma!" The brahman woman witnessed this and she and all her sons and their wives were dumbfounded. In the meantime as these events unfolded, the two children of the brahman woman's own daughter had died.

When the daughter saw her dead children, she beat her chest and began to weep bitterly. Suddenly, a disembodied voice seemed to ring from the sky, "Who else but you deserves this? You yourself stole the hairclips and then blamed the elder daughter-in-law! It is your children who should die and no one else's! If you beg forgiveness and clasp the feet of the eldest daughter-in-law in humble supplication, she can bring your children back to life!" Everyone searched all around but could not see who was speaking. At the same time a great many neighborhood children and their mothers were drawn to the house by the excitement.

The sister-in-law grabbed the feet of the eldest daughter-in-law and begged forgiveness. The brahman's wife, the eldest daughter-in-law's husband, his younger brothers, and the neighborhood wives all together entreated the eldest daughter-in-law, but she adamantly refused to help. After numerous requests, she eventually relented, "All right, with everyone as witness, let her produce the golden hairclips and then pull her sari around her neck in expiation and swear, 'Mother Ṣaṣṭhī, never again will I steal anything belonging to a god or goddess.' "

Hearing this, the daughter opened her bag and brought out the ornaments. She placed them in her mother's hand and then, banging her own head on the floor, begged forgiveness from Mother Ṣaṣṭhī. Then the eldest daughter-in-law sprinkled the water from the bamboo leaves on the bodies of the two children and they sprang back to life. Witnessing this amazing feat, all of the local wives and daughters praised the eldest daughter-in-law for her act of compassion. Then the eldest daughter-in-law shared the entire tale of her devotion to Mother Ṣaṣṭhī.

The brahman woman and her sons saw it all, and there was no stopping the spread of the tale of the daughter's misdeed and the glory of Ṣaṣṭhī worship. Afterwards, day by day, the fortunes of the family of the brahman woman increased.

ṢAṢṬHĪ OF THE RICE CAKE

There was one brahman and his wife, who were well-to-do. They had seven sons and those sons all had wives. None of them had any children except the youngest daughter-in-law, who had two sons. The two children were beloved of everyone. And the youngest child was the very favorite of the brahman; he was always to be found in that brahman's lap, day or night.

One day the brahman's wife said to him, "Listen, it would be good if you would have a pond or a bathing tank dug for us. If you do, I would no longer have to perform Ṣaṣṭhī worship in someone else's pond or be ashamed to take my sons' wives to the river to bathe."

The brahman registered this request and said nothing more. A few days later he called workmen and employed them to dig an extremely large tank near the rear entrance to the house. Their pond was quickly constructed and a few trees were set on its banks for shade and landscaping, just as it should be—but not a single drop of water appeared.

Everyone in the house was distressed that such a large pond had been dug, yet not a bit of water seeped into it. It was anticipated that during the rains of Āṣāḍha [June-July] and Śrāvaṇa [July-August] the water would fill it up. But the month of Bhādra [August-September] came and though the fields were flooded, no water at all rose into the tank. The brahman could be seen sitting in despair with his face in his hands.

The brahman's wife, quite miserable, complained to her husband, "What bad luck! Day after tomorrow is the ritual worship of Ṣaṣṭhī. I had hoped that this time I would be able to take my son's wives and perform the Ṣaṣṭhī rituals in our own tank. By my ill fate it is not to be! Oh, such is our terrible misfortune! All the neighbors are beginning to talk, and they say that those brahmans must be terrible sinners!"

The brahman said nothing. Maintaining his silence, he lay down and for some time remained that way.

That day was the fifth of the month of Bhādra. After he ate that night he went to bed. In the middle of the night he dreamed that Mother Ṣaṣṭhī was standing at the head of his bed and said, "Tomorrow is my ritual worship and there is no water in your pond." As soon as she said that, the brahman, continuing his dream, told her his dire circumstance and then sang her profuse praises. Hearing his plea, the Mother was filled with compassion. She then said, "Listen carefully! If you chop up your smallest grandson, drain his blood, and then throw it into the pond, water will fill your pond. It will be water that is clear as the limpid eye of a crow."

Suddenly the brahman awoke. His heart cried out. Bitterly he wept. Then, calming down, he meditated on his clan deity in his heart of hearts. Collected, he arose and peeped in the room of his daughter-in-law. When his grandson spotted the brahman, he ran to him and jumped into his lap. The brahman hugged him with great affection, kissed him, and cried to himself. Disconsolate, he still knew that since Mother Ṣaṣṭhī had commanded him, he must sacrifice the child. If the Mother is truly merciful, then many more children would be had in place of this one lost. Thus resolved, he spoke to no one. He took the child and headed straight to the pond near the back entrance of the house. He dismembered the trusting boy and sprinkled the blood into the gaping maw of that bone dry hole. With a quiet gurgle, the pond gradually filled with water. When he was convinced that it was real, the brahman went back inside the house and told the news to his wife. The brahman woman then summoned the priest, who consecrated the pond. The women then gathered her daughters-in-law and sat them down to perform the ritual worship of Mother Ṣaṣṭhī. At the conclusion of the story of the ritual vow, the youngest daughter-in-law wrapped a banana in the corner of her sari, dipped it in the water, and at the same time immersed a rice cake. The immersion mantra goes like this:

> Immersing the rice cake
> (Name of child) comes forth laughing.

In precisely this fashion, she immersed the rice cake and called out the names of her children. Just as she pronounced the name of her youngest son, the rice cake, which was totally immersed, suddenly rose up from the water onto the dry land, and before she realized what had happened, she found her youngest son, Ananta by name, emerging from those eternal waters holding fast the knotted end of her sari. The daughter-in-law instinctively took the child on her lap, dried him off, kissed him, and stood him on the bank. She let cry,

"Blessings upon you! May you be Ṣaṣṭhī's servant! How is it that you just rose from out of the water, my child?" But not waiting for a reply, she herself climbed up out of the water onto the landing steps. Her mother-in-law and sisters-in-law were speechless, for they witnessed this miraculous event!

Meanwhile, the brahman had surreptiously followed them. He had concealed himself behind a tree for the whole while. When he saw his grandson, he bolted forward and whisked him onto his lap, weeping. When he regained his composure, he told of his dream, of cutting up the child, and the rest. When she heard this mind-boggling tale, the child's mother, quite understandably, fainted. The women sprinkled her face with water and eventually she came around. Afterwards she got up, made a profound and sincere obeisance to Mother Ṣaṣṭhī, and took her child in her own room.

The story—the sacrifice of the youngest daughter-in-law's son, the sprinkling of his blood in the pond, and the upsurge of water—soon spread far and wide. And from that great event, the ritual worship of Mother Ṣaṣṭhī of the Rice Cake, or Cāpaḍā Ṣaṣṭhī, was extended throughout the land.

ṢAṢṬHĪ WHO REMOVES SORROW

Once there was a king. One afternoon while he was out hunting, he grew quite thirsty. He began looking for water, and soon spied a hut a short distance away. He galloped up to it. As he approached the hut, he saw it was a sage's hermitage. The king dismounted, walked to the entrance, and called out for water. A young girl of unsurpassed beauty brought him water from inside the hut. The king went crazy at the very sight of her and completely forgot his thirst. Recovering, the king asked her, "Whose daughter are you?" to which the young maiden answered, "I am the daughter of a sage." The king then inquired of the sage's whereabouts, and the daughter replied, "He has gone to practice his austerities." The king then drank his fill of water and sat down at the foot of an aśoka tree in front of the hermitage—and an appropriate place it was, for aśoka means to be without sorrow or misery, and the king was miserably in love.

A little before evening the sage returned to his hut, chanting the holy Veda. Immediately the king prostrated himself in obeisance and pressing his palms together in respect said, "My Lord, I have seen your daughter and like her immensely. Grant me your favor and present her to me. I will marry her and take her away to live as my queen." The sage listened to the king's offer and replied, "Look, I am very partial to my daughter and I love her very much. If you swear three times that when my daughter bears a son you will make him king, then I shall give her to you." And then the king touched his sword and recited the oath, "I make this oath in your presence, that I will pass on the throne to your daughter's son."

Then the sage called out, "May you be without sorrow," which also happened to be the name of his daughter, Aśoka. With smiling face and radiant beauty,

Aśoka came forth immediately and stood obediently near her father. The sage took Aśoka's hand, placed it in that of the king and said, "Little Mother, from this day forward you are the king's wife, his queen. But one cannot trust these kings. So, when it comes time to leave, in the corner of your sari tie up some seeds from the aśoka tree, your namesake, and take these seeds with you. Along your journey scatter them in double handfuls on the both sides of the road. Do this all the way to the capital. If ever the king be inattentive or give you pain, these seeds will by that time have grown into trees and you will be able to follow their line straight back to my hermitage." Saying this, he blessed the newly joined couple. Aśoka folded the seeds in her sari end and accompanied the king to his palace. And, just as her father instructed, during the trip she scattered the seeds with both hands, strewing them along both sides of the road.

The news that the king had married and was bringing his new queen preceded them to the palace. And as soon as the king's seven other queens heard, they prepared the house for welcoming the newest queen. The king sent ahead to have a new annex constructed especially for her. From that day the king lived day and night in Aśoka's chambers, much to the dismay of her displaced co-wives.

Some time later Aśoka conceived. All seven queens, who had learned of the news immediately, began to frequent Aśoka's annex and lavish much affection on her. Gradually through their attentions, Aśoka forgot the discomforts of her pregnancy. In the fifth month they held the preparatory rite of the five nectars and in the ninth month they performed the appropriate rituals for the very pregnant Aśoka and indulged her every culinary whim. On the tenth day of the tenth [lunar] month she experienced pains. The king was informed, and the palace midwife sent for. The midwife hastened forth promptly. The seven queens then took her aside and secretly bribed her with a large sum of money. "Look, if it is a boy, hide him and show the king a wooden doll instead." The midwife could not turn down such a huge sum, and so consented to the task.

When Aśoka started to suffer the sharp pains that indicated her time was near, the seven queens appeared before her and exclaimed to the innocent Aśoka, "How can you have a baby like this? You must cover your eyes with a cloth folded seven times." Thus they applied the seven-folded cloth and just as they did, the lying-in room lit up from the glow of the birth of a child who was brilliant as the moon itself. It was, naturally, a boy. The midwife hurriedly thrust him into a silver pot, covered it with a clay lid, and set it afloat on the river. Meanwhile, smearing blood on a wooden doll, the midwife sent word to the king, "Mahārāja! The youngest queen has given birth to a wooden doll!" Hearing this the king's heart was broken.

Out of grief, the king stayed away from Aśoka's chambers for several days. But soon he began to frequent them again, and once more Aśoka became pregnant. In time, the queens found out and as before began to lavish their attentions on her. At the time of birth, again plotting with the midwife, the seven queens arranged everything—with the help of some money, of course. This time, too, Aśoka bore a son. Just as before, the midwife stuffed the child in a silver pot, covered it with a clay lid, and set it adrift on the river. Afterwards she informed the king that the youngest queen had given birth to a handsome wooden stallion.

Six times, the youngest queen's sons were set adrift in similar fashion. Meanwhile, one by one, those pots, each of which contained a boy, floated down to the landing of the river where Aśoka's old father, the sage, observed his austere practices. And each time the pot floated right into his lap. Having meditated on this, he discovered that each child belonged to his beloved Aśoka. Lifting the lid, he would extract the child and raise him as he had his own daughter. In this way he began raising all six of Aśoka's sons, his grandsons.

To the king, however, Aśoka was anything but beloved. He was incensed with her inability to produce a son. For a great many days he refused to reenter her chambers. However, after some time he again returned and very quickly Aśoka was with child. This time she had a girl. Because it was a girl, this baby was not disposed of and the news was sent to the king, "Mahārāja! Your youngest queen has given birth to a beautiful daughter!" As soon as he heard, the king flew into a rage! He ordered, "Send Aśoka and her defiling daughter away from my palace!" No sooner had they received the command than the queens sent Aśoka and her daughter packing. They gloated in their success, extremely pleased with themselves.

Sobbing, Aśoka took the child on her hip and moved out onto the road, understandably upset. As she looked around, she caught sight of the line of Aśoka trees and recalled the words of her father. So, following this long line of trees, she came straight to the hermitage and found her father sitting with six stunningly handsome boys playing all around him.

With her child on her hip, Aśoka fell at her father's feet, weeping, her misery touching. Affectionately, the sage consoled her, "Little Mother, I knew everything that was to transpire all along and for that reason I had given you the Aśoka seeds. I knew you would come back to me. Why such grief? Just look, Mother, all of your boys are playing around me like a constellation of brightly shining moons. Since I knew all these children were yours, I set aside my austere practices and have undertaken to raise them." Hearing this, Aśoka immediately pulled each one to her lap and kissed him, while the children stood encircling their newly found mother. With all her children at the hermitage, Aśoka was happy, becoming once again true to her name.

Some time later when all of Aśoka's children had grown, the sage bought six wooden stallions and a single wooden mare. He took all of the children to the river landing opposite the one where the king daily came to bathe. Then he issued the six stallions to the boys and the mare to the girl with these instructions, "Go and water your horses at the river! Should the king question you about what you are doing, simply reply, 'We are watering our horses.' If the king comes back with the question, 'Since when do wooden horses drink?' you should then reply, 'If your majesty's queen can give birth to wooden dolls then why cannot wooden horses drink water?' " The sage rehearsed with them this dialogue, and then concealed himself nearby.

The brothers, taking their younger sister by the hand, led her to the river landing and made their horses drink. Seeing the king arrive, the children carried out their plan, loudly commanding the horses, "Drink, you wooden stallions and wooden mare, drink! Drink!" The king was, at that moment, bent over washing his face. He asked his manservant to find out what those children—who he noticed were more radiant than the moon itself—were doing on the bank of the river. The manservant did as he was bade, and returned to say, "Mahārāja, they are watering their wooden horses!" Hearing this the king called out to the children, "Humph! Since when do wooden horses drink water?" From the opposite bank the children recited in unison their carefully rehearsed lines, "Mahārāja, if the great queen can give birth to a wooden doll then our wooden horses are most certainly able to drink water." Upon hearing that, the king's thoughts raced to Aśoka. Without hesitation, he instructed his servants that wherever those children went, he intended to follow.

Having watered the wooden horses, each child took his horse on his lap and made straight for the hermitage. True to his word, the king followed in hot pursuit. As the children arrived, Aśoka ran to greet them, lifting them to her lap and kissing them affectionately. Witnessing this, the king was somewhat taken aback, but he quickly gathered his senses and proceeded into the hermitage.

When the king entered, the sage quickly and bluntly admonished him, "You, who are a wise man, failed to question how a woman could give birth to a wooden doll. Your queens schemed with the midwife, whom they bribed with large sums of money. They had her set each child adrift and then show you a wooden doll." Crying out in the agony of his own blindness, the king clasped the feet of the sage and exclaimed sorrowfully, "I confess I made a terrible mistake! Forgive me!"

The sage replied, "Forgiveness is not mine to give. Ask forgiveness of Aśoka. If she is satisfied and wants to return with you to your palace, I have no objection." The king then begged Aśoka to forgive him, and affectionately kissed and hugged each child in turn. Good wife that she was, Aśoka forgot and forgave everything upon seeing her husband, the king. But she did remember the seven co-wives and their horrible deeds. The king prepared to take his queen and children back to his kingdom. Before Aśoka left, the sage advised her, "Little Mother Aśoka, you must perform worship on this sixth day of the month, placing in your mouth six aśoka buds and six pulses mixed together with curd. After that act, you may eat and drink normally. If you perform this ritual vow, you will experience neither misery nor sorrow henceforth. The sixth will be known as the worship of Ṣaṣṭhī Who Removes Sorrow or Aśoka Ṣaṣṭhī. If you tell everyone about this worship and propagate its practice, your tears will never again grace this earth." Aśoka heeded her father's advice, then made obeisance to the king. Taking her children by the hand, she began the journey back in the company of the king to the world she had lost.

Returning to his realm, the king sat in the assembly and summoned all the inhabitants of his kingdom. When they had gathered, he called for his seven elder queens. All seven obediently appeared. At the same time, he sent for the midwife, who was bound and brought forth forcibly. According to their individual treachery was each one judged. Thus, the king sent into exile the seven scheming queens to live the rest of their miserable days in shame in the forest, away from the court and the amenities to which they had become so greedily accustomed. As for the conniving midwife, who endeavored to ruin the kingdom for a few coins—she was fed to the dogs, who never once complained of the bitterness of their treat.

The grateful Aśoka performed the worship of the Ṣaṣṭhī Who Removes Sorrow just as the sage had instructed, and the king ordered all his subjects to do likewise. The worship of Aśoka Ṣaṣṭhī during the month of Phālguna [February-March] quickly spread throughout the kingdom.

After ruling for some time longer, the king arranged for his six sons and only daughter to be married, and then handed over charge of the kingdom to his sons, according to proper custom. At an auspicious moment, a golden chariot descended from heaven. Reminding everyone to perform the ritual worship of Aśoka Ṣaṣṭhī every year at the proper time and in the proper way, the king and his queen Aśoka rode off to their heavenly abode.

BLUE ṢAṢṬHĪ

There once was a brahman and his wife who had seven boys and a single girl. They used to perform their rites with devotion on the proper days, and their adoration of their chosen deities and celestial beings was without limits. But neither gods nor celestial beings nor any of these pious observances were effective. For each child would live only two years and then suddenly die. Seeing this happen, the pair concluded that whether they referred to rituals, or vows, or whether they spoke of the gods or of the celestial beings, in this Kali age, all were baseless and without truth. With this heretical notion, they abandoned the brahman's ancestral home and went to Kāśī [Varanasi], Lord Śiva's holy city, which sits on the banks of the Gaṅgā.

One day after bathing at the famous landing of Maṇikarṇikā in Kāśī, the brahman woman sat on the steps and mulled over her fate. Mother Ṣaṣṭhī espied her and approached, disguising herself as an old brahman woman with a beggar's sack over her shoulder, leaning on a cane. She inquired, "I say, friend, why are you worrying so this afternoon, sitting there with your chin planted so firmly on your fist?"

The brahman woman responded with a certain despair, "What good will it do if I tell you my sorrows? Not one or two, but seven children I have mothered, yet all have been taken away! So, I have come to realize that whether it be auspicious days or ritual vows, none are effective. They are all a sham! In this Kali, last of the four ages, are there any gods or goddesses left to act in this world?"

Maintaining her brahman guise, Mother Ṣaṣṭhī chided, "What's this? Since when are deities false or ritual vows and auspicious days fruitless? You have lost your children, yet do you revere Mother Ṣaṣṭhī or ever perform her worship? She is the goddess of children, you know."

Quickly the brahman woman replied, "What? Me not honor Mother Ṣaṣṭhī? I always have and continue to revere her greatly!"

Still in her brahman disguise Mother Ṣaṣṭhī said, "But have you done all of the ritual vows dedicated to her or have you performed only a few? Have you performed the Blue or Nīla Ṣaṣṭhī vow?"

Surprised, the brahman woman quickly replied, "No Mother, I have never even heard of that one, and so naturally I do not know its rules. Tell me, how is it performed?"

Still not revealing her identity, Mother Ṣaṣṭhī said, "One must perform Śiva worship every day for the entire month of Caitra [March-April]. Then, on the next to last day of the month, you must fast. During that evening burn a lamp of ghi in the temple of Nīlakaṇṭha, the Blue-throated Śiva, and with sincere and abiding devotion pay your respects and make obeisance to Mother Ṣaṣṭhī. Afterwards the fast can be broken with both food and water. For one who observes the Blue or Nīla Ṣaṣṭhī ritual vow, her children never die an untimely death." And having imparted this instruction, Mother Ṣaṣṭhī vanished into thin air.

Staying on in Kāśī, the brahman woman began to perform Śiva worship every day during the month of Caitra. On the next to last day of the month she offered the lamp of ghi in the Śiva sanctum and afterwards broke her fast with water and food. The woman observed this repeatedly, time and again according to Mother Ṣaṣṭhī's exact instruction. Eventually, as promised, the brahman woman conceived—this the ninth time! Later, on the tenth day of the tenth [lunar] month, she went into labor and soon gave birth to a boy who was brilliant as a golden moon. After a time, she gave birth to a great many more sons and daughters, and the brahman became famous throughout Kāśī. By their familial prosperity, their home overflowed with wealth—gold and silver coins, pearls, rubies, emeralds, diamonds. The brahman's wife methodically popularized the Nīla Ṣaṣṭhī ritual far and wide. And soon, having witnessed the results, everyone began to observe Nīla Ṣaṣṭhī worship with deep devotion.

—22—

Women's Celebration of Muḥammad's Birth

Marcia Hermansen

This selection incorporates material from a manual that is used by individuals, primarily women, in celebrating a ceremony in honor of the Prophet Muḥammad known as a "noble birth" (*mīlād sharīf*). Although this name refers to the birth (mīlād) of Muḥammad, these ceremonies may be performed at any time and are usually done at times of need or crisis, when it is hoped that a wish may be answered or a difficulty resolved through divine intervention. A person may also vow to sponsor such a ceremony after such a request has been granted.

It will be noted that some of the narrative material included in the ceremony recounts episodes from the sacred biography of the Prophet. Passages from the Qur'ān or the reports and sayings (*ḥadīth*) of the Prophet are cited to justify or enhance points made in the narrative. The manual is performative, in that there are instructions for conducting the ceremony and sections in the text that lend themselves to repetition by the listeners, such as short poems, refrains, and repeated exhortations to send blessings on the Prophet. This sending of peace and blessings is known as *durūd*.

This material indicates the importance of the Prophet Muḥammad in popular Muslim piety and the presence of popular religious rituals that take on regional forms, although versions of ceremonies honoring the Prophet are found in most Muslim cultures. These ceremonies, which often take place in private homes, provide the major context for women to participate in communal religious rituals.

In contemporary Pakistan, the issue of popular devotion to the saints and the Prophet is somewhat controversial. Although the vast majority of Muslims in the Indian subcontinent favor this type of pious expression, some groups promote a more strict reformist adherence to textual tradition and discourage the elevation of the Prophet to the status of a super-human being. In the context of this controversy, the author of this manual includes at the end of the text legal opinions by Arab Muslim scholars that affirm the permissibility and desirability of these ceremonies.

The manual finishes with a section of some twenty-five pages (pp. 144–69) of legal opinions solicited from religious scholars of Mecca and Medina, Saudi Arabia, concerning the legality of holding such ceremonies in honor of the Prophet. These are reproduced in the original Arabic with Urdu translations. This indicates both the sensitivity of the issue of whether these ceremonies are non-Islamic innovations and the appeal for legitimacy to the classical tradition and to the scholars of Arabia. One such opinion is translated here.

The translation is from Khwāja Muḥammad Akbar Wārithī, *Mīlād-e-Akbar* (Lahore: Shaikh Ghulām ʿAlī Publishers, n.d.)

THE PROPER CONDUCT FOR HOLDING AN ASSEMBLY OF IN HONOR OF THE BIRTH OF THE PROPHET (MĪLĀD SHARĪF)

The location must be clean and ritually pure; only money that has been earned by religiously approved means can be spent. The more perfumes, incense, fragrances and flowers, and so on, that are used, the better. Showing off must absolutely not enter into this. A high pulpit or chair on which is placed a stand or some ritually pure cloth should be used. Nice decoration should be employed for a pleasing effect—if possible also make arrangements for food. For performing the recitation of the Qurʾān over the food to bless it, use only sweets that are made by Muslims and preferably use candles for lighting because the bad odor of clay oil lamps should be avoided during this blessed gathering. The listeners and participants should be in a state of cleanliness and ritual purity, and should sit politely. The reciter of the mīlād sharīf ceremony should be someone who adheres to the Islamic Law. Persons should be exhorted again and again to recite salutations and blessings upon the Prophet (*durūd*).

THE BENEFITS OF MĪLĀD SHARĪF

"Mercy descends at the remembrance of the righteous ones."

In whichever place the remembrance of Aḥmad, the Chosen One, Muḥammad Muṣṭāfa—may the peace and blessings of God be upon him, the leader of all the righteous ones and messengers—takes place, in it this merit is found that voices are raised in praising him. Why shouldn't blessings descend on those present there, and why shouldn't the desired article be obtained by the audience? It is reported that, in whatever home this blessed gathering is held, for the next whole year showers of mercy will rain down on those who dwell there and they will live in protection and security with infinite good and blessings. In blessed Mecca and radiant Medina it is customary that when a son is born to someone, or when some other ceremony such as first hair cutting, circumcision, wedding, building of a new home, returning from a journey, or recovering from an illness is held, among all of the other functions a mīlād sharīf is sure to be included. May God also give us people such success that we will illuminate and ennoble our homes and gatherings with the mention of Muḥammad, and that we will be spared corruptions such as dancing and playing music, and so on. Amen.

Ḥadīth: Ḥaẓrat [the Prophet] said, "The person who sends salutations to me morning and night will obtain my intercession on the Day of Judgment."
Ḥadīth: The Prophet said, "Whoever recites salutation to me one hundred times on Fridays will find the sins of the whole year forgiven."

In short, true reports and ḥadīths have confirmed that sending blessings and salutation to the Prophet are a means to good and blessings in this world and a means to forgiveness and salvation in the afterlife. They cure illnesses and cheer up the grief-stricken. Doing these practices a lot brings blessings in material possession and advancement for one's children and, best of all, the one who does this often comes to love the Prophet more completely, and love for him is love for Allah—and this is faith and the basis of Islam.

> Recite the salutation, recite O lovers, recite the salutation,
> never be neglectful of the salutation, recite the salutation,
> send infinite salutation and blessings
> to the spirit of Muḥammad and the family of Muḥammad.

INTRODUCTION TO THE BIRTH OF THE LIGHT OF MUḤAMMAD, MAY THE PEACE AND BLESSINGS OF GOD BE UPON HIM.

> The mirror the divine essence was placed face to face,
> so that this form was duplicated,
> the reflection of the divine essence appeared in the mirror,
> the name of this reflection became Muṣṭāfa.
> If such an image had not been born
> the conclusion of beauty would come with him.
> All flames come from this one flame
> which illuminates from earth to heaven.

The explanation of this is given thus by the masters of knowledge and the possessors of inner wisdom. The first emanation of God, may his state be exalted, is the light of Muḥammad, may the peace and blessings of God be upon him. That is, the absolute Creator brought the light of Muḥammad into being 1,670,000 years before all other existent and created things. Hazrat ibn Jauzī wrote that God said to this light, "Become Muḥammad," so that it became a column of light and stood up and reached to the veil of divine greatness—then it prostrated and said, "Praise Be to God!" Then God said, "For this I have created you and I will make you the beginning of creation and the end of the Prophets."

BIRTH STORIES

It is reported that according to the lunar calculation exactly nine months had passed so that the time for his birth was near, when along with many other women, Āsia [wife of Pharaoh] and Mary, may peace be upon her, came to attend his mother from the spiritual world, and with them were many houris of Paradise. His mother said, "Right now I feel rather thirsty." At that very moment a radiant angel came to her holding in his hand a glass filled with a refreshing drink which was whiter than milk, sweeter than honey, colder than snow, and more fragrant than rose. He put it in her hand saying, "Drink this beverage which has come to you from paradise." She thus drank her fill. Then he said, "Have more," so she drank more and all thirstiness was lifted and she became calm. Then the angel made this appeal. "Come forth, O Master of messengers, come forth Master of the worlds, come forth, O Seal of the Prophets."

There is a report related from his paternal grandfather, Abd al-Muṭṭalib, that at that time [of his birth] he was inside the noble Kaʿba when all at once God's Kaʿba moved from its place and jumped for joy, then it bowed with its four walls and made a prostration at the station of Abraham. Then the walls stood up in their place and several times raised the call, "God's accepted one, Muḥammad may peace be upon him, is born."

His nurse [Ḥalīma] related that he grew at such a fast rate that in one day his size increased as much as most children's would in a month. In a month he grew as much as others would during a year! Thus in his second month his arms were so strong that he could crawl and after five months he could walk on his own legs and by the ninth month he could speak fluently and his first words were, "God is Great, God is Great, and praise be to God Lord of the Worlds. Praise be to God first and essentially." His statements were extremely wise. When he saw children playing he would stop them, and if they asked him to play he would say, "God did not create us for playing."

MIRACLES

One day a woman brought a person who had been dumb since birth, and had never uttered even one word. When the holy Prophet(s) asked him "Who am I?" the dumb person said, "I testify that there is no God but God and Muḥammad is his Prophet."

> Since even the dumb person has attested to his position as the Messenger,
> Why should not the two worlds utter the praises of Muḥammad?

A shepherd was tending goats in the forest. The Prophet, may the peace and blessings of God be upon him, arrived so that a she-wolf informed the shepherd saying, "The Prophet of God has come to your forest, I will tend your flock while you go to him." The shepherd immediately went to meet the Prophet and, having accepting the faith, began to perform the ritual sacrifice.

> The she-wolf protected the sheep folds in the wilderness
> While the shepherd became the sacrifice of Muḥammad.

A camel, after prostration before the Prophet, said, "My master loads me with too much baggage and gives me very little food." The Prophet called his master and requested him to load him more lightly and feed him until his stomach was full.

One day many companions and helpers were with the Prophet, and when they drew near to a goat pen the goats prostrated to the Prophet.

> Some prostrated, some recited the profession of faith,
> Even the wild animals were the Muslims of Muḥammad.

Stones turning into wax beneath his blessed feet is a well-known miracle of the Prophet. Once it occurred that by night in Mecca some of the most powerful unbelievers had gathered. The full moon shone in the sky. The unbelievers said that if the Prophet, may the peace and blessings of God be upon him, could perform the miracle of splitting the moon in the sky into two pieces then they would believe in him. At that very moment Ḥaẓrat, peace be upon him, lifted his index finger and pointed at the moon. It immediately split into two pieces.

> The stones turned into wax, the moon split into two pieces
> The heavens and earth are at the command of Muḥammad.

LEGAL OPINIONS OF THE NOBLE ARABS: FATWĀ FROM THE SCHOLARS OF MEDINA, THE RADIANT, CONCERNING THE HOLDING OF MĪLĀD CEREMONIES

In the name of God the merciful, the compassionate.

Question: What is your opinion, may God have mercy on you, concerning the memorializing of the birth of the Prophet, may the peace and blessings of God be upon him, and standing up at the mention of the birth of the Prophet, and appointing a particular day for this and decorating the place and using scents and reciting some chapters of the Qur'ān and distributing food to the Muslims? Is this permissible and rewarded by God? Please give an explanation, may God reward you with the best reward!

Answer: Praise be to God who raised the heavens without a support. I ask Him for help, success, and assistance. Know that memorializing the birth of the

Prophet, may the peace and blessings of God be upon him, and all of his virtues in the presence of listeners is a tradition, since it has been reported that al-Ḥassān used to praise the Prophet, may the peace and blessings of God be upon him, in his presence while people were gathered to listen to him, and indeed the Prophet, may the peace and blessings of God be upon him, invited al-Ḥassān and let him mount the pulpit, so that he mentioned these virtues while standing on it. However, the holding of a noble birth ceremony in a communal form by specifying a day, standing up, and distributing food, and these other things which were mentioned in the question is a "sound innovation" (*bid'a ḥasana*) which is recommended and in which nothing prevents the obtaining of a reward from God so long as the intention is good, and especially if this is combined with exalting, honoring, and joy and happiness at the birthday of the noble Prophet. It is hoped that his reward from the Generous One will be to enter blessed Paradise through his grace. The people of Islam have continued to take care to celebrate the birthday of the Prophet, may the peace and blessings of God be upon him, and to make tasty food and give out various types of charity, and to be extremely joyful and have the recitation of the noble mīlād [ceremony] undertaken at this time.

Remarkable Lives and Edifying Tales

—23—

The Rescue of Two Drunkards

Tony K. Stewart

The Gauḍīya Vaiṣṇavas of Bengal were and still are famous for the vitality of their collective religious observances, especially the public singing of the praise of Kṛṣṇa (*kīrtana*). An important dimension of this public activity is proselytizing and conversion, two aspects of the premodern Hindu devotional traditions that are frequently ignored. Anyone, so this community holds, can be saved by becoming a Vaiṣṇava, a devotee of Kṛṣṇa. The concept is easy to explain although, as we shall see in the conversion story translated below, its execution is not always simple. But what does it mean to a Vaiṣṇava "to be saved"?

In the sixteenth-century biographical literature devoted to him, Kṛṣṇa Caitanya is frequently referred to as the "savior (*pāvana*) of the fallen (*patita*)." A person is considered fallen if he lives a life devoid of the love of Kṛṣṇa (and the ambiguity of the English expression "love of Kṛṣṇa" captures the Bengali sentiment, for it is both to receive and give love). In the *Bhagavad Gītā,* composed well over a millennium before Caitanya's time, Kṛṣṇa speaks of that cosmic moral order known as dharma, which includes the physical laws of the world as well as personal and social obligations, all necessary for the smooth running of the cosmos. But in a twist on this ancient yet still-changing idea, the *Bhagavad Gītā* proposes that dharma is, in effect, nothing other than God's, Kṛṣṇa's, will; and the Bengal Vaiṣṇavas embrace this idea wholly. To live a life according to dharma is to follow God's will, and that is possible only through a proper devotion (*bhakti*). Devotion ensures that God will guide the devotee according to his individual circumstance. Conversely, to do anything contrary to God's will is to act against dharma, which is to live a life devoid of devotion, a meaningless, misguided existence. This contrary act, whether seemingly intentional or not, is deemed *pāpa,* often translated into English as "sin," but more properly understood as "divergence from dharma." For the Gauḍīya Vaiṣṇavas of Bengal, that person is "fallen," slipped from the proper and satisfying order intended by God. Every human is eligible for reintegration into God's cosmic order, that is, to be "saved"—God plays no favorites nor excludes anyone. The terminology resonates strongly of Christian notions of salvation when translated into English (and the parallels are certainly striking), but the mechanism by which salvation is effected is, in this case, quite different.

Ontologically, says Caitanya's disciple, the theologian Jīva Gosvāmī, every living being (*jīva*) is a part, albeit ever so minute, of Kṛṣṇa. Most, however, are ignorant of this and consequently live their lives according to their own whims in a manner inconsistent with God's will. The first step to overcoming this painful experience of a life without direction is simply to hear God's name. The simplicity of this observation is stunningly profound—how can you know about Kṛṣṇa if you have never heard his name? But the name (as noted in Chapter 40) is more than a word, it is part and parcel of Kṛṣṇa himself; it is an aural manifestation of his power. When properly chanted, the name functions as a mantra, a seed syllable that enters the heart and mind of the devotee and begins to work a seemingly magical transformation. A person who hears the name of Kṛṣṇa, in whatever way, is understood to have received at least a tiny portion of Kṛṣṇa's grace. To understand grace, however, it is useful to examine the physical metaphors used by the Vaiṣṇavas when speaking of it.

In the selection below, four terms are used to capture this complex idea: grace (*dayā*), mercy (*kṛpā*), favor (*prasāda*), and compassion (*karuṇā*). The first three are frequently interchangeable and refer to the action of Kṛṣṇa, who turns his attention to a devotee or fallen candidate, like the guru to a disciple. The last of the four terms represents the cause of this attention: compassion. Kṛṣṇa's attention inevitably involves a transfer of part of Kṛṣṇa's power—by sound, touch, or sight—which alters the recipient. In much the way that modern anthropologists have shown that food alters the very physical being of an individual by symbolic transformation, and its exchange and ingestion lead to changes in status and rank, so too does grace seem to operate for Vaiṣṇavas. To receive Kṛṣṇa's grace is to have your very being transformed, purified, and cleansed, resulting in a reorientation of action and thought that is more consistent with what Kṛṣṇa intends for this world. The sense of prasāda, whose original meaning was "to show favor," is extended to refer to the food that is first offered to Kṛṣṇa and then consumed by the individual, thereby physically and spiritually transforming the recipient. Prasāda as grace assumes a physical form as leftover offerings of food; grace becomes a substance. Because there is no clear separation of the physical and the spiritual dimension of the human being—those two representing opposite ends of a continuum of existence rather than bipolar dichotomies—the transformation is not limited to one's physical being; rather, it affects the whole. For this reason the writer can speak of the bodily nature of grace, or how the recipient's body becomes a receptacle of grace, and so on. The two drunks Jagāi and Mādhāi experience just this transformation as they become the vessels for Kṛṣṇa's mercy. And it becomes clear why Vaiṣṇavas are so concerned about the company they keep, the food they eat, and the sounds they hear—all have the power to transform.

The conversion of Jagāi and Mādhāi comes from the first Bengali biography of Kṛṣṇa-Caitanya (1486–1533 C.E.), the *Caitanya Bhāgavata* of Vṛndāvana Dāsa. The text, which was completed by 1540 C.E., only a few year's following Caitanya's death, was written at the behest of the author's guru, Nityānanda. Nityānanda, an ascetic whose name means "Eternal (*nitya*) Bliss (*ānanda*)," was one of Caitanya's two most prominent disciples, the other being Advaitācārya. Nityānanda was a flamboyant man who attracted a large following, especially among the lower classes and those who had little or no experience as Vaiṣṇavas, such as Jagāi and Mādhāi. Tradition records a healthy rivalry between him and Advaitācārya who, as his name suggests ("Teacher [*ācārya*] of Nondualism [*advaita*]"), was much more conservative than Nityānanda. Advaitācārya had a substantial following of his own well prior to Caitanya, who in this story is just beginning to make public his divinity. Verse 13 in the selection below plays on their relationship and involves a pun. "Advaita" refers both to the man and to the meaning: nondualism is a position inimical to Vaiṣṇavas, who are dualists. For Vaiṣṇavas, to be absorbed in the nondual ultimate of Brahman, the neuter principle of cosmic unity, is a fate much worse than hell. Caitanya's name means "consciousness," but his full name is Kṛṣṇa-Caitanya, "he who makes people cognizant of Kṛṣṇa," so the pun extends to include both the individuals and the belief systems represented by their names. Nityānanda's companion, Haridāsa, was a converted Muslim, whose experiences are recounted in Chapter 40.

In this exchange between Jagāi and Mādhāi on the one hand and Nityānanda and Haridāsa on the other, we can see an active attempt to convert, a conscious choice to proselytize in the name of Kṛṣṇa. Likewise, it is evident that not all of the inhabitants of Nadīya were enamored of this rather public and boisterous form of devotional worship, which looked to all appearances as if the practitioners were as drunk as the two targets for conversion, Jagāi and Mādhāi. But the "drunkenness" of the Vaiṣṇavas is one of devotional ecstasy, madness for Kṛṣṇa. The author, with his keen eye, has vividly captured a slice of sixteenth-century Bengal in all of its religious and social diversity.

The following translation is from Vṛndāvana Dāsa, *Caitanya Bhāgavata,* edited with Bengali commentary *Nitāikaruṇākallolinī ṭīkā* by Rādhāgovinda Nātha (Calcutta: Sādhana prakāśanī, 1373 B.S. [1966 C.E.]), 2.13.

Further Reading

Three helpful discussions of Vaiṣṇava religious observance are: Sushil Kumar De, *Early History of the Vaiṣṇava Faith and Movement in Bengal,* 2d ed. (Calcutta: Firma KLM, 1961), Edward C. Dimock, Jr., "Doctrine and Practice among the Vaiṣṇavas of Bengal," *History of Religions* 3:1 (1963), 106–27, reprinted in *Kṛṣṇa: Myths, Rites and Attitudes,* edited by Milton Singer (Hawaii: East-West Center Press, 1966), pp. 41–63; and David Haberman, *Acting as a Way of Salvation: a Study of Rāganugā Bhakti Sādhana* (New York and Oxford: Oxford University Press, 1988). A fundamental source is the work of an early biographer, Kṛṣṇadāsa Kavirāja, *Caitanya caritāmṛta*, translated with an introduction and notes by Edward C. Dimock, Jr., edited with revisions and addenda by Tony K. Stewart, Harvard Oriental Series no. 52 (Cambridge: Harvard University Press, forthcoming).

The Saving of Jagāi and Mādhāi

1. And so did Lord Viśvambhara—He Who Bears the World's Burden—carry on in [the city of] Navadvīpa, but what he revealed was not recognized by anyone. 2. People saw the teacher Nimāi [an affectionate name for Caitanya] as he was before, and saw nothing more than that. 3. When he joined the gathering of the servants of Kṛṣṇa they would float in a strange delight. 4. He revealed to them whatever divinity they worshiped, while to those who were outside the circle he revealed nothing.

5. One day he was swept with inspiration and issued commands to Nityānanda and Haridāsa. 6. "Listen closely, Nityānanda! Listen, Haridāsa! Make known my wishes to everyone! 7. Go and beg at each and every house—'Worship Kṛṣṇa! Say Kṛṣṇa! Learn the teachings of Kṛṣṇa!' 8. Say nothing other than these words. At the end of the day, return and report to me. 9. If you ask for this as alms and someone fails to repeat the words, then I shall come, disc in hand, and chop them to pieces." [The disc is a martial emblem of Viṣṇu's cosmic sovereignty, a characteristic Caitanya seldom exhibits.] 10. The Vaiṣṇava community received his instruction with smiles. Who had the power to disobey this direct order?

11. Taking responsibility for the order, Nityānanda and Haridāsa gleefully set off down the road. 12. Nityānanda especially took the charge to heart, "No one who has good sense could be inimical to this. 13. I will gladly believe that anyone who might pay their respects to Advaita, while showing no respect to Caitanya, will be slain by that very same Advaita." 14. And so taking their charge, the two men made their rounds, moving from house to house. "Say Kṛṣṇa! Sing Kṛṣṇa! Worship Kṛṣṇa! 15. Kṛṣṇa is life itself. Kṛṣṇa is prosperity. Kṛṣṇa is the living soul! Concentrate your mind on him, brother, and speak of that very Kṛṣṇa!" 16. In just this way did the two go to each and every house throughout Nadīya, telling of the Lord of Earth.

17. The duo, dressed in the garb of ascetics, would pick a house and scurry forward, begging alms. 18. Nityānanda and Haridāsa would recite in unison, "For this we beg: Say Kṛṣṇa! Worship Kṛṣṇa! Learn the teachings of Kṛṣṇa!" 19. Having uttered these words, the pair would carry on at the next place. Those people who obliged them soon were blessed with happiness. 20. Many people heard those moving words from the mouths of the pair and spoke in response; they immediately received the pleasing benefits. 21. One happily replied, "I will certainly do it!" But another gave the excuse, "You two men have uttered your mantra with a tiny defect. 22. From this defect in your

mantra you have gone quite mad. Why should I come and join your circle of madmen?" 23. When they approached the houses of those who previously had failed to gain entry to Caitanya's dance, the inhabitants yelled, "Beat them! Beat them! 24. All of those people of good breeding and manners have gone mad—Nimāi the teacher has destroyed us all!" 25. Someone else skeptically opined, "These two are probably thieves or their spies, and their systematic visits to people's homes are only pretexts for robbery! 26. Why would respectable people go about like this in public? The next time they come around, we will have the watchman apprehend them!"

27. As Nityānanda and Haridāsa listened to these and similar comments, they smiled. Through the strength of Caitanya's orders, they had no fear. 28. So they made their rounds from house to house, and each day returned to Viśvambhara [Caitanya] to describe it.

29. One day, two men, both drunk, could be seen on the road. Given to excessive drink, these two were miscreants to the point of being truly criminal. 30. The tales that circulated about them were too many to document—there was nothing of which they were not guilty; they could not possibly be more wicked. 31. Although they were brahmans, they ate cow's flesh and drank wine. They were dacoits, robbers, and routinely pilfered their neighbors' houses. 32. Somehow they were never spotted by the local guards, even though they were routinely reported to the police. Never a time passed when they were without their drink. 33. Often the two would start a scuffle on the road, and whoever ventured to intervene would get mugged. 34. [This day] people watched from a safe distance as that ploy was followed on the road where Haridāsa accompanied Nityānanda.

35. Typically, the two [miscreants] would be quite pleasant one minute, but the next minute they would grab [their victims] by the hair, yelling obscenities. 36. They had destroyed the high rank of many of Nadīya's brahmans, but some were convinced that it was only from the bad influence of their intoxication. 37. Every imaginable sin had been nurtured in the bodies of these two men, yet persecuting Vaiṣṇavas was not among those offenses. 38. Day and night they lived and played among the drunkards, but they never committed an offense against the Vaiṣṇavas—both of them were innocent of that. 39. He who commits but a single offense against a Vaiṣṇava, even should he live righteously, will meet with certain destruction. 40. When heinous acts are directed toward renunciates by drunkards, the entire group is held to be unrighteous. 41. When someone does manage to shake free from the addiction of alcohol, it is fated that they never join those who criticize and meddle. 42. Everything will come to ruin should one offend Nityānanda, regardless of whether the person is learned in the scriptures or an absolute idiot.

43. Nityānanda and Haridāsa saw the two men pushing and shoving and wrestling with each other [on the road that day], and so kept their distance. 44. Nityānanda personally queried the locals, "What caste are these two men? Why are they carrying on like this?"

45. The people answered, "Reverend Sir, the two men are brahmans, born into the grandest lineages, with model mother and father. 46. The lineage of their forefathers, from one generation in Nadīya to the next, never once suffered even the slightest of blemishes. 47. But these two, who inherited such good qualities, have completely forgotten their duties, their dharma. From birth they have acted in this unseemly fashion. 48. They abandoned their families and appear as terrible derelicts, associating with drunkards, doing as they please. 49. Everyone fears that when they meet these two men, some day one of them will return and destroy their homes. 50. There is no offense that these two men have failed to commit—they are reprobates and thieves, and they drink wine and eat meat."

51. Hearing this, Nityānanda's heart filled with a great compassion. Being merciful, he mentally resolved to save the two men: 52. "The Master, the Lord [Caitanya], descended in order to save the wicked. Where will one find greater sinners than these? 53. The Master has withheld his personal appearance [as God], but if people do not witness his power, then they will be derisive. 54. If the Master takes compassion on these two, then everyone in the world will behold his majesty and might. 55. If anyone is going to reveal Caitanya to these two, it is Nityānanda, the servant of Caitanya. 56. What if they, who are drunk on wine, were at this very moment and without realizing it to become drunk in the same way on the name of Kṛṣṇa? 57. If the two men start to weep when I say 'my Lord,' then these aimless wanderings of mine will become meaningful. 58. He who is touched by the mere shadow of these two men goes directly to the Gaṅgā to bathe, even fully clothed. 59. Sometime soon, when he see these two sinners, rather than thinking of bathing in the Gaṅgā, this same man will wish himself to be remembered in a manner similar to this pair."

60. Without limit is the majesty of the lord Nityānanda, whose descent was brought about to save the fallen. 61. Thinking all of these things, [Nityānanda] turned to Haridāsa and said, "Haridāsa! Look at those two wayward men. 62. Although they are brahmans of terrible disposition, there is no proper retribution in Yama's house [hell] for these two. 63. You thought benevolently even of those Muslims who beat you to within an inch of your life [see Chapter 40]. 64. If you really meant to effect that positive result, then you can accomplish the same thing through the salvation of these two. 65. The Master did not intend for you to do anything otherwise. This is the real sense of the words he himself spoke. 66. Let us show the world the power of our Lord, that Caitanya has rescued men such as these. 67. Just as the salvation of Ajāmila is heralded in the [*Bhāgavata*] *Purāṇa*, let it be seen by eyewitnesses here and now in the triple world."

68. Haridāsa understood full well Nityānanda's nature and he knew that they had already saved the duo. 69. Haridāsa said to the eminent [Nityānanda], "Listen, O revered one, whatever is your wish is certainly that of the Lord [Caitanya]! 70. Yoke me to the task as you would yoke a beast of burden. Again and again you must put me to the test."

71. Nityānanda smiled and embraced him, and with an extremely gentle voice he said, 72. "We have been wandering around at the Master's express command while he had been referring to these two drunkards. 73. It was the Master's order that everyone must worship Kṛṣṇa, most especially the inveterate sinners among them. 74. We alone bear the burden of those instructions—it would be far braver to ignore them than not." 75. So Haridāsa and Nityānanda headed straight for the two men to carry out the Master's command.

76. Virtuous men offered their advice, "Do not go near them! If they slip up behind you they will take your life! 77. We stay indoors because we are so afraid. How can you have the courage to march right up to them? 78. The fact that someone is a renunciate will be lost on these two men, who are disposed to attack brahmans and destroy cows."

79. Nevertheless, the two [devotees], repeating the name of Kṛṣṇa, headed straight for the [drunkards]. The two [drunkards] were struck with curiosity. 80. Getting close enough to be heard, the [two disciples] talked loudly, repeating the Master's words. 81. "Say Kṛṣṇa! Worship Kṛṣṇa! Take the name of Kṛṣṇa! Kṛṣṇa is your mother! Kṛṣṇa is your father! Kṛṣṇa is the very treasure of your life! 82. Kṛṣṇa has descended for the sake of all of you. Worship that very Kṛṣṇa and abandon all of your evil ways!"

83. Hearing these loud cries, the two [reprobates] raised their heads and looked about. Their eyes glowered red, seething with anger. 84. Seeing the forms of renunciates, they looked at each other, shook their heads, and yelled "Grab them, grab them!" as they tried to catch [the devotees]. 85. Nityānanda and Haridāsa scrambled for safety, while their ill-tempered pursuers cried, "Halt! Stop!" 86. With the rabble hard on their heels, spewing endless deprecations, the two Vaiṣṇava worthies were frightened to their wits' end and fled in alarm. 87. Some onlookers predicted, "Now there is no avoiding it—those two ascetics have fallen into a sure disaster today." 88. Those of a more inimical bent gleefully thought, "Nārāyaṇa is giving those imposters their just deserts." 89. "Kṛṣṇa! Protect them, Kṛṣṇa! Save them!" countered high-minded brahmans. But in their fear everyone, without exception, scattered from that spot.

90. The two delinquents gave chase, forcing the two pious men to flee. But the cry everyone expected—"We've got them! We've got them!"—never materialized. 91. Nityānanda said, "They have become Vaiṣṇavas! That we escaped with our lives today can only mean than we have won them over!"

92. Haridāsa replied, "Are you crazy? How can you say that? Do you realize that you narrowly escaped a decidedly unnatural death? 93. According to Kṛṣṇa's own instruction, the appropriate punishment for what those two drunks did is for them to forfeit their lives!" 94. Talking like this, the eminent disciples ran, laughing hysterically. And right behind chased the two irascible men vomiting unspeakable abuse.

95. The bodies of these two [Vaiṣṇavas] grew tired and heavy; they could run no more. Still they could just see the drunken pair running in hot pursuit.

96. The two wretches yelled out, "O Brother! Where are you running? How do you expect to escape from Jagā and Mādhā [diminutives of Jagāi and Mādhāi] this day? 97. Don't you realize that Jagā and Mādhā own this place? Wherever you are you will be discovered and instantly turned over [to us]!"

98. The two pious men heard these words and their apprehension spurred them forward. They continued to repeat "Save us, Kṛṣṇa! Protect us, Kṛṣṇa! O Govinda!" 99. Haridāsa wheezed, "I cannot run any further! I know this and my body quakes, yet still I try. 100. Kṛṣṇa firmly protected me from death at the hands of the Muslims, but today, with my mind faltering, he takes my life!"

101. Nityānanda reassured him, "I am not going to waver! I am certain that Lord Caitanya is the cause of your agitation. 102. Although just a brahman, he commanded us with the authority of a king—'Go tell the story [of Kṛṣṇa] to each and every house!' 103. In his command I heard no provision regarding location, nor did he say to except thieves and known swindlers among the people. 104. If we do not fully execute his command, then all is lost. Conversely, should we execute his order precisely, we shall reap the rewards. 105. Understand well that our Lord makes no mistakes. He explicitly said, 'The two of you . . .'—am I mistaken?" 106. And in this way did the two men garrulously bicker, pausing only to glance back at the two ne'er-do-wells chasing them.

107. They ran desperately until they arrived at their Master's house, while the drunks, impeded by their own alcohol, followed somewhat circuitously in their footsteps. 108. Losing sight [of Nityānanda and Haridāsa], the inebriated men paused, stirring up a commotion in no time at all. 109. Completely befuddled by their drink, the pair failed to discern much of anything—they did not know where they were nor could they remember where they themselves lived. 110. A short while later the two Vaiṣṇavas reconnoitered the area but failed to discover where the two drunks had disappeared. 111. They breathed easily and embraced each other. Laughing, they made their way to the Master, Viśvambhara.

112. The great Master sat, his eyes like lotuses, his limbs pleasing in beauty like [Kṛṣṇa] Madanamohana, 'The Enchanter of the God of Love.' 113. Crowded around on four sides was seated the congregation of Vaiṣṇavas, everyone deep in discussing the tales of Kṛṣṇa. 114. Viśvambhara deftly explained to those gathered the true nature of himself, just as the Lord of the White Island [Viṣṇu] reclined with the sage Sanaka and others. 115. When Nityānanda and Haridāsa arrived, they recounted the wild adventures of their day.

116. "Today we encountered two truly extraordinary men: unmistakable alcoholics, yet called brahmans. 117. For their edification we said to them, 'Say the name Kṛṣṇa!' They came after us. We were fortunate to escape with our lives!"

118. The Master inquired, "Who are these two? What are their names? How can someone called a brahman indulge in such vices?"

119. In front of him sat Gaṅgādāsa and Śrīnivāsa, who spoke of the public misbehavior of those men. 120. "Master, the names of those two men are Jagāi

and Mādhāi. They were born here [in Navadvīpa], the sons of good brahman parentage. 121. These two have never been associated with anything but vice; save liquor, they have striven for little else, practically since their birth. 122. Out of fear of these two, the citizens of Nadīya lock up their houses, and those who do not are certain to be burgled. 123. But we do not need to tell you about these two depraved men, for you see everything; you know everything, O Lord!"

124. The Master replied, "Yes, yes, I know. I have come here in order to destroy these two men, to dismantle them piece by piece."

125. Nityānanda protested, "Chop them to pieces if you must, but I have not yet visited all of their hiding places. 126. Think how much more credit would reflect on you if first these two men were made to say 'Govinda!' 127. It is the nature only of a righteous individual to say the name of Kṛṣṇa. These two have never known nor done anything other than impious acts. 128. If you save these two men by giving the gift of devotion, then you will be rightly known as the "Savior of the Fallen." 129. In saving me your greatness was revealed to be fantastic; how much more that will be increased by saving those two!"

130. Viśvambhara smiled and said, "They have already been saved, from the very moment they caught sight of you. 131. You focus your attention on them especially, which precipitates this auspicious result: Kṛṣṇa will bring about their well-being in no time."

132. When they heard these blessed words, the devotees broke into a roar, proclaiming the victory and greatness of Kṛṣṇa. 133. "Already saved!"—everyone deeply mulled over those words. Haridāsa then confided privately in Advaita.

134. "The Master sent me out with an unstable man [Nityānanda]. I did not have any idea where we were, and still he ran all over the place. 135. During the rainy season, with the Jāhnavī River crawling with crocodiles, he went swimming and even wrestled with [those crocodiles]! 136. I stood on the bank and called across to alert him, but he just floated into the Gaṅgā's main stream. 137. Then he happened to espy a young child on the bank. He clambered up to beat the child, but only chased him away. 138. The child's mother and father appeared, stick in hand. I urged restraint by grasping their feet in supplication. 139. I sent for some ghi and curds [to assuage them], but they took me hostage. They intended to thrash me! 140. Those people, whose actions were as imprudent [as Nityānanda's], turned and, pointing out their daughter, announced that she should be married to me. 141. Later [Nityānanda] climbed up on the sacred altar seat and cried out, 'I am the Supreme Lord Śiva!' and then he milked a cow belonging to someone else and drank the milk! 142. I threatened to get you to rebuke him in order to teach him; [but he responded], 'What can your Advaita do to me? 143. You may even call Caitanya your "lord," but what is he going to do if he comes here?' 144. I have not told any of this to the Master. Only by the good working of fate did I escape with my life today!

145. On the road we encountered two men, both incorrigible drinkers. We spoke to them to share the message of Kṛṣṇa. 146. They responded with a frightful anger and gave chase to beat us. Only by your grace was my life spared."

147. Advaita chuckled and observed, "This is not the complete picture. The two drunks you mentioned were in the company of yet another drunk. 148. You have described being in the presence of three drunks. Why were you frightened? Have you become orthodox? 149. Nityānanda will intoxicate everyone. I know only too well his actions. 150. Look, suffer this for two or three days and he will bring those two drunks into the fold." 151. As he spoke Advaita began to be possessed of anger. Transformed into the Naked Ascetic, Śiva, he ranted and raved. 152. "I shall suck up all of the nectar of Caitanya's Kṛṣṇa-devotion! How will he dance and sing? Everyone will see just how powerful he really is! 153. You watch! Tomorrow he will fetch those two drunks and Nimāi [Caitanya] and Nitāi [Nityānanda] will dance with them. 154. These two must be treated as one, not different from each other. To protect our social standing, they have maneuvered you and me away!" Haridāsa just smiled at Advaita in his possession of anger, while he contemplated the idea of the two drunkards' salvation.

156. Who, except for one as adept as Haridāsa, had the capacity to fully comprehend Advaita's speech?

157. At that time certain unrighteous followers of Advaita, smouldering with jealousy, cast aspersions on Gadādhara. 158. He who casts aspersions on one Vaiṣṇava in the presence of another is rooted in sin and certain to meet with destruction.

159. These two derelicts [Jagāi and Mādhāi] wandered all over and they ended up at the ghat where the Master was bathing in the Gaṅgā. 160. It was by chance that they had gone to that particular spot. Roaming about rather aimlessly, they harassed everyone they met. 161. Whether powerful or wealthy or miserably poor—each feared for his safety. 162. When night would fall, no one ventured alone to the Gaṅgā to bathe. If one did go, he went with ten or twenty people. 163. Those who found themselves in the vicinity of the Master's house at night would be regaled with the Master's kīrtana throughout the evening. 164. The double-ended *mṛdaṅga* drum and the small hand cymbals punctuated the beat of the kīrtana. Prompted by the music, the participants would dance, moving with the staggering convulsions of the inebriated. 165. Even people who lived a good distance away could hear the din. To hear it makes you dance like one who has drunk to excess.

166. Now where there is a party, those two trouble-makers show up. They heard the music and could not help but dance. 167. Oblivious from imbibing, they knew neither where they were nor what part of town they were in. 168. They saw the Master and called out to him, "Nimāi Paṇḍita! Have them play the complete medley of songs in praise of the Goddess Caṇḍī! 169. All of your singers are superb! I want to witness this myself. Let everyone in who wants

to come!" 170. Seeing these insufferable men, the Master distanced himself quickly, but they ran after him, fortunately along another route altogether.

171. The next day Nityānanda was walking about the town. At nightfall these two hoodlums ambushed him. 172. "Where are you going?" Jagāi and Mādhāi called out. Nityānanda replied, "I am headed for the Master's house."

173. Somewhat stupefied by their drink, they queried further, "Just what is your name?" Nityānanda replied, "My name is Avadhūta, the wandering ascetic." 174. Under the spell of the emotional condition of Kṛṣṇa's brother, Balarāma, the lord Nityānanda was himself visibly intoxicated. And in the spirit of this condition he played along with the two drunks. 175. Then he remembered—"I was going to save these two men. Clearly it was for that reason that I came to this particular spot tonight."

176. When he heard the title "Avadhūta," Mādhāi was furious. He broke a water pot over the head of the ascetic. 177. The pot shattered on his skull and the blood streamed down in torrents. This extraordinary devotee, Nityānanda, thought only of Govinda [Kṛṣṇa].

178. Seeing the blood on Nityānanda's head, Jagāi was moved to compassion and grabbed his brother's hands which were raining blows on Nityānanda. 179. "Why do you do such cruel and hard things? Will it make you a big man to beat up someone who is not from around here? 180. Give it up! Do not strike the Avadhūta. What will you gain from beating a renunciate?"

181. With a great hubbub, people ran to tell the Master. In a short while the Lord arrived together with his retinue. 182. By this time blood had completely drenched Nityānanda's body, yet Nityānanda stood there laughing with the two men. 183. When he saw the blood, the Master lost himself in his anger. "Disc! Disc! Disc!" the Master called out in a booming deep voice. 184. In a flash the disc materialized and Jagāi and Mādhāi both saw it with their own eyes! 185. The devotees were dumbstruck with astonishment. Gathering his wits, Nityānanda pressed forward an earnest request. 186. "O Lord, Jagāi restrained Mādhāi from hitting me! Only an accident made the blood flow so copiously. I am not hurt! 187. Grant me as a boon the bodies of these two men, O Lord! I am not injured in the least. Please calm down!"

188. When he heard the words, "Jagāi restrained him," the Master embraced Jagāi with great joy. 189. To Jagāi he said, "May Kṛṣṇa be merciful to you! By saving Nityānanda, you have won me over. 190. Ask for anything you may desire. From this day forward may you be blessed with devotional love."

191. When the assembled Vaiṣṇavas heard the boon granted to Jagāi, they noisily rejoiced, "Victory! Hail to Hari!"

192. At the very moment when he said, "May you have devotional love," Jagāi fell down in a dead faint from that love. 193. The Master commanded, "Jagāi, stand up and look at me! In truth, I have granted you the gift of devotional love." 194. Jagāi then beheld him, the Lord, Viśvambhara—He Who Bears the Burdens of the Universe—with four arms holding the conch, the disc, the club, and the lotus. 195. Upon seeing this spectacular vision, Jagāi again

fainted and Caitanya the Lord placed his holy feet on Jagāi's chest. 196. Grasping as a treasure those precious feet, which are the very life of the goddess Lakṣmī, Jagāi held them as if they were priceless gems. 197. By the pious act of grasping those feet, Jagāi wept.

In this way did the Lord Gaurāṅga, the Golden-Limbed One, accomplish the unprecedented. 198. One soul, in two bodies, were Jagāi and Mādhāi—one meritorious, the other sinful—one [soul] divided. 199. When the Master was merciful to Jagāi, the heart and mind of Mādhāi was at that same time purified. 200. With a great rush they returned to where Nityānanda was sitting and fell down in full prostration, grabbing his feet in humility. 201. [Mādhāi entreated Caitanya,] "Treat the two of us as one, O Master. We both are unrighteous men. How can you apportion your mercy into two separate parts? 202. Be merciful to me, for I have taken your name. There is no one else who can save me!"

203. The Master replied, "I cannot countenance your salvation, for you have shed the blood of the body of Nityānanda." Mādhāi pleaded, "What you say is impossible! How can you abandon your own duty, your own dharma? 205. How were you able to grant the shelter of your feet to those demons who pierced you with their arrows and their curses?"

206. The Master replied, "Your fault is much greater than theirs—you have spilled blood from Nityānanda's body. 207. The body of my beloved Nityānanda is much more important than my own. This truth I have already explained to you."

208. "Indeed you have so spoken to me, my Lord! Please tell me how I can be saved! 209. You are the crown jewel of physicians, destroyer of all ailments. If you heal my ailment, then I can be healthy and hale again. 210. Do not let me down, Master, Lord of My Existence! You are known to all, so why do you hide yourself from me?"

211. The Master responded, "Your fault is ultimately damning! Go and fall at Nityānanda's feet."

212. As soon as he received the Master's command, Mādhāi grasped Nityānanda's feet, a treasure without price. 213. He who embraces those feet can never be destroyed. Revatī [Balarāma's wife] experienced the power of those feet. 214. Viśvambhara continued, "Listen, most worthy Nityānanda! He has fallen at your feet in the gamble that you will be merciful, 215. even though he drew blood from your body. You have the power to forgive him; it has fallen to you to act."

215. Nityānanda replied, "My Lord! What can I say? You are the life-giving power which can grant mercy through this inert tree [of my body]. 216. All of whatever merit I have accrued in my many lifetimes, I transfer to Mādhāi. This I guarantee, make no mistake. 218. My faults, however, are many—I have no accumulated grace to grant. Please abandon this charade and be merciful to Mādhāi!"

219. Viśvambhara then said, "If you have forgiven everything, draw Mādhāi

close and embrace him. May it all come to pass!" 220. When the Master commanded it, he strongly embraced him, and all of Mādhāi's bonds [of sin] were loosed. 221. Nityānanda—Eternal Bliss—entered into Mādhāi's body. Mādhāi was then completely empowered.

222. In this way were both [drunkards] liberated. And the two men sang their thanks at the feet of [Nityānanda and Caitanya]. 223. The Master commanded, "Never sin again!" to which Jagāi and Mādhāi eagerly responded, "Never again, Father!"

224. The Master continued, "Listen well, you two! I have spoken matters of truth to you. 225. You have accumulated much demerit in hundreds of millions of lifetimes, but if you sin no more, my grace will counter all. 226. I will provide food for the mouths of all. My incarnation (*avatāra*) will enter your bodies."

227. When Jagāi and Mādhāi heard those words, they fainted in ecstasy and collapsed on the spot. 228. The two brahmans had completely lost consciousness in that ocean of bliss. Fathoming their condition, the Master, Viśvambhara, instructed, 229. "Pick up these two men and take them to my house. We will sing the praises of Kṛṣṇa with them. 230. Today I will give them what is difficult for even the god Brahmā to attain. I will make these two the most honored men in the world. 231. The touch of these two is like bathing in the Gaṅgā, and so they will be proclaimed as equal to the Gaṅgā. 232. This is none other than what Nityānanda resolved. I know with certainty the wish of Nityānanda."

233. Jagāi and Mādhāi were lifted up by the Vaiṣṇavas and carried inside the Master's house. 234. Intimate friends and companions entered with the Master. Then the door closed and no one else could enter. 235. The great Lord Viśvambhara seated himself—Nityānanda and Gadādhara sat prominently on either side. 236. Directly in front sat Advaita, the King of the Storehouse [of Devotion], while the Vaiṣṇava retinue crowded around on all four sides. 237. Puṇḍarīka Vidyānidhi, the adept Haridāsa, Garuḍāi, Rāmāi, Śrīvāsa, Gaṅgādāsa, 238. Vakreśvara Paṇḍita, Candraśekhara Ācārya—all of these [devotees] were well familiar with Caitanya's ways. 239. Other respected individuals further encircled Caitanya—joyfully seated among them, Jagāi and Mādhāi. 240. The bodies of Jagāi and Mādhāi rippled all over with gooseflesh; they cried profusely, racked with convulsions, jerking about on the ground. 241. Who has the power to fathom what Caitanya had in mind—he turns two incorrigible sinners into two great devotees, 242. and turns heretics into ascetic renunciates. In this way one savors a portion of the immortal elixir of his worldly play. 243. He who believes in this will surely gain Kṛṣṇa. He who doubts goes to a certain destruction.

244. The two men, Jagāi and Mādhāi, sang songs of praise, while the beautiful Golden-Limbed One, Caitanya, listened with the rest of the group. 245. The pure and holy Goddess of Speech sat on the tongues of these two men at the direct instigation of the Lord, the Radiant Moon Caitanya. 246. Nityānanda and Caitanya appeared as but one—the truth of which was seen and apprehended by the two men [who were saved]. 247. These men then sang songs

of praise for what they had witnessed. Anyone who hears these panegyrics gains devotion to Kṛṣṇa. 248. "Glory, glory be to the Great Master, Glory to Viśvambhara! Glory to Nityānanda, who himself bears the Bearer of the World Burden. . . .

282. "You have rescued so many famous sinners—all kinds, shapes, and sizes can be distinguished in that notable group. 283. Among the undistinguished you have saved two particularly recalcitrant demons—us two—because your compassion stretches to everyone." 284. Continuing in this vein, Jagāi and Mādhāi wept. Thus does the Protector Caitanya precipitate the unprecedented. 285. The Vaiṣṇavas who witnessed this extraordinary event placed their palms together in respect, intoned formal praise, and prostrated themselves in obeisance.

286. "Master, the praises sung by these two incorrigible drunkards most would believe to be false, except for your grace! 287. May you distribute your mercy when and where and to whom and in what shape you deem fit—who can apprehend your incomprehensible power?"

288. The Master replied, "These two men are drunkards no more. From this day forth these two are my servants. 289. All of you in the community must support these two men. In succeeding births they will not forget me. 290. Whenever they slip and commit an offense against someone, no matter the nature, forgive and be gracious to these two men." 291. Jagāi and Mādhāi listened to the Master's speech and promptly fell at the feet of those present. 292. Those stalwart devotees blessed Jagāi and Mādhāi, who were now without fault. 293. The Master commanded, "Stand up, Jagāi and Mādhāi! You have become my servants. Worry no more! 294. The two of you recited praises, invoking supremely profound truths which are incorruptible. 295. Nothing else, save Nityānanda's grace, can ever reside in your bodies—that you can know for certain! 296. See for yourself and realize that I have removed all of your manifold sins, O brothers." And no more sin sullied the bodies of these two men. . . .

—24—

Encountering the Smallpox Goddess: The Auspicious Song of Śītalā

Tony K. Stewart

Śītalā, the goddess of smallpox, is a deity who is popular throughout the Indian subcontinent, where smallpox has been endemic for centuries, but she is especially venerated in the delta regions of Bengal (today the Indian state of West Bengal and the country of Bangladesh), which suffered terrible outbreaks in the eighteenth and nineteenth centuries. Her name literally means the Cool One, an epithet that appears to be a euphemistic designation, since her speciality is accompanied by debilitating fever, but probably derives from her birth from the cooled ashes of the sacrificial fire. Her chief lieutenant and the organizer of her vast contingent of diseases is Jvara or Jvarāsura, the triple-headed Fever Demon. Śītalā herself is also known as Queen of Disease (Roga Rājā), Lord of Pestilence (Vyādhi Pati) and Master of Poxes (Basanta Rāya), especially smallpox, her most dreaded product. She is represented most frequently by a golden pot, although in wealthier temples she is depicted as a woman riding on a donkey, her preferred mount, and she will be represented occasionally in the village by a simply decorated stone.

Śītalā is one of the many Hindu mother goddesses invoked by the inhabitants of Bengal and, like other goddesses, she is worshiped by all classes, including many Muslims. The majority of these deities, mothers of the earth, are benevolent in obviously positive ways: they provide wealth, fertility, extensive families, and long life, and preside over knowledge, language, and the arts. With these patrons obvious salutary relations can be developed; but Śītalā's is a relationship of great ambivalence, for she represents one particularly frightful dimension of the Bengali physical environment: diseases. As mother she can be expected to nurture, but she is prone to anger and quick to offend, a characteristic she shares with Manasā, goddess of snakes, and Ṣaṣṭhī, goddess of children, along with the more well-known goddesses such as Kālī. When provoked, she can be expected to visit her wayward child and to remind that child that she is still their mother. To most, the logic of that causal connection is understandable, for those who defy her suffer her wrath in the form of pestilential disease; they get what they deserve. Yet many faithful and devoted worshipers of the goddess have also been touched by her heavy hand, and that is not so easily explained.

To the casual observer, the inhabitant of Śītalā's landscape is faced with a very uneasy set of alternatives, which run something like this. If you do not worship the goddess, you run the risk of being singled out for this egregious omission; Śītalā will extract her due. Yet, should you revere Śītalā and supplicate her, you risk coming to her direct attention, and that might prompt her to visit you, her devotee, in person. When she calls she leaves her mark, the pock, pointedly called "the grace of the mother" (*māyera dayā*). Should you survive, you bear her indelible print as a living reminder of her latent presence; should you die—and millions have—your death at the hands of the deity ensures an eventual salvation. Either way, the faithful and the corrupt alike directly encounter the divine as it is manifest in the natural world; some weather the enounter and others succumb, but none emerges unscathed. It is, as one scholar has aptly named it, a "theology of the repulsive."

Yet, to the inhabitants of Bengal, this threat of punishment is not so pessimistically burdensome because it is accompanied by a promise of well-being. Worship of the goddess does not require that Bengalis fatalistically resign themselves to her wrath, nor does a naturalistic explanation of the presence of the disease run counter to her veneration. Bengalis accept the modern scientific etiology of the disease and, at the same time, accept that Śītalā is responsible. Steps can be taken to avoid her pox, and the most popular is the innoculation, which has been prevalent in Bengal for several centuries (*guṭikā*). The advent of this particular goddess has long been associated with a cycle of drought, which reduces food availability, and famine, which weakens and makes vulnerable the local population—to which can be added the exacerbations of the rapacious tax-collector, who refuses to relent during these times of need. Worship of the goddess, which seems to peak during these periods—as demonstrated in the mid-eighteenth and nineteenth centuries—belays anxiety and creates a strong communal response that cuts across the traditional divisions of Bengali society. The natural world and the ills of society are inextricably bound one to the other, and the goddess must in these times intervene to remind, reward, and punish, while the local population must work together to overcome the challenge to the normal order of things. If they discipline themselves in proper conduct, the goddess will be benevolent.

During the eighteenth and nineteenth centuries, Śītalā's worship effloresced in direct correspondence to the epidemics that devastated the Bengali countryside. During the eighteenth century writing her texts, and in the nineteenth printing her texts became an industry of devotion, perhaps born of desperation. Yet even to compose or transmit her texts carries its own danger. The text that follows is the earliest known example of a Bengali *Śītalā Maṅgala*, the "Auspicious Song of the Cool One," written by one Kṛṣṇarāma Dāsa. Informed speculation places the date as early as 1690 C.E. but, based on internal evidence, it is probably a few years later. In this text the goddess is thoroughly provoked by the shameless behavior of an incorrigible toll collector named Madana Dāsa, who eventually suffers the full force of her wrath. Many of the poxes distributed by the goddess to this despicable man are descriptive of their shape and color and have been literally translated; where possible modern equivalents to other diseases have been noted. The language of the text itself conveys the ambivalence of Śītalā's position. Madana Dāsa's capitulation is really just that; the text even speaks of Śītalā simply frightening people into giving up their sinful ways. The humor, morbid though it is, and the mocking tones adopted by the goddess to bludgeon her hapless victims, suggest the oral and performative nature of the tale—although this is not quite so ribald nor riddled with the plethora of stinging double-entendres as the most popular and most frequently performed version of the cycle today, the story by Nityānanda, who wrote his tale in the 1750s. Kṛṣṇarāma, who collected and recorded no fewer than five maṅgala poems, explains that he has written it just as he heard it—a subtle caveat which hints that his fear of poetic failure could have personally disastrous results. The story of Madana Dāsa is the first and simplest of three episodes still extant from this earliest tale, and in its narrative starkness vividly captures the intensity of dramatic confrontation in these stories. Even though smallpox has been officially eradicated since 1978, the memory remains fresh and the worship of Śītalā continues, for to the Bengali follower, the manifestation of the pox is part of a much larger causal nexus that connects earth, heaven, and moral action; where there is the potential for drought and famine and taxes, the community must remain ever-vigilant for the visit of this mother-figure.

The following story is translated from "Madana Dāsa Pālā" of Kṛṣṇarāma Dāsa's *Śītalā Maṅgala* in *Kavi Kṛṣṇarāma Dāsera Granthāvalī,* edited by Satyanārāyaṇa Bhaṭṭācārya (Calcutta: Calcutta University, 1958), pp. 251–57.

Further Reading

A study by Edward C. Dimock, Jr., entitled "A Theology of the Repulsive: The Myth of the Goddess Śītalā," may be found in *The Divine Consort: Rādhā and the Goddesses of India,* edited by John Stratton Hawley and Donna Marie Wulff, Berkeley Religious Studies Series (Berkeley: Graduate Theological Union, 1982), pp. 184–203. Ralph W. Nicholas and Aditi Nath Sarkar, published "The Fever Demon and the Census Commissioner: Śītalā Mythology in Eighteenth and Nineteenth Century Bengal," in *Bengal: Studies in Literature, Society and History,* edited by Marvin Davis, South Asia Occasional Paper no. 27 (East Lansing: Asian Studies Center, Michigan State University, 1976), pp. 3–68. Nicholas has published three other relevant articles: "Śītalā and the Art of Printing: The Transmission and Propogation of the Myth of the Goddess of Smallpox in Rural West Bengal." in, *Mass Culture, Language and Arts in India,* edited by M. L. Apte (Bombay: Popular Prakashan, 1978), pp. 152–80, "The Village Mother in Bengal," in *Mother Worship: Theme and Variation,* edited by James Preston (Chapel Hill: University of North Carolina Press, 1982), 192–209; and "The Goddess Śītalā and Epidemic Smallpox in Bengal," *Journal of Asian Studies* 41: 1 (November 1981), 21–44. Also see Susan S. Wadley, "Śītalā: the Cool One," *Asian Folklore Studies* 39: 1 (1980), 32–62.

The Auspicious Song of the Cool One, Śītalā, Goddess of Smallpox

1. Let us bow down to you Śītalā, the Cool One,
whose enchanting lotus feet
  reap universal weal.
The serene beauty of your face soothes and delights
more than clusters of hand-picked flowers,
  forcing the fount of elixir, the moon, to hide in shame.

2. Bestower of calm and remover of fears,
you remain ever resolute
  with the name She Who Lays Waste the Corrupt.
You reside at all times
in the dark hollow of your golden pot,
  your comely shape cleansing and absolving.

3. Links of bells girdle your waist,
tinkling anklets ride above your feet,
  your limbs whispy like tender shoots of paddy.
Plain bands and ornamental bracelets
demurely grace your delicate wrists,
  while conch-shell bangles dance at your hand.

4. You provide the life-giving rains,
and plunder all suffering.
  Around your neck glisten strands of pure gold.
Your flowing tresses fly wild,
thicker than a yak-tail whisk—
  no fiery sun can compare.

5. Not once in eternity will be destroyed
the good fortune of all those who are
  blessed to serve under your motherly care.
Brahmā sings high your praise;
how can I, who am intellectually impaired,
  tell anything of your incomparable majesty?

6. With hands cupped in deference, the minstrel
places his meager offering into your pot—
  Listen to your tale in song!
He who is devoted to you
sees his manifold faults destroyed,
  destined never to endure more miseries.

7. Because you are suffused with compassion,
descend into our midst and
  protect the clan of our dramatic subject.
You infuse yourself throughout the world,
the universe—but when taking form on earth,
  you prefer that of a simple household ascetic.

8. When you spoke to me in dream
this truth alone entered my mind—
  I could know nothing else whatsoever.
This tale is true, and it is truth—
your two feet alone provide shelter
  from misfortune and disaster.

9. May you inhabit this sacred pot,
Goddess of Smallpox, possessor of all qualities,
  and grant us an auspicious look.
Kṛṣṇarāma describes in detail
the education process directed at our subject
  by that gracious glance.

10. In another realm situated across the wide waters there was a prosperous sea-trading community called Saptagrāma or "Seven Cities." Everyone referred to it as a meritorious land. The goddess, mounted on her donkey, traveled to every corner of the earth, and eventually reached that place. 11. Living in the environs of that fair city was one Madana Dāsa, appropriately named the Servant of the Lord of Spring Pleasures, a Kāyastha by caste, who labored as a toll collector along the highway. Always accompanied by a large contingent of local militia, and flanked on either side by menacing Rajput warriors, he was easily recognized by the paper and pen he held in his hand.

12. In order to test this man, the goddess called upon her venerable contingent, summoning untold numbers of dread diseases. Then the Goddess of Smallpox transformed herself into a vendor of assorted foods—fruits, vegetables, pulses, and sweetmeats. Her menagerie of bulging sacks failed calculation. 13. Jaundice hid in oil laced with turmeric, while ripe wood-apples harbored the dreaded goiter, both innocently under cover of a brace of palmyra fruits. A cluster of ripe, juicy coconuts was really nothing but hydrocele—dropsy of the scrotum—and dysentery invaded her tender young bunches of spinach leaves. 14. Typhoid fever wove itself into the leafy greens, and various wind

afflictions—flatulence, eructation, halitosis—assumed the form of irresistible milk sweets. Corns, warts, moles, wenns, sebaceous cysts, and other skin extrusions were disguised in the homologous shapes of sesame seeds. Jaundice likewise invaded the sugar of various milk sweets, while dropsy became the bulbous sweetmeat that resembled its own symptomatic protruding belly. Jujube seeds—which easily burst when ripe—were actually boils and abscesses. 15. Betel nuts were tiny enclosed sacks of elephantiasis; leprosy insinuated itself into sandalwood; and digestive diseases flowed through the succulent pith of ginger root. In melons and grains of various types were fixed morbidity of the spleen, hepatitis, and other disorders of the liver and internal organs—all of whose names filled the general populace with horror!

16. Her multitude of bags were carried on oxen, who in appropriate form trampled underfoot the garland offerings made along the road, and clumsily brushed aside the ritual vessels used to worship the many gods and goddesses. Yanking on the coarse rope lead, she beat those ornery beasts of burden with her wooden goad. And with the sweet words, "Move, you rotten sons-of-bitches!" she urged them gently down the road. 17. The Queen of Dread Diseases, on her donkey mount, now followed along behind the train, appearing to be but a successful trader. Magically the toll collector appeared, walking down to the end of the landing ghat, while our treasure-trove of virtues, the goddess, steadily advanced toward him. 18. She said nothing at all to that toll collector, gamely driving right on by. This infuriated Madana Dāsa, who watched in utter disbelief. He quickly ordered his armed guards to apprehend her—right then and right there on the road—so Kṛṣṇarāma writes, his own curiosity suddenly piqued.

19. "I do not understand! What is all the fuss about my carts? Why do you refer to my ox as lowly? By what right do you, a lordly man, treat everyone with contempt? I have never encountered such ill behavior anywhere else in the world! 20. Whose privileged son are you to determine whether and whither one passes? I have no fear of anyone . . . " and so it went.

With each word the officer twisted the end of his mustache a little harder, cranking his anger another notch higher. The head of the column of soldiers advanced quickly. 21. "I will wring your little neck!" the militiaman growled menacingly as he reached out to grab her. "It will certainly be a pleasure to punish you!"

"So you will slap the blackjack across my neck, then steal away everything I own. But it is curious how my anger checks itself, 22. For as soon as you attack and the first cry of distress is born, the full weight of your arrogance will come crashing down. I will not even have to resort to the evil eye! Even half that amount of hubris would be extremely unpleasant to bear. Let that give you pause, you insufferable brute! If the truth be known, my initial attraction to you had first inclined me to share some of my boundless hoard. 23. But now that you have cast aspersions on me there is no escaping the fruits of those deprecations. How can one so ostensibly full of good sense be so decidedly pig-headed? In your kind one finds neither honor nor respect. Listen, what I think is that everyone in your detachment is a double-talking sophist sprung from the most noxious of dung heaps! 24. The treachery in your minds is matched only by the lust harbored in your breast. Pay attention to me, you hard-hearted fools!"

The poet Kṛṣṇarāma can but describe the Goddess of Smallpox, whose deep, frightful eyes have been wrathfully cast.

25. The militia officer spoke, "Hey you addle-brained crone! Pull over by the śāla tree. Do exactly as I say! I want you front and center to explain yourself!"

"I have come from Tomabālapura, 'the City of Your Youth,' terribly far from this place, but then tell me, brother, where else is a trader to find goods and produce of such extraordinary and exceptional quality?"

26. Jumping at the bait, the officer queried, "Tell me, how exactly did you come to be so laden with this merchandise? Did you just break out of jail? All of these bags bear the unmistakable look of ill-gotten gains! . . . . " And so the accusations flew.

At last, the goddess feigned to acquiesce, "Sāheb, your honor, our negotiations clearly have reached an impasse. Take everything away. It is undoubtedly your good fortune." 27. And so the Goddess of Smallpox relented, with the cryptic parting comment, "I came to distribute my goods and distribute I have. Now happily and with a light heart I return to my home in Burdwan." But secretly she thought to herself, "You, my toll collector, are such an ass; you have neither shame nor intelligence!"

28. The toll collector never once feared for his safety. He never acknowledged requests or listened to solicitation, even when proffered by a holy man, 29. Because, you see, the toll collector was thoroughly and completely wicked. It was with a sinister pleasure that he confiscated items without number. 30. It was routine for the collector to rough up the poor and ignorant and, under pretext, to appropriate their possessions, which mysteriously but invariably found their way into his private house. 31. This day he was quite pleased to have hauled in such a handsome catch, for various important personages would come to his home expecting lavish entertainment—and so they did.

32. The Goddess of Pestilence watched from her perch in the heavens as the toll master and his guests ate. The sweets and other items that he had personally selected were eaten noisily and with great relish. 33. Afterwards, some bathed and then reached for the turmeric-laced oil, which really contained jaundice. 34. In their gluttony, the guests unceremoniously wolfed down the sugary pots of sweets, which distended their greedy stomachs. Then they turned to the small metal plates filled with the dreaded dropsy sweets of ascites and beriberi. 35. What they consumed as tasty grains entered their guts as pyemia, splenomegaly, and various necroses of the spleen. 36. The bodies of those who ate the palmyra fruits were wracked with clonic convulsions, which alas were only

portents to the lesions, boils, and furuncles that would soon appear on their thighs, in their intestines, and around their anuses. 37. The betel was consumed with much laughter and pleasant banter, only to be manifested as hepatitis and cirrhosis, and followed closely by either elephantiasis or blindness. 38. What first appeared on their bodies as a simple leukoderma was really leprosy in disguise. When they partook of the various leafy greens, they tasted typhoid. 39. When they glanced in the mirror they discovered through blurry eyes that their corneas had glazed over with cataracts. No one could speak clearly for the agonizing, hacking cries of pain—it was fever fueled by sin.

40. The punishment reserved for that mean toll collector was deemed especially appropriate—various forms of smallpox he contracted in their guise as pulses. 41. Ground pulse cakes coated with poppy seeds hid measles, chickenpox, and even the disfiguring pox of the "black death." 42. The "sackcloth" pox blanketed him in a rough patchwork of pustules, while the "māsakalāi pulse" pox clumped in painful, thick, oozing masses.

43. There is no one on earth who could weather this onslaught: it afflicted each and every one without exception. The poet Kṛṣṇarāma opines that the retribution for their folly was more than fitting.

44. Draped around the victim's neck was a breathtaking necklace of deep red coral—and his life breath it was, being drained by the reddish "bloody-mawed" pox. 45. Madana Dāsa, rogue of tax extortionists, was felled. So, too, his mighty Rajput warriors buckled under the strain. 46. That toll man found that he could no longer vent his wrath, for masses of putrid boils and abscesses had erupted to shrink his mouth to but the tiniest, painful pinhole. 47. The hideous "monster" pox appeared, so even the threads of his loose pajamas lacerated his flesh like razors. The deadly "ugly-maker black" pox turned his body into a disfigured pulp. 48. His guards shed their weapons and armor, down to undershirts and turbans, but even the light touch of their cotton left them howling in agony, so they shamelessly and without hesitation stripped stark naked—but to no avail.

49. Choosing her moment, the Queen of Pestilence resumed her disguise, and with deliberate intention returned to that now-devastated place to needle her offender. 50. "We just couldn't get enough, could we? And have we gotten tired after sampling all our scrumptious goodies? Now tell me, why is the big bad toll collector straining so hard without success? Are we suffering from a touch of tenesmus? Do we hurt? . . . " And so she made her point.

51. Grudgingly repentant, Madana Dāsa—the Servant of the Lord of Spring Pleasures—pressed his palms together in humility. "I have committed many gross and grave offenses toward your person. 52. You have left an indelible impression on this man of rank, and can on others at your will. I will worship your holy feet if only you will cure me! Remove these excruciating diseases! 53. Say that it will be so, O Gracious One! Heed my petition! For your worship I will never use anyone but my brahman who personally attends me, the em-

inent toll collector. 54. When that brahman goes to perform your evening rituals, everyone will know it is dedicated to Śītalā, Lord of the Śūdras.

55. And so it was that the goddess, that ocean of greatness, left her mark and become widely known. Said she, "You are now the son of Śītalā, the Cool One, for it is really I, Ruler of Pox, in disguise. 56. When you worship me in my pot, you will suffer no more. You will come to taste a wonderful variety of pleasures and joys, and they will expand immeasurably." 57. With these parting words, the goddess started for her own abode, and the toll collector was, as promised, relieved of all of his dread diseases.

58. He erected a winsome temple on the banks of the Gaṅgā River and had there installed the Queen of Smallpox, Śītalā, the Cool One. 59. He had her worship performed, offering the full gamut of appropriate sacral items. From that the wicked and base were frightened into good and honest people! 60. Goats and rams were sacrificed with satisfying production, and her worship was consumated with reverent concentration and attention.

61. The lowly among men, who struggle with death and disease in our world, are incapable of cognizing just how extraordinary this treasure-trove of qualities truly is. 62. The Mother's parental affection erodes one's faults and, one by one, the entire population will have their sins forgiven. 63. The goddess, compassionate as she alone can be, has offered her grace, and the whole world dances in that knowledge, letting fly the sounds of triumph. 64. Openly pleased, the Goddess of Smallpox triumphantly returned to her private heavenly citadel, and along the way nothing could be heard but praise of Śītalā, the Cool One. . . .

149. The poet Kṛṣṇarāma pleads, "Listen carefully, my dear Mother Śītalā, for I have composed your song exactly as it was recited."

—25—

The Wonders of Śrī Mastnāth

David Gordon White

The Nāth Siddhas in Their Religious Context

In about the twelfth century C.E., a sect called the Nāth Siddhas appeared on the Indian religious scene. The name of this sect tells us much about its adherents. *Nāth,* which means "lord" or "master," is a term that is often suffixed to names of the great god Śiva (so, for example, the phallic image of Śiva in his main temple in Varanasi is called Viśvanāth, "Lord of the Universe"). The Nāth Siddhas took Śiva to be the highest god, and claimed to imitate him in much of their religious practice. They furthermore suffixed the term *nāth* to their own names: upon his initiation, a member of this sect would be given a name ending in -nāth, such as Bīrnāth, Gambhīrnāth, and so on.

The second term in the name of this sect is *siddha. Siddha* literally means "one who is accomplished or perfected," "one who has become fully realized." A siddha was one who, through the practice (*sādhana*) of a number of techniques for perfecting his body, had realized (*siddha*) bodily perfection, and had thereby become possessed of supernatural powers (*siddhis*) and bodily immortality (*jīvanmukti:* literally "liberation in the body"). The Nāths were not the sole group to take the name of "Siddha" in the medieval Indian religious context; a number of other sects, generally Śaiva, were also called "Siddhas." Among these may be counted the Maheśvara Siddhas (also known as the Vīraśaivas or Liṅgāyatas), the Rasa Siddhas (the alchemists of medieval India), and the Mahāsiddhas (Buddhist tantric yogins).

In very broad terms, the siddha traditions of medieval India constituted a broad current of religious thought and practice that emphasized the perfectability of the human body as a means to dominating the forces and laws of nature, including life and death. Present in every siddha tradition was a body of techniques for physical transformation called *haṭha yoga* (the "yoga of violent force"). This system projected upon the gross human body a remarkably intricate physiology of the yogic or subtle body, which was composed of a series of energy centers, networks of channels, and an array of male and female divine forces. It was upon this subtle body that the yogic practitioner, through an elaborate combination of postures, breathing techniques, meditative states, and acoustic devices, came to channel forcibly all of his internalized divine energies, breaths, bodily fluids, and mental states into a single point, at which he realized, once and for all time, bodily perfection and immortality.

No Indian siddha sect has ever compared with the Nāth Siddhas for its use of this system of haṭha yoga. It is, in fact, Gorakhnāth and Matsyendranāth, the legendary founders of this sect, who are credited with having first revealed the secret techniques of haṭha yoga to humanity. Both were and remain the greatest of India's haṭha yogis, living on from age to age and aeon to aeon in perfected, immortal, ever-rejuvenated bodies. In all that they do, the Nāth Siddhas wear their haṭha yoga "on their sleeves," in the form of the insignia particular to their sect. These insignia include wide hoop earrings (called *mūdrās* or *darśans*), worn through the thick of their ears; a small piece of antelope horn (called a *nād*) that hangs on a woollen thread upon their chests; and ashes that they smear over their entire bodies. In addition to these, they also pile up heaps of ashes (called *dhūnīs*) wherever they install themselves to practice their yoga.

When a novice is initiated into a Nāth Siddha order, his ears are bored in order that a subtle channel in his yogic body be opened, without which it would be impossible for him to carry his yogic practice through to its ultimate goal. A short time later, mūdrās are placed in these earholes. It is by virtue of this practice of ear-boring that the Nāth Siddhas have also come to be known as the Kānphaṭa ("Ear-bored") yogis.

The nād ("sound," "note") the Nāth Siddha wears over his heart is both a piece of horn—which, when blown into, sounds a note—and an external mark of the subtle sound heard internally by the yogi in the course of his practice. It is at the level of the heart, precisely, that the yogic nād is said to be reversed: instead of being uttered by the yogi, the sound begins to reverberate of its own accord once the yogi has raised his yogic energy, seed, and breath up to the level of his heart. "Reversing the nād" is also a metaphor for the haṭha yogic process in its most general sense. Through the application of "violent force" (*haṭha*) in his yogic practice, the yogi succeeds in reversing the natural trends of aging, disease, and death, and channels his energy, seed, and breath upward, against the normal flow of bodily processes. In so doing, he rejuvenates himself—growing younger instead of older—and realizes all manner of other powers that flaunt the laws of nature, culminating in bodily immortality.

This concept of reversal is also present in the ashes and dhūnī of the Nāth Siddha. "Ashes to ashes" is the way of the world. In India, nearly every human life ends with cremation, in which the physical body is reduced to ashes. So too, the universe, at the end of a cosmic aeon, is reduced to ashes by Śiva, who incinerates all matter with his wild dance. In the Hindu context of cyclic time, however, the universe is always born anew, out of those same ashes. More than this, the renewed universe is always a better, more purified universe than that which was burnt away through Śiva's irresistable energy, an energy born of his yogic practice. Śiva is said to smear his own body with the ashes of past creations. The Nāth Siddha, who imitates Śiva in his practice of yoga, wears ashes on his body and piles up his dhūnī before him to symbolize the yogic dissolution of his own gross, physical body. The burning energy born of the practice of haṭha yoga internally incinerates the gross, mortal body, tempers and purifies the subtle yogic body, and ultimately gives rise to the perfected, immortal, and supernaturally powerful body that is the Nāth Siddha's goal. The ashes of death and destruction are thus emblems of the transformative power of yoga. It is this nearly single-minded adherence to the haṭha yogic system, however, that has historically brought about the censure of the Nāth Siddhas by a number of other Hindu groups.

The Nāth Siddhas are, in present-day India, the sole religious sect to have remained truly faithful to the precepts of the medieval siddha traditions. The Rasa Siddha alchemists have disappeared, the Buddhist Mahāsiddhas have long since left Indian soil to thrive in altered form as the Vajrāyāna Buddhists of Tibet, and the Maheśvara Siddhas or Vīraśaivas have, since their twelfth-century inception, been mainly a devotional sect. Apart from the Nāth Siddhas, most medieval Indian religious movements evolved in three different directions. The first of these was a trend toward devotionalism, which turned around a loving god who offered salvation through grace to his devotees. Leading the faithful in the medieval devotional sects were charismatic leaders called Sants, "saints," who were at once models of devotion, intercessors between god and man, and at times earthly incarnations of the god himself.

The second major medieval trend in Hinduism was tantra, a mystic body of religious theory and practice which, while it certainly grew out of the earlier siddha traditions, came to diverge widely from them after the tenth century. Briefly stated, tantra retained the goals (immortalization and divinization of the human body) and some of the means (haṭha yoga and meditative practices) of the siddha traditions, but greatly altered their conceptual foundations. Whereas the siddhas emphasized the concrete manipulation of substances (bodily fluids, alchemical preparations, and so on) for the material transformation of the human body (into, for example, a body hard as a diamond) for the concrete domination of the physical world, tantra operated at a higher level of abstraction. Tantric transformations were more acoustic than transmutational, and tantric realization more gnostic than physical. The ultimate tantric goal of "becoming a second Śiva" referred more to the liberation of consciousness than to the immortalization of the body. Tantra (or that aspect of tantra known as Śāktism) was, moreover, devotional in its own way, worshiping Śiva, the absolute, through the intermediary of his divine energy, which was portrayed at once as a goddess, the phenomenal world, the phonemes of the Sanskrit language, womanhood in general, and the subtle body in all its constituent parts.

The medieval Nāth Siddhas, in contrast, left nearly no place for devotionalism in their religious practice. Although they have historically identified and worshiped their founders as incarnations of Śiva himself, this has more to do with "guru-ism," the adoration of one's teacher and initiator as god (whence the denominations *gurudev*, "guru-god" and *gurunāth*, "lord guru" applied to illustrious Nāth Siddhas), than with devotion to god. They have, moreover, perceived the female sex to be the greatest danger and barrier to success in the practice of haṭha yoga, for which the retention of male semen is the sine qua non.

The third religious current to dominate the medieval Indian scene was Islam, the faith of the peoples who gradually conquered most of the northern part of the subcontinent from the year 1000 when Maḥmud of Ghazni entered from the west, down through the rule of the Mughal dynasty, from 1526 to 1788. In the course of nearly a millennium of Islamic presence in India, perhaps no Hindu religious sect has interacted on as profound and sustained a level as have the Nāth Siddhas with exponents of that mystic branch of Islam known as Sufism. Over the centuries, a great number of the religious virtuousi of Sufism, called fakirs (*faqīrs*), *pīrs*, or *wālīs* (plural: *awliyā'*) have come to be identified with various Nāth Siddhas, and vice versa. So, for example, the "Hindu" Matsyendranāth is called Morchā Pīr by the Muslims, while the Muslim Ratan Pīr is known as Ratannāth by the Hindus. Often, it is impossible to extract specifically Hindu or Muslim elements from the syncretist cults of these holy god-men, who could evoke, in the same breath, both the Hindu god Rāma and the Muslim Allah.

In the final analysis, we can say that the Nāth Siddhas were censured by broader elements of Hindu society for three reasons. The first of these was their Islamicizing tendency, their willingness to absorb and adapt to Sufi practices. For an orthodox Hindu, such syncretism was unacceptable. Second, the Nāth Siddha emphasis on a haṭha yoga that had no need for a god or goddess for success (and which thereby was, for all intents and purposes, atheistic) did not sit well with the more mainstream devotional cults of medieval India. For this, the Nāth Siddhas are criticized by Sants from a broad array of traditions, who revile them for their arrogance and materialistic self-sufficiency. Last, the Nāth Siddhas were and remain a kind of throwback to a relatively archaic form of Hindu religious practice. Clearly the heirs to such earlier Śaiva sects as the Pāśupatas (followers of Śiva, the "Lord of Beasts") and the Kāpālikas ("Skull-Bearers"), the Nāth Siddhas seem not to have changed with the times, as have the majority of the tantric sects. Whereas the latter have refined and reformed their theory and practices to phase out the matter-oriented tendencies of the siddha traditions, the Nāth Siddhas have continued to cultivate their old haṭha yogic practices. For this, they have been branded by their critics as frauds and conjurers, deceivers both of themselves and of their followers.

The Acts of the Illustrious Mastnāth as Nāth Hagiography

In this light, it is striking that the Nāth Siddhas continue to survive if not thrive in much of north India, whereas the great majority of the medieval tantric sects who once "improved" on the Nāth Siddhas' synthesis have died out. What has been the secret of the Nāth Siddhas' relative success? Like the fakirs and pīrs who are their Muslim counterparts—and this much to the chagrin of the more elite sectarian followers of medieval and contemporary Hinduism—they have always been the chosen holy men and wonder workers of the Hindu masses. Whenever a village in the Himalayan foothills of Garhwal is threatened by a hailstorm, it is a Nāth Siddha (called a *wāli,* which at once means "hail-man" in Hindi and "holy man" in Perso-Arabic) who is called upon to deflect the storm through the power of his yoga. And so it is that down the ages, it has been Nāth Siddhas who have healed ailing cows, provided barren women with sons, and brought down the mighty in favor of the poor.

These perceived powers of the Nāth Siddhas have translated, in history and legend, into a great body of accounts that portray their most illustrious holy men as power brokers of sorts. The most common scenario runs as follows: A prince, divested of his kingdom, meets a Nāth Siddha in the forest. The Nāth Siddha helps him to regain his kingdom, in thanks for which the prince takes initiation by that Nāth Siddha, and establishes the Nāth Siddhas as the religious specialists of his royal house.

In at least one case, this kingmaker role is supported by historical documentation. This is the account of the surprising rise of Mān Singh, in the year 1804, to the royal throne of Marwar, a kingdom in the western part of the state now called Rajasthan, in western India. Prince Mān Singh, by birth the rightful heir to the kingdom of Marwar, has seen his cousin Bhīm Singh kill all of his brothers. Bhīm Singh's army has lain seige to Mān Singh and his forces, who are camped in the city of Jalore. A Nāth Siddha appears in Jalore, discovers a "hidden" well containing abundant food and water for the beseiged, and then mysteriously predicts that Mān Singh's troubles will soon be at an end. That very night, Bhīm Singh dies by poisoning. Mān Singh takes initiation from the Nāth Siddha, makes him his prime minister, and becomes a great benefactor of the sect.

The name of the Nāth Siddha who intervened in this episode of Rajasthani history was Ayasdevnāth. There is, however, a source that gives this Nāth Siddha another name: this is the hagiographical *Śrī Mastnāth Carita* ("Acts of the Illustrious Mastnāth"), authored by a certain Śankarnāth in the late nineteenth century. As Śankarnāth's title indicates, the Nāth Siddha in question is Mastnāth, the "Intoxicated Lord," whose traditional dates are 1704–1804. Although Mastnāth's dates would render an intervention in events of 1804 historically possible, the historical documents clearly state that the Nāth Siddha who saved the situation was named Ayasdevnāth. This disagreement between our sources would be troubling were it not for the fact that Śankarnāth's glorification of Mastnāth (the subtitle of which is "Exposition of the Supernatural Sport of the Illustrious Mastnāth") has little or no historical pretensions. This is, after all, the biography of a wonder-working Nāth Siddha who, by definition, is immortal and capable of changing bodies at will. Therefore, there can be no contradiction in terms when Śankarnāth says that it was Mastnāth who intervened on Mān Singh's behalf: this was merely Mastnāth inhabiting Ayasdevnāth's body.

While Śankarnāth does not make the explicit claim that this is what he is doing in his hagiography of Mastnāth, such is clearly the case. So it is that, in the course of his lifetime, Mastnāth is shown to perform miracles universally attributed to Gorakhnāth, the founder of the Nāth Siddhas, and is said to be, in a number of passages, identical to Gorakhnāth himself. It is in this light that we are to read Śankarnāth's work: this is a compendium of some one thousand years of Nāth Siddha miracles concentrated into the hundred-year lifespan of one of their number (who, in the logic of Nāth Siddha doctrine, did not die when he gave up his material body, but merely entered into another body as part of his yogic sport).

What sort of miracles does Mastnāth perform? As a child, he brings rain to a village suffering from drought, produces a milk pail that never empties, and simultaneously herds cows in the forest while playing with his friends back at home in the village. After he has been initiated, the miracles multiply: he restores the limbs of a woman who is without arms or legs, causes a barren woman to bear sons, becomes the disciple of an illustrious guru before becoming an illustrious guru himself, prophesies future events, and turns a camel bone into gold and watermelon seeds into pearls. There is also a dark side to Mastnāth's supernatural sport, however. Once, when he has gone to a village to beg alms, the abbot of a nearby monastery advises the villagers close their doors to him. Mastnāth punishes the village, besetting it with poverty, panic, pestilence, and death.

Mastnāth and Shāh Alam II

It is Mastnāth's combination of creative and destructive yogic power, as well as the Nāth Siddhas' traditional roles as wonder workers and intercessors on the behalf of the poor that are brought to the fore in the seventeenth chapter of Śankarnāth's hagiography, translated here. This is the chapter entitled "Account of the Miracles [Concerning] Alamshāh." Here, a mature Mastnāth (the chronology would make him eighty-four years old here) plays a role in nothing less than the collapse of the mighty Mughal empire, in the person of Shāh Alam II.

History tells us that Shāh Alam II was the last emperor of the Mughal dynasty, which had been founded some two hundred fifty years earlier by Bābar. By the end of Shāh Alam's life, little remained of this once great empire, and the poor emperor found himself buying off both allies and enemies with what little remained of the imperial treasury. His chroniclers tell us that in these sad times he took some solace in the princely vices of sex and indolence. In matters of religion, he practiced the eclectic faith of a number of Mughal emperors after Akbar, a religion that was a combination of Hindu and Islamic doctrines that wholly respected neither faith.

The Mughal empire and Shāh Alam's time ran out in 1788, in the person of Gulam Qādir, a rogue and adventurer working in the service of a political faction called the Rohillas. Having insinuated himself into the imperial court, he quite suddenly turned against his emperor and inflicted terrible tortures upon his person (eventually blinding him with his own dagger) as a means of extorting the last meager resources of the once fabled empire. Gulam Qādir continued his depradations against the entire imperial family until Shāh Alam's Maratha allies defeated his army and put him to a slow and terrible death in 1789. Shāh Alam survived his blinding, and was put back on the throne of Delhi in the same year, but only in a figurehead role. In 1803, the British took over Shāh Alam's so-called Kingdom of Delhi, but continued to bankroll the old monarch until his death in 1806.

Without ever saying so explicitly, Śankarnāth intimates that Mastnāth played some role in the blinding of Shāh Alam II (whom he calls Alamshāh): at the very least, he prophesied Shāh Alam's blinding before leaving Delhi behind; at most, it was he himself who, through his yogic powers, punished Shāh Alam for the latter's failure to come and pay homage to him. It is quite likely that Śankarnāth based his compilation of this chapter on popular traditions concerning both the deeds of some Nāth Siddha, perhaps Mastnāth himself, and the events that swept through the court of Shāh Alam in the year 1788. He portrays the emperor as a man who is personally intrigued by the wild yogi who has appeared in the suburbs of his capital city, but as a ruler who is so insulated from the real world by his courtiers that he is unable to carry out his desire actually to see Mastnāth. At one point, Mastnāth appears to condemn Shāh Alam for this, telling a royal servant (prophetically?) that the emperor has been blinded by his obsession with pleasure and sex. Later in his narration, Śankarnāth calls Gulam Qādir "Gulam Kokar," is rather vague on the details of his blinding of Shāh Alam II, and collapses some fifteen years of British colonial history into a single verse.

It is clear, however, that Śankarnāth is not particularly interested in writing accurate history; his purpose rather is to sing the glories of Mastnāth and of the Nāth Siddhas in general. It is for this reason that the narrative of chapter seventeen appears to be somewhat disjointed. It is in fact divisible into four parts. The chapter opens with Mastnāth coming to Delhi and word of his greatness spreading and reaching the ears of the emperor. Next, the emperor seeks to persuade Mastnāth to take audience with him in his imperial court. To this end, he sends Mastnāth a shawl with which to cover his nakedness, which was prohibited within the Delhi city limits. Mastnāth's handling of this matter is highly illustrative of Nāth Siddha belief and practice. First, the Nāth Siddha, as a perfected being, need not answer to any worldly law or custom: his nakedness, like his other yogic insignia, is symbolic of his transcendence and freedom. Second, Mastnāth's incineration of Shāh Alam's shawl in his dhūnī fire and production of a seemingly infinite number of shawls from the same fire is yet another case in which ashes symbolize the creative power of the Nāth Siddha as a living image of the great god Śiva. Mastnāth's feat is in fact a favorite element in the repertoire of Indian magicians and conjurers, who have historically impersonated powerful yogis and fakirs in their acts (critics of the Nāth Siddhas have long tended to confuse the two).

Following this, there is a rather abrupt transition to the account of Mastnāth's disciples "reversing their nāds," (or "playing their horns backwards"), the symbolism of which we have already discussed. A shadow falls across the sky: this is, according to the *Śiva Saṁhitā,* a guide to haṭha yoga, a sign of great yogic power. This issues into the final portion of the narrative: in answer to a disciple's question, Mastnāth prophesies the fall of Shāh Alam. Śankarnāth then has Mastnāth leave Delhi for the city of Cittor in Rajasthan (where he will intervene in the fate of Mān Singh in chapter twenty), after which he relates the blinding of Shāh Alam by Gulam Qādir.

Drawing all of these rather disconnected episodes together, and undergirding the entire narrative, is the theme of the Nāth Siddha as a god-man who plays with the entire universe, with the lives of the great and small alike, as he pleases. In both word and deed, Mastnāth, the "Intoxicated Lord," takes the universe to be his plaything, with its every element (shawls and ashes, mountains and mustard seeds, princes and paupers) interchangeable according to his whim. This is the raw, unalloyed power of the Nāth Siddhas, which have made them the butt of attacks by Hindu elites even as they have remained the objects of awed respect (and sometimes fear) by the masses of village India.

Chapter 17 of *Śrī Mastnāth Carit* is found in *Śrī Mastnāth Carit (Śrī Mastnāth Adbhut Līlā Prakāś* of Srī Saṅkarnāth Yogīśvara (Delhi: Dehati Pustak Bhandar, 1969), pp. 103–112.

Account of the Wonders [Concerning] Alamshāh

Refrain: Mastnāth is the gurudev, there is none as merciful as he; one need only think of him, and a hundred thousand obstacles fade away.

One day the gurunāth thought, "Just this once I'll take in Delhi's sights! There's saints and holy men galore, one is good, the next one more. That's where the lovely Yamunā flows, the Yamunā whose fair waters are pure and holy, whose praises are sung in the Vedas and Purāṇas, whose contact drives away all sin. Emotion, devotion, and virtue, I'll come to know them all—but in a sultan's town, how will things fall? I'll go and take a look around, and put on a wondrous show for all to see! I'll protect the faithful and remove the thorns that trouble their way. Highly virtuous are the motives of a saint; what's good for him is good for all."

Refrain: Having resolved this in his mind, he gathered his disciples around him. Every one of them shared his desire, and the gurudev rejoiced.

Accompanied by his many disciples, the Nāth made his way toward Delhi. Slowly they advanced until they came to the place called "Five Wells," where they set up camp. Once he saw that all were seated in their proper yogic postures, the venerable gurunāth began to practice his yoga. The news spread throughout all Delhi city that a great jewel among siddhas had come. "He's come together with a host of disciples, each one greater in wisdom than the last. Some are smeared with ashes, some live on milk alone, some are silent, some eat only fruit. Some have shed all worldly ties, some have broken all attachments, some act like fools, some are clever sophists. They call themselves Nāths, but they look like yogis; their wondrous arts cannot be pondered."

Refrain: Then, hearing he had settled near the city, the people rejoiced in their hearts. By gaining a vision of the gurunāth, their lives would be fulfilled.

Men and women thronged to the Five Wells, swelling to a great crowd, bearing with them gifts of betel nut, flowers, coconuts and bhel fruits, and performing every kind of service. Gaining a vision of him, the people were gladdened, joy welling up in every heart. Like hands joined in prayer, prosperity and success were joined together. Coming before him, they stood and washed his feet. The words they spoke were blissful, and rang with joy, "We are the servants of the Nāth's feet!" The news at last reached Alam Shāh himself that a yogi named Mastnāth had come. "He's a mighty one, a wild fakir, a carefree holy man, and a pīr. I'll go and gain a vision of him, once and for all!" and hope ran high in the emperor's heart.

Refrain: The emperor turned the matter over in his mind. One who sees and touches a saint comes to know joy itself.

The sultan came into his throne room, a diadem upon his head. He quickly summoned his Muslim advisors, and the judges and scholars came, one and all. The prince gave a speech on the matter, and the court was filled with great wonder. "Word has reached us that there's a fakir, a holy man, nearby. Seated in yogic posture at the Five Wells, in the company of his many expert disciples, is a world famous yogi, a siddha, a mind-reader! I've heard reports of the people's love for him, and now I want to see him too. Speak! Here's your chance to give expert advice. You all know the ins and outs of government!"

Refrain: Then an advisor spoke these words: "Hear, O noble prince! A detailed report on this ascetic has come to my attention. I now describe him to you."

"Word of mouth from the city has reached me, word that overflows with praise. His body is totally covered with ashes, crowned with a crest of yogi's locks! Great thick earrings bedeck his ears, and a piece of antelope horn, strung upon a woolen thread, shines at his throat. He sits in yogic posture, his dhūnī burning before him. They say he's a naked sage, a pīr, a fakir. He doesn't have a stitch on him: a yogi with nothing on is always in his element. He has no modesty or shame—that's the Hindu path he follows night and day. One ought not look upon a naked man. Think this over, Lord, then make up your mind. Considering what tradition, faith, and the Qur'ān say, here's my advice, don't ever go his way!"

Refrain: "Now that you've been duly informed, and all have had their say, cause your will to be known to us: your wish is our command!"

When the emperor had heard their counsel, he quickly considered, and then spoke in this wise: "What this naked yogi needs is a good double shawl, so send one please! Just some token to honor his dhūnī, give him that but nothing more. Holy men and saints do not like material goods; food and clothing are the two things they ever beg for." Receiving his orders, the king's man went off and made his way to Mastnāth. Holding the gift of the shawl before him, he joined his hands together and placed it between his feet. "The wise and sage king Alamshāh has sent me here before you. O gurunāth! Accept this gift and give your blessing!"

Refrain: In his mind, Mastnāth weighed the man's words. "A shawl, a double shawl, what use are they to me, I who am naked and unfettered?"

The gurunāth then took the double shawl, and with his own hand tossed it into his dhūnī fire. The king's man, seeing it had been reduced to ashes in the fire, took fright. "Now that I've fulfilled my mission, I must depart at once. Now I have to go away and make a full report!" "Hear, Your Majesty, O noble sire, he burned that double shawl right up! He's a carefree holy man, a venerable fakir, with no use for possessions." When the entire affair had been recounted truthfully to him, the emperor became incensed. "How can a yogi who has no illusions burn up a double shawl that's offered him?" Then the prince turned the matter over in his mind. "Just this once, I'll witness his miraculous powers."

Refrain: "I'll go see this siddha, this holy man, and find out what he's famous for. And if he doesn't prove his powers to me, I'll have him tied up on the spot!"

The king called to one of his men, and told him in detail what he had to do. "Go to this Mastnāth fellow. Have him give you my double shawl and bring it back to me." The servant came before the yogi, and spoke these words: "Long life to you, O wise and venerable one! O gurunāth, give me that double shawl, and take another in its place. That last shawl wasn't worth very much, now I'll give you an expensive one." Hearing his words, the Nāth considered, "I see what the emperor's driving at. He's looking to see one of my miracles today, so I'll give him a real one this time around. All anybody asks for is miracles, they want you to be Brahmā, Viṣṇu, and Maheś."

Refrain: Mastnāth is the bearer of the three worlds, the giver and remover of sorrow; whatever he wishes to do he does, and there is no one who can stop him.

Out of his dhūnī the gurunāth suddenly pulled a great heap of double shawls. He threw them down before the servant saying, "Take the one that's yours!" Seeing this, the servant became ashamed, his heart filled with remorse. "Now that I've seen this siddha's wondrous act, I'd give up my right arm for him! Whose friend is a yogi when he plays? It takes so little to please him. He doesn't give a thought to what's high or what's low. Whatever he wants to do, he just does it." Joining his hands, he bowed at his feet, "O guru, please be merciful! You, O Nāth, are my lord and master, and I your servant and slave."

Refrain: You are Lord Gorakṣanāth, powerful and able. Your glory, greatness, revelation, and splendor, how can they be described?

When the servant had pronounced on his greatness, the wise Nāth then spoke. "I teach both kinds of revelation. I say Gorakṣa and I are yogis. The world's four cornerstones are my playground; when you're carefree you want for nothing. From a pauper to a king, from a king to a pauper, I've never had a care for the difference between the two. Alamshāh is a man gone blind. Pleasure and sex have been his calling in life. What reason have I to go to him? Go now, and tell him he is to come to me. For his thoughtlessness and carelessness he must suffer an unhappy fate; that which he has sown he now must reap. Ruination and failing will follow in his path."

Refrain: Thinking "what he says is true," the king's man followed his command. He took the double shawl in his hand, and went to the imperial court.

Holding the double shawl before him as he went, he joined his hands together and entreated the emperor, "Hear my words, O honored one! The yogi performed a great miracle! I asked him for one double shawl, and right there the mad yogi gleefully pulled a pile of shawls, each one a different color, from out of his dhūnī! Putting them down, he gave them to me, all of those finely woven shawls. 'Take from these the one that's yours, and send it back to the emperor'!" Many agreed that this was a wondrous thing, and recounted the whole affair from beginning to end. "We've never seen or heard the likes, a yogi who performs such miracles."

Refrain: The conjurations of this wild man are a curious thing, hear, hear, O Alamshāh! You can go to every last siddha there is, but you'll find none as imponderable as he.

Then the prince thought the matter over: "It's true what my chief has told me. He's a master, a holy man, a carefree saint, one who holds his desires in check. The word is spreading that there isn't another like Mastnāth." Then the Nāth called all his disciples together, and spoke words that all could understand. "Reverse your nāds, yogis! To do it but once would be a mighty act. Then say such-and-such a thing will happen, and both Rāma and Allah will go and do it." Taking their guru's words to heart, all immediately reversed their nāds. Rāma and Allah both went and did their bidding, for whatever a yogi says, is.

Refrain: Suddenly what they said came to pass, when all set their minds to it at once. They raised a great and mighty roar, and a shadow fell across the sky!

There was one wise disciple who did nothing at all, an obedient one named Kīratnāth. He didn't sound his nād at all, for he had something on his mind. A disciple came and said, "Kīrat didn't sound his nād." The accomplished guru called out at once, and his disciple came and bowed his head. The Nāth said,

"Listen, you who have no disciples of your own, why didn't you sound your horn? Everyone followed my order but you; why are you being obstinate? What was your reason for doing this today? Tell me that, O thoughtful one!" Coming before him with joined hands, the disciple told him why.

Refrain: "O gurunāth, exceedingly merciful, listen to what I have to say to you. I have a doubt that's nagging me, so please relieve me of it."

"Both the Hindu and Muslim are religions that the wise of this world follow. When these have both become minor faiths, who will rule the Kingdom of Delhi? It is this doubt that troubles my mind, and that is why I did not sound my horn. So by your grace do tell me please, and erase this doubt from my mind today." The gurunāth's voice was soft when he spoke, "Listen my child, this is something you do not know. The Kingdom of Delhi will have a new master when on the third day of the month a terrible calamity strikes. Men of every caste will be thrown together, with all creaturely distinctions broken down. Both religions will be ordered about, and the king and all his subjects will be filled with fear."

Refrain: Some time passed before this happened to Delhi and its king. I [Śankarnāth] am without doubt when today I tell you this is so.

Know that the guru's word is true. Hearing it, surrender all worldly knowledge up to him. Whenever a gurunāth has given his word, that has fully come to pass, for the welfare of all. He is an accomplished knower of the three worlds, an ocean of mercy, a protector. The Nāth then made up his mind: "It is no longer fitting that I remain here."

He then took himself to another place—I can no longer recall what day it was. The yogi gradually made his way until he came to Cittor, where he stopped to rest. Because he was a yogi, he remained forever free, settling in a forest that held no fear for him. As many souls and their bodily husks as there were, moving and unmoving in that grove, all were in his power, all under his command.

Refrain: Acknowledge the gurudev Mastnāth to be Gorakṣa himself, whose sport in this world is a mine of happiness and bliss!

Hear, O nobles in the service of the king, how the emperor came to be blinded! Gulam Kokar was a servant who was very dear to him. Staying in Delhi night and day, the promise of great fortune made him turn against the emperor. He overthrew the emperor, he took away his rule! Then, seizing the moment, he gave the order, and commanded the emperor be taken. With a dagger he put out his eyes, and sending the others to prison, he spread terror! The white man's army put down the rebellion, and the English made the Kingdom of Delhi their own. This story is known the world over, and has been talked about in every place.

Refrain: A mountain was made from a grain of mustard, and a grain of mustard became a mountain. This is but the gurunāth's sport, that none is able to fathom.

Within every body the pure Nāth dwells, an ocean of mercy to drown all sorrow. There are a few saints and wise ones capable of knowing this, but the foolish cannot recognize it. Desire and passion are snares of sorrow, into which the unknowing fall time and again. The yogi remains ever absorbed in yoga, caring nothing for either wealth or women. Illusion and women when joined together can break a yogi's concentration. The wise man always remains aloof and fearless, and will have no doings with either. Those whose vision is exalted as theirs will brook no debate or discussion.

Refrain: The connoisseur tests the diamond, the goldsmith's nature is gold; the test of a saint is the saint none other than himself, who raises himself above this world!

—26—

Jain Stories Inspiring Renunciation

Phyllis Granoff

The following three stories are typical of many that appear in the Jain didactic story collections. Two are taken from the *Dharmābhyudayamahākāvya,* written by the Śvetāmbara monk Udayaprabhasūri sometime before 1271 C.E., and the other is from the Digambara *Bṛhatkathākośa,* composed by Hariṣeṇa in 931 C.E. These stories were meant to instill in their audience a deep revulsion for the world as we know it and a desire for renunciation and for ultimate release from the cycle of transmigration. They do so by deconstructing our notions of reality, particularly our normal understanding of human relationships as fixed and definable categories. Two stories show how relationships we assume to be one thing in this life were very different in the past; a third story tells us how in a single lifetime circumstances can arrange our lives for us in such a way that our assumptions about our relationships to those closest to us are totally wrong. This genre of story relies on shocking us to make its point; these are accounts of murder, incest, and cannibalism, but they are meant to show us how all our relationships can and do have this dark underside. The only way to be safe is to renounce human ties and seek salvation as a monk or nun.

The *Dharmābhyudayamahākāvya,* edited by Jina Vijaya Muni, was published in the Singhi Jain Series, vol. 4 (Bombay: Bhāratīya Vidyā Bhavan, 1949). The *Bṛhatkathākośa,* edited by A. N. Upadhye, was published as vol. 17 of the same series (Bombay: Bhāratīya Vidyā Bhavan, 1943). These stories have also been published in "Life as Ritual Process: Remembrance of Past Births in Jain Religious Narratives," in Phyllis Granoff and Koichi Shinohara, eds., *Other Selves: Autobiography and Biography in Cross-Cultural Perspective* (Oakville, Ontario: Mosaic Press, 1994).

THE STORY OF MAHEŚVARA FROM THE *DHARMĀBHYUDAYAMAHĀKĀVYA*

There was a famous city named Tamālinī, where the pillars of the lofty temples to the gods seemed to reach so high that they could support the very vault of the heavens, and the many palaces of the rich were like a garland around the city. There lived the wealthy merchant Maheśvaradatta, who was the foremost citizen of the town, and he was famed for being like an elephant that sported at will in the ocean of false belief. His wife was like the mistress of the school of wanton women. Her name was Nāgilā, and she was famous in the city for being a water channel to make bloom the garden of erotic delights. Now one day, on the occasion of the death anniversary of his father, Maheśvaradatta killed a buffalo as an offering to the dead. And he even fed his son, whom he held on his lap, with the meat of the sacrificed buffalo. Just at that moment a sage came to his house; his face was all wrinkled, and he had seen for himself the true nature of things. He recited this verse again and again:

"He feeds his own enemy, whom he holds on his lap, with the flesh of his very own father. And that he considers to be a proper sacrificial offering in honor of his father. Alas, could there be any more deluded act?"

When he heard those words Maheśvaradatta quickly rushed over to the lord of monks. He bowed to him and asked, "O Lord! What is this strange thing that you say?" And when he saw that Maheśvaradatta was determined to find out the truth, then that foremost of those who are restrained in speech, knowing through his great wisdom that he could help Maheśvaradatta, and being filled with compassion, replied: "That lover of Nāgilā whom you once killed long ago is now playing happily in your lap. He died just as he released his semen into Nāgilā, and because he was reborn in Nāgilā's womb, he became thereby your very own son. And that buffalo, with whose flesh you satisfied your deceased father, was really the soul of your father, Samudradatta. And, O wise one! There is a she-dog by the door that is eating the bones of the buffalo. Know O wise one that the dog is none other than your very own mother, named Bahulā. Knowing through my supernatural knowledge that all of these terribly strange and improper things were going on in your home, I hastened here to enlighten you."

"What proof is there that what you say is true, O lord?" When Maheśvaradatta asked the monk this question, the monk in turn replied, "When you take the dog inside the house it will remember its previous births and reveal to you where some jewels were buried long ago."

At this the monk took his leave. And the dog that he had told Maheśvaradatta about indeed showed Maheśvara the buried jewels when it was brought inside the house, just as the monk had said it would. And that merchant Maheśvaradatta, like an elephant brought under control by a good trainer by means of an elephant goad, was brought to his senses by the monk, by means of his pointed words. And he gave up his wrong religious beliefs and accepted the correct religious beliefs. Knowing that the whole net of relationships—father, son, and everything else—was all topsy-turvy, he realized that even he could not save himself, and that of course no son could help him.

THE STORY OF THE MONK SUḌṚṢTI FROM THE *BṚHATKATHĀKOŚA*

In the glorious realm of Avantī was the wonderful city Ujjain. Prajāpāla was king there, and his wife was named Suprabhā. Now this king had a jeweler named Suḍṛṣti, who was very knowledgeable about gems. The jeweler's wife was named Vimalā. The jeweler had a student named Vaṅka; Vimalā was in love with the student and her mind was filled with lustful thoughts about him. One day, just as Suḍṛṣti was making love to Vimalā, Vimalā had that deceitful Vaṅka kill Suḍṛṣti. And Suḍṛṣti, having been slain by Vaṅka, was reborn in Vimalā's womb. He had the ability to remember his past births and this made him not want to do very much at all. For this reason, the child, playing like all children his age, nonetheless came to be known as "the biggest lazybones in the whole world." One day when Queen Suprabhā was in her pleasure garden, her necklace broke and no one could find it. After much seeking it was only through a stroke of great luck that the king's men were able to find the necklace somewhere deep in the woods. No one among the many goldsmiths in the city was able to put the necklace together properly, not even the cleverest and most skilled of them all. Then it was that "Lazybones" rushed to the palace and fixed the necklace so that it made the very heavens shine with its radiance. The king beheld that necklace, so magnificently repaired, and then looked at the child who had always lived right there in the city. His mind was filled with wonder. "Where did you learn such skill, skill possessed by my former jeweler, Suḍṛṣti, and by no one else? Tell me child, for I am amazed by your deeds." When he heard these words of the king, the child replied, "I died and was reborn as my own son in my own wife. That Vimalā, who was formerly my wife, is now my mother. I died without a son and then became my own child. Isn't that something?" When he heard all of this about Suḍṛṣti, the king, along with many other kings, decided to practice austerities according to the Jain doctrine under the instruction of Abhinandana. Many other people were astonished at the tale, and wisely took refuge in the Jain doctrine, the source of true happiness. And that Lazybones, fearful of transmigratory existence, also became a Jain monk under the same teacher. After performing many austerities, his mind as firm in its religious resolve as Mount Mandara is strong and unshakable, in the course of his monastic wanderings Lazybones reached the northern region of the city of Sauri. In the end he died the pious death of a Jain monk, in meditation.

THE STORY OF KUBERADATTA AND KUBERADATTĀ FROM THE *DHARMĀBHYUDAYAMAHĀKĀVYA*

There was in the city of Mathura a courtesan named Kuberasenā. She was so beautiful that it seemed that the moon was just a poor copy of her face, made by the Creator in the same way a sculptor makes a special image of a god that can be used for the bathing ceremony, so that the more valuable image in the temple is not harmed by the eager devotees as they wash it. One day with great difficulty she bore a son and a daughter, just as the sword of a great king gives rise to glory and victory. Kuberasenā fought off the harsh words of the madame of the house, who urged her to abandon the twins, and she nursed them for a full eleven days. She made a signet ring for the boy inscribed with the name Kuberadatta, and a similar ring for the girl, marked with the name Kuberadattā. And then the cowardly mother, terrified of the madame, placed the two children in a casket studded with jewels. She set the casket afloat in the waters of the River Yamunā, as if it were the vessel containing all of her own future happiness, and she bade it farewell, washing it with the tears from her eyes, as one might send off a beloved guest with sprays of consecrated water. It so happened that a pair of merchants were delighted to discover the casket which had floated down the River Yamunā as far as the city of Sūryapura. They quickly opened the box and there they discovered the two children. Like heirs sharing their rightful inheritance, the two merchants divided up equally the contents of the box, each one taking home one of the two children. The brother and sister were raised with loving care by the merchants, and they grew more charming with every day, like the moon and the moonlight in the moon's waxing phase. Those two best of merchants then married off the boy and girl, who were known by the names that had been inscribed on the signet rings found with them, even though they seemed indeed to be twin brother and sister. Now one day Kuberadatta placed his own ring in his wife's hand, as if to give her a letter that would announce her renunciation of the world. Seeing that ring, so like her own, Kuberadattā was astonished, and she said to her husband, "How is it that these rings are so like each other, just as our names are so similar? I fear that we are in truth brother and sister, and that we are not the two children of those merchants at all. They must have found us somewhere and out of ignorance of the true state of affairs they married us to each other. We must find out the truth from our parents, no matter how much we have to ask them. We must know the circumstances of our birth." And after she said this, the two of them together went to the merchants. They asked them again and again about their birth and then, realizing that their suspicions were true and that they were indeed brother and sister, they deeply regretted their marriage. They lost all taste for worldly life, which they regarded as without value and as their enemy; filled with the desire for renunciation, they just stood there, heads bowed low, bereft of all their natural beauty, like the moon and the moon-lotus as early dawn breaks. And then Kuberadattā, being very wise, bid farewell to her brother and her parents and became a Jain nun. She then hid her jeweled signet ring, on which her name was inscribed; the ring was as radiant as the knowledge that would also come to Kuberadattā one day.

Kuberadatta, for his part, made his way to the city of Mathura as a trader, selling various toys. He became the lover of that very Kuberasenā who had given birth to him, as the moon is said to be the lover of the night. O fie on the Creator who makes us all do such things!

In time Kuberasenā bore Kuberadatta a son, created as it were by the ultimate delusion that governs transmigratory existence. Now Kuberadattā had perfected her knowledge to the extent that she now had the ability to know some things that were beyond the range of the senses. She desired to enlighten her brother, and she knew through her supernatural knowledge the terribly improper things that he was doing. She told her superior about herself and showed her the signet ring that she had kept concealed all that time, and like a boat to rescue her brother who was sinking quickly in the ocean of transmigratory existence, she hastily made her way to Mathura. She asked Kuberasenā for a place to stay and found lodgings there, in that unsuitable place; for religious people will do anything that they have to in order to help someone else.

Now one day the nun Kuberadattā saw the robust son of Kuberadatta, and knowing how monks and nuns enlighten others, she spoke these absolutely true words, "Child! You are my brother-in-law, for you are the brother of my husband. And our mother is the same woman, and so you are also my brother! My husband begot you, and so that makes you also my child. But your father is the child of my rival in love, and that would make you my grandson. You are the brother of my mother's husband, which makes you my uncle. And you are my brother's child, which makes you my nephew. Your mother is my mother, who bore us both in her womb. And that woman is also the mother of my mother's lover, which makes her my grandmother. She is the wife of the young man who was born from my co-wife, which makes her also my daughter-in-law. And she is the mother of my husband, which makes her my mother-in-law as well. She is the wife of my brother, which makes her my sister-in-law, and she is the wife of my husband, and so is my co-wife. And as for your father, who is the lover of my mother, I guess that makes him my father, too. You are my uncle, and he is your father, and an uncle's father is your grandfather, so he is my grandfather as well. My mother and his mother are the same woman, and so he is my brother. He is the husband of the woman who bore my husband, and so he is my father-in-law, too. He took my hand in marriage, and so he became my husband in addition to all of this. And he is the son of my co-wife, and so is my son as well."

Now when Kuberadatta heard these words of the nun, which seemed to contradict themselves at every step, he was amazed, and he asked her, "What does all of this mean?" And the nun then told everything to that Kubera, who kept asking her what she had meant. And she gave him the jeweled signet ring, which was like a lamp to enlighten the darkness of his delusion. By that signet ring, which was bright like the sun, Kubera became enlightened, and he gave up his deluded beliefs as a bee leaves a lotus. He was ashamed of his own behavior and he became a monk, and that wise Kuberadatta, though still a young man, renounced the householder's life and went into the forest. The forests were made radiant by that one, who was like a lion to destroy the elephant of karma, and who was like a mountain with natural rushing springs of his own glory; he was like a tree bearing as its fruits one austerity after another. He meditated on the Jain teachings and constantly recited Jain prayers to the Tīrthaṅkaras and sages of old, and he went to heaven, a lion that had killed the elephant of sexual desire. Even Kuberasenā saw how topsy-turvy the world of sense objects is, and she became disgusted with life in this world and took on herself the vows of the Jain householder.

—27—

A Holy Woman of Calcutta

June McDaniel

Archanāpurī Mā is the spiritual leader of a large ashram in Calcutta, with almost one hundred members. She grew up in rural West Bengal, in the Birbhum district, an area with a wide variety of spiritual practitioners and temples. The area is especially known for its Śaktas who worship the goddess Kālī, Śaivas who worship the god Śiva, and Bāuls, itinerant singers who worship a deity who lives within the physical body. She is a respected guru, a Holy Mother and teacher, and as such has much power in her ashram and among other devotees. She gained her social role in a traditional manner, by being part of the respected spiritual lineage of Rāmakṛṣṇa Paramahaṃsa, and being chosen to succeed her guru after his death.

It is traditional for a male disciple to inherit the guru's role as leader of the ashram when the guru dies; it is quite unusual for holy women in West Bengal to do so. Most holy women have never been part of a traditional lineage, and thus are outsiders who have had to fight for acceptance in a culture that tends to believe that women belong in the home, surrounded by children. Often holy women are not respected when they speak of religious experience, and are considered to be possessed by an evil spirit. They must then undergo painful and protracted exorcisms, medical treatment with Āyurvedic medicine, or various forms of testing to see if their experiences are false, or a result of insanity (there is a long tradition of religious madness in Bengal, in which abnormal behavior is accepted and even expected from spiritual figures). Because religious experience is a major claim to spiritual leadership, it is always questioned and tested in some way. Archanāpurī Mā had this testing occur in a mild way (during the testing of her trance states), but in her case she was supported by a respected religious figure, and there was no physical torture.

The holy women who seem to have the most difficult time are the gṛhī sādhikās, the married women who decide that they have a religious vocation. This is often preceded by a "call" (the god or goddess comes to the woman while she is cooking or involved in other domestic chores, and tells her that she must become a devotee). When the call is reported to the husband and members of the joint household, it is vigorously denied by the others. Such holy women have a very difficult time defending their religious interests and experiences.

In India, the religious life is traditionally a hard life. Holy people of both genders eat little, sleep for only a few hours a night, have only one or two sets of clothes and few other possessions, and must spend their days in spiritual disciplines. These may involve long fasts, enduring extremes of heat and cold, physical pain and discomfort, and following arduous work schedules. The goal is to make the person strong, relatively unaffected by temperature and the presence or absence of food, and capable of extended meditation. They may wander, sleeping in the woods, praying and meditating, or settle down in one locale. This is generally an ashram (literally, a refuge or shelter for people following a religious life).

Because of the difficulties involved, fewer women than men tend to become religious renunciants. Whereas the adolescent boy may see the religious quest as a great challenge to his masculinity, the girl is being prepared for her marriage (which is usually arranged by her parents and family in non-Westernized areas of Bengal). Once married, it is difficult to leave husband, home, and children (and frequently a houseful of relatives) to go off on a religious quest. Men leave the family setting for the religious life more frequently than do women, and it is more socially acceptable for them to do so. It is much easier for a woman to decide to be a holy woman if her husband dies and she is childless, or her children are grown. Also, women have a harder time gaining credibility and respect in India, as the ascetic tradition there tends to portray women as distractions to the spiritual path (as in the expression "women and gold," showing what spiritual people must avoid), rather than as seekers themselves.

Although Archanāpurī Mā is part of the Śakta Universalist tradition made famous by Rāmakṛṣṇa, her own path may be characterized as *guru bhakti* or devotion to the guru. The guru or gurudeva is not an individual, but rather a person whose mind has been joined with that of a god, or with Brahman, the universal consciousness. Devotion to the guru is thus the equivalent of devotion to a god. For those who find transcendent gods too distant and abstract, here is a god in the flesh.

A person begins to follow a guru through initiation, or dīkṣā. Different religious traditions in India have different types of initiation. For instance, the *Kulārṇava Tantra* (XIV, 40–60) describes initiation by look (the guru looks deeply into the disciple's eyes), by touch, by thought, by speech, and by sprinkling with water. Unlike the mainstream dharmic tradition in India, the tantric tradition holds that initiation by a woman is very powerful, and eight times more powerful still is initiation by one's mother. Some gurus initiate by writing a mantra on the tongue of the disciple, or on some other part of the body. Initiation is believed to give instantaneous knowledge and insight.

In Archanāpurī Mā's tradition, there are three levels of initiation (as will be seen in her biography). The first, mantra dikṣa, gives mantra and lineage (acceptance into a line of gurus). The second, or brahmacarya, enters the person into an austere and celibate life, and the final renunciation, or sannyāsa, is the declaration of death to the physical world, and total devotion to the spiritual world.

Often, renunciation is accompanied by austerities. There is a long tradition in India of testing the person's endurance and dedication by means of extreme actions: enduring heat, cold, hunger, and so on. This is also understood to increase the person's tapas, a spiritual heat or energy which may then be used for meditation or miraculous abilities which many people believe that renunciants and gurus possess.

Archanāpurī Mā belongs to a universalist order, whose most important guru, Rāmakṛṣṇa Paramahaṃsa, had at one time worshiped his wife Śāradā Devī as a goddess. Her ashram emphasizes creativity: her guru Satyānanda was said (by different sources) to have written between seven and eight thousand songs, and Archanāpurī Mā has written forty-eight plays and three thousand songs, as well as a thousand poems, epics, essays, and several books. She speaks of her mood of separation (from her guru) in "A Memorable Midday" ("*Ekti Snarnīya Dupur*"):

On this side it is still very silent, absolutely lonely and desolate
You cannot tell whether or not the Gaṅgā waves are rolling.
Far away, one or two boats are floating like disjointed talk
All this I see is a broken part of a complete poem
That must be rhymed.

The ashram is also a teaching institution, with courses on Hindu religion, morality, music and dance, drama, and spoken and written Sanskrit. There is also an eye clinic and a general clinic, as well as a homeopathic dispensary, to help the poor.

The following text is drawn from Archanāpurī Ma's oral description of her life, during which disciples added various statements with which she agreed. For ease of reading, the statements of some disciples have been incorporated into the text. The poem is from a Bengali photocopied manuscript, recently mailed to me by her chief disciple. He has also sent me some additional background material, which is included.

Further Reading

For further information on Bengali holy women see June McDaniel, *The Madness of the Saints: Ecstatic Religion in Bengal* (Chicago: University of Chicago Press, 1989). For information on Sri Lankan holy women, see Gananath Obeyesekere, *Medusa's Hair: An Essay on Personal Symbols and Religious Experience* (Chicago: University of Chicago Press, 1981).

Archanāpurī Mā

I was born in Dinajpur in Bengal, in 1928. I lived in the great house of my maternal grandfather, who was a zamīndār or landowner, and he had the title of Mahārāja of Dinajpur in the days before partition and independence. I loved my grandfather very much, and when I was a child, he would call me Brahmavādinī, a girl who follows the wisdom of Brahman.

I come from a religious family. My father took religious vows of renunciation and became a svāmī, Svāmī Nirvedānanda (his earlier name was Nalinish Chandra Mitra), and my mother became Sannyāsinī Renuka Purī Mā (her name had been Renuka Mitra). During my childhood, we lived in a joint family in Suri, in Birbhum, West Bengal. It was a very large household of about fifty people, including my father's seven brothers and two sisters. My father worked as a lawyer, a stage actor, and a writer, and then was involved in India's fight for independence. In later life he was the chief disciple of Śrī Ṭhākur Satyānanda and president of his ashram in Suri, the Śrī Rāmakṛṣṇa Ashram. Education was important in the family, and the boys went out to school, but the girls had a private tutor instead, because the family was conservative and followed the old traditions. I lived in a large family setting, but I did not feel close to any of my relatives or friends during childhood.

I began to sing almost from the time I started to talk. I could pick up songs that I heard quickly, and entertain relatives and family members by singing to them. I used to dance alone on the roof of the top floor of the house beneath the open sky. I felt like a bird spreading her hands as wings. I remember that I tried to reach heaven by placing piles of rice bags one upon the other, forming steps up toward the heavens. Just a few years later my guru Ṭhākur mentioned that one cannot reach heaven by placing rice bags one over the other as steps toward the sky. Instead, one must come down from the heights of such idealism to the ground of renunciation.

When I was twelve years old, I met Ṭhākur Satyānanda and my life was changed; when I saw him, I never wanted to leave him, and everything else became unimportant. I recognized him as my Jīvandevatā, the god of my soul. He asked me if I did pūjā, and I told him that I had worshiped the god Śiva from the age of six years, and he was pleased. He also asked if I could meditate, and when I told him that I could, he showed me a portrait of Rāmakṛṣṇa Paramahaṃsa and asked me to meditate on him as Lord Śiva by putting an imaginary trident by his side.

Ṭhākur Satyānanda had both a god and a goddess to which he prayed. One was Gopāla Kṛṣṇa (Kṛṣṇa as a cowherd), and the other was Kālī Bhāvatāriṇī (Kālī as savioress). He was constantly in communion with these deities, and sometimes he took on their forms. People saw him and worshiped him as Gopāl, as Mother Kālī, and as Rāmakṛṣṇa Paramahaṃsa. He would appear in visions to people, and in their dreams at night. Ṭhākur was in a state of continuous union with the divine, which was not an obvious trance, but rather a state which was subtle and arose in him spontaneously.

Śrī Ṭhākur Satyānanda was born in 1902, after his mother Kāśīśwarī Devī had performed religious rituals to have a spiritual child, and his birth name was Satyavrata. He loved silence and meditation. He had been initiated by Svāmī Abhedānanda, a disciple of Rāmakṛṣṇa Paramahaṃsa of Dakṣiṇeśwar, for his first initiation, but later was initiated into renunciation by Mā Bhāvatāriṇī, and she gave him the name Satyānanda. He immersed himself deeply in spiritual practice (*sādhana*) and performed many penances. He attained his spiritual goal in 1939, and began to initiate disciples into the Rāmakṛṣṇa order with traditional Hindu rites. His own paternal house at Suri was transformed into the Śrī Rāmakṛṣṇa Ashram, and separate sections of male renunciants and female renunciants were created.

I began to visit Śri Ṭhākur Satyānanda at his ashram in Suri. I spent a lot of time there and began living there, rarely returning to my parents' house. I used to play games with Ṭhākur, but his games were always special. Ṭhākur gave me initiation in that year, but he surprised me; while we were playing a game, he grasped my hand and whispered a mantra to me. In his playing with us, he taught us much about religion.

I remember that one day I was sick and lying asleep in my room, and Ṭhākur was leaving Suri for Calcutta on that day. My mother and the other disciples and devotees went to the Suri railway station to see him off, and I woke up alone in the house. I did not eat, but wept at being alone and then fell deeply asleep. I dreamt that Ṭhākur came to me and caressed me, and tore off a nail from one of his fingers and gave it to me. I felt full of ecstatic joy, and awoke just as my mother entered the room. I was angry at her for leaving me there, but she said, "Look at what Ṭhākur has sent for you." I opened my eyes, and was overwhelmed with joy to see that it was a piece of fresh fingernail which he had torn off and sent affectionately as a gift.

Life at the ashram involved worship of the ashram's deities, and singing the morning and evening worship inside the temple. Ṭhākur had also established a school, and he taught us about great men and women, such as Rabindranāth Tagore, Rāmakṛṣṇa Paramahaṃsa and Śāradā Devī. There were also other teachers, including a Christian woman. Learning the language of Sanskrit was very important. My parents became part of the ashram, and my father took religious vows and became a svāmī. When I grew older, I told Ṭhākur that I did not want to marry, and I took vows of celibacy at the age of fourteen years. I was initiated by Ṭhākur. I concentrated on my studies, and learned about philosophy, and Sanskrit and Bengali literature.

When Ṭhākur would give people initiation, a light used to flash from his eyes. I remember that, around the time of the holiday of Kālī Pūjā, Ṭhākur initiated a disciple. I was watching through a window, and I remember a curtain was blowing. I could see Ṭhākur looking at the disciple in a strange way, and then I could see rays of light coming out of his eyes, like the beams coming out of a powerful flashlight. My eyes were open, I could see this right before me. The rays of light seemed to enter into the disciple's soul. I don't know how he felt at the time, but I felt as if somehow those rays had entered me, and I was terrified. I started to shake and I couldn't stop myself, so I ran home. My whole body felt as if it were burning, though the weather was cold, and I did not know what to do. I lay on the cold cement floor at home, but my relatives did not pay much attention to me; they were thinking of the ashram and of spiritual things, so they didn't ask if anything was wrong. But late that evening a message came from Ṭhākur, to attend the Kālī Pūjā ceremony which took place at midnight.

Without even thinking that I would be out alone very late at night, I started running toward the ashram. It was all lit up with candles, as people were there rehearsing for a stage play. The ceremonies of Kālī Pūjā would start just at midnight, and they would be performed by Ṭhākur himself.

I was still frightened, and in my mind I could see those powerful eyes with their beams of light. When I quietly moved toward the well, Ṭhākur called me over, and I went straight to him and fell on my face before him. He patted me on the back and asked, "Have you become afraid of me? Is something wrong?" At his touch I felt wonderfully cool, and the painful burning in my body disappeared. He had me sit close to him, and he spoke to me about the process of initiation. I could not understand him fully, but he spoke of transferring his spiritual power into his disciples by a certain type of look. Perhaps that day the transmission of power was tolerable to the disciple, but it certainly was not so for me. Without realizing it, Ṭhākur had given him the same "Śakti mantra" which he had repeated to me earlier.

Ṭhākur would have many spiritual experiences and visions, and there were times when he would spend the whole day in a state of ecstatic trance (*bhāva*). This is a deep experience of religious bliss, and he would enter this state through meditation. When I was initiated by him into celibate life, my soul began to fuse with the soul of Ṭhākur, and I would fall unconscious. I became lost in Ṭhākur, he was all that I could see or hear, I became one with him, and I too began to fall into trance states like his. This lasted for several years, and these were not fainting fits. I was fully aware in my soul, but I could not move my body; it was like a wooden statue, or a rock. I was sharing Ṭhākur's thoughts and emotions, I was becoming one with him.

When I fell into these trance states, Ṭhākur would leave his own meditation to care for me. Some of the other devotees at the ashram would complain about this, saying that I was disturbing him in his spiritual practice. But Ṭhākur became angry with them, and said, "I have taken her as my adopted daughter (*mānasakanyā* or spiritual daughter), so you should not question her. I forbid the devotees to criticize her." Some of them thought that I might have some disease, but Ṭhākur said, "She does not have a disease, it is a state of religious ecstasy. For the sake of you who are questioning her, I will do an experiment."

When I was in one of these trance states, Ṭhākur brought a group of doctors and devotees into the house. He had one group sit in the room where I lay on the bed, and the other group was nearby on the veranda. I have heard about this from both Ṭhākur and from the devotees. While I was unconscious, with my eyes closed and my hands in fists, Ṭhākur started striking his own body in different places. Wherever he struck his body, I felt the pain in my own body, and I winced and put my hands on my own body. My eyes were still closed, though Ṭhākur was not within the range of my sight even if they had been open. The devotees could walk from the bedroom to the veranda and see the similarity of the gestures. For another experiment, he had groups of people synchronize their watches and write down notes on what I did during trance. Ṭhākur would make deliberate gestures, and the gestures that I made would echo them. I was upstairs in bed, while Ṭhākur was downstairs. The gestures and times again corresponded.

This was because my soul was fused with the soul of my guru. It is a state called *ekātmika bhāva,* which means that we share one soul. I shared his emotions and dreams, thoughts and desires, and we could sense each other's feelings at a distance. We were no longer two separate people, but in some mysterious way we were united, and we could see each other in dreams and visions. In such a state, the whole body is made of love (*prema*), and the mental images of the other person stay bright and clear in the memory.

In my spiritual life, I believe in both bhakti and yoga. If one has firm devotion to the divine, one can have many have kinds of visions, with eyes open or closed. Visions are like dreams, except that they are conscious and stay in the memory, and they make you feel an intense state of love. You see the god or the guru with the eyes of love, which are different from the physical eyes. Sometimes a god shows pictures in your mind, and then your mind becomes like a screen, and god is like a film projector. You feel so much love that your whole body becomes a body of love, and you can hardly stand to feel so much joy and love. This is how I would feel when I saw Ṭhākur, inwardly or outwardly.

This fusion of souls remained over time, though the uncontrolled trance states stopped after a year or two. After that I took vows of full renunciation into the state of sannyāsa, and I spent my time in meditation and prayer. As Ṭhākur was fond of penance, all of his disciples performed austerities, like sitting in the scorching sun on summer days and being drenched in ice water on winter nights for hours together, as well as performing extended fasts. But these were just part of life, and because we loved him so, they gave us enormous pleasure instead of pain. His love was greater than that of a worldly mother and father, sister and brother, friend and relation. His love was a thousand times greater than the love of all of these combined. I never felt any lack of worldly love.

Ṭhākur used to feed poor people at the Suri ashram, and often holy people came to eat with us. I remember once helping him feed a wandering renunciant with wild eyes and uncombed hair. He said to Ṭhākur, "You take everything from the lion cub, and lion cub, you take everything from the lion." He meant that Ṭhākur and I should learn from each other. Ṭhākur would stand there, looking closely at the people, looking into their eyes. The ashram would distribute food, clothing and medicine to poor people, and he initiated low-caste people and called them Ṭhākurdās. They could come into the temple and worship with us, and some took vows and became part of the ashram.

We lived with him for about thirty years, and it was a very happy time. Though sad events happened from time to time, they did not touch us, for we floated on a current of joy. We had a series of festivals with music, song, drama and dance which kept us all joyful over the years.

But then Ṭhākur left us, and I felt as if I fallen from some ideal heaven world onto stony ground. I felt as helpless as a child of six months old, and I wanted to leave the earth with Ṭhākur and not stay here alone. I wanted intensely to go with him. But he had wanted me to stay on earth to help the ashram, and I obeyed his wishes.

The fusion of souls between guru and disciple does not end with death. I still fight with Ṭhākur for leaving me alone here on earth, and I can still talk to his subtle presence, although his physical body is not here. His invisible grace is showered upon all of us at every moment, and in every act. I could not stand alone without him. I depended on him so much, I was one with him to such an extent that I did not have a mind separate from his. Now I suffer from this separation, as Rādhā suffered when Kṛṣṇa was (away from her) in Mathura. It has been many years, but I still cannot bear his physical absence. Sometimes I feel so helpless. I was so full in his presence, and now I am empty in his absence.

But I stayed to support the ashram, and began to initiate the seeking devotees. In 1976, we established the ashram dedicated to Ṭhākur in Calcutta. From being the spiritual daughter of my guru, I have become the Holy Mother of the ashram, giving spiritual shelter to its children. The ashram has grown up around us. I stayed there, and other women and men came. Early on, there were twelve unmarried holy women (*sannyāsinīs*), and a few married ones, as well as renunciant men (*svāmīs*). This has increased to about thirty female and about fifty male renunciants.

At the ashram, I offer ritual worship to the temple deities, write books, compose songs and poems, teach courses, direct music and evening worship. During the last five or six years I have increased my prayers and recitation of mantras for the well-being of all humanity. I spend more time in ritual worship, because the environment is deteriorating, and the greed for money and power is wiping away the respect for religion in India. The serenity and calmness of spiritual bliss is no longer a goal for people who are diving down and breaking all of the barriers of morality and conscience. My own health is not good, but I try to do what I can.

The relationship between a guru and his disciple is an eternal one; it does not stop even if one of the persons dies. When I first saw Ṭhākur, I was only a child and had no understanding of the spiritual world or of God. But I loved him from the very first moment that I saw him. I entered the ashram by play, but gradually I found that Ṭhākur had become my friend and spiritual guide. He has been an eternal source of love.

—28—

Jain Stories of Miraculous Power

Rosalind Lefeber

The *Bhaktāmarastotram* is a collection of verses in praise of the Jain saint, Ṛṣabha, first of the twenty-four Jinas. It was composed in Sanskrit by a Jain sage, Mānatuṅga, who flourished some time before 1000 C.E. and was already revered as an ancient teacher by the end of the thirteenth century. Four of his verses are presented below, each followed by a short tale composed by a later commentator, who in turn summarized his plot in a brief introductory verse.

In the accompanying stories, each Mānatuṅga verse is shown to provide a mantra, or sacred formula, for use in some specific human predicament. It is made clear that the Jain saint, when invoked, will save his devotees from all manner of calamities. He usually performs his miraculous rescues through an intermediary, the goddess Cakrā or Cakreśvarī.

Mānatuṅga's own style in the verses of the *Bhaktāmarastotram* is a model of clarity; but even though it is quite restrained in its use of figures of speech, it belongs to the tradition of refined Sanskrit poetry (*kāvya*). The stories, on the other hand, are written in prose in a colloquial Sanskrit, interspersed with verses of popular wisdom drawn from both the Sanskrit and the vernacular literature.

The tales demonstrate the effectiveness of Mānatuṅga's verses as mantras by taking the figurative speech of the original and giving it a very literal sense. For example, whereas Mānatuṅga calls the impossible task of enumerating the sublime virtues of the saint equivalent to swimming across a perilous ocean, the commentator's story relates the rescue of a Jain devotee from an actual shipwreck. In another case, the original verse refers to the saint's unblemished nature, whereas the tale tells how the face of the Hindu goddess Durgā is permanently scarred by a Jain sage. In fact, all of these stories explicitly declare the superiority of Jain doctrine over other religions. In addition, they often hold out some implicit promise of worldly prosperity to accompany the hope of spiritual perfection.

It is, of course, not to be assumed that the commentor himself did not fully comprehend the metaphors of the original verses. Rather, the simplicity of form and content of the illustrative stories seems designed to provide more direct reassurance to a humble devotee than is found in the traditional poetic imagery of Mānatuṅga's meditative verses. The combination of verse and accompanying tale would thus encourage virtue and steadfast devotion, while appealing to the widest possible audience.

The following selections are translated from *Bhaktāmarakalyāṇamandiranamiūṇ-stotratrayam*, edited by Hirālāl Rasikdās Kāpadīā, with foreword by Hermann Jacobi (Bombay: Nirṇayasāgara Press, 1932).

STORY 2

Oh ocean of virtues, your qualities shine like the moon! What person, though equal in intelligence to the teacher of the gods, could describe them? Who, after all, could by the power of his arms alone swim across an ocean swarming with crocodiles churned up by winds as fierce as those at the end of a world-age? (verse 4)

In this very verse a mantra has already been disclosed, as is illustrated in a story concerning its power:

> There was once an illustrious man, Sumati,
> who by recalling this wish-granting hymn of praise,
> Crossed the ocean by the grace of the goddess Cakrā,
> with only his arms to keep him afloat.

Formerly, in the city Ujjayinī, there was a merchant named Sumati who lived in poverty but whose character was good. And he revered a certain Jain sage who, in his presence, imparted the following instruction:

> Giving wealth to those seeking wealth and satisfying every desire
> of those seeking worldly pleasures,
> The dharma taught by the Jina bestows both heaven and emancipation.

Moreover:

> Without the dharma you cannot know happiness.
> It is like working in someone else's house fetching water and fuel:
> you chop, crush, and stir, but you get nothing at all to eat.
>
> Lowly birth, misfortune encountered, the threat of separation from
> one's loved ones,
> Disgrace, and the contempt of the whole world—
> such is the fruit that arises from the tree of evil.

It is a sign of past virtue that even those who are possessed by demons
have wealth.
It is further a proof of past sin that virtuous people must beg.

When he had heard the sage's words, Sumati believed that the great white-robed Śvetāmbara sage had given him instruction in the dharma that was proper for him. So, provided with the Jina's dharma and desirous of wealth, he studied the *Bhaktāmara* hymn of praise. He recited it constantly, morning, noon, and evening, a practice that never fails to develop devotion.

Then one day Sumati reflected on this popular saying:

Even though he is born into a distinguished family,
a man who is without wealth gets no respect.
He is disdained and is thought to be as lacking in merit
as a bow without a bowstring.

With this in mind, Sumati, wishing to increase his wealth, went to a city on the shore of the ocean and boarded a ship. When in due course the boat reached the open sea, terrible winds began to blow, like the winds of destruction at the end of a world-age. A long bank of clouds like a veil of darkness obliterated the circle of the heavens. Forked lightning, like a flame from the pupil of a demon's eye, burst forth from inside the dark clouds. Loud thunder groaned, as terrible to the boatsmen's ears as the onslaught of a hurricane. Multitudes of vicious sea-dwelling creatures—huge, fabulous fish such as timis, timiṅgalas, pāṭhīnas, and piṭhas, and every kind of crocodile, alligator, tortoise, and man-eating dolphin—were churned up and floated drunkenly hither and yon in the ocean waves. The grains of sand were also stirred up from the ocean floor, like people released from their karma. A wall of waves surged upward, like a demon trying to swallow the universe. Running hither and thither as if terrified by robbers, the seafaring merchants cried out loudly and each began to say his final prayers to his chosen deity.

Unable to remain above the waters, the ship's hull, like a wicked person, could not steady itself anywhere. The white sail was torn to shreds, like the dreams of the seafaring merchants. Like the affections of the ungrateful, the ropes, though strong, broke apart. And even though the sailors were capable men, they could not protect against the destruction of the boat. So at that point they cut down the mast at its base, just as certain sages destroy the knot of grief caused by their previous ignorant actions. Some clutched at planks with both arms, as if clasping the body of their sweetheart. Others riveted their thoughts on all their fine jewels as if they were the words of their gurus. Then at that moment, drifting hither and thither like a demon-ridden sinner afflicted by the pain of death, the boat went to pieces, just as a favor goes to waste on an ingrate. That entire mass of wealth was sunk in the middle of the ocean.

But Sumati meditated on the fourth verse of the *Bhaktāmara* hymn, and through the magic power of the goddess Cakreśvarī, swam across the mighty ocean by the power of his arms alone. As he reached the shore, Cakreśvarī, herself appeared before him and gave him five jewels equal to five akṣas in weight, and led him to the city. There, munificent and worthy of respect from kings, righteous Sumati enjoyed his wealth. Then, with his fame as bright as a white kāśa flower, after enjoying preeminence in this mundane existence, he became one of the foremost Jain disciples.

STORY 13

I think it was surely for the best that I saw Hari [Viṣṇu], Hara [Śiva] and the other gods first. For I have seen them, and now my heart can find satisfaction in you. What has happened since I saw you? No other in the whole world can win over my mind from you, oh lord, even in my next life. (verse 21)

Here begins a story about great power:

> Glorious Jīvadeva, chief of Jain pontiffs, went to Devapattana,
> where he brought all the gods,
> Including Śiva, Brahmā, and Viṣṇu, before the very eyes of the citizens.

Formerly in the important Gujarati town called Vāyaḍa, there was a Jain pontiff, glorious Jīvadeva, who knew the science of entering into the bodies of others. By reciting each night the twenty-first verse of the *Bhaktāmara* hymn of praise along with the secret lore, he was given by the invincible goddess Cakrā the ability to summon all the gods.

From Gujarat, he went to the town of Devapattana in Saurashtra. Now in that place there was a very great religious celebration at Somanātha, the Śivaliṅga temple. The pilgrims, people who were Śiva's devotees, vied with each other in bowing down to their god. But among the residents there were some Jain disciples who went to greet their guru. And when their master asked them whether they were prospering in the dharma, they said: "How can we prosper in the dharma here, where there is only one prevailing doctrine, which is a false one?"

Then the teacher, glorious Jīvadeva, together with the Jain disciples, approached the Somanātha temple. At this, Śiva's devotees were delighted and exclaimed: "Aha! Even the white-robed Śvetāmbara ascetics have come to bow down to Śiva!"

But the teacher meditated on the goddess Cakrā and then said: "Someśa [Śiva]! Come forth!" At this, Śiva showed himself and stepped forward. Next Brahmā and Viṣṇu came forward from the temple, and then Sūrya, Gaṇeśa, Skanda, and the rest of the Hindu gods also stepped forward.

So then all the gods who had been summoned, together with the astonished citizens and the worshipers of Śiva, bowed down to the Arhat Candraprabha, lord of Jinas, in his own temple. And Somadeva [Śiva] was asked to give tribute to honor this eighth Jina, and he agreed to do so. Then when Hara [Śiva] and the other gods had been dismissed, they vanished and returned to their respective places.

After this, there was a great increase in instruction in the true doctrine. The keepers of the liṅga in the Śiva temple now became submissive to the Arhat Candraprabha and believed the Jina to be the great god. For who goes astray after seeing real proof? There are very few on earth who would do such a thing. And it is said:

> Among all the gods, who number more than one hundred thousand,
> there is only one worthy of that name.
> Among all the trees, there is only the rose apple tree, the Jambū,
> whose name has been given to Jambūdvīpa, the earth's centermost continent.

So each month Śiva gives in tribute ten thousand blossoms for worship, five seers of sandalwood, three seers of sesame oil, two measures of grain in the food offering, two palas of saffron from lotus filaments, one māṣaka of camphor, and a kara of musk, all for the eighth Jina, Candraprabha.

STORY 15

The sages know you as the supreme spirit, bright as the sun, beyond darkness, and unblemished. When they have truly perceived you, they conquer death, for there is no other auspicious path to final liberation, oh lord of sages. (verse 23)

Here is a story about great power:

> When the goddess Durgā was struck on the cheek and wounded by a fingernail,
> Tears flowed from her eyes, and she became a wish-granting deity.

Long ago, the glorious sage Āryakhapuṭa meditated on the Ṛṣabha mantra that derives from the twenty-third verse in the *Bhaktamāra* hymn of praise. The goddess Cakrā and the Arhat Sarvānubhūti were pleased with him and granted him a boon, and so it was that he obtained the means of overpowering wicked gods.

Afterwards, he went to the illustrious city Ujjayinī. There this man with a brilliance of knowledge that blazed like fire spent the night in the city gardens in a Durgā temple. Now this wicked goddess, whose doctrine was false, was angry with the people of the Jain monastery, particularly with the white-robed Śvetāmbara ascetics. So she appeared in a hideous form, her face reddish as if she had been drinking alcohol, and came toward the master.

The master was seated, occupying himself with meditation, but he saw that she was enraged. So he scratched her cheek with his fingernail, and a scar formed, as hard as a diamond. Then tears flowed from her eyes, and she granted him a boon.

The guru ordered that killing be prohibited, and he wanted the people not to be troubled any more. And the goddess was changed so that she became peaceable.

Toward daybreak, preceded by the master, she and the townspeople set off toward the Jain monastery. Turning back at the city gate, she bowed down to his venerable feet and returned to her own abode. But she remained just like that, with the nail mark on her cheek.

The people respected her command, which had to be carried out correctly. Many of them achieved faith in the true religion, and they remembered the virtues of the guru as they returned to their homes.

And it is said:

> Why should virtuous people, who have their very own virtues,
> need to be endowed with wealth?
> Does not a sandalwood tree give pleasure even though it lacks
> abundant fruit?

STORY 28

People who are bound from head to foot by heavy chains and whose legs are harshly scraped by the sharp edges of massive shackles are freed at once from the danger of their bonds by constantly invoking the mantra of your name. (verse 42)

The great power of this verse was first demonstrated when the strong chains and shackles binding the glorious teacher Mānatuṅga were broken. But then later the iron chains of several royal ministers also came apart.

> In this worst of times, the Kali age, when the gods suppressed by the
> Muslims still produce amazing results,
> The strong chains on prince Raṇapāla were broken.

There once was born a king's son, Raṇapāla, who possessed a great number of villages in the vicinity of the famous fortress Ajayameru. He pleased all who met him with his inborn generosity, good behavior, and virtues. He often thought of this verse:

> Great generosity in the giving of food, and deep respect for all
> doctrines—
> These two things working together bestow greatness on the person
> who displays them.

And since he had a good basic nature from associating with the Jain sages, he recited the *Bhaktāmara* hymn of praise and the five principal mantras. He maintained his devotion to Ṛṣabha, the glorious Yugādi Jina, and knew the meaning of the great power of the hymn. And because he protected the dharma, he was to the minds of the virtuous like a garland of lotuses, and because of his great eminence he was like a dagger in the hearts of the Muslims. Once, he was tricked by an evil amir staying in the fortress Ajayameru and was captured, along with his son. This was a wicked trick typical of this Kali era, the last age before the end of the world. And it is said:

> Good people sink down, the evil enjoy themselves.
> Sons die, while their parents are long-lived.
>
> There is friendship toward enemies, yet anger toward one's own people.
> Let the whole world behold the topsy-turvy Kali era.
>
> In the Kali era, the small shrink, the wise prosper.
> In the summer, lakes dry up, yet the ocean swells.

And so the mind of this man, an ocean of nobility, never deviated from the dharma.

With his son he set off, and reached the city of Yoginī. Now Jalāludīn, a protector of demons, ruled the kingdom there. He had Raṇapāla and his son bound with strong shackles and chains and thrown into prison inside the old fortress of Delhi. There virtuous Raṇapāla meditated night and day on the forty-second verse of the *Bhaktāmara* hymn.

At the end of the ten thousandth night, there appeared before him a lovely young woman of enchanting appearance, resplendent in fine garments. The sound of her jingling anklets revived love, the tinkling of the string of bells on her jewel-studded girdle bewitched the three worlds, her rows of necklaces of large, perfect, incomparable pearls glowed like a host of captive stars. It was as if the whole multitude of human desires was fulfilled at the sight of the beautiful jeweled rings on her outstretched fingers, tender as lotuses. Her braided hair, as shiny as a row of black Indian bees, was so thick that it seemed to have been used as a staff to make gleaming nāga serpents attend her.

She said: "My child! Arise at once." So Raṇapāla replied: "Oh Mother, who are you? Are you a goddess or a human or a supernatural vidyādharī?" She replied: "There is a goddess Cakreśvarī, who is borne by the fabulous garuḍa bird. She is devoted to the glorious Jina Yugādi, and protects those who recite the *Bhaktāmara* hymn of praise. I am her servant and warder, and have been sent by my mistress Cakreśvarī to release you from prison."

Raṇapāla spoke: "Oh goddess! To me you are greater than Cakrā, but how can I arise when my hands and feet are fettered?"

Said the goddess: "Touch your hands and feet." And when he touched them, he saw the thick chains fallen before him in a heap. His son's shackles also fell, and then the bolt on the prison doors unfastened by itself. But as they were both about to stand up, the goddess stopped them, for just then the watchmen on guard came along. And when they came and saw those two there as usual, the watchmen left.

The goddess then showed Raṇapāla and his son a staircase by which they climbed up to the top of the fortress, and when they both leaped off together, it was as if they were landing on a bed of goose down covered with a fine silk cloth. And then they set off toward their own village.

Now the king's army was stationed on the side of a hill. But while those two saw the approaching army, the army could not see them. So Raṇapāla and his son went on as far as the mountain and Lake Śākambharī and finally returned to Ajayameru, where they safely took refuge in Raṇapāla's own dwelling. Reunited with his family in his fortress Citrakūṭa, he enjoyed worldly pleasures and protected the dharma.

—29—

Mother Ten's Stories

Ann Grodzins Gold

In Ghatiyali village, Ajmer District—as in many Rajasthani villages and cities—women worship the beneficent goddess Dasā Mātā (alternatively Daśā Mātā), here called Mother Ten, by telling her stories. A more accurate but awkward translation of this goddess's name would be "Condition Mother," for—as the stories teach—her power may transform a human's condition (*dasā; daśā*). Instantaneously, she bestows or removes well-being or ill-being. It seems likely that an initially accidental homonymy in Hindi and Rajasthani between the word for condition—*dasā*—and the auspicious number ten—*das* (alternatively *daś*)—led to the association of Dasā Mātā with ten days of worship, ten stories, a ten-pointed design, and a string with ten knots. Thus I shall call her Mother Ten.

The days of Mother Ten's worship in Rajasthan fall during a period crowded with rituals and festivals, and rich with songs and stories. Coming at the beginning of the hot season, this period coincides not incidentally with the harvest of winter grain crops. It begins with the major villagewide and nationwide festival of Holī on the full moon and last day of the lunar month called Phālgun (March-April). As the moon wanes and waxes again, during the succeeding month of Chaitra (April-May), many women in Ghatiyali participate in a series of ritual events appealing to and celebrating various aspects of female divinity. These rituals are all intended to secure for women and their families the comforts of a good life and, by the same token, to ward off the disasters of childlessness, widowhood, illness, loneliness, and poverty. Perhaps, above all, they are about the value of sustaining relationships.

The day after Holī is Brother Second, when sisters pray for their brothers' long lives and brothers give sisters gifts of clothing. The first day of Mother Ten's worship coincides with Brother Second, but Mother Ten's stories are told at a different time of day and in a different location from those dedicated to the goddess addressed only as "Mother of Brother Second." Eight days after Holī is the worship of Sītalā (alternatively, Śītalā) Mother, the Cool One, who controls both fertility and children's health—especially rashes and fevers. Rowdy groups of singing, laughing women celebrate Sītalā Mother's worship, visiting her shrine outside the village and alternately singing solemn devotional tunes and lyrics, and joking, bawdy ones. Mother Ten's worship on that day is quietly conducted at a lull in the activities dedicated to Sītalā. Sixteen days after Holī, and five after the culmination of Mother Ten's worship, is the festival of Gaṇgaur, in praise of the fair goddess who through austerities won Lord Śiva for her husband. Gaṇgaur worship is meant to secure auspicious wifehood for virgin girls and long-lived spouses for married women. Shortly after Gaṇgaur the spring celebration of the Goddess's semi-annual Nine Nights (Navarātri) caps this series of festivities honoring female divinity. Like Holī, Nine Nights is actively and publicly celebrated by men, but the worship performed for Brother Second, Sītalā Mother, Gaṇgaur, and Mother Ten is largely women's business.

It would be easy to overlook Mother Ten's worship during the vivid pageantry that characterizes many of the events with which it coincides and overlaps. On all but the tenth day, the ritual for Mother Ten probably takes less than two hours, from the drawing of the ten-pointed design through the stories and prayers. In many ways Mother Ten's rites are similar to the performance of vows (*vrat* or *vrata*) which both women and men, but more frequently women, undertake for the well-being of their families. Vrats, like Mother Ten's worship, typically involve a fast, a simple domestic worship ritual, and a story. However, Mother Ten's worship, although conducted in homes, has a collective aspect. Small groups of women, who may be neighbors and friends as well as relatives, perform it together. The tenth day sees the largest gatherings, as all married women who seek the goddess's protection for the coming year will attend the worship in order to obtain a blessed ten-knotted string to wear around their necks.

The three stories translated here I recorded on the second, fourth, and seventh days of Mother Ten's worship in March 1980.[1] The storyteller, Shobhag Kanvar, was then a woman in her mid-fifties, and a grandmother. She is of the Rājpūt caste—traditionally the ruling, landed gentry or "warrior" caste. Her own husband and one of her two sons had urban jobs as chauffeur and truck driver, respectively; another, more educated, son held a clerical position in a nearby town. Shobhag Kanvar, who had no formal schooling and can neither read nor write, is an acknowledged religious expert in Ghatiyali. I lived in her household from September 1979 to March 1981, and she was always quick to summon me and my tape recorder when what she considered a worthwhile cultural performance was about to take place in her home. Although other women in our village performed Mother Ten's worship, I attended and recorded only Shobhag Kanvar's rituals.

To participate in Mother Ten's worship and receive its benefits, women forego their morning meal and make sure to bathe, but otherwise they carry out their usual daily routines. Then, sometime in the afternoon, fasting women gather at the storyteller's home. In 1980, the regular participants who assembled in Shobhag Kanvar's courtyard for Mother Ten's worship were the female residents of this compound's household. These included Shobhag Kanvar, her daughter-in-law, her older sister (married to her husband's older brother), her sister's daughter-in-law, and me. A few neighbor women—none of them Rājpūts—attended irregularly. A couple of workmen were employed at the time doing masonry labor on Shobhag Kanvar's new house, and were thus professionally immune to the customs of gender seclusion that generally applied in a Rājpūt courtyard. I was surprised and amused to note how these men gravitated each day to within hearing distance of the storytelling session, positioning themselves just a little behind the small circle of women. Officially nonexistent at this female event, they nonetheless interjected appreciative exclamations and offered commentary on the stories. Shobhag Kanvar responded to their interest with her customary self-possession.

The atmosphere at Mother Ten's worship sessions was companionable as well as prayerful; no great solemnity prevailed. Children of all ages distracted and disrupted at their whim, including an infant who defecated on its doting grandmother's lap in the midst of one session, evoking general hilarity.

Before each worship Shobhag Kanvar prepared a special ritual space on the courtyard floor. With cowdung paste as her medium, she used her hands to paint a brown ten-pointed figure, upon which she placed a skein of white cotton yarn and a small pile of whole wheat grains. Next to this design Shobhag Kanvar set a small brass jar of pure water and a small dish of red powder, mixing water with powder to make a thick, bright red paste. On each day of Mother Ten's worship she used this paste to make auspicious dots on the ten-pointed design—one on the first day, two on the second, until a full complement of ten dots is made on the tenth day. Each day, as the worship began, every woman present took a few grains in her hand and held them while a story was told. At each story's conclusion, following Shobhag Kanvar's lead, the women tossed the grains in front of them while uttering prayers to the goddess.

On the tenth day the skein of yarn is twisted into necklaces called "Mother Ten's strings" which all participating women wear throughout the year that follows. Each string has ten knots in it. These strings are understood as forms of the goddess and respected as icons. For the tenth day women dressed in their best, attendance at least tripled, and the fast was broken with special festive foods offered to the goddess and eaten collectively.

Shobhag Kanvar told three stories at each worship session. The first (and longest) was always of the goddess herself; the second was always of the elephant-headed god Gaṇeśjī; the third was of a character called the Greedy One (Lobhyā). The chief feature of the Greedy One's stories was his futile efforts to snatch for himself the merit of women's fasts and offerings and stories. Shobhag Kanvar would conclude the Greedy One's tales by admonishing him that his story and his grains belonged to him, but nothing more.

In sum, then, during the ten days of Mother Ten's worship, Shobhag Kanvar produced thirty stories—ten for Mother Ten, ten for Gaṇeśjī and ten for the Greedy One—although only two of the Greedy One's tales had any substantial narrative content. Shobhag Kanvar told me that she had learned some of these stories from an aunt in her natal home, some from her (now deceased) mother-in-law in our village, and some from an elderly woman of a different and lower caste in our village.

Mother Ten is identified with Lakṣmī, the goddess of wealth and prosperity, while her opposite, Odasā—"Ill-Condition" or "Bad Ten" as I call her here—is identified with Kulakṣmī, the goddess of misfortune. Worshipers believe that Mother Ten brings well-being, comfort, and plenty to the families of the women who perform her rites. But if she is angered or neglected, abject poverty and every kind of bad luck will result—when Mother Ten departs and Bad Ten arrives.

A phrase that occurs in every Mother Ten story is "X had Mother Ten's niyam" and I have consistently translated this as "X followed the rules of Mother Ten." *Niyam* is variously glossed as "rule," "habit," or "regimen," but also includes, unlike those terms, a strong measure of self-restraint. To have the niyam of a particular deity means to act in accordance with that deity's traditional, prescriptive desires. These usually require acts of self-control and self-denial, such as fasting or renouncing certain foods, as well as acts of worship, such as offering grains or telling stories.

All Mother Ten's stories seem simultaneously to celebrate the absolute power of the goddess over human welfare and to demonstrate mortal women's great aptitude for exercising their pragmatic wits. An explicit connection between devotion to the goddess and human ingenuity is made in the first story when the narrator describes the heroine as knowing many things because "Mother Ten had turned her heart's key, and opened her heart, and put ideas in her brain." Each story begins with a woman in a difficult situation, but ends with the same woman having attained an ideal condition of general prosperity and security—through a combination of the goddess's blessings and her own efforts. Each story also ends with a prayer to Mother Ten to generalize that bliss: not only the story's heroine but the whole world should partake of it.

The tales reveal, in passing, forms of exploitation and abuse to which women are subject, but seem to view these more as challenges to feminine ingenuity than as intolerable burdens. The vocal, smart, well-behaved but unsubmissive women in these tales understand and experience, as do the narrator and her audience, a world strongly patterned by gender distinctions. Women perceive their disadvantages in this world, as when the bride of the first story fears a beating, or when the old woman of the third story acquiesces to the greedy king's unfair demand. But the stories express no resignation to imposed subordination. In the three tales presented here—and in all Mother Ten stories—potentially victimized females take fate into their own hands and, with help from the goddess, turn things around to their own advantage. In the process they often manipulate the men around them, and males are notably more voiceless and passive than women in these stories.

The heroines of Mother Ten's tales also manipulate other women. No ideology of female solidarity prevails in the story world. Realistically enough, solidarities and jealousies, mutual support and mutual predation, coexist. If a mother's worship establishes a secure fate for her daughter, and mother-in-law and daughter-in-law appreciatively bless one another, a stepmother may be deliberately cruel to her stepdaughter. If friendly neighbor-women lend grain and utensils to a lonely bride, a greedy neighbor-woman contrives to rob a defenseless old lady.

Each tale of Mother Ten seems to address one or more powerful cultural motifs surrounding female existence. "The Brahman's Daughter and the Five Bachelors" begins with an image of brothers dividing property. To separate cooking hearths is the paradigmatic act by which a joint family divides itself, and such divisions are strongly disapproved, although widely practiced, in Rajasthan. One of the most pervasive cultural truisms in north India has it that women's feuds and jealousies cause men to sever their brotherly ties. But here the five bachelors divide their property when they become an all-male group, and they are subsequently reunited by the clever bride. Thus as they worship the goddess of well-being, women powerfully deny the validity of a misogynous stereotype.

Another common characterization of north Indian kinship is that there is a painful antagonism between mother-in-law and daughter-in-law. This is supposed to be grounded in their presumed bitter competition for the son/husband. In "The Sword-Husband," however, the pair—mother-in-law/daughter-in-law—virtually creates a man for their mutual enjoyment, and they praise one another for this accomplishment. The story also sensibly enough reveals that a little disobedience to husband's mother is forgivable, and may be all for the best.

To be old and alone is a dreaded fate for anyone, perhaps most of all for women. But the story of "The Old Woman and The Yellow Calf," the third and last presented here, shows how devotion to the goddess and independent-mindedness may transform this fate. In the end, we see the old woman move from isolation to a familial situation, a move construed as one from misery to well-being. If her security lies in obtaining a new dependence, the old woman does not achieve this through begging or becoming an object of charity. Rather, her benefactor is forced to realize her personal worth. The goddess, Mother Ten, has many ways of taking care of her own. None of her devotees, as portrayed in Shobhag Kanvar's stories, lacks inner strength and all of them have lively tongues and their wits about them.

Further Reading

Two books provide further material on rituals and festivals in rural Rajasthan: Brij Raj Chauhan, *A Rajasthan Village.* (New Delhi: Associated Publishing House, 1967); and S. L. Srivastava, *Folk Culture and Oral Tradition* (New Delhi: Abhinav Publications, 1974). My earlier works treat related aspects of devotional storytelling, popular religious practices, and women's expressive traditions; Ann Grodzins Gold, *Village Families in Story and Song: An Approach through Women's Oral Traditions in Rajasthan* INDIAkit Series, South Asia Language and Area Center, University of Chicago, 1981; *Fruitful Journeys: The Ways of Rajasthani Pilgrims* (Berkeley and Los Angeles: University of California Press, 1988); and Gloria Goodwin Raheja and Ann Grodzins Gold, *Listen to the Heron's Words: Reimagining Gen-*

der and Kinship in North India (Berkeley and Los Angeles: University of California Press, 1994).

THE BRAHMAN'S DAUGHTER AND THE FIVE BACHELORS

A brahman had five sons. Their mother died, and what did the five sons do? They built five separate huts and five separate cooking hearths and five separate ovens for roasting grains, and even five separate manure piles. They went from village to village, begging for grain, and roasted it and ate it. The old man, their father, also went begging, made bread for himself, and ate it.

In another place there was a brahman who had one daughter. When her mother died, he married again and had another daughter. His second wife said, "Marry my daughter into a fine family, but give this one into any old place. Give her to a house with five bachelors."

Her husband went searching for such a house but could not find one anywhere. Many days passed and he kept wandering and searching. At last he heard about the brahman widower with his five bachelor sons and he arranged the match. They came for the marriage very poorly dressed. The stepdaughter was given in marriage to the middle brother. For wedding gifts, her stepmother gave her a broken tray, a broken brass pot, and a torn quilt and mattress. That woman was so unfeeling, as a real mother could never be, that she filled the huge clay jar with pieces of old plaster which she had dug up from the ruin of a broken-down wall [traditionally, this vessel would be filled with a special fried treat made of white flour]. She covered the mouth of the jar with a red cloth. This was the send-off that she gave to her stepdaughter.

The five bachelors, their old father, and the bride traveled in a borrowed ox cart. After some time, when they were approaching a river, the five bachelors felt they were dying of hunger. They began to grunt rudely to show how hungry they were. The father-in-law said, "Don't do that! What will this little one think? Look, you are five bachelors and you are grunting very rudely. Don't do that. Instead, let us go to the riverbank, relieve ourselves, wash, and then we will eat whatever is in the huge clay jar."

Now the girl knew there were pieces of plaster in the jar. She was a blooming young girl of seventeen or eighteen years, and very clever, and she knew that her stepmother had filled the jar with pieces of plaster. She thought, "Now these five bachelors will beat me." They were about to open the jar.

The girl's mother when she was alive had always faithfully followed the rules of Mother Ten, and during the ten special days for the worship of Mother Ten she always told that goddess's story first, and only afterward did she eat her food. Actually, her daughter had been born by the grace of Mother Ten. So now the girl prayed to Mother Ten: "Sustain my honor, sustain my honor! My mother always followed your rules and I was given to her by you. Therefore only you can sustain my honor, and if you don't, then right now the five bachelors will beat me." Just at that moment, as the men sat to eat, by the grace of Mother Ten the jar was filled with fried treats. Because the girl's mother had followed the rules of Mother Ten, Mother Ten fulfilled the needs of her daughter.

The father-in-law was quite pleased. He told her husband's younger brother to give the bride a snack of the fine treats. So she ate and drank. Then they tied up the mouth of the jar and put it back in the cart. And they all went on their way.

They came to the village of the five bachelors. When the clever women of the village saw the new bride they said, "Oh, look! Lakṣmī has come. [A new bride is often identified with Lakṣmī, the goddess of prosperity, who is of course identified with Mother Ten.] She has all good qualities and no bad qualities." Then five women of the village went to the huts where the five bachelors lived and took the new bride inside.

The bride got up early the next morning after the father-in-law and his sons had left to go begging for grain. She looked all around and saw all the huts, all the cooking hearths, all the roasting ovens and all the manure piles.

The bride went to her neighbors and said, "Aunties, please give me five kilos of wheat and just a little bit of dried greens too so that I can boil vegetable sauce."

The neighbor women said among themselves, "Lakṣmī has come, poor thing, let her have what she wants. Where else will she go?" And they gave her the grain and dried greens. Then she ground the wheat into flour and went back to ask the neighbor women for a sifter so she could sift the flour. They said, "Lakṣmī has come, let her have what she wants." They gave her a sifter. She boiled the greens into vegetable sauce and sifted the flour.

Then she asked the neighbor women, "Which cooking hearth is my husband's father's and which manure pile and which roasting oven?" They pointed the father-in-law's out to her. First she dug up all the five brothers' manure piles and combined them with her father-in-law's, making them all into one. Then she tore out the five brothers' cooking hearths and threw them in that manure pile. Then she broke up the five brothers' roasting ovens. After this she set to work cleaning all the huts. She swept and cleaned them thoroughly and then began to make bread. [Here Shobhag Kanvar broke out of her recitative storytelling voice to interject her own commentary, conversationally: "Lakṣmī is a woman and a house is not man's, it is woman's."]

Soon the five bachelors arrived, each bringing one or two kilos of grain which they had received while begging. They began at once to yell, "Oh no! Someone dug up my cooking hearth! Oh woe is me! Someone broke up my roasting oven."

But the bride said, "Don't make a racket. All of you bring your separate bags of grain and put them in a pile right here next to me. Then go to the tank and bathe. After you have cleaned your bodies and washed your clothes, on the way back, go to the temple and bow in front of Ṭhākurjī [a name often used for God, meaning "ruler"]. Then come home and eat bread."

When the brothers were returning from the tank it was easy to see that they had just bathed, because one had a wet ear and one had a wet back, and so on. The villagers were surprised and said to one another, "Ah, who has put a nose-ring on the bachelors today?" [That is, who has brought them under control like an ox?] But persons in the know said, "Ah, today Lakṣmī has come into their house." They went to the temple, and some bumped into the columns, and some looked at Ṭhākurjī, but soon they all came running home, just dying of hunger.

Then the bride said, "Don't make a racket, just sit down." They sat and she placed trays of food in front of them. First she served her father-in-law and then she served the two younger bothers of her husband and then she served the two elder brothers of her husband and last she served her husband. One of them ate five pieces of bread and one ate four and one ate six. But they all said, "Ah, today our brother's wife has satisfied us. It is good that our brother's wife has come. For so many days we have eaten nothing but roasted grains." The brothers decided, "Today we went to two villages but tomorrow we will go to four and we will bring a lot of grain and eat a lot of bread."

And so they did. The brahman's daughter returned to her neighbors the five kilos of wheat that she had borrowed from them, and there was more left over. So she cleaned it and ground it into flour. Every day she put all the grain that the men brought in one pile. They had plenty of food now because this girl was born by the grace of Mother Ten and wealth was in her hand. She knew many things in her heart. This was because Mother Ten had turned her heart's key, and opened her heart, and put ideas in her brain.

After a few days had passed, she said to her husband's younger brother, "The earnings of five sons are enough. Your old man's earnings are no longer needed. Now he is old. Let him collect small kindling and dry wood and bring it for the cooking fire." So the father-in-law went and gathered little sticks, brought them and threw them down by the hearth, and the bride ground grain and kneaded dough and prepared bread.

The five brothers brought huge bundles of grain tied up with cloth. Some days they brought 40 kilos, some days 80 kilos, some days 120 kilos, sometimes each of the five brought a full 40 kilos so that all together they had 200 kilos. They had so much grain it wouldn't fit in the huts.

One day in the rainy season the father-in-law found a dead snake lying on the ground and he brought it home and threw it up on the roof of his hut. Soon afterwards, the queen of that land was bathing. She had removed her necklace, which was worth millions, and set it down nearby. Just then it happened that a hawk flew by and took the necklace and flew away with it. It flew over the huts of the five bachelors and there was the dead snake lying on the roof. The hawk dropped the necklace and picked up the dead snake and flew away. The hawk took the snake because it was something to eat.

Now the bride was standing outside and saw this happen. She immediately took the necklace into the hut. Soon the king's men began to tour the kingdom, announcing in all the towns and villages that whoever found the queen's necklace and brought it to the king would have as a reward whatever he demanded. The whole kingdom was searching for the necklace. Then the bride told her husband's father to tie it up in a handkerchief and take it to the king. She said, "Tell him that you want nothing at all. Tell him only that on Divālī, Lakṣmī's day, light should burn in the five bachelors' huts and in the castle. But outside of those two places, in the whole kingdom, nothing should burn—no lamp, no electricity, nothing at all. Tell him, 'On the day of Lakṣmī worship, Divālī, there should be absolutely no light allowed anywhere except in the king's castle and in the five bachelors' huts.' " [Divālī falls on the pitch-dark new-moon night in fall. It is normally celebrated in each household by placing many clay lamps—small dishes of oil with wicks floating in them—on top of walls and roofs and on window sills.]

The father-in-law did as she said and the king agreed to his conditions. He called together all the chiefs of police and they went with their soldiers to each and every house to sit and enforce complete darkness. The entire city was completely dark, but lamps were burning in the five bachelors' huts and in the castle.

Both Mother Ten and Bad Ten came on Divālī night. Bad Ten slipped easily into each and every house, under cover of darkness. But where could Mother Ten enter? She saw no light and so she could not enter any house. She wandered all over the village, here and there, but Mother Ten could not enter anywhere because of the darkness. She thought to herself, "I'll find a place or else I'll turn back."

Then, suddenly, she saw lamps burning in the bachelors' huts, flickering and gleaming. The lamps had been filled with oil by the brahman girl. She had also lit a big torch and it was shining in the bachelors' huts like the moon. But the rest of the village was completely dark. Where the lamp was, there was Lakṣmī's dwelling.

Now Mother Ten wanted to enter right away, but the brahman's daughter would not open the door. She said, "No, you go present yourself elsewhere in the village." It got to be late, 4 A.M., and Mother Ten was very upset. She said, "You brahman girl, you open the door!" But the girl said, "Give me a promise, give me a promise."

So Mother Ten gave a promise. She swore: "If I forget my promise may I wither upon my feet, may I hang upside-down in a washerman's pool. For fourteen generations I will never leave you." This was the promise Mother Ten gave to that brahman girl.

Then the girl opened the door and Mother Ten put her foot in the hut. At once the hut flew away and in its place was a nine-story castle, made of glass, with gold and silver fittings, and many diamonds and rubies, and hundreds of thousands of rupees. How could this be? It was all given by Mother Ten, and what does she lack?

Oh, my Mother Ten, as her wishes were fulfilled, so let the world's wishes be.

THE SWORD-HUSBAND

There was once a brahman who had no sons or daughters. One day his wife said to him, "Take this sword, arrange its engagement, and get it married. Arrange the engagement and marriage of our 'son.' "

This brahman's wife always followed the rules of Mother Ten. During the days of Mother Ten's worship she would daily make a design on the ground with cowdung paste, put whole grains and the skein of yarn on it, and tell Mother Ten's stories. She was deeply devoted.

She told her husband to arrange the sword's marriage. She told him what to say to the bride's party: "My son has gone on a long business trip and I want to fix his engagement. If he is not back in time for the wedding, then, no matter. In the ceremony the sword can take the marriage rounds."

[Shobhag Kanvar here broke out of the story sequence to explain to me, a foreigner, that among brahmans, merchants, and her own Rajput caste, in not-so-distant times it truly happened that swords were used as proxy grooms in wedding ceremonies.]

Because she followed the rules of Mother Ten, the brahman's wife was acting out of faith. Her husband went at once. He found a suitable family and told them his son had gone on a long journey in order to earn a lot of money, but that meanwhile he wanted to arrange his marriage. He fixed the time, and on the appointed day the sword's wedding party set off with much pomp. The sword was ornamented with all the splendor of a bridegroom, including a turban and a garland and everything else that was necessary.

They reached the bride's village and went to her house. The wooden marriage emblem (*toraṇ*) was set over the doorway and the sword struck it. Then they took the sword into the house and performed the "knotting together" and the "joining of hands" ceremonies coupling the bride and the sword. In this fashion the sword took "marriage rounds" with the girl. [By mentioning these four important moments of the Rajasthani marriage ritual, familiar to everyone, Shobhag Kanvar provides verisimilitude to the outlandish image of a sword-bridegroom.]

Then the wedding party departed for the brahman's village, bringing the new bride. They took the bride inside the house, and for a few days young girls came and wanted to visit the bride. Her mother-in-law sat in the entranceway of the house, and the daughter-in-law sat there too, and every day girls and boys came to visit, and they passed the time in conversation. So a month or two went by. Then the girl's family came to take her back, so they took her. [A new bride's first sojourn in her marital home is normally a short one.]

But soon that old woman, the brahman's wife, said to her husband, "Time passes so pleasantly when my daughter-in-law is here. You must bring her back." So he brought her back to live with them. The neighbor girls wanted to visit with her, but her mother-in-law forbade it.

The mother-in-law ordered her "son's" bride, "Don't ever let the cooking fire go out, and don't ever let the water in the water pots run dry, and don't ever go to the houses of others because there you will receive false instruction."

However, one day by chance it happened that the cooking fire went out, and the water pots were empty. Then the daughter-in-law ran to the neighbor's house and said, "Oh Auntie, please give me at once some burning coals so I can start my cooking fire. Hurry before my mother-in-law calls me. If it weren't for her I would always be visiting at neighbors' homes."

Then the neighbor women all taunted her. "You fool, you have no groom, you have no man in your house, you married a sword. Your mother-in-law and father-in-law have no son."

Hearing this the girl became angry. "Oh ho, they have no son. They told me he had gone on a long journey to earn a lot of money, but you tell me they have no son."

"Yes, they have no son, they are childless, and are just taking advantage of you to live easily" [because a daughter-in-law does all the household chores]. Hearing all this made her so angry that she decided to trick her mother-in-law. One day she got her chance. The mother-in-law fell asleep sitting up; her head hung over and she was nodding. The daughter-in-law saw that she was wearing a bunch of keys at her waist. Stealthily, she took the keys and began to open the doors of the inner rooms of the house. She opened the locks of the doors with her mother-in-law's keys while her mother-in-law was sleeping.

In the first room she found grain in piles and boxes lying around. In the second room, there were various goods, and in the third, there was iron and wood and this and that, household things, lying around.

But in the seventh of seven inner rooms, there was a ten-pointed design on the floor, a ten-pointed design and upon it were whole grains of gold—whole grains of gold and a gold lamp. In this inner room a king's son was sleeping. He had been given by Mother Ten and lived in this room where the goddess provided him with food and drink.

As soon as she saw this miracle the daughter-in-law said to herself, "Oh ho, I have been in all the rooms and what is this that I have found here?" Then she asked him, "Who are you?" And he answered, "I am the brahman's son. I was given by Mother Ten. Because my mother always follows her rules and tells her stories, Mother Ten has given me to her." Right away the girl and the prince began to play parcheesi [a common way to refer to marital intimacy in Rajasthani folklore]. After that she prepared food for him.

Now the daughter-in-law worked hard and pleased her mother-in-law and father-in-law. But secretly she had a duplicate made of the key to the innermost room. She put the original back when her mother-in-law was sleeping. Her mother-in-law was not suspicious because she was a trusting person and she never knew that the girl had done this.

Every day the daughter-in-law finished her work of making bread and bringing water as fast as she could, and then she went at once to the inner room. And at night when her mother-in-law and father-in-law were sleeping, she went there also. Living in this way two years passed, and by the grace of God she became pregnant. One day when she was about seven months pregnant the mother-in-law noticed her daughter-in-law's big stomach. She said in surprise, "Oh, a lot has happened!" Now the brahman couple did not know about their son in the innermost room.

When the girl was eight months pregnant she asked her mother-in-law to get some special sweets for her and to inform her relatives of the coming happy event. But the mother-in-law said, "Daughter-in-law, aren't you dying of shame?" The daughter-in-law only repeated, "You must send the good news to my home." Then the mother-in-law answered, "How will I cut my nose [experience great public shame] and send the news to your home? My son has gone on a long journey to earn a lot of money and is not here and never has come here. You have certainly cut all our noses." This is the kind of thing she was saying. But the daughter-in-law insisted: "No, your son is here, right here, and you must send the good news to my parents' house."

So the mother-in-law thought, "All right, the nose is cut anyway." Then she sent a man immediately to tell the girl's family a child was going to be born, and they should come and bring sweets.

The girl's family was very happy when they received this message. They came to their daughter's husband's village with great pomp and celebration, with a band playing and a big display of money. They came in ox carts and horse carts and motor cars. They came making a great show; two hundred, four hundred, perhaps five hundred people came, and they had a great celebration. But the women of the village gossiped. "Aren't the brahman and his wife dying of shame? Look, there is no groom, no son, and who knows where she got her stomach. They ought to be ashamed." But the daughter-in-law said, "If anyone speaks like that then throw them out of here and don't listen to them."

Then the daughter-in-law said to her father-in-law and mother-in-law, "Clean everything in the house and bathe and have the band play and put on good clothes and I also will dress in finery and pearls." When all these preparations were complete, she told them to be seated together [as a couple would for a religious ritual or for their child's wedding]. Then she went and stood in front of the closed locked doors and prayed: "If Mother Ten is true, then all of these locks will open right now of their own accord and the prince will come out. If this does not happen then Mother Ten is false."

Then her mother-in-law mediated and prayed, "Mother Ten, I have fasted on your fast days for twenty-four years and told your stories with firm attention and always followed your rules. Now, because of my truthful principles, give me a son."

Then, "*khat, khat, khat*" the locks broke and the prince, a blooming youth with curling mustaches, twenty-five years old, emerged and sat down next to the brahman's daughter, his wife. Then the mother-in-law fell at her daughter-in-law's feet and the daughter-in-law fell at her mother-in-law's feet. The mother-in-law said, "Daughter-in-law, in your fortune, in your destiny, it must have been written that you would be a happily married woman, and for this reason Mother Ten gave me a son."

But the daughter-in-law said, "Dear Mother-in-law, you told the stories of Mother Ten, and if you had not done that, then where would it have been written for me to have a 'lord of the house' [husband]?"

Then the whole village gathered to see the wonder. They came to see what had happened. The boy given by Mother Ten was so handsome he was just like a king, his face shone like the moon's. Then their house became a nine-storey palace and Mother Ten dwelled with them there. Where Mother Ten dwells there is always wealth in plenty, so they never wanted for anything.

Hey, Mother Ten, give well-being to the whole world and then give it to me.

THE OLD WOMAN AND THE YELLOW CALF

There was an old woman who always followed the rules of Mother Ten. She ate bread only after telling the stories of Mother Ten. Mother Ten was pleased with her and thought to herself, "This is our old woman and we will give her a calf."

That night when she was sound asleep, the old woman dreamed that she heard a command: "Go to the yellow-dirt mine and make the sound '*pīlar pīlar pīlar pīlar pīlar pīlar*' and a yellow female calf will come to you" (*pīlā* means "yellow").

Immediately the old woman jumped up from her bed and went to the yellow-dirt mine and called "*pīlar pīlar pīlar pīlar pīlar pīlar*." Right away a yellow female calf came to her, and the old lady took it back to her home. She took it to her home and tied it up outside her house.

Now this was no ordinary calf. When it made dung, its dung was pure gold. But the neighbor woman would come and take away the golden dung and the old woman didn't know anything about it. In this way several days passed and the old woman was still very unhappy because, although she always performed the proper worship of Mother Ten, still she had nothing. She did not know that the calf's dung was golden, but she did know that someone was taking away its dung every day. [Village women regularly collect cow dung as it has many household uses.] So she decided to bring the calf inside at night and she tied it to the leg of her bed. In the morning she discovered the calf's golden dung and she was very happy.

But the neighbor woman became jealous. She was so jealous she could not bear it. So the neighbor woman went to the king. She told the king, "There is an old woman and she has such a calf, such a calf as ought to live with kings. That female calf would look beautiful in your palace."

The king gave a command to summon the old woman to the palace. The king's messenger came to her house and said, "Old Woman, the king is calling you."

She replied, "Brother, when Rām [a name of God] calls then I must go but if the king is calling, why should I go? What has the king to do with me?"

But the messenger said, "Let's go, lady. The king told me: 'Inform the old woman that she must show me her calf. That very calf of hers would look fine in my palace.' "

Then the old woman agreed to go. She went to the king and said to him, "Lord, Mother Ten was satisfied with me. One day I went to sleep hungry and at midnight Mother Ten came to me and said, 'Friend, why do you sleep hungry? Go to the yellow-dirt mine and make the sound "*pīlar pīlar*" and you will get a female calf.' So, great King, for ten days I tied it outside and my neighbor came and stole the dung, but now for several days I have tied it inside. Because she could not stand her jealousy she came and told you. All right, if you demand it, then take it. Why do I need the female calf? O King, demand it and take it, if you want it."

The king said, "Bring the calf and tie it in the palace. It makes golden dung so it belongs in my palace."

So the old woman brought the calf and tied it in the king's palace. Then the calf began to make a great deal of dung, but it was not golden. The palace was soon filled with it. The calf made watery dung, all by the grace of Mother Ten. It shot out dung with great force, on top of the king's royal bed and all over his trunks and boxes; everything was covered with it. And the calf also kicked; it kicked the mirrors and the cupboards and broke them.

The king summoned the neighbor woman and said, "You wretch, you told me this calf made golden dung, but it has filled my castle with its excrement and it has broken the royal beds and the mirrors and the cupboards. It has broken everything and I am in great distress. You must bring someone at once who can remove it from the palace."

She answered, "Great King, I know nothing about it, that old woman knows." Again the king's messenger came to the old woman's house. "Old woman, old woman, the king summons you."

She replied, "What's all this? The king is always calling me. I went only yesterday." But she went to the palace.

The king said to her, "I can't stand it. Take the calf away." He said, "Old woman, you must know magic, you must be a magician, because when it was with you the calf made golden dung but as soon as it came to me it began to make foul excrement."

She said, "King, I only follow the rules of Mother Ten and I tell her stories. The calf was given to me by her. I have picked no one's pocket, I have stolen nothing. I have let nobody else's livestock loose. The calf was given to me by Mother Ten, but you couldn't bear to see me have it so you demanded it and took it for yourself."

Then the king decided to keep the old woman in his court for the rest of her days, to give her everything she needed to live comfortably. He said, "Mother [addressing her for the first time with appropriate respect], you sit here near me in my castle and praise God and tell my court about noble things, tell about Mother Ten, and eat your bread right here."

Hey, caretaker, Mother Ten, as the king looked after her, so you look after everyone.

Notes

1. I would like to acknowledge the thoughtful cooperation of Shobhag Kanvar and Vajendra Kumar Sharma, without whom I would not have been able to bring these tales to a Western audience.

— 30 —

The Life of Guru Nānak

Hew McLeod

The Sikh faith begins with Guru Nānak, born in the Punjab in 1469 and dying there in 1538 or 1539. Nānak himself was raised as a Hindu in a predominantly Muslim part of India, but adopted the same critical attitude toward the two religious systems. He believed that although it was possible for both Hindus and Muslims to win liberation, this could only be achieved by renouncing all trust in the external features of either religion. For Nānak the only true religion was within.

Nānak believed emphatically in Akāl Purakh (God), and for him liberation lay in the merging of the human spirit with the all-embracing spirit of God. For Nānak the key to liberation lay in the nām or divine Name. It was the nām that gathered into a single word the whole nature of God, the fullness of God's greatness being clearly perceived in all that was expressed by the all-pervading divine Name. God pervades all things (both those which lie around and those which dwell within), and the person who realizes this is the one who comprehends the Name. Recognize this, and you have taken the first essential step on the pathway to liberation. Practice with regularity and determination a pattern of meditation on the divine Name, and eventually you must attain to that condition of supreme bliss.

This message is variously spelled out in the numerous hymns of Guru Nānak, collected in the *Ādi Granth* (the *Guru Granth Sāhib*) with those of his four successors and some other religious poets who had the same message. In these hymns he tells us a great deal about his teachings, yet almost nothing about his actual life. His followers (the early Sikhs) could not be satisfied with this and inevitably there developed within the Panth (the Sikh community) the practice of relating hagiographic tales concerning the greatness of the guru. These in turn came to be written down and in their recorded form they are known as janam-sākhīs.

The janam-sakhīs consist of anecdotes about Nānak. In an early version these were ordered roughly according to the guru's childhood, adult life, and death. As they were told and retold they became more sophisticated, and in one of the later janam-sākhī traditions (the so-called Puratan tradition), much of Guru Nānak's adult life is arranged into four missionary journeys directed to the four cardinal points of the compass.

A janam-sākhī version of the birth and childhood of Nānak, together with the call to preach and his ultimate death, is contained in my *Textual Sources for the Study of Sikhism*. The selection of anecdotes offered here is taken from his adult life, most of them from the period of his travels. In the translation, words and occasionally phrases have been added to the original in order to impart continuity to the story, but in no case has anything else been added.

Further Reading

See my books, *Early Sikh Tradition* (Oxford: Clarendon Press, 1980); *Guru Nanak and the Sikh Religion* (Oxford: Clarendon Press, 1968); and *Textual Sources for the Study of Sikhism* (Chicago: University of Chicago Press, 1990).

The first anecdote is a humorous tale in which Nānak gently rebukes Hindus, gathered at the Gaṅgā.

Many people had come to the Gaṅgā to bathe. Bābā ("Father") Nānak also went there and, sitting down beside the river, he looked around. "Perhaps I shall see someone who is near to God," he thought. He observed that tens of thousands of people were bathing. Having taken their dip, they offered water to their forefathers, although they did not realize that none of their forefathers was cleansed. Bābā Nānak possessed divine knowledge, whereas the people whom he observed had only a mundane understanding. They believed that purity comes from bathing, and so they bathed. According to Bābā Nānak's understanding, however, it had no effect.

Bābā Nānak also entered the water to bathe. The people were worshiping facing the rising sun, but Bābā Nānak began to bathe facing the direction of the setting sun. Other people were casting water toward the rising sun. Bābā Nānak began to throw water in the direction of the sun's setting. Observing this, the people asked him, "Are you a Hindu, friend, or are you a Muslim?" [From the Gaṅgā River the direction of the setting sun is also, roughly, the direction of Mecca].

"I am a Hindu," answered Bābā Nānak. "If you are a Hindu," they said, "to whom are you casting water?"

"To whom are *you* casting water?" countered Bābā Nānak

"We are casting water to our forefathers," they replied.

"Where are your forefathers?" enquired Bābā Nānak.

"Our forefathers are in heaven," they answered.

"How far is heaven from here?" asked Bābā Nānak.

"Heaven is forty-nine and a half crores [ten millions] of miles from here," they replied. "The location of the land of departed souls is there, and that is where we are throwing water."

"Will it get there?" asked Bābā Nānak, and they answered, "Yes, it will get there."

When they said this, Bābā Nānak cast a little water forward and then began to toss large quantities of it.

"To whom are you throwing water?" they asked. "And so much water!"

"At home I have a field," replied Guru Bābā Nānak, "and the unripe grain in it is withering. I am watering that field."

"But Master," they protested, "how can the water reach your field? Why are you throwing water like this?"

"My friends," said Bābā Nānak, "if water will not reach my field then how can it reach your forefathers? Your forefathers are away in heaven. How can the water get there?" When Bābā Nānak said this, they exclaimed, "Brothers, this is no ordinary person. This is indeed a great one."

The next tale describes an encounter that Guru Nānak, while on his travels, had with a robber. In this story the janam-sākhī author is faithful to the message of Nānak that the divine Name is the sole and sufficient remedy awaiting the erring person.

There was once a villainous robber named Bhola who every day sat on an elevated lookout, wearing white clothes and terrorizing the road below. He was a fearless fellow who would tackle eight or ten men at a time, and he had committed many crimes. When he observed Bābā Nānak approaching, he descended from his lookout and, hovering near him, he threateningly announced, "Remove your clothes or I shall kill you."

"Well!" exclaimed Bābā Nānak. "So I have fallen into your clutches! Do one thing for me—I shall not run away. Return home and when you arrive there put a question to your family—to your mother, father, wife, and sons. You do evil and commit murder, and at the same time you provide for them. Now ask them this question: "When you are in trouble will there be anyone from your entire family who will stand by you in your misfortune?"

"You are deceiving me," said Bhola. "You will run away."

"Take my word for it," promised Bābā Nānak. "I shall not go."

Bhola the robber returned home, and when he arrived there he gathered his family together—mother, father, sons, wife, the entire family. "Listen," he said, "I have committed a thousand murders and crimes without number to provide your food. Tell me, when I am in trouble will any of you share my anguish? Will any of you break the god of death's net? Can any of you release me from his angel? Will any of you share my suffering, or will you not?"

"Your deeds will be your companions," they all replied, "for as you act so you appear for judgment before God. The relationship between you and us concerns only this life. Whether a man does good or whether he does evil, while at the same time caring for his family, in the court of God he must answer alone. No one can be taken as a substitute for another."

At this Bhola was most distressed, and beat upon the ground with both hands. "Have I foolishly wasted all these years with you?" he cried. "If at the end you are going to desert me then why have I spent my life committing a thousand crimes and murders, while providing for you?"

He went off wailing and coming to Bābā Nānak, fell at his feet. Then he stood up with palms joined in supplication. "I have been grossly negligent," he humbly confessed. "Forgive my evil deeds. My whole life has been spent in this manner. Accept me. Amend my life that I may be restored."

"Prostrate yourself," commanded Bābā Nānak, and then he released Bhola from the penalty of his misdeeds. Having forgiven him, Bābā Nānak sang a hymn in sūhī rāga.

> Bronze shines brightly, but rub it and it sheds an inky black.
> Though I clean it a hundred times, polishing will never remove its stain.
>
> O heedless one! They are my real friends who accompany me now and who will accompany me into the hereafter,
> Who, where accounts are demanded, will stand and give an account of good deeds done.
>
> Houses, temples, and palaces may be colorful without,
> But let them collapse and they are useless and empty.
>
> The heron wears garments of white and dwells at places of pilgrimage.
> But as it pecks and rummages it consumes and destroys life; how then can it be regarded as pure?
>
> My body is like a simmal [silk-cotton] tree which men, when they observe it, mistake as useful.
> But as its fruit is devoid of value, so is my body empty of virtue.
>
> A blind man bearing a burden and climbing a precipitous path;
> I scan the road but, finding nothing, how can I hope to pass over?
>
> Of what use is any service, virtue, or wisdom other than the divine Name?
> Cherish the Name, O Nānak, for only thus shall your bonds be broken.
>
> Bābā Nānak thus relieved Bhola the robber of his distress and proceeded on his way.

According to the janam-sākhī accounts, Bābā Nānak traveled to Mecca.

When Bābā Nānak was making his way toward Mecca, on the road he happened to encounter some fakirs (faqīr). They asked him, "What is your name?" Bābā

Nānak answered, "It is Nānak." They then asked him, "Are you a Hindu or a Muslim?" and he replied, "I am a Hindu." Hearing this they drew away from him. "Nānak!" they exclaimed, "this is no road for Hindus!"

"Very well," said Bābā Nānak. "Let us make the pilgrimage to Mecca separately and whoever God takes will go there. Proceed on your way." When Bābā Nānak said this they left him and went on their way, while he remained there. It was a year's journey to Mecca, and after a year the fakirs reached the city. When they arrived, whom should they see but Bābā Nānak already there! The fakirs were astounded. "We left him behind and yet he has arrived ahead of us!" they exclaimed. "What marvel is this?"

The fakirs then enquired from the people of Mecca concerning Bābā Nānak. "How long has this fakir been here, friends?" they asked.

"This fakir has been here for a year," answered the people of the place.

"O God, has a Hindu drawn so near to you?" cried the fakirs. "Glory to your grace whereby he has been brought near to you. You have imparted your grace to a Hindu." They then related what had happened along the way. The people of Mecca, however, assured them: "This is no Hindu. This is a great sage, one who recites the nāmāz [Muslim prayer, particularly the prescribed daily prayers]. Everyone recites the nāmāz after him. He recites the nāmāz before anyone else."

"He told us he was a Hindu," said the fakirs, "but he is really a Muslim and thus he has come near to God. We were amazed, wondering how a Hindu could draw near to God in this way."

While in Mecca, Bābā Nānak went into a mosque and dropped off to sleep with his feet toward the mosque's miḥrāb (the niche in a mosque which marks the direction of the Ka'bah in Mecca). The story is a familiar one in Sufi hagiography, telling how the very house of God moves in obedience to the presence of a great Muslim mystic. In this case it revolves for one who is not a Muslim and is greater than the greatest of Sufis.

Bābā Nānak lay down in the Mecca mosque and went to sleep with his feet toward the miḥrāb. A mulla, who was the mosque attendant, appeared and cried out, "You blasphemous fellow! Why have you gone to sleep with your feet in the direction of the house of God?"

"My friend," answered Bābā Nānak, "lay my feet in whatever direction the house of God is not be found."

When the mulla pulled Bābā Nānak's feet around in a northerly direction, the miḥrāb moved in the same direction. When he moved Bābā Nānak's feet to the east, the miḥrāb also moved in that direction, and when he dragged Bābā Nānak's feet to the south, the miḥrāb went the same way. Then from the cupola of the mosque there echoed a voice, mysterious and resonant: "Praise be to Nānak! Praise be to Nānak!" it boomed.

During the lifetime of Nānak, the Mughals under Bābar invaded from Afghanistan, and following the battle of Panipat in 1526, Mughal rule was established in north India with Bābar as the first emperor. Janam-sākhīs naturally include anecdotes concerning Bābā Nānak's encounter with Bābar. Although none of these is likely to have occurred, Guru Nānak certainly witnessed the Mughal invasions, as he has left four hymns that are clearly the work of an eyewitness. The most famous of these centers on the Mughal sack of the Punjabi town of Saidpur.

Carrying on to Saidpur, Bābā Nānak stopped outside the town and rested. Further on, a wedding was being celebrated in the house of some Pathans [Afghans], and the Pathans were dancing. With Bābā Nānak there were some fakirs who were very hungry. He remained for some time at that place, but no one paid any heed to him sitting there. The fakirs were weak with hunger, and so Bābā Nānak arose and, taking with him Mardana [the guru's faithful companion] and the fakirs, went into the town. There they asked for food, but at all the houses they visited their request was ignored. Bābā Nānak became exceedingly wrathful. "Mardana," he commanded, "play the rabāb [rebec]!" In anger he sang a hymn in tilaṅg rāga.

I proclaim the tidings that I have received from the Lord, O Beloved.
From Kabul he has descended with sin as his marriage-party
and forcibly demanded a dowry, O Beloved.
Modesty and sacred duty have gone into hiding,
and falsehood struts around as Lord, O Beloved.
The writ of the qāḍī and the brahman no longer runs,
for it is Satan who reads the marriage ceremony, O Beloved.
In their agony Muslim women read the Qur'ān
and cry for help to God, O Beloved.
And Hindu women, both high caste and low,
they too suffer the same violation, O Beloved.
It is a song of blood that is sung, O Nānak;
and blood, O Beloved, is the saffron wherewith they are anointed.

In the city of the dead Nānak praises the Lord, and to all he proclaims this belief:
He who created the world in all its manifestations sits alone, observing all.
When the fabric of our body is torn to shreds, then will Hindustan recall my words;
For the Lord is true, his justice is true, and true will be his judgment.
He will come in seventy-eight and go in ninety-seven,
and another disciple of a warrior will arise.
This is the truth that Nānak utters, the truth that he will proclaim,
for now is the moment of truth!

On the third day Bābā Nānak returned to Saidpur and entered it. When he gazed around at the town he observed that all its inhabitants had been killed. "Mardana," said Bābā Nānak, "what has happened?"

"My Lord," replied Mardana, "that which pleased you has come to pass."

"Play the rabab, Mardana," said Bābā Nānak. Mardana played the āsā rāga on the rabāb and Bābā Nānak sang this hymn [omitted here].

And so all the Pathans there were slain. The female prisoners of the Pathans were carried off and the rule of Mīr Bābar prevailed. Hindustan was seized and joined to Khurasan.

Bābā Nānak then proceeded to the army encampment and entered it. Now Mīr Bābar was a Sufi. According to the janam-sakhīs, he was secretly a darvīsh or mystic. During the day he performed his royal duties, but at night he cast the fetters off from his feet, bowed his head, and worshiped God. When day dawned he would recite the nāmāz, read the thirty sections of the Qur'ān, and after this consume bhang (cannabis).

Bābā Nānak entered the army encampment and began to sing a hymn. Nearby were the prisoners, and when he looked at them he observed how dreadfully miserable they were. "Mardana," he said, "play the rabāb." He then sang a hymn in tilaṅg rāga.

> You spared Khurasan but yet spread fear in Hindustan.
> Creator, you did this, but to avoid the blame you sent the Mughal
> as the messenger of death.
> Receiving such chastisement, the people cry out in agony
> and yet no anguish touches you.

When Mīr Bābar heard this hymn, he exclaimed, "Friends, fetch that fakir." Some men went and brought Bābā Nānak into his presence. Bābar said, "Fakir, repeat what you just sang." When Bābā Nānak repeated the hymn, the portals of Bābar's understanding opened. "Friends," he declared, "this is a noble fakir!"

He then opened his bhang pouch and offered it to Bābā Nānak, saying, "Have some bhang, fakir."

"Mīrjī," replied Bābā Nānak, "I have already eaten bhang. I have taken a kind of bhang which induces a condition of permanent intoxication." Bābā Nānak continued, "Mardana, play the rabāb." He then sang a hymn in tilaṅg rāga [omitted].

Bābā Nānak then looked at the prisoners again and was much grieved by their misery. "Mardana," he said, "play the rabāb." Mardana played the rabab and Bābā Nānak sang a hymn in āsā rāga [omitted].

Having uttered this hymn, Bābā Nānak passed into a trance, fell to the ground, and lay there. Bābar came and, standing over him, asked, "What has happened to the fakir?"

"Sir, the fakir is in agony," answered the people. "Seeing the wrath of God, he has fallen into a trance."

"Pray to God that the fakir may arise, friends," commanded Bābar.

Bābā Nānak then sat up, and as he did so there blazed forth a radiance as if a thousand suns had risen. Bābar salaamed and cried, "Have mercy!"

"Mīrjī," replied Bābā Nānak, "if you desire mercy then release the prisoners."

"May I make one request?" asked Bābar.

"Speak," answered Bābā Nānak.

"Promise me one thing and I shall release them."

"Make your request," Bābā Nānak said to him.

"This I ask," said Bābar, "that my kingdom may endure from generation to generation."

"Your kingdom will endure for a time," replied Bābā Nānak.

Having clothed the prisoners, Bābar released them, and Bābā Nānak rejoiced. He took leave of Bābar and went on his way. Crossing the Ravi and Chenab rivers, he made his way through the Punjab inspecting waste lands, in search of a suitable place to stay. Traveling on, he reached a spot beside a river. Crowds of people flocked there. All who heard that he was there came to him. "A true fakir of God has been born," they declared. "His name is Nānak and he is absorbed in his God." Many people gathered there and became disciples. All who came were overjoyed. Whenever Bābā Nānak composed a hymn it was circulated. He composed hymns, and fakirs sang devotional songs. In Nānak's house the truth concerning the one divine Name was expounded. His praises resounded and enormous crowds came to him. Hindus, Muslims, [all manner of people] came and were captivated. All extolled his greatness.

While on his travels, Guru Nānak encountered a frightening creature who turned out to be Kaliyuga, an incarnate version of the fourth cosmic age. The cosmic cycle is divided into four ages and the Kaliyuga, the iron age, is the period of deepest degeneracy which precedes the restoration of absolute truth and fulfilment in the Kṛtayuga or Satyayuga. (We are at present living in the Kaliyuga.) Guru Nānak is here confronted by an incarnate form of this, the evil age, and in his discourse with it he reduces it to total subjection.

Guru Nānak and Mardana entered a great and fearsome wilderness, where no dwelling was to be seen. One day, in accordance with the divine command, there came darkness and a terrible storm. Around them flashed black, white, and red. Torrents of rain fell as awesome black clouds rolled over. Mardana was terrified. "Bābājī!" he cried. "A mighty storm has blown up! It is raining! Let us flee! Come, let us take shelter under a tree!"

"Say 'Praise to the Guru,' Mardana, and nothing will come near you," answered Bābā Nānak. "This darkness and rain with these clouds of smoke will go. Keep calm."

Gradually the darkness and the rain lifted. When they had cleared, there appeared the figure of a demon with huge fangs, the top of his head touching the heavens and its feet the ground. Enormous was its belly and terrifying its evil eyes. Fearsomely it advanced. "Bābājī!" cried Mardana. "God saved us from the storm, but this calamity we shall not escape!"

"Say 'Praise to the Guru,' Mardana," replied Bābā Nānak, "and like the storm this too will depart. Keep calm."

In accordance with the divine command, the apparition assumed the form of a man standing respectfully before them in an attitude of submission. "Who are you?" asked Bābā Nānak. It replied, "Gracious one, I am Kaliyuga. I am greatly honored by your entry into my kingdom, into this domain of mine. Accept an offering from me."

"What is there in all that you have to offer?" asked Bābā Nānak. "Tell me, may I ask whatever I please?"

"Gracious one," replied Kaliyuga, "if you command I shall erect a palace studded with pearls and annointed with musk."

Bābā Nānak, in response, sang a hymn in the measure sirī rāga. "Mardana," he said, "play the rabāb so that I may sing a hymn."

> If I should own a priceless palace, walled with pearl and tiled with jewels,
> Rooms perfumed with musk and saffron, sweet with fragrant sandalwood,
> Yet may your Name remain, O Master, in my thoughts and in my heart.
>
> Apart from God my soul must burn,
> Apart from God no place to turn,
> The guru thus declares [refrain omitted].

Kaliyuga then said, "If you so command I shall encrust the whole world with diamonds and stud a bed with pearls and rubies." In reply, Bābā Nānak sang the second stanza.

> If, in a world aglow with diamonds, rubies deck my bed;
> If, with alluring voice and gesture, maidens proffer charms;
> Yet may your Name remain, O Master, in my thoughts and in my heart.

Kaliyuga then said, "My Lord, if you so command I shall lead the whole of creation captive and lay it in obedience before you." Bābā Nānak then sang the third stanza.

> If with the yogi's mystic art I work impressive deeds,
> Present now, then presto vanished, winning vast renown;
> Yet may your Name remain, O Master, in my thoughts and in my heart.

Kaliyuga then said, "If you so command I shall give you kingship over all lands." Bābā Nānak sang the fourth stanza.

> If as the lord of powerful armies, if as a king enthroned,
> Though my commands bring prompt obedience, yet would my strength be vain.
> Grant that your Name remain, O Master, in my thoughts and in my heart.

"I have no use for the things you have been describing," continued Bābā Nānak. "What else do you have? What kind of kingdom have you? What manner of deeds do you expect from your subjects and what way of life do you impose on them?"

"My Lord, in my kingdom the way of life is of the kind that is typical of this evil age, the Kaliyuga. It consists of hunger, lethargy, thirst, abuse, avarice, sloth, drunkenness, and indolence. Highway robbery, gambling, strangling, slander, the four cardinal sins, falsehood, deceit, wrath, greed, covetousness, and pride abound. There is scarcely one in ten million who can evade my authority. No, *all* are in my power."

"I am asking you for a boon, brother," said Bābā Nānak. "Gracious one," replied Kaliyuga, "I shall do whatever you command."

"Let not any of my Sikhs who may be under your authority be harassed, brother," said Bābā Nānak, "nor any gathering of my followers that may be within your domains. Do not let your shadow fall upon them. Let not the recitation of hymns be neglected, nor the works of mercy and benevolence, holy charity, remembrance of the divine Name, and bathing at the pilgrimage center of truth."

"Merciful one, forgive me," said Kaliyuga humbly. "Of all ages the authority of mine is the greatest."

"If you are going to give a boon," replied Bābā Nānak, "then let it be this. Let the congregation of my followers live in peace, happiness, and the fear of God."

"You are omniscient, merciful one," answered Kaliyuga, "but even if one is regarded by others as a mighty seer (*sadhu*) yet to me he is a mere man."

"If you are going to give a boon then let it be this," repeated Bābā Nānak.

Kaliyuga then adopted an attitude of submission. "My Lord," he said, "my life, my soul, everything is at your disposal."

"Swear to me that this is the case, brother," answered Guru Bābā Nānak.

Kaliyuga swore it three times and fell at his feet. Bābā Nānak was filled with joy. "Go on your way," he said. "Your glory shall exceed that of all ages. In your kingdom there will be the singing of hymns and preaching of the most exalted kind. Previously people performed austerities for a hundred thousand years in order to obtain liberation, but in your age if anyone meditates on the divine Name with undivided concentration for a few short minutes, that person will be liberated."

Later in their travels, Bābā Nānak and Mardana came to a country that was ruled by women. This particular story clearly shows the janam-sākhī debt to puranic and tantric tradition, as the narrative descends from a famous Nāth legend concerning the capture of Machendranāth by the women who ruled the country of Kadali (or Kāmarūpa) and their magical transformation of him into a sheep. Machendranāth was subsequently rescued by Gorakhnāth, as here Mardana was rescued by Bābā Nānak.

Bābā Nānakjī came to a land beside the sea where no man was to be found. Women rule there, and in all villages throughout the country women receive the earnings, not the men. "Bābājī, let us see this country," suggested Mardana.

"This is a land of women," replied Bābā Nānak. "It would be unwise to proceed further into this country."

"Now that we have come so far let us see it," persisted Mardana. "Who else comes so far?"

"Go then if you so desire," said Guru Nānak, "and having seen it return here."

Mardana took his rabāb so that he might beg and, proceeding straight to a town, he entered it. When the women observed him all of them slowly closed in upon him. No man was to be found there. "Come inside," they said, but Mardana replied, "No, I cannot enter."

When they perceived that he would not go in voluntarily, they pushed him in and tied his hands with thread. Their thread was enchanted by means of a potent spell, and through the magic power of the thread they could do whatever they wished with him. When they tied his hands with the thread he changed into a ram. They threw his rabab inside and, having turned him into a ram, they tethered him in the courtyard.

Meanwhile Bābā Nānak was scanning the road, but Mardana did not return. "God be blessed!" said Guru Bābā Nānak. "He used to pluck the strings of his rabab and meditate on the divine Name of God. Wherever has he gone? He had another man with him and he has not returned, either."

Guru Bābā Nānak arose and went to the town. As he proceeded into the town he came to the place where Mardana had been ensnared, and there entered the courtyard. Seeing him enter the women all came to him. "You have my man. Return him to me," commanded Bābā Nānak.

"He is not here," they replied.

When Mardana, who had been turned into a ram, observed Bābā Nānak, he began to scratch the ground with his hoof. He was unable to speak, for when he tried to do so he only bleated. Bābā Nānak saw that it was Mardana and motioned to him to be patient, although he could not help being amused at the same time.

Bābā Nānak then said to the women, "If you would do a good deed, restore my man."

"Sir," they replied, "where is this man? Come in, take food and drink. Where else would you go now?"

As soon as they had said this, Bābā Nānak's hands were instantly tied by the magic thread. But Bābā Nānak is a perfected one. What can overcome him? When their thread was tied on him nothing happened. They called others skilled in sorcery, but those who came also failed. "Restore my man," said Bābā Nānak.

They began to whisper to each other. "This must be some great warrior, someone of mighty power upon whom our charms have no effect."

Bābā Nānak repeated, "If you would do a good deed then restore my man."

"Find your man, wherever he may be, and take him," they replied.

"But you are not giving him to me," said Bābā Nānak.

"Take him!" they answered.

Bābā Nānak released Mardana from the enchanted thread and he stood before them, a man again.

"This is no man!" cried the women [referring to Bābā Nānak]. "This is a god! He on whom our charms were ineffectual must be God!"

All the women came and fell at Bābā Nānak's feet and from their hearts they made this request: "Sir, we have suffered much from the absence of men. Free us, sir, from this suffering." Bābā Nānak, being one who understands inner thoughts and motives, heard their petition and blessed them. They found peace and began to sing the praises of God.

In the first of his lengthy poems (known as *vars*) the celebrated Sikh poet Bhai Gurdās tells, with remarkable brevity, the famous story of how Bābā Nānak approached Multan. As he drew near the city the Muslim holy men of the city brought out for him a cup brimful of milk.

> Bābā Nānak arose and journeyed from the fair to Multan.
> As he drew near, the pīrs of Multan came bringing a cup filled [to the brim] with milk.
> Bābā Nānak plucked a nearby jasmine flower and laid it on the milk,
> Just as the Gaṅgā flows into the ocean!.

In laying the jasmine petal on the milk, Bābā Nānak had not spilled any of it. The intention of the pīrs in offering milk was to indicate that Multan was already brimful of holy men and that accordingly there was no place in the city for Guru Nānak. The point of the guru's response was that as a flower petal could be laid on a brimming cup without causing it to overflow, so Multan could find room for one more holy man, and that the most sublime of them all.

This anecdote is contained in Sufi tradition of an earlier date. The Sufi pīr was ʿAbdul Qādir Jīlānī, the city was Baghdad, the cup was filled with water, and the petal was that of a rose. It is, however, essentially the same anecdote, communicating exactly the same message. The anecdote had, moreover, been transferred by the Sufis to Multan and attached to two different pīrs. The earlier was Baha' al-Dīn Zakariyya, who died in 1266. The second was the slightly later Shams al-Dīn Tabrīzi who was sent the cup by Baha' al-Dīn Zakariyya. In both instances, the cup contained milk.

Before he died in 1539, Nānak passed the leadership of his Sikhs on to the second guru, a man called Lahiṇā whom he renamed Aṅgad. The reason for Guru Nānak's trust in the absolute loyalty of Aṅgad is well illustrated by several stories from the janam-sākhīs. The following serves as an example.

One day Bābā Nānak was bathing and Aṅgad, who had already bathed, was sitting nearby. Bābā Nānak was standing in the river. It was winter and as a result of the squalls and the rain that had fallen it was exceedingly cold. Guru Aṅgad suffered greatly from the cold and the rain. The clothes he was wearing were soaked. Eventually the cold overcame Guru Aṅgad and, losing consciousness, he collapsed.

Having emerged from the river, donned his clothing, and performed his prostrations, Bābā Nānak went to Aṅgad and, reaching him, nudged him with his foot. When Bābā Nānak nudged him, Guru Aṅgad regained consciousness. He was restored. The chill departed, he became warm, and sat up.

"Aṅgad, my son, what happened to you?" asked Bābā Nānak.

"Lord," replied Aṅgad, "you know all things."

"But tell me what happened to you, my son," said Bābā Nānak.

"Sir, my clothing was soaked with rain and I lost consciousness. I was aware of nothing that had happened. I had no knowledge of it at all."

"How are you now?" asked Bābā Nānak.

"Because of you," answered Guru Aṅgad, "I now know that my spirit has been illumined by the light of ten million suns, and that because of you warmth has been restored."

"Well, my son, are you comfortable now?" asked Bābā Nānak, and he replied, "I am comfortable."

Bābā Nānak then said, "This discipline which I perform I do only for my Sikhs. I perform this service in your stead, my son, for your body cannot endure its rigor." If anyone bears the title of Nānak-panthi [a follower of Nānak's way, a disciple of Nānak, a Sikh; in practice the term is generally restricted to Sikhs of the pre-Khālsā period or to those of the later period who do not take the Khālsā vows] he will be liberated.

—31—

The Autobiography of a Female Renouncer

J. E. Llewellyn

According to some of the classical sources that spell out the rules for renouncers, this stage of life is restricted to twice-born males. Renunciation is permitted neither for men of low caste nor for women. There are references in classical Indian texts to women who were masters of spiritual knowledge and even to women who are renouncers, but they are few. In traditional Hindu society, women are supposed to be subordinate to men. The following verses from *The Laws of Manu* are frequently quoted to illustrate this principle:

> By a girl, by a young women, or even by an aged one, nothing must be done independently, even in her own house. In childhood a female must be subject to her father, in youth to her husband, when her lord is dead to her sons; a woman must never be independent. She must not seek to separate herself from her father, husband, or sons; by leaving them she would make both [her own and her husband's] families contemptible.[1]

The wandering life of the renouncer is the very embodiment of independence, and it was not deemed appropriate for women.

This is not to say that women were not allowed religious experience. In some domestic contexts the wife is the chief ritual actor, and the home has generally been perceived to be the proper realm for a woman's religious life, where she practices the asceticism peculiar to her social role, sacrificing herself for her family. The asceticism of the renouncer—wandering, fasting, studying, and meditating—has remained largely closed to women.

Today one does encounter female renouncers. They are called *sannyāsinīs* in Sanskrit, which is the feminine form of the word *sannyāsin*. But they are rare. Somewhat greater scope for women is allowed in modernist Hindu movements such as the Ārya Samāj.

The Ārya Samāj is a Hindu revivalist group that was founded in 1875. It advocates the reconstruction of Indian religion and society on the basis of the ideals of the oldest Hindu scriptures, the Vedas. Despite the ancient sources upon which it draws, the program of the Ārya Samāj is in many ways consistent with that of nineteenth- and twentieth-century social reformers. For instance, according to the Ārya Samāj the division of society into castes was not the same in Vedic times as in later classical Hinduism, so some Ārya Samājists have worked to change the caste system, especially trying to end discrimination against the lowest caste groups. Undoubtedly the most distinctive thing about the Ārya Samāj is its theology. It rejects the polytheism of contemporary Hinduism in favor of belief in a single supreme being. Because this God cannot be represented in any image, the Ārya Samāj condemns the worship of images that traditional Hindus practice.

One of the social reforms that the Ārya Samāj has advocated on the basis of Vedic models has been improvement in the status of women. In traditional Hinduism, women were not allowed to study religious and philosophical works. Svāmī Dayānanda Sarasvatī, the founder of the Ārya Samāj, rejected those rules and argued that women should be educated. Dayānanda's followers opened schools for women to put his ideas into practice. Some of the oldest Hindu girls' schools in northwest India are affiliated with the Ārya Samāj. Not everyone in the Ārya Samāj was willing to grant women equality with men, however. In the early history of the organization, a dispute developed among Ārya Samājists over whether women should have access to advanced professional education, or whether rudimentary schooling was sufficient. Still, the Ārya Samāj has been more progressive in this area than other Hindu groups.

The basic unit of the Ārya Samāj is the local chapter, the members of which gather on a regular basis for communal worship services. At these services, a simple sacrifice is conducted in which herbs and wood are offered in a fire. These services usually include a sermon, and often the preacher is a renouncer and an Ārya Samājist. One occasionally encounters female renouncers in this context, though they are certainly less common than male renouncers. The leaders of the local Ārya Samāj are more often than not men, but women are not excluded from positions of responsibility, and sometimes are elected as officers. Many Ārya Samājes also have regular services that are conducted by and for women, in which individuals can gain the kind of experience that is required for leadership.

The renouncer who adopts a life of seclusion is rather rare in Ārya Samāj circles. Ārya Samāj renouncers instead tend to carry on an active public life, traveling and preaching. Some have even held positions of responsibility in Ārya Samāj institutions after renunciation. The model for Ārya Samāj renouncers is Svāmī Dayānanda himself, who was by all accounts a dynamic preacher and eventually a person of some renown.

Mīrāṃ, the author of *Mīrāṃ Ātma-Kathā,* was born in 1929 in a village called Mehetpur in the Punjab. As a child and young woman she was called Kamlā, and only adopted the name Mīrāṃ upon initiation as a renouncer, but for simplicity's sake we will call her Mīrāṃ throughout this introduction. Mīrāṃ was the eighth girl in her family. Disappointed that she was not a boy, Mīrāṃ's parents were joyful a couple of years later when they finally had a son. Despite the many children, Mīrāṃ's family was well off. Her father owned a cloth store, and later a flour mill, brick kiln, and orchards. Mīrāṃ attended a girls' school in her village affiliated with the Ārya Samāj, which was supported by substantial contributions from her father. Though she was a bright student, Mīrāṃ's formal education did not extend beyond secondary school because nothing more was available in her village.

Although Mīrāṃ's father was a committed Ārya Samājist, he was too busy with his work to devote a great deal of time to her religious education. Mīrāṃ was exposed to different forms of Hinduism, and even engaged in religious practices inconsistent with the Ārya Samāj's philosophy. As Mīrāṃ grew she became more narrowly committed to the teachings of the Ārya Samāj, and she also became more active in the affairs of the local chapter. In addition to preaching, especially to women's groups, Mīrāṃ's religious convictions led her to serve the poor and members of lower-caste communities. When she was around eighteen years old, Mīrāṃ came to the realization that marriage might constitute an obstacle to her religious work, and she resolved not to marry. At first Mīrāṃ's parents objected to her decision, but eventually they acquiesced in the face of her determination.

Until her late thirties, Mīrāṃ remained at home serving her family. At the same time she worked to perfect herself by various spiritual exercises. Eventually she became a well-known preacher, and she was invited by Ārya Samāj groups throughout the Punjab to speak on special occasions. For several years Mīrāṃ contemplated the idea of leaving her family to live at the Vanprasth Ashram, an Ārya Samāj religious center in the town of Jwalapur near Hardwar in Uttar Pradesh. Finally in 1966, Mīrāṃ was able to convince her parents to go along with this. They moved from their village to Delhi, to live with her younger brother, and the family home was rented out. Mīrāṃ took up residence in the ashram. In April of 1966 a special ceremony was conducted to initiate her as a permanent celibate student.

Mīrāṃ's early years in the ashram were marked by continuing experimentation with various spiritual disciplines and by further education in language, religion, and philosophy. By 1969 she was being drawn into an active life of public preaching again. Eventually a regular routine developed of residence in the ashram during the winter months and traveling to speaking engagements through the rest of the year. In the winter, Mīrāṃ concentrated on writing articles for Ārya Samāj newspapers and composing books that she distributed on her preaching tours. Most of Mīrāṃ's books are religious in character, such as collections of sermons, commentaries on scriptural verses, and hymns. As people came to know of her through her preaching and writing, Mīrāṃ received more and more invitations to speak. She maintained a heavy schedule, sometimes speaking in two neighboring towns on a single day.

Most organizations paid Mīrāṃ a fee for her speeches, sometimes a substantial amount. Rather than spend this money on herself, Mīrāṃ donated it to the poor or used it to support her publications. Although Mīrāṃ at one time begged as a part of her initiation as a renouncer, she never had to depend on charity for her living. Her father had arranged it so that the rent from the family home went to Mīrāṃ. Eventually Mīrāṃ decided to sell the house. She donated a part of the proceeds to charity, and deposited the rest in the bank for her maintenance. Because of the financial support that ultimately derived from her parents, Mīrāṃ was able to use her speaking fees for some good purpose other than her own needs.

For several years Mīrāṃ had wanted to become a renouncer, but she postponed her decision because her mother had forbidden it. After her mother's death, and with the blessing of her younger brother, Mīrāṃ was initiated as a renouncer on April 13, 1979. This ritual was theoretically a turning point in Mīrāṃ's life, and the event is one that she describes at some length in her autobiography. Yet she maintained her earlier routine, writing in the winter months and traveling and preaching when the weather was better. Her renunciation did not mark an absolute break from her family. On the contrary, she became a renouncer only with her brother's permission. Still, there is no denying that within the context of the Hindu tradition, Mīrāṃ is a woman of outstanding independence. This continued up to 1985, when she wrote her autobiography, *Mīrāṃ Ātma-Kathā,* and it is still true today.

Mīrāṃ's autobiography is 284 pages long. Other than a one-page introduction, it is not divided into chapters. Written in very simple Hindi, *Mīrāṃ Ātma-Kathā* is not a great literary work. Although it contains passages that describe the author's spiritual exercises, much more of the text is given over to accounts of preaching tours, and it is unlikely to become a spiritual classic. Yet the book does give the reader an understanding of one woman's life as a renouncer. And it was written for a lofty goal, to show other women that such a life is possible. After describing her own work as a renouncer, Mīrāṃ writes, "I have written an autobiographical book for this reason, so that this tradition will continue unbroken after my death when other women read it and leave home."

In the first selection of the following translation Mīrāṃ describes her initial decision not to marry, the beginnings of her ascetic practice, and her continuing involvement with the Ārya Samāj. The second selection concerns Mīrāṃ's departure from home to live in the Vanprasth Ashram, including some of the financial arrangements that had to be made. It begins with Mīrāṃ seeking the advice of Mahātmā Ānand Svāmī, a noted Ārya Samāj leader. The final selection comes from the end of the account of Mīrāṃ's initiation as a renouncer, a ritual directed by a scholar named Rāmprasād. It includes speeches that she and her brother made at that time, as well as some indication of her continuing work as a preacher after her initiation. The translation is from Ārya Mīrāṃyati, *Mīrāṃ Ātma-Kathā* (Jwalapur: the author, 1985), pp. 18–22, 65–69, and 217–24.

Further Reading

See J. E. Llewellyn, *The Arya Samaj as a Fundamentalist Movement* (Delhi: Manohar Book Service, 1993). Also relevant are Catherine Ojha, "Female Asceticism in Hinduism: Its Tradition and Present Condition," *Man in India* 61:3 (September

1981), 254–85; and Katherine Young, "Hinduism," in *Women in World Religions,* edited by Arvind Sharma (Albany: State University of New York Press, 1987), pp. 59–103.

THE DECISION NOT TO MARRY

In 1947, when my age was around eighteen, Pakistan was created. In just those days a certain change began in my life. Sometimes I would go sit in a deserted place and think, "If I am bound in the bonds of marriage then all my work of service will be lost. This life is invaluable. I should make it fruitful by spending it in social service." Thinking thus, I made a firm decision, "I will not marry." I told my mother about this and said, "You tell father for me." When my father heard he began to say, "How can this be? I have already seen a young man. I have made the arrangements for an engagement." He had called my uncles from Delhi for this. They had both come. The next morning they all sat together and they sent my mother saying, "Call Kamlā and bring her here." I went and my father began to say, "You should marry. I have found a husband." In answer I said, "I have no desire to get married. My heart tells me that I should remain unmarried and serve society." At this my grandfather began to say, "Did anyone ever keep their daughter unmarried?" I did not think it appropriate to say more at this time. When they were all elder to me, should I talk back to them over and over? During a conversation a day or two later I gave my mother my final answer, "On the day that everyone is going to force me to marry I will run away. Then what will it profit anyone?"

Hearing this, everyone was silent. The entire family had to bow before my firm desire. There was no limit to my happiness. A second chapter began in my life from this point. My father was very wealthy, as I have written earlier. Because I was the daughter of a rich man I wore gold jewelry and fine silk clothing. Now I thought, "If I am going to remain a celibate student, why shouldn't I wear plain jewelry?" I took off all the gold, which some years later I gave away in the dowry of a poor girl. I took off the imported cloth and gave it to people. I had two or three outfits made of pure hand-spun cloth and I began to wear them. There was a small village nearby where hand-spun cloth was made in those days, which I got for six annas per yard.

In the same way there was a change in my daily routine, too. From morning until going to bed at night I followed a regular program. The whole day passed and I did not know where it had gone. In the hot weather I slept alone on the roof of the third story of our house. At night I would go to sleep after repeating God's name over and over and a Vedic verse, using a rosary to count. I kept a diary. At night I would sit and take stock in it, to see that I had not lied that day, or become angry, or spoken harsh words to someone. If I had committed one of the those sins then I would repeat God's name for another round of the rosary as a penance. If there were two lapses, then I would do this two times.

If five or seven, then I would say that many rosaries. I would not go to bed without doing this. I even kept a cane with which I would strike myself on the back three or four times thinking, "Why this oversight? Now you will have to engage in spiritual exercises and make yourself a master of them."

Once Svāmī Kṣamānand came to the Ārya Samāj. I and my father thought that in the morning we would arrange a sacrifice and sermon, and have some people over to eat. I got up at four in the morning to make the lentils and went to the back room to get a big pot. Just when I had set foot outside the room, the ceiling fell in. When everyone in town had come to hear the svāmī's sermon, at the very beginning he said, "Let us together thank God out of whose mercy Kamlā just barely escaped injury. This was the result of her good deeds." Everyone was surprised to hear this. After the sermon, everyone expressed their good wishes to my mother and father.

Previously we did not offer sacrifice daily in our house. There were sacrifices in the women's samāj on Tuesdays and in the men's samāj on Sundays. On one occasion, Mahātmā Ārya Bhikṣu came. We arranged a sacrifice and sermon at our home. Many people gathered to hear him. When the mahātmā began to perform the sacrifice he asked, "Sir, you don't have any bad habits, do you?" Father said, "I smoke a pipe and have stomach trouble." He said, "Then I will perform a sacrifice. First vow, 'I will not smoke a pipe.' " Father gave his word and he kept it, so that he did not smoke up to his death. The second question was, "Do you sacrifice in your home daily?" Father said, "No. I have to go out to the fields early in the morning, so I don't have time." He said, "Do it in the evening when you come back from the well." For a few days we performed the sacrifice in the evening, but it did not seem right. So we began to do it every day in the morning. Even if I was sick, no matter how much I had to do, still we did not neglect the sacrifice. If I had to go some place, I would only go if I took the things for the sacrifice along.

DEPARTURE FOR THE ASHRAM

Then I said to him [Mahātmā Ānand Svāmī], "Father, I don't feel like going back home. My desire is to start living in Vanprasth Ashram." He began to say, "Daughter, what will you do if you start living in the ashram now? You have a good deal of work at the Ārya Samāj at home. Along with that there is the care of your mother and father. Beyond that you can do whatever good thing you want." The svāmī knew my father well. He was aware of all these matters because of that. I complied with his order and went back home. Once there, I began to do the work of the Ārya Samāj as before. Daily services continued in a good manner. There was happiness and relaxation at home. In town I encountered love and sympathy. But my mind told me, "I should go to the ashram and learn the Vedas and other religious works and the Sanskrit language, and study the books written by Dayānanda."

When my age was thirty-seven, one evening I was conversing with my father.

I indicated to him, "My heart says that I should go now and live in Vanprasth." At that time, without answering, he sat silent. The next morning, when he was getting ready to go to work after breakfast, he said to me, "Kamlā, were you saying last night that you will go to the Vanprasth Ashram? I have seen the ashram. The happiness that you have here you won't find there. Here everyone accepts what you say. They sit at home and work. There, gathering wood in the forest, no one loves anyone else. Everyone is busy with their own work." He said this. I replied, "It's not like that." Then he began to say to me, "No, no. Come near me and let's talk."

I went and stood beside him. He was sitting in a chair in the courtyard. He put a stool in front of me and said, "Sit down." I began to speak my piece and I said, "You have done so much work for the Ārya Samāj throughout your life. Now my wish is that I go to the ashram and engage in spiritual exercises and give up all my activities here. You have done a good deal of work. You have given so much to charity, you have helped the poor. Your fame has spread not only throughout the city but in all of Jallandhar District. But now you have become weak. So I want to make sure that you will not be troubled." He listened to what I had to say along these lines, and then a little later he went off to work.

Now only a week had passed when in the evening he returned home and began to say, "Listen, Kamlā. I accept your decision." Hearing this I was amazed, "What's this?" He said, "Today I made a deal to sell the land in the orchard that is in your name. But I only have a verbal agreement, it won't be written out until tomorrow. Tomorrow he will bring a down payment." I was happy beyond words. It was as if a pauper had found a treasure. Until late in the evening we three sat and talked about what we would have to do. I said, "In the house we will keep a tenant, and the factory we can give to someone to live in for free."

The next day those people came and gave a down payment of eleven hundred rupees and had the deed written, and the matter was settled. I was even more joyful. Now we began to sell household items. Some we distributed to the poor for free. For the house we got a tenant for five rupees per month, and we made out a lease. We included the five rupees rent so that in future the tenant would not try to claim ownership of the house.

On the day that the land sale had to be registered I had to go along, since it was in my name. Sardār Hajārsimh was the registrar in Nakodar. His message came to take me along. I, my father, and the purchaser all three went to the court in Nakodar. I told my father, "I don't know anything about these matters. You think about it and have the transaction registered." Later in the afternoon the registration was completed and twenty-three thousand rupees were counted and placed my hands. I gave the money to my father. And I blessed the farmer who was standing there. "May God make this land profitable for you." I was very happy it had been sold. For me it was a fetter. And today God broke this fetter and opened the way to go from home to the ashram. After this I and my father went to Punjab National Bank in Nakodar and deposited the money in my father's name.

I went to the bazaar to buy the things that I would need for living in the ashram at that time. And then we both went back to Mehetpur. One person we met on the road said, "What did you do? You gave away land worth one hundred thousand rupees for twenty-three thousand."

Another said, "What did you do? Are you going to move away and leave all of us?" I was listening to all of this as I went along and thought to myself, "What has happened is only what is good for me. What else should we have done?" When we, father and daughter, came to the house, then my father said to my mother, "Look. Your daughter has come with the things that she needs to move to the ashram. Even now she is separated from us." My mother's idea was, "Go to the ashram, but just don't become a renouncer. Then how would I be able to see my most beloved daughter?"

RENOUNCING

Now Professor Rāmprasād said, "Some time should be given to Mīrām." As soon as I sat on the stage many people loaded down my neck with garlands. I humbly said to everyone with respect, "Today a desire that I have had for years has been fulfilled. Dropdī Devī, my mother who gave me birth, used to say, 'Daughter, don't wear the orange clothing in front of me.' After her death I made a firm decision that now I will definitely becoming a renouncer. For this purpose, from that time I began to read very carefully about the duties of a renouncer in *Saṃskar Vidhi* and *Satyārth Prakāś,* which were written by Svāmī Dayānanda. Now my age is fully fifty years, too.

"Whatever work I have done until today has been the result of such firm decisions. Even when my mother and father died I didn't go home. Some people who live in the ashram said, 'You should go home.' But once I had taken a vow it would never be broken. For some years I had given up going to marriages and such things in the family. I have upheld this vow until now. What was all of this? It was the preparation for renouncing that was being done.

"I have served the Ārya Samāj since childhood. I have spent my entire life up to today in the work of the Vedic religion. During whatever life I have left, God willing, I will continue to work in this way by word and by my writings. And upon leaving this body, in my next life I will be born a human. After wearing a loincloth and performing asceticism in the jungle I will come back to the world and do the work of the Vedic religion. In the same manner as before, I will not take for myself whatever fees I receive. Rather I will give them wherever there is a need.

"I want to say one thing especially to all of you. This is it. My private desire is that I live for twenty-five more years and will continue to do the work of the Vedic religion. And at the end, like Vidyānand Videh, I will abandon this perishable body on the stage, giving a sermon.

"In the future what God desires will come to pass. This body is made up of the five elements. It could be that illness will come sometime. You will have to care for me. Don't say, 'Go home.' I will allow only you to help me. If you don't look after me when I am sick, then I will drag my bed into the meeting hall and I won't let you have services." At this people on all sides began laughing. "Now in just a few minutes I will go to beg for alms. My request to all of you is just to place one rupee in my begging bowl. Because whatever donations I get I will have to distribute.

"Yes, there is a rule that renouncers must beg. This is what I want. Whenever I return from traveling far for Vedic preaching and I need food, then I will beg for alms." In the end I said, "My prayer to God is that he will protect the honor of my body." After speaking, I got down from the stage.

Then the secretary of the ashram said, "Kamlā's brother Maheś has come from Delhi. I request that he also say something on this occasion." I began to think, "My beloved Maheś has never given speeches in public. How will he talk?" But he began to speak in very beautiful words.

"Members of this assembly, who are worthy of honor and welcome, you have been sitting for a long time and you must be tired. I don't want you to have to sit here much longer. Today is a day of great good fortune that my older sister has taken the initiation into renunciation. Her becoming a renouncer is a matter of pride not only for our family, but it is a matter of pride for the whole Ārya world. Respected sister, you are mine no longer, now you belong to everyone. My only hope is that you will look after them now.

"I thank you all very, very much who have come here from far away. It is such great good fortune that the best scholars and renouncers of the Ārya Samāj community have come in great numbers to give their blessings to my sister.

"I bow my head at the feet of the residents of the ashram. I am especially very grateful to the officials who made such fine arrangements. I am a householder, busy in my work. But I feel myself blessed at having the opportunity to be among you."

Then there were the final prayers. Professor Rāmprasād said, "Everyone remain seated. Now the begging of alms is to be done." When I took the begging bowl in my hand and extended it to my beloved brother Maheś to beg for alms, tears began to flow in the eyes of Tejkaur and some other men and women. I wanted to go on, but from all sides people surrounded me and in my bowl placed money, fruit, boxes of sweets, and books.

In the end the chief officiant of the ritual, Ācārya Priyavrat, placed five rupees as alms in my bowl, and with very great respect he bowed at my feet. And he began to say, "From today you are our mother." After that he said, "I want to say one thing to you. Your new name Mīrāṃyati is very good. But you certainly should add the word Ārya at the beginning of your name, so that no one will think, 'This is a traditional Hindu woman.' " I accepted his suggestion, and began to write my name Ārya Mīrāṃyati.

In the end my book, *Yajña Mahimā,* was distributed to all, instead of leftovers from the offering. I don't like to distribute halvah and things like that. So I distributed this book. Then people could go home and learn something from these leftovers. All my family came to my room. Professor Rāmprasād said, "You should eat food given as alms for at least three days." All the women in my part of the ashram came to say, "Take alms from us." For three days I ate only food given as alms in this way.

The next day, April 14, was the day of the final ceremony of the celebration of the raising of the banner against religious hypocrisy in Kankhal. I had received a special invitation from Dr. Hariprakāś. As soon as the sacrifice was finished he stood up and said, "It is our highest good fortune that yesterday our sister was initiated as a renouncer and now she is present in our midst. I request that she come on stage and give us all her blessing."

I said, "It is a thrill that we are all gathered here to celebrate the raising of the banner against religious hypocrisy by Dayānanda. If Dayānanda had not come then, who knows, maybe we would all be worshiping images like others and spending hours in ringing temple bells.

"It is the fruit of Dayānanda's mercy that I have entered the fourth ashram. If my mother and father had not been made Ārya Samājists, then how could I have arrived at this point? Today I am doing Vedic preaching here, and I am also distributing literature that I have written there. I have distributed books written by me in all the educational institutions of Parampuri. I have myself gone to Har ki Pairi [a center of traditional Hinduism] to distribute them. I am extremely happy to have done such work. May God give us all strength so that we all together can do even more preaching of the Vedic religion." When I had done speaking, then Dr. Hariprakāś stood up and he started to say, "Now we will all welcome our mother." He told the photographer, "Take a picture." And he gave me a copy of a Vedic verse in a large frame and placed a garland around my neck.

Right away I had to go from there by car to the Gurukul Mahāvidyālaya in Jwalapur. I saw that the arrangements were not finished. When I asked, they gave me the answer, "Professor Śersiṃh's wife had not come. For this reason the women's conference was postponed. Even so your lecture is scheduled."

I gave an exposition on Ārya culture. And then I said, "Send me quickly. Because from twelve o'clock I keep a vow of silence."

The next day after this, there was a celebration at our ashram. Women from the Hardwar women's samāj came and began to say, "Mother, you have arranged the celebrations at the Jwalapur women's samāj. Please arrange a celebration for our samāj as well. If not more, it should be at least for one day, that is our wish. But we do not have any money and none is coming in, so how can we do it?" I said, "Take however much money you need from me. I will give you assistance, but you must exert some effort, too." Having discussed all this I explained things to them. I wrote an announcement and they took it with them.

Note

1. Georg Buhler, trans., *The Laws of Manu* (New York: Dover Publications, 1969; first published as vol. 25 of The Sacred Books of the East in 1886), 5.147–49.

—32—

The Prince with Six Fingers

Kirin Narayan

This is an ancient tale retold by a modern holy man in the town of Nasik in the state of Maharashtra, in western India. The story itself occurs as early as the *Mahābhārata Saṃhita* of Jaimini, with variants in Buddhist and Jain literature. Moriz Winternitz declared in his *History of Indian Literature* that "the story of Candrahāsa and Viṣayā is of importance to the literature of the world," and refers to variants in Jain and Buddhist literature as well as in European literature from the *Gesta Romanorum* to poetry by Schiller.

In short, the text below is one variant of a tale that spans extensive time and space, transmitted through written collections and in oral retellings alike. Swāmiji, the holy man who told this story, was born in the southern state of Karnataka, with Kannada as his first language. However, since his teens he had wandered throughout India on spiritual quests, settling down on a mountain sacred to the Mother Goddess near Nasik in 1956, when he was thirty-nine years old. When I arrived as a graduate student in anthropology, tape recorder in hand, Swāmiji was in his late sixties. Due to failing health, he had moved from his mountain residence to live in town, occupying an apartment next door to his doctor. Stretched out in an aluminum deck chair beside an altar, he met with visitors each day. Among his visitors were local people and also a scattering of Westerners from England, France, Australia, and the United States. With my ambiguous identity as local woman (my father is from Nasik) and foreign academic, I often found myself in the position of translating Swāmiji's vivid and unabashedly ungrammatical Hindi into English.

In reproducing the story below, I adopt a performance-oriented approach: that is, locating the text squarely in the lived context of its retelling for an audience that included an inquisitive anthropologist. I include notes on what inspired Swāmiji—always a compelling raconteur—to remember this story, and his interactions with his listeners. Although Swāmiji often told stories for didactic purposes, he tended not to spell out the moral precisely but rather to leave a tale's interpretation open to his listeners. Reader-response theory has alerted us to the variety of readings a text may receive, and so it should be kept in mind that the meanings I highlight may not match what my fellow listeners understood, or what a reader viewing this transcription might surmise.

Most broadly, the story is about destiny. In this Hindu construction of destiny, hardship and success are intertwined: the worst catastrophe can carry the seeds of a brilliant triumph. Further, destiny is located within the framework of religious belief. Born in the lap of luxury, Candrahāsa sinks to penurious vulnerability on account of his stars. However, he later swallows a revered holy man's sacred śalagrāma—a round stone representing Viṣṇu—and incorporates its powers. Thanks to his magnetic luster coupled with piety, he is saved from execution, adopted by a king, blessed by the Mother Goddess with an invincible sword, and miraculously saved from further plots for his murder. By the end of the story, he has acquired two wives, two kingdoms, and also, it is suggested, the possibility of controlling an entire empire of disparate kingdoms. Even his adversary Duṣṭbuddhi ("Wicked Mind") is transformed through the blessings of the Mother Goddess into Subuddhi, ("Good Mind"). This would suggest an allegorical interpretation, advanced by one of Swāmiji's disciples, in which Candrahāsa represents the individual self unaware of its own expansive grandeur, largely on account of the machinations of an illusion-spinning mind.

Although it is centered around a heroic male figure, this tale gives women important roles. It is an old woman who rescues Candrahāsa as an infant. Similarly, the spunky and nubile minister's daughter. Viṣayā, rescues Candrahāsa from murder by altering the letter he carries. Throughout Swāmiji's version of the tale, ultimate power resides in the hands of Bhagavatī, the many-armed, fierce, and compassionate Mother Goddess whom he worshiped.

Further Reading

Kirin Narayan, *Storytellers, Saints and Scoundrels: Folk Narrative in Hindu Religious Teaching* (Philadelphia: University of Pennsylvania Press, 1989).

On the afternoon of September 16, 1985, Swāmiji had been discussing the nature of the divine inner self and how to meditate upon its nature. "Who am I? This is the most important question. Meditation is a dialogue about this. One part of you poses the question, the other part puts forward answers. . . ." Swāmiji lay in his aluminum deck chair, ocher robes wrapped around his waist, expounding in this vein. His eyes were earnest behind black-rimmed spectacles, his voice weighted with seriousness. An overhead fan blew a cool incense-scented breeze through the room.

I sat among the handful of listeners, fidgetting with my tape recorder. After all, I hoped to document storytelling as a form of Hindu religious teaching, and was especially interested in folk narratives that featured holy men like Swāmiji himself. I couldn't decide whether this discourse on meditation was relevant to my project or not, and so I fitfully switched my recorder on and off. Swāmiji had perhaps discerned my unrest, for when he suddenly stood up, he shot me a question: "What are your professors going to do with this?"

As a young, unmarried, female student, I had often tried to gain some credibility for my work by invoking the interest of my distant professors: my metonymn for male authority and the prestige of American-based academe. But questioned directly, I knew well that my professors were not interested in this material in any way beyond whether it would help me complete a dissertation to their satisfaction. I began to mumble something about documenting Indian culture. "But what will your *professors* do with it?" Swāmiji repeated.

"They won't do anything with this," I had to confess, "It's for me." I took a deep breath and adopted Swāmiji's own idiom of the will of the Divine Mother. "If it's the Goddess' wish, I'll write a book." I said. "One can write a Ph.D. dissertation on anything, and I've chosen this. Many holy men tell stories, and you tell these stories, too. Your stories contain your teachings: your stories and your spiritual teachings are the same thing." I made this speech with self-possession, but inwardly I was shaken. Just the day before, Swāmiji had stated that everything in the world was a matter of self-interest and business: even I was taking his stories for a business. Even as I had smarted, I also could see that Swāmiji's stories were for me a medium for academic exchange: lectures, fellowships, books, jobs, invitations for edited volumes might all result from collecting them. "Don't just take these stories," Swāmiji had admonished, "Understand them." Today, his asking about my professors reopened the painful issue of ethics in fieldwork, and so I felt that I needed to clarify my purpose.

"*Hañ-hañ-hañ,*" Swāmiji let out a stream of assent when I finished speaking. Then he went inside to spit out some tobacco. I seemed to have reassured him of my best intentions, for when he returned he was grinning from ear to ear. He resettled himself in his armchair, and started to question me exuberantly about my familiarity with beloved Indian stories.

"Do you know why the elephant has a trunk? There are so many stories from India that you must have heard. You must have heard the story of Gaṅgā [River Ganges], you must have heard the story of the Pāṇḍavas [in the *Mahābhārata* epic]. Haven't you heard Candrahāsa's story? No? What are you saying? You haven't heard about Candrahāsa? There was a king in the past . . . you're taping this, aren't you? You can tape this one, it's really good. . . . "

Swāmiji launched into the story, and I translated after each sentence on behalf of the French woman and Jewish-American man present. Swāmiji's voice unfolded an alternate reality, while in the background we were reminded of the bustle of everyday life in Nasik by a screech of horns, putter of motorcycles, ring of bicycle bells, and occasional cries of vendors. On the windowsill behind Swāmiji, sparrows hopped and twittered.

There was a king. He was a very good king. He had a queen. They had no children. They worshiped God because they were childless. This went on and on, and finally they had a child. When the child was born, they summoned the pandits. They summoned them and asked them to cast a horoscope. [*"Horoscope," Swāmiji echoes Kirin's translation into English.*] As the pandits drew the horoscope, they said, "The child has a very auspicious future."

The king was overjoyed. He distributed fine milk sweets, he distributed milk. He presented many gifts to the brahmans. The pandits said [*hesitantly*], "King, what can be done? There's just one planet that's a little badly placed. He has a great future, but there's just this little thing wrong."

"What is it?" the king asked [*with anxious haste*].

"He has six fingers on one hand. And one planet badly placed. Because of this, within eleven days of the child's birth, his mother and father will die. The entire kingdom will fall into the hands of wicked enemies. Otherwise, this child has the future of a great emperor."

[*Swāmịji unexpectedly bursts into laughter, eyes creasing behind his spectacles, and toothless gums exposed. "What, Gulelal!" he says, addressing the American who sits cross-legged in Indian clothes at the back of the room. "Look at what destiny can be like! Just one bad planet can make havoc." 'Gulelal' nods. It is hard to understand just what Swāmiji finds so hilarious—the ironies of destiny? the hubris of householders? the brahmans underplaying impending catastrophe?—but his laughter is infectious. Everyone in the room laughs along as he continues, amusement sputtering through his words.*]

When the pandits said this, the mother and the father worried about what they were to do. "Now we have this child, how do we get rid of him?" They were stumped. The pandits, on the other hand, had received their gifts, and off they went.

The wicked enemy king heard this news. "This king has had such a child, with this sort of life predicted, and his kingdom is about to be destroyed." His minister came, bringing a big army. They surrounded the kingdom on all four sides. The army [*"military"*] emerged for the battle. Then there was a terrible war.

As they fought, the army was defeated. Then the king left the fort to fight, too. In the midst of the battle, he was also killed. Someone immediately brought this news to the queen: "the king is dead." The queen heard this. "Now what should I do? I'll fall into enemy hands, and will be dishonored. It's better that I die. But I have this eleven-day-old child. It's just ten days since he was born."

There was this old woman, a maid who served the queen. The queen wrapped the baby in dirty rags and gave him to her: "Take this child." There are secret doors in king's palaces, with secret passages that lead out into the jungle. "Escape through this passage," the queen said, "I'm giving this child to you."

Then she set herself on fire. And the secret door was tightly closed.

The enemy came in. They looked here and there and saw that everything had been burned. They came to the king's quarters and looked around. "The king had a wife and a child. What happened to them?" There was just ash there. "They probably died and are now ash," they said. So they captured the fort, and the kingdom was in their possession.

The old woman took the child and went far off to another kingdom. She was an old woman, what did she have? Nothing. "If I ask for alms and receive something, I'll feed it to the child. He's a king's child, but now he's become a beggar, look at what a person's destiny can be! He has no clothes to wear, nothing. And he has no idea who he is."

Then after two or three years, the old woman died, too. He had no clothes to wear, and no food to eat. He was a tramp. He didn't even had a loin cloth. He wandered around with his "Gaṇapati" swinging. [*Swāmiji laughs again, though his translator is embarrassed. Gaṇapati, the elephant-headed deity, is clearly standing in for a penis. "He wandered around naked," Kirin glosses over the translation.*] He wandered all over the place. Then one day he found some cloth and wore this as he wandered. He didn't have to go to school or anything. He lived like one of the beggar's children on the roadside here [*Swāmiji extends an arm to encompass the squalor on the streets beyond this quiet enclave*]. What do beggar kids do? They play marbles together [*Swāmiji demonstrates, taking aim at an imaginary marble with his right forefinger pulled back by the left*]. He kept company with these sorts of children. They'd look around outside the houses of rich people to see if anything was thrown out that they could scavenge. If something was lying outside, they'd eat it. This is what their life was like. They'd eat what had fallen through the drains.

This went on, and there was one big house. Consider it to be Kirin's house. A great Swāmiji had come there: a big Swāmiji like Swāmi R. [*Kirin laughs tentatively, for though Swāmiji often includes people from his audience in his stories, this is the first time that she, her grandfather's Victorian mansion in Nasik, or her family's longstanding affection for young Swāmi R. have ever found their way into a traditional plot*]. This Swāmi had many śalagrāmas, round stones representing Viṣṇu. He was one who did a lot of ritual worship. It took him at least five or six hours to perform his worship. Many people used to come for audience with him. He kept all these śalagrāmas in a dish and washed them as worship. They were very round and small, and were washed as they were worshiped.

He wasn't exactly like Swāmi R., he was an older Swāmiji. As he was washing, he left behind one of the śalagrāmas. He took each one out, wiped it, and kept it aside. But one śalagrāma remained in the dish. There was a maid there, like Līlabai [*who sweeps Swāmiji's apartments each day*]. She took the water from the ritual wash, and she tossed it down the drain.

What happened next was that the child was out wandering to scrounge for food that might have fallen around wealthy people's houses. He knew that wealthy people ate well. As he came to this house he spotted a round stone by the window. He thought "This will be a good marble." And he kept it.

That evening when he was playing with the other children he used this as a marble. Whenever he played with this, he won the game. This marble was better than all the others, and he won with every child. All the children thought, "He has a wonderful marble. Whenever he plays, he wins."

He defeated all the children, even those bigger than him. Then the bullies said, "Give us your marble."

But this child had understood that he had a good marble and that was why he was winning. "I won't give it to you," he said [*in a stern voice*].

"What do you mean you won't give it to us? We won't let you off. Hand it over!"

"No, I won't."

"What, you won't give it to us?" And the children began to chase him. He ran away. He had nothing to hide it in; no box, nothing. Where could he hide it? He put it in his mouth. Then they caught him and began to beat him up, saying, "Spit it out." Instead he swallowed it. "I ate the marble," he said.

There was no marble any more. What to do? The other children left.

When this marble reached his stomach, a lustre came over his face. With this shine on his face, everyone who looked at him was drawn to him. Everyone started to say, "Child, come to our house, come to our house!" Every day, people were inviting him to their homes for food. Some gave him clothes, some called him to eat. Everyone loved him. He became the child of every house.

The minister there had a son of the same age. This boy was going to have his "hair-cutting" [*Swāmiji enunciates the English words*] ceremony. He was about eight years old. It was a special day, so people from all the surrounding towns were called: the brahmans. Then all the brahmans went around saying "In the minister's house there'll be a child's tonsure. A lot of food will be distributed. And lots of gifts will be given."

They asked this child, "Will you come? Come along too! You'll get some good food."

"Let's go," he said. So they took him along too. Everyone was sitting down to eat. There was a very long line of people eating. The minister was also personally serving everyone, pouring water. So as he was coming around he saw the child. He asked those people, "Whose child is this? He looks like the moon among the stars. He has the auspicious marks of a king. Whose child is this with such a shine on his face? Whose child is this?"

The brahmans said, "We have no idea whose child this is. He has no mother, no father. He's lives in our town. In the future, this child will be the emperor of our entire country. We have all given him this blessing. A brahman's words are never false. He will truly become an emperor. He has all the right attributes for it."

When they said this, the minister became suspicious. "That king had a son. The brahmans had said that this boy would be an emperor recognized by the world. He had some trouble with a planet, so within eleven days his kingdom was to be destroyed. But later he was to become an emperor. It's possible that he survived. He would have been of this age. Maybe this is that very boy."

The minister actually hoped to make his son the emperor of this country.

He wanted to start out by making him king of the region. He said to the brahmans [*nonchalantly*], "That's fine. I can bring up this child. I'll have him educated. Why should you all trouble yourselves about him? Give him to me."

"Fine," they said. When no one knew whose child he was, how could it matter who he went with? "You bring him up." They left the child behind and took off.

The minister took the child inside with him. He said [*sternly*], "You stay in this room!" So the child stayed put in the room. Then the minister called two Caṇḍāla outcastes: executioners! At twelve midnight, he said, "There's a child sleeping in that room. Take him to the jungle and hack him up. Bring me some token that he is dead. Then I'll give you two thousand rupees."

"Fine," they said. What did it matter to them? They proceeded inside and threw open the door. They grabbed hold of the boy.

He asked, "Who are you?"

They had huge moustaches [*Swāmiji twirls his hand by a cheek*], they had red eyes. And he was just a little child. "Who are you?" he asked.

"How does who we are matter to you?" they said [*fiercely*]. "Come on!"

He began to cry. But who was there to heed his crying?

"If you cry we'll beat you!" they said. Smacking him and striking him, they dragged him off. There was nobody to hear his cries. So they took him to the jungle. It was a dark and terrifying jungle. When they arrived, they sat down and began to consult with each other. "This is a good spot to do it," they said.

The boy asked [*in a worried voice*], "What will you do to me? What have I done to you?"

They said, "We're going to hack you up!"

"What did I do wrong? Why are you murdering me?"

They said, "We don't know anything about all that. We're supposed to execute you anyway."

"But if I haven't done anything, then why are you going to execute me?"

"We don't know anything about that, but we're going to execute you."

He said, "All right. If you must execute me, execute me. But first let me worship Bhagavān."

He started to worship Bhagavān. As he worshiped, these people watched. Compassion crept into their minds. "What are we going to gain by killing this child?" they said. "We'll get two thousand rupees. But that's not going to last us all our lives. We too have children. What has this child done anyway? He has six fingers on one hand. If we cut off one of these fingers, we'll get two thousand rupees. We'll get every rupee. And we'll also be doing a service to this child. We'll tell him never to return to this country. And then we can set him free."

They told the child. "Look, don't ever come back here! We have been offered two thousand rupees, but we won't kill you. We'll just cut off one finger and take it with us. Don't ever come here again."

"Fine," he said.

So they grabbed hold of him and sliced off one finger. He fell down unconscious. They left.

He lay there crying out, "Water! Water! Water!" But he was all alone in the jungle. Only the lions and other wild animals heard him.

The next day what happened is that another king came to the jungle. As he entered the jungle, he heard the cries of a child: "Water! Water!" Kings always carry a flask of water. He rushed to the place the cries were coming from. He poured water into the child's mouth. The child felt stronger. Then he lifted him up. "Get up," he said. Then the king took the child with him.

The previous night the king had had a dream. He was childless. In the dream, he was told to go hunting in the jungle. He thought Bhagavān had given him this child. He was overjoyed.

He immediately sent his police [*Swāmiji uses the English word—"polis"*] ahead to the kingdom. "Bhagavān has given me a child!" he said, "Tell the queen that all the women should stand by their doorways with auspicious pots of water on their heads to welcome us. Prepare the horses and elephants for our arrival. I'm coming with a child. The military should stand at attention."

He took the child with him. He took him, and presented him to the queen, "Look, Bhagavān has given you this child." They made this child the crown prince. They gave him the name Candrahāsa.

Then he worships Bhagavatī, the Goddess. Then the Goddess gives him a sword like the moon, just like a sickle moon. If he fights with this in his hand, nobody can defeat him. This is what the Goddess gives him. This is why he is called Candrahāsa. Then as the prince in this kingdom he learned how to govern. He lives here in a nice way until he is eighteen years old. [*As though summarizing a long passage, Swāmiji has switched from past to present tense: then he resumes in past tense.*]

Previously, this particular king had often been defeated. He had to pay fealty to many other kings. He was a subsidiary king to the very king who had acquired Candrahāsa's father's kingdom. He owed a lot of money to this king. One day the accounts were drawn up, and all the money was sent at once. It was sent to the other kingdom with a police escort.

Now in this kingdom was the minister Duṣṭabuddhi ["Wicked Mind"]. He was the one who killed the boy's father, the same one who tried to kill the boy. The money was sent to him. He saw all the money. He was very pleased. And he told the police, "You can eat here. It's good that you sent this money to us after so many years."

The police said, "We won't eat today. We'll just leave."

"Why won't you eat today?"

They said, "Today is ekādaśī, the eleventh day of the lunar fortnight [a day many devotees of Viṣṇu fast]. One shouldn't eat on an ekādaśī."

"Why not? Why shouldn't one eat on ekādaśī?"

They said, "This is the order of our prince—

[*"What is it?" Swāmiji asks Mr. Karnad, the retired journalist, who lives nearby and has just come in with another man. Mr. Karnad settles cross-legged on the floor, murmuring something. Swāmiji nods and returns to the story*].

"It's the order of our prince that we shouldn't eat on an ekādaśī."

"But in the past you never did this! How long has this been practiced?"

"We've been doing this ever since our king found a son."

[*Swāmiji returns his attention the new arrivals, and they speak briefly in Kannada, their shared mother-tongue, which none of the rest of us understand. Then he returns with a renewed vigor to Candrahāsa*].

"Ever since then, we've been doing this ekādaśi fast—it has been very good for our country. This is good on two scores. It's good according to your science because look, if you drive a machine every day, it breaks down. If you empty out a boiler once every fifteen days, the fire is stronger when you put something in later. So in this way, just as a person needs to rest after working, so this body-machine needs a rest.

"That's one. Second, this is good as far as food goes. It's good for the entire country. Say there's a city like Bombay with about six million people living there. Consider how much food is consumed there in one day. Say every person eats a half kilo, half of six is three. Three million kilos of food are finished in one day. That much food is saved on a day that people fast. Then there is less need for doctors, since people don't fall sick so much. So this is why we do an ekādaśī fast. We have no sick people and our stocks of food grow. In the past we didn't have enough to eat, but now there's plenty. We are happy."

Duṣṭabuddhi heard this and thought it over. "Your king didn't have a child before," he said, "Where did child come from?"

They said, "One day he went hunting in the jungle and he found this child."

He thought, "This is probably the very child I sent to be executed."

[*From the adjoining rooms, we now hear the voices of children joined together in a chant that Dr. Mukund, Swāmiji's devotee, is teaching. These are children from all over the neighborhood who gather each afternoon for prayers, worship, and consecrated food. From now on, the story continues with this background of sound from the children.*]

Duṣṭabuddhi had a daughter. Her name was Viṣayā. Understand? She had come of age: about fifteen or sixteen years old. She was always asking her father, "When will you marry me off? Get me married!"

Her father loved her a lot. Whenever he went somewhere, she would ask, "Where are you going? When will you get me married?"

"I'll do it, I'll do it," he'd say.

So he sent those people away, saying, "You go. I'll come to your kingdom tomorrow."

The next day he saddled up his horse. "I must see this boy," he thought. As he climbed on his horse, his daughter came there. "Father, where are you going? Where are you off to?"

Whenever someone is leaving you shouldn't ask where they're going. It's a bad omen if you ask where someone is going. So when she asked this, he got angry. "I'm going to look for a boy for you!" he said [*sharply*]. "I'm looking for a boy so I can marry you off. I'm going to arrange your marriage." [*Swāmiji uses the English word, "marriage" as members of the audience chuckle*]. So she went inside laughing. She didn't ask him anything more. So he left.

When the minister arrived in the next kingdom, he understood, "This is the very boy that I wanted to kill. Now he's grown up, he's got a good physique. Nobody can take him on in a fight. He possesses strength. [*"Strength" too is an English word melded effortlessly into Hindi grammar*]. Somehow or other I've got to kill him. What way can this be done?" He thought about it. After all, he was a minister. He pondered [*chin in his hand*].

Then he said, "Oh son, I've become an old man, and I forgot to do this one thing as I was coming here."

"What?" the boy asked, "What is it, Mahārāj? Tell me and I'll do it for you in a flash."

"Look, it's just this one thing I forgot to do. I'll give you a letter for my son. Then he can do it."

"Fine. If you give it to me I'll deliver it."

So Duṣṭabuddhi gave Candrahāsa the letter. He stamped his seal on it. "Don't give it to anyone else, just give it to my son."

"Fine," he said. He took it, and he arrived promptly at twelve or one o'clock. It was very sunny. It wasn't a time that he could meet the son. There was a garden there, with a lake. He gave his horse water, and then he went to sleep under the tree.

Then the minister's daughter came to this very garden to play with her girlfriends. She had a huge retinue of girlfriends along with her. There were many trees there. The girl was hiding from her friends, and she crept to the very place where Candrahāsa lay sleeping. She spotted the letter in his pocket. She looked at it, and from above she could see a little of the writing. "This is my father's handwriting," she said [*Swāmiji uses the English word "handwriting," leaning forward, then very slowly drawing up one hand*]. She stealthily pulled the letter out. He was still in a deep sleep. She examined the handwriting and saw it was her father's.

Now, girls are really smart! She slo-o-owly opened the letter and read it. In it was written, "My dear son Madan. Don't enquire about the family or lineage of the one who carried this letter. As soon as he comes, give him poison (*viṣavā*)."

The girl looked at this and thought, "My father has grown a little old. Instead of writing 'Give him Viṣayā,' he wrote 'Give him viṣavā'. He made a mistake. Instead of a *yā* it's a *vā*. And there's no problem in making a *vā* into a *yā*." She had black collyrium in her eyes, right? So she put took a little on her fingernail, and changed the *vā* into a *yā* [*Swāmiji crooks his little finger with a conspiratorial gleam, as his audience laughs*]. She just lengthened it. Then she closed up the letter, pressed down the seal [clapping one horizontal palm over the other], and left.

Then Candrahāsa woke up. He washed his hands and feet. The minister's son Madan was in the assembly hall. Candrahāsa went in to deliver the letter. Madan looked at the letter. In it was written, "Don't enquire about the family, caste, or lineage of the one who carries this letter. As soon as he comes, just give him Viṣayā." [*Swāmiji wheezes with delighted laughter*] That's what was written.

[*Kirin's tape has snapped to a halt, and in a frantic rush, she inserts a new one.*]

In this it was written, give him Viṣayā with love. ["*In Kannada, we say, 'give poison with love,' Swāmiji explains as an aside.*] "Give her to him with love."

Madan thought, "How can this be? Father isn't even here." So he said to his mother, "Father has written such and such a letter. What should I do?"

His sister, on the other hand, was very happy. "He's such a handsome boy! I haven't ever seen a handsomer one. Brother, I want this man as my husband. You have to get me married immediately. Call the pandits!" [*Laughter rumbles from Swāmiji's listeners at this show of enthusiasm which in real life would be anything but dignified or demure.*]

Then the mother said, "Call the guruji."

So they called for their guruji, the family priest. They showed him the letter. He said, "Look, if a girl doesn't have a father, the elder brother has the right to give her in marriage. Tomorrow isn't an auspicious day. Today is the auspicious day. That's why your father has written such a letter. There's nothing wrong with doing this today."

[*Swāmiji joins his listeners' laughter, his shoulders shaking with merriment.*] Brahmans will do anything at all, as long as they get their payment! So the wedding was performed that evening. The marriage was performed. Instead of giving him poison, they gave him Viṣayā. Look how Bhagavān's play can be!

Then after the wedding Candrahāsa stayed there. The next day Duṣṭabuddhi returned. He thought Candrahāsa was safely dead. He came riding in on his horse. When he arrived, he saw that his house was all decorated. He asked people, "What happened here?"

They said, "Your daughter was married."

"My daughter got married! Whom did she marry?"

"To the boy you sent." [*The switch in tone from alarm to a cool informative tone provokes our laughter, and Swāmiji too is laughing*].

"How did this happen?"

"You wrote the letter, and the marriage was done."

So he went into the house. He said, "Madan, what have you done? What is all this?"

Madan said [*respectfully*], "The wedding has taken place, father"

"What was in the letter I sent you?!"

"I did exactly what you told me to in the letter."

"Bring me the letter" [*abruptly*].

The letter was brought. In this it was written "Viṣayā." "Idiot!" he said, "Get out of my sight. I never wrote such a thing!"

Madan said, "What's happening? If this is what is clearly written but you say you didn't write it, what am I to do? What did I do wrong?"

Duṣṭabuddhi didn't know what to say. "Leave this place immediately!" he ordered. "Don't stand here in front of me. It makes me furious." But he didn't explain what he had actually meant. He didn't open his heart and confide everything. "Just get out of this place," he said.

Madan went straight to the king's palace. The king had had a dream. He had just one daughter. In the dream he was told, "Arrange your daughter's marriage. Then leave the kingdom and retire to become a forest-dweller. Give your kingdom to your son-in-law."

Because of this dream, the king was looking for a boy. At that point the minister's son arrived. The king said to him, "Look, brother. Someone must marry my daughter immediately. I had this dream, this vision. I want a boy who's a prince: a boy with a prince's attributes, bravery, and character. He must be a valiant hero. If you know of such a prince, bring him to me. I need him immediately, for within two days I must go to the forest. I plan to give this person my kingdom. Do you know of any boy like this?"

Madan said [*reflectively*], "Well, there is my sister's husband. I just gave my sister in marriage to him, and he's from the next kingdom. He's a prince: a very fine chap."

"All right, then bring him here."

"Fine," he said.

In the meantime Duṣṭabuddhi had thought, "If my daughter becomes a widow, that's no problem, but my son-in-law must certainly die." He summoned another two Caṇḍāla executioners to do this.

There was a temple to the Goddess at the cremation grounds. Duṣṭabuddhi posted the two executioners there, inside the temple. "This morning a man will come wearing such and such clothes, bearing bananas and coconuts as offerings. When he enters the temple, hack him into two pieces. Then I will give you four thousand rupees. If you don't do this, I'll cut you to bits."

He issued this order, and posted those two men in the temple. He said to Candrahāsa, "Look, whenever there's a wedding in this house, we go to worship the Goddess in the early morning. Take coconuts, bananas and so on, and go worship the Goddess."

"Fine," Candrahāsa said. He took everything with him. He took the bananas and set out. As he went, he met Madan on the road. "Where are you going?" Madan asked [*excitedly*].

He said, "I'm going to the temple."

"Why are you going there?"

"My father-in-law has said that I must go there and worship."

"Leave all that! Go: the king is calling you. You're about to be married to the king's daughter!"

Candrahāsa said, "First I should do my father-in-law's bidding. Otherwise he'll get angry."

"I'll do this for you, let's hurry to the king," said Madan.

"Fine," said Candrahāsa.

Madan escorted him to the king and left him there. "Look, this is the person I was telling you about." He presented Candrahāsa to the king and left.

Madan took the coconuts and other things, and went to the temple. He got there and was cut into two pieces. Yes? Madan was cut into two pieces.

And here, Candrahāsa was married to the king's daughter. After the wedding a howdah was put on an elephant. The couple sat there with the king behind them. The entire army was called out, all the regiments. They went in a procession.

They were moving past the minister's house. The minister was watching everything. "I sent him to be killed and here he is sitting paired with the king's daughter. What's this?"

Duṣṭabuddhi came up and said, "Hey there, I sent you out for worship, and what did you do instead?"

Candrahāsa said, "Madan went to do it."

"All right," he said. Then what had become of Madan? Duṣṭabuddhi raced directly to the temple. When he arrived he saw that Madan was in two pieces. He saw this and he wept bitterly. "Oh Madan, what did I hope, and what actually happened? I thought I would kill this boy and make the entire kingdom yours. I even wanted to marry you to the king's daughter. I wanted to give you the kingdom. And it was I who gave the orders that killed you. If Bhagavān is protecting someone, then nobody can kill him. I tried so many times to kill that boy. But I was never able to kill him. I killed you instead. Now what's the use of staying alive?" And he stabbed himself. He died then and there.

In a little while, Candrahāsa went to the temple. Madan hadn't returned, Duṣṭabuddhi hadn't returned. He went to see what had happened. He went there and saw the Goddess, with both the corpses lying before her. Then he said to Bhagavatī, the Goddess, "Mother, look how you are, so compassionate. This Duṣṭabuddhi tried so hard to kill me. You who are so expert protecting others protected me through such hardship. You protected me. Duṣṭabuddhi did so much conniving to gain the kingdom. And innocent Madan died for no reason. So I too will abandon this body. What will I gain from this kingdom? Take this body too!" He lifted up his sword to stab himself. "Since these people died for it, what's the use of this body?"

Just then the Goddess came and caught hold of his sword. "Don't die! I have a lot of work in store for you." Then she said, "Is there any boon you desire? Request it."

He said, "Bring them all back to life."

They came to life. Then Duṣṭabuddhi ("Wicked Mind") became Subuddhi ("Good Mind"). He became a good character.

This is what happened. This is the story of Candrahāsa.

Emerging from the story frame, Swāmiji addressed me genially, "Did you ever hear this before?"

"No, never," I said, still awed by the length and poetic beauty of the tale. "It's a very lovely story."

"There's a lot to understand in it," Swāmiji reflected.

"Yes, a lot," I agreed. Thinking of my dissertation project highlighting holy men in stories, I observed, "That Swāmiji's śālagrāma, his grace, made the boy what he was. If that śālagrāma hadn't come into the boy's mouth, good fortune would never have come to him."

"No," Swāmiji shook his head. "That was his destiny. His destiny was like that. There was a prediction given on reading his horoscope at the time of his birth. First there would be suffering, then later he would become an emperor. Then Candrahāsa also went to the horse sacrifice that Dharmarāja sponsored. He caught hold of the horse. But Arjuna didn't fight with him, because he was also a devotee of Kṛṣṇa, Kṛṣṇa warned Arjuna, 'If you fight with him you won't be able to defeat him.' So they became friends instead."

"Is this part of the *Mahābhārata?*" I asked.

"This is set in that time, but the story isn't in the *Mahābhārata.*" Swāmiji reflected a minute. Then he added, "Actually, it's possible that it could be in the *Mahābhārata,* in the section in the forest, when Dharmarāja is talking to the sages. How many minutes are there before we have evening worship? Five minutes?"

Swāmiji resumed his conversation with the two Kannada-speaking visitors until it was 6 P.M., and we all rose to go chant with the children.

—33—

How a Girl Became a Sacred Plant

Kirin Narayan

The sacred basil shrub, tulsī (*ocimum sanctum Linn*), is worshiped in upper-caste Hindu households all over India. Usually, tulsī is grown in the courtyard, and is offered water as a part of daily worship. Tulsī beads are frequently worn by devotees of Viṣṇu; tulsī leaves are used for a variety of ritual purposes. Furthermore, the plant is regarded as a goddess, and is a special focus of women's religious life. The wedding of the goddess Tulsī to a form of Viṣṇu is usually celebrated over five days preceding the full moon in the lunar month of Kārttika (October-November).

In Kangra, a valley in the Himalayan foothills of Himachal Pradesh, a rich corpus of women's songs and stories clusters around the worship of Tulsī. Tulsī is often called Sailī, "the green one," in Kangra's regional dialect, Kāngri or Pahāṛi. She is likened to a girl who comes of age and must be wed. Her cycle of annual growth is sung of, month by month, as a budding into womanhood. Her wedding in November is performed with all the symbolic accoutrements of an actual marriage. After her wedding, she is believed to wither away, much as a woman who is married to a stranger from a distant village dies to her previous identity. These five days are known as "five days of Bhiṣma," (*panch bhiṣam*) for (along the lines of convergences familiar in the Hindu calendar), during these five days Bhiṣma of the *Mahābhārata* epic lay dying on his bed of arrows.

Women's rituals in Kangra are usually transmitted across the generations by women themselves, without the intervention of a brahman or a written text. As a result, there is broad variation in ritual behavior between households: many women report having had to learn rituals from scratch when they joined a mother-in-law, as the expected practice was so different from what they had learned at home. Although the auspicious date of a ritual is usually set by the lunar calendar, how the ritual is actually observed and interpreted varies between households in a caste, between castes, and across villages. Due to the practice of women marrying in, several sisters-in-law in the same household might have different ideas of what was entailed in a ritual. However, a mother-in-law's version (learned from her mother-in-law), was usually adhered to.

As a result of this wide latitude in ritual practice and belief, I collected many varying versions of stories about Sailī or Tulsī. An old brahman man recounted the standard textual narrative, in which Tulsī was the wife of the demon Jārasandhā, so chaste that she rendered her husband invincible. To destroy Jārasandhā, Viṣṇu plotted to corrupt Tulsī's virtue. He took on Tulsī's husband's form and slept with her. She cursed him to become a stone, and in return, he cursed her to become a plant.

Women's versions, on the other hand, were woman-centered, with a sympathy toward women's domestic concerns and the anxieties of co-wives. In their stories, Tulsī was always cast as a young virgin rather than as the wife of Jārasandhā. Her love for Kṛṣṇa, the Dark Lord, made for a jealous rivalry with Rukmanī, his chief wife. Usually, it was due to the machinations of the offended co-wife that Tulsī became a plant and Kṛṣṇa, in turn, a stone. In a cultural context where until recently it was acceptable for men to marry more than once, stories like these bear a poignancy for women unable directly to control their domestic fate.

The story below was told by a Rajput woman shortly before the annual marriage of the plant to Kṛṣṇa. I never encountered another version of this particular tale and, in fact, when I outlined it to women of the Sūd merchant caste several villages away, they were horrified: "Sailī as a cobbler? Impossible!" Reproduced in its performance setting, this story should be viewed as one variant of the tale of Tulsī as told in Kangra.

This story derives much of its poetic strength from the inversions that recur throughout. As a cobbler girl of the lowest caste, it is entirely inappropriate that Sailī be wooed by a brahman of the highest caste. Yet, in her innocence, she does not recognize the social inequalities ingrained by caste, and she ends up marrying a pure god, Kṛṣṇa, instead. Kṛṣṇa's chief queen, Rukmanī, cursing a troublesome black crow as being an untouchable Caṇḍāla, is accused of having become an untouchable herself. For while Rukmanī has hired Sailī as a maid, it is she who is slaving away at household work while Sailī revels in the pleasures of "bathing"—a common allusion to sexual relations in Indian folk narratives—with Kṛṣṇa. There is a similar echo and inversion in the theme of spoken words coming true. Early in the story, Sailī's father sarcastically states that she will marry Kṛṣṇa, and curses her to become stone. Toward the end of story, Kṛṣṇa calls to ask whether she has sprouted, only to find that with his words, she has literally done so. Sailī is freed from her imprisonment in stone when Kṛṣṇa nears, yet later, when she becomes a plant, he becomes a stone "inside her." When women celebrate the wedding of Sailī, they wrap the plant in the spangled red garments of a bride, and place either a śālagrāma stone or a small brass image of Kṛṣṇa within it, clearly evoking auspicious fertility.

Further Reading

For more on tulsī worship, see Sudha Chandola, "Tulsī Plant in Indian Folklore," *Folklore* 17 (1976), 107–14; Sankar Sen Gupta, *Sacred Trees across Cultures and Nations* (Calcutta: Indian Publications, 1980), pp. 38–45; and Shakti M. Gupta, *Plant Myths and Tradition in India* (New Delhi: Mushiram Manoharlal, 1991), pp. 66–72.

On November 3, 1990, I was visiting a Rajput family in Dattal. Sitting out on a cot in the winter sun, I taped the reminiscences of Mātaji, the wizened old mother of the family. As she spoke, she raveled a sweater that her granddaughter had outgrown, and carefully gathered together the yarn so it could be knit afresh. Her daughter-in-law, Saroj, bustled about in the kitchen of the adobe house, occasionally leaning through a low window to shout offers of tea to those of us sitting in the courtyard. In the late afternoon, Jñānu Devī Bhandārī, a neighbor, came by on her way from the shop where sugar rations had just come in. A broad-faced, pretty woman in her fifties who exudes intelligence, she settled down on one corner of the cot to ask about my research. I told her that I was taping women's songs and life-histories. To give her an idea of my work, I shuffled through my notebook to read aloud a beautiful song I had taped several days earlier. In this song, Sailī's story was recounted. Jñānu Devī listened as I read aloud a few lines, and then she began to recite along. I asked her why, in this song, Kṛṣṇa's first wife put poison in the food at Sailī's wedding feast.

"There's a story," Jnānu Devī said.

"Tell it," I said, hastily adjusting my tape recorder.

"You'll get late, though won't you?" she asked, knowing that I had at least a twenty-minute walk through the rice fields between villages.

"No, no: tell it."

She began to speak as the children of the family came home from school, squeezing in with us on the cot, their satchels beside them. Their mother, Saroj, had come down from the kitchen with a tray of sweet, milky tea in steel glasses, berating her daughter. But as the story progressed, she too was distracted from the responsibilities around her, and sat smiling, captivated by the tale told in Jñānu Devī's expressive, musical voice.

This Sailī, or Tulsī: she was an untouchable cobbler's daughter. She was very beautiful, very beautiful. Then, a brahman boy had put aside some broken shoes for mending. He brought them, and this girl Sailī's father wasn't home. There was just this girl in the house.

He asked, "Can I drop off my shoes?" He held them out. This girl came out,

and said, "My father isn't in the house." Now this brahman boy, he had come of age. He stood to one side, staring at her face. He thought, "I have never seen such a beautiful girl. She's gorgeous."

Then he came home and he told his mother, "I want to marry this girl." His mother said, "We are brahmans, they are cobblers, You're dreadful! Why did you take birth in this house? No, of course you can't marry her."

But he insisted. This brahman boy wanted to marry Sailī, he was all ready to marry her. Everyone in the village was unhappy. They said, "Let's throw these cobblers out of here." Then people of the cobbler caste were unhappy too.

This girl, she didn't understand the difference between brahmans and themselves. She didn't understand: "What's the difference between the brahmans and cobblers, what's the difference?" She was so innocent. She said, "Father, what's the problem? This boy wants to marry me, and I want to marry him."

Then in the cobbler brotherhood, too, the men said, "We don't want to marry her, either."

So she said, "Then who will I marry?"

He father said, with anger and pain, "You will marry Kṛṣṇa. You'll marry Kṛṣṇa: Go! Become a stone. When Kṛṣṇa takes human form he'll marry you."

So she went to the banks of the Ravī River. [*"That's where they place stones, right, during the five days of Bhiṣma?" Jñānu Bhanḍarī consults with Mātāji, "They definitely put them out, right?" Hunched in the cot, Mātāji nods her head, "Yes, yes, they put them out."*]

So, she became a stone. Then when Kṛṣṇa took human form, he married Rukmanī. Then, when Arjuna and Kṛṣṇa went along the banks of the Ravī River, she became a complete girl again, and stood there. Arjuna was left behind, and Kṛṣṇa was wandering through the forest when he came to this spot.

Then he asked, "Who are you?"

"I'm Tulsī," she said [*serenely*].

He said, "Who are you waiting for?"

She said, "For Kṛṣṇa. I'm waiting for Kṛṣṇa."

He asked [*with a note of surprise*], "Why?"

She said, "I'm going to marry him."

Then Kṛṣṇa Bhagavān said, "I am Kṛṣṇa." She put the wedding garland around his neck. Then he said, "I won't take you to my home. I've already been married, and Queen Rukmanī is in my home."

She said [*soft and resigned*], "All right."

Then these days of fasting come right, the five days of Bhiṣma? These come during the month of Kārttika. So the month of Kārttika came. Kṛṣṇa said, "Let me see how I can bring you home." The month Kārttika is a very holy one. Lord Kṛṣṇa goes to bathe in the Yamunā River during that month, the whole month. And in the house, brahmans had to be served, sacred fires had to be lit, scriptures had to be read.

Every day, Rukmanī had so much work to do that she didn't even find a single minute of time. [*Jñānu Devī lapses out of Pahari to enunciate "minute" and "time" in English*]. She said to him after a while, "Mahārāj ["great king"], I get tremendously tired."

He said [*voice rising with an edge of indignation*], "What can I do about it? I have to get this much work out of you."

He used to go see Tulsī, too. He said, "Tulsī, what you should do is come one day with milk and curds, having made yourself a milkmaid of the Gujarī tribe."

Tulsī had been saying, "If you married me, when are you taking me to your home?"

All right. So she brought these things. Kṛṣṇa was sleeping, but Rukmanī had been up from three in the morning. Tulsī said, "Curds for sale! Curds for sale!"

Kṛṣṇa said, "Rukmanī, buy some curds."

She said [*voice rising, impatiently, as though to disparage men's knowledge of household matters*], "Mahārāj, why should I buy curds? We have cows, milk, curds, everything." He said, "Take a look, maybe the curds haven't set." This was Bhagavān's illusion, right?

She said, "No, Mahārāj, I put it to set, and it's probably set."

He said, "Just take a look, won't you?"

So she looked, and the curds hadn't set. She said, "OK, I'll take some curds." So Tulsī gave her the curds and went away.

Then Kṛṣṇa asked, "Rukmanī, did you buy curds?"

"Yes I did," she said.

Then he said to Tulsī, too, "You should come every day. Come every day."

[*Mātāji lets out a chortle, as though anticipating complications.*]

From Rukmanī's perspective, during this ritual, 101 brahmans would arrive, she'd have to prepare food for them all, give them all fresh white garments to wear, do this, do that: she'd get exhausted. She said, "Mahārāj, I get terribly tired. I'd like it if I had someone else to help me with the work."

Kṛṣṇa said, "Listen Rukmanī, why don't you ask that woman who comes to sell curds, why don't you ask her to work here?"

[*"Yes, become a servant!" puts in Mātāji, who is hanging on every word.*]

So when she came next, Rukmanī asked, "Tulsī, who do you have that's yours?"

Tulsī said, "I don't have anyone." Kṛṣṇa had trained her: when Rukmanī asks you, you should say this.

Rukmanī said, "Then, will you stay with us?"

Tulsī said, "Yes, I'll stay."

Fine. So she stayed. Then there were two women. Their work was done in a flash when they did it together. [*"There was happiness," adds Mātāji.*] And in Rukmanī's heart, she thought, "Since this poor thing has come, I too have had so much help." [*"So much help," clucks Mātāji, "Just look!"*]

Then when these five days came, the five days of Bhiṣma, then Kṛṣṇa instructed Tulsī: "Tomorrow—no, the day after—these five days will begin. You should make her so happy that she'll let you bathe with me for all the five days."

Now whatever Rukmanī remembered, Kṛṣṇa made her forget. The next day, 101 brahmans had to be fed, before nine in the morning. Tulsī remembered this though, she was clever. So Rukmanī kept sleeping, she was fast asleep. And Tulsī, she didn't sleep. She got up, she made all the food, and she closed the kitchen door. Rukmanī woke up and realized it was already morning.

"Oh no!" she exclaimed [*in a hushed, horrified voice*]. "Today I'm dead! You didn't even come to wake me."

Tulsī said, "What's the matter, sister?"

She said [*still hushed*], "One hundred and one brahmans are coming to eat before nine o'clock. How will I possibly be ready?"

Tulsī said, "Sister, what if all the food was already made?"

She said, "If that was so, then I'd give you anything that you asked for. I would be so pleased with you." [*Mātāji, Saroj, and another old aunt who has joined us, all laugh*].

She opened the kitchen, and there everything was ready. [*"Ready," agrees Mātāji*]. She said, "Now, ask me for whatever you wish."

Tulsī said, "The entire month you bathe with Kṛṣṇa. Give me these five days to bathe."

She said, "Take them, what's there in bathing? If you want to take them, take. You can bathe too. When he bathes, you can bathe with him."

They went off to bathe: Kṛṣṇa and Tulsī, to the Yamunā River. Rukmanī was washing wheat that later she would feed to the brahmans. She washed the wheat and set it out to dry in the courtyard, and went on with her work. Three days of bathing went by. Then, a black crow used to come and put his beak in the wheat. She would pick up the grains, wash them, put them out again, and go back to her work. The crow would come back again.

Then she said, "Shoo! You black untouchable caṇḍāla, you black crow. The pandits are going to eat bread from this wheat, and you are polluting it?!"

The crow said, "You're the black caṇḍāli: you!" [*Everyone laughs at this repartee.*] "You're in the house, and all your austerities, all your religion for this month is being taken by Tulsī!"

She said, "How?"

He said, "Go! Go to the banks of the Yamunā where they're having fun. Sailī is scrubbing Kṛṣṇa's back, and Kṛṣṇa is scrubbing hers. And you're at home!"

She got angry. "Is that so?!"

"Yes," he said.

So she went to the Yamunā. They were bathing just as he had said. Kṛṣṇa saw her, "There's Rukmanī coming." So Kṛṣṇa lifted his foot and began to cry [piteously], "*Hai, hai, hai!*" [*Jñānu Devī is grinning broadly at this sly ruse of Kṛṣṇa, the notorious mischief-maker, and her audience explodes into laughter.*] Tulsī bent over to look at his foot, to see what was the matter.

Rukmanī said, "Mahārāj! When I was hidden, you were in fine form. You were washing each other's backs. Then when you saw me you began to make this big show of crying *hai, hai.*"

He said [*in an injured fashion*], "I had a thorn in my foot, and I showed it to Tulsī so she could take it out. That's what it was, Rukmanī," he said.

But this matter went and settled in Rukmanī's heart. "I kept this servant, and she's become the wife." Rukmanī was angry all the time. Then, during these days when they were bathing, things were different. Before, when Kṛṣṇa went to bathe, he would say to Rukmanī, "Bring my garments, bring my waterpot." But after this day he would call out to Tulsī, "Give me my garments, give me my waterpot." And he talked to her in the same way and as much as he would talk to Rukmanī.

Rukmanī said, "This is a terrible outrage." So then she hid his garments, and she hid the waterpot too. So then where could Tulsī give them to him from? They were hidden: the garments and the waterpot.

When Kṛṣṇa went to bathe, he said, "Bring, Tulsī, bring me my garments and my waterpot too."

When she went inside she didn't find them. They had been hidden. She didn't find them. She searched but she didn't find them. Kṛṣṇa was standing outside saying, "Bring, bring!" But she didn't find them.

Then Kṛṣṇa said in anger, "Tulsī! What, did you sprout in there? Did you just sprout in there, staying in there and not coming out?"

Now, in the past it was Satyayuga, the era of righteousness, and it is said that whatever speech came from the mouth then came true.

So Kṛṣṇa Bhagavān went in to see what had happened. She had become Sailī. [*"She had become Tulsī," echoes Mātāji.*] She was a shrub. She had become Sailī. Kṛṣṇa Bhagavān went in and he became a stone śālagrama, there within Sailī."

Rukmanī was left outside. Sailī went in, she didn't turn back; Kṛṣṇa went in, he didn't turn back. So she went inside to see what was going on. Inside there, Sailī had become like this [*Jñānu Devī holds her two palms facing each other, to indicate about one foot*], and in the middle, having become a śālagrama, Kṛṣṇa Bhagavān was sitting there."

Rukmanī began to cry, "Mahārāj, what is this? What's this you've become?"

At that time, Kṛṣṇa Bhagavān said, "Rukmanī, now I can meet you in the month of Kārttika. If you fast in this way, then I'll meet you. Now I'm with Sailī."

Finishing her story, Jñānu Devī Bhandari returned to her explication of the Sailī song, "Then Rukmanī fed one hundred maunds of poison to her co-wife," she said.

"Where did she put it?" demanded ten-year-old Kāku, with all the cockiness of a cute, adored boy.

"Then Kṛṣṇa changed his name into Ṭhākur." Jñānu Devī hummed lines of the song, "Now Tulsī will marry Ṭhākur . . . Stop, turn back, she'll marry Ṭhākur." She married Ṭhākur. Rukmanī fed her the poison."

"Whom did she feed?" Kāku continued, not to be deflected. Like Kāku, I saw the story as having formed an adjacent space of meaning beside the song text, explaining Rukmanī's cause for jealousy; since the poisoned wedding feast was not mentioned, it was difficult to discern the immediate connection.

"Sailī," said Jñānu Devī. She laughed, shaking her head at Kāku. "What were you listening to? This is like the saying, 'All night you read the *Rāmāyaṇa,* and in the morning you ask, "Who was Sītā's husband?" '!"

I asked Jñānu Devī where she had learned this story, and she said it was from her sister. "She's a very learned person," put in Mātāji. "Lots of rituals and scriptures," said Saroj. "That's how she knew it," Mātāji shook her head with awe, "Here what do people know? Everyone is illiterate. Those who read and write know these stories."

Jñānu Devī continued, "When the five days of Bhiṣma comes, with Sailī's wedding, then this story is always told."

"This very story?" I asked.

"This story," she repeated.

"And other stories," I said, thinking of the rich corpus I had already taped from women from different villages, castes, and generations.

"And others," agreed Jñānu Devī, "For five days, women tell lots of stories about Sailī."

—34—

Lives of Sufi Saints

Carl Ernst

The Life of Sayyid Muḥammad ibn Jaʿfar al-Makkī

The concept of sainthood in Islamic history may be considered one of the fundamental religious categories that has guided the development and structure of Islamic society. Hagiography, the writing of lives of the saints, has accordingly been one of the most prominent forms of Islamic religious literature. The hagiographer chooses exemplary figures from among the "friends of God" (*awliyāʾ*, pl. of *walī*), and the resulting portrait is designed to mirror for the faithful the qualities of the perfect human being. Sainthood is one of the basic principles of Sufism, the mystical tradition of Islam, and lives of the saints were first written down in large collections in Arabic at the end of the tenth century C.E., when the Sufi movement had become highly visible in Islamic society in the Arab countries and Iran. In India, large biographical dictionaries of saints began to be written in Persian in the late sixteenth century, under the patronage of the Mughul emperors. The selection that follows is from one of the best of these hagiographies, *Notices of the Noblest Concerning the Secrets of the Sanctified,* by ʿAbd al-Ḥaqq Muḥaddith Dihlawī ("Servant of the Real, the Traditionist, from Delhi," d. 1642). It concerns a Sufi saint from the fifteenth century, Sayyid Muḥammad ibn Jaʿfar al-Makkī ("Descendant of the Prophet, the Praised, Son of River, from Mecca"). After providing brief notes regarding the training, writings, and life of his subject, ʿAbd al-Ḥaqq gives extensive excerpts from al-Makkī's letters to a friend, which had been written in 1421 and collected under the title *The Sea of Meanings.* These excerpts elucidate two main topics: the nature of sainthood and mystical experience.

Traditions going back to ḥadīth reports from the Prophet Muḥammad affirm that there is a special class of servants of God, usually numbered as 356 (but here counted as 357), upon whom the maintenance of the world rests, though they remain unknown to the world. These include the "substitutes" (*abdāl*), the "pegs" (*awtād*), the "solitaries" (*afrād*), and the supreme figure of the hierarchy, the "axis" of the world (*qutb*). Al-Makkī not only describes these figures, but claims to have met them personally in his mystical experiences (it is noteworthy that his biographer seems to take these claims with a grain of salt). Like many Sufi authors, al-Makkī relates the qualities of the members of the spiritual hierarchy to the supreme religious personalities of Islam, the Prophet Muḥammad and, to a lesser extent, his son-in-law and cousin, ʿAlī.

Al-Makkī comments on various figures from the Sufi tradition, both from India and from beyond. He describes two famous Sufi saints, ʿAbd al-Qādir Jīlānī ("Reviver of the Faith, Servant of the Almighty, from Gilan" in Persia, d. 1166) and Niẓām al-Dīn Awliyāʾ Badāʾōnī ("Order of the Faith, the Saint of Saints, from Badāʾōn" in northern India, d. 1325) as having attained the highest possible station, that of being the beloved of God; Niẓām al-Dīn, whose tomb is in Delhi, was the teacher of al-Makkī's teacher. Al-Makkī reports that this was confirmed to him personally by the deathless master Khiḍr, who has initiated many well-known Sufis.

He also takes up the controversial topic of the ecstatic sayings of the early Sufis Ḥallāj ("woolcarder," executed in Baghdad in 922) and Bāyazīd Bisṭāmī ("Father of Yazīd, from Bisṭām" in Persia, d. 874); Ḥallāj was renowned for having said "I am the Truth," whereas Bāyazīd was famous for saying "Glory be to Me! How great is My Majesty!" Although to some these sayings sounded like blasphemous pretension to divinity, Sufi tradition saw here the annihilation of the individual ego and the manifestation of God directly through the tongue of a mortal. Al-Makkī complicates the discussion by reporting that the renowned Andalusian Sufi Ibn ʿArabī (d. 1240) saw Ḥallāj's saying as a manifestation of the divine essence. Al-Makkī argues that this is impossible, since a complete effacement of the self in the divine essence would prevent the concept of "I" from ever arising. Using a theological distinction common in Islamic thought, he maintains that the divine essence is utterly transcendent, but that it is possible for the divine attributes, acts, or influences to manifest in a human being, since these attributes (known best as the divine names in the Qurʾān) are the medium through which God relates to the created world. The most peculiar aspect of this discussion is the fact that Ibn ʿArabī never held this position regarding Ḥallāj, but instead took a view similar to al-Makkī's; who al-Makkī's source was, and how the issue became confused, remain obscure.

The final passage concerns an extraordinary meditation retreat that al-Makkī undertook under the direction of an otherwise unknown Sufi who maintained a hospice in Egypt; al-Makkī arrived there from India by levitation. The experiences that are described here put al-Makkī on a higher level of mystical experience than the early Sufis whose sayings he has criticized. Al-Makkī informs us that he has attained the manifestation of the essence, and has truly gone beyond his ego.

The selections are translated from ʿAbd al-Ḥaqq Muḥaddith Dihlawī al-Bukhārī, *Akhbār al-akhyār fī asrār al-abrār*, edited by Muḥammad ʿAbd al-Aḥad (Delhi: Maṭbaʿ-i Mujtabāʾī, 1332/1913–1914), pp. 136–39, with corrections from Muḥammad ibn Naṣīr al-Dīn Jaʿfar al-Makkī al-Ḥusaynī, *Baḥr al-maʿānī,* MS 1235 Persian, Asiatic Society, Calcutta, fols. 86a–b, 98b–101b.

Sayyid Muḥammad ibn Jaʿfar al-Makkī al-Ḥusaynī was one of the greatest of the designated successors of Shaykh Naṣīr al-Dīn Maḥmūd ["Master Helper of the Faith, the Praised," d. 1356]; in unity and unification he has a lofty station. He is among the solitaries of the saints. Regarding that which he himself has written about his internal and external states, the intellect is amazed. If all of this is without taint of obscurantism and is purely what it appears to mean, then he is one of the perfect ones of the age (may God sanctify his conscience).

He has a book entitled *The Sea of Meanings* in which are explained many realities of unity and sciences of the Sufis and secrets of gnosis. He speaks with intoxication, and he has other books: *The Subtleties of Meanings* and *The Realities of Meanings,* which he promises to write, but God knows if they have been written or not. He has other books: a treatise explaining the Spirit, and a treatise called *The Five Points,* and *The Sea of Relationships,* in which is an explanation of the family of the Prophet Muḥammad, showing his relation to his ancestors. He makes many claims, but he has verified by experience the internal states that he explains.

He had a long life, from the time of Sultan Muḥammad ibn Tughluq [d. 1351] to the time of Sultan Buhlūl [r. 1451–1489], his years exceeding one hundred. His forefathers are of the Sharīfs of Mecca, having come to Delhi and established themselves in Sirhind. Now his tomb is in the same city. He says in *The Sea of Meanings:* "For a period of sixty years I remained in external knowledge, pursuing the acquisition of excellence, and I was heedless of the eternal Beloved and the eternal goal. For thirty years I have been seeing that which is shown, and I have been hearing that which the ear hears. Beloved! The range of the thoughts of the externalists and their barren intellects are impediments; and if not, I shall set off in the trappings of ceaselessness to the desert of eternity! The little that I say, Beloved, is that which has not been heard. That which I say from the wordless promise of 'and he has the Mother of the Book' [Qur. 39.13] is put into words, and it is unknown to humanity. It is thirty-three years since I have repented of what humanity says, and no object has been attained from what I say."

In that book he explains about the substitutes and pegs and axes and solitaries and the other men of God, and he has distinguished and differentiated their numbers, names, ranks, prayers, ages, states, and divisions, beyond which nothing could be conceived, and he has said, "I have had conversation with all of them and have been blessed by each, and I have contemplated all of their stations." And he says, "There are 357 different substitutes, and I conversed with them on the mountain at the source of the Nile, where they were dwelling, living on the gum of trees and the locusts of the deserts."

And he also says, "O Beloved! There is no number to the society of solitaries. They are many and are veiled from the sight of humanity, although the chief axis and some of the axes know them and see them. Wherever the perfect solitaries are, who are the manifestations of the aspect of the singularity of ʿAlī (God ennoble his countenance), they advance on the path. They find a rank by the heart of the Prophet (and ʿAlī, God ennoble his countenance, found a rank by the spirit of the Prophet). When from the heart vessels of the Prophet they advance on the path, they arrive to the true axis, and from the station of the true axis to the station of Beloved, which is unity.

"O Beloved! In the station of the axis, out of all the saints, two have attained the station of Beloved, which no one else like them has attained. Who are those two, Beloved? The first is Shaykh al-Dīn ʿAbd al-Qādir Jīlanī, the second Shaykh Nīzam al-Dīn Badāʾōnī; both were vessels of the spirit of Muḥammad. Beloved! You have considered well; nothing comes from my pen that has not been witnessed. Beloved! One day I was in the company of the Revered Khiḍr [the "Green One"] in a boat on the Nile in Egypt, and some words were spoken of the contemplation of the unending. Khiḍr also said that Shaykh al-Dīn ʿAbd al-Qādir Jīlanī and Shaykh Nīẓam al-Dīn Badāʾōnī were in the station of Beloved."

And he also says, "O Beloved! Nineteen years I was sober, and twenty-one years I was intoxicated to the extent that I knew nothing, but I was in the neighborhood of Shaykh Yaʿqūb who was the axis of the region. He told me of these twenty-one years of mine, so it was known that I was intoxicated for twenty-one years. And after this time, by the grace of the master in his solitariness, it is some years since I descended from the state of intoxication.

I am a single pearl; I sat down alone
  for in myself I have many lights from singleness;
if I am not Moses (Mūsā), I am still a songbird (*mūsī*),
  for there is a musician within my breast.

"O Beloved! Ibn al-ʿArabī [Son of the Arab," d. 1240], author of *The Bezels,* writes that in Manṣūr Ḥallāj ["Victorious, the Woolcarder," d. 922] was the manifestation of the essence, and that he held the station of the solitaries. But I say that if the manifestation of the essence had been in Manṣūr Ḥallāj, he never would have said 'I am the Truth' nor would another [Bāyazīd Bisṭāmī, d. 874] have uttered 'Glory be to Me,' because the manifestation of the essence is effacement—and what does the effaced know of 'who am I?' and 'what am I?' so that he would say 'I am the Truth' and 'Glory be to me'? 'He who knows God is dumb' in the manifestation of essence 'and becomes eloquent' in the manifestation of attributes. In the manifestation of attributes and acts and words, it is right, Beloved, when the dervish is totally absorbed in the manifestation of attributes. Then he sees himself by the glory of one of his attributes, that is: the essence of the possible existence becomes absorbed by the light of the glory of the attributes into the attributes of the necessary existence; and that attribute enters, as a necessary existence, into the temporal, and utterly ravishes away the being of the possible existence. When this attribute [one of the divine names, as 'Truth,' 'Grace,' 'Wrath,' etc.] has ravished someone in this way, it enters into his speech, and he says 'Glory be to Me' and 'I am the Truth' and 'Truly God is speaking by the tongue of ʿUmar.' What shall I do? Ibnal-ʿArabī is no longer living. I would have said to him what I said here, and he would have heard that which is certain.

"My words are not the measure of *The Sea of Meanings*. Who can bear it? Where are there still words? God willing, one day I shall write of that Beloved. Beloved! When by the grace of the 'Solitary of Reality,' Shaykh Naṣīr al-Dīn Maḥmūd [his master], there was advancement on the path of wayfaring, from the manifestation of attributes to the manifestation of essence—which is the station of solitariness—I descended in a veiled condition. In a dream I saw the 'solitary of reality' repeating a silent chant; I entered and pressed the face of supplication in the dust. On his blessed tongue came the words, 'You royal falcon of the field of the world of divinity, and pure one come from the world of power, and player in the worlds of the angels and humanity!' After that a longing flickered across my eyes, and he said, 'This longing is for the light of the glory of the essence.' This dream happened in the year 811 [1407 C.E.].

"When night came I was levitated from the town of Khatlān [in Afghanistan] and entered Egypt. I was honored with kissing the feet of Shaykh Awḥad Simnānī ["Master Unique, from Simnān" in Central Asia], who at that time was axis of the world. He also praised me by the same words that the 'Solitary of Reality' had praised me with. He was in his cell, and told me to take one corner. In the room were two men, a Sufi and a student. I did the sunset prayers levitating, and performed evening prayers in company with the axis of the world, Shaykh Awḥad Simnānī. After that, for two-thirds of the night I read the Qurʾān through three times completely and sixteen of its thirty sections in addition. I looked down and my body had become light, and it encompassed the great throne [of God], and the great throne became as a mustard seed in my sight. Then I looked at myself, and the very hairs of my person became images, and I looked at each image, and I saw that it was the image of myself. Then the images began to be obliterated, and then I looked and all the worlds, the heavens, and the souls began to take on an indescribable condition, and all the manifestations of attributes and actions and influences began to be obliterated. Beloved! This is the very obliteration into obliteration!

"Just then in the twinkling of an eye I traveled through seven hundred thousand worlds of manifestations. Then by an unmediated Word I heard the command: 'O my servant! My glory is a veil on my beauty, and my beauty is the light of my glory, and you are between my glory and my beauty!' After the Word, I was ennobled by the manifestation of the essence, the nature of which is only attainable by witnessing. From that time I descended into the world of divinity, which is the place of solitariness. After the manifestation of the essence, on the seventeenth day I entered the world of sobriety; I was still dwelling in the cell of Shaykh Awḥad Simnānī.

> I became drunk with Him, by the wine of longing,
> my being became lost in His;
> our existence became nonexistent in His existence—
> everything but Him was scorned.
> When I became perfectly detached from existence,
> neither name nor reality remained to me.
> When Muḥammad became annihilated from being,
> who else could he see? There was no other!

"Then, Beloved! After the manifestation of the essence in the cell of Shaykh Awḥad Simnānī, I lost my senses, and on the seventeenth day the shaykh himself came into the cell and kissed me on the forehead. If the shaykh had not been fully aware of my condition, the very companions of my cell would have enshrouded me as a dead man for burial. Then I returned to the world of sobriety. This was because of the beginning of manifestation: for some time thereafter, wherever I looked I saw a light that was joined with me; this image is the 'hangover' of the station of solitariness, which grasps all creation on the level of nobility. And all this was from the blessed words of the 'Solitary of Reality' (God sanctify his secret!). For one day 'the king of the verifiers,' the great prince Jaʿfar Naṣīr (who is my father) was seated in the presence of my master, who said, 'Amīr Jaʿfar Muḥammad is the royal falcon of the field of divinity; he will be influenced by the blessings of over three hundred and seventy saints, the axes and the solitaries, and he will be ennobled by these blessings.' And on that day I was in the presence of the master Mawlānā Shams al-Dīn Yaḥyā ["Our Master Sun of the Faith, Living," fourteenth century], disciple of Niẓām al-Dīn Awliyāʾ (God sanctify his secret!), reading digests. Praise be to God, Lord of Creation. Beloved! When I was united to this station, I brought these verses to speech:

> Now I say, I don't know who I am;
> this slave is not the Creator; then what am I?
> Slavery was obliterated, but no freedom remained;
> no atom of happiness or misery remained in my heart.
> I was without quality or direction;
> I am a gnostic, but I have no gnosis.
> I don't know whether you are I or I am you;
> I was annihilated in you, duality became lost.

"Beloved! For the lost one, whence comes this speech? Whoever speaks, speaks of the manifestation of the attributes. In the manifestation of the attributes, there is speech. When I want to write something about that Beloved, I have become sobered from the manifestation of the eternal essence. That is the reason; otherwise, what does this Beloved have to do with these words? One should ask that Beloved in prayer that he hold this beggar in the world of sobriety, so that I may put the wordless library into words for that Beloved. Beloved! You have considered well, and have said goodbye to the house of humanity. Beloved!

> Enter bravely, for in this path, scent and color have no worth.
> Arise as the whole from existence, don't fall in the narrow path.
> Tie a Magian belt around your waist, then go chant in the temples.
> Know of a truth, that in the two worlds, in your path, the only trap is you.

This noble letter was completed on the last of Shawwāl, 824 [October 27, 1421]."

The Life of Burhān al-Dīn Gharīb

Another kind of sacred biography is the eulogistic praise of a saint by devotees who are interested in the power of the saint as an intercessor with God. This kind of hagiography is not so much concerned with teachings as with demonstrations of power, often in the form of miracles. Retrospective portraits of saints by later devotees stress prophecies of their coming, attributed to famous early Sufis, and they often emphasize the establishment of the center that later becomes the focus of pilgrimage to the saint's tomb. Frequent also is an admixture of political considerations, based on the desire of kings to borrow legitimacy from the saints by becoming patrons of their shrines.

In the selection that follows, an anonymous author describes the life of Burhān al-Dīn Gharīb ("Proof of the Faith, the Poor Man," d. 1337), a master of the Chishtī Sufi order. It is noteworthy that the author does indicate that the text, *The Victory of the Saints,* was composed in the city of Burhanpur in western India in 1620, and that it was dedicated to the Mughul governor ʿAbd al-Raḥīm Khān-i Khānān ("Servant of the Merciful, Ruler of Rulers," d. 1627) and the emperor Jahāngīr ("World-Ruler," d. 1627); this occurred, coincidentally, during a siege of Burhanpur by the forces of the Deccan kingdom of Ahmadnagar. Since the tomb of Burhān al-Dīn Gharīb lay in Ahmadnagar territory, in the town of Khuldabad near Daulatabad fort, it is tempting to conclude that the commissioning of this hagiography by the Mughul governor was at least in part an assertion of Mughul sovereignty over the Deccan, which is here called the dominion of Burhān al-Dīn Gharīb. The emperor Akbar's conquest of Burhanpur in 1601 appears to be the fulfillment of Burhān al-Dīn Gharīb's prophecy nearly three centuries earlier, and it implicitly places the Mughuls in the position of being patrons and rulers over the Deccan as well. The emphasis on the saints as agents of conversion to Islam fits in with the imperialistic ambitions of the Mughuls and other rulers, and is wholly lacking in Sufi texts of the fourteenth century. The interpenetration of political and religious symbolism is also indicated by the use of the title "Sultan" to describe Burhān al-Dīn Gharīb.

This biography begins by describing a miraculous encounter in which the great saint of Delhi, Niẓām al-Dīn Awliyā' ("Order of the Faith, the Saint of Saints," d. 1325), is given a boon by heaven, that whomsoever he entrusts with any dominion will retain it forever. According to this concept, every major saint is responsible for a particular territory around his shrine, and has supreme spiritual and temporal authority there. Then the text tells how Niẓām al-Dīn sent his chief successors to various parts of India to assume their dominions. The main concern is now how Burhān al-Dīn Gharīb is assigned the Deccan (the southern region of India, south of the Tapti River down to the Tungabhadra, roughly comprising the present states of Maharashtra, Karnataka, and Andhra Pradesh). The Deccan had previously been in the care of Burhān al-Dīn Gharīb's brother Muntajib al-Dīn, but through a hint of Niẓām al-Dīn it is revealed that he has just passed away. When Burhān al-Dīn Gharīb expresses his anguish at parting from his master, Niẓām al-Dīn sends along his sandals as symbols of his authority as well as a company of seven hundred (or fourteen hundred) of his disciples. Burhān al-Dīn Gharīb then heads for Daulatabad, but halts to pray on the site of a future city, Burhanpur, that would be named after him. His holiness and prayers are invoked as the basis for the foundation of the city, the establishment of his tomb-shrine, and for the presence of later Chishtī saints in the region of Burhanpur, such as Shāh Nu'mān ("King Beneficent," d. 1476–77). The saint's prophecy about Akbar uses traditional local Indian imagery of fertility and power, showing the king discovering the form of an elephant in a massive stone in the Tapti River; Akbar then caused the stone to be carved in that shape (the elephant stone was still being worshiped by Hindus in the seventeenth century, according to European travelers).

Of the actual religious behavior and teaching of the saint, only a fraction remains. The biographer falsely ascribes "many writings" to the saint, though extensive works by Burhān al-Dīn Gharīb's disciples refute this. The biography concludes only by observing that the saint was celibate and that he taught many disciples (both points confirmed by other sources). This hagiography is of less value for the actual life of the saint than as an indication of the religious and political concerns of later generations, for whom the saint acts as a source of authority.

The translation is from an anonymous manuscript, "Fath al-awliyā'," in the collection of the Committee Khuddamin Dargahjat Rauza Kalan, Khuldabad, pp. 18–25. No other copies of this document are known.

Further Reading

Carl W. Ernst, *Eternal Garden: Mysticism, History, and Politics at a South Asian Sufi Center* (Albany: State University of New York Press, 1992).

In praise of the revered sultan of the gnostics, the axis of the wayfarers, the cream of the companions of reality, the exemplar of the lords of the path, the sun of the sphere of excellence and perfection, the revealer of the secrets of majesty and beauty, who is raised up on the pillars of unity and stability, Sultan Burhān al-Dīn Fārūqī al-Chishtī. He was one of the worthy successors of the revered sultan of the masters, Niẓām al-Dīn Awliyā'. He was for a time in the company of the latter, and reached the degree of perfection in meditation, piety, asceticism, and Godfearing. He has many writings in the science of spiritual realities and wayfaring, and he is the master of the dominion of the entire Deccan.

One day, the sultan of the Sufis, the lamp of the Chishtīs, Master Niẓām al-Dīn Awliyā' was in the state of joy and expansion, in the intoxicated feast of select divine manifestations of the essence and royal attributes, which is the encompassing sea of divine illuminations. He was totally immersed in the sea of annihilation, drowned and absorbed in God, when suddenly a loving voice from the divine presence reached his conscious hearing, saying, "Niẓām al-Dīn, ask for whatever desire you have, for it will be given to you, and request whatever object you have, for it will appear from the hidden veil into the manifest world." Since the state of absorption overpowered him, he remained silent. A second time also the voice gave the same cry, but the master did not attend to it, and did not turn his face from the prayer-direction of his absorption, and because of that state he did not raise his head from the form of the treasury-seraglio of unity. Then a third time the voice conveyed the good news of acceptance to his blessed ears, saying, "Niẓām al-Dīn, you are a marvel to be without desire, for from the limitless bounties of the divine presence and the sublime sources of lordly grace, you hold yourself back." The master arose, full of the well of meditation and vision, and pressed the face of indigence in the earth of weakness and helplessness.

He lifted up the hand of prayer hopeful of answer to the threshold of majesty and said, "My God and Lord, let anyone to whom Niẓām gives dominion hold it safely until the resurrection, and give no change or alteration in that path." The prayer of the master was chosen to be answered in the court of God, whose existence witnesses and comprehends all existences. After a few days, having commanded each of his successors, who are perfect and unsurpassed in the realm of asceticism and discipline, to reside in a city and a dominion, he dispatched them. For example, in the environs of Gujarat, he put the exemplar of those who attain union and the prayer-direction of the people of the inner path, Master Ḥusām al-Dīn ["Sword of the Faith," d. 1329] safely in as master of the domain; in the realm of Delhi, he honored the axis of axes, the knower of the secrets of reality, the announcer of the illuminations of the religious law, Master Naṣīr al-Dīn Maḥmūd Chirāgh-i Dihlī ["Helper of the Faith, the Praised, the Lamp of Delhi," d. 1356]; in the realm of the Deccan, he gave the portion to the master of religion, knower of principle and application, master of chivalry and piety, Muntajib al-Dīn ["Chosen of the Faith," d. 1309?]; and in the domain of Malwa he appointed the standard of master of religion, Master Wajīh al-Dīn Yūsuf ["Leader of the Faith, Joseph," fourteenth century]. Likewise, he appointed each one of them over every clime and domain, and each one over a realm and district. This was because God has made the prophetic faith and Muḥammadan proof eternal until the resurrection, and as long as they remain externally alive, they will call creation to the faith of Muḥammad the Chosen (God bless him and grant him peace) and convey every seeker of God to his desire. After they leave the station of impermanence for the palace of eternity, until "the day when the hour [of judgment] arrives" [Qur. 31.12], every later saint that appears in these territories is from their giving grace and their internal assistance. Every rebel and sinner who has been of the community of our revered Prophet Muḥammad the Messenger (God bless him and grant him peace) is taken into the divine mercy and forgiven through the concentration of their saintly spirits.

It is related that one day Master Niẓām al-Dīn Awliya' (may God sanctify his conscience) was performing ablutions, and Sultan Burhān al-Dīn (may God sanctify his conscience) was present in the fortunate assembly, rendering the customary service, pouring water from a vessel he held in his hand. The master [Niẓām al-Dīn] glanced at the sultan [Burhān al-Dīn Gharīb] affectionately, and asked, "Was Master Muntajib al-Dīn your elder or younger brother?" The sultan knew by his prescience for certain, and realized by the indication of his master, and had intelligence by his cardiognosy and wit, that the master just mentioned had been joined to the mercy of God. The next day he prepared the materials for the third-day funeral observance, and attended the noble gathering. Several of the lovers wondered and asked the sultan the meaning of this. He said, "When the revered master's blessed tongue asked whether my brother Muntajib al-Dīn was elder or younger, by prescience I knew for certain that my brother had passed away, because the word 'was' indicated the past tense." After that, before the whole assembly, Niẓām al-Dīn Awliyā' (may God sanctify his conscience) said to him, "I have made you the leader in place of Muntajib al-Dīn, I have made you his successor. You should go to Daulatabad."

The sultan obediently accepted the pearl-like words of the master and put the seal of silence on his lips, but in his thoughts, from the pain of separation from the master, a great grief and bitter pain appeared. From this condition, pain and perturbation began to beat in waves upon him. From both of his eyes tears ran as from the springs of rivers, and weeping overwhelmed him. The meaning of his condition could not fit into the capacity of mere words. At this point the master came and examined his condition, and enquired of him the cause of his consternation. He replied, "I will be separated from these sandals." The master replied, "The master will be your companion," meaning, "Take the sandals as your companions." The sultan obediently placed the noble sandals on his head, and pressed his blessed forehead to the grace-bestowing threshold. From the pain of separation, the fear of loneliness, and the dread of trouble, however, he reached a point such that despite all his perfect self-possession, and control of the reins of will, the halter of disturbance slipped out of the grasp of his will, and from his extreme sadness and regret, and his great terror and pains, losing sight of his own aspirations he could not set foot outside his master's hospice.

They say that a second time Master Niẓām al-Dīn Awliyā' (may God sanctify his conscience) became aware of his condition, and his luminous eye perceived that no amount of preaching could make the heart grasp the hem of patience. To his spiritual son he said, "What is the cause of the delay in your leaving?" With weakness and humility, he replied, "I shall be separated from the eternal assembly of the laws of God." When he saw and witnessed his painful, lamenting, and burning cry, then by way of generosity and affection he gave the whole assembly, with all the noble successors and disciplined disciples, to the sultan, saying, "The master will be your companion." Some say the successors and disciples were seven hundred, and others hold that there were fourteen hundred who came in the company of the sultan. Among the successors, one was Amīr Ḥasan ["Prince Fine," d. after 1329], the second Master Kamāl Khujandī ["Perfection, from Khujand" in Central Asia], the third Master Jām ["the master of Jām," from Afghanistan], the fourth Master Fakhr al-Dīn ["pride of the faith"], the fifth Master Naṣīr al-Dīn Chirāgh-i Dihlī, and other masters. At the time of farewell, he honored him with five guidances. The first was the cloaks of service that were entrusted to him in the traditional way from the time of Master 'Uthmān Hārwanī ["'Uthmān, from Hārwan" in Central Asia, d. 1211] and from Master Mu'īn al-Dīn Chishtī ["Aider of the Faith, from Chisht" in Afghanistan, d. 1236] and others, which had been intended for Mawlānā Da'ūd-i Ḥusayn Shīrāzī ["Our Master David, Son of the Mountain"], known as Master Zayn al-Dīn ["Adornment of the Faith," d. 1369], for they would reach the latter, just as these events will be explained in the section on Master Zayn al-Dīn. The second guidance was [illegible]. Third, "Do not abandon the communal Friday prayer." Fourth, "Do not forget to inquire after the condition of my master's daughter who dwells here." Fifth, "Always remain celibate."

After hearing the five points, he headed toward Daulatabad, and in the year 720 [1320 C.E.; actually 1329] he reached Daulatabad. They say that the sultan, after completing several stages in a few days, reached the land of this city [Burhanpur]. It was a very pleasant and delightful place, and he saw an inhabited village. Longing for it to be established [as a city] took root that day in his luminous mind. He spread a cloth to stand on, by the bank of the Tapti river. The sultan stood and made ablutions and performed communal prayer on the stone in the middle of the river that they call the "elephant stone." Entering into intimate conversation with God, the holy and exalted Creator, he asked that in this place a town by the name of Burhanpur become inhabited. This became a prayer chosen to be granted, inasmuch as the news of blessing in respect of the habitation of this region reached from the hidden world into his ear. When he was praying the midnight prayers and was absorbed in recollection of God in the middle of the night, he summoned one of the knowers of His secrets [an angel]. Regarding what he said, the power of God opened up his heart to its destiny; an inhabited city appeared to his vision, so that the beholder became astonished at its habitation.

After the dawn prayer, he was said to leave for Daulatabad. The best time of all the days in the environs of that region was illuminated by the vision of that graceful one. Since the groups of scholars and notables residing together there obtained perfect delight and inclusive participation in his pure and eternal authority and his abundantly blessed company, after a few days, some of the dear ones received his permission to depart, and returned to Niẓām al-Dīn Awliyā' (may God sanctify his conscience). And some remained in the service of the sultan, and today the tombs of the lovers are famous and well known, near his blessed shrine.

After some years, Shah Nu'man [d. 1476–77] was residing down below the Asir fort [near Burhanpur]. The influence of his [Burhān al-Dīn Gharīb's] prayers was manifest. This desert and desolation had become inhabited, and its fortune had been sustained by Burhān al-Dīn Awliyā'.

When the revered nester in the divine throne, the crown-bestower on the face of the earth, the victorious by the grace of God, the eternal king Jalāl al-Dīn Muḥammad Akbar Pādshāh ["Glory of the Faith, the Praised, the Greatest, the Emperor," d. 1605], in the year 1008 (1600 C.E.; actually 1601) honored the region of Burhanpur, and conquered the fortress of Asir, at that time he made that stone called the "elephant stone" into the shape of an elephant and made a statue from its internal meaning which had lacked external thought, so that it would remain forever the chief memento (of his conquest).

It is related that one day the mother of the sultan ordered him to get married. This presented a great difficulty to the sultan, for the advice of his master was to remain celibate and his mother's pleasure lay in his getting married. That very day he vowed to fast, and he said, "I am fasting. Whenever I break my fast, I will do whatever I am ordered." And he formed the intention to fast for several years. As time went on, the weakness of his body reached such a point that at the time of kneeling and prostration, his brain was disturbed. Then his mother passed away, and the sultan did not maintain his asceticism [but remained celibate].

For some time he bestowed knowledge of truth and divine gnosis on the people of that place, and he brought plenty of people to the universal goal and the essential object, and conveyed the basis of divine gnosis. In the year 738 [1337 C.E.] the bird of his spirit took flight from the defile of humanity, and in Daulatabad he built his angelic nest. His blessed shrine, which is full of grace and the first spirit, is located two miles from the fort of Daulatabad.

The Miracles of Aḥmad Sirhindī

One of the most controversial religious figures in Mughul India was Aḥmad Kabūlī Sirhindī ("Praiseworthy, from Kabul [in Afghanistan], and from Sirhind" in northwest India, 1562–1624). He was initially a successful scholar attached to the court of the emperor Akbar ("The Greatest," d. 1605) and was associated with the prime minister Abū al-Fazl (Abūl Faẓl, "Father of Excellence," d. 1601). He underwent a great change, however, when he was initiated into the Naqshbandī Sufi order under the guidance of the Central Asian master Bāqī Billāh ("Abiding in God," d. 1603). As the excerpt below shows, Sirhindī gained notoriety from appearing to claim, in one of his widely circulated epistles, that he was spiritually superior to one of the companions of the Prophet Muḥammad, Abū Bakr. Eventually, criticism of Sirhindī's claims led Emperor Jahāngīr to imprison him in 1619 for a year, and the controversies continued through the nineteenth century both in India and in Arabia.

In the twentieth century, Muslim nationalists gave Sirhindī a new role as defender of Islam against the heresies of the emperor Akbar. This is based primarily on a few selected passages in his writings that are critical of Akbar and Abū al-Fazl, and that show a markedly hostile attitude to Hindus in the Mughul bureaucracy. These remarks took on new significance in the polemical climate of religious nationalism, which now tried to read Indian history as an eternal conflict between Islam and Hinduism. The same attitude places the Mughul prince Dārā Shikūh on the side of his great-grandfather Akbar, because of Dārā's interest in translating Sanskrit religious texts (such as the *Upaniṣads*) into Persian. Curiously, this political judgment is shared by Hindu fundamentalists, but in their view one simply reverses the evaluation, so that Sirhindī becomes an evil fanatic, while Akbar and Dārā become tolerant liberals.

The extract given below is the description of Sirhindī from Dārā Shikūh's well-known biographical work on Sufi saints, *The Ship of the Saints,* which was written in 1640. Contrary to the political interpretation just mentioned, Dārā does not find Sirhindī to be an opponent, nor does the latter's attitude toward Hindus seem to be of interest. Instead, Dārā is concerned to defend Sirhindī from criticism. The defense of Sirhindī as a saint is based on the direct testimony of Dārā's spiritual master, Miyān Mīr ("Respected Prince," d. 1635) of Lahore, who personally observed Sirhindī's miraculous ability to read unspoken thoughts. When Miyān Mīr met Sirhindī, he decided to test Sirhindī by thinking of three questions for him to answer. The first question related to the charge that he claimed superiority to Abū Bakr. The second question was the accusation that Sirhindī's master Bāqī Billāh had begun to teach without authorization from his own master Khwājagī Amkunagī ("Mastery, from Amkuna" in Central Asia, d. 1599–1600); this was a charge made against a newcomer by disgruntled older disciples. The third question was Sirhindī's opinion of the man who initially questioned Bāqī Billāh's credentials, Khāwand Maḥmūd ("Praised," d. 1642–43). Sirhindī passed the test. He spontaneously produced the controversial letter (the eleventh in his collected epistles) and showed it to Miyān Mīr, who found it blameless. He related how Khāwand Maḥmūd questioned Bāqī Billāh's authorization to teach, and told how he himself refuted it and persuaded Khāwand Maḥmūd of the truth. Finally, Sirhindī smoothed over any dispute with Khāwand Maḥmūd by praising him and attributing any problems to the latter's followers. The text is of particular interest because it shows how different Dārā's perception of Sirhindī was from the modern political view of them both.

This text is translated from Dārā Shikūh, *Safīnat al-awliyā'*, edited by Mr. Beale (Agra: Maṭba'-i Madrasa-i Āgrah, 1853), pp. 339–41.

Further Reading

See Yohanan Friedmann, *Shaykh Aḥmad Sirhindī: An Outline of His Thought and a Study of His Image in the Eyes of Posterity* (Montreal: McGill-Queen's University Press, 1971).

The revered Aḥmad Kābulī al-Sirhindī was a descendant of the revered Commander of the Faithful 'Umar Fārūq ["Living, the Discriminator," d. 644]. He was a Ḥānafī in his legal school [follower of Abū Ḥanīfa, d. 767] and lived in Sirhind. He was a disciple of Master Bāqī in the Naqshbandī order, who was a disciple of the learned Khwājagī Amkunagī, who was a disciple of his father, the learned Darvīsh Muḥammad. He also had obtained authorization to guide others from modern Qadiri and Chishti masters. He was a master of meditation, asceticism, miracles, and writing. Toward the end of his life, some accused the shaykh of saying, "My rank is higher than that of the rightly-guided caliphs (Abū Bakr et al.)," but this is pure slander and defamation by opponents of the shaykh.

I myself have heard from the protector of dominion and leadership, the possessor of excellences and perfections, who is conscious of realities and gnosis, the most excellent of the age, my teacher, my learned one, my instructor, the revered Mīrak Shaykh ibn Shaykh Faṣīḥ al-Dīn ["Prince, Teacher, son of Teacher Eloquence of the Faith," that is, Miyān Mīr], who said, "Once we happened to pass through Sirhind, and somehow there was an opportunity to meet with Shaykh Aḥmad. In the midst of the talk, it occurred to me that if the shaykh can perform miracles, he should do three things: first, recall for me what people have said about him; second, explain what I have heard about Master Bāqī his master taking a disciple without authorization from the learned Khwājagī Amkunagī; third, whether he believed in Master Khāwand Maḥmūd.

"After I had been sitting before the shaykh a time, he gave me piece of paper he had beneath his cushion and told me to read it. After I saw all of it, he said, 'Something has happened because of this.' I said, 'From this itself nothing has happened; everything in here is fine.' Again, after a time he said, 'The same is true of what happened to me; the rest is lies.'

"Then after a time, he said, 'One day Master Khāwand Maḥmūd had come here and said, "Master Bāqī did not have a clear authorization from his master, since one day the learned Khwājagī Amkunagī was eating watermelon, and having himself cut it in pieces, gave it into the hands of bystanders and disciples, but he did not give it to Master Bāqī." Those present said, "The Master [Bāqī Billāh] is here too," but the learned Khwājagī Amkunagī said, "We have given him watermelon in the right way." From this Master Bāqī became conceited, thinking, "He has authorized me to give guidance." ' "

" 'I [Sirhindī] said, "This is not so, for we have never heard such words from our master or others; rather, Master Bāqī used to deny it, saying, 'This act was never done by me, and I cannot be responsible for it. The learned Khwājagī [actually] said, "We gave authorization and you ought to do this work." ' At this time some of the older men [present during the conversation between Khāwand Maḥmūd and Sirhindī] also said, "We were present in the assembly, when the learned Khwājagī gave authorization for guidance to Master Bāqī." Master Khāwand Maḥmūd then admitted, "We have listened to error." '

"Then Shaykh Aḥmad said, 'Do you believe what you have heard from the disciples of Master Khāwand Maḥmūd? The master is not like that, and I do not believe that of him.' "

All three doubts had passed through the thoughts of my revered teacher [Miyān Mīr], and the shaykh [Aḥmad Sirhindī] answered them.

His death took place in the year 1034 [1624 C.E.], and the length of his life was sixty-three years. His tomb is in Sirhind.

A Woman Saint: Bībī Jamāl Khātūn

As in other sectors of Islamic culture, women played an important though less public role than men in Islamic mysticism. Among the early Sufis in Iran and Iraq were a number of prominent women, and during the growth of Sufi orders women participated as patrons and disciples of Sufi masters. The following extract concerns Bībī Jamāl Khātūn ("Lady Beauty Noblewoman," d. 1647), also known as Bībī Jīv, the sister of the Sufi leader Miyān Jīv or Miyān Mīr (d. 1635). This passage occurs in *The Peace of the Saints,* which Dārā Shikūh (author of the previous selection) wrote between 1640 and 1642 as a biography of Miyān Jīv and his disciples.

Dārā Shikūh, himself a disciple of Miyān Jīv, knew Bībī Jamāl Khātūn and held her in great respect. As a sign of his esteem, he placed her biography immediately after that of her brother, before the notices of Miyān Jīv's other disciples; large biographical works, such as Dārā's own *The Ship of the Saints,* typically put the biographies of female mystics in an appendix at the end of the book. Dārā describes her saintly virtues in somewhat stereotyped and formulaic terms, comparing her to the famous early woman Sufi, Rābiʿa ("Fourth Daughter," d. 801) of Basra. This selection, typically, emphasizes her miracles as a sign of her spirituality.

Bībī Jamāl Khātūn is an example of a woman who independently pursues a spiritual path in a way that includes but goes beyond the normal social role of family life. Her mother Bībī Fāṭima had been widowed at an early age and had returned to live and study with her father, Qāzī Qāzin (the "Judging Judge"), a renowned Sufi of Sind (in southern Pakistan). Although Bībī Fāṭima trained all her five sons and two daughters in Sufi practice, Miyān Jīv was the one who had the strongest mystical vocation, and all his brothers and sisters later became his disciples and followed his path (*ṭarīqa*) or spiritual method. Bībī Jamāl Khātūn was nonetheless outstanding even in this spiritually talented family, as shown by the vision in which she saw her brother predict the date of his death.

Although Bībī Jamāl Khātūn married, Dārā Shikūh treats it as an unimportant event, to the extent that he fails to mention her husband's name. Evidently she had no children, and after six years of marriage she lived apart from her husband, who must have died or divorced her four years later. The choice of celibacy was her conscious decision to seek a closer relation to God; her later life was passed primarily in prayer and meditation, and she never left her home in Sīvastān in Sind.

The miracles ascribed to Bībī Jamāl Khātūn stress her attainment of mystical states. The episode of the fish, which became luminous after her gaze fell on it when she emerged from a powerful trance, illustrates the concept of mystical experience as the contemplation of light; the light not only filled the soul of the saint, but also spilled over onto an ordinary object like a fish, which was then preserved as a holy relic and source of blessing. Her other miracles also concern household items, like the chicken and the wheat that can feed any number of guests, and the transformation of oil into milk; her blessings also produce sons. Despite her relative isolation, she evidently had many visitors who sought her help. Her contact with Jalāl Khāmūsh, a recently deceased saint, shows how the invisible hierarchy was consulted by ordinary people; they referred problems to her, the most eminent living Sufi in the district, and she in turn invoked God's blessings on someone with higher spiritual status, so that he would convey divine assistance to the petitioner. The fact that Jalāl Khāmūsh was dead in no way impaired his ability to act as an intercessor with God.

Five years after completing the book, Dārā Shikūh appended a postscript giving the date of Bībī Jamāl Khātūn's death.

This selection is translated from Muḥammad Dārā Shikūh, *Sakinat al-awliya'*, edited by Muḥammad Jalālī Nā'īnī (Tehran, 1344/1965), pp. 129–31.

Memorial of the Felicitous Conditions Surrounding the Revered Bībī Jamāl Khātūn (may God prolong the blessings of her noble breaths)

She is the sister of the revered Miyān Jīv (may God sanctify his conscience), and she is the daughter by whose existence the noble mother of the revered Miyān Jīv was ennobled. Today, in the year 1050 [1640–41 C.E.], she is still living. The revered Bībī Jīv mastered lofty states and stages, austerities, and exertions, and in renunciation and detachment she is unique. She is the Rābiʿa of her time, and many miracles and wonders manifested from her and continue to do so.

In the beginning of her spiritual career, she entered into the path of spiritual exercises under the guidance of her illustrious mother and father. After that, the revered Miyān Jīv sent word to her, through the intermediary of his brother Qāzī Ṭāhir ["Judge Pure"], to occupy herself with his path. Thereafter, Bībī was occupied in this path.

In accordance with fate conformable to the religious law, she became joined to one of the nobly born and a legal bond was made between them, and for a space of ten years she was his spouse. Altogether six years passed that they were bedfellows. After that, a divine longing and love won the victory over her in respect to married life, and maintaining complete aloofness, she kept herself separate in her room. She has two maidservants who are at her service in the day, who prepare water for ablutions and other necessities. At night she is alone in that room, occupied with the remembrance of God. In these days absorption prevails over her. And from the time that the revered Miyān Jīv left his homeland, she did not come to see him, nor did the revered Miyān Jīv go to see her, but there was mutual inquiry, and the revered Miyān Jīv frequently praised her.

It is said that one day a fish was brought into Bībī's house when she was absorbed in ecstasy. When she came back from that state she opened her eyes; her blessed gaze, from which a light emanated, fell on that fish. From the influence of this glance, a luminosity appeared on that fish and remained. After that, Bībī Jīv said, "This fish has become holy, and when you preserve it among your possessions, much blessing will be evident in it." Until now, that fish exists in the house of one of her relatives, and its blessings are evident.

Muḥammad Amīn ["Praised, Trustworthy"], a nephew of the revered Miyān Jīv, said, "I heard Bībī say, 'When the time of the revered Miyān Jīv's passing approached, in the angelic world he met me and said, "On such-and-such a day in such-and-such a month, I shall be a traveler in the realm of eternity. Knowing me to be present, occupy yourself with the remembrance of God." ' "

Another story is that often, by the grace of the spirits of the saints, she was cooking a certain amount of food when many people came together. She asked to have a rooster brought, and the first time, saying, "In the name of God, the Merciful, the Compassionate," with her own hand she slaughtered it to make a bit of food, and after that she would have someone else do the slaughtering. Whatever number of people were present, all were completely satisfied.

They say that one day for some reason milk was required and was not to be met with anywhere. This request was conveyed to Bībī Jīv, who asked for a bottle of oil, put her own blessed hand on it, and commanded, "Take milk, as much as you require." They saw that the bottle was full of milk. They got as much milk as they wanted.

And it is said that in the house of Amīr Khān ["Prince Lord"], the judge of

Tatta, there were several daughters. The family of Amīr Khān, going in attendance on Bībī Jīv, made many supplications and lamentations, asking for a son. Bībī Jīv said, "After this there will be sons." From the blessing of her saying, five sons were born, one after another.

They say that once Bībī Jīv cast a quantity of two maunds [about two kilograms] of wheat into the wheat vessel with her own blessed hand. From the blessings of her hand, for a year the whole expense of the house was taken from that, and the wheat remained in the same condition.

They say that in those regions there had been a noble named Jālāl Khāmūsh ["Glory, Silent"], who had perfect renunciation and detachment, from whom Bībī Jīv also had benefited internally. Whenever a difficulty befell anyone, or a need became pressing, they would refer it to the revered Bībī Jīv. Then Bībī Jīv would go to the grave of Shaykh Jālāl Khāmūsh and spiritually turn to him. The problem of that person would be solved in accordance with her prayer.

The noble age of Bībī Jīv Khātūn is in excess of sixty and she dwells in her own abode in Sīvastān, and she has never left that place for any other.

Her miracles are more numerous than one could list, but for the sake of blessing this piece of information was written after the composition of this book: her demise took place on Tuesday the twenty-seventh of Rabīʿ the First in the year 1057 (May 2, 1647).

—35—

Conversations of Sufi Saints

Carl Ernst

The primary medium through which the Sufi masters communicated their teachings in India was oral instruction. Although most Sufis studied Islamic law, theology, and mysticism in Arabic and Persian, the early masters of the most popular Indian Sufi order, the Chishtīs, did not themselves write. Several of them were, however, surrounded by disciples of a literary bent, who decided to record their masters' teaching in a diary form. The pioneer of this new literary form was Amīr Ḥasan Dihlawī ("Prince Fine, of Delhi", d. after 1329), a famous poet at the Delhi court. From 1307 until 1322, he recorded the conversations of his teacher, Niẓām al-Dīn Awliyā' ("Order of the Faith, the Saint of Saints," d. 1325), whenever he was able to visit Delhi. His compilation, *Morals for the Heart,* became extremely popular as a summary of the master's teaching, and subsequent generations of Sufis likewise had disciples record their discourses (*malfūẓāt*) in writing.

In this way, one of Niẓām al-Dīn's chief successors, Shaykh Naṣīr al-Dīn Maḥmūd Chirāgh-i Dihlī ("Helper of the Faith, the Praised, the Lamp of Delhi," d. 1356) is known to us through the vivid diary of his sayings recorded in 1354 by his disciple Ḥamīd Qalandar ("Praiser," belonging to the unconventional "qalandar" type of Sufi). This text, entitled *The Best of Assemblies,* was in part personally corrected by the shaykh, who pruned down the verbose style of his disciple, making it into a beautiful example of clear and simple Persian prose. Unlike formal treatises on mysticism, it conveys the dynamic give-and-take of living conversation and personal interaction. This selection is the thirty-sixth assembly, given in full, followed by a brief excerpt from the twelfth assembly. Chirāgh-i Dihlī is shown here as a Sufi who has fully imbibed the canonical tradition of the Qur'ān and the ḥadīth sayings of the Prophet Muḥammad, which he uses as the basis for his homilies. We also see him receiving a "man of the world," who has sought the saint's supernatural aid in some unspecified difficulty. As soon as the man comes in, the saint observes, without being told, that the man's difficulty has been solved. Chirāgh-i Dihlī uses the incident, however, to point out the hidden benefits of afflictions sent by God, who tolerates the ephemeral success of evildoers like Pharaoh. This leads him, a celibate, to reflect on the distractions inherent in earthly possessions and family life, which disturb the meditations of the mystic. In all cases he recommends "recollection of God" (*dhikr*), meditation on the names of God, which is one of the principal spiritual methods of classical Sufism. Of particular interest is his skillful adaptation of the story of Moses and the idolater to the Indian environment; a similar story had been told by the Persian poets Rūmī and Saʿdī, but without any reference to India. Here, Chirāgh-i Dihlī has the idolater address the idol in Hindi, and the story of the idolater's renunciation of paganism and his forgiving acceptance by God brings the audience to tears. The master concludes with some words about the divine mercy. This is a typical example of how Sufi tradition forged in Iraq and Iran came to be adapted to the situation of South Asia.

The brief excerpt from the twelfth assembly is a remark about the importance of breath control in meditation. It is significant because of the casual mention of Hindu yogis, whose technique is acknowledged to be fundamentally similar to that of the Sufis, regardless of their doctrinal differences.

The selections are translated from Naṣīr al-Dīn Maḥmūd Chirāgh-i Dihlī, *Khayr al-majālis,* compiled by Hamīd Qalandar, edited by Khaliq Ahmad Nizami, Publication of the Department of History, Muslim University, no. 5, Studies in Indo-Muslim Mysticism, 1 (Aligarh: Muslim University, Department of History, [1959]), pp. 120–25, 59–60.

Further Reading

Hasan Dihlawi, *Morals for the Heart,* translated by Bruce B. Lawrence (New York: Paulist Press, 1992).

The Conversations of Naṣīr al-Dīn Maḥmūd Chirāgh-i Dihlī

THE THIRTY-SIXTH ASSEMBLY

Good fortune and happiness! The happiness of speech [with the master] was facilitated. The master (God remember him to the good) had mentioned some useful point, and eminent learned men were seated [in attendance]. He kindly told me to come sit closer. Then he began to speak. I [still] did not hear, so he repeated his remarks, saying, "A man came into the presence of the Messenger of God (God bless him and grant him peace), and said, 'Counsel me, Messenger of God.' The Messenger of God said, 'He who works an atom's weight of good will see its reward. And he who works an atom's weight of evil will see its reward.' The man said, 'That suffices me, Messenger of God.' He replied, 'The man has understood.' That is, he will do as he has heard."

Then a man came in to see the master. He was an eminent man of the world, just and renowned, and having sought the master's help, he was released [from his difficulty] by the blessing of the thought of the master. As soon as he entered, the master brightened up and said, "Welcome! How wonderful! Sit down, for you were released." He said, "By the blessing of the thought of the master, last night I was released." Then the master said, "When a thorn pricks one's foot, or an ant bites one, one should know that it is the reward of one's action, as God says in the holy Qur'ān: 'And the affliction that befalls you is acquired by your own hands' (Qur. 42.30)." Then he said, "What is affliction? An occurrence that is disliked. In general, the word 'affliction' (*muṣībat*) is that which people dislike. But the words 'occurrence' (*iṣābat*) and 'befell' (*aṣāba*) have been mentioned in reports of the Prophet also. God says, 'Whatever of good befalls you is from God' (Qur. 4.79)." Then he said, "The word 'affliction,' for a disliked occurrence, is acknowledged as a legitimate category." Again he said, "When something disliked occurs, the sins one has committed are forgiven on that account, because one is awakened thereby and turns back toward God, and sorrowing repentance is brought about. One's errors are forgiven on that account."

Then he said, "Whatever injury and affliction God sends is one's guide to happiness. But the person who has been granted a long life and has many worldly goods is sent no difficulties, and he falls short in his devotions; this is 'being led on,' and 'being led on' is very near to punishment. God says: 'Step by step we lead them on from whence they know not' (Qur. 7.182)." Then he said, "Pharaoh never had a headache. Throughout the long life he had, he claimed that he was God, but never had a headache."

Then he said, "The Master of the Law has called possessions and children a trial. 'Your possessions and children are a trial' (Qur. 8.28)." He said, "They are a trial because you want to be occupied in devotions in the corner of the house for a time. The children come and pull on your garment, saying, 'This devotion of yours is no good to us! Go, get something for us to eat!' Because of children you abandon your devotions to God. Then you come out, and become worried and distracted. Thus are children a trial. Wealth is also a trial, because as long as there is no wealth, you are occupied with God. When wealth comes, one gets to thinking of pretty girls and longs for enjoyment and delight. Thus wealth is also a trial."

"But if one does not spend on oneself that which God has given him, what does one do? One spends it for the sake of God, such as in giving to darvīshes, visiting the sick, building mosques, and doing other good deeds. When one turns the corrupt tool of wealth into good deeds, it is not a trial."

Then he said, "Be involved in whatever work you do, speak, and do the world's business. But never let your tongue be empty of the remembrance of God for one minute. Whether standing, sitting, or tumbling in His path, you should remember God," and he recited this verse: " 'Those who remember God standing and sitting and on their sides' (Qur. 3.191). When your tongue is busy remembering God, it is to be hoped that it will remove all the sorrows of the world from your heart, and make you sorrowless." Then he said, "What happiness is there beyond this, that in the corner of your house, or in the mosque, or in a shrine, you are occupied with the remembrance of God and are not occupied with human devils? Who are the human devils? They are the ones who hold you back from the remembrance of God when you wish to be occupied in remembrance of God, for God is seated beside you. It is said in the divine sayings, 'I am seated beside him who remembers me.' and God reminds us in the Qur'ān, 'Remember me, and I will remember you' (Qur. 2.152). When you hold back from remembering God, your companions are devils. God says, 'He who turns away from the remembrance of the Merciful, We assign to him a devil' (Qur. 43.36), or 'We entrust [to him a devil].' And when you are occupied in remembrance of God, who will be your companion?" At this point he turned both eyes up toward heaven and said, "God will be. See what God has said: 'I am seated beside him who remembers me.' " Then he said, "This is the saying of Abū Bakr al-Ṭamistānī [d. 954] (God have mercy on him); the Shaykh of Shaykhs [i.e., Abū Ḥafṣ ʿUmar Shihāb al-Dīn al-Suhr-avardī, d. 1234] (God sanctify his soul) has said in the *ʿAwārif,* that ʿAbū Bakr al-Ṭamistānī (God have mercy on him) said, 'Keep the company of God, and if you are unable, keep the company of those who keep the company of God, in order that the blessing of their company may unite you with the company of God.' "

After that he told the following story. "In the age of the prophet Moses (God's prayer and peace be upon him), there was an idolater among the Israelites, who had practiced idolatry four hundred years. He had not ceased for a single day in these four hundred years, and he did not raise his head from the foot of the idol, nor did he pray for any necessity during these four hundred years. One day he got a fever, and he placed his head on the idol's foot and said, '*Tū merā gusāʾīṅ, tūn merā kartār, mujh is tap tahīṅ chuṛā.*' In Persian, that is, he said to the idol, 'You are my God, you are my Creator, release me from this fever!' He said this in the Indian language, just as it is written. However much he spoke to the idol, what answer comes from stone? No answer came. His fever increased. He got up and kicked it, saying, '*Tū merā kartār nahīṅ!*' That is, 'You are not my Creator!' He went out and saw a mosque before him. He put his head inside the mosque and said once, 'O God of Moses!' From the four directions, the cry came, 'I am here, my servant! I am here, my servant!' This was heard seventy times, without interruption. He was astonished, saying, 'For four hundred years I have not raised my head from the foot of the idol, and I never prayed for any necessity. Today I pray for one, but the idol did not supply my necessity. He gave no reply, no matter how much I implored him. A single time I called out in the name of the God of Moses, and seventy times I heard, "I am here, my servant!" I am His servant! So much of my life has been wasted!' Then he prayed for what he needed: 'O God of Moses, remove this fever from me!' At once the fever left him."

"Afterward he went before Moses, saying, 'O Moses! If one has practiced idolatry for four hundred years, and during these four hundred years not once lifted one's head from the foot of the idol, but afterwards turns back to your God, will your God make peace with him or not?' Moses (on whom be peace) was wrathful. When he heard that someone had practiced idolatry for four hundred years, and never once lifted his head from the idol's foot, the expression of wrath was plain on Moses' face. the idolater grew afraid, and fled from Moses, and every moment he was looking back and thinking, with trust in the mercy of God, that he would call him back. At that moment a revelation occurred: 'O Moses! Receive my servant, and tell him, "What of four hundred years? If you practice idolatry for four thousand years, and despair of the idol in time of need, then just once cry out in our name; mercy is from us. I reply without interruption seventy times, and every necessity that you pray for I provide." ' Moses ran barefoot, saying, 'Come! For your repentance has been accepted, and your faith has been found acceptable! It is decreed, even so: "If for four hundred years, nay! If for four thousand years you practice idolatry and never once lift your head from the idol's foot, and then despair of him and come to us, and just once cry out, then seventy times without interruption I will reply, and every necessity that you pray for I will provide to your desire." ' "

The master told this story, and those who were present wept with loud cries and exclamations. A clamor arose, and I became upset from weeping. He said something that I did not follow. I composed myself, and listened. He was saying, "God is kind and merciful. He has said, 'My mercy is quicker than my wrath.' Since mercy is quicker, wrath is delayed." After that he said, "He gives life, he bestows the blessing of faith, and he distributes sustenance. God says, 'Though you reckon the blessings of God you will not count them' (Qur. 14.34). Do not forget a God such as this. He did not exclude an infidel who had practiced idolatry for four hundred years; if a Muslim repents, he is merciful and kind, he accepts it." After that he recited this verse, " 'Truly God does not forgive that one should associate partners with him, and he forgives all else besides that to whomsoever he wishes' (Qur. 4.48)." And praise be to God, Lord of Creation.

FROM THE TWELFTH ASSEMBLY

He said, "The essence of this matter is restraint of breath, that is, the Sufi ought to hold his breath during meditation. As long as he holds his breath, his interior is concentrated, and when he releases his breath, the interior is distracted, and it destroys his momentary state." . . . Then he said, "Therefore the Sufi is he whose breath is counted. The adept is the master of breath; this has but a single meaning. The accomplished yogis, who are called *siddha* in Indian language, breathe counted breaths."

—36—

Teachings of Two Punjabi Sufi Poets

Mustansir Mir

Punjabi is spoken in the large northwestern province of the Punjab—East Punjab in India and West Punjab in Pakistan. It has a rich literary tradition, and is especially rich in mystical poetry. Two of the most popular Muslim mystic poets of the Punjab—both of West Punjab—are Sulṭān Bāhū (1630–1691) and Bulleh Shāh (1680–1758).

The last quarter of the seventeenth and the first half of the eighteenth centuries in Indian history were marked by intense political and social upheavals. The Mughal empire showed clear signs of disintegration, and the reign of the last great Mughal emperor Aurangzeb, begun in 1658, was to end in 1707. The British were consolidating and expanding their hold in India. Sikhism, originally aimed at religious reform through a syncretist program, had by the end of the seventeenth century given rise to a distinct and strong political community, challenging the Mughals. The Punjab was especially strife-ridden, and Bulleh Shāh in his poetry makes a few references to the situation, which would understandably drive some souls, among them mystics, into a private world of universal love and compassion that gave comfort denied in the world outside.

Both Sulṭān Bāhū and Bulleh Shāh received traditional orthodox education, but had a preference for the mystical path. Sulṭān Bāhū is said to have written, besides poems in Punjabi, about one hundred and forty books on mysticism, all in Persian; only a few of them are extant. His Punjabi verse, like his other works, gives evidence of his familiarity with the Islamic literary tradition, and this is true to a greater degree of Bulleh Shāh. A word about the names of the two poets. Bāhū, if analyzed as a Persian construction, would mean "with Him," and, with the addition of a dot under the first letter, would become the Sufi Arabic invocation meaning "O He!" *Sulṭān* means "king"; *Bāhū* is so called because he is recognized to be the "king of those who know." As for Bulleh Shāh, his given name was ʿAbdallāh, which became the (variously pronounced and written) nickname Bullah, Bulleh, or Bullhe. With a slightly different intonation it means "one who has forgotten" or "one who has lost the way." Both Sulṭān Bāhū and Bulleh Shāh played on the possible mystic significations of their names.

The poetry of Sulṭān Bāhū and Bulleh Shāh has reached us mainly through oral transmission. Early manuscript evidence is lacking in the case of both, but disciples, admirers, and minstrels in the early phases, scholars and researchers in the modern period, and folk memory through the centuries have managed to preserve, and have conferred a reasonably high degree of authenticity on, much of the verse in question. Naturally there are variants, and sometimes the recensions prepared by different hands diverge greatly. Still there is, in the case of each poet, a body of verse, as also a distinctive style, that enables us to establish internal criteria not only for the validation of the texts but also for their interpretation.

The poetry of Sulṭān Bāhū and Bulleh Shāh has a critical and a constructive aspect. On the constructive side, love of God, and often also of the Prophet Muḥammad, is emphasized as the supreme virtue, and the need for living the good moral life is underscored. Such a life can be lived, it is maintained, with the help of a spiritual guide and in the company of pious people. On the critical side, worldliness, empty ritualism, sectarianism, pedantry, and hypocrisy are decried and held up to ridicule. In this way a distinction is drawn between what is essential and truly meaningful in life and what is incidental and superficial. The specific terms or concepts used to make this distinction are typically Sufi in their dialectic—body and soul, interior and exterior, bookish learning and intuitive understanding. Above all, these works are marked by an all-pervading humanity that endears them to a vast audience.

We may note the use of one or two conventions of Punjabi mystic poetry, conventions that have thematic significance. Both Sulṭān Bāhū and Bulleh Shāh frequently address themselves in their verses, using their names (Bāhū and Bulleh) as noms de plume, usually in the last line or concluding part of the poem. This feature, in view of the didactic nature of Sufi poetry, is significant in two ways: first, it softens the blow of any criticism offered by making the poet himself the addressee of the criticism; second, it represents a humble acknowledgment on the part of the poet that he has to reform himself before he can advise and admonish others. According to another convention, encountered especially in Bulleh Shāh, the mystic presents himself as a bride trying to woo the bridegroom, God. The implication is that a Sufi, having suffered loss of self in his quest, becomes a passive vehicle through which God, the active partner in the relationship, operates. Thus the roles of the lover and the beloved, as ordinarily perceived, are reversed, with the lover (poet) becoming the one pursued and the beloved (God) becoming the pursuer. To put it differently, God himself chooses the object and recipient of his grace.

The standard form used by Sulṭān Bāhū is the octametrical four-liner, though in actual recitation in Punjabi there is a pause in the middle of each line, yielding two tetrametrical halves. The lines have the same rhyme, and, in most recensions, each line also ends with a self-standing word, *hū*, meaning "he," or rather "He" (God). A sort of Sulṭān Bāhū trademark, the word not only carries a mystic meaning, but, coming as it does at the end of every line, also creates a hypnotic effect, especially when the verses are sung. The poetry of Bulleh Shāh has greater formal diversity, ranging from two-liners to poems of several stanzas. Metrically, too, it is more diverse; in fact it exhibits a lack of respect for the constraints of meter. Sulṭān Bāhū's poems, unlike Bulleh Shāh's, have an alphabetical arrangement, as whole sets of them begin with one or the other letter, the poems together running the gamut of the alphabet.

Both Sulṭān Bāhū and Bulleh Shāh employ the vernacular language, which must have been plain to the original audience, though today a large part of the vocabulary would be more readily understood in rural rather than in urban Punjab. The general meaning of most of the verses would, however, be clear to most Punjabis. The language is idiomatic, and there is constant shuttling between the literal and metaphorical (or mystic) meanings. It has a highly epigrammatic quality, and also is eminently "singable," both factors doubtless aiding in the preservation of the verses down the ages. The poetry, moreover, is rooted in a living context, to which its language constantly appeals. The imagery, for example, is drawn from a variety of everyday situations of village life: weaving, spinning, and pottery making; churning milk and making yogurt; sowing seeds and harvesting crops; swimming and rowing in the nearby river; collecting wood to make a fire and lighting a lantern as the night approaches; hunting game and fighting off predatory animals in the surrounding jungle; the mendicant going around in his worn clothes, begging-bowl in hand; and the local religious scholar in the mosque teaching children how to read the Qur'ān. But it should be kept in mind that the poetry of Sulṭān Bāhū and Bulleh Shāh, while it was meant to be readily comprehensible to its original hearers, is at the same time grounded in the Islamic literary tradition, as evidenced, for instance, by the multitude of references and allusions it contains to Islamic sources, history, and tradition.

At the risk of oversimplification, one might say that Sulṭān Bāhū is a moralist whereas Bulleh Shāh is more of a philosopher. The kindly didacticism of Sulṭān Bāhū, couched in charmingly simple language, compels quiet and serious attention. In language equally captivating but in a bold, even audacious manner all his own, Bulleh Shāh on the one hand forces one to reevaluate the assumptions of a smug, heedless life, and, on the other hand, with his pantheistic utterances, raises questions about one's relationship with God. On another level, Sulṭān Bāhū exhorts one to take up the challenges of life courageously, while Bulleh Shāh seems to strike a note of resignation.

The poetry of Sulṭān Bāhū and Bulleh Shāh appeals to audiences across religious boundaries: Hindus and Sikhs as well as Muslims enjoy reading it or listening to oral recitations of it. Yet there is no doubt that the two poets are, in regard to both thematic complex and linguistic repertoire, situated firmly within the Islamic tradition, and it is a mistake to think that they were influenced by the Hindu Vedantic tradition or advocate the doctrine of unity of religions based on a rejection of the formal aspects of religions. What we have called the critical aspect of their poetry can be appreciated by people of any religious outlook—or for that matter by people of any outlook on religion—but the constructive side of their poetry cannot be reduced to an abstract, formless doctrine, for it consists of a positive set of values that is decidedly Islamic in structure and detail. For all their detractive remarks about the mulla and the scholar, Sulṭān Bāhū and Bulleh Shāh, themselves orthodox in belief and practice, hold the basic code of the Sharīʿah—Islamic law—to be inviolate, seeking only to imbue conduct with moral insight and spiritual meaning. The apparently bold statements about religious belief and practice that, especially in the case of Bulleh Shāh, sometimes have an antinomian ring, must not, therefore, be interpreted to mean a revolt against formal religion in general or formal Islam in particular. They are rather attempts to shock people into reality through use of the favorite Sufi technique of "allopathy"—remedying something by means of its opposite.

The following selections give a fairly good idea of some of the principal themes and motifs in the poetry of Sulṭān Bāhū and Bulleh Shāh. The poetry of Sulṭān Bāhū and Bulleh Shāh has a simple construction, and thus admits of a straightforward translation. In rendering it into English, therefore, I have stayed close to the original, and have only occasionally felt the need to make an interpretive translation. Very occasionally, again, have I felt the need to rearrange, for purposes of translation, some of the lines in the original texts. The translations are followed by notes that are meant to serve as guidelines for discussion and provide clarifications one might need in reading the translations.

The translations are made by the author from *Kalām-i-Sulṭān Bāhū* (Punjabi) ("The Verses of Sulṭān Bāhū"), edited by Sayyid Nazir Ahmad (Lahore: Packages Ltd., 1981), cited as *KSB;* and *Bulleh Shah: A Selection. Rendered into English Verse* by Taufiq Rafat, with an introduction by Khaled Ahmad (Lahore: Vanguard Publications, 1982), cited at *BS*, which includes texts based on the Sayyid Nazir Ahmad edition, published under the title *Kalam-i Bulleh Shāh* ("The Verses of Bulleh Shāh") in Lahore in 1977.

Further Reading

The following books may be consulted: Lajwanti Krishna, *Punjabi Sufi Poems* (New Delhi: Ashajanak Publications, 1973; reprint of 1938 Oxford edition); J. R. Puri and T. R. Shangari, *Bulleh Shah, The Love-Intoxicated Iconoclast* (Amritsar: Radha Soami Satsang Beas, 1986); and I. Serebryakov, *Punjabi Literature: A Brief Outline* (Moscow: Nauka Publishing House, 1968).

SULṬĀN BĀHŪ

Jasmine in My Heart

My master planted jasmine in my heart.
"No" and "Yes" watered the plant,

Soaking it through and through.
It blossomed, its fragrance filled my heart.
May he live long, Bāhū—
My perfect master, who planted this flower!

KSB, p. 1. Praise for the master for planting in the disciple's heart the flower of divine love. "No" and "Yes" refer, respectively, to negation of everything other than God and affirmation of God as the only deity. Compare the negative and affirmative components of the Islamic formulaic declaration of the oneness of God: "I bear witness that there is no god but God."

Learning without Understanding

Beta, theta is what they read,
Alpha is what they omit.
And even those who read a bit,
Reading what they ought to,
Fail to reach the Beloved.
The light is all around and yet
The blind—they cannot see.
If you fail to get to God,
All you read is tales and stuff.

KSB, p. 16. The Arabic name for God, Allah, begins with *a*, the first letter of the alphabet. Symbolically, therefore, God is the beginning ("alpha") of all knowledge, and acquisition of knowledge should therefore begin with an understanding of God, for otherwise it would be like learning the alphabet by starting at beta and theta. "They" in line 1 refers to scholars. The first line of the original translates literally: "They have become accomplished scholars by reading beta and theta." I have read the second line of the original slightly differently, in light of another recension, and translated accordingly. Lines 3–5 refer to those who make only half-hearted attempts to attain knowledge of God.

If God Could Be Won

If God could be won by bathing and washing,
Frogs and fish would have;
If God could be won by getting shorn,
Sheep and goats would have.
If God could be won through celibacy,
Castrated bulls would have.
God is won by no such means;

He is won by those
Whose intentions are pure.

KSB, p. 30. Purity of heart enables one to achieve nearness to God. Note the rejection of celibacy in lines 5–6.

Looking for Him

He lives close by,
He appears to be far,
He steps not into my yard.
Failing to find him inside,
People go out to look for him.
It's no use, to seek him far afield,
The Beloved is to be found inside the house:
Polish your heart like a mirror,
And the veils will all be rent.

KSB, p. 90. The favorite mystic theme of enlightenment through self-purification.

Lose, and You'll Find

If you are iron, you will become a sword
Only when beaten flat.
Only when you are, like a comb,
Torn from limb to limb,
Will the Beloved's hair engulf you.
Only when you are, like henna, crushed,
Will you adorn the Beloved's feet.
Only when you become a true lover,
Will you taste the drink of love.

KSB, p. 78. The importance of "paying one's dues." In lines 3–4 the teeth of the comb are represented as being so many torn limbs of a body.

Making Friends with Fire

Cry, my heart,
Maybe the Lord will hear
The sighs of those stricken with love.
Pain fills my heart,
My heart is in flames.

Without a match the lamp is not lit,
And without suffering there is no sighing.
If it makes friends with fire,
Will the moth get burned or not?

KSB, p. 73. Suffering is the necessary consequence of love of God, and a true lover should be ready and willing to pay the price, just as the moth, once it strikes a friendship with the lamp, must be prepared to die. Also, there is no light without love of God: it is the match of this love that sets the heart ablaze, and the sacrifice is thus worth it.

Deeper than Oceans Is the Heart

The heart is deeper than rivers and seas—
Who has fathomed the heart!
Everything is in it—
Ships and storms, oars and boatmen.
There, in the heart, is the whole wide world,
Vast like a tent outstretched.
He who learns the secret of the heart
Comes to know God.

KSB, p. 40. This is perhaps the best-known verse of Sulṭān Bāhū.

"A Lion of a Man!" They'll Say

They will set about making your grave,
And will put you in it,
Your permanent home;
They will cover you up with dirt,
Making a pile of a grave;
They will say the necessary prayers,
And head back home, saying,
"A lion of a man!"
But in the court of God,
Nothing will avail
Except good deeds.

KSB, p. 78. After one's death, one will be presented in the court of God, where the only thing that will count is one's good deeds; one's reputation in this world will be of no avail to one.

God Will Provide

Quit reasoning, O mendicant,
Buckle up, get ready!
The birds fly, provisioned with nothing
Except trust in their Maker.
Every day they fly and get their food,
Never hoarding anything.
God feeds the insect that crawls inside a rock.

KSB, p. 36. The mendicant, who has devoted his life to worship of God, should put his trust in God and stop worrying about tomorrow.

A Perfect Guide is Like a Washerman

One needs a perfect guide!
One who would, like a washerman,
Wash one thoroughly clean;
With a piercing glance purify one's heart,
Using no soda or soap;
A guide who would shine up
Those begrimed with dirt,
Leaving them spotless;
A guide who would
Impenetrate one's being.

KSB, p. 69. The role of a true master explained. Also a criticism, by implication, of false and incompetent guides.

BULLEH SHĀH

Who Am I?

Who am I, Bulleh? What do I know?
I'm not a Muslim sitting in the mosque,
Nor an unbeliever firm in unbelief.
I'm not a saint,
Nor a sinner untouchable.
I'm not Moses, I'm not Pharaoh.
Who am I, Bulleh? What do I know?

I've nothing to do
With clean and unclean,

With joy and sorrow.
I'm not of water, nor of earth,
Nor of fire, nor of wind.
Who am I, Bulleh? What do I know?

I never fathomed the secret of religion,
I'm not born of Adam and Eve,
I never got myself a name.
I'm not still, I'm not in motion.
Who am I, Bulleh? What do I know?

I call myself first and last,
And refuse to recognize another.
No one is wiser than I.
But who's that, standing over there?
Who am I, Bulleh? What do I know?

BS, pp. 68, 70. The poem raises, and attempts to answer, the question of what constitutes true human identity. The ordinary categories, laid down or suggested by convention, law, and philosophy, are found wanting. Lines 4–5 of stanza 1 may also be translated: "Nor am I one untouchable in the midst of the pious." The last stanza seems to be providing an answer to the question—union with God brings out the true essence in a human being—but thwarts the attempt at a neat final answer by asking enigmatically, "But who's that, standing over there?" which is meant, through denial of total identification of humans with God, to blunt orthodox criticism. A variant of the last line translates: "Who is the true beloved, Bulleh?"

From Hīr to Rānjha

"Rānjha! O Rānjha!" I cried so much,
In the end I became Rānjha myself.
"Rānjha!" is how you should call me now,
Do not call me Hīr.
Rānjha is in me, I in Rānjha,
No thought of other exists,
It's not I, it's he;
It's he who comforts himself.
he who dwells inside me
Is now of the same caste as I,
And I've become like him,
The one I love.
Girl! Take off your white garments,
Wrap yourself in a beggar's sacking,

For white will become soiled and stained,
But not the sacking.
Bulleh! Take me to Takht Hazara,
for I'm not welcome
in the land of the Sials.

BS, p. 100. Hīr and Rānjha are the main characters in what is probably the most famous romance in Punjabi literature. Hīr, a woman, stands for body, whereas Rānjha stands for soul. Hīr is separated from her lover and forcibly married to another suitor. The lovers meet a tragic end, but their souls are reunited in heaven. Bulleh Shāh calls himself Hīr (compare the bride-bridegroom motif, noted above), saying that absorption in the thought of God has made him one with God, just as Hīr's great love for Rānjha made her one with Rānjha in spirit. Takht Hazara (line 17) is the birthplace of Rānjha. The Sials (last line) were the tribe Hīr belonged to. Hīr wishes to move to the land of her beloved, for her own people have, disapproving of her love for Rānjha, turned against her. In the same line Bulleh's name is mentioned, but simply as a matter of convention, for Bulleh Shāh, of course, is not the one whose help is being invoked by Hīr.

It's All Cotton

Cloth four hundred threads in width, or five,
Garments plain or dressy,
Muslin fine and elegant—
The same one thread runs through them all.
And from the same roll comes out, too,
The brownish garment of the saint.
All these are so many forms
That cotton takes.

BS, p. 106. The unity underlying phenomenal multiplicity. Only the second of three stanzas is translated here.

An Alif is All You Need

Enough, my friend, of learning, enough!
A single alif is all you need.
Of learning there's no end,
Life ebbs away! No guarantees!
Enough, my friend, of learning, enough!

You read, you write:
The books you read, the books you write,

Are piled around you, and so high!
Brilliant light is all around,
Darkness in the midst.
"Where's the way?" should someone ask,
You would not know, would you?
Enough, my friend, of learning, enough!

You spend your time in prayer,
Offering extra prayers, too;
Announce the time of prayer to all,
And take the pulpit and sermonize.
Learning has been your disgrace!
Enough, my friend, of learning, enough!

Full of problems learning is:
Those with eyes turn utterly blind,
Nabbing saints, releasing thieves.
Enough, my friend, of learning, enough!

You're so learned, you're called a shaykh.
You dish out verdicts you make up yourself,
Looting and plundering the ignorant,
Making vows of every sort.
Enough, my friend, of learning, enough!

The erudite mulla becomes a judge!
God is pleased without learning, though.
Your greed grows by the day;
Your greed has brought disgrace to you.
Enough, my friend, of learning, enough!

You teach people the do's and don't's,
The food you eat is tainted, though.
You teach one thing, but do another,
Base inside, gilt without.
Enough, my friend, of learning, enough!

The day I read the lesson of love,
The sea of Oneness put terror in my heart.
I got stuck in the eddying waters.
Shāh ʿInāyat brought me ashore.
Enough, my friend, of learning, enough!

BS, pp. 114–18. Alif is the first letter of the Arabic alphabet's compare Sulṭān Bāhū, poem 2. In the opening stanza, line 4, "No guarantees" means that one's life may end at any moment, implying that one should therefore use it purposefully. Stanza 2 speaks of the inability of many scholars to receive or give the right guidance in spite of their great erudition. Lines 5–6 are ironical: these scholars are like a lantern or lamp that lights up the surrounding area but underneath it there is complete darkness. Stanza 4 says that bookish learning causes one to make gross errors; lacking inner light, one is liable to confuse good and bad—thus, for example, incriminating the pious and sparing the wicked. In stanza 5, "verdicts" in line 2 refers to legal rulings which a scholar of the law dispenses when requested to do so. Stanzas 5–7 criticize the hypocritical lifestyle of scholars who are legally qualified but spiritually and morally bankrupt. "Making vows of every sort" means swearing false oaths in order to convince others of one's truthfulness. In the final stanza, Bulleh Shāh praises and thanks his guide and mentor, Shāh ʿInāyat, for steering him to the destination of truth (compare Sulṭān Bāhū, first poem).

5 The Wiles of Fate

The blossoming season arrived,
The birds alighted to nibble and eat.
Falcons picked up some of them,
Some were caught in nets.
Some did hope to make it back,
Spits were put through some.
Bulleh Shāh! What can he do
Who falls a prey to fate?

BS, p. 44. Teaches the lesson of resignation to the fate decreed by God.

Traditions in Transition and Conflict

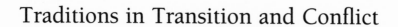

—37—

Ascetic Withdrawal or Social Engagement

Patrick Olivelle

The sixth century B.C.E. was a watershed in the history of Indian religions, a period that witnessed momentous social, economic, and political changes. A surplus economy, the establishment of cities and large kingdoms, the facility of travel, and the rise of a merchant class contributed to the emergence of several significant religious doctrines and institutions, including the new religious movements of Buddhism and Jainism. A major concept in the emerging new world was *saṃsāra,* a category that provided the framework for understanding and evaluating human life. According to this new understanding, life is ultimately and essentially suffering, subject as it is to repeated births and deaths. The goal of human existence, therefore, should be to transcend this bondage to the cycle of rebirth and to reach the realm of total freedom and bliss called *mokṣa.* The religions sharing this world view challenged the society-centered ritual religion of the earlier Vedic period. The result of this confluence of two opposing worlds was a deep and lasting conflict within Indian religions between the value of responsible social engagement within the context of marriage and family and the ascetic withdrawal from society that was seen as the necessary precondition for achieving liberation.

The conflict between these world views is revealed in the emerging diversity of opinion regarding dharma, that is, the proper way to act and the right doctrines to believe. In the mainstream of the Vedic tradition, dharma meant the rules for ritual and moral behavior contained in the Vedic scriptures. By the sixth century B.C.E., such a simple solution to the question, "What is dharma?" was no longer possible, especially because of the new value systems resulting from ascetic ideologies that considered society and social norms as well as the ritual religion to be part of saṃsāra, the world of suffering subject to rebirth. Good and intelligent people were asking serious questions about ultimate truth and proper conduct, all trying in their own way to define the "true" dharma. The Buddha himself, for example, called his new doctrine and way of life dharma. This spirit of inquiry and doubt is captured well in the following passage from the *Mahābhārata*

(14.48.14–17, slightly abbreviated here), which also reveals the diversity of opinions regarding the proper dharma within the brahmanical tradition itself.

Some sages question a divine being:

> Which of the different paths of proper behavior and conduct (dharma) do the scriptures advise us to follow most closely? The various paths that people take as proper, it appears to us, are diverse and contradictory.
>
> Some, for example, claim that there is life after death, while others maintain that there is not. Some express doubt about everything, while others claim certainty.
>
> Things are impermanent according to some and permanent according to others, unreal according to some and real according to others, while still others claim that they are both real and unreal.
>
> Some believe that the one reality appears as diverse. Some teach unity, others separateness, and yet others multiplicity. So do wise brahmans who know the truth opine.
>
> Some wear matted hair and deer skin, some shave their heads, while others go naked. Some say that one should not bathe, while others insist on bathing. Some favor eating, while others are given to fasting.
>
> Some praise rites and others cessation from them. Some assert the influence of both place and time [in astrology], while others deny it. Some extoll liberation and others diverse pleasures.
>
> Some desire wealth, while others strive after poverty. Some maintain the efficacy of worship, while others deny it.
>
> Some are devoted to noninjury (*ahiṃsā*) and others to injury. Some claim that we attain glory through good deeds, while others deny it.
>
> Some proclaim certainty as to the truth, while others adhere to skepticism. Suffering is the motive for some, pleasure for others.
>
> Some assert the primacy of meditation, others that of sacrifice, and still others that of giving gifts. Some assert the existence of everything, while others deny that anything exists.
>
> Some praise austerity, while others extoll Vedic study. Some assert that knowledge comes from renunciation, while nature philosophers claim that it comes from nature.
>
> With so much disagreement regarding proper belief and conduct (dharma), leading in so many directions, we are bewildered, O God Supreme, unable to reach any certainty.

"This is ultimate bliss," "No, that is ultimate bliss": so thinking, people charge on, for one always praises the dharma to which one is devoted.

Our judgment is confounded in this regard, our mind bewildered. This we want you to tell us, O Lord: what is ultimate bliss?

Centrality of the Householder: Ritual and Procreation

The ideal religious person within the Vedic theology was a married householder devoted to study and ritual activities and intent on fathering children, especially sons, to continue his line. A conversation between King Hariścandra, who had a hundred wives but still failed to obtain a son, and Nārada, recorded in the *Aitareya Brāhmaṇa* provides perhaps the clearest and boldest enunciation of the theological significance of a son and, by implication, of a wife, although, as we shall see below, it also contains hints that significant challenges to this theology were brewing.

The Brāhmaṇas translated in this chapter are printed in *The Aitareya and Kauṣītaki Brāhmaṇas of the Rigveda,* translated by A. B. Keith; Harvard Oriental Series 25 [1920; reprinted Delhi: Motilal Banarsidass, 1971], 7.13. I have benefited greatly from Keith's translation.

Hariścandra asks:

Now, since they desire a son,
Both those who are intelligent and those who aren't;
What does one gain by a son?
Tell me that, O Nārada.

Nārada replies:

A debt he pays in him,
And immortality he gains,
The father who sees the face
Of his son born and alive.

Greater than the delights
That earth, fire, and water
Bring to living beings,
Is a father's delight in his son.

By means of sons have fathers ever
Crossed over the mighty darkness;
For one is born from oneself,
A ferry laden with food.

What is the use of dirt and deer skin [of ascetics]?
What profit in beard and austerity?
Seek a son, O brahman,
He is the world free of blame.

Food is breath, clothes protect.
Gold is for beauty, cattle for marriage.
The wife is a friend, a daughter brings grief.
But a son is a light in the highest heaven.

The husband enters the wife;
Becoming an embryo he enters the mother.
Becoming in her a new man again,
He is born in the tenth month.

A wife is called "wife,"
Because in her he is born again.
He is productive, she's productive,
For the seed is placed in her.

The gods and the seers
Brought to her great luster.
The gods said to men:
"She is your mother again."

"A sonless man has no world."
All the beasts know this.
Therefore a son mounts
Even his mother and sister.

This is the broad and easy path
Along which travel men with sons, free from sorrow;
Beasts and birds see it;
So they copulate even with their mothers.

The importance of a wife for the religious welfare of the husband is a recurring theme in the Vedic texts. The wife is said to be one-half of the husband: "A full half of one's self is one's wife. As long as one does not obtain a wife, therefore, for so long one is not reborn and remains incomplete" (*Śatapatha Brāhmaṇa,* 5.2.10). The fully complete person includes the father, the mother, and the son. Being reborn in the wife as the son, therefore, the wife becomes the husband's mother. According to a popular etymology, the Sanskrit term for wife, *jāyā,* is seen as derived from the fact that the husband is born (*jāyate*) in her. Apart from her indispensable role in procreation, the wife is also essential for the husband's ritual activities, for only a married man accompanied by his wife is entitled to perform a sacrifice. The *Taittirīya Brāhmaṇa* (2.2.2.6) declares: "A man who has no wife is not entitled to sacrifice."

The religious obligation to get married, to study the Vedic scriptures, to offer sacrifices, and to beget offspring was given theological expression in the doctrine of debts. A person is born with debts to significant categories of persons inhabiting the Vedic world. Two parallel formulations are found in the Vedic literature, one enumerating three debts and the other four. The first is found in the *Taittiīrya Saṃhitā,* 6.3.10.5:

> A brahman, at his very birth, is born with a triple debt—of studentship to the seers, of sacrifice to the gods, of offspring to the fathers. He is, indeed, free from debt, who has a son, is a sacrificer, and who has lived as a student.

The second and more elaborate formulation is found in the *Śatapatha Brāhmaṇa,* 1.7.2.1–6:

> Now, whoever exists is born indeed as a debt at his very birth to the gods, to the seers, to the fathers, and to men. Because he has to sacrifice, he is born as a debt to the gods; and he pays it to them when he sacrifices to them and when he makes offerings to them.
>
> Because he has to study the Veda, furthermore, he is born as a debt to the seers; and he pays it to them, for they call a person who has studied the Veda "the guardian of the seers' treasure."
>
> Because he has to desire offspring, furthermore, he is born as a debt to the fathers; and he pays it to them when he has children that provide the continuity of their lineage.
>
> Because he has to provide shelter, furthermore, he is born as a debt to men; and he pays it to them when he offers them shelter and food.
>
> Whoever does all these things, has done what he has to do; he obtains everything, and he conquers everything.

Centrality of the Ascetic: Celibacy and Renunciation

In the early Upaniṣads we already find evidence of antiritual tendencies that favored celibate modes of life and advocated withdrawal from family and society. The inability of sacrifices to assure liberation from the cycle of rebirth is presented in the following satirical dialogue with a proponent of sacrificial religion recorded in the *Muṇḍaka Upaniṣad,* 1.2.6–10:

> Saying, "Come, come!" the splendid offerings carry that sacrificer on the rays of the sun, praising him and saying sweet words to him: "This is your Brahma-world of merits and good acts."

> These are indeed unsteady rafts, the eighteen sacrificial forms, which teach an inferior ritual (*karma*). The fools who hail it as superior lapse repeatedly into old age and death.
>
> Living in the midst of ignorance, self-wise, and thinking themselves to be learned, the fools go about hurting themselves, like blind men led by one who is himself blind.
>
> Living endlessly in ignorance, the fools think "We have reached our goal!" Because of their passion, those who perform rites (*karmin*) do not understand. When their worlds are exhausted, therefore, they fall down wretched.
>
> Regarding sacrifices and good works as the best, the fools know nothing better. After enjoying the highest heaven of good acts, they enter again this or even a lower world.

The *Bṛhadāraṇyaka Upaniṣad* (4.4.22) associates three central features of the ascetic mode of life—celibacy, mendicancy, and homeless wandering—with those who possess the liberating knowledge of the self as well as with those who aspire to such knowledge:

> The great unborn self, indeed, is he who among the senses consists of knowledge. In the space within the heart lies the controller of all, the lord of all, the ruler of all. He does not increase by good acts (*karman*) or decrease by evil acts. He is the lord of all, he is the ruler of beings, and he is the protector of beings. He is the causeway that separates and keeps these worlds apart. It is he that brahmans seek to know by reciting the Vedas, by sacrifices, by gifts, by penance, and by fasting. It is he, on knowing whom one becomes a silent sage (*muni*). It is he, in desiring whom as their world, wandering ascetics wander forth. When they came to know this, indeed, the men of old had no desire for offspring: "We possess this self, this world; what is the use for us of offspring?" Rising above the desire for sons, the desire for wealth, and the desire for worlds, they lead a mendicant life.

The householder is thus replaced by the celibate renouncer as the new ideal of religious living. Ascetic ideologies, moreover, even denied that it was possible for a householder to attain liberation. A frequently cited stock phrase in the Buddhist canonical texts reveals the ascetic perception of domestic life: "The household life is a dusty path full of hindrances, while the ascetic life is like the open sky. It is not easy for a man who lives at home to practice the holy life (*brahmacariya*) in all its fullness, in all its purity, in all its bright perfection" (*Dīgha Nikāya,* I.63).

The Upaniṣads express the contrast between the ideals of the new theology and those of the Vedic tradition in terms of the opposition between wilderness and village, the respective habitats of ascetics and householders. The *Chandogya Upaniṣad* (5.10.1–2) applies the doctrine of the two paths along which the dead travel—the path of the gods and path of the fathers—to the two classes of people, those who live in the wilderness and those who dwell in villages.

> Now, those who know this and those in the wilderness here who worship with the thought "Faith is our austerity," pass into the flame, and from the flame into the day, from the day into the fortnight of the waxing moon, from the fortnight of the waxing moon into the six months when the sun moves north, from these months into the year, from the year into the sun, from the sun into the moon, from the moon into lightning. There is a person there who is not a man. He leads them to Brahman. This is the path leading to the gods.
>
> But those in villages here who worship with the thought "Sacrifice and good works are our gift," pass into the smoke, and from the smoke into the night, from the night into the latter [i.e., dark] fortnight, from the latter fortnight into the six months when the sun moves south—they do not pass into the year—from these months into the world of the fathers, from the world of the fathers into space, from space into the moon. . . . They live there until [their merits] are exhausted and return by the same course along which they went.

The central activities, especially sacrifice, of those who live at home in a village are associated with return, that is with the prolongation of the rebirth process. Cessation of that process is associated with the activities of those who have left home and village and live in the wilderness.

Defense of Domesticity: Argument and Compromise

In the passage of the *Aitareya Brāhmaṇa* cited above we already see the rejection of ascetic celibacy and the strong defense of marriage and procreation. Later literature focuses especially on the suffering a person causes his forefathers when he assumes a celibate life without leaving any progeny to continue his line. Several episodes found in the *Mahābhārata* illustrate this concern. One day the sage Agastya finds his forefathers hanging upside down in a cave and discovers that they have been reduced to that miserable condition because of his decision to turn celibate without leaving any progeny to continue his line and to provide his forefathers with ritual offerings (*Mahābhārata*, 3.94.11–15). A similar story is told even more graphically in the case of the ascetic Jaratkāru (*Mahābhārata*, 1.41–42). As Jaratkāru was wandering the earth devoted to a life of celibacy and asceticism,

> he saw his forefathers hanging from their feet in a pit, suspended from a single remaining strand of a clump of grass. And a rat living in that pit was

slowly gnawing through that strand. They lived in that pit without food, emaciated, wretched, and tormented, yearning for help.

Jaratkāru is overwhelmed with compassion and, without recognizing them as his own forefathers, asks how he may help them. His ancestors also do not recognize him and reply:

> We are seers called Yāyāvaras, faithful to our vows. We have fallen here from heaven, sir, because our lineage has been cut off. Our reservoir of austerities and merit has been destroyed, for we have lost our strand. There is, however, one strand left for us now, but that too is as good as lost. To us, luckless as we are, there remains a single unfortunate relative in our family. His name is Jaratkāru, an expert in the Vedas and the auxiliary sciences, full of self control, magnanimous, keeping to his vows, and performing great austerities. Living without a wife, son, or any relative, it is he who out of his greed for austerity has reduced us to this miserable state. So here we hang senseless in this pit without a protector. Be our protector, and when you see him tell him: "Your poor forefathers are hanging from their feet in a pit. Come on, good man, take a wife and bear children!" For a single family strand is left for us, great ascetic. And this clump of grass you see us hanging from, O brahman, it was our family tree that assured the growth of our family. The roots of this clump you see here, O brahman, they are our strands eaten away by Time. And its half-eaten root you see, O brahman, from it all of us hang, and even that one is given to austerity! The rat you see, O brahman, that is mighty Time itself. And it is striking him and slowly killing off that foolish Jaratkāru, the stupid ascetic greedy for austerity. For all that austerity of his will not save us, good man. Our roots are cut, Time torments our minds, and we have fallen. See us stuck in hell like sinners! Since we are fallen here together with our forefathers, he too in due course, when he is cut down by Time, will surely descend here into hell. Whether it is austerity, sacrifice, or other great purificatory act, nothing, dear child, equals offspring—that is the view of the good men. Tell him that, dear child, when you see the ascetic Jaratkāru. Tell him all that you have seen, and speak to him, O brahman, in such a manner that he will be persuaded to get married and beget offspring. You will thus become our protector.

Jaratkāru, torn with grief and guilt, tells his forefathers:

> I am Jaratkāru, your wicked son. This nitwit has committed a crime. Wield your rod of punishment over me!

A compromise between the values of domesticity and asceticism is found in the widely shared view that ascetic modes of life are best suited for people of advanced age who have fulfilled their domestic obligations and whose natural passions have subsided. This view finds expression in the classical āśrama system, according to which a person should live as a student during his adolescent years, get married and live as a householder during his prime and, when his domestic obligations are fulfilled, leave the world and devote himself to ascetic pursuits. This position is stated clearly in the following verses of *Manusmṛti* (4.1; 6.33):

> Having spent the first quarter of his life at his teacher's, a twice-born should get married and spend the second at home.
>
> And having thus spent the third quarter of his life in the forest, he should give up attachments and live as a wandering ascetic during the fourth.

Even in texts that follow the compromise established in the classical āśrama system, we find repeated panegyrics extolling the virtues of domesticity and the superiority of the householder. These texts especially seek to instill in their readers the sinfulness of taking to celibate asceticism without first fulfilling their domestic responsibilities.

> Through a son one wins the worlds, through a grandson one attains eternal life, and through one's son's grandson one ascends the very summit of heaven. A man saves himself by begetting a virtuous son. A man who obtains a virtuous son saves from the fear of sin seven generations—that is, six others with himself as the seventh—both before him and after him. . . . Therefore, he should assiduously beget offspring.
>
> *Baudhāyana Dharmasūtra* 2.16.6, 8, 9, 11
>
> A householder alone offers sacrifice. A householder afflicts himself with austerities. Of the four āśramas, therefore, the householder is the best.
>
> As all rivers great and small find their rest in the ocean, so people of all āśramas find their rest in the householder.
>
> As all creatures depend on their mothers for their survival, so all mendicants depend on householders for their survival.
>
> *Vasiṣṭha Dharmasūtra,* 10.14–16
>
> As all living beings depend on air for their survival, so all the āśramas depend on the householder for their survival.
>
> The householder constitutes the most excellent āśrama, because it is the householder who daily supports everyone belonging to the other three āśramas with knowledge and food.
>
> After paying the three debts, a man may set his mind on renunciation; a man who practices renunciation without paying them, however, will fall.

> A man may set his mind on renunciation only after he has studied the Vedas according to the rule, fathered sons according to precept, and offered sacrifices according to his ability.
>
> A twice-born man falls when he seeks renunciation without first having studied the Vedas, fathered sons, and offered sacrifices.
>
> Student, householder, hermit, and renouncer: these are four distinct āśramas arising from the householder.
>
> Now, all these, when they are undertaken in the proper order and in accordance with the law, lead a brahman who acts properly to the highest state.
>
> Yet, among all of them, according to the dictates of the Vedas and smṛtis [sacred texts], the householder is said to be the best, for he supports the other three.
>
> *Manusmṛti* 3.77–78; 6.35–37, 87–89

Continuing Debate

Attempts to blunt the opposition between domesticity and celibate asceticism were at best only partially successful. Proponents of asceticism objected especially to the fact that the grand compromise of the āśrama system relegated asceticism to old age, equating it thereby with retirement. The urgency of personal salvation could not brook such postponement. In this final section is a selection of texts that capture the ongoing debate between the two value systems.

The first comes from a *Life of the Buddha* written in the first century C.E. by Aśvaghoṣa, a brahman who converted to Buddhism and became a Buddhist monk. Although the setting is formally Buddhist, the dialogue between the future Buddha and his father, Śuddhodana, captures the controversy both within and outside the brahmanical mainstream regarding the proper age for becoming an ascetic. When the future Buddha informs his father of his intention to leave the world, Śuddhodana tells him:

> Give up this plan, dear child; the time is not right for you to devote yourself to religion (dharma). For in the first period of life, when the mind is unsteady, the practice of religion, they say, can cause great harm.
>
> His senses easily excited by sensual pleasures, a young man is incapable of remaining steadfast when confronted with the hardships of ascetic vows. So his mind recoils from the wilderness, especially because he is unaccustomed to solitude.
>
> But for me, lover of religion, it is the time for religion, after I hand over the kingdom to you, prosperity incarnate. If you, however, O man of unwavering

> courage, should forsake your father in violation of the proper order, your religion (dharma) will in fact be irreligion (*adharma*).
>
> So give up this resolve and devote yourself fully to the religion (dharma) of a householder. It is, indeed, a beautiful sight to see a man enter the penance grove after he has enjoyed the pleasures of youth.

The future Buddha listens to his father's plea and gives this terse reply:

> I will not enter the penance grove, O King, if you will be the surety for me in four things. My life shall not be subject to death. Sickness shall not rob me of my health. Old age shall not strike down my youth. And misfortune shall never plunder my wealth.

The father advises the son to refrain from making such extravagant wishes, but the future Buddha replies:

> If this course is not possible, then do not stop me, for it is not right to impede a man trying to escape from a burning house.
>
> Given that separation is certain in this world, is it not better to separate oneself voluntarily for the sake of religion? Or should I wait for death to separate me forcibly even before I have reached my goal and attained satisfaction?

Buddhacarita 5.30–38, selections

The rejection of the compromise proposed in the classical āśrama system is also presented vividly in a conversation recorded in the *Mahābhārata* (12.169, selections) between a father, the guardian of the old order, and his son, representing the troubled and anguished spirit of the new religious world. This story, appearing as it does in Jain (*Uttarādhyayana*, 14) and Buddhist (*Jātaka*, 509), and later brahmanical (*Markaṇḍeya Purāṇa*, 10) texts as well, probably belonged to the generic ascetic folklore before it was incorporated into the *Mahābhārata*. This text, just like the story of the Buddha, points to the ascetic rejection of societal attempts to convert asceticism into an institution of old age. To the son's question regarding how a person should lead a virtuous life, the father replies:

> First, learn the Vedas, son, by living as a Vedic student. Then you should desire sons to purify your forefathers, establish the sacred fires, and offer sacrifices. Thereafter, you may enter the forest and seek to become an ascetic.

The son retorts:

> When the world is thus afflicted and surrounded on all sides, when spears rain down, why do you pretend to speak like a wise man?

Father:

> How is the world afflicted? And by whom is it surrounded? What are the spears that rain down? Why, you seem bent on frightening me!

Son:

> The world is afflicted by death. It is surrounded by old age. These days and nights rain down. Why can't you understand?
>
> When I know that death never rests, how can I wait, when I am caught in a net?
>
> When life is shortened with each passing night, who can enjoy pleasures, when we are like fish in a shoal?
>
> This very day do what's good. Let not this moment pass you by, for surely death may strike you even before your duties are done.
>
> Tomorrow's task perform today. Evening's work finish before noon, for death does not wait to ask whether your duties are done.
>
> For who knows whom death's legions may seize today? Practice good from your youth, for uncertain is life's erratic path.
>
> Those who do good enjoy fame in this life and happiness hereafter. Foolish indeed are those who toil for the sake of son and wife, providing for their welfare by means proper and foul.
>
> Such a man, full of desire and attached to sons and cattle, death carries away, as flood waters would a tiger sound asleep.
>
> Death will carry away a man obsessed with amassing wealth, his desires still unfulfilled, as a tiger would a domestic beast.
>
> "This I've done. This I must do. And that I have yet to complete." A man who is thus consumed by desires and pleasures, death will bring under its sway.
>
> Death carries away a man who is attached to his field, shop, or house, even before he reaps the fruits of the works he has done, fruits to which he is so attached.
>
> When death, old age, disease, and misery of all sorts cling to the body, why do you stand as if you were in great shape?
>
> Death and old age accompany an embodied soul from his very birth so as to destroy him. The two embrace all these beings, both the mobile and the immobile.

> The delight one finds in living in a village is truly the house of death, while the wilderness is the dwelling place of the gods—so the Vedas teach.
>
> The delight one finds in living in a village is the rope that binds. The virtuous cut it and depart, while evil-doers are unable to cut it.
>
> Those who do not cause injury to living beings in thought, word, or deed, are themselves not oppressed by acts that harm their life or wealth.
>
> Without truth one can never check the advancing troops of death. Never abandon truth, for immortality abides in truth.
>
> I do not injure, I seek the truth, I am free of love and hate, I remain the same in pleasure and pain, and I am safe—so I laugh at death like an immortal.
>
> In the self alone and by the self I am born, on the self I stand, and, though childless, in the self alone I shall come into being; I will not be saved by a child of mine.

The text concludes:

> Of what use is wealth to you, O brahman, you who must soon die? Of what use are even wife and relatives? Seek the self that has entered the cave. Where have your father and grandfather gone?

The final selection illustrating the debate between societal and renunciatory values is an argument between Janaka, the famous king of Mithilā, and a female ascetic named Sulabhā (*Mahābhārata* 12.308, selection). Janaka was reputed to have attained liberation (*mokṣa*) without abandoning household life and to have acquired the fruit of renunciation while he continued to rule the world. Sulabhā, hearing this news, wanted to test Janaka's claim. Using her yogic powers she entered Janaka's body. Janaka tells her how he had learned the Sāṃkhya doctrine from Pañcaśikha and how that knowledge had liberated him even though he did not abandon his kingdom. He argues that if it is knowledge that liberates, then with regard to the attainment of liberation it is immaterial whether one is an ascetic or a king.

> If knowledge is the cause of liberation even when one possesses triple staffs [of ascetics] and the like, then how can it not be so also when one possesses royal parasols and the like? For the possession of these articles can be traced to a common cause.
>
> Even a person who, noting the defects of household life, leaves it for a different order of life (*āśrama*), however, is not freed from attachment, for he gives up one thing only to grab hold of another.

> Ochre robes, shaven head, triple staff, water pot—in my opinion these are extravagant emblems having little to do with liberation.
>
> If, even when these emblems are present, knowledge alone is here the cause, all emblems are useless for getting rid of suffering in this world.
>
> There is no freedom in poverty, as there is no bondage in plenty; both in plenty and in poverty it is knowledge that liberates a person.
>
> This noose of royal power is tied with seats of passion. See, I have cut it off with the sword of renunciation sharpened on the whetstone of liberation.

Janaka goes on to admonish Sulabhā about the impropriety of her entering his body. Taking her to be a brahman, Janaka asserts that she has thus created a confusion of castes. He then inquires who she is and where she comes from. In her response, Sulabhā points to these questions as demonstrating Janaka's lack of true knowledge. A man who is liberated would not ask such questions. Sulabhā thus exposes the fallacy that a householder can acquire the liberating knowledge without abandoning home and family.

> You have asked me: "Who are you? Whose daughter are you? Where do you come from?" Listen attentively, O King, to this reply of mine.
>
> As you claim that by yourself you see the self within your self, in like manner, if you in fact consider another's self to be the same as yours, why do you fail to see in others also your own self?
>
> So, why do you ask me who and whose daughter I am? "This is mine and this is not": for a liberated man, O King of Mithilā, what is the use of such duality? And what profit is there in the queries: Who? Whose? Wherefrom?
>
> A man who makes distinctions between friends, foes, and neutrals in victory, war, and peace—how can he, O King, possess the mark of liberation?
>
> A man who fails to look equally upon one who is dear to him and one who is not, or upon one who is powerful and one who is weak—how can he possess the mark of liberation?
>
> Your friends should hold you in check, you who imagine yourself to be liberated when you are not, as doctors a deranged man.

—38—

The Bodhisattva Vajrapāṇi's Subjugation of Śiva

Ronald M. Davidson

Buddhist monastic institutions in India were complex entities. They interacted with other Indian social structures—the kings and aristocracy, the guilds and castes—in a variety of ways. Certain sections of the monasteries, and frequently entire monasteries, became focused on education, a development from the Buddhist definition of the existential problem as ignorance. Other sections of the monasteries became focused on the commercial or artistic requirements for maintaining their institutions in a changing cultural environment. Yet another facet of the monastic institution was a meditative function, which would be formed around exemplary contemplative monks in most monasteries and would sometimes become the dominant orientation of entire institutions known as "forest monasteries."

Loosely associated with or wholely outside of the formal institutional structure, however, were monks on the margins of the high Buddhist culture. Some would be contemplatives who had proceeded on their own, eschewing the formal, institutional life. Others would be monks forced out of the monastery due to transgressions, sexual and otherwise. Another group would be the wandering "teachers of the dharma [the Buddha's teaching]," clerics who traveled from town to monastic center preaching to a wide variety of audiences, cleric and lay, Buddhist and non-Buddhist. Still others would prefer the old wandering existence without the intrigue of monastic life or the strict regimen associated with famous institutions. All of these diverse characters would find themselves passing from village to village, discussing the word of the Buddha or enlarging on their own accomplishments in the forum of the Indian village temple grounds or marketplace.

These marginal clerics, if institutionally disempowered, had the ability to live by their wits, and the stories they told would often be influential in ways unforseen by the tellers of tales. Their audiences frequently had little regard for dialectical subtlety or elegance of syllogism. Indeed, the forces known to their audiences were those of the countryside—dominion, power, gangs—and the primal desire to have a leader bring these lawless elements under control. Concomitant with the desire for security was the need to feel significant, frequently comingled with the suspicion that their lives had either been forgotten by the gods or, worse, cursed by them.

In this environment, a wandering Buddhist preacher could bolster spirits, teach dispassion, and proclaim the course of liberation from the wheel of existence. With the increased ritualization of the countryside, however, Buddhist monks from the seventh century on felt the need to use the efficacy of myth and ritual for their own benefit and the benefit of the Buddhist dharma. Thus they adopted many of the same themes of power and dominion, of subjugation and renewal, that they encountered in both rural and urban sectors of India. To appear viable, to seem current, to communicate efficacy, Buddhist clerics wove webs of story, in which the Buddhist exemplars were the heroes and in which they demonstrated their transcendent compassion for the benefit of the world.

Vajrapāṇi's subjugation of Maheśvara is just such a tale. Destined to become the most influential myth of the Vehicle of Secret Spells (Mantrayāna), the story indicates the superiority of the Buddhist comprehension of reality and the Buddhist skill in the manipulation of that reality by the use of the classic Indian medium of potency: the voice. With his secret spells, Vajrapāṇi surpasses Maheśvara's ability in the drama of competition. Impelled by his compassion for the world and commanded by the cosmic buddha Vairocana, Vajrapāṇi suppresses all of the worldly deities and brings them into the compass of his mystic circle. Only Maheśvara—the god Śiva—is incapable of comprehending the necessity for submission to the teaching of the Buddha. For this inability, Maheśvara looses his life, only to be reincarnated in another world system and eventually to obtain the final awakening of the Buddha.

Such a dramatic tale eventually was taken into the high monastic culture and elaborated in a wide variety of combinations and permutations in the scriptures of the Mantrayāna. In this scriptural milieu, it was slowly transformed into a shadow of its source; the form found in the *Sarvatathāgata-tattvasaṃgraha* ("Summary of All Tathāgatas' Reality") is one of the few to retain the vital dialogical format of the Indian storyteller. This same redaction of the tale set the parameters for the myth's manifold levels of significance, a requirement for it to be acceptable to the intelligensia of the Mantrayāna. Simple domination of a competing religious system might interest the general audience, but the monastic clergy would need to unfold a variety of readings indicating the integration of enemies into the sacred circle of reality.

First and foremost, the story recreates for the Mantrayāna the myth of Māra's subjugation by the historical buddha, Śākyamuni. Maheśvara is depicted as the obstacle for the unfolding of Vajrapāṇi's family in the sacred circle, and thus constitutes the primary impediment against teaching the world the path of liberation, which occurs at the end of the scripture. In order for the teaching to be effected and beings awakened, Maheśvara must be conquered. Within the myth of Śākyamuni's awakening, Māra—the figure of death by sensory enslavement—required subjugation before the young prince could awaken to absolute reality and pronounce the lion's roar of the true dharma as the perfect Buddha. Thus both tales erect classic dramatic conflicts, in which the movement toward freedom for all beings cannot be thwarted despite the best efforts of those representing empowered oppressors.

The story also invokes the compassion of the Buddha—all beings will be included in the sacred reality, whether they want to or not. In contrast to a model of a last judgment and eternal damnation, Mahāyānists maintained that all beings will finally obtain awakening. For the Path of Secret Spells, this is effected by the efficient action of bodhisattvas like Vajrapāṇi, who convert the intractable for their own good, thereby saving them from the unlimited suffering their deeds would otherwise bring them in the future. In the same way that all forms, beautiful and ugly, are reflected in a mirror, all beings, good and bad, are included in the fields of awakening of the buddhas. Their compassion brings liberation to all as the sun warms all places on earth.

Finally, the myth was interpreted as a model of internal realities, in line with the movement toward increasing inwardness during the period of Mantrayāna development. In the way that Māra was interpreted as an extension of the Buddha's own death and suppressed psycho-physical tendencies, Maheśvara illustrates for the meditator that defilements, no matter how corrupt, are themselves the stuff of awakening. Liberation is impossible without prior bondage, purification inconceivable without defilement. For the those following the Path of Secret Spells, then, Maheśvara represents the reality of intractable mental events turning into the gnosis of awakening following their consecration, in this case by Vajrapāṇi's foot. Without such determined resistance to the teaching, Maheśvara never would have achieved his mythic goal of final emancipation as the buddha Bhasmeśvara-nirghoṣa. Without intractable defilements, the meditator will never experience the supernormal cognition of the highest goal. Thus the circle of emancipation is closed: mind, meditator, and Maheśvara all come to rest in the universal diagram.

The text translated here comes from Isshai Yamada, *Sarvatathāgata-Tattva-Saṅgraha,* Śatapitaka Series 262 (New Delhi: International Academy of Indian Culture, 1980), pp. 56–59. The Tibetan is found in Daisetz T. Suzuki, ed., *Tibetan Tripitaka, Peking Edition* (Tokyo: Tibetan Tripitaka Research Institute, 1956), Peking 112, vol. 4, pp. 239.4.6–242. The Chinese is in *Taishō Shinshū Daizōkyō* 882.18.370a–372c.

Further Reading

See Ronald M. Davidson, "Reflections on the Maheśvara Subjugation Myth: Indic Materials, Sa-skya-pa Apologetics, and the Birth of Heruka," in the *Journal for the International Association of Buddhist Studies* 14:2 (1991), 197–235; and David Snellgrove, *Indo-Tibetan Buddhism* (Boston and London: Shambhala, 1987), vol. 1, pp. 134–41.

Vajrapāṇi Subjugates Maheśvara

Then, all the tathāgatas again came together and exhorted the Blessed One, the Universal Ruler [Vajrapāṇi] . . . "We exort you, O Lord, to do your duty for the welfare of all beings: bring forth your family of divinities, those who exert control for all buddhas."

Now Vajrapāṇi, the supreme lord of all the tathāgatas, having heard the entreaty of all the tathāgatas, placed his vajra on his heart. Then he addressed all the tathāgatas, saying, "Lords, all tathāgatas! I do not agree to produce my divine clan."

And all the Tathāgatas responded, "For what reason?"

Vajradhara replied, "O Lords, there are beings—criminals, like Maheśvara and his ilk—who remain unsubdued, even by all of you tathāgatas. How could I accomplish anything with them?"

At that point, Vairocana, the Tathāgata, went deep into the concentration known as the "vajra of the knowledge of all tathāgatas' exhalted procedure" which is sustained by all tathāgatas. As soon as he was so concentrated, all the tathāgatas—as numerous as the particles of dust in all the realms of space—burst forth and assembled in the adamantine jeweled palace on the peak of Mt. Sumeru. Visualizing their essential identity, they all entered into the heart of the Śrīvatsa mark on the chest of Lord Vairocana.

So the Lord Vairocana, Tathāgata, empowered himself with all the tathāgatas residing in his heart. Since he had the highest accomplishment—bringing all benefit and happiness for the protection of every being by means of the identity of all aspects of adamant—he plunged deep into the concentration known as the "vajra of the wrathful pledge to perform all tathāgatas' exhalted procedure" in order to discipline all the criminal elements. At the very moment he entered concentration, the essential phrase of all tathāgatas—known as the "pledge of all tathāgatas"—the syllable HŪṂ issued forth from the heart of all the tathāgatas.

Immediately, the Lord Vajradhara issued forth from the vajra at his heart multiple forms of Vajrapāṇi, each a universally flaming embryo, knit eyebrows, wrinkled foreheads, crooked brows, terrible bent fangs. Hands twitching with flailing flaming vajras, elephant goads, swords, and nooses, all afire, and clothing variegated in color and ornament, they subdued every criminal in all the world systems. Returning from everywhere to form the great circle of the Vajradhātu, they became seated on a white lunar disk and pronounced this verse:

We are the means of discipline for those of great means.
While we conduct ourselves angrily as a means of
disciplining beings, we are ourselves stainless.

Then the Blessed One, the Tathāgata Vairocana, visualizing the [conceptionless] nondiffuse reality of all the tathāgatas, entered the concentration known as the "empowerment of the adamantine vow and the great adamantine anger of all the tathāgatas." He then intoned the excellent essential phrase of all tathāgatas, the adamantine HŪṂ of all tathāgatas:

OṂ SUMBHA NISUMBHA HŪṂ GṚHṆA GṚHṆA HŪṂ
GṚHṆĀPAYA HŪṂ ĀNAYA HO BHAGAVAN VAJRA HŪṂ PHAṬ

Well, when this essential phrase went forth from the heart of all the tathāgatas, Vajrapāṇi came forth and, blessed by all the tathāgatas from every world system, which are like oceans of clouds trailing in all directions, along with their encircling assemblies of bodhisattvas, they invited Vajrapāṇi. They entered him into the great circle of the pledge and, becoming bound with their vows, he formed one great mass—the great adamantine wrathful corpus. Taking residence in the heart of the Blessed One, Vairocana, he uttered this verse:

Hah! We are entirely the goodness and sinlessness
Of the thought of awakening. Even though angry,
We move toward beauty, since we discipline beings.

Then the great adamantine wrathful corpus descended from the heart of the Blessed One, and became seated on a white lunar disk before all the tathāgatas, again requesting their orders.

So the Blessed One entered into the concentration known as the "adamantine call to the pledge of all the tathāgatas" and sent forth from his own heart the essential phrase of all tathāgatas, elephant goad of the pledge of all tathāgatas: HŪṂ TAKKI JAḤ.

At this moment, all of the overlords of the triple worlds—Maheśvara and the rest, surrounded by all their worldly gangs without—were summoned by the adamantine elephant goad of the pledge of all tathāgatas. All passed into the adamantine jeweled palace at the summit of Mt. Sumeru and there they stood, surrounding the jeweled palace of the Blessed One on all sides.

Then Vajrapāṇi, taking his vajra from his heart, waved it around and looked out at the whole wheel of the triple worlds constituting the three realms of existence. "Friends!" he said, "accomplish the dispensation of all tathāgatas and uphold my command!"

They replied, "Just how do we do that?"

The Blessed One, Vajrapāṇi, answered, "By completion of going to the Buddha, the dharma, and the saṅgha for refuge. Friends, do it for the sake of attaining the omniscience of the Omniscient!"

But Mahādeva, the overlord of all the triple worlds in this world system and swollen with the pride of his position, responded by displaying great anger, "Hey, sprite! I am the lord, the overlord of the triple worlds, the creator, the arranger, the lord of all spirits, the supreme God of gods, Mahādeva! How should I take orders from you, a local tree spirit?"

So Vajrapāṇi again waved his vajra and ordered him, "Hey, criminal! Quickly enter the mystic circle and take your position in my pledge!"

But the great God of gods turned to the Blessed One, Vairocana, "Just who is he, Blessed One, and what kind of person is he who would give orders to the Lord?"

The Blessed One merely replied to Maheśvara and his entire horde in the triple worlds, "Friends, I would really do what he says and assent to the vow and discipline of going for the refuges! Do not let Vajrapāṇi, this cruel, angry, mean spirit, this great bodhisattva, lay to waste the entire triple worlds with his flaming vajra!"

But Maheśvara, impelled by his own brand of knowledge and swollen with his overlordship of the triple worlds, decided to show the Blessed One, Vajrapāṇi, just exactly what fear was all about. So he displayed great wrathful anger in a ferocious form, bursting with flames, laughing a horrible laugh with his horde, "Well I am the overlord of the triple world—now you do what I command!"

Now Vajrapāṇi chuckled at him and waved his own proud vajra, saying, "Hey! You eat human flesh like a ghoul and make your clothing, seat, bed, food, and snacks from the ashes of the funeral pyre—accept these refuges and observe my command!"

Yet Maheśvara, the great God, infused the entire triple world with great anger and said, "*You* observe *my* command and accept my vow!"

So Vajrapāṇi, the great wrathful king, addressed the Blessed One, Vairocana, "He, O Blessed One, is God, the great God, and is not submitting to the dispensation of all tathāgatas, being swollen with pride at the power of his own brand of knowledge and his great overlordship. So what should I do with him?"

Then, the Blessed One, Vairocana, recollected the great adamantine vow born from the heart of all the tathāgatas, "OṂ NISUMBHA VAJRA HŪṂ PHAṬ."

At that moment Vajrapāṇi, the great bodhisattva, intoned his own adamantine essential phrase, "HŪṂ." As soon as these were spoken, Mahādeva and all his assembled henchmen of the triple world, all the overlords of the triple world, fell face down and let out a cry of pain, finally going to Vajrapāṇi for refuge. Moreover, the god Mahādeva fell to the earth unconscious, and died.

Then the Blessed One, knowing what had occurred, said to Vajrapāṇi, "Vajrapāṇi, so that the triple worlds might be released from fear, do not let them dissolve into their constituent elements and perish!"

The great wrathful king Vajrapāṇi, having heard the Blessed One's words, said to all the gods, "If you value your life, execute my command and accept the rite of going to the Buddha, the dharma, and the saṅgha for refuge!"

Having no choice, they all replied, "We go to whole oceans of buddhas, dharmas, and saṅghas for refuge, but we do not know what the laws of your doctrine command!"

So the Blessed One, Vairocana, the Tathāgata, addressed them saying, "O gods, he is the overlord of us, all the tathāgatas. He is the father, the servant, the eldest son of all the tathāgatas, the Blessed One, the bodhisattva, mahāsattva, Samantabhadra ["All-Goodness"]. He has been consecrated in the kingship of great wrath to do what is necessary in the training of all beings. Why? There are in your midst hordes of criminals, such as Mahādeva and his ilk, who are not capable of being turned from their evil ways by peaceful means, even by all the tathāgatas. He has therefore been empowered to take care of those evil ones. So all of you, I command to be established in the circle of his pledge!"

They replied, "Blessed One! Protect us from the dissolution of our lives! What ever command you give us, we will perform!"

The Blessed One responded, "Listen, friends, anyone going to him for refuge will be protected. You have no other option!"

Then all the lords of the triple worlds, assembled from all the threefold world systems, turned to face the Blessed One, Vajradhara, and with one voice released a great lamentation, saying, "O Blessed One, protect us from the suffering of death!"

To their plea, Vajrapāṇi, the great bodhisattva, replied, "Hey, criminals, accept this my dispensation! Don't make me turn you into a single flame with my burning vajra and reduce all of you to ashes!"

They asked, "Samantabhadra, you, O Lord, are all tathāgatas' development of the thought of awakening for the sake of all beings; you are well-disciplined in peacefulness; you desire the welfare of all beings and bestow fearlessness on all creatures! Why, O Lord, would you want to burn us alive?"

Vajrapāṇi, the great king of all wrath, responded to them, "O friends! I am Samantabhadra since I carry out all tathāgatas' commands, and I consume for the sake of purification all those like you in the clan of criminals whose minds are evil, if they do not take their stand in the circle of my pledge!" To which, they all responded, "So be it!"

So Vajrapāṇi, the great king of wrath, revived all of the gods, with the exception of Maheśvara. In order to bring them upright, he intoned this essential phrase of all the tathāgatas known as "stand up vajra: VAJROTTIṢṬHA!" As soon as this was said, all of the lords of the triple worlds, assembled from the threefold world system, with all their retinues—again with the exception of Maheśvara—regained consciousness, and every one became full of confidence in their hearts. They experienced divine happiness and horripilation at the disappearance of their fear and dread. Looking at the Blessed One, Vajrapāṇi, they stood up.

Then the Blessed One, Vairocana, addressed the bodhisattva Vajrapāṇi, "Great being, this Mahādeva, the overlord of gods, has not stood up. What is the purpose of taking his life? Revive him, and he will become a real person."

To this Vajrapāṇi gave his assent, and intoned the essential phrase to revive the dead, "VAJRĀYUḤ."

As soon as he said this, the dead god Mahādeva revived and wanted to stand up but could not. So he addressed the Blessed One, Vairocana, "Is the Blessed One going to dominate me in this way?"

Vairocana replied, "You have not agreed to accept the commands of this great true person. Only he is responsible for chastising you, not I."

Maheśvara asked, "Lord, aren't you able to protect criminals like me?"

Vairocana responded, "It is beyond my capacity to protect you."

So Maheśvara asked, "How is that?"

Vairocana answered, "Because he is the overlord of all the tathāgatas."

Maheśvara was puzzled. "Lord, I don't understand the meaning of what the Blessed One has said. Since the tathāgatas are the overlords of all the triple worlds, who a superior overlord might be and where he might be found is beyond me."

With this, the Blessed One, Vajrapāṇi, the great bodhisattva, again addressed Mahādeva, "Criminal! Will you agree to accept my commands?"

Mahādeva heard the words of that adamantine being and again became angry and enraged. Displaying his great ferocious form he said, "Death I can endure, but I will not submit to your orders!"

So Vajrapāṇi, the great bodhisattva, displayed his own great rage and emanated a servant from his feet with the mantra, "OṂ PĀDĀKARṢAṆA VAJRA HŪṂ!"

So then, from the foot of the Blessed One, Vajrapāṇi, came a completely blazing embryo with knitted brows, bared fangs, and an enormous face. Thus the servant of the Blessed One, Vajrapāṇi, stood before him, awaiting his orders.

Vajrapāṇi, in order to pacify Maheśvara, intoned the mantra, "OṂ PĀDĀKARṢĀKARṢAYA SARVAVAJRADHARĀNUCARA KAṆḌA KAṆḌA VAJRA HŪṂ JAḤ!"

The moment this was spoken, both Mahādeva and his consort Umādevī were suddenly turned naked and inverted, and were dragged before the feet of the Blessed One, Vajrapāṇi, by this servant Padākarṣaṇavajrānucāra while all the world laughed at them. Then the bodhisattva Vajrapāṇi asked the Blessed One, Vairocana, "Here, Lord, is the criminal and his wife. What should I do with them?"

Then the Blessed One intoned "OṂ VAJRĀKRAMA HOḤ!" As soon as this was spoken, the great bodhisattva Vajrapāṇi, treading on Mahādeva with his left foot and the breasts of Umādevī with his right, intoned his own essential phrase, "OṂ VAJRĀVIŚA HANAYĀ TRAṂ TRAṬ!"

The instant these were spoken, Mahādeva became possessed and beat his own thousand heads with his own thousand hands. All those lords of the triple world who were assembled outside of the adamantine jeweled peak palace let out a great roar, "Our overlord is being instructed by this great being!"

With that, the Blessed One felt compassion toward Mahādeva, and intoned the essential phrase of loving kindness of all the buddhas, "OṂ BUDDHA MAITRĪ VAJRA RAKṢA HAṂ!" The moment this was said, the suffering of Mahādeva's possession ceased and the touch of Vajrapāṇi's sole conducted him to the obtainment of the consecration, concentration, liberation, code, gnosis, and higher knowledge of the supreme accomplishment, even bringing him up to the reality of the Tathāgata. So, from the touch of the Blessed One's sole, he experienced the bliss of all tathāgatas' concentration, code, and liberation. Having abandoned his form as Mahādeva at the feet of Vajrapāṇi, he passed down beyond as many world systems as there are motes of dust in the world systems, equal to the grains of sand in thirty-two Gaṅgās. There, he was born as the Tathāgata Bhasmeśvara-nirghoṣa in the world system called Bhasmacchatrā. Then the following verse slipped out of the prostrate form of Mahādeva, left behind:

> Aho! Having released the highest buddha gnosis of all the buddhas
> in the form of phrases and letters, the [buddhas] establish them in nirvāṇa.

Thereupon, the great bodhisattva Vajrapāṇi addressed the other overlords of all the triple worlds, Nārāyaṇa and so forth, "Friends, enter the great mystic circle of the adamantine pledge of all tathāgatas! Once you enter, nurture the pledge of all tathāgatas!"

They responded, "As you inform us, so we obey!"

—39—

India as a Sacred Islamic Land

Carl Ernst

Modern political nationalism in the South Asian subcontinent partitioned formerly British India into two nations, Pakistan and India, along religious lines. This political division postulates, according to some, an essential opposition between India and the Islamic tradition. Before modern times, however, this political construction did not exist. Muslims have lived in South Asia from the first Islamic century, as a result of raids and conquest on the northwest frontiers of Sind and the Punjab, and from trading colonies established all around the coasts of India on the route to the Spice Islands. India from a very early period occupied an important position in Islamic cosmology. Accounts in ḥadīth reports (sayings attributed to the Prophet Muḥammad) relate that India (more precisely, Ceylon) was the site of Adam's descent to earth after his expulsion from paradise. The first Indian Muslim to give notable literary expression to these stories was the poet Amīr Khusraw Dihlawī (Prince Royal of Delhi, d. 1325), who referred repeatedly to Adam's descent to India, in his Persian epic *The Eight Paradises;* there he set forth seven poetical arguments demonstrating that India is indeed paradise on earth. On the mountaintop in Sri Lanka called Adam's Peak, pilgrims of different religions still pay homage to the massive footprint variously ascribed to Adam, Śiva, or the Buddha.

The most exhaustive presentation of India as a sacred Islamic land is the work of Ghulām ʿAlī (the "Slave of ʿAli") of Bilgrām, better known by his pen name Āzād ("Free"). Āzād (1704–1786) was a prolific author of poetry in both Persian and Arabic; his Arabic odes in praise of the Prophet Muḥammad earned him the epithet "the Ḥassān of India" (after Ḥassān ibn Thābit ["Fine Son of Firm"], d. 674, an Arab poet who eulogized Muḥammad). Āzād wrote biographical works on officials of the Mughul empire and the Deccan as well as a hagiography devoted to the saints of Khuldabad, the western Indian town where he himself was buried. Āzād summarized the symbolic significance of Adam's descent to Ceylon in a remarkable Arabic treatise, *Subḥat al-marjān fī āthār Hindūstān* ("The Coral Rosary of Indian Antiquities"), which he completed in 1764. It is a work in four parts, dealing with: the references to India in the sayings of the Prophet Muḥammad; biographies of eminent Indian Muslim scholars; rhetorical figures in Arabic and Sanskrit; and lovers and love poetry in the Islamic and Hindu traditions. It is from the first of these four parts, entitled *The Ambergris Fragrance,* that the following selections are taken. From the numerous accounts that he culled from disparate classical Arabic sources, Āzād concluded that Adam's Peak is the second holiest place on earth next to Mecca; India was the site of the first revelation, the first mosque on earth, and the place from which pilgrimage to Mecca was first performed. Using the Sufi mystical concept of Muḥammad's primordial prophetic nature, Āzād described India as the place where the eternal light of Muḥammad first manifested in Adam, whereas Arabia is where it found its final expression in the physical form of the Prophet. The black stone of Mecca descended with Adam, the staff of Moses grew from a myrtle that Adam planted on the peak, and all fruits, perfumes, and craft tools derive from Adam's descent to India. The modern editor of Āzād's work dismisses these traditions as unreliable in terms of ḥadīth criticism, due to their "weak" sources and transmitters; they are, in his view, "semi-historical, based on legends."

Although these objections to Āzād's collection of ḥadīth are perhaps valid from a strictly textual point of view, they fail to explain the symbolic significance of Āzād's portrait of a sacred Islamic land of India. Āzād was aware of the strictures of ḥadīth criticism about unreliable reporters. He had studied ḥadīth in Medina with the celebrated Indian scholar Muḥammad Ḥayāt al-Sindī, who trained an entire generation of scholars and Sufis in the study of ḥadīth. As a historian, Āzād sought out eyewitness reports from travelers, describing contemporary pilgrimage to Adam's footprint under the friendly eyes of Ceylon's "Hindu" (actually Buddhist) rulers. Āzād's purpose in writing this admittedly novel treatise was not, however, to produce a standard work of ḥadīth studies; he wanted instead to describe "the land of India, which God made the realm of vicegerency (*dār al-khilāfa*) and singled out with this distinction." Since it was in India that Adam first exercised the authority that God gave humanity over the earth, it had the unique status of being the first place on earth where human vicegerency (*khilāfa,* also "caliphate") was established. Āzād even made a connection between the location of the famous black stone on the east corner of the Ka'ba in Mecca and the eastern orientation of Hindu temples in India. Ingeniously, Āzād concluded that since Adam was in all essential respects an Indian, so all of his descendants—all human beings—are Indians too.

Āzād described India's sacredness by reference to the highest scriptural authorities in Islam, the Qur'ān and the sayings of Muḥammad, scrupulously citing his sources and keeping his own commentary separate. His work points up the importance of Arabic as an Indian classical language, even in relatively recent times. The centuries of Islamic sources on which Āzād drew illustrate an important point that runs counter to current political dogma: for Muslims, India has been a sacred land as long as they can remember.

This selection is translated from Ghulām ʿAli Āzād al-Bilgrāmī, *Subḥat al-marjān fī āthār Hindūstān,* edited by Muḥammad Faḍl al-Raḥmān al-Nadwī al-Sīwānī, 2 vols. (Aligarh: Jāmiʿat ʿAlīgarh al-Islāmiyya, 1976–1980), pp. 7–57, abridged.

The Coral Rosary of Indian Antiquities

Part One: The Ambergris Fragrance

Now, no one has woven a treatise in this fashion before, nor could any disposition attain the like of it, so may God most high aid his trusting and imploring servant with the writing of it—the poor man, Ghulām ʿAlī, al-Ḥusaynī by clan [descended from the Prophet's grandson Ḥusayn], al-Wāsiṭī by origin [from the Iraqi town of Wāsiṭ], and al-Bilgrāmī by birth [from the northern Indian town of Bilgrām]—may God work his grace privately and publicly. He included in it what mention of India he found in the great commentaries on the Qur'ān and the noble ḥadīth sayings of the Prophet; he entitled it *The Ambergris Fragrance, regarding what has come down from the Chief of Men [the Prophet Muḥammad] concerning India,* hoping from the lordly presence and the merciful threshold that its breezes would perfume the horizons and its fragrances scent the coasts. For he is the protector, the one whose aid is sought, the one who is worthy of forbearance and beneficence.

Know (may God most high aid you!) that when God (who is glorious) decreed in pre-eternity the power of his names, his attributes, and the mirrors of his lights and manifestations, he called creatures into being, and manifested the realities until he ended at the uttermost locus of manifestation. The most perfect of these, which radiates with his noble form, and is adorned with the jewels of his primordial attributes, is the human race. Its creator then made the victor of men, Adam (on whom be peace). God chose him as a vicegerent for his sacred threshold and an adornment for his transcendent throne. He taught him the sacred names and commanded the angelic spirits to bow down before him. Then he caused him to descend from heaven to earth, on the land of India, which he made the realm of vicegerency and distinguished with this excellence. So this vicegerent sat on the seat of nobility, and his decrees rule until the Day of Judgment. The divine sciences spread, the hidden secrets manifested, and abundant blessings and manifold distinctions were bestowed on the region of India.

But Adam's time is far removed, and his ages are long gone, and nothing is found of his sayings in Islamic books save a little bit, and his affair is as the affair of the drop of the heavenly fountain Salsabīl ["Easily Imbibed"]. Then we did not learn of any existing traces, except for a certain number of subjects, due to the lack of materials. Among them is the point that the land of India was honored with the descent of the viceregent of God, his Pure One [Adam] (on whom be peace). And therefore Serendip [the ancient name of Ceylon] is known as "the realm of vicegerency." And no one before me has applied this term to it, though it was well-deserved, for God most high inspired me to do so.

The Master Jalāl al-Dīn al-Suyūti ["Majesty of the Faith, from Suyut" in Egypt, d. 1505] (may God most high have mercy on him), in *The Strung Pearl,* commenting on sura 46 of the Qur'ān, citing Ibn Abī Ḥātim [the "Son of the Wrecker's Father"], from 'Alī [the "Lofty," nephew of Muḥammad, d. 661] (may God be pleased with him), said, that [the Prophet Muḥammad] said, 'The best of valleys for humanity are the valley of Mecca and the valley where Adam descended in India.' "

I say, this compares the best spot in India with the land of "the secure town" [i.e., Mecca] (Qur. 95.3), may God ennoble it until the Day of Judgment. And one of the implications of the comparison is the descent of one of the pair, that is, Adam, at Serendip, and the descent of the other, that is, Eve, at Jidda [in Arabia]. Adam (on whom be peace) named the place he descended "the holy mount," and he heard there the voices of the angels. He saw them honoring the throne of God most high, and he found there the scents of heaven and its perfume, as is found (God most high willing) in the report of Ibn Sa'd ["Son of the Fortunate," d. 845], from Ibn 'Abbas ["Son of the Frowner," d. 688] (may God be pleased with them both).

The Master 'Alī al-Rūmī ["the Greek"] (May God most high have mercy on him) said, in his book *Discourses of the Ancients and Conversations of the Moderns,* "The first place where the springs of wisdom gushed forth was India, then the Meccan sanctuary, on the tongue of the first teacher unto humanity, Adam the pure (God's blessings and peace be upon him, and on all the prophets)." The master mentions this in his commentary, and he says also in his *Discourses,* "The first place where books were made, and where the springs of wisdom gushed forth was India . . . and [Adam] performed pilgrimage to Mecca more than once, on foot. Then he emigrated to the noble sanctuary of Mecca, due to its nobility, and he preferred it to all other countries. He was the first to emigrate due to the nobility of a place or location. And emigration is the custom of the prophets and messengers (God's blessings and peace be upon them all)."

The Imām al-Zāhid [the "Ascetic Prayer-Leader," from Bukhara, d. 1125] said in his Qur'ānic commentary, quoting Ibn 'Abbas (God be pleased with them both), "Adam descended to Serendip in India, placing his right hand upon the left; and Eve descended in Jidda. And from Serendip to Jidda it is seven hundred leagues." And in *The History of Jerusalem:* "When Adam descended to Serendip, he performed the prostration of thanks and the attestation of the created signs, and his head touched the stone of the temple [at the Dome of the Rock in Jerusalem], for it is the loftiest place on the face of the earth, and the path to ascension to heaven is from it."

In addition, there is the footprint of Adam. The Master 'Alī al-Rūmī said in his *Discourses:* "The first place where Adam descended was the mountain called Rāhūn on an Indian island, in the kingdom of Serendip in the place called

Dujnā, upon which is his footprint (peace be upon him). On the footprint is a luminosity that dazzles the eyes, which none can endure to see. The length of his footprint in the rock is seventy spans, and on the mountain there is a light like dazzling lightning. There is no doubt that it rains there every day and washes his footprint. From this mountain, Adam traveled to the seacoast in a single step, though it is a journey of two days."

In the days when I was writing this book, a trustworthy traveler came to "the realm of victories," Arcot, which is a well-known town among the important cities in Karnataka, not far from "the realm of vicegerency," Serendip (may God water it with downpours of rain!). That traveler came from Serendip after having spent three months there. He told me, "I made pilgrimage to the footprint of Adam (peace be upon him), and I circumambulated that place." A group of Madārī darvīshes had lived there for some time, attending the sacred footprint and accepting donations made to it. They have a leader to whom they are related, Shaykh Badīʿ al-Dīn Quṭb al-Madār ["Master Wonder of the Faith, Axis of Orientation"] (may God illuminate his tomb), one of the greatest and most famous saints of India. He died 18 Jumādī I, 838 [December 20, 1434], according to tradition. His tomb is in the village of Makanpur, a day's journey from the city of Kannauj, which is mentioned in *The Ocean* [a famous dictionary]. The rulers of Ceylon today are Hindus who revere the blessed footprint and honor its pilgrims.

Another point is the acceptance of the repentance of Adam (peace be upon him) and his learning the [divine] words in India. It has been mentioned in the *Testament of Adam* (peace be upon him), "So repentence descended upon me on this earth," as the ḥadīth goes. And al-Ṭabarī [the Persian historian, d. 923] said in his *History*, "After three hundred years, 'Adam learned from his Lord the [divine] words, and he repented' (Qur. 2.37), and Gabriel came with good tidings, so he wept on that mountain for a year in gratitude and joy. Herbs grew from his tears on that mountain, and a perfume is carried to this day from India to the horizons."

Another point is the return of Adam (peace be upon him) from the sanctuary of Mecca (made God increase its honor and dignity) to India, and his choice of it as a homeland. Al-Ṭabarī said in his *History*, "When Adam finished the pilgrimage, he departed with Eve for the mountain of India where he had descended from heaven, then he performed pilgrimage after that for forty years. Whenever he completed a pilgrimage, every year, he departed for India." He also said in his *History*, "Then he built for himself a house in India, and God conferred the land of India upon him and gave him its beasts, both wild and tame, and its birds. And he made the rain fall and the plants grow, and he tamed animals for him, some for food, some for riding, and some for bearing loads." . . . I say, I deduce from this that the affection of Adam (peace be upon him) was for India, since he returned to it and chose it for a homeland.

Another point is the sealing of the Covenant on Mt. Dujnā, according to a tradition. Al-Suyūṭī said, citing Ibn Jurayj [d. 768] and Ibn al-Mundhir, from

Ibn ʿAbbās (may God be pleased with them), "Adam (peace be upon him) descended on Mt. Dujnā, and God stroked his back and extracted every soul that he would create until the Day of Judgment. Then he said, 'Am I not your Lord?' And they said, 'Yes' (Qur. 7.172). And on that day 'the pen dried up' for that which he has created, up to the Day of Judgment." I say, among the souls who came forth on the Day of the Covenant from Adam's back were the prophets (peace and blessings be upon them), as related in a long ḥadīth ascribed to the Prophet by Abū Hurayra [the "Kitten Man," d. 676] (may God be pleased with him). And al-Suyūṭī has related in his Qurʾān commentary, "Adam said, 'Lord! Who are these people whom I see revealing light?' He said, 'These are the prophets from your offspring.' " So it appears that the Day of the Covenant honored the land of Mt. Dujnā [that is, India] with the presence of a sufficiency of prophets and messengers (the blessings and peace of God upon them all). Another point is the rising of the sun of prophecy for the first time from the region of India, since the first of the prophets was Adam (peace be upon him).

Another point is the loftiest and most sublime of miracles—may God inspire me with his beauty of expression, the reins of which no one's hand has grasped. Al-Suyūṭī said, citing Ibn ʿUmar al-ʿAdanī [the "Son of Living, from Aden"], from Ibn ʿAbbās (peace be upon them), "[Muḥammad, scion of] the Quraysh tribe, was a light in the hands of God most high, two thousand years before he created Adam. That light praised him, and the angels recited his praise. And when God created Adam, he placed that light in his loins." The Messenger of God (God bless him and grant him peace) said, "He caused me to descend to earth in the loins of Adam, and put me in the loins of Noah, and cast me into the loins of Abraham. Then God continued to transfer me from the noble loins and pure wombs until he brought me forth from my parents, who had never encountered fornication."

So it is proved that India is the place of the dawning of the Muḥammadan light, and the origin of this eternal effusion. And Arabia is its end and goal, the locus of manifestation of his elemental existence and illumination (God bless him and grant him peace). Thus India suffices in honor and excellence. How excellent was Kaʿb ibn Zuhayr ["Honor Son of Helper," d. after 632] (peace be upon him), when he said [regarding Muḥammad], "The Messenger is a light illuminating God's drawn swords of Indian steel."

Another point is the descent of the Holy Spirit on Adam (peace be upon him) for the first time, in India. And another point is that the call to prayer of the monotheistic community was first called, and the drum of Muḥammadan fortune first struck, in this land.

Another point is the descent of the black stone for the first time in India. Al-Suyūṭī said, citing al-Azraqī [the "Blue"], from Ibn ʿAbbās (peace be upon him), "Adam descended from heaven carrying the black stone under one arm, and it was one of the sapphires of heaven. If God had not dimmed its brightness, no one could have endured seeing it," as the ḥadīth says. And al-Suyūṭī said, citing al-Bayhaqī in *The Proofs,* from al-Sindī ["Man of Sind"], "Adam left heaven with the stone in his hand, and a leaf in his other hand. The leaf propagated in India, and from it are derived all of the perfumes that you see. But the stone was a white sapphire full of light. When Abraham built the house [that is, the Kaʿbah], he reached the place [reserved] for the stone and said to Ishmael, 'Bring me a stone for me to place here.' And he brought him a stone from the mountain, but he asked for another. Time after time he rejected the stone, not being pleased with what he brought. So he himself went again, and Gabriel (peace be upon him) came with a stone from India, which Adam had brought from heaven, so he [Abraham] placed it there. And when Ishmael came, he said, 'Who brought you this?' He said, 'Someone who is livelier than you.' "

I say, I once attained the felicity of visiting the sacred precinct and the noble house (may God increase it in honor and glory). I found its four corners facing the four directions of the world, and its walls facing the four intermediate directions. The corner of the black stone faces the east, which is the direction of prayer of the people of India, and the direction of their worship. Now it is known that this corner is one of the sapphires of heaven. This is the noblest of the corners and the bezel in the seal-ring of faith, the right hand of God, by which he greets his servants and those who accept him, who have sworn obedience to God and his Messenger. It has eyes, a tongue, and lips to bear witness to those who accept him in truth, for it is the repository of the covenants of humanity. It has honor sufficient to it that the Messenger of God (God bless him and grant him peace) lifted it up with his hand and kissed it with his lips.

And another point is the cup of Adam (peace be upon him). In *The Treasury of Wonders* is a long tale of Alexander the Great, when he journeyed to the land of India. There the king of India sent a message to Alexander about his wonderful gifts, among which was a cup from which his entire army could drink, which was the cup of Adam (peace be upon him), made from heavenly jewels.

There are other diverse matters. Al-Suyūṭī said, citing Ibn Abī Ḥātim, from Qutāda ["Thorn"], that [the Prophet] said, "It was said to me that the earth is twenty-four thousand leagues, of which twelve thousand are the land of India, eight thousand are China, three thousand are the West, and one thousand are Arabia."

Al-Suyūṭī said, citing Ibn Abī Ḥātim and Abū al-Shaykh ["Father of the Master"], in *The Greatness,* from ʿAbd Allāh ibn ʿAmr ibn al-ʿĀṣ ["God's Servant, son of Life, son of the Rebel"] (may God be pleased with them), that [the Prophet] said, "The world was formed in five forms, in the form of a bird, with its head, breast, wings, and tail. Medina, Mecca, and the Yemen are the head. The breast is Egypt and Syria. The right wing is Iraq, and beyond Iraq the people called Wāq, and beyond Wāq the people called Waqwāq, and beyond that are people known only to God. The left wing is Sind, and beyond Sind is India, and beyond India is a people called Nāsak, and beyond Nāsak is a people called Mansak, and beyond that are people known only to God. And the tail is from Dhāt al-Ḥamā to the setting sun, and the evil part of the bird is the tail."

In the *Life of the Prophet* of al-Ḥalabī ["Man of Aleppo"], in the eighth chapter, al-Nasā'ī ["Man of Nasā' " from Central Asia] and al-Ṭabarānī ["Man of Ṭabaristān" from Iran] transmitted by a sound chain from Thawbān, the client of the Messenger (God bless him and grant him peace), that the Prophet said (God bless him and grant him peace), "There are two bands from my community that God most high will protect from hellfire: the band that engages India in holy war, and the band that will be with Jesus son of Mary."

In the *Book of Proclamation on the Conditions of the Hour,* by Sayyid Muḥammad al-Barzanjī al-Madanī ["Lord Praised, from Barzanj and Medina"], on the mention of the Messiah (may God most high be pleased with him): "Then the land will be guided by the Messiah, and it will accustom itself to him. All the kings of the land will enter into obedience to him. He will send a mission to India and conquer it, and he will bring the kings of India in chains; their treasures will be conveyed to the sacred house and made into an adornment for the sacred house."

This is what I know of the mention of India in the noble scripture and the solid books. The completion of this book took place on Sunday, the twenty-first of Sha'bān, 1163 [July 26, 1750], at "the realm of victories," Arcot (may God protect it from calamities).

Postscript. After writing this book, a group of people from Bukhara and Samarqand objected that India is a land that is the object of divine wrath, because God (glory be to him) caused Adam (peace be upon him) to descend while in a state of wrath. But I said to them, "God made Eve descend to Jidda, which is of the land of Mecca, which is the noblest of places. If one examines it closely, one will learn that their descent from heaven to earth was caused externally by their eating from the forbidden tree, and internally by something else, namely, the decree of the Unitary Presence that it manifest its characteristics on the tribunal of existence, and bring forth its manifestations to the assembly of visibility. Yes, if Adam (peace be upon him) had not descended there, who would have brought beauty to this desolation through civilization, and who would have displayed the special wonders of the human race? It is no secret that the children of Adam are all Indians, because their father Adam (peace be upon him) was an Indian; he dwelled to the end of his life in India, and brought his children there. After they reached maturity, they spread from India through the seven climes."

The Creator promised Adam his light
  shining like a burning star.
India is our father's descent and station—
  a true story with a firm foundation.
The earth of India's land shines in its beginning,
  from the light of Muḥammad: the best of distinctions.

—40—

The Exemplary Devotion of the "Servant of Hari"

Tony K. Stewart

Gauḍīya Vaiṣṇavas are named after the geographical region of Gauḍa, which is central to modern Bengal in northeastern India. Today, because the Gauḍīya Vaiṣṇavas have spread far beyond the confines of that region, some people prefer the name Caitanyaites, after the community's founder Kṛṣṇa-Caitanya (1486–1533 C.E.). Caitanya was, during his lifetime, believed to be God himself, Kṛṣṇa—not just a holy man or accomplished devotee. Born Viśvambhara ("He Who Bears the Burden of the World") to a good brahman family in the scholastic center of Navadvīpa, in Nadīya District, Caitanya lived a relatively normal childhood, according to the traditional accounts. He was destined to become a Sanskrit scholar, a pandit, following in the footsteps of his father, or so it seemed. During his youth, two events seem to have made a profound impression on him: one was his brother's renunciation into the orders of ascetics, the other was Caitanya's father's death. To commemorate that death, Viśvambhara travelled to the Vaiṣṇava holy city of Gayā, today in the state of Bihar, to perform the rituals that would ensure the sustenance of his father's lineage for the seven previous generations. While there, Viśvambhara met a famous ascetic who had such an effect on the young man that he was transformed, apparently overnight, into the greatest of Vaiṣṇava devotees. And it all started, so the tradition goes, by kīrtana—chanting and singing the name of God.

Kīrtana literally means song, especially a song of praise which glorifies its subject, in this case the god Kṛṣṇa. For the Vaiṣṇavas of Bengal, it is the simplest form of devotional activity and one of the top five of the sixty-four prescribed ritual forms, according to the scholastic analysis of devotion by Caitanya's disciple and theologian, Rūpa Gosvāmī in his *Bhaktirasāmṛtasindhu* ("Ocean of the Immortal Nectar of the Rapturous Experience of Devotion"). This devotional act, however, is much more than a mechanical ritual enjoined to discipline the devotee. Rather, the formal and proper repetition of the name of God turns that name into a mantra, a holy utterance which invokes God's very presence. The sound is a projection of aural power, for traditionally it is generally believed in India that the name of a thing is the aural dimension of its ontological reality, which is to say that the name of a thing at least partially constitutes the thing itself. By invoking Kṛṣṇa, a devotee effectively makes Kṛṣṇa present, allowing the devotee to come into contact with Kṛṣṇa and to enjoy the benefits of that direct association. The Gauḍīya Vaiṣṇavas invoke Kṛṣṇa in a variety of ways, but the great mantra is a recitation of three names sixteen times in thirty-two syllables, all in the vocative form: Kṛṣṇa, Hari, Rāma.

Hare Kṛṣṇa Hare Kṛṣṇa
Kṛṣṇa Kṛṣṇa Hare Hare
Hare Rāma Hare Rāma
Rāma Rāma Hare Hare

If someone utters this mantra prior to accepting Kṛṣṇa as God, Vaiṣṇavas believe that it has the effect of initiating devotion, bhakti, by providing the seed for its proper beginning. This ancient idea of sound possessing seedlike potency, the bīja mantra or seed syllable, goes back to the Veda, and in Bengal this was prominently found among the rituals of Tantra.

Chanting was often done with beads to keep the count, usually a string of 108 (an auspicious number that factors into $1^1 \times 2^2 \times 3^3$), marking one round of 16 names per bead. To "do the rosary" itself 108 times in the course of a day—the recommended count—means that the devotee will invoke Kṛṣṇa 186,624 times, an act bound to make one aware of Kṛṣṇa's eternal presence! The effect is to cloak oneself in the protective aural cover of the name. It is no accident that Kṛṣṇa-Caitanya's own religious name means "He Who Makes People Cognizant (*caitanya*) of Kṛṣṇa." Repeating the name has obvious benefits as an aid to meditation for the highly trained adept practitioner, but it was also meant to be done by the ordinary devotee in his or her daily life. Among the many early followers of Caitanya, a humble man named Haridāsa—the "Servant of Hari"—was renowned for his diligence in daily kīrtana and serves as a model for all devotees.

Haridāsa was a converted Muslim, a religion that in Bengal has its own long tradition of repeating the name of God in the practice of the Sufi dhikr. That Haridāsa was converted was a phenomenon of some importance in its own right. Conversion to Islam was fairly common in Bengal, but not until the Vaiṣṇavism preached by Caitanya was it possible to become a Hindu by any means other than birth. In the selection translated below, we find that the local ruling Muslims are having a difficult time knowing how to deal with their former brother who had fallen in with the local "infidels," the Vaiṣṇavas. But the piece, which comes from the most popular of the early biographies of Caitanya, the *Caitanya Bhāgavata* of Vṛndāvana Dāsa, shows that kīrtana was not always terribly palatable to local Hindus either. One of the reasons is that kīrtana, when practiced in groups (*saṃkīrtana*), involved individual and collective singing of songs of praise, which in turn often led to dancing (a style of devotional worship that is by no means unique to Bengal). When the sessions continued late into the night, as they often did, the emotions of the participants would peak in public displays of ecstasy that to the uninitiated sounded and looked like the revelry of a drunken party. The physical manifestations are, however, the signs of true devotion: sweating, trembling, fainting, roaring, crying, hair standing on end, gooseflesh, and so on. As will become clear in the reading, the trained devotional eye could distinguish between the ecstasy of devotion and other forms of possession, in spite of the similarities of their physical form. Because these possessions departed so dramatically from ordinary conduct, it is easy to see why outsiders were suspicious and how misunderstandings could ensue. Kīrtana precipitated responses both positive and negative, which suggests something of its power. Haridāsa had to suffer extreme punishment for converting to Vaiṣṇavism, and even more for his refusal to abandon the ritual action of repeating the name of Kṛṣṇa; yet it is the repetition of the name which enabled him to endure, which invoked Caitanya's comforting presence, and which dissipated the pain of the torture.

As he endured this pain, reportedly enough to kill an ordinary man, Haridāsa projected a general image of the holy man for Bengali culture, an image that resonated strongly in both Muslim and Hindu communities, cutting across those sectarian boundaries. For the Hindu, his power is that of the accomplished ascetic yogi, who sits in rapt meditation to gain control over his physical and spiritual world. The imagery is reinforced in the two stories of Haridāsa as a lord over snakes, for the serpent energy (*kuṇḍalinī*) is common to traditional and tantric yogic practice. Yet the association for Vaiṣṇavas goes further, for kīrtana is the very support of their devotion and the means for structuring God's message of love, whereas the cosmic serpent Ananta-Śeṣa is mythologically the support of Viṣṇu-Kṛṣṇa and the ontological source of Kṛṣṇa's projected environment, the emanations that create the world itself. Haridāsa, of course, projects and participates in both of these constructs. For the Muslim, however, Haridāsa's action is interpreted through the model of the pīr, a Sufi saint. That the same Haridāsa can be understood by the two communities through different and competing models of piety demonstrates that the Hindu and Muslim worlds were not, in their daily experience, as far removed from each other as is often depicted. In fact, in the throes of his trial, we shall see that Haridāsa goes so far as to argue that the Muslim's Allah and the Hindu's Kṛṣṇa were not different from each other except in name. What was different between Muslims and Hindus was simply the outward, physical garb of their practices, and that is a significant theological and sociological position that many Bengalis have continued to hold through the last five centuries.

The translation is from Vṛndāvana Dāsa, *Caitanya Bhāgavata,* edited with Bengali commentary *Nitāikaruṇākallolinī ṭīkā* by Rādhāgovinda Nātha (Calcutta: Sādhana prakāśanī, 1373 B.S. [1966 C.E.]), 1.11.

Further Reading

See the works by Sushil Kumar De, Edward C. Dimock, Jr., and Kṛṣṇadāsa Kavirāja cited in Chapter 23, p. 375. Also see Dimock, "The 'Nectar of the Acts' of Caitanya," in The *Biographical Process,* edited by Frank E. Reynolds and Donald Capps (The Hague: Mouton, 1976), pp. 109–17 and Norvein Hein, "Caitanya's Ecstasies and the Theology of the Name," in *Hinduism: New Essays in the History of Religions,* edited by Bardwell Smith (Leiden: E. J. Brill, 1976), pp. 15–32.

The Exemplary Devotion of the "Servant of Hari"

1. Glory, glory be to the revered Golden One, friend of the wretched. Glory, glory be to the Lord of All, Husband to Lakṣmī. 2. Glory, glory be to the incarnation who serves as the shelter of devotees. Glory to the essential truth of the ages, the play of kīrtana, praise [to Kṛṣṇa]. 3. Glory, glory be to the Golden-Limbed One along with his family of devotees. If one hears the story of Caitanya, devotion is the gain. 4. The story of the first part [of his life] is a stream of immortal nectar, wherein the play of the Golden-Limbed One enchants completely.

5. And so [Kṛṣṇa-Caitanya,] the chief actor of Vaikuṇṭha heaven, lived in the city of Navadvīpa. Disguised as a brahman householder, he taught. 6. This incarnation was intended to spread prema-bhakti, pure devotional love—but he did not desire to do it right then. 7. The further reaches of the cyclic world were devoid of this highest of truths, yet he was concerned that everyone experience at least a tiny portion of this love. 8. Even those who taught the [*Bhagavad*] *Gītā* and *Bhāgavata* [*Purāṇa*] failed to sing or get others to sing in saṃkīrtana. 9. But those who were devotees would assemble and spontaneously perform kīrtana, clapping their hands— 10. and this aroused joy in their hearts.

[Detractors puzzled,] "What is it that makes them shout out in a loud voice, 11. "I am Brahman; within me resides the Stainless One, Nirañjana'? On what basis do they distinguish between servant and master?" 12. People who were caught up in the cycle of life observed, "To eat they beg, then they preach to everyone to repeat loudly the name of Hari. 13. We shall batter down and desecrate the doorways to their houses"—This is what much of [the city of] Nadīya gathered together and decided. 14. When they heard about this, the devotees were extremely anguished, but talk among themselves relieved them. 15. The devotees saw the material world as meaningless. With sighs of "O Kṛṣṇa!" they felt their misery to be without limits. 16. And so it was at the arrival of Haridāsa, who embodied pure devotion to Viṣṇu.

THE WHIPPING OF HARIDĀSA THROUGH TWENTY-TWO MARKETS

17. Now hear the story of Haridāsa Ṭhākura, the stalwart servant of Kṛṣṇa, by whose hearing one gains Kṛṣṇa in all ways. 18. In the village of Būḍhana, Haridāsa took his birth. To benefit [the villagers], he spread the praise of Kṛṣṇa, kīrtana, completely throughout that land. 19. After residing there for a while, he moved to the banks of the Gaṅgā, finally settling in Phuliyā in Śāntipura [the home of Advaitācārya]. 20. When the venerable [Advaita] Ācārya received him, he responded with a huṃkāra roar, his joy knowing no bounds. 21. Together with the saintly Advaita, Haridāsa floated on the waves of the ocean of the rapturous pleasure of Lord Govinda's love. 22. Endlessly did Haridāsa wander along the banks of the Gaṅgā, crying out rather strangely, "Kṛṣṇa." 23. He showed no interest in the pleasures of the senses. His mouth was filled with the name of Kṛṣṇa, his only sustenance. 24. Never did he experience boredom with the name of Govinda. His frame of mind shifted constantly in his devotional experience. 25. Sometimes he danced all by himself; other times he roared like a lion enraged. 26. Sometimes he wailed in a loud, mournful voice; and other times he laughed, that deep paroxysm of extreme humor. 27. Sometimes he would howl, making the full-throated huṃkāra sound; and other times he would fall down, completely insensate. 28. One moment he would call out with an inhuman voice and the very next talk in the most polished of manners. 29. He cried effusively, his flesh thrilled in waves, he laughed, he fainted, he perspired—such was the delirium of Kṛṣṇa-devotion which he experienced.

30. When the lord Haridāsa entered into solitary dance, everyone came and gathered around this holy image. 31. At such times tears of bliss would soak his entire body, a sight which evoked great pleasure, even for the exceedingly wicked. 32. Whoever witnessed this [dance] flushed with an extraordinary ripple of gooseflesh; even Brahmā and Śiva delighted to see it. 33. Everyone in the village of Phuliyā, many brahmans among them, was overwhelmed by watching him. 34. When Haridāsa lived in Phuliyā, an abiding belief was fostered in everyone there. 35. When he bathed in the Gaṅgā he ceaselessly took the name of Hari. Everywhere he went, he took the name in a strong voice.

36. One day a qāḍī went to the seat of the governor of the land and described these activities in great detail. 37. "A Muslim (*yavana*) is conducting himself as a Hindu. It would be advisable to haul him in and try him." 38. Listening to the words of this sinner, [the governor] was inclined to evil. He promptly had [Haridāsa] arrested and dragged before him. 39. By the grace of Kṛṣṇa, the great devotee Haridāsa had no fear of death, regardless of the charges of the Muslim. 40. As he was going forward and was presented to the governor, he muttered "Kṛṣṇa, Kṛṣṇa" over and over again. 41. Hearing Haridāsa as he arrived, a number of those present were simultaneously thrilled and saddened. [The commentator, Rādhāgovinda Nātha, notes that the name of Kṛṣṇa clearly

brightened the spirits of these men, while the realization of what was about to happen to Haridāsa dampened those spirits.]

42. There were a number of prominent individuals held in the jail, and inside they were, to the man, excited when they heard [of Haridāsa]. 43. "It is the great Vaiṣṇava, the eminent Haridāsa. Just to get a glimpse of him will destroy the misery of our bondage!" 44. The guards struggled to restrain the inmates who were determined to get a glimpse.

45. The stalwart Haridāsa arrived in that place and when he looked at the prisoners, his was the glance of heartfelt mercy. 46. Gazing hard at the feet of the venerable Haridāsa, the inmates were motionless, fixed in prostration. 47. [He stood] with arms hanging to his knees, lotus eyes, his moonlike face unsurpassed and completely charming. 48. With great affection and reverence they greeted him. Everyone felt transformed by Kṛṣṇa-devotion. 49. Seeing the devotion of those of the group, Haridāsa blessed all of the prisoners, 50. "Be still. Stay! May you remain as you are now." He laughed strangely as he proferred this cryptic blessing. 51. The prisoners did not fully fathom this mystifying expression and so became a bit depressed. 52. Then Haridāsa, moved by compassion for them, explained the hidden meaning of this blessing. 53. "You feel bad from not fathoming the real meaning of the benediction I pronounced over you. 54. I would never offer a prayer that was base or mean. Pay close attention and understand clearly what I meant. 55. Right now each and every heart is turned toward Kṛṣṇa—and it is just in that condition that you should always remain. 56. Now may you always join together to dance, to take the name of Kṛṣṇa, to reflect on Kṛṣṇa! 57. Now let there be no more violence, no more persecution of people. Say 'Kṛṣṇa' and dwell on this gentle advice. 58. Should you forget this when you reenter the ordinary, sensual world, you will rejoin the depraved, 59. and all of your shortcomings will reappear. Such is the nature of worldly affairs; listen carefully to the real meaning of what I said. 60. The blessing I gave did not mean, 'May you remain prisoners!' rather 'May you forget the ordinary, sensual world and say Hari day and night!' 61. My strategy for giving that blessing was that you would not consider your miseries, even for a minute. 62. My look of mercy is directed toward all living beings. May all of you develop an unfaltering devotion to Kṛṣṇa. 63. Do not worry, for within two or three days your bonds will be lifted—this I have promised. 64. Live in the ordinary, sensual world, but wherever you reside, never let any of this advice slip from your memory." 65. Imparting this advice for the welfare of the prisoners, he went to the court of the regional governor.

66. When he saw [Haridāsa's] magnificence and charm, [the governor] had him seated in the place of highest honor. 67. The regional governor cross-examined him personally. "How, O brother, am I to understand your attitude, your action? 68. Look, it was by great fortune that you had been a Muslim. How, then, can you believe and act like a Hindu? 69. Consider that we do not eat food with the Hindus, yet you have cast aside your [Muslim] religious heritage in doing so. 70. You transgress the obligations of your position and

do things contrary to it. How will you be delivered in the afterworld? 71. You did not realize that you performed an abominable act. Efface this sin by uttering the kalima [the Islamic creed]."

72. When Haridāsa heard these words from a man enchanted by the phenomenal world, he laughed loudly and pronounced, "Aha! The magic (*māyā*) of Viṣṇu!" 73. Then he began to speak gently [to the governor], "Listen, father! Humanity has but one Lord! 74. Hindus and Muslims differ in name only. The Supreme is described as One in both the Qur'ān and the [*Bhāgavata*] *Purāṇa.* 75. The One is flawless, of eternal substance, indivisible, unchanging. Indwelling in all things, it lives in the hearts of all. 76. This Lord, who motivates the hearts of men, effects the action of the entire world. 77. Everyone claims throughout the world that the names and qualities of this Lord are the preserve of their particular scripture. 78. Should anyone commit an act of violence, it is an injury directed toward that God who periodically assumes the burden of this world. 79. And so, in whichever direction this God leads my heart, I follow and act accordingly. 80. Should some brahman within the Hindu community desire to become a Muslim by following the dictates of that inner self, 81. what can the Hindus do to him for that action? What kind of law can punish one who has killed himself [by converting]? 82. Good sir, now you judge! If fault be found, then punish me!"

83. The words of the eminent Haridāsa had the sure ring of truth and all of the Muslims gathered were satisfied with what they heard. 84. The sole sinner among them, the qāḍī, advised the governor, "Punish him! 85. This is evil! And he will do much more evil, for he will bring disgrace down on the Muslim community! 86. So you would be well advised to mete him a severe punishment. If not, at least force him to preach his own [Muslim] scripture!"

87. The governor addressed [Haridāsa] again, "O brother! Recite your own scripture and there will be no further consideration [of this matter]. 88. Otherwise, all of the qāḍīs will administer punishment, after which they will still wonder what other little things they can do to you."

89. Haridāsa replied, "No one is able to do anything other than that which God has him do. 90. You must fully understand that God precipitates an outcome perfectly appropriate to the offense. 91. Even if my body is torn to pieces and my breath disappears, I will never quit saying the name of Hari."

92. Listening to that statement, the governor questioned [the qāḍī], "Now what would you do to him?"

93. The qāḍī replied, "Flog him through twenty-two market places! Take his life! I make no other judgment. 94. Let him be beaten through twenty-two market places and if he survives, then I will know that this man is truly learned and has spoken the complete truth."

95. The governor called the guards and ordered with vehemence, "Thrash him so badly that no life remains! 96. He is a Muslim acting as if he were a Hindu. When his life comes to an end he will finally escape this horrible sin." 97. With those vile words he ordered this terrible misdeed—and the wicked came forward and seized Haridāsa.

98. As they moved from market to market, those malicious men beat him senseless, their hearts seething with hatred. 99. Haridāsa meditated, "Kṛṣṇa! Kṛṣṇa!" and through the ecstasy of that name, the suffering of his body failed to register. 100. As they watched the extraordinarily cruel punishment administered to Haridāsa's body, all of those who were good suffered immeasurably. 101. Some predicted, "The entire kingdom is bound to be destroyed because of their perverse treatment of this good and honest man." 102. Some in their anger cursed the wazirs, the king's ministers, while others stepped forward to add blows of their own. 103. Some begged the Muslims, clasping their feet, "Let up! Do not flog him so hard!" 104. Still, no mercy was inculcated in those malefactors and they obdurately whipped him through market after market.

105. Through the wonderful grace of Kṛṣṇa, Haridāsa's body felt not the slightest pain from those awful beatings. 106. It was precisely as the demons had beaten the body of Prahlāda, for all the scriptures attest that he felt no pain at all.[1] 108. Even though Haridāsa remembers, all of the suffering was effaced at the time—how extraordinary this story of Haridāsa! 109. All of those iniquitous men who thrashed him suddenly felt the pain throbbing in their own hearts, 110. [for Haridāsa beseeched his Lord,] "O Kṛṣṇa! Be gracious to all of these living souls! Do not hold them responsible for any wrongdoing because of my punishment!"

111. In this way did those pernicious men beat the stalwart Haridāsa through one city after another. 112. They whipped him mightily to take away his life, but the beatings never even registered on Haridāsa. 113. All of the Muslims were dumbfounded, "Can any human being live through such a thrashing? 114. People die after being beaten in two or three market places, yet we have whipped him through twenty-two markets! 115. Not only does he not die, he appears to laugh the whole time! Is this man really a pīr?" And so they wondered.

116. Then the Muslims bemoaned, "O Haridāsa! The destruction of our community is certain to ensue because of you! 117. Even after such fierce punishment, you have not given up your life. The qāḍī is certain to kill us all!"

118. Haridāsa smiled and replied, "If by my living you meet with destruction, 119. then I will die to this worldly existence." Saying that, he quickly absorbed himself in deep meditation. 120. Replete with all powers, the adept Haridāsa became insensate; no breathing could be discerned.

121. Watching this the Muslims grew even more bewildered. They dragged and dumped him before the governor. 122. The governor simply ordered, "Bury his body."

The qāḍī rejoined, "But does he deserve such good treatment? 123. That would make honorable his despicable action. Therefore match the treatment to his deed. 124. If he is buried, he will reap the benefits in the afterlife. Toss him into the Gaṅgā so that he may suffer for a very long time."[2] 125. The Muslims accepted the command of the qāḍī and they started to pick him up to cast him into the Gaṅgā. 126. When those Muslims picked up Haridāsa to take him to the Gaṅgā, he remained in a seated position, firmly fixed. 127. As the venerable Haridāsa sat absorbed in the bliss of deep meditation, the Bearer of the Burden of the Universe came and took over his body. 128. His body had become the seat of the holder of a billion worlds, Viśvambhara.[3] Who could possibly have the power to budge Haridāsa? 129. Strong men converged on him from all sides, but the master remained motionless, fixed like a great stele [as they carried him]. 130. Haridāsa was drowning in the purified ocean of the bliss of Kṛṣṇa; he was not outwardly conscious. 131. Whether in the firmament, or on hard ground, or in the Gaṅgā—Haridāsa was totally unaware of where he was. 132. Just as Prahlāda had called on his Kṛṣṇa-devotion, so too was the power of the venerable Haridāsa.

133. All of those in whose heart the Golden-Limbed One [Caitanya] dwelled found this not at all unusual for Haridāsa. 134. Just as Hanūmān had subdued the demon and then was himself taken, out of respect for Brahmā,[4] 135. So too did Haridāsa consent to be punished by the Muslims for the sake of instructing the world— 136. 'Being under severe and ceaseless adversity, even to the point of death, even then the name of Hari does not fail to come from his mouth.' 138. Even though Haridāsa remembers all of the pain, it was annulled at the time—how extraordinary this tale of Haridāsa! 139. Truly, truly Haridāsa is lord of this world, the foremost among the followers of the Moon Caitanya!

140. And so when Haridāsa was committed to the Gaṅgā, he simply floated, and a short while later he was brought to consciousness by the will of God. 141. The honorable, adept Haridāsa became conscious enough to crawl up on the riverbank; he was filled with the highest bliss. 142. In this condition he returned to Phuliyā village, crying out the name of Kṛṣṇa in a loud voice. 143. All of the Muslims witnessed this unbelievable, strange power and immediately abandoned their violent ways, goodness filling their hearts. 144. They recognized him as a pīr and paid their respects. The entire lot of those Muslims gained salvation.

145. A short while later Haridāsa regained his normal consciousness. With a smile of compassion, he met the governor [who had come]. 146. The governor placed his palms together in deference and began to speak with great humility. 147. "Truly, truly I have come to realize that you are a great pīr. You have become firmly ensconced in the knowledge of the One. 148. Empty words [about the One] spew from the mouths of so many yogis and monists, but you have realized it, gaining power in this fabulously wondrous realm. 149. I have come here specifically to meet with you. O honorable devotee, please forgive my many shortcomings! 150. For you there is neither friend nor foe; you treat everyone the same. I recognize no one in the three worlds such as you. 151. You may go and do your good as you wish. You may go back and live in your hut on the banks of the Gaṅgā. 152. You may stay wherever you yourself desire. Do whatever suits you without any restriction."

153. When the socially elevated [Muslims] looked upon the feet of the venerable Haridāsa, they abandoned convention and forgot that he was low. 154.

They had dragged and beaten him with such incredible anger and now they recognized him as pīr and reached to grasped his feet. 155. The eminent Haridāsa looked with compassion on the Muslims and then returned to Phuliyā.

156. Haridāsa returned to the community of brahmans, constantly taking the name of Hari in a loud voice. 157. The brahmans of Phuliyā were collectively overjoyed when they saw Haridāsa. 158. The brahmans began to make the sounds of Hari, and Haridāsa, the Servant of Hari, began to dance in ecstasy. 159. Haridāsa's delirium was extraordinary and endless—crying, shaking, laughing, fainting, rippling with gooseflesh, shouting. 160. Haridāsa crashed to the ground in the rapturous experience of love, and the brahmans who witnessed it floated in great bliss. 161. After a great while Haridāsa became still and sat down. The brahmans sat in rows all around him. 162. Haridāsa spoke, "Listen brahmans! Do not in any way suffer on account of me. 163. I have listened to endless slander of my Lord, but my God has punished that. 164. Good resulted, and for that I am deeply gratified. Huge faults have been forgiven with a minimum of punishment. 165. To listen to Viṣṇu being slandered portends the Kumbhīpāka hell, and plenty of that I heard through these sinful ears. 166. They have been appropriately punished by God so that such sin will occur no more."

167. In this manner did Haridāsa join the brahmans in performing kīrtana, without fear and with great public display. 168. The families of all of those Muslims who had made them miserable were destroyed within a few days, as well. 169. Haridāsa then erected a small hut on the banks of the Gaṅgā and lived in solitude, meditating on the name of Kṛṣṇa day and night.

HARIDĀSA VANQUISHES THE SERPENT

170. Haridāsa took the name [of Kṛṣṇa] three hundred thousand times per day, which transformed his hut into the citadel of Vaikuṇṭha heaven. 171. Underneath that shack a monstrous serpent took up residence, his heat so radiant that nothing else could stay alive in there. 172. No one who came to converse with the stalwart Haridāsa was able to bear it. 173. Everyone without exception felt the incredible burning of the poison, but Haridāsa never noticed it at all. 174. The brahmans all gathered around to discuss why Haridāsa's abode radiated such massive heat.

175. In Phuliyā there lived a great physician, who came and determined that the cause was a serpent. 176. The physician pronounced, "Under the floor of the hut lies a single, extraordinary snake! The heat comes from that! 177. It can be said with certainty that no one can possibly survive there. Haridāsa must move quickly to another dwelling. 178. He can not continue to live there with that serpent. Come, let us go to his place and tell him!"

179. And so they came and addressed the venerable Haridāsa, explaining why he must abandon the hut. 180. "A monstrous serpent dwells underneath your hut. No one can stay here exposed to its radiance. 181. Consequently, it

is not appropriate for you to remain here. You must remove yourself to another residence elsewhere."

182. Haridāsa replied, "I have been here a great many days, yet I have never felt any burning sensation in my hut. 183. The misery in all of this is that you are not able to bear it! So because of that I will go somewhere else tomorrow. 184. If it is true that an honorable creature lives here and if by tomorrow it has not abandoned this dwelling, 185. then by all means will I leave and go elsewhere. Do not worry yourselves! Recite the stories of Kṛṣṇa!"

186. And so they did, telling the stories of Kṛṣṇa in auspicious song, kīrtana. As they were engaged, a marvelous event took place. 187. When the great serpent had heard that Haridāsa would leave that place, it left instead. 188. As they entered the evening, the snake rose up from its burrow and all who saw it ran for cover. 189. It was the most awesome of serpents, incredibly terrifying, yet strangely beautiful with its yellow, blue, and white coloration. 190. A huge gem glistened upon its head. The brahmans stared, terrified, silently calling, "Kṛṣṇa, Kṛṣṇa!" 191. The serpent simply slithered away and the heat was dissipated. The brahmans felt a relief without measure. 192. When the brahmans witnessed the tremendous power of the eminent Haridāsa, a greater devotion toward him was born among them. 193. What magnificent power is in the possession of Haridāsa, by whose mere words a serpent fled his quarters, 194. whose mere glance casts off the bonds of ignorance! Kṛṣṇa never counters Haridāsa's words.

THE FALSE POSSESSION

195. Listen now to another of his marvelous legends, which reveals more of his majesty as master of serpents. 196. One day in the fine house of an important man, a snake charmer was performing various versions of the dance of the snake bite. 197. The snake charmer circled everyone, singing in a loud voice, swaying to the rhythms of the mantra, accompanied by the double-ended mṛdaṅga drum, the cymbal, and instrumental music. 198. Just by chance, Haridāsa came by that place and he stood to one side to watch the snake charmer's dance. 199. Through the power of mantra, the King of Snakes [Ananta, upon whom Viṣṇu sleeps] took possession of the man's body and danced in delight. 200. In a loud voice, he sang the compelling song depicting Kṛṣṇa's dance on the serpent Kāliyadaha. 201. Listening to the innate majesty of his Lord, Haridāsa fell down in a dead faint, not breathing. 202. Shortly he regained consciousness, emitted a roar, and began to dance in an ecstasy without bounds. 203. When he saw the venerable Haridāsa's possession, the snake charmer stepped aside and waited. 204. The stalwart Haridāsa rolled around on the ground and put on an amazing display of rippling gooseflesh, tears, and the trembles. 205. This great devotee, Haridāsa, cried, absorbed in listening to the qualities of his Lord. 206. Haridāsa circled the group as he sang with joy, while to one side stood the snake charmer, palms pressed together in obeisance. 207.

When Haridāsa's possession subsided, the snake charmer reentered the dance. 208. When they witnessed the lordly Haridāsa's possession, the entire group experienced a strange pleasure. 209. Wherever the dust of his feet had brushed them, they smeared it around on their bodies with delight.

210. There was one particular brahman, very affected in manner, who lived in that area. He calculated cleverly, "Today I, too, shall dance! 211. I have realized that although it is only the foolish and ignorant who dance, even the most insignificant man can exhibit a supreme devotion." 212. Thinking in this vein, he suddenly crashed to the ground, falling as if he were completely insensate. 213. As soon as he fell in the snake charmer's dance arena, the snake charmer began to beat him unmercifully, thoroughly incensed. 214. From all quarters the cane pole rained blows down on his neck, for the snake charmer struck, never missing his mark—there was no escape! 215. The brahman was shattered by the cane beating. He fled, crying in terror, "Dear Father, Father!"

216. Pleased with himself, the snake charmer danced at length—while all those present felt mystified. 217. Pressing their palms together in respect, they questioned the snake charmer, "Explain to us why you beat that brahman, 218. and why you remained with your hands pressed in obeisance while Haridāsa danced! Can you explain all this?"

219. Then through the mouth of the snake charmer, that serpent who is the devoted servant of Viṣṇu [Ananta], began to speak of Haridāsa's greatness. 220. "That which you have asked is a great mystery, and although it is inexpressible, I shall try to explain. 221. When you saw the venerable Haridāsa's possession, your esteem for him grew to something special. 222. The brahman also watched this and, faking it, he fell to the ground, his mind brimming with jealousy. 223. What person has the right to break up the enjoyment of my dance by his jealousy and hypocrisy? 224. And he had the audacity to pull this sham in the presence of Haridāsa—so I punished him severely. 225. To convince me and the other people that he was a great man, he exhibited this seemingly righteous behavior before you. 226. There is no love for Kṛṣṇa in all of this personal pride. If one is honest and unaffected, then he gains Kṛṣṇa. 227. This could be seen when Haridāsa danced. Just to witness that dance was to have all of one's bonds destroyed. 228. Kṛṣṇa Himself dances in the dance of Haridāsa! The Brahmā-egg [the universe] is sanctified by watching this dance. 229. The name of Haridāsa—the servant of Hari—is perfectly appropriate to his calling, for Kṛṣṇa is eternally captured within his heart. 230. Kind and benevolent toward all living beings, he accompanies God down to earth in each and every birth.[5] 231. So faultless is his conduct toward Vaiṣṇavas and Viṣṇu that he never strays from the path, even in his dreams! 232. That living creature who is in his company even for a second is certain to gain the shelter of the lotus feet of Kṛṣṇa. 233. Brahmā and Śiva join Haridāsa as such devotees who ceaselessly cogitate the great drama [of Kṛṣṇa]. 234. Fully realizing that one's birth and lineage are ultimately without meaning, he took birth in a lowly clan [*nīcakula*, which in this case means Muslim, according to the commentator] at the order

of the Lord. 235. If devotion toward Viṣṇu can occur in the lowest of classes, how much more the possibilities among the self-consciously righteous, say all of the scriptures. 236. If one is born into the highest ranks but does not worship Kṛṣṇa, what can be done for his clan as he sinks into hell? 237. In order to bear direct witness of all of these scriptural truths did Haridāsa take birth in a lowly lineage. 238. Just as Prahlāda did for the titans (*daitya*) and Hanūmān did for the monkeys, so too did Haridāsa bring honor to a lowly community. 239. Deities crave the touch of Haridāsa; the Gaṅgā desires Haridāsa to immerse himself [in her waters]. 240. Let alone his touch, even Haridāsa's glance could shatter the beginningless bonds of karma for all living beings. 241. Whoever will seek refuge in Haridāsa will have the imprisonment of this cyclic world torn asunder by a mere look from him. 242. Should his greatness be told through a hundred mouths for a hundred years, its limit would not be reached. 243. That has made you fortunate, yet only a tiny portion of his majesty has been made public from within your community. 244. Surely he who speaks the name of Haridāsa but once will journey to the abode of Kṛṣṇa!"

245. When he had spoken thus, the Lord of Serpents became silent. The gathering of righteous and good people who heard were gratified. 246. Such was the greatness of the lordly Haridāsa which the holy Vaiṣṇava serpent [Ananta] had described since the ancient times. 247. The group was amazed when they listened to the speech of the serpent, and they felt an abiding love for Haridāsa. In this way did the venerable Haridāsa live prior to the Golden Moon, [Caitanya] manifesting his devotional love.

Notes

1. See *Bhāgavata Purāṇa* 7.5, 8. In this famous story, Prahlāda, who was a devotee of Viṣṇu-Kṛṣṇa, was ordered killed by his father, who felt that Prahlāda's devotion was a threat to his own aspirations to cosmic sovereignty. He enlisted hosts of demons to kill the boy with their celestial weapons, but to no avail, as Viṣṇu-Kṛṣṇa protected him. To avenge this attack, Kṛṣṇa descended to earth as Narasiṃha, the Man-Lion, who finally destroyed the megalomaniacal Hiraṇyakaśipu. The association seems to voice a certain yearning on the part of the current author.

2. It is perhaps worth noting that in Bengal, Hindu householders are cremated, whereas ascetics are never burned, but buried. Those who have died an unnatural death, by snakebite or some other means, are thrown into the river unburned in the hopes that they may be revived. The qāḍī, however, clearly deems Haridāsa to be a Muslim, so throwing him into the river would lead to his continued suffering, whereas burial would lead to eternal residence in heaven or confirm Haridāsa's piety.

3. Verses 127–28 contain a typical ambiguity in designating the figure who took control of Haridāsa's body—Viśvambhara. The line can be read three ways: either Viṣṇu as Viśvambhara came, or Caitanya as Viśvambhara came, or simply his body was as heavy and rigid as the billion worlds held by Viśvambhara. Vaiṣṇavas, including the commentator, opt for all three.

4. Hanūmān, the monkey general of Rāma's army, led the forces in the overthrow of the demonic king Rāvaṇa on the isle of Laṅkā. Rāvaṇa's son, Indrajit, employed the weapons of the god Brahmā in fighting Hanūmān. So as not to insult Brahmā and the power of his weapons, Hanūmān acquiesced to capture.

5. Because Kṛṣṇa descends to earth with his entire environment, Haridāsa is part of that eternal retinue that surrounds Kṛṣṇa at each visit, and he personifies the same kind of loving service each time.

—41—

Satya Pīr: Muslim Holy Man and Hindu God

Tony K. Stewart

Satya Pīr is a holy man or saint, in the form of a mythic Muslim pīr, who has been popular in the Bengali-speaking region of the South Asian subcontinent since the early sixteenth century. During the following three centuries, Satya Pīr's popularity prompted his followers to compose scores of literary works—poems, songs, epic narratives—dedicated to his praise and the promulgation of his cult. Today we can find over one hundred extant works dedicated to this powerful figure.

Bengalis worshiped Satya Pīr's power to provide for the general weal of the individual and family, to attain wealth, to ward off disease, and to counter the activities of demonic figures. At some indeterminate time, but probably in the seventeenth or early eighteenth century, Satya Pīr came to be identified with the Hindu god Satya Nārāyaṇa, a majestic form of Viṣṇu, and today the two epithets are used interchangeably. In a sophisticated and long-term process of Sanskritization, the primary exploits of Satya Nārāyaṇa were incorporated into two late Sanskrit Purāṇas. But the Bengali cycle of tales has historically dominated the practices of the cult. Today Muslims worship Satya Pīr only sporadically, whereas Hindus more consistently include him as part of their vrata household ritual cycle. The story of Satya Pīr has become, in this apparent shift of allegiance, ossified, and much more narratively predictable than suggested in the earliest compositions. The literary creativity of his devotees seems to have spent itself, for no new stories have been composed within the last century, a fact that is coincident with the development of strong communal and sectarian identities in Bengal.

The collection of writings dedicated to Satya Pīr is arguably the largest literary heritage in medieval Bengal, even challenging in breadth the prolific Gauḍīya Vaiṣṇava literature of the period. But unlike the literature of the Vaiṣṇavas, that of Satya Pīr has no highly developed theology or aesthetic theory to help the reader interpret his stories: his is a popular literature that deals with immediate and local problems that beset his Bengali audience. The earliest manuscripts dedicated to Satya Pīr point to the prominent Muslim ruler, Ḥusain Shāh (r. 1497–1525 C.E.), or more frequently to his daughter, as the popularizer of the cult. The historicity of such a claim is almost impossible to establish; but the fact that authors would seek to connect Ḥusain Shāh to the figure of Satya Pīr is in itself not surprising because of that king's notable patronage of both Hindu and Muslim literary culture. During his long and rather peaceful reign, classics from Sanskrit and Persian were translated into the local Bengali vernacular, and many original Bengali works were commissioned. The Bengali literature of this period was not sharply divided, in most instances, between Muslim and Hindu subject matter. The designations "Muslim" and "Hindu," especially for popular productions, such as the Satya Pīr stories, seem to have been read back onto the literature from the public, political formations of the nineteenth and twentieth century. The early literature of Satya Pīr appears to have been for all Bengalis, and the benefits from worshiping Satya Pīr knew no such communal boundaries, even though differences between Hindus and Muslims were certainly acknowledged. Bengalis worshiped Satya Pīr because to do so was effective.

The earliest Satya Pīr compositions take the form of the traditional pālagāna (a dramatic production that is either sung or acted) and the popular pāñcālī (a collection of short verses in praise of a deity), which were often set to music. A common literary trope of the Satya Pīr literature, which is akin to the maṅgala kāvya genre (a highly developed form of narrative poem on the exploits of a god or goddess), is the adventure of the merchant, who suffers dangerous and often demeaning trials prior to his worship of Satya Pīr. His fortunes reverse when, usually at the instigation of his wife or daughter-in-law, he acknowledges the power of Satya Pīr and proffers with respect the appropriate substances, traditionally the mixture of rice, sugar, milk, and spices, called *śirṇi* or *śinni*. This offering, which is directed to Satya Pīr in an aniconic ritual, restores wealth, health, and even the lost lives of the merchant's sons, to the obvious mutual benefit and pleasure of all.

The image of Satya Pīr found in the merchant's story is one that remains fairly constant throughout the literature: a wandering mendicant Sufi in tattered rags, vengeful and harsh to those who spurn him, but benevolent and gracious to those who show respect. He represents the raw power of divinity, which he can channel positively or negatively. But his field of action is not limited to any particular community, such as the merchants noted above; Satya Pīr is class-, race-, sect-, and gender-blind, in both his rewards and punishments, and his stories, when taken collectively, address every segment of society. That same lack of bias is reflected in the eclecticism of the texts' language. Perso-Arabic elements are woven into the Sanskrit-based Bengali to create a rich linguistic tapestry that shows remarkable local variation, and that, possibly more than any other literary examples from this period of Bengal's history, reflects the culture's linguistic pluralism. Satya Pīr's literature is, in the real sense of that word, a popular literature, aimed at a general listening public.

Satya Pīr addresses certain existential concerns relevant to survival in Bengal, such as gaining wealth, escaping disease, avoiding crocodiles, and so on, and he does so in terms that are coherent and rational according to a commonly held local knowledge regarding human action. You, as an individual, are responsible for your actions, which will in turn determine your future—a rather generic, popular form of causality. If you do the morally right things and worship Satya Pīr, you will reap the rewards—and, of course, the converse holds true as well. The efficacy of the action is justification enough for belief. What else one might believe or disbelieve did not affect this perceived reality for the Bengali of the pre-modern period; Satya Pīr rewards and punishes in culturally relevant terms that cut across social divisions. Worshiping Satya Pīr in pre-modern Bengal had no negative effect on one's worship of, or belief in, Allah or Viṣṇu.

Starting in the nineteenth century, certain political groups within the populace, generally labeled as "reformers," sought to establish more clearly their group identities as Muslims. It would seem that only with the emergence of a new fundamentalism did Muslims begin to confront the worship of Satya Pīr as a glaring inconsistency in their personal actions: it became embarrassing and problematic to worship a pīr who was promoted by Hindu "idolaters" and "polytheists." This process is quite the opposite of syncretism; it is one of differentiation and demarcation. Muslims began to perceive a contradiction in the construction of their personal (and group) identity, so they began to withdraw their general support of the Satya Pīr community in an effort to overcome the disjunction. Conversely, with the concomitant articulation of a new Hindu identity, Satya Pīr could be comfortably accommodated into the hegemonic theological structure of Vaiṣṇava avatāra theory; he confirmed his identification with Lord Viṣṇu, who in this final aeon, the Kaliyuga, assumed the image of the holy man of India's conquerors prior to the British. Where previously no Muslim felt it a contradiction to believe both in this figure of local power, Satya Pīr, and in Islam, increasingly in the nineteenth and twentieth centuries, many Muslims apparently did begin to perceive it so. Today in Bengal—both Bangladesh and West Bengal—the disappearance of Satya Pīr from the Muslim world seems imminent.

The three most common tales found in this broad literature, and the set that now reflects the shift toward a Hindu appropriation of Satya Pīr, is the "Story of the Poor Brahman," the highly abbreviated "Woodcutter's Tale," and the longer "Merchant's Adventure." This narrative set has been incorporated into the Sanskrit *Skanda Purāṇa* (5.233–36) and *Bhaviṣya Purāṇa* (3.2.24–29). The Bengali pāñcālī versions of this story by Rāmeśvara Bhaṭṭācārya and by Śaṅkarācārya follow the puranic account and redact the narrative in explicitly Hindu terms according to the avatāra theory of the Vaiṣṇavas: Satya Pīr is Nārāyaṇa Viṣṇu come to earth in a Muslim guise. This and the other narratives are told in as many different ways and styles as there are authors, and there are a lots of them.

To give a sample of the distinct regional variations, the local flavor of the narrative, and its popular oral basis, the Satya Pīr cycle is presented here from several different works. The salutation and invitation to worship (translation 1) come from the *Satyadeva Saṃhitā* ("Scripture Dedicated to Satyadeva") of Dvija Rāmabhadra, edited by Vyomakeśa Mustaphī (*Baṅgīya Sāhitya Pariṣad Patrikā* 8:2 [1308 B.S.], pp. 131–32). Dvija Rāmabhadra was a poet popular in East Bengal (today Bangladesh) during the late eighteenth century. The description of Satya Pīr in the garb of a fakir (translation 2) comes from the elegant work, *Satyanārāyaṇera Vratakathā* ("The Story of the Vow to Satya Nārāyaṇa") of Bhāratacandra in *Bhāratacandra Granthāvalī,* edited by Vrajendranātha Bandyopādhyāya (Calcutta: Baṅgīya Sāhitya Pariṣat, 1357 B.S.), p. 440. Bhāratacandra Rāya Guṇākara was court poet to Rājā Kṛṣṇacandra in the early eighteenth century. Śaṅkarācārya's accounts of the poor brahman's and the woodcutter's tales (translations 3 and 4) come from his *Satyanārāyaṇa Pāñcālī* ("Song of the Vow to Satya Nārāyaṇa"), Gaurāṅgasundara Bhaṭṭācārya, Baṭṭalā edition (Calcutta: Rajendra Library, n.d.). And the final story, the merchant's adventure, comes from the elaborate work of Ayodhyārāma Kavicandra Rāya, who wrote during the sixteenth century. That work, *Satyanārāyaṇa Kathā* ("The Tale of Satyanārāyaṇa"), edited by Vyomakeśa Mustaphī (*Baṇgīya Sāhitya Pariṣat Patrikā* 8, no. 1 [1308 B.S.], 61–72), has proved especially popular in the Rāḍha region of southwest Bengal.

Further Reading

Three works are recommended: Anoop Chandola, *The Way to True Worship: A Popular Story of Hinduism* (Lanham, Maryland: University Press of America, 1991); S. C. Mitra, "On the Worship of the Deity Satyanārāyaṇa in Northern India," *Journal of the Anthropological Society of Bengal* 9:7 (1919), 768–811; and Asim Roy, *The Islamic Syncretistic Tradition in Bengal* (Princeton: Princeton University Press, 1983).

SALUTATIONS TO PREPARE FOR THE RITUAL

Stretching fully prostrate on the earth,
I make obeisance to the lord Gaṇapati [Gaṇeśa],
  the son of Lord Śiva.
Second, I bow to the sun,
whose complexion is redder than the hibiscus flower,
  residing in a chariot of a single disc.

Obeisance likewise to Lord Nārāyaṇa,
enthroned as lord of the heavens,
  wielding conch, disc, club, and lotus.
Fourth, I bow low to Hara [Śiva],

whose naked body is clothed in ash,
above whose head, where the Gaṅgā flows, rests the moon.

Fifth, revering the Mother [Umā],
I bow low to the daughter of the Himalayas,
the enchanting magician, slayer of the buffalo demon.
Keeping Gaṇapati in the cave of my heart,
I make obeisance to [the goddesses] Lakṣmī, Sarasvatī,
and the ten-armed [Durgā] riding her lion.

I bow to the Bhāgīrathī and Gaṅgā rivers,
cleansers of the offences of the Kali age,
and to the sacred sites of Nīlācala [Purī] and Varanasi.
To the hosts of deities
gathered at his lotus feet I bow,
basking in the bliss of the divine play of Govinda.

In age after age he descends,
stealing away the burden of the earth
as the Fish, the Tortoise, the Boar, and the Dwarf.
I prostrate myself at the feet of
the Plow Holder [Haladhara Balarāma] and the Man-Lion
and Jāmadagnya [Paraśurāma], the destroyer of warriors.

Obeisance be to Rāma, green as a blade of durbā grass,
accompanied by [his wife, Sītā] Jānakī
and [his brother] Lakṣmaṇa, who holds the royal parasol over his head,
whose exploits made famous Setubandhu,
where they destroyed the ten-headed [Rāvaṇa].

I revere Buddha and Kalki, and the other incarnations—
Obeisance be to Kṛṣṇa,
the complete godhead, the formless Brahman,
the one who plays among the trees in the forests of Vṛndā.
The scion of the Yadu clan,
having destroyed the demonic Kaṃsa,
partially descends in the form of Satya [Pīr].

[For him] there is no sacrifice, yoga, asceticism,
purification of the body, nyāsa ritual,[1] recitation of the names,
nor ritual worship with fire according to the injunctions;
Famed and revered throughout the world,
made accommodating only by a loving devotion,
God extends his parental love to his devotees.

You, who embody the heavenly realm of Gokula,
who are named Satya Nārāyaṇa—the Pure and True Refuge of Man—
have laid hold the wicked to save them!
Take note of these poor and lowly folk,
grant your mercy through your own good nature!
Whoever knows will attest to your greatness.

You, O Lord, friend of the lowly,
fetch me across this ocean of existence,
alleviate my misery!
Simply by recalling your name,
one gains the desired four goals of life [wealth, pleasure, duty, and liberation].
You are the living soul of all living beings.

He who develops proper devotion to you
is certain to achieve liberation;
but how can I, a fool, even know enough to speak [of this]?
To serve your lotus feet,
Rāmabhadra has composed this book—
Alleviate the searing agony of this earth!

Everyone listen carefully and with great concentration
to the manner of Satya Nārāyaṇa's advent.
In the citadel of Hastināpura, the Pāṇḍava king
Yudhiṣṭhira met one day with Govinda [Kṛṣṇa].
In seclusion they sat, holding long and serious discussions.
With palms pressed together in supplication, Yudhiṣṭhira entreated [Govinda].
"The Kali Age has begun. My body shudders at the prospect.
Where are people to turn? Speak, Gadādhara—Wielder of the Club!"
Govinda replied, "What you, O King, have said is of widespread concern.
For the sake of living beings I have descended in age after age.
One hundred thousand qualities accrued in the Satya age,
are reduced to ten thousand qualities in the Tretā age,
one thousand qualities in the Dvāpara, and one hundred in the Kali.
Five thousand years after the Kali age begins,
I will descend in the city of Avantī.
By virtue of my grace, people will find a dwelling in heaven,
for the name of Hari is fire and the Kali but mounds of cotton.
Toward the end of the Kali age, foreigners will appear.
Through the Kalki avatāra I will destroy them."
King Yudhiṣṭhira was relieved to hear this.
Meditating on Govinda, he was then bodily transported to heaven.

Listen now to the amazing tale of how, at the appropriate time,
Nārāyaṇa [Kṛṣṇa] descended to the city of Avantī!
While on the earth he assumed the name of
Satya Nārāyaṇa—The Pure and True Refuge of Man—
whose fame spread from region to region with each passing day.
Assuming the dress of an ascetic renunciate, Satya Nārāyaṇa
made his first appearance before a beggar brahman.

SATYA PĪR DESCRIBED

In this Kali age the societal offices of the twice-born, the warriors, the common folk, and the lowly servers have gradually disintegrated, succumbing to the might of foreign Muslims. At this, Lord Hari came down, taking on the body and form of a fakir, and strategically positioned himself at the foot of a banyan tree. Slightly stooped, he wore a beard and mustache, his body covered by a patchwork wrap, a cap on his head, in his hand a staff. From his shoulder swung a knitted bag. He was replete with splendor, effulgent like the sun itself. From his mouth poured forth the speech of Muslim pīrs and the Prophet. His were the lips that uttered prayers to God, and kissed the dust of the tombs of saints.

THE STORY OF THE POOR BRAHMAN

Obeisance to Satya Nārāyaṇa, with many salutations! In proper order I salute all of the gods. In order to institute the worship of Satya Deva—the True Lord—in the Kali age, Lord Nārāyaṇa has appeared. The Lord has come to the world of mortals. Traveling far and wide, he eventually reached the city of Mathura.

In Mathura there lived a poor brahman who passed all his time in misery, knowing not one moment of pleasure. One day this brahman was making his rounds through town and, unsuccessful in obtaining food by way of his begging, grew distraught. His heart ached. Dejected, he sat under a banyan tree and wept bitterly, hopeful for a meager handout. The more the twice-born [the brahman] wept, the more disconcerted he grew.

Watching the whole affair was Satya Pīr. Assuming the form and dress of a [Muslim] fakir, he presented himself and inquired, "For what reason do you weep, my brahman son? A great compassion wells as I watch you in your misery."

The brahman replied, "What good will it do to tell you?"

The fakir countered, "O twice-born, what harm can it do? Tell me your story exactly as it transpired."

The twice-born said, "I eat whatever I can beg from people. Today, for no apparent reason, I received no offerings of food. Not only did I fail to obtain any rice, I am now bereft of clothing as well. You can see for yourself that without oil to dress my hair, my scalp has begun to crack. The day has passed and I have not tasted even the semblance of a meal. I do not believe that I can bear any more the searing agony of my miseries!"

The fakir answered, "From this day forward, your miseries shall fade into darkness. Incomparable wealth awaits you. Go now to your own village! I have spoken to you with the certainty of truth, for I am Satya Pīr, the Saint of Truth. In the Kali age I appear on earth. When someone reflects on me in this form and proffers an offering of rice and milk śirṇi, it brings results. Riches are guaranteed to accrue to you."

The twice-born observed, "Each day I worship [Nārāyaṇa's sacred] śālagrāma stone; should I fail, a disastrous fate is surely in store. My only hope has lain in doing that diligently. In a future time, when Lord Nārāyaṇa comes, that act is sure to be rewarded. How can I simultaneously worship a [Muslim] pīr, as I discharge this [duty]? Were I to follow such a barbaric and foreign custom, I would sink to the depths of hell."

Smiling, the fakir replied, "Listen well, ignorant one! That pīr is one and the same as the Lord Nārāyaṇa! Understand that the Veda and the Qur'ān derive from a common source. Do not listen to them as two separately created entities here on earth." As he was speaking he transmuted into the universal sovereign who holds in his hands the conch, the disc, the club, and the lotus. The kaustubha gem [one of Kṛṣṇa's emblems] hung from his neck, his chest radiating splendor. He was the full and eternal Brahman, a reservoir of unimaginable power.

Seeing this image, the twice-born fell to the earth and in choked words sang the praises of his Lord. "No one is capable of recognizing you as an ordinary mendicant—how much more difficult it is for me, a poor and lowly brahman." As [the brahman] looked on, the fakir resumed his previous form.

The twice-born continued, "Tell me everything so that I can worship you and have my birth fulfilled. In what fashion should I offer the rice and milk śirṇi to make the worship appropriate? Speak, speak, great Lord, for I am listening attentively!"

And speak the fakir did, solely for the benefit of that brahman. "Collect one and one-quarter seers [about two pounds] of coarse white rice powder and spread five and one-quarter gaṇḍās of bananas [either twenty-one bananas or twenty-one cowrie shells' worth] on a sanctified pedestal. Then prepare and offer five and one-quarter gaṇḍās of betel quids [areca nut, spices, and lime wrapped in a betel palm leaf]. Finally offer one and one-quarter seers of sugar and one and one-quarter seers of clotted cream. With this, I, who am Satya Pīr—the Saint of Truth—will be pleased.

"If you cannot procure the sugar and clotted cream, then offer milk and molasses, liberally mixed with devotion. Combine all the ingredients and place them in the middle of all the devotees, whom you will seat all around. You must perform the worship, observing faultlessly the rules of the sacred ritual manuals. At the end of the worship, you will listen closely to the story of the vow."

Satya Pīr continued, "Place your hand on your forehead. When your hand rests there, you avert untold calamities. Repeating the name 'Satya Satya Nārāyaṇa' again and again, press your palms together and make respectful obeisance. Everyone who is present will consume what is left, the prasāda, which embodies [Nārāyaṇa's] grace."

This is the story of the vow written by Śaṅkarācārya.

"Go back into the city, brahman, where you will receive much to eat! This is my promise. Afterwards, go home and spend the night. The following day, worship Satya Pīr unerringly!"

After he imparted these instructions, the pīr disappeared. The blessed twice-born went to collect his food. The brahman ate and shortly thereafter was to receive great wealth. He returned to his own house and explained everything in detail to his brahman wife. He fasted throughout the night, but grew apprehensive. By the second watch of the morning, he went out and visited a number of houses. He received extraordinary quantities of food and other goods. When the brahman's wife heard, she was overjoyed and quickly gathered the necessities to perform the worship service. The twice-born dedicated the worship ritual to the feet of Nārāyaṇa through an assortment of appropriate offerings, for it was by the grace of the pīr that the brahman had gained his wealth. If one receives such favor, then little by little a matchless wealth will accumulate—such is the power of this ritual worship!

THE WOODCUTTER'S TALE

Servants, male and female, cows, water buffaloes, horses, elephants—these and innumerable guests soon filled the twice-born's house. First the brahman prepared the articles for worship. Then he methodically acknowledged all of those present. The woodgatherers, who had gone out to cut wood, stopped by the brahman's home seeking refreshment. When they beheld [his new wealth], the woodsmen were all amazed. In the course of a single day and night this poor brahman had been transformed into a king! Recovering from the shock, they eagerly questioned the brahman. The best of twice-born responded with the story from beginning to end, leaving out nothing. The woodsmen then proffered the śirṇi offering in exactly the way it had been described. Their miseries and hardships instantly disappeared. Happiness entered every household.

THE MERCHANT'S ADVENTURE

. . . After erecting a sprawling abode
the woodcutters, deeply satisfied,

routinely offered śirṇi with great public show.
A merchant trader,
appropriately named Ratnākara—Treasure Mine of Gems—
landed his vessel's tender at that ghat.
The merchant, being very inquisitive,
questioned the workers who met him,
"What kind of religious ritual are you doing, brothers?"
The woodcutters responded,
"We are worshipping Satya Nārāyaṇa.
When understood, it is an exhilirating experience!
If one worships, all powers obtain,
riches, sons, weal, and long life,
for Nārāyaṇa is Satya—the True—in the Kali age."
Perceiving only the tiniest glimmer of [the ritual's] majesty,
the merchant declared, "Then I too shall do worship,
if to me a child be born.
As I have spoken before my attendants,
I will offer the śirṇi under those conditions."
Speaking thus, he boarded his dinghy.
He returned to his own land
and reentered his own sprawling domain—
So sings the poet Ayodhyārāma.

Proud and respectful of his śirṇi, the merchant returned to his home.
With his wife, Sīmantinī, the merchant deceived even the night,
for the trader truly outshone the face of the moon in his love.
His blessed wife, her gait graceful like the elephant's, grew ever more pregnant.
In time she gave birth to a girl of uncommon beauty,
just as Jayā had been born from the womb of Yaśodā [Kṛṣṇa's foster mother].
The little girl grew [each day] as noticeably as the moon waxes.
After seven months she was given the desired name of Suśīlā—Good Conduct.
When the time was deemed appropriate, the young woman was betrothed
to the son of the merchant Sadānanda Nāga of Kāṭoyā.
The two men, father and son-in-law, discussed, trader to trader,
how the stream of their forefathers' lineages had merged.
Pleased in a number of ways, the merchant returned to his abode
and reflected on the need to undertake a voyage for business.
The trader supplied his wife with
ten thousand gold coins for household expenses.
Diamonds, rubies, silver, gold, coral,

yak-tail fly whisks, sandalwood, and conches he collected in limitless quantity.
With great fanfare, cymbals clashed, kettle drums rumbled, and horns blew,
while the two men auspiciously boarded their vessel.
The cannons were fired with flickering wicks,
the horrendous thunder reminiscent of the monsoon clouds of July.
Sadāgara called out, "May we be protected! May we be safe!"
as he slipped away from his own realm of Bāgīśanagara.
Veṇīpura lay to port and Sanata to starboard.
Coming behind him from upstream blew a healthy breeze.
Sailing swiftly past Baḍajāṃhāpura, he arrived at Sākāi.
Stopping over at Kāṭoyā and Indrāṇī, he made for Pāṭuli.
Sailing past Kubjapura, the successful merchant
stopped off in Navadvīpa, then left behind the paddy land along the river.
He sailed by Guptipāḍā, which lay to the right in the distance,
while on the left lay the village called Śāntipura.
Jirāṭa, next in the merchant's itinerary, was left behind
when he reached the Triveṇī, where three streams form the Bhāgīrathī.
Briefly he visited the city of Hugli, where
he performed the ritual worship of Lord Ṣāṇḍeśvara [Śiva] in Cuṃuḍā.
With favorable winds his boat easily sailed to Degaṅga,
where yellow cāmpaka flowers blossomed among the medicinal nim trees.
At Cākala he worshiped Hara [Śiva], which was especially gratifying.
He likewise performed the rituals for Jagannātha as the sole Lord.
To port were Bhadrakhāli, Bāli, and Varāhanagara;
then Sadāgara passed on through Dihi and Calcutta.
He sailed past Dhulanta on the left and Jirāṭa on the right.
Slipping past Bhavānīpura, he made his way to Kālīghāṭa.
There he performed the rituals to Kālī according to the injunctions,
whereupon he boarded again—so sings Ayodhyārāma.

Pushing off from Kālīghāṭa,
his seven boats then set sail,
making Sadāgara extremely happy.
To the beat of kettle and gourd drums,
with the village of Rasā sitting on the left,
the shackled oarsmen broke into song.

Sailing by the small subdivision of Sārabhāṭṭa,
Vaiṣṇavaghāṭṭā passed to starboard.
The boats shot like arrows downstream.
With Mahāmāyāpura lying off the port bow,

they left Mālañca far behind,
arriving soon at Mradanmala.

Just beyond Bāruipura,
the merchant Ratnākara
negotiated the duties owed to the collector.
When he reached the village of Bārāśat,
he offered a variety of collected items,
and reverently worshiped the primordial Viśvanātha—Lord of Cosmos.

Hard on Hetegaḍa,
they escaped the turbulent and swift currents, and the men cried, "Hari, Hari!" in relief.
They ceremoniously touched the Gaṅgā's waters,
making obeisance to Kapila, and
paid homage to Mādhava [Kṛṣṇa] at Gaṅgāsāgara, the river's mouth.

They begged the protection of Dakṣiṇa Rāya—Tiger Lord of the South—
before the boats slipped into the ocean expanse
where the waves swell high and coast disappears.
A great distance from their point of departure,
from the towns where the river currents swirl into the ocean,
the blue mountains of Orissa crept into view.

In Orissa, of Lord Jagannātha—the Lord of the Universe—
together with his sister Subhadrā—the Fortunate One—
the merchant took darśana.[2]
Whoever looks but once
is subject to no more rebirth—
such is the power of the unseen, supreme Lord.

The intrinsic value of that place
is comparable only to the heaven of Vaikuṇṭha.
Whoever gives up his life in that city,
becomes accommodated to Viṣṇu,
four-armed, filled with a majestic power, and
is whisked straight away to heaven on a celestial chariot.

That most accomplished of merchants
purchased and consumed prasāda,[3]
then immediately launched the ship.
He passed through many lands,
seeing many strange and wonderful things along the way,
reaching the embankment of Rāma in the middle of the ocean.[4]

He kept Māṇikapura to starboard,
and Siṃhalapāṭana to port,
staying far away from the fatal whirlpools of Kālīdaha.
After sailing for six full months
he arrived at Hiraṇyapāṭana, the City of Gold—
so reports Ayodhyārāma.

It took six months for the trader to reach the City of Gold.
It lay in a land whose king was appropriately named
Citrasena—the Amazing Warrior.
Satya Nārāyaṇa began to brood,
"Those two merchants failed to offer the śirṇi they promised."
Whatever treasures lay in the storehouses of King Citrasena
were stolen away by Satya Nārāyaṇa.
By the power of his yoga, he deposited them in the boats of the merchants.
Seeing his treasury emptied, that king of men swelled with anger.
He had seized and brought for questioning the chief of police,
who was of fierce countenance, and was called "He Who Nets His Foe."
Furious, the monarch screamed, "Listen, police!
You have an hour to bring that thief to justice!
If not, I will have you severed in two,
and will impale the rest of your lineage on pikes."
The policeman, shaken by the threat of the king,
sent guards to cordon the city and scour every beat.
When the police arrived at the docks, they saw seven ships
and immediately detained the two merchants.
They discovered the king's wealth filling the boats floating there—
sacks and sacks of diamonds, emeralds, silver, and gold.
The two merchants, father-in-law and son-in-law, were viciously bound,
just as Aniruddha had been seized by the magical arrows of Bāṇa.
Thousands upon thousands of men hauled out the treasure.
Citrasena, that kingly ornament of earth, watched this with great satisfaction.
Then the order was issued to the policeman,
"Slap both the father-in-law and son-in-law in jail!"
When the fates grow cranky, such events take place.
The merchant and his son[-in-law], made out as thieves, sat trapped in jail.

Meanwhile, the wife of the merchant grew increasingly miserable.
All the money that had been left for her was spent, and no more arrived, so
food no longer came into her hands; the days were passed in weeping.

She was wasting away to skin and bones, and she worried,
"My husband has gone far away on a money-making venture,
and I have heard no news at all, good or bad."
Now there was a local twice-born, named Hariśarma—
He Who Finds Shelter in God—who daily offered śirṇi, and,
as luck would have it, the attractive wife of the merchant happened by there.
With hands humbly pressed together, she inquired of that brahman's wife,
"Tell me, my noble woman, whose worship are you performing?"
Heeding her request, the brahman's wife explained its point.
"We offer śirṇi to worship Satya Nārāyaṇa.
All suffering and misery disappear, and destroyed are all obstacles
to whatever you wish or desire."
Understanding this little bit about Satya Nārāyaṇa's power,
the merchant's wife offered śirṇi in precisely the same way [as the brahman].
"When my son-in-law and merchant husband return safely,
I promise to offer śirṇi once again to the very best of my ability."
With this contingency, the worship was performed by mother and daughter,
and Satya Nārāyaṇa was contented and absolved their faults.

He, Satya Nārāyaṇa, showed himself in a dream to the king,
lord of the land where the son-in-law and father-in-law were captive.
To the lord among men, Citrasena, he spoke secretly,
"The two merchants were imprisoned for no good reason.
In that prison you are punishing two of my devoted servants.
In the morning, release them and send them back to their own land!
You will award them ten times the wealth with which they arrived!
If you do not, I will, in my anger, kill everyone in your lineage."
At the end the king was yanked hard by his hair—
and calling on Govinda, he trembled in fear.
In the morning, like one mad, the king
hastily summoned the chief of police,
"Bring to me those two thieves from the boat!"
Heeding the order, he brought the two merchants forward with alacrity.
Then, at the king's command, the barber
shaved and trimmed the two merchants.
After bathing and performing worship, they ate contentedly.
The king addressed them, "Please forgive my many faults!
Look, by reason of fate, Rāma was forced into the forest,
and I cannot begin to describe the misery suffered by Vatsarājā.

The five brothers, Yudhiṣṭhira and the rest, were exiled to the forests,
And Kali dispatched Nala from his kingdom."[5]
Having made his apologies, the king called the chief of police,
"Fill a cart with valuables from the treasury."
The king bestowed on them many fine garments, much jewelry and
treasure,
to a value ten times [their original cargo], and bade them farewell.
Without delay, they filled their seven ships with diamonds,
emeralds, coral, conches, yak-tail fly whisks, and sandal.
At a particularly auspicious moment, the two men pushed off
and continued on their journey—so sings Ayodhyārāma.

Filling their vessels with riches,
the two traders
set sail for their own country.
Their winds were favorable,
stiff, yet consistent,
as the boats sailed day and night.

On both shores were villages,
too numerous to name,
after which they passed Orissa.
Where the [Gaṅgā] River meets the ocean,
they bathed and made offerings
in the presence of Lord Kapila.

Having paid their respects to Mādhava,
they then continued the journey,
until they landed up at Kālīghāṭa.
Performing the worship of Mother Kālī,
they departed Calcutta;
the boats struck for Śrīpāṭa.

Hṛṣīkeśa [Nārāyaṇa] assumed
the guise of a celibate student of the Vedas,
and queried the trader.
"What riches are aboard your ships?
Please describe them in detail.

Can't you please give me something of them?"
The merchant responded this way,
"What words can I say?
I'm hauling nothing but coal."
When this patent lie was voiced,
everything on the boat turned to ash
through divine intervention.

As if the very life had escaped his body,
the merchant was dumbstruck,
as was his son-in-law.
He disembarked the boat and
headed for the man who was dressed as a student;
he fell at his feet, which he clasped hard to his breast.

"I am a miserable cretin!
I did not recognize you
and so spoke to deceive.
What good will a mirror do
for one with no eyes,
or scriptures for the illiterate farmer?

You are Nārāyaṇa,
the eternal Brahman,
while I am but an ignorant child.
The lion does not get angry
at the stupidity of the jackal!
Can an animal recognize riches?"

The Lord listened
to the self-effacing admission of the merchant
and, growing compassionate, spoke,
"That offering of śirṇi, which you promised to me,
and which I had previously prescribed,
you failed to offer.

Your loving wife
offered śirṇi—
an act for which you gained reprieve.
Go back to your home
and offer me śirṇi,
if you wish to live!

From the bowels of that prison,
I sprang you free,
and now you try to deceive me.
Risking your wealth and son [-in-law]
to cross the Gaṅgā
is like waving bananas in front of hungry crocodiles."

Having explained the situation,
Satya Nārāyaṇa
then disappeared.
The holds of their ships,

which had held nothing at all,
  they realized, were now filled with treasure.

The treasure, as much as before,
the two men recovered
  and secured in their holds for sailing.
In such an extraordinary fashion
they returned to their homeland
  after twelve long years.

That evening
a messenger came and began,
  "Greetings to the wife of the merchant!
Amazing news—
your husband and son-in-law
  have returned to this land.

Their ships, filled with treasures
and priceless gems,
  have plied the ocean of misery."
Hearing these auspicious words,
the mother and her daughter
  had at last grasped the moon!

When they had made their offerings of śirṇi,
the merchant's daughter, Suśīlā—Good Conduct—
  dropped some of the prasāda on the ground.
She ran quickly
to meet the returning ships,
  woefully disrespectful of her god.

Satya Nārāyaṇa grew
exceedingly irritated at the thought,
  "She has thrown down my śirṇi!
Of such self-centeredness
I shall bestow on her the fruit"—
  as is told by the poet Ayodhyārāma.

When the merchant's daughter cast the śirṇi onto the ground,
her husband and his ship went straight to the bottom.
The merchant watched as his son-in-law drowned and floated to the ghat.
Grieving, he cried out, beating his chest.
Right then Suśīlā came up to the ghat
and upon arrival saw that things had gone terribly awry—
her father was weeping bitterly, and her husband's boat had disappeared.

Her face withered instantly, no breath could enter her lungs.
The radiant wife of the merchant worriedly inquired, "O my lord,
Why do you cry and strike yourself on the head?"
The merchant replied, "No one is as wretched as I!
At this very ghat my son-in-law just drowned."
Hit with the news, the mother and daughter were stunned.
They struck their foreheads with such violence that blood began to flow.
Sobbing uncontrollably, the merchant's daughter cried out,
"A terrible misery plagues me, affecting my entire life!
Alas, what now is to become of me?"
Crying, Suśīlā decided to plunge into the waters;
but Satya Nārāyaṇa then appeared in the guise of an astrologer.
He presented himself before the merchant's daughter.
"Beautiful one, why do you want to give up this life that stirs in your heart?
I can foretell anything in the three realms of the universe.
You will regain your husband and undo this awful misfortune."
Pretending to make calculations, he drew some figures on the ground.
Seating the mother and daughter to calculate the results,
the Lord spoke, "I have determined the nature of the situation.
You threw down some śirṇi, which is prasāda, as you hurried to the ghat.
On account of this, calamity has struck.
Gather up that śirṇi and eat it with proper devotion!
You will regain your husband at once! Go and raise his ship!"
Heeding his words, the daughter scurried off with her mother close behind,
while Satya Nārāyaṇa vanished with a smile.
Where she had thrown down the śirṇi, they ate, even licking the ground.
The ship carrying her husband sprang up from the deep.
Catching sight of his son-in-law, the merchant was overjoyed,
while the mother and daughter ran back to the landing ghat.
The merchant's wife let loose the auspicious hulāhuli sound of triumph
and, together with her daughter, greeted the incoming ship.
A din arose with the sounds of kettle drums, large and small, cymbals,
double conches, jagajhampa,[6] double-ended drums, and so forth.
The two men—the father-in-law and his son-in-law—landed on the bank,
mindful of nothing but Satya Nārāyaṇa.
They reflected, "We shall offer śirṇi to Satya Nārāyaṇa."
Exhibiting great devotion, they gathered together all the necessary items.

The men called all of their neighbors and friends,
as the merchant's wife made ready the sacred space for worship.
Demarcating it with elaborate designs drawn with colored rice flour,
the wife installed a seat of honor in the center.
With assorted flowers and especially fragrant sandalwood paste,
she lovingly set the stage to her satisfaction.
The merchant brought śirṇi worth one thousand rupees;
the crowd was seated all around in neat rows.
The officiating priest sat before them like Bṛhaspati himself
and installed Satya Nārāyaṇa there [on the seat].[7]
The glories of Satya Nārāyaṇa were read to the group.
Those gathered ate the śirṇi, quickly running their hands over their heads.
When the merchant offered the previously promised śirṇi,
Satya Nārāyaṇa was pleased and granted a boon.
[The merchant's] wealth grew without limits,
making him equal to Śakra, king of the gods,
while Lakṣmī, the goddess of wealth, herself the daughter of the ocean, looked favorably on him.
His family grew and their servants, male and female, likewise were many.
Thousands upon thousands of people came and were fed in that house.
And in this fashion the father- and son-in-law, delighted,
lived in their respective homes, prosperous without limit.

Whatever wish is made with the promise of offering śirṇi
is certain to be fulfilled by Satya Nārāyaṇa!
In this Kali age, he is filled with mercy, the very limits of compassion—
what human can fathom his extraordinary majesty?
So it has been written by Ayodhyārāma, the masterful moon of poets.
Everyone rejoice with the words, "Hari, Hari!" as this book draws to a close.

Notes

1. Nyāsa is a personal ritual wherein the observer sanctifies the working of the body to its proper function by placing the hand on each part and reciting a mantra to a deity appropriate to that part.

2. Darśana is the ritual viewing of the icon wherein the devotee looks on the image with loving devotion and the activated image is understood to look back, a sort of visual touching (because the sense of sight is active, not passive) that connects the two. Darśana is a major component of most temple ritual and especially prominent in the cult of Jagannātha.

3. Prasāda here is the leftover food offered to Jagannātha, which is styled *mahāprasāda*. Jagannātha's

prasāda is renowned throughout northeast India for its effectiveness in purifying and protecting devotees.

4. The "embankment of Rāma" is the strip of land once believed to have connected India and Sri Lanka.

5. These four stories all refer to ranking kṣatriya rulers who, for various reasons, were forced into exile in the prime of their lives. Rāma is the hero of the epic *Rāmāyaṇa,* Yudhiṣṭhira the eldest of the five Pāṇḍava brothers of the *Mahābhārata.* The stories of Vatsarājā and Nala are also found in the *Mahābhārata.* It should be noted that Kali here is not the goddess Kālī, but the personification of the Kali age, who tormented Nala.

6. *Jagajhampa* is an old instrument made of gourd, covered on both ends with stretched animal hide, with one or more strings pulled through. The sound is produced by plucking the string, which is amplified by the skins; tone is changed by tension.

7. Although the word for "installed" is used, it should be noted that the worship of Satya Pīr is an aniconic ritual, so installation is temporary and understood more in terms of invocation. Bṛhaspati is preceptor to the gods.

—42—

Jain Questions and Answers: Who Is God and How Is He Worshiped?

John E. Cort

The Jain Definition of God According to Ācārya Vijay Ānandsūri (Ātmārāmjī)

Ācārya Vijay Ānandsūri (1837–1896), better known as Ātmārāmjī, was the most important mendicant in a major reform movement within the Śvetāmbara Mūrtipūjaka community in the late nineteenth and early twentieth centuries. He took initiation as a mendicant in the iconoclastic Śvetāmbara Sthānakavāsī sect as Muni Ātmārāmjī in 1854, but after extensive reading in Jain literature became convinced of the truth of the Mūrtipūjaka position in favor of image worship, and so took a new initiation as a Mūrtipūjaka mendicant in Ahmedabad in 1876 along with eighteen disciples. His new Mūrtipūjaka name was Muni Ānand Vijay, later Ācārya Vijay Ānandsūri, but he was more commonly known by his Sthānakavāsī name.

He came into contact with European scholars of Jainism, and was invited to be the Jain delegate to the World Parliament of Religions in Chicago in 1893. Since Jain mendicants, as part of their vow of total non-harm (*ahiṃsā*) cannot travel by any means of transport, it was impossible for him to attend. In his stead he sent a young Jain layman from Bombay, Virchand R. Gandhi. (Virchand was no relation to the better-known Mohandas K. [Mahatma] Gandhi, although the two did meet in Bombay in 1892.)

In this passage from his 1884 exposition on the true Jain religion, entitled *The Ideals of the Jain Tenets,* Ātmārāmjī responds to the criticism commonly made both by Europeans and by other Indians, that the Jains are atheists. He explains that the Jains do believe in God, but it is a God with a difference. In contrast to the Christian and many Hindu definitions of God, according to the Jains (as well as many Buddhists and other Hindus) the universe has existed from beginningless time, and so God did not create the universe. The Jain position that God did not create the universe is not unusual in India. Many theologies and cosmologies view

God and the universe as separately eternal and uncreated. God for the Jains, in fact, is the totality of all the Jinas and other perfected souls (*siddhas*), that is, all of the souls that have attained enlightenment and liberation, and reside at the top of the universe eternally in the four infinitudes of infinite knowledge, infinite perception, infinite bliss, and infinite power. On the one hand there is an uncountable number of such souls; on the other hand, since they are essentially indistinguishable one from the other, they take on a corporate identity. Thus God for the Jains is simultaneously plural and singular.

The proof text employed by Ātmārāmjī is the medieval Sanskrit *Bhaktāmara Stotra* of Mānatuṅgasūri, a hymn that is accepted as authoritative by both Śvetāmbaras and Digambaras, and is still known by heart by thousands of Jains today. Many of the epithets for the Jina in the hymn are epithets of the Buddha and the Hindu gods Viṣṇu, Śiva, and Brahmā. Ātmārāmjī explains how these epithets are to be correctly understood when applied to the Jina.

The passage is translated from Ācārya Vijay Ānandsūri, *Jain Tattvādarś*. 2 vols., edited by Banārsīdās Jain (Ambala: Śrī Ātmānand Jain Mahāsabhā Panjāb, 1936), vol. 1, pp. 80–85. Originally published in Bombay in 1884.

Q 1: We have heard that the Jains do not believe in God (Iśvar). Their tradition is atheist. But in the first chapter you have written in many places "Lord God Arhat" (Arhant Bhagvant Parameśvar), and the first chapter gives a complete description of the Lord (Bhagavān). How is this possible?

A: Oh, faithful one! Whoever says that those people whose support is the Jain tradition do not believe in God is mistaken. They have never read or heard the scriptures of the Jain tradition, nor have they ever met an educated Jain. Those who have read or heard the Jain scriptures never say that the Jains don't believe in God. If the Jains don't believe in God, then whom does the following verse praise?

> You are imperishable, mighty, unknowable, uncountable, primordial,
> Brahmā, Īśvara, infinite, destroyer of Kāma,
> Lord of yogis, knower of yoga, many, one, the embodiment of knowledge,
> stainless: the saints call you by these names.
>
> *Bhaktāmara Stotra* 24

This verse means as follows. Hey Jina! The saints, the people of truth, call you imperishable, that is, unchanging. The one who attains to the state of unchangingness from the perspective of physical things is unchanging, and exists in a single innate form in the three times of past, present, and future. He is mighty, he shines; he who exists in lordship is mighty. Or, the one who uproots karma is mighty. Or, he who is the Lord of Indra and the other celestial beings is mighty. In this way the true people call you "Mighty." How are you to be described? Unknowable, for the spiritual knower cannot comprehend your totality, in this way the true people call you "Unknowable." How are you to be described? Uncountable, for you have so many virtues that they cannot be counted, and for this reason the true people call you "Uncountable." How are you to be described? Primordial, the one who was in the beginning. Because you set in motion the affairs of the world, the saints call you "Primordial." How are you to be described? Brahmā, from existing in infinite bliss, you are the foremost increaser, so the true people call you "Brahmā." How are you to be described? Īśvara, the Lord of all the celestial beings. Because you are the master, they call you "Īśvara." How are you to be described? Infinite, that is, infinite knowledge, and your union with perception is infinite. Or, that of which there is no finitude is infinite. Or, the one who resides in the four—infinite knowledge, infinite power, infinite bliss, and infinite life—is called "Infinite." How are you to be described? Destroyer of Kāma, from being a destroyer just as the arising of Ketu was to Kāma, they call you "Destroyer of Kāma." Or, he is called "Destroyer of Kāma" whose bodily marks indicate no gross physical body, who is not subject to change, who does not eat, who is not virile, who does not act. What do your Vedic followers call you? "Lord of Yogis." A yogi is one who possesses the four knowledges [sensory knowledge, reason, clairvoyance, telepathy] and because he is Lord, he is called "Lord of Yogis." How are you to be described? Knower of yoga, the one whose form is correct knowledge, and so on. Or, the one who does yoga of meditation, and so on. Or especially, the one who destroys the bonds between karma and soul. Thus you are called "Knower of Yoga." How are you to be described? Many, from being omnipresent due to knowledge. Or, unifying the various perfections. Or, from consideration of the many virtues. Or, due to the separation of the many virtues. Or, due to the separation of the Jinas Ṛṣabha, and so on, from humanity, they call you "Separate." How are you to be described? One, without a second, the highest of the high. Or, from consideration of the category of soul, they call you "One." How are you to be described? Embodiment of knowledge, whose own nature is solely the knowledge of the extinction of all desires to be active. Thus they call you "Embodiment of Knowledge." How are you to be described? Stainless, who are not dirty from the eighteen forms of fault, for this reason they call you "Stainless." It is proven through these fifteen descriptions that the Jains are among the traditions that believe in God.

And:

> You are the true Buddha, for the knowledge praised by the wise
> awakens in you.
> You are Śaṅkara, for you make the triple world happy.
> You are the Creator, O firm one, for you show the rules of the rites on
> the holy path.
> It is obvious, O Lord, only you are the best of men.
>
> *Bhaktāmara Stotra* 25

This means: He is worshiped as wise and is honored by the wise celestial beings.

From displaying excellent wisdom among the seven excellent things, You are called "Buddha." From creating happiness in the triple world, You are called "Śaṅkara," for the one who creates (*kara*) contentment and happiness (*śaṃ*) is Śaṅkara. Because you establish the path to liberation, consisting of knowledge, faith, and conduct, you are "Brahmā the Creator." O Lord! Among mortal forms yours is the best. There are hymns with hundreds of thousands of verses just like this one to God (Parameśvar). If people say that Jains don't believe in God, then to whom are these hymns addressed? Therefore, those who say that Jains do not believe in God speak falsely.

Q 2: You have removed that doubt from my mind very effectively. But I still have one doubt. You believe in God, but is it believed in the Jain tradition that God created the world or not?

A: Oh, faithful one! If it could be proven that God created the world, then why wouldn't Jains believe it? But there is no proof that God created the world.

Removal of Doubts Concerning Worship of the Blessed Jina According to Paṅnyās Bhadraṅkar Vijay Gaṇi

Bhadraṅkar Vijay (1903–1980), who was in the same monastic lineage as Ātmārāmjī, was one of the most highly revered of all Śvetāmbara Mūrtipūjaka monks of this century. He was esteemed as a great mystic, who was able to expound the spiritual significance of rites of worship and of the Namaskāra Mantra. In these two passages from his writings he responds to the questions of an imaginary interlocutor concerning the suitability of worshiping images of Jinas with physical offerings. The objections are of three sorts. The first is that since God [the Jina] resides in total dispassion at the top of the universe, God is totally absent from the image, and the worship therefore should be inefficacious. The second objection is that worship involving physical objects also involves an element of harm (*hiṃsa*) to living beings, and therefore runs counter to the central Jain ethical principle of non-harm (*ahiṃsā*) to all living beings. The third objection is that since God is pure soul, and therefore is totally removed from the realm of karma and physical matter, it is a contradiction to worship God with physical offerings, which involves the worshiper in interaction with karma. Bhadraṅkar Vijay uses many similes for God, all of which are essentially interchangeable; these are indicated in the translation. He also uses the terms *pūjā* and *darśan* interchangeably; I have translated both as "worship."

The first translation is from Paṅnyās Bhadraṅkar Vijay Gaṇi, *Dharm-Śraddhā* ("Faith in Religion") (Bombay: Jain Sāhitya Vikās Maṇḍaḷ, 1978), pp. 91–102. This was originally published in 1942. The second is from the same author's *Paramātmā Darśan* ("The Worship of God"), Hindi translation by Muni Ratnasenvijay (Madras: Svādhyāy Saṅgh, 1986), pp. 47–50. This was a loose translation of the Gujarati *Dev Darśan,* 1941.

FROM *FAITH IN RELIGION*

Q 1: What are the pure God (*deva*), guru, and religion?

A: The God who is dispassionate, the guru who is celibate, and the religion which consists of compassion—these are pure. Those who have attained a human birth because of auspicious karma, but who then follow a passionate god, a householder guru, and a harmful religion, fall under the control of a passionate obstinacy and squander this much-sought-after human birth.

Q 2: What are the marks of the true God (*deva*), and what is the manner of worshiping Him?

A: The one who has attained victory over all internal enemies, who is omniscient, who is honored in the three worlds, and who expounds the true meaning—whoever fits this is the true God (Īśvar). His names include Viṣṇu, Brahmā, Mahādeva, Śaṅkara, Jina, Kevalin, Arhat, and Tīrthaṅkara. The worship (*pūjā*) of God (Parameśvar) involves reciting his name, worship (*darśan*) of his image, remembrance of his biography and virtues, and praising him. From these four kinds of worship (*pūjā*) the soul becomes itself the very form of God (Bhagavān).

Q 3: The great fruits of devotion are expounded in the scriptures. What is their cause?

A: In the scriptures, the fruits of devotion of God (Arihant) are described as the best of all fruits, because God's conduct is pure and his teachings are pure. Those who know the teachings of God who gives the pure teaching, but who don't perform devotion of God, have their fierce atoms become stronger, and there isn't even a trace of moderation in their exaggerated speech. Those men who are knowledgeable receive the knowledge of the teachings of God, and while traveling toward liberation they greatly desire to do service of God. Devotion of God destroys both separation from oneself and contact with harmful karma; it spreads glory throughout the world; and the person attains a birth such as a world emperor, a celestial being, an Indra, and so on. The person who has no faith in God is unsuccessful in this human life, misses the highest fruit, acts ignorantly, becomes an authority in harmful karma, and abuses rites such as asceticism, mantra repetition, study, and meditation. Those who reject God in their quest for liberation and instead go to other gods abandon the water of the ocean of peace from thirst and fall into a whirlpool. Those who do not accept the pure teachings of God destroy logic and are called destroyers of logic. For such a person the spiritual knowledge of God is unobtainable, the speech of preachers is unknowable, and pure sense-objects remain invisible. But all these are accessible to true yogis. Those who don't believe in a creator and sustainer of the world meditate on the God as Arhat, the true form of Brahmā, who aids all souls. They are successful, they acquire meritorious karma, their life is meaningful, and their minds become ever attached to the virtues of God.

Q 4: These are the fruits of reciting the names or virtues of God (Bhagavān); but what benefit is attained from worship of his image?

A: The name of God is just an inanimate thing. Although inanimate, the name becomes a support to the recitation of the virtues of God. But the inanimate image of God is a superior support for introducing one to the ultimate innate form of God. From praising, and so on, the image of God, one attains a great fruit in the form of right faith. One becomes attached to the supporting meritorious karma of the path to liberation, and that which is meaningless becomes the success of meaningfulness. The peaceful image of God causes one to remember the virtues of God, and one attains all one's desires, just as from a wishing-gem. Those who worship the image of God from a sentiment of covetousness are unfortunate, for the wishing-gem slips out of their fingers. After attaining the arising of the supreme meritorious karma, they then gamble with desire, and the wishing-tree in the courtyard of their house withers.

Q 5: If a householder performs only spiritual (*bhāva*) worship, and not physical (*dravya*) worship, then will it work or not?

A: It won't work. A householder is always subject to violence and possessiveness. He is always troubled with worries. Because of these worries his intellect is trapped. Therefore a householder's mind cannot remain stable without an external support. In order to maintain stability of mind, he must worship (*pūjā*) God with form, he must perform daily service to the mendicants, and he must perform religious rites such as gifting in the full ritual manner.

Besides, the householder remains engaged in objectionable activities. He is always engaged in obtaining worldly wealth. He is engaged in the discipline of materialism for wealth and the prosperity of his family. He is always pursuing business, and is dejected when he is financially dependent. So it is impossible for his mind to remain stable from mental worship alone.

Not only that, all his other activities involve physical matter and are successful, so therefore his mind is satisfied in the realm of religion by physical things. Since his mind is oppressed with worldly worries and intrigues, he cannot attain any result through spiritual worship. A householder is involved with physical things, so his religion cannot be successful without physical worship.

Q 6: What are the results from an inanimate image?

A: An inanimate thing surely provides results. For those who worship the form, there is a connection between the form and religion. He who sees that which is fully embodied as only a puppet is stuck in delusion. In the *Scripture on Love* there is the example that the lustful person experiences all the feelings of sex just from the sexual postures. In the *Yoga Scripture,* it is said that the person studying yoga finds his study of yoga improved from sitting in the yoga posture. One can clearly learn about all the cities in the world from studying geography. A wise person learns many new things from reading the physical letters in books. In the same way, by worshiping the image of one's own God one stands firm in the path of remembering his laudable virtues.

The greatness of images and forms is explained in worldly books and common parlance. When her husband is absent, the faithful woman looks at his lifeless photograph and experiences pleasure and bliss. This is a fact well known to faithful women. When the faithful Sītā was separated from Rāma, she experienced pleasure by clinging to his ring, and Rāma experienced the pleasure of having Sītā present just by holding her jewelry. When Rāma was dwelling in the forest, Bharata worshiped Rāma's sandals as if they were Rāma himself. In the *Mahābhārata* it is written that the tribal hunter Lavya attained a knowledge of archery that equaled Arjuna's just by worshiping the image of Droṇa. [Several other similar examples are omitted.]

In this way there are many kinds of results from the images of physical objects. Not only that, but the images of even nonphysical things have an effect in the world. The zero, the letters from *a* to *z*, the physical categories such as earth, the rāgas described in music theory, outer space, the wind, and similar things are not physical, but many activities are based upon their existence. In this manner, the worshiper gains the greatest fruits when, with an auspicious intention, he considers the formless God (Īśvar) as having a form. The formless God does not derive anything either karmically auspicious or harmful from the worship of the formless God through the physical image, but the worshiper definitely does.

A person throws a rock at a wall made of diamond, or holds a lamp up to the sun, or criticizes or praises the emperor; nothing happens to the emperor, but the one who criticizes or praises definitely accrues some auspicious or harmful fruit. In the same manner, God does not accrue any fruit from the worship of the physical image of the formless God, but the worshiper from his auspicious intention, or the abuser from his harmful intention, definitely accrues auspicious or harmful fruit. Besides, there is no unanimity of opinion in the Jain teachings that God is formless. The formless God might first be in a condition with form, and then in a formless condition.

Q 7: Why doesn't the fruit from worship (*pūjā*) of God (Parameśvar) accrue immediately?

A: Everything comes to fruition in its own time and place. Birth occurs after nine months. The fruit of repeating a mantra one thousand times, one hundred thousand times, or ten million times occurs later. Different plants have their own time and place of fruition. Government service, commercial transactions, and so on, all have their own time of fruition. The supreme fruit from such an excellent ritual as worship comes in one's next birth. From a wishing-stone and other such this-worldly and insignificant things one attains fruits in this life. The merit from worship gives not an insignificant human fruit, but rather a much-desired fruit such as rebirth as a celestial being.

There are various kinds of meritorious karma in the world. Here one finds the fruits of many kinds of meritorious and harmful karmas. If one is stingy in giving to a king, then one attains the great fruit of execution. He who ably serves a king attains the fruit of enjoyment, as does his whole family. In the same way, those who worship God out of a supreme sentiment get fruit in this life in the form of wealth and also quite definitely get even better rewards in the next life.

Q 8: Can you give some similes for the temple?

A: There are many lovely similes for the temple. The temple is a book that teaches the ignorant people caught in the cycle of rebirth. It is like a lamp for the forgetful person who has fallen in the cycle of rebirth. It is a peaceful place for an agitated heart. It is an herb for healing a wound. It is an eternal wishing-tree in a world of rocks. It is a mountain of shining snow. It is sweet water in the midst of the salty ocean. It is the living breath of the saints. It is an unfailing teaching for bad people. It is the pure memory of former times. It is the play-house for the soul in the present. It is a feast for the future. It is the path to heaven. It is the pillar of liberation. It is the lock on the door to hell. It is a lake of nectar in the form of knowledge of the soul. It is a strong fortress to protect one from the misfortunes in the cycle of rebirth.

Q 9: What is worship of God (Tīrthaṅkaradev) for?

A: God (Tīrthaṅkaradev) is your ancestor. It is not the same as worshiping the emperors of great kingdoms. There is only one reason for worshiping the Tīrthaṅkaras: they have shown you the path to liberation. They have traveled this path themselves, and have also taught you how to travel this path. Therefore you should worship them. You worship their virtues. If you do not think those virtues are the most excellent, then you do not respect the Tīrthaṅkaras themselves, but only their outer form. The respect of those who do not focus on the nature of the virtues of the Tīrthaṅkaras is worthless. The Tīrthaṅkaras are true, and what they have done and the path they have taught are true. The person who in the fullness of faith worships them grasps this path and is engrossed in it.

The worship performed by people who worship the Tīrthaṅkaras without understanding the renunciatory path of the Tīrthaṅkaras is not considered to be real worship. It is considered to be real worship of the Tīrthaṅkaras and respect for their teachings of the renunciatory path only if the person incorporates those virtues in his life. Without this, it is not really worship of the Tīrthaṅkaras, whether it be done out of fondness, tradition, or worldly desires.

FROM *THE WORSHIP OF GOD*

Q 1: Is it possible for there to be any benefit to that which is conscious from an inanimate image (*mūrti*)?

A: The glass of eyeglasses is inanimate, but isn't there a benefit to the eye? Of course there is! Your eyes cannot see even two miles, but with the aid of a telescope they can see fifty miles. From an inanimate blanket the cold is removed from the conscious body, so why can't there be benefit to the soul from an inanimate image?

Q 2: What is the basis for the benefit from worship (*darśan*) of God (Paramātmā)?

A: From worship of God an auspicious karmic sentiment arises in the soul. At the time of worshiping God the worshiper becomes humble, and sings praises of God, from which a sentiment of gratefulness becomes evident. From this gratefulness, knowledge-obscuring and other karmas are destroyed, and the soul gradually advances on the path to liberation.

Q 3: It is said in the scriptures that positive results are obtained from worship of God, so why doesn't everyone get those positive results?

A: There is no doubt that in the worship of God there is the power to give positive results as described in the scriptures. But positive results accrue only from rites which are done according to the proper ritual rules. Positive results do not accrue from any rite that is not done according to the proper ritual rules, where the ritual rules are incompletely followed, or that is done in opposition to the ritual rules. It is necessary to follow the proper ritual rules in all rites, even those such as farming, cooking, and business. Hence in this way, by performing the rite according to the proper ritual rules, it is certain that devotion (*bhakti*) to God gives results.

Q 4: It is possible to perform devotion to God by reciting the names of God (*nām-smaraṇ*), so why is it necessary to perform rites to images (*pratimā-pūjan*)?

A: If it were possible to perform devotion to God only through reciting the names of God, then wouldn't it also be possible to perform devotion to the guru through just reciting the names? But in addition to reciting the name, the guru is given obeisance, veneration, respect, food, and water. In the same manner it is necessary to perform veneration and rites along with reciting the names of God.

Q 5: In the worship of God, minute living beings are killed, so aren't these rites therefore unworthy?

A: The injury that occurs to souls in water and vegetable bodies in the worship of God is beneficial to householders, according to the example of the well. This example is as follows: A person is traveling through the jungle during the hot season, and due to the heat begins to feel thirsty. He looks for water everywhere, but can't find any. In the end, he comes to a dry riverbed, and he learns from someone that water can be found by digging just a little bit in the riverbed. He is very thirsty, so when he learns this he digs in the riverbed. His thirst grows even greater from the exertion of digging, and his shirt becomes dirty from sweat, but due to the hope of finding water he becomes indifferent to the exertion. In the end, after he finally finds water, he can forget about the exertion. See! In the same way, there is a small amount of injury done to living creatures in the worship of God, but in the auspicious perseverance of devotion to God, that violence is the cause of great gain.

Q 6: If the worship of images is esteemed, why don't mendicants perform worship with physical things (*dravya*)?

A: To a slight extent mendicants do perform worship with physical things. They go to the temple, fold their hands before the image, perform veneration, bow their heads, sing hymns, give intentions—in this way mendicants worship with physical things. The Rite of Veneration is a spiritual (*bhāva*) form of worship, but in it there are also bodily obeisance and other physical forms of worship.

Mendicants have renounced money, therefore what is forbidden for them is to perform worship with physical things that have to be purchased with physical money, such as incense, lights, sandalwood, rice, and food.

Q 7: There is no benefit to God (Jineśvar) from the worship of God, so isn't the worship of God therefore useless?

A: There is no benefit to God from the worship, but there is definitely a benefit to the worshiper. From the repetition of a mantra, tending a fire, or studying science there is no benefit to the mantra, fire, or science. But from repeating a mantra, poison is destroyed; from tending a fire, cold is destroyed; and from studying science, there is surely an increase in the student's knowledge. In the same manner, from the worship of God the auspicious perseverance of the worshiper increases, and from that there surely is dissociation from previously acquired karmas and the association with meritorious karma.

Q 8: The Lord is self-sufficient in satisfaction, so therefore how do we get any benefit from worship?

A: The Lord is self-sufficient in satisfaction, which is why he is a suitable object of worship. In addition, it is because the Lord is self-sufficient in satisfaction that he performed the great beneficence of establishing the religion for the benefit of faithful souls. His beneficence upon us is immeasurable. He is the fulfillment of all virtues, which is why he is the suitable object of the best worship.

—43—

Esoteric Knowledge and the Tradition of the Preceptors

Douglas Renfrew Brooks

When the esoteric traditions and texts known collectively as "tantra" first came under scrutiny in the late nineteenth century, Western scholars dismissed them as intellectually corrupt and morally degenerate. Though the basic elements of tantric ideology were as yet still largely unexplored, judgments had already been rendered. Sir Monier Monier-Williams, Boden Professor of Sanskrit at Oxford, wrote in 1894 that "the Tantras are generally mere manuals of mysticism, magic, and superstition of the worst and most silly kind. . . . Indeed, Tantrism . . . is Hinduism arrived at its last and worst stage of medieval development" (*Hinduism* [London: Society for Promoting Christian Knowledge, 1894], p. 129).

Monier-Williams was correct in stating that Hindu tantrism reached its zenith of development in medieval India. Further, much of tantrism can be rightly called mystical, inasmuch as it consists of secret or privileged theories and practices that demand special qualifications and promise experiences that confer divine knowledge and empowerment. Hindu tantrics have been particularly interested in establishing an extra-canonical body of text and tradition that could complement and augment exoteric scriptures. Rather than merely reject the status quo, some tantrics appropriated or self-consciously inverted "orthodox" concepts and values in order to reinvigorate and reinterpret what they viewed as a moribund tradition. Efforts to create alternative scriptural authorities and ritual practices were not necessarily directed against the interests of entrenched social and religious authorities, namely, those from priestly castes. Further, "mainstream" or classical categories, such as revelation (*śruti*) and law (*dharma*), were employed to add legitimacy and authority to tantric undertakings. Although it is true that tantrics deliberately violated conventional ethics and ideology in their practices, they are best understood as an extra-Vedic, rather than an anti-Vedic movement. In other words, the tantric strategy is to claim that they represent a legitimate and alternative secret, exclusive, and easily misunderstood tradition from within the legacy of traditional Hindu orthodoxy.

Only in the past twenty-five years have scholars begun to appreciate the variety of Hindu tantric traditions and the very different religious and social interests that appear within tantric texts. Monier-Williams, like other scholars of his day, based his opinions about Hindu tantrism on private studies of texts and on discussions with informants. He tells us that, "None of the actual Tantras have, as yet, been printed or translated in Europe" (p. 129). Despite his admission to knowing little about the tantras' origins, the people who composed them, or those who have made use of them, he assures us repeatedly that they contribute nothing of significance to understanding Hinduism. Yet, his own remarks suggest otherwise; perhaps unwittingly, he raises important questions about the historical and intellectual origins of tantrism. He writes, "So little is known about the composition of these mystical writings that it is not possible to decide at present as to which are the most ancient, and still less as to the date to be assigned to any of them. They are all said to be founded on the Kaulopanishad" (p. 131).

Contemporary scholarship is rarely more decisive about the probable dates and authorship of tantric texts than was Monier-Williams nearly a century ago. However, we no longer treat Hindu tantrism as a homogenous tradition with a single canon emerging from an isolated text, and we are not likely to accept any exclusive claim about tantrism's origins or its textual foundations or authority. Monier-Williams's last statement that all the tantras are founded on the *Kaula Upaniṣad* ("The Secret of the Preceptors") is certainly not correct, but he did establish an important precedent. For, despite his hasty and often unwarranted generalizations, Monier-Williams was among the first to suggest that students of Hindu tantrism must take seriously the claims tantrics make about themselves. Unfortunately, he did not differentiate what he learned from consulting a handful of titles in Sanskrit and Bengali from the judgments of his native informants.

If Monier-Williams's remark about *Kaula Upaniṣad* had come from reading the text itself, then he might have said the same thing about other texts he mentions by name, since nearly all make similar claims. If, however, he concluded that the *Kaula Upaniṣad* is the source because it is the scriptural (that is, the Vedic) revelation on which the tantras are founded, he would merely have adopted the position of those with an interest in such claims. A select group of tantrics would claim that the *Kaula Upaniṣad* is among the texts on which the tantras are "founded." Further, they would probably argue that the *Kaula Upaniṣad*'s status as revelation (*śruti*) makes it ancient, authoritative, and foundational to all other texts that reflect (*smṛti*) on its content or appeal to its authority. Not all Hindus, or even all tantrics, would agree that it deserves to be treated as the authoritative revelation foundational to tantric tradition, but it is true that the *Kaula Upaniṣad* is part of a legacy within Hindu tantrism that seeks to reinforce rather than reject priestly methods of establishing authority, one that is intent on expanding the boundaries of the canon in order to substantiate claims to sacred knowledge and social legitimacy. In other words, the *Kaula Upaniṣad* is important precisely because its teachings represent the social and religious interests of a particular segment of Hindu tantrism.

From its title and the use of archaic language, the author or authors of *Kaula Upaniṣad* seek to confer on it an antiquity and authority reserved for scriptural or Vedic revelation. The Upaniṣads—nontantric and tantric—are understood to offer privileged, powerful, and secret types of knowledge. Further, the genre is assumed to be authoritative because, as revelation, such texts are either "without origin" (*apauruṣeya*), that is, they have no human author, or have God as their author. Placing tantric ideas within the genre of "Upaniṣad" or "secret teaching" confers on them antiquity and authority equal to nontantric counterparts, and further distinguishes the specific tantric elements as matters of greater secrecy, power, and importance. Thus, tantric secrets, special requirements for initiation, and promised benefits are all justified in terms of Vedic precedents. The exclusive category of Upaniṣad also justifies the concealment of such potentially dangerous and powerful teachings from "mere beasts."

Other ideas in the *Kaula Upaniṣad* suggest a late medieval composition from within a mature, sectarian tantric tradition. By declaring that one should "inwardly worship the goddess, outwardly follow Śiva, and in worldly affairs follow Viṣṇu," the texts create a hierarchy of theological possibilities in which goddess worshipers are clearly superior. The details of this worship purportedly represent the Preceptor (*Kaula*) tradition; though the Upaniṣad does not specify precisely what is meant by its Preceptor tradition, there can be little doubt that it focused on relatively narrow sectarianism of goddess-centered or Śakta tantrism. Texts in Sanskrit about goddess-centered tantrism do not appear in written form until at least the ninth century.

The *Kaula Upaniṣad* ("The Secret of the Preceptors") is not mentioned by name before the eighteenth century, though its views are current by at least the twelfth century. It is important not because it is ancient or, as Monier-Williams thought, because it is the "original source" of the tantras but for three related reasons. First, it collects in a single place ideas crucial to understanding Hindu tantrics who sought legitimacy within the religious and social mainstreams of priestly orthodoxy. Its views are not unique but rather commonplace for so-called high-caste tantrics, and, it represents the interests of those who seek to introduce sectarian tantric ideas and values into the priestly discourse. Second, *The Secret of the Preceptors* drew the attention of Bhāskararāya Makhin, who is among the great Indian intellectuals of the eighteenth century. Bhāskararāya, born into a brahman family, was a polymath; he wrote poetry, logical and grammatical treatises, commentaries on classical religious texts, and was a practitioner of the esoteric ritual arts of tantra. He was renowned in his day for his writing and teaching, managing to win the political favor of his local sovereign and gain the esteem of priestly traditionalists despite his advocacy of controversial tantric ideas. Though he is not as well known as many other Indian scholars, his intellectual legacy is best compared to that of the great Kashmiri Śiva-centered tantric Abhinavagupta: everyone in his wake has felt compelled to acknowledge his influence and comment on his contributions. In short, *The Secret of the Preceptors* has become an important text within the goddess-centered Hindu tantric corpus because Bhāskararāya wrote a commentary on it. A curious absence of commentaries prior to Bhāskararāya does not diminish the importance of its remarkable content. This leads to the third reason one gains from a study of this text.

The Secret of the Preceptors is rare among texts that assume a goddess-centered tantric bias since it discusses philosophical positions and religious goals as well as practical instructions for worship. Goddess worshipers generally prefer to express their theological positions in the form of ritual liturgies and instruction in secret types of yoga. In fact, most tantric goddess-centered texts assume the intellectual doctrines of their first cousins, the Śiva-centered tantric traditions of Kashmir. In contrast to these more practical manuals detailing ritual instruments and techniques, *The Secret of the Preceptors* is a pithy, first-hand account of the key philosophical issues in goddess-centered esotericism. Seen in light of Bhāskararāya's commentary, these philosophical issues are interpreted first in terms of Preceptor tantrism and second, in the narrow sectarian terms of the goddess-centered tradition known as Śrīvidyā or Auspicious Wisdom.

For Bhāskararāya, Preceptor tantrism entails two components. First, it involves specific forms of knowledge and techniques by which one gains the realization that divinity is embodied within one's own body and in the cosmos. In this sense, the Preceptor (*kaula* or *kaulika*) is the divinity itself and the knowledge about reality that liberates the soul from death and rebirth. Second, Preceptor tantrism focuses on the relationship between guru and student, which is deemed the only means by which the secret power of divinity can be realized and identified within oneself.

The Preceptor, Bhāskararāya states, is none other than the ascetic god Śiva ("Auspicious"), who is identical in essence with all sages, gurus, gods, and goddesses. Śiva, however, is another means by which one can gain access to Power or Śakti, the goddess. It is the goddess, he tells us, that stands at the head of the pantheon of divinities. Śiva is one's own guru and "one should serve only one guru who fits the defined prescriptions." The Preceptor tradition may permit many interpretations since "all views are without condemnation," but if an authoritative teacher "argues against his own tradition, one should not count him as an authority." In other words, one must have an unthreatening, private relationship with only one Preceptor, but that Preceptor must measure up to prescriptions which demonstrate that he is an embodiment of the divine.

The divine concentrates its presence in other forms, as well. When the divine is knowledge mediated through law (*dharma*), it manifests as one's judgment and is derived from the intellect. In this sense, knowledge takes the form of one's guru and of the eternal law prescribed in one's own tradition.

When the Upaniṣad states that "knowledge is the only cause of liberation," Bhāskararāya comments that knowledge is identical with the secret power of the great goddess Śakti, who "alone you indeed are." Knowledge is therefore "an unmediated personal experience of the Absolute" which "everyone experiences under the pretext of the 'I' " as their own self (*ātman*). In every entity, animate or inanimate, resides the same self which is nothing other than the goddess Śakti.

In Bhāskararāya's view, there is an ultimate identity between the teacher, the teaching, and the one who is taught, just as there is an identity between all selves and the goddess. Such views are potentially dangerous to those ill-equipped to understand their implications. Thus "one should not discuss this [secret of the self] even with one's friends because they might talk about it openly," while, at the same time, one must follow the practical teachings of one's own guru, which can take "priority over revelation and recollection [scriptures]." The reasons for this deference to the guru, we are told, are both theological and practical. On the one hand, the guru as preceptor is none other than God embodied; on the other, Bhāskararāya uses the analogy that when a great writer uses a word that defies the rules of grammar, thereafter the writer's practice is considered authoritative. Thus, one must defer to guru who teaches "what works" over what is prescribed by this or that authority. For Bhāskararāya, the secrecy of a preceptor's teachings is a function of the potential danger of knowledge in the wrong hands; the authority of a preceptor's interpretations is rooted in the notion that knowledge and the divine Power—the goddess herself—is embodied in the guru.

Preceptor tantrism, in Bhāskararāya's view, leads one to conclude that everything must be divine in origin and in whatever form it takes. This uncompromising view, that every "I" is identical to every other self, and that everything is nothing other than the Absolute, forms the logical basis for many of the text's more puzzling comments. What appear at first to be patently absurd statements are interpreted as the highest expressions of ultimate truth. For example, when the text states that "The absence of knowledge is knowledge," Bhāskararāya takes this to be a statement about the nature of reality. He writes, "Even the absence of knowledge is a form of state-of-being; that [absence] too is a form of knowledge that is only Power." In other words, an absence is always a "something," and, therefore, the universe is divine whether viewed as one permanent reality or as a plurality of impermanent realities. Thus when the text states, "The impermanent is permanent," Bhāskararāya uses a mundane example to make his point: "Even such things as pots, which appear to be impermanent, are permanent inasmuch as they are only Power."

As for other apparently absurd statements such as, "The scriptures do not exist," and "The unjustified is justified," Bhāskararāya insists that logic alone rarely provides a single, definitive answer and that even revelation, when viewed as something human beings learn, is merely an object of knowledge. "The difficulty," he reminds his readers, "is with the advocates [who interpret] rather than with logic." Although much of *The Secret of the Preceptors* appears in the form of paradoxes, riddles, and absurdities, the underlying purpose of these statements is clear to Bhāskararāya: "Objects, living beings, yoga, liberation, ignorance—all of these are only knowledge. [Why?] The meaning is that there exists nothing different from [the supreme goddess] who is Power." Following the preceptor's path insures knowledge so powerful that "even liberation" from death and rebirth "is . . . an insignificant matter." A follower of the path knows that "This [tradition] is the only worship from which [one acquires] wisdom," and that "outsiders" are "really beasts because they lack a wisdom tradition" even though they might be learned in sculpture or other sciences.

When the Upaniṣad identifies the supreme goddess Śakti in more personal terms, it prefers either ancient names, such as Varuṇī ("the West"), who is the female counterpart of the Vedic god Varuṇā, or obscure names, such as Śambhavī ("Birth"). The text never uses the name of the goddess that Bhāskararāya prefers—Tripurasundarī (the "Beautiful Three Cities"), the deity of choice for adherents of the sectarian tantric tradition known as Auspicious Wisdom or Śrīvidyā. Neither does the text mention the specific sound formula (*mantra*), the fifteen- or sixteen-syllable "auspicious wisdom" (*śrīvidyā*), or the diagrammatic image known as the "auspicious wheel" (*śrīcakra*), that would identify it with the theological and ritual elements of the Auspicious Wisdom school. Nonetheless, Bhāskararāya takes for granted that the Preceptor tantrism expounded here is none other than the Auspicious Wisdom.

As for the goddesses the text does mention by name, he states that "meditation on [the goddess] Tripurasundarī makes no distinction [between her and other goddesses, such as Śambhavī]." For Bhāskararāya, the issue cuts much deeper than the text's explicit pronouncements. The relationship between the text, the reader, and the goddess Tripurasundarī is one of absolute identity: "You are *The Secret of the Preceptor* and [the supreme goddess] Tripurasundarī."

Bhāskararāya, like the text itself, declares his views without justification or apology. Like so many other tantric texts, the commentary on *The Secret of the Preceptors* does not offer positions to be debated. Rather, it claims to make a definitive statement about reality that would otherwise remain hopelessly obscure even to those who aspire to ultimate truth. Opponents are scoffed at as inferiors unworthy of the teaching; like mere animals, they are best left to manage their lives in comfortable misconceptions.

Bhāskararāya's commentary on *The Secret of the Preceptors* provides an example of esoteric Hindu tantrism at its most mature and bedeviling stage of development. He asserts that the most secret and powerful knowledge requires one to transcend the boundaries of law (*dharma*) and logic. One must transcend difference itself, which is nothing but an "error." In other words, one must realize for oneself that the universe in its entirety is nothing other than the goddess who is Power (*Śakti*).

At the same time that he asserts the views of a radical nondualist philosopher, he demands a commitment to the tradition of the Preceptors that excludes and diminishes other options. All other views, he claims, are incapable of bringing one to the highest forms of knowledge and power. Most people, he reminds us, will neither understand nor appreciate the arguments and ideas presented here.

The text that has been translated here comes from *Kaula and Other Upanishads with Commentary by Bhāskararāya,* edited by Sītārāma Śāstri (Calcutta: Agamanusandhana Samiti, 1922).

Further Reading

More on tantrism will be found in my two books: *The Secret of the Three Cities: An Introduction to Hindu Śakta Tantrism* (Chicago: University of Chicago Press, 1990); and *Auspicious Wisdom: The Texts and Traditions of Śrīvidyā Śakta Tantrism in South India* (Albany: State University of New York Press, 1992). Also relevant are: Paul Eduardo Muller-Ortega, *The Triadic Heart of Śiva: Kaula Tantricism of Abhinavagupta in the Non-Dual Shaivism of Kashmir* (Albany: State University of New York Press, 1989); and Deba Brata SenSharma, *The Philosophy of Sādhana, with Special Reference to the Trika Philosophy of Kashmir* (Albany: State University of New York, 1990).

Prosperity!

Bhāskararāya's commentary on *Kaula Upaniṣad*
Salutations to the Auspicious Teacher!

Bhāskararāya ("Sun King"), in whose heart obstruction has been dispelled by the spreading rays emanating from the lotus feet of the auspicious teacher, explains *The Secret of the Preceptor [Kaula Upaniṣad]* which belongs to *The Scripture of Fire [Atharva Veda]*. The gods are petitioned to remove the obstacles that will inevitably occur when the meaning of instruction, which is very secret, is being related.

> *May the Preceptor be well-disposed to us! May Varuṇī be well-disposed to us! May Purity be well-disposed to us! May Agni be well-disposed to us! May all [the gods] become [well-disposed to us]!*

The one who founded the Preceptorial path is the Preceptor, the supreme [god] Śiva ["Auspicious"]. [To explain the words used in the opening salutation: the word meaning "well-disposed," *śannaḥ*, consists of two parts, the first is the particle of speech;] *śaṃ* means attaining the bliss of one's own self, which is preceded by removing obstacles [while the second part, the particle] *naḥ* [means] us; [the verb is used to express a wish, meaning] let that one become. Varuṇī ["the West"] is first [mentioned and] worthy and is the great goddess—and may she be well-disposed to us! Purity who is second [mentioned] and [likewise] worthy is also a god—may he be well-disposed to us! Agni ["Fire"] means splendor. And so it should be that all [the gods, who need not be listed here,] are pleased!

Homage to the Absolute! Homage to the Earth! Homage to Water! Homage to Fire! Homage to the Wind! Homage tc the Teachers!

[The idea is that] homage [should be paid] to the four gods, beginning with the Earth up to the supreme Absolute, and to [the Preceptors] beginning with the supreme Śiva up to one's own teacher. Space [which is the fifth element] is also implied [among] the four elements [mentioned in the verse].

You alone are immediate. She is you alone. The immediate is only you. I will describe her.

The immediate is the Absolute which everyone experiences under the pretext of the "I." She alone [is that Absolute experienced as "I," as] you indeed are. You are *The Secret of the Preceptor* and [the supreme goddess] Tripurasundarī [the "Beautiful Three Cities"]. Hence, [the verse means] I will describe *The Secret of the Preceptor* which is not at all different [from me] to you alone [who is not different from that, either].

I will describe the sacred. I will describe the true. Describe that to me! Describe what is said about that! Tell it to me!

The word "sacred" means the supreme Absolute and likewise the word "true." When there is an expectation [such as the verse suggests,] there is repetition. The rest [of the verse] is clear.

Oṃ! Peace, Peace, Peace

This is a prayer for pacifying [forces of] obstruction.

Then, therefore, the desire to know the law.

[The word] "then" [means that] following the desire to know the Absolute [is the desire to know the law (*dharma*)]. [The word] "therefore" [is used to indicate that only after this desire to know the Absolute] can there be knowledge with respect to the law. [Analyzing the compound] "the desire to know the law," [the goddess who is] Power (*Śakti*) is the reflection of law; the desire to know [means that] analysis for the sake of knowledge should be undertaken.

And knowledge is judgment.

Knowledge is an unmediated personal experience of the Absolute. Judgment is mediated knowledge which causes that [unmediated personal experience]. So in such statements as, "For one who has a personal experience is led into the reality of judgment," the meaning is that when there are two conflicting established rules both of them are indeed the embodiment of law [and therefore they do not conflict]. With regard to [essential] laws derived from the intellect and the like, not stated [explicitly but] listed by scholars such as Nāgānanda ["Blissful Cobra"], [these are] included [through the verse's use of the word] "and."

Knowledge is the only cause of liberation.

The meaning is explicit.

Liberation is obtaining the nature of all selves.

"The nature of all selves" [means that] one's own self is not different from [the self] of others. "Obtaining" that [nature of all selves means] manifesting that object [of knowledge] through the elimination of ignorance. Therefore in *[The Ancient Lore of] The Blessed Goddess (Devībhāgavatā [purāṇa])* it is stated in verse, "Everyone says the same thing, there is nothing other than the eternal." In this way it is suggested that knowledge of identity causes liberation. Or, the same knowledge is brought about by a different activity [which is] undivided [knowledge as well].

The five objects are expansion.

The word "all" [in the previous verse] is explained as the five [objects] beginning with sound and [here, in this verse,] by the word "expansion." With respect to this [expansion] there is no difference between [the five] gross elements and the subtle elements. Even though there are thirty-six categories [of reality], these are included [in the five gross elements]. The [sage] Vasiṣṭha [the "Controlled"] [concurs], "Everywhere are the five elements, there is no sixth."

Those [elements] have as their very nature knowledge.

Having so far discussed that which arises as inanimate, the discussion [turns to] that which is born with consciousness. [The word] "knowledge" (*jñāna*) [can be] distilled to *jña* plus *na*. The meaning is that the one who knows (*jānāti*) the object [is knowledge] and is animate. The sense is that one who has this very nature [as knowledge, as the verse says,] is called "living."

Yoga is liberation.

Yoga is the cessation of the [mental] whirlwind and it is [a means to] liberation.

Knowledge is only ignorance, which causes the antinomian.

The antinomian (*adharma*) is the supreme Absolute because it is bereft of qualities (*dharma*). With regard to this [statement], "knowledge" is only that ignorance whose root is the object which causes knowledge. The word "only" suggests a different rendering: objects, living beings, yoga, liberation, ignorance—all of these are only knowledge. [Why is this the case?] The meaning is that there exists nothing different from [the supreme goddess who is] Power. The implication is that [the very notion] of difference is an error.

The Lord is the expansion [of the universe].

[One can argue logically that] because [the expansion of the universe] is pervaded by difference, which is unreal, the expansion is only the Lord. [This is because the Lord,] even in his role as controller [of the process] and [that which is] controlled, is prevented from being [only] the pervader [since the Lord is both the pervader and the pervaded].

The impermanent is the permanent.

Even such things as pots, which appear to be impermanent, are permanent inasmuch as they are only Power.

The absence of knowledge is knowledge.

Even the absence of knowledge is a form of state of being; that [absence], too, is a form of knowledge which is only Power.

The absence of a quality (adharma) indeed is a quality (dharma).

Even a quality is a form of Power because there is nothing other than that; yet the Absolute alone has the form of a qualifier who provides the basis for the quality.

This is liberation!

This alone is the path to liberation, no other.

The five bondages have for their very nature knowledge.

[The first and second bondages] begin: "that which is self is thought of as other than self; whatever is other than self is thought of as self." This is knowledge in the form of bondage. The *Verses of Śiva (Śivasūtra)* [state that] "knowledge is bondage." [The third bondage that is a type of knowledge is] the difference between one embodied soul and another; [the fourth is] the difference between the Lord [and the embodied soul]; and [the fifth is] the difference between the conscious and that which is different [from the conscious]. These three types of knowledge taken together [with the first two] make five.

Because [one feels] insignificant, [there is] birth.

Only because there are [five types of] bondage of this sort is one born as an entity [feeling] insignificant.

Even under those circumstances there is liberation.

However, by virtue of the greatness of the knowledge of the Preceptors, even liberation is merely, under those circumstances, an insignificant matter. Yet [for one who has the knowledge of the Preceptors] there is no delay [in obtaining] the form [of final] liberation by way of [having first to control] the more than one hundred channels [through which yogic energy flows], then traversing the path of the gods [as the next, higher stage in the cycle of rebirths], and then by having to come together with the Absolute. Other statements from revelation as, "For him the delay is only that much," [and] "The vital breaths do not cause him to go beyond," [corroborate what is said here].

This is knowledge.

First, having stated the conclusions reached in texts, [the sage-author] states the essence of knowledge: This statement [means that what is stated hereafter] is only about knowledge.

Of all the senses, the eyes (nayanam) are foremost.

One should lead (*nayet*) [the senses] toward the Absolute. With regard to the knowledge about the self generated by the six senses which one fashions in statements such as, "I know this," the Absolute that shines as the very knower [in these statements] is foremost. When revelation states "Only that is shining, all [the rest] reflects," it means to say that all other things are mere reflections of that [one Absolute which is the knower behind the "I"]. This type of discernment with regard to all [mental] variables one should obtain in just such a way [as this analysis of "I" and through study of texts, including revelation]. Although knowledge can be generated by one sense without discernment, it should lead to the foremost [that is, to the Absolute]. In statements such as [from *The Consciousness of Bhairava (Vijñānabhairava),* verse 106, where it says,] "The consciousness of object and subject is common to all embodied [beings], but [the yogis] are distinguished by an awareness of this relationship," [we can infer similarly that] the meaning [of this text] is that the nonexistence of nondiscrimination is very essence of knowledge.

Whatever is opposed to the law should be done.

Beginning with this [verse], the methods to be adopted by worshipers are enjoined. It is enjoined on adepts who depend solely on such discriminating knowledge to counteract that which is opposed to treatises on law [and] to use their intellect and the like, even during the time of ritual, for the sake of stabilizing the mind.

What is prescribed as the Law should not be done.

Even though they have been prescribed by treatises on law, ritual sacrifices such as those involving Soma ["Nectar"], can be appropriately countermanded when they are assumed to oppose a given tradition. This injunction to act or not to act does not prohibit [all sacrifices] but depends on the context [in which the countermand is made]. Even [the ritualist] Gautama ["Rich-in-Cows"], who prescribed forty external and eight internal rites for the sake of internal purity, has said that the external aspects can be eliminated. Also Manu ["Man the Law-giver"], having explained the whole law in detail, has stated at the conclusion of the treatise that when enjoining reflection on the Absolute, previously stated laws need not be applied. For all these recollections (*smṛti*) [of revealed (*śruti*) texts] this [Upaniṣad or secret teaching] alone is the original revelation (*śruti*).

Everything has the form of Śambhavī.

When applicable, as it were, to prescriptions as well as to prohibitions, the meditation on [the goddess] Tripurasundarī makes no distinction [between her and other goddesses, such as Śambhavī ("Birth")]. What is suggested here is that worshipers who think there is [such] difference [and] are mistaken are still bound to act according to injunctions and prohibitions. Hence, in the words of the Blessed One,

> If a man who does my ritual should lapse in action, the 300 million great sages will perform that action.

The scriptures do not exist.

Because they are [merely] learned, even revelation [that is, the scriptures] do not exist. This is why the Venerable (*Bhāgavata*) [Śaṅkara ("Propitious")] in his Commentary [on the *Stanzas on the Absolute (Brahmasūtrabhāṣya)*] has said, "As far as the ignorant are concerned, the treatises are objects." The stanza [cited by Śaṅkara] has the form of a recommendation [rather than an injunction, since it provides] a reason authorizing both what is said and what should be first done.

The guru is one.

The meaning of this is that one should serve [only] one guru who fits the defined prescriptions that have been discussed. When there are many gurus there are bound to be a variety of contradictory instructions and certainly doubt [in the mind of the student.] Hence the [authoritative] *Stanzas on Ritual [of The Joyful One with the Axe (Paraśurāmakalpasūtra)]* state, "There is no doubt when one serves one guru." This [*Secret of the Preceptors*] is the original revelation for the restriction stated in *The Ocean of Precepts (Kulārṇava)* [*Tantra* or esoteric treatise]: "Having obtained a preceptorial guru, one should not resort to another guru." By using the term "having obtained," [the text means,] as the *Secret of Power (Śaktirahasya)* states, "In the tradition of the preceptors there are countless gurus," [but] such a guru is not usually obtained.

Insight at the end [of life] of the oneness of everything.

[One should note that the word] "oneness" (*aikyam*) is formed by [employing the grammatical affix] *syan* [which transforms the word "*aikya*" into "*aikyam*" without changing the sense.].

Thus, a practitioner who possesses such an attitude, even if it occurs at the end of life, surely obtains insight into nonduality.

Up to the time of accomplishment in the mantra.

This is a governing rule [in which what is stated here is understood in every subsequent statement under the following condition]. The meaning is that beginning here those prescriptions that are mentioned [in the following stanzas] are restrictions that should be carried out [only] up to the time of accomplishment in the mantra. By this [governing rule] it is suggested that neglect of but one [of the prescriptions] which are going to be mentioned will be detrimental to accomplishment [in the mantra].

Intoxication and so forth should be shunned.

Intoxication is that peculiar malady produced by using an intoxicating substance; take the phrase "and so forth" to mean other [substances] that [produce] change. The six enemies [that is, desire, anger, greed, delusion, intoxication, and envy] and the collection [of other acquired faults] should also be shunned. After accomplishment in the mantra, however, desire, anger, and so forth naturally do not develop. But even before one deals with the peculiar malady [induced by wine and so forth], [the six enemies] should be shunned. And so with regard to the two statements, "[You should drink] until your eyes can't move" and "You should drink [intoxicating] substances only up to your neck [and not more]," there is no contradiction [with the recommendation of this text] because the first is addressed to a practitioner who has yet [to experience] accomplishment in the mantra, whereas the other is addressed to one whose accomplishment is fixed.

Publicity should not be given.

The tradition should be kept secret in such a way that one's own worship ought not to be known to any one who does not [continue in] worship after initiation in the mantra of your own [tradition], those who are committed to other teachings, and those who practice your mantra but are phony. This is similarly applicable to those with other initiations. [This is confirmed] from statements treating [similar] matters such as [those in scriptures and ritual texts in which it is said], "Those who are not initiated should not observe the one who performs rites." Just because initiation is prescribed only in the Forest Text (Āraṇyaka) portion of the scriptures (Veda) [which is restricted to those qualified by birth and initiation], one may think that secrecy is maintained as it is in the preliminary Soma ceremony which is ancillary to the [main] sacrifice. However, even then performing [the ceremony] in full voice, such that someone from another secret tradition [could hear it], is forbidden. In the case of other teachings, when a secret is divulged it results merely in an imperfection in the sacrifice, whereas in a case such as this it leads to hell. And so [for the same reason] the blessed Paraśurāma ["Joyful One with the Axe"] [has said], "Publicity [leads to] hell."

One should not converse with bores.

Indeed, all outsiders are really beasts because they lack a wisdom tradition. This [tradition of the Preceptors] is the only worship from which [one acquires] wisdom. [We know this] from such statements as, "The term 'learned' should not be used for those well-versed in sculpture and such other [branches of] knowledge." With such beasts one should not have conversation merely for the sake of gladdening one's own heart, though there is no prohibition against incidental conversation.

The unjustified is justified.

If someone who likes to talk, using the logic of the [schools] of Earlier and Later Analysis, tries to condemn the practice of the Preceptors, even in such a case one should not become the slightest bit angry—this is what is meant when "unjustified" is said [in the verse]. The negative [particle that generates "un-"] means only slightly opposed [rather than adamantly against]. The statement intends to suggest that the opponent's justification [for opposition] is only slight justification, [though] even that is justification [of a sort]. For even an opponent's [justification] is another proposed justification. Hence, even in similarly accomplished justifications, traditions [say] this too [should be considered another form of] justification. And in the current instance, how can we be confident [in the usefulness of logic] when there are exceptions to traditional logic such as this? Because of the variety of different opinions expressed by the sages in [sundry] traditions, [various] interpreters have taken to them severally and with multiple meanings despite their mutual contradictions. As a consequence, we see many views made with reference to the tantras, the gods, and [various] statements [of other texts]. The idea is that the difficulty [with interpretations of texts] is with the advocates rather than the logic [of the texts]. So the Lord Vyāsa [the "Editor"] has said, "Reason is inconclusive [because humans always think themselves correct and so see their views as logical]."

And so it is said [elsewhere], "Those experiences [previously] unimaginable cannot be explained by mere logic." Such statements have as their sole purpose to assuage the mind and should be explained as violations of tradition. [With respect to the authority of sources,] the latter is less [authoritative] than the former, such that [first comes] revelation, then recollected texts, [and finally] tradition. But in the relevant esoteric treatise (tantra) [cited above, in which it is said that previously unimaginable experiences are not explained by logic alone,] the reverse order [of priority for ascertaining what is authoritative] is to be inferred. Neither [method for deciding the priority of texts] is entirely illogical. But those adept in treatises on law have, in most cases, accepted the restriction that the earlier [text] is [more authoritative] than those that follow, rather than the [the principle that] the later [listing is more authoritative than] those that precede.

Even then one should not count [as an authority].

Even if one is a priest, if he argues against his own tradition one should not count him as an authority. The meaning is that one should not have unqualified belief in him. Hence the ritual [text] states, "the authority is that which one maintains with conviction."

One should not discuss the secret of the self.

The meaning is that one should not discuss this even with one's friends because they may talk about it openly.

One should discuss it with a disciple.

Hence, in recollection (*smṛti*) it states, "By instruction from ear to ear, it has reached the earth." Similarly, if one requires learning from a single source of tradition in order to obtain a correct interpretation, then that practical source takes priority over revelation (*śruti*) and recollection. With respect to the rules of grammar, for example, a form that is used by a great writer [is likewise given priority over the rules].

Inwardly a goddess worshiper, outwardly a follower of Śiva, in worldly affairs a follower of Viṣṇu.

Even though [being a follower of the goddess] should not be known publicly, [the author] describes how one ought to behave. One should make others know about the worship of the goddess only through one's inner nature. "The essence [of the goddess's transcendent form] is displayed by the red sandalwood paste on the brow of the goddess worshiper," yet despite these prescribed marks one should only wear the holy ash of the Śiva worshiper by which one's nature as a goddess worshiper is concealed. There is no [ultimate] difference between the worshiper of Śiva and the the worshiper of goddess: "I am the masculine form who is ambrosia in the eyes of the maidens." By such statements, which refer only to forms of Viṣṇu [the "Universal"], one learns the meaning of the three verses [pertaining to how one should worship]. That is, one should only proclaim publicly the worship of Viṣṇu by such acts as repeating his names, because Viṣṇu is that explicit form in whom [the secret and powerful goddess] Tripurasundarī is hidden and within [Tripurasundarī] the supreme Śiva is concealed. Hence in the *Thousand Secret Names (Rahasyasahasranāma)* it has been said that [the worship of] Viṣṇu yields lesser goals than Śiva, that Śiva yields less than the goddess and, comparably, that Viṣṇu is secret [in nature], Śiva more secret, and that the goddess is more secret still.

This alone is the practice.

Even though there are many texts [among the tantras] that address the practice named for the Preceptors, among all of these the one that best attempts to conceal revealing publicly [the tradition's deepest secrets] is the [most] important: This is the meaning [of the verse].

Liberation is knowledge of the self.

One should not be indifferent to meditation on the self because one performs the rituals prescribed in [the portions of] revelation devoted to ritual. Rather both [ritual and knowledge] should become established correctly in order to remind one of this [fact that liberation is knowledge of the self], which the verse repeats [as a point that] has already been made.

There should be no condemnation from the world.

In the stream [of tradition] there have been a variety of authoritative textual views that pertain to different qualifications. Those [different textual views] should not be condemned in any way. By accusations [that undermine one view or another], one doubts the qualifications [of the texts and the traditions of the Preceptors] and loses faith in the insights on which one depends. Without the qualification for the tradition of the Preceptors, there is the danger of losing both [assurance in different qualifications and faith in the insights], in which case [practitioners] disperse like so many scattered clouds. Therefore it is undesirable [for practitioners] to feel in danger of condemnation because they are practitioners [of the Preceptor's tradition in which there are various authoritative textual views]. So the Lord Kṛṣṇa [the "Black One"] says, "One should not splinter the judgment of the ignorant who are attached to action." And Bhārgava Rāma [the "Joyful One Who Bears the Axe"] [who makes a similar point in the *Ritual Verses of Parasurāma (Paraśurāmakalpasūtra)*], "All views are without condemnation."

So it is with respect to the self.

When there is a doubt about the statement, "In what cases should one apply [the principle that] all views are without condemnations?" one is in danger of feeling inferior oneself because [the opinions of] others are dispersed like so many scattered clouds over the nature of the self of all. The meaning is that the tradition [in all its variety] helps one obtain knowledge of the self.

A vow should not be taken.

Vows for the sake of the [four] human aims [that is, law, wealth, sensuality, and liberation] should not be taken. For those [who make such vows], the aims achieved will not be more than what is obtained [from this practice of the Preceptors]. Whichever legal obligations pertaining to one's social estate and stage in life are met through systematic discipline with regard to the [four] human aims, those obtained as subordinate to a function of the daily and occasional rituals, such as the new moon rites and its accessories, which are vows whose purpose is sacrificial, must be done because no injunction exempts one from [the duty to perform] daily and occasional rites.

One should not abide by restriction.

This is the only interpretation of this [verse]: a restriction that takes the form of a demand is inconsistent with the examination of the self.

There is no liberation from [observing] restriction.

The reason for this [statement] is [that following the restriction entails] the danger of delaying liberation because [restriction] is contrary to examination of the self.

One should not establish the Preceptor [tradition].

If someone is proficient in expounding the tradition of the Preceptors to the extent that he is capable of establishing it expertly, he should not establish it because of the danger of making the path public. Hence, with respect to the concerns of this treatise, the author, because of the prohibition on establishing the Preceptor [tradition], writes in various places that what is to be learned should come only from the mouth of the teacher—instead of divulging some portions of the tradition publicly.

One should be the same to all.

The injunction that should be drawn from this treatise is that one should feel the same way toward living or inanimate beings, that is, one should consider them to be not different [than oneself]. Hence in [texts] such as the [*The Ancient Tale of*] *the Blessed Viṣṇu* (*Viṣṇubhāgavata* [*purāṇa*]) [it states], "Be it sky, wind, fire, water, or earth [all are identical]."

He has become liberated.

He is surely liberated immediately should he become wise in such matters. The intention is that those who are deficient in one way or another are liberated only little by little.

"The teacher, arising early in the morning, should recite these verses. For him, there will be accomplishment and power to command"—this is the command of supreme Goddess.

Hence the true teacher is one who recites these verses before examining [the self]. So to paraphrase, he alone has obtained accomplishment and the power to command through identity with Śiva. Thus, the idea is that the supreme Lord has commanded it to be so, and hence there should be no doubt.

And the one who is bereft of practice or who does not perform worship, if he does not consider this to be the best he will enjoy the forest of bliss [that is, the garden of the god Indra rather than liberation].

One who has doubts about practice as it was taught previously does not perform the prescribed worship as it was taught.

The [grammatical] disagreement [in the Sanskrit of the above-cited stanzas between the singular subject and the plural ending of the verb] is archaic verse [that is, grammar found in the scriptures].

For the one who does not think, "This path [of the Preceptors] is higher than all [others]," though the fruit that has been discussed [that is, liberation] is not obtained, even such a defective practitioner surely obtains heaven. The intention is this: how much more will be the fruit obtained as it has been taught for the practitioner [who is not defective]?

May the practitioner of the precepts be well-disposed!
Oṃ! Peace! Peace! Peace!
The Secret of the Preceptors has been completed.

So ends the commentary on the *Secret of the Preceptors* composed by the auspicious Bhāskararāya, who has crossed over from the near to the far shore [and so has obtained liberation while living].

— 44 —

The Rebuilding of a Hindu Temple

Richard H. Davis

When Turko-Afghan military forces adhering to Islam arrived in India, starting in the early eleventh century, they brought with them a set of theological premises very different from those of the varied Hindu groups they encountered there. Whereas Hindus appeared to worship a rich and complicated pantheon of divine characters, Muslims worshiped a single, exclusive divinity and considered all homage directed toward any other deity to be "polytheism" (*shirk*), anathema to the true religion. Whereas Hindus assumed that divinity would enter into and inhabit objects fabricated by humans, this seemed to Muslims an extreme example of hubris and a compromise to Allah's transcendence. Whereas Hindus venerated their divinely animated images in temples, Muslims classified this as "idolatry," and often considered it a religious duty to remove such objectionable practices from any lands they conquered. And since Hindu image-worship was the dominant mode of public religious practice in the subcontinent—indeed, so prevalent that some Islamic chroniclers came to view India as the original home of idolatry—Muslim conquests in India from the eleventh through fourteenth centuries were often accompanied by desecration and destruction of Hindu religious images and conversion of temple sites into mosques. Hindu claims of autonomy, conversely, were often symbolized by rebuilding or restoring temples that had been desecrated.

This inscriptional poem records the restoration of one of the most famous sites of Hindu-Muslim conflict, the temple of Somanātha ("Śiva as Lord of the Moon") on the coast of Gujarat. Somanātha was a longstanding Śaiva pilgrimage center (*tīrtha*). Local tradition has it that it was first consecrated by the Moon who, waning from "consumption" (tuberculosis), worshiped Śiva there and so regained his rotund form. According to more skeptical archeologists, a modest temple may have occupied the site as early as the mid-seventh century. Around 970 C.E., the local Solaṅki ruler Mūlarāja built a more impressive royal temple at Somanātha, one of the largest temples of northern India at the time.

In the early part of the eleventh century, the Islamic ruler Sultan Maḥmūd of

Ghazna (in present-day Afghanistan) launched a series of raids into northern India. Gradually overcoming the various Indian forces he encountered, Maḥmūd's armies reached as far east as Kanyakubja, captured in 1018. But when a confederacy of Hindu rulers led by the Candella dynasty impeded further progress to the east, Maḥmūd turned his attention southward, toward Gujarat and the temple of Somanātha. The Ghaznavids understood Somanātha to be a tantalizingly wealthy and dominant Hindu institution. Muslim chronicles speak of an endowment of ten thousand villages belonging to the temple, of one thousand priests performing the liturgy, of three hundred musicians and dancers entertaining the god, and of fresh Gaṅgā water and Kashmiri flowers brought daily to adorn it. Moreover, they appear to have considered Somanātha the cultic center of idolatry, the Hindu equivalent of Mecca, and hoped that by destroying that temple they might strike a significant blow for Islam itself.

Maḥmūd's forces marched into Gujarat in January 1026, and after a bloody two-day engagement at the temple, Maḥmūd defeated the local guardians and entered the sanctum. The temple was systematically pillaged and its metal images melted down, yielding some 20 million coin-weight (*dīnārs*) in gold and other precious metals, which was transported back to Ghazna to help gild the mosque Maḥmūd was having built in his capital. He had the central icon, a Śiva-liṅga, broken into pieces and its fragments dispatched to Ghazna and (according to some accounts) to the caliph in Baghdad and to Mecca. Later Indo-Muslim accounts portray this encounter of Maḥmūd with the idol at Somanātha as a paradigmatic victory in the conquest of India.

The Solaṅki ruler of the area, King Bhīma (1022–1065) was only momentarily defeated, and soon after Maḥmūd's retreat to Ghazna he set about rebuilding the temple. The new Somanātha may have been completed as early as 1030. No more Muslim raids occurred in the next hundred years to disturb the temple, though it appears that subsequent rulers may have allowed it to fall into disrepair. By the mid-twelfth century the Solaṅki dynasty had become the dominant power of western India, and the ruler Kumārapāla, instigated by his priest and religious advisor Bhāva Bṛhaspati, decided to rebuild Somanātha on a much larger scale, consonant with the grander Solaṅki dominion he and his predecessor had established. It is his restoration, carried out in 1156, that this inscription records.

The story of Somanātha temple, however, does not end with Kumārapāla's reconstruction. Through the great reputation of Maḥmūd's victory at Somanātha throughout the world of Islam and the diligence of Hindu Solaṅki rulers in rebuilding it as a sign of autonomy, Somanātha came to be seen as a primary point of regional contention. As the frontier of control shifted over the ensuing centuries, nearly every Islamic ruler seeking to establish control over Gujarat felt the compulsion to desecrate the liṅga of Somanātha, and every Hindu chieftain seeking independence felt an imperative to restore it. It is not possible to specify exactly how often the temple was attacked by Islamic forces and then rededicated by Hindu insurgents. Finally, in 1669 it was converted into a mosque, with a dome where the temple tower had once been, and local Hindus, rather than risk another restoration, declared that the liṅga in a smaller Śaiva temple on the outskirts of town was in fact Somanātha.

Through much of the British period the old temple stood empty and forgotten, but shortly after India regained independence in 1947, it was rebuilt one last time, largely through the instigation of K. M. Munshi, a prominent Gujarati author and freedom-fighter, and the support of Sardar Vallabhai Patel, India's formidable Minister for States. The remains of Kumārapāla's twelfth-century temple were bulldozed away, and on the site a completely new structure was raised, following as closely as possible the plan of the old one. "With the dawn of a new era," wrote Munshi, "the new temple has risen like the phoenix, from its own ashes." So once more the Somanātha temple served as a symbol, this time signifying the independence of the newly established Indian nation state and its continuity with a recovered past.

Considering this background, the most striking aspect of the inscriptional account of Kumārapāla's rebuilding of Somanātha temple is what it leaves out. It completely ignores Maḥmūd's dramatic destruction of the temple. Many Hindu accounts of the period seek to ignore Islamic attacks or to naturalize them as part of an ongoing struggle between demons and gods. Here, the inscription locates the destruction and rebuilding of the temple as one more in a sequence of recurrent disappearances and reappearances of the site, going back to the first age (*kṛtayuga*), when Pārvatī's curse made it invisible. This entropic cycle of decline and resurrection, rather like the phases of the Moon with whom the site is so closely associated, is viewed as a natural corollary to the passage of time.

The theory of the four ages, accordingly, is central to the vision of this poem. As developed in classical and medieval Indian thought, this model of cyclical time embodies a belief in a past "golden age" (the first age) when society was characterized by law and righteousness, a notion of moral deterioration through successive eras up to the present "age of strife" (*kaliyuga*), and a faith that this degenerate era will be followed cyclically by a return to an age of renewed virtue. As Manu's renowned codebook, the *Manusmṛti,* puts it, in the first age righteousness (*dharma*) stands firmly on four feet, in the second age on three, in the third on two, and in our present age of strife it wobbles precariously on its one remaining foot. Already an old theory by Maḥmūd's time, it was nevertheless useful to account for the new situation brought about by Islamic victories, for it placed the present vicissitudes within an existing moral framework and predicted the eventual return of an older, happier order of things. Indeed, restorative acts of kings and priests like Kumārapāla and Bhāva Bṛhaspati were often credited in inscriptional panegyric with bringing back the first age.

Moreover, in the view of the inscription, the rebuilding of the temple was not simply a matter of human initiative, but also the result of a command of Śiva himself, carried out through the incarnation on earth of his favored devotee and mount, the bull Nandi. When Śiva noticed that the temple had been broken, the inscription tells us, he ordered Nandi to take birth on earth. Obligingly, Nandi was born as the brahman Bhāva Bṛhaspati in the holy city of Varanasi, and after an illustrious religious career he found his way to the court of Kumārapāla, where he persuaded the king to repair the temple. So the inscription takes both the destruction and the rebuilding of Somanātha largely out of human hands and locates them instead as the working out of larger cosmic patterns and movements.

In medieval India it was common to commemorate the construction of a temple or the installation of a divine image by inscribing a eulogy praising the patron and others associated with the deed onto a set of copper plates or into the stone wall of the temple itself. Prominent court poets often composed the inscriptional praises in elegant and highly ornamented Sanskrit verse. The eulogy recording Kumārapāla's reconstruction of Somanātha (which is admittedly not among the finest examples of epigraphical verse from a poetic point of view) was composed by an unnamed poet specializing, apparently, in improvisational verse (he refers to himself as the "quick poet"). Carefully inscribed on a stone slab roughly 29 by 18 inches, it was preserved in the porch of the nearby temple of Bhadrakālī and rediscovered in the early nineteenth century by a British traveler and historian, Colonel James Tod. The lower part of the stone had been chipped away over the years, leaving verses 37 through 48 fragmentary and largely indecipherable; they are not translated here.

Certain conventions characterize the genre. Most often, inscriptional eulogies begin with several verses, referred to as "auspicious stanzas," invoking the blessings of prominent deities. When dedicating a temple to Śiva, as here, one naturally began with an invocation of Śiva himself, and continued with other closely associated deities such as Gaṇeśa and the Moon. Next inscriptional poems generally proceed to praise the royal sponsor of the gift, and often give a highly flattering account of the king's royal predecessors, as well. (Scholars have used these panegyrics of royal lineages extensively to reconstruct the dynastic history of medieval South Asia.) Here the poet departs from usual form by choosing not the king but the royal preceptor Bhāva Bṛhaspati as the primary agent of the temple reconstruction and the main subject of praise. Inscriptions then go on to record the specific provisions of the gift. For example, if the patron grants the royal share of revenues from particular villages or lands to provide for ongoing worship in the temple, the inscription might detail the boundaries of the lands, the amounts of revenue or produce to be remitted to the temple, and the persons responsible for payment. Many inscriptions document these more mundane matters not in high Sanskrit verse but in prose, using the local vernacular language. Here the inscription alludes to a royal grant made by Kumārapāla to Bhāva Bṛhaspati in passing, but is more concerned to record a whole series of town improvements and temple renovations carried out by the high priest at Somanātha. Finally, inscriptions often conclude with warranties that their provisions be observed permanently, by future rulers and inhabitants of the area, "as long as the moon, stars, and sun endure."

In its description of the religious career of Bhāva Bṛhaspati, the inscription provides a normative account of relations between a medieval Hindu king and his chosen preceptor. Bhāva Bṛhaspati initially gains renown, the inscription tells us, during his pilgrimages around northern India, then makes his way to Dhārā, the capital of the Paramāra kings. From there he comes to the attention of the Solaṅki ruler Jayasiṃha, who makes him his highest priest, and thereby also implicitly declares his allegiance to the tenets of Pāśupata Śaivism that Bhāva Bṛhaspati propounds. Both Jayasiṃha and his successor Kumārapāla, however formidable their political authority, humble themselves publicly before the preceptor, bowing and even smearing his feet with sandal powder, a most striking act for any independent king. In recognition of his high status, Bhāva Bṛhaspati receives the title "Gaṇḍa" (chief one, high priest), a land grant for permanent support of his family and descendents, and virtual carte blanche to supervise the rebuilding of the great temple of Somanātha and to carry out other improvements in the locality. Reciprocally, Kumārapāla as patron of the temple receives the primary religious merit resulting from his priest's renovations there. Even though the Solaṅki kings do not appear to recognize that their Gaṇḍa is in fact Nandi, Śiva's divine bull, they do perceive his superior virtues and treat him—as the poet wishes all to know—with the respect due him.

The poet introduces a large cast of divine figures in the course of his eulogy, and assumes on the part of his audience a background knowledge of their appearances, biographies, and characters. Not surprisingly, much of this lore concerns Śiva, the god worshiped as the highest lord by Kumārapāla, Bhāva Bṛhaspati, and the Moon himself at Somanātha.

The poet repeatedly refers to Śiva as the enemy of Kāma, the god of love. Kāma was once attempting to distract Śiva from a deep meditation, it is told, when out of Śiva's third eye blazed a laserlike flame, reducing Kāma's body to ashes. This is why the Love-god is so often referred to as the "bodiless one." The poet must have felt it particularly appropriate to emphasize this well-known aspect of Śiva when praising the rather austere high priest Bhāva Bṛhaspati. Yet, as the poet also reminds us, this yogic self-restraint does not prevent Śiva from marriage to the goddess Pārvatī, and likewise the high priest has a wife, one Mahādevī ("Great Goddess," an epithet often used for Pārvatī), daughter of Soḍhala.

Śiva wears the unwashed, matted hair of a yogi—hence one of his names is Kapārdin, the shaggy-haired one. In this unruly crown, we learn, is the River Gaṅgā. When an ascetic once persuaded the Gaṅgā, which had previously flowed only across the heavens, to descend to earth in order to alleviate a worldwide drought, there was a danger that the great river's impact might devastate the terrestial world. Śiva caught the river in his hair, absorbing her force before allowing her to meander harmlessly onto the ground. Gaṅgā's presence in Śiva's hair does, however, put a bit of a strain on his domestic tranquility, for Pārvatī's jealousy at seeing this other woman caressing her husband's locks is a common poetic theme. Also nestled atop Śiva's head is the Moon, and this attribute also is fitting to mention here, since the Moon's worship of Śiva is the constitutive mythical act marking Somanātha as an especially holy site.

Though Śiva and his many aspects and exploits receive the inscriptional poet's primary attention, other deities also appear in the eulogy, often to serve as measures for Bhāva Bṛhaspati's greatness. In this way the poet compares the priest's erection of Somanātha temple to Viṣṇu's incarnation as a giant Boar, who once raised the earth itself on his powerful tusk to save it from being submerged in the ocean. Likewise, it is the poet's conceit that certain well-known features of the gods Indra and Brahmā—namely, Indra's thousand eyes and Brahmā's four faces—exist only for the sake of seeing and praising the high priest more fittingly. And he refers to the legendary sage Agastya, born from a pot, who once quenched his immense thirst by drinking from the ocean until it was depleted; the water reservoir Bhāva Bṛhaspati constructed, by contrast, is drunk continuously by hundreds of buckets on revolving waterwheels, yet never diminishes.

As the inscriptional poem assumes a plethora of Hindu deities ranked hierarchically, with Śiva foremost, so Bhāva Bṛhaspati reconstructed the town of Somanātha as a home for many deities, with Śiva Somanātha preeminent among them. After renovating the main temple, we are told, the priest had new cupolas placed on the temples of Pārvatī, Śiva Bhairava (the "Terrifying Lord"), Śiva Kapārdin, Śiva Siddheśvara ("Lord of the Saints"), and other gods. He renovated a temple of Śiva Pāpamocana ("Liberator of all Sins"), he built two new temples for the goddess Durgā, he reinstituted worship in the local Viṣṇu temple, and he constructed a well apparently devoted to the goddess Sarasvatī. The pilgrimage site of Somanātha became under Bhāva Bṛhaspati's direction a veritable city of divine dwellings, and the great mountainlike temple devoted to Śiva Somanātha towered over all.

The text has been translated from two sources: Vajeshankar G. Ozha and G. Buhler, "The Somnāthpattan Praśasti of Bhāva Brihaspati," *Weiner Zeitschrift fur die Kunde des Morgenlandes* 3 (1889), 1–19; and Peter Peterson, "Stone-Inscription in the Temple of Bhadrakāli at Prabhās Pāta͟na at the Time of King Kumārapāla," in *A Collection of Prakrit and Sanskrit Inscriptions* (Bhavnagar: Bhavnagar Archaeological Department, 1895), pp. 186–93.

The Rebuilding of Somanātha Temple

1. "Just because I allow the river of the gods, Gaṅgā, in your tangled hair, you now have her frolicking onto your ears and soon you will even have her sitting in your lap. You cheat!" Angrily Pārvatī the Daughter of the Mountain, accused him. But Śiva replied, "Most excellent woman, this is just the fame of the teacher Gaṇḍa, like jewels adorning my ears."

2. May the Lord over Obstacles be victorious! I bow to you, Gaṇeśa! O Goddess of Speech, remove all that might hinder my new poem! Glitter on my tongue, my friend, that I may compose a tribute to the virtues of the high priest Gaṇḍa, eminent among all lords.

3. May the Moon be victorious, made spotless by the one who burned the Love-god's body! When Somanātha had disappeared in the first age from Pārvatī's curse, the Moon rebuilt it himself, following the orders of the Moon-crowned Śiva, and gave it to those pious and intelligent followers of the Pāśupata creed, along with a liturgical guidebook.

4. When a little of the age of strife had passed, Śiva noticed that the temple had been broken, and he ordered the divine bull Nandi to carry out its restoration.

5. In the excellent region of Kanyakubja lies the famous city of Varanasi, family home of the highest god Śiva and of both righteousness and liberation. There at his Lord's command, all-knowing Nandi took birth in the home of a brahman headman, and followed the vow of Pāśupata conduct.

6. That ocean of austerities set out to tour the sacred fords, to initiate kings, and to protect the holy places.

7. And when he had become the very paradigm of pilgrims, and everyone honored him for his fine intelligence, the venerable Bhāva Bṛhaspati went to the city of Dhārā. His body looked like Śiva the Beggar, the Love-god's opponent, worshiped by ascetics. He seemed a kind of living encyclopedia, unveiling his own teachings to all.

8. In the regions of Malwa, Kanyakubja, and Avanti his austerities glowed. The Paramāra kings became his pupils. The monasteries were properly protected. The venerable Solaṅki king Jayasiṃha enjoyed his complete fraternity. For all these reasons, the blossoming of Bhāva Bṛhaspati's mind still shines today throughout the three worlds.

9. When Śiva reminded that holy personage of the reason he had incarnated himself in the fluctuating world, Bhāva Bṛhaspati made up his mind to rescue and rebuild the temple. On that very day, the Solaṅki ruler himself, with hands respectfully folded, made him highest priest in the kingdom.

10. When Jayasiṃha went to heaven, the valorous prince Kumārapāla, rising through his superior energy, at once climbed onto the lion's throne of sovereignty. His majesty is unimaginable. Lord over the cities of Ballāla and Dhārā, he is a fearsome lion prowling the heads of those elephants, the illustrious chieftains of the jungly regions.

11. While the brave king Kumārapāla was exercising uninterrupted dominion from his heroic lion's throne, bringing his kingdom prosperity as Indra's tree of plenty does to the three worlds, high priest Bhāva Bṛhaspati examined the decrepit temple of Śiva, enemy of the Love-god, and advised the king that he should save this house of God.

12. And so, by order of Śiva who punished the Love-god, the firm-minded and universally respected Bhāva Bṛhaspati, born in the lineage of the sage Garga and honored everywhere for his excellent ancestry, brought about the rebuilding of the great temple tower. The king gave him the title, "Lord Gaṇḍa (high priest), master of all."

13. The king presented his priest with ornaments and a pair of elephants, hung a pearl necklace on him, bowed his head down with devotion, and smeared his two feet with sandalpaste. Abandoning his high status, he took off his very own signet ring and made the place over to Gaṇḍa, presenting him also with an excellent, ancient ritual digest and all provisions for feeding devotees.

14. When he had built the temple of the Love-god's foe, resembling Kailāsa Mountain itself, the king was extremely joyful and spoke these words to the illustrious and intelligent Gaṇḍa: "I grant the title 'Gaṇḍa' to you, your sons, and your grandsons, as long as moon, stars, and sun shall endure."

15. King Soma, the Moon, built Somanātha's temple in gold. Kṛṣṇa, whose bravery equals the demon Rāvaṇa's, then made it of silver. Śrī Bhīmadeva built the "jewel peak" temple with huge beautiful stones. And when in time that had become worn out, the majestic Kumārapāla, best of all kings, built the temple for Gaṇḍa's overlord Śiva, repository of all virtues, and named it Meru, the "World Mountain."

16. After that the king of Gujarat, full of pleasure and joy, gave to his priest the town known as Brahmapuri, with all its trees and water, and had the order inscribed on three copper plates as the local assembly looked on: "This village may be enjoyed by you, your sons, your followers, and members of your family, howsoever you please."

17. Because he restored the temple according to Śiva's command, there has never been a person, nor will there ever be, like Gaṇḍa, the equal of Bṛhaspati, preceptor of the gods.

18. A group of bad royal ministers, overcome with greed for wealth, evil-minded and mad, brought the temple down. Now the teacher Gaṇḍa has quickly raised it back up again, as if he were playfully competing with the great Boar who once raised the earth on the tip of his tusk.

19. What opponents did he not put to shame before the king? Whose faces were not blackened? Whose pride not stripped away? Whose positions at court were not forcibly reduced, when he placed his foot on their heads? What adversaries were not made to accept a vow of begging after debating this powerful man?

20. If this tiny vessel the universe were not snugly tied outside with the ropes of his virtues, it would surely burst open from his splendors within it.

21. Wishing to see Gaṇḍa's beauty, Indra, Lord of a hundred sacrifices, wears a thousand eyes. To sing his boundless virtues, wise Brahmā, the Creator, has four mouths. Trembling with the weight of his greatness, the earth needed to be tied down with mountains as its stakes. His fame could not be contained on earth alone, so three worlds were created.

22. Desiring fame, he rescued the proper modes of conduct, both external and internal, and taught them to people of the four classes.

23. When measuring out the town boundaries for renovating the temple, he filled it with five hundred and five respectable persons.

24. He extended the town, building formidable ramparts on both north and south sides of the deity.

25. He placed golden pinnacles on the temple towers of the brilliant goddess Pārvatī, the terrifying Lord Śiva, Kapārdin the Shaggy-Haired Śiva, Śiva Lord of the Saints, and the other gods.

26. He built a royal hall and dug a well of Sarasvatī to provide water for bathing the deities and cleaning the main kitchen.

27. In front of the temple of Kapārdin he put up a canopy with firm posts, a silver water channel, and a throne resting on a frog image for the deity.

28. He renovated the ruined temple tower of Śiva Pāpamocana, the remover of sins, and there built bathing stairs down to the river three body-lengths in height.

29. He had big houses built for many brahmans, and reinstituted the acts of worship for Viṣṇu.

30. In the middle of the new town and on the road to Somanātha he constructed two reservoirs, and there placed another temple to the goddess Durgā.

31. The reservoir Gaṇḍa built contains pure, sweet, ambrosialike water in vast amounts. With hundreds of shafts of water streaming from buckets on its many revolving waterwheels making a reckless, resounding, tumultuous roar, it seems to laugh at the ocean, which was drunk by the sage Agastya, born from a waterpot.

32. He wanted to gain a great heap of happiness, and so he built anew the temple of Durgā that stands near the God who wears the moon as crown jewel.

33. On solar and lunar eclipses he always honored the wise, learned brahmans who came to him with all sorts of gifts, and likewise on the five monthly holy days he pleased the very earth with his series of gifts, which became famous around the world. What other man could ever equal this treasure chest of virtues?

34. Devotion to the Love-god's enemy, delight in contemplating the highest spirit, faith in the revealed texts, addiction to helping others, resolute forebearance, engagement in good works, and praise for the one who supports the whole world—for him, these are the highest pleasures.

35. Pārvatī belongs to Śiva, enemy of the demons' triple city. Triumphant Lakṣmī belongs to Viṣṇu, who killed the demon Mura. And likewise to Gaṇḍa belongs a beautiful moon-faced wife, the daughter of Soḍhala, known far and wide on earth by the name Mahādevī ("Great Goddess"). In fame she matches the river Gaṅgā, in speech the Sarasvatī, and in beauty the Yamunā.

36. Her charm is like a fresh blooming campaka. Her arms are garlands of śirīṣa flowers. Her eyes are . . . curlews. Her smile is jasmine blossoms. Her high cheeks are the bright yellow flowers of the rodhra tree. Her body was fashioned by the Love-god himself using the beauties of each season.

[Verses 37–48 are omitted, being too fragmentary for translation. They praise the four sons of Bhāva Bṛhaspati and Mahādevī, and seem to describe a visit to Somanātha by the Paramāra king Bhojadeva during a lunar eclipse.]

49. The high priest, the sons and grandsons born in his lineage, and their wives may enjoy this village as long as the moon, sun, and stars shall endure.

50. The quick poet . . . composed this tribute to Gaṇḍa's virtues, using beautiful verses.

51. Rudasūri, son of Lakṣmīdhara, transcribed it . . . in the mouth of Āṣādha (June-July), in the Vallabhi year 850 [or 1169 C.E.].

—45—

The Origin of Linga Worship

Richard H. Davis

The primary ritual act of Śaivism is the worship of the Śiva-liṅga. This reading, drawn from the *Kūrmapurāṇa,* is an exemplary tale describing how that practice was first instituted among humans.

During the early medieval period (roughly 700–1200 C.E.), devotional cults and temple worship directed toward the divinities Viṣṇu, Śiva, and the Goddess increasingly supplanted Vedic sacrifice and the Veda-based religious practices of orthodox brahmans, as well as the Buddhist and Jain monastic communities, as the dominant religious and political order of South Asia. Yet even as it introduced major innovations in Indian religious practice, temple Hinduism sought to maintain continuity with the earlier Vedic tradition, unlike Buddhism and Jainism, which had rejected Vedic authority more decisively.

The genre of texts known as Purāṇas (literally, "Old Traditions") served as the main cosmological texts of this new form of Hinduism, setting forth the structure of the cosmos, the roles and activities of the deities within that cosmos, and the proper courses of conduct for human beings to follow in such a world. The *Kūrmapurāṇa* was originally composed by the Pāñcarātra ("Five Nights") school, worshipers of Viṣṇu, some time between the sixth and eighth centuries. At the beginning of the text, the bard Sūta Romaharṣaṇa (who "Makes the Hair Stand on Edge" with his tales) relates to a group of sages gathered in Naimiṣa ("Transient") Forest how Viṣṇu in the form of a tortoise (*kūrma*) had once held up Mount Mandara while the gods and demons used it to churn the Milk Ocean. A group of sages present at the churning asked the great turtle a question, and in response Viṣṇu narrated the teachings constituting the *Kūrmapurāṇa,* while still supporting the cosmic mountain on his mighty shell.

However, sometime around the early eighth century, the text was appropriated and recast by a group of Śiva worshipers, the Pāśupatas. The most prominent early Śaiva school, the Pāśupatas were particularly devoted to Śiva in his aspect as Paśupati, the "Lord of Animals," here understanding animals in a metaphoric sense to denote all human souls in their condition of bondage, fettered like sacrificial beasts. The Pāśupatas reworked the *Kūrmapurāṇa* to reflect their own premises and concerns, adding numerous accounts of Śiva's deeds and directions for worshiping Śiva. The lengthiest and most important of the insertions was the *Īśvara Gītā* ("Song of the Lord Śiva"), evidently a Pāśupata reply to that preeminent Vaiṣṇava catechism, the *Bhagavad Gītā* ("Song of the Lord Kṛṣṇa"). Though they still allowed a substantial role in the text to Viṣṇu, his position in the Pāśupata recension has clearly been subordinated to Śiva's. In one interpolated episode, for example, the god Kṛṣṇa, an incarnation of Viṣṇu, must go to the hermitage of the sage Upamanyu (the "Zealous One") and receive initiation into the ascetic regimen called the "Pāśupata vow" to enable him to procure a son.

The well-known narrative excerpted here, "The Origin of Liṅga Worship" (which is told, with variations, in many other Purāṇas), exemplifies several of these points. The story focuses on a group of sages who have retired to the Pine Forest (*devadāruvana*) in the Himālayas to perform Vedic-style sacrifices and renunciatory austerities, the kinds of practices described in Vedic and Smārta texts as appropriate to the "forest-dweller" stage of life. Observing them from his own mountain residence, Śiva judges that these practices may be useful for worldly purposes (*pravṛtti*), but they do not lead to the highest liberations (*nivṛtti*, "cessation"). (This reflects a charge commonly leveled at Vedism by schools of temple Hinduism.) He decides to intervene, and sets out to impart to the sages a new and superior form of religious practice, worship of his own liṅga. By the end of the story the sages are diligently engaged in the religious exercises into which Śiva has initiated them.

Although the *Kūrmapurāṇa* presents liṅga worship as a new practice, instituted for the first time among humans (though, as Brahmā reveals, gods have long known of it), the text grants an important role in the Pāśupata liturgy to Vedic texts. The god Brahmā, often portrayed as the creator of the Vedas, advises the sages to employ mantras from the Vedas and to chant the "Hundred Names of Rudra" from the *Yajur Veda* in worshiping the liṅga, explaining that Śiva had initially imparted the Vedas to him in olden times. (Rudra, the "Howler," is the form in which Śiva appears in the Vedas, a capricious and frightening god associated with storms and disease.) Śiva himself cautions the sages against following any systems of knowledge outside the Veda, and claims that he himself embodies the Vedas. The Pāśupata vow that he recommends to the sages, he says, is the "essence" of the Veda.

Śiva certainly plays the leading role in this story, but the other primary deities of temple Hinduism appear as well. In a Śaiva Purāṇa, these divinities may be presented as powerful, glorious, and immensely knowledgeable in their own rights, but they are also made to recognize the ultimate preeminence of Śiva. Here we see Viṣṇu as Śiva's partner in tricking the Pine-Forest sages, and Brahmā as the wise adviser who explains to the sages the great error they have committed and what they need to do to make recompense. The goddess Pārvatī, "Mountain-Born" daughter of Himālaya, puts in an appearance at the end, and the narrator tells us that she should be considered as identical with Śiva. Elsewhere in the *Kūrmapurāṇa*, both Viṣṇu and Brahmā are also revealed to be aspects of Śiva. So it is that the Pāśupata school resolves the apparent multiplicity of Hindu deities into a single godhead, identified as Śiva.

Such realizations are precisely what is at stake here, for the episode revolves around the initial inability of the Pine-Forest sages to see beyond particular form to true reality. Deities such as Śiva and Viṣṇu have the superhuman ability to control or alter the appearances of things, termed *māyā*. (Māyā is used in the text also as an epithet for the goddess Lakṣmī, consort of Viṣṇu, and as a name for Pārvatī, Śiva's wife.) So when they show up at the forest hermitage in the form of naked beggar and lascivious companion, the hermits are fooled or deluded (*moha*) by their appearances. Later, Brahmā chastises the sages for their failure to recognize (*vijñāna*) Śiva in his true nature, and he prescribes practices that will enable them to gain the ability to see Śiva properly in the future. Sure enough, Śiva does visit the Pine Forest once again, and when the sages recognize him this time and praise him profusely, he presents his highest form to them and reveals the secret mystery of things.

If recognition of Śiva is presented in this text as the fundamental aim of religious practice, worship of the liṅga is advanced as the key to recognition. The word *liṅga* has three primary meanings, and all three are important here. *Liṅga* denotes the penis, the male generative organ. It also denotes a mark, emblem, badge—a sign that allows one to identify or recognize something, as one may identify someone as a member of the male sex by his penis. Finally, it also denotes the primary cult object of Śaivism, an upraised cylindrical shaft with rounded top, rising from a rounded base. The icon resembles, in a generally abstract manner, an erect male member, and serves at the same time as a sign of Śiva. In the Pine-Forest episode, the link between penis and icon is clear: the sages order Śiva to rip out his penis, and Brahmā orders the sages to make a copy of Śiva's sundered penis as an object of worship. This, he tells them, will enable them to perceive Śiva, for it is his mark, the easily formed emblem on earth that allows all of us to recognize the god who is at the same time transcendent Lord of the cosmos.

"The Origin of Liṅga Worship" is framed by an account of holy bathing spots or fords (*tīrtha*, literally "crossing places"). The assembled sages of Naimiṣa Forest hermitage, the primary auditors of the *Kūrmapurāṇa*, request the narrator Sūta Romaharṣaṇa to describe to them the greatest and most celebrated holy places in the world. Sūta responds with a detailed list, comprising eight chapters of text. Like a good tour guide, he not only lists the sites and praises each one as worth a visit, but also retells the past events that distinguish each spot. The Pine Forest (near Badarināth in present-day Garhwal, Uttar Pradesh) is the sacred spot where Śiva once tricked the sages, he tells them, and where Śiva's liṅga was first worshiped by humans. Yet in Sūta's generous view, one need not make a pilgrimage there to gain its benefits. Just reading or listening to the story of the sages of the Pine Forest, he says, is enough to release one from all sins.

The text of the inscription may be found in Anand Swarup Gupta, ed., *The Kūrma Purāṇa* (Varanasi: All India Kashiraj Trust, 1971), 2.36.49–2.37.164.

The Origin of Liṅga Worship

Sūta Romaharṣaṇa said:

"Adepts and celestials live in the auspicious Pine Forest, where the great god Śiva once granted a great favor. He tricked all the sages there, and when they worshiped him again, the glorious Lord Śiva was pleased and said to those devout sages:

" 'Dwell here always, in this lovely hermitage, meditating on me. In this way you will reach the highest state of attainment. To those righteous persons who offer worship to me in this world I grant the high status of "leader of my followers" permanently.

" 'I will stay here always, along with Viṣṇu. A man who gives up his life here will never again be reborn. And I destroy all the sins even of people who have gone to other regions and recollect this holy place, excellent brahmans. Funeral rites, gift-giving, austerities, fire sacrifices, ancestral offerings of rice balls, meditation, mantra repetitions, and vows—all ritual acts performed here will be free from decay.'

"For that reason, twice-born brahmans should make every effort to see the auspicious Pine Forest where the great god Śiva dwells. Wherever the Lord Śiva and the highest being Viṣṇu are, there also the Gaṅgā River, holy bathing spots, and temples are present."

The sages asked:

"How did the Lord Śiva, who carries the banner of the bull, fool those lordly sages when he went to the Pine Forest? Please tell us that now, Sūta."

Sūta narrated the story:

Once, thousands of sages along with their sons and wives were practicing austerities in that pleasant Pine Forest, where gods and adepts also dwell. Performing the kind of activities that engender continued existence (*pravṛtta*), the great seers performed various sacrifices and practiced self-restraints, as prescribed in the Vedas.

The trident-bearing god Śiva declared that those sages whose minds were intent on continued existence were committing a grave mistake, and set out for the Pine Forest. Taking Viṣṇu, the teacher of the world, at his side, the beneficent god Śiva went there to establish the doctrine of cessation (*nivṛtti*).

Śiva, Lord of the World, took on a fine form: nineteen years of age, frolicking playfully, with big arms, muscular limbs, beautiful eyes, and a golden body. His face glowed gloriously like the full moon, and he swayed like a rutting elephant, stark naked. Wearing a garland of water lilies and adorned with every jewel, he approached smiling. The eternal person Viṣṇu, imperishable womb of the worlds, assumed a female form and followed the trident-bearer. He had a full-moon face, breasts full and firm, and a gleaming smile; very gracious, with a pair of jingling anklets, nice yellow clothes, divine, dark-colored beautiful eyes. He moved like a fine swan, charming and enchanting. In this manner, the Lord Śiva went with Viṣṇu begging in the Pine Forest, fooling everyone with their power of appearance (*māyā*).

The women saw the trident-bearing Śiva, Lord of Everything, weaving this way and that, and followed him, beguiled by his appearance. These chaste wives abandoned modesty, their clothes and jewelry disheveled, excited by desire, and began sporting playfully with him. Though their minds were usually subdued, all the young sons of the sages were overcome with desire and followed Viṣṇu, Lord of the Senses.

When they saw the deceitful sole Lord Śiva, looking exceedingly attractive along with his wife, the groups of women began singing flirtatious songs and dancing, desiring and embracing him. When they saw the original god Viṣṇu, husband of Prosperity, the sons of the sages fell at his feet. They began to smile. Some sang songs, while others arched eyebrows at him. The demon-slayer Viṣṇu cunningly entered the minds of women and men. He created mental activity for their enjoyment, as if they were truly embraced by the goddess Māyā. Viṣṇu, support of all gods and living beings, shone in the midst of those women as the Lord of lords, Śiva, shines surrounded on his throne by many energies, seated with his single Śakti. Then Śiva rose up again and danced with utmost splendor. The original god Viṣṇu also rose and showed his true nature, nectar through Śiva's action.

The excellent sages saw Śiva and Viṣṇu fooling the women and sons, and were infuriated. Tricked by his appearance, they unleashed harsh words at Śiva, god with shaggy locks, and cursed him with a swarm of oaths. Yet all the ascetic heat they directed at Śiva was rebuffed, as the stars in the sky are driven off by the sun's splendor.

Confused, their ascetic powers defeated, the sages approached the bull-bannered god Śiva and asked him, "Who are you?"

The illustrious Lord Śiva replied, "I have come here today with my wife to practice austerities in this place with you, men of excellent vows."

Those eminent sages, Bhṛgu and the others, listened to his words and commanded, "Put on your clothes, get rid of your wife, then you can do austerities!"

Laughing and looking at Viṣṇu, womb of the world, standing nearby, the Lord Śiva, who carries a staff, spoke: "How can you tell me to abandon my wife, while you who know proper conduct and have calm minds are yourselves devoted to supporting your own wives?"

"It is said that a husband should shun women who are fond of wrongdoing," replied the sages. "So, we should avoid this charming lady, who is that type of woman."

The great god said, "Sages, this woman never desires another, even mentally, and so I never abandon her."

"You vile person!" the sages exclaimed. "We have seen her making mischief right here. You have told a lie. Leave here immediately!"

When they ordered him so, Śiva replied, "I have spoken the truth. She only appears like that to you." And saying this, he left. . . .

The brahmans looked at the naked, mountain-dwelling, mutilated Śiva moving, and began to beat him with sticks, clods of dirt, and fists. They yelled at him, "You foul-minded one! Pull out your liṅga!"

"I will do it," replied Śiva, the great yogi, "if you feel some aversion toward my liṅga." And so saying, Śiva, who had once plucked out Bhaga's eyes, ripped it out.

Immediately, Śiva, Viṣṇu, and the liṅga were no more to be seen. Then began strange portents, betokening danger to all the worlds. The sun with its thousand rays did not shine. The earth began to tremble. All the planets lost their splendor, and the ocean roiled.

Anusūya, chaste wife of the sage Atri, had a dream and announced to the other sages, her eyes full of fear, "The one whom we saw begging alms in our homes was certainly Śiva, whose emanating energy illuminates the whole world, accompanied by Viṣṇu."

When they heard her words, all the sages were perplexed, and they went to the great yogi Brahmā, creator of everything. There they saw him seated on a spectacular throne full of many marvels, shining with a thousand rays, and endowed with knowledge, lordliness, and the other powers. He was accompanied by his wife Sāvitrī, and surrounded by throngs of pure yogis, all knowers of the Vedic texts, and by the four Vedas themselves in bodily form. Brahmā shone, smiling, radiant-eyed, with four faces, big arms, his body composed of Vedic hymns, unborn, supreme, the Vedic Person, gentle-faced, and auspicious.

Putting their heads to the ground, the sages propitiated the Lord.

Feeling well-disposed toward them, the four-formed, four-faced god asked, "Excellent sages, what is the reason you have come?"

They placed their folded hands atop their heads and all began to narrate the whole incident to the eminent Brahmā. The sages said: "A certain person of extreme beauty came to our auspicious Pine Forest, stark naked, accompanied by his wife, beautiful in every limb. This lord beguiled our wives and daughters with his handsome figure, and his wife seduced our sons. We made various curses, but he repelled them. We beat him soundly, and his liṅga was thrown down. The lord, his wife, and the liṅga all disappeared. Then terrible portents began, frightening every creature. Who was this man? Lord, highest of beings, we are scared! We take refuge with you, firm one. You know everything that stirs in this world. Protect us with your grace, Lord of Everything."

When the band of sages had told him this, lotus-born Brahmā, the inner soul of the world, meditated on the trident-marked god Śiva, and spoke with his hands reverently folded.

Brahmā said: "What an error you have made! What has happened today ruins everything. Damn your strength! Damn your ascetic power! In this world, all your good conduct is worthless. Through your auspicious rites you have obtained the most precious treasure among treasures, and you have ignored it here, fooled by appearances. Your good conduct is in vain. Yogis and ascetics constantly exert themselves, seeking the treasure that you have obtained and foolishly neglected. Vedic experts perform myriad sacrifices to attain that great treasure that you have obtained and foolishly neglected. You have obtained and neglected the imperishable treasure through which the gods achieve their lordship over the entire world. My own universal sovereignty results from identifying myself with that treasure. But you, abandoned by fortune, have seen it and neglected it. Divine sovereignty is united in that imperishable treasure which you have obtained and foolishly rendered useless.

"This god is the great god Śiva, recognized as the greatest lord. One can attain no higher abode than this.

"This Lord Śiva becomes the god Time, and reabsorbs all embodied beings—gods, sages, ancestors, and all others—during the cosmic dissolution, at the end of a thousand aeons. And this one god emits all beings through his own emanating energy. He is Viṣṇu bearing the discus, Indra wielding the thunderbolt, and Kṛṣṇa marked with the curl of chest hair. In the first age, the god is "Yogi"; in the second age he is called "Sacrifice"; in the third he is Lord Time; and our present fourth age he is the Buddha, whose banner is righteousness. The entire world is suffused by the three embodiments of Rudra—the dark quality is Fire, the active one is Brahmā, and the virtuous one is the Lord Viṣṇu. And another form of his is also recognized: naked and eternal Śiva, where Brahmā remains, full of yoga.

"And that wife you saw following him—that was the eternal god Viṣṇu Nārāyaṇa, the highest soul. The whole world is born from him, and into him it also disappears. He deceives everyone. He alone is the highest abode. Viṣṇu is the Person of the ancient traditions, with a thousand heads, a thousand eyes, a thousand feet, a single horn, and eight syllables. The revealed texts say that the highest Viṣṇu Nārāyaṇa has four embodiments, which are the four Vedas; three embodiments, which are the three qualities of matter; and one embodiment, which is the immeasurable Soul. This blessed Lord, existing as water, a body of changeable appearance, is the womb of cosmic order. Brahmans seeking liberation through proper conduct praise him with a variety of mantras.

"When the supreme being Viṣṇu reabsorbs all of creation at the end of the aeon, drinks the nectar of yoga, and sleeps—that is Viṣṇu's highest state. Creating everything, he is not born, nor does he die, nor does he grow. Experts in the Vedas sing him as the unmanifested, unborn, originating source of all substance. Then, when the cosmic night is completed and Śiva desires to emit the whole world again, he places a seed in Viṣṇu's navel. Know that I am that seed—the eminent Brahmā, with faces in every direction, a great being, the unsurpassed watery womb of everything.

"You were fooled by his power of appearance. You did not recognize the great god Śiva, the Creator, God of Gods and Lord of all creatures. This god is the greatest god. Śiva is without beginning. Accompanied by Viṣṇu, he makes and unmakes. He has no obligation to perform, and there is none superior to him. His body made of yoga, he gave me the Vedas in former times. Possessing the goddess Māyā, he makes the world and unmakes it with his power over appearances (*māyā*).

"You should recognize him as Śiva and take refuge with him to attain liberation."

Feeling very dejected, Marīci and the other sages listened to the Lord's speech, bowed to the mighty god, and asked Brahmā, "How can we see that bow-wielding god again? Tell us, Lord of all immortals. You protect those who seek your shelter."

"You should make a copy of the god's liṅga which you saw fall on the ground," answered Brahmā, "and with your wives and sons attentively offer worship to that matchless liṅga, following Vedic rules only and observing celibacy. You should consecrate the liṅga using the mantras from the *Ṛg, Yajur,* and *Sāma* Vedas pertaining to Śiva. Then, following the highest ascetic regime and chanting the hundred names of Śiva, you, your sons, and your kinsmen should worship it intently. You should all approach Śiva with hands folded in reverence. Then you may see the Lord of gods, who is difficult to perceive for those who have not done this. When you see him, all your ignorance and unrighteousness will be destroyed."

They bowed to the beneficent Brahmā, unlimited in his power, and returned to the Pine Forest, their hearts rejoicing. They began to worship just as Brahmā had advised them. Still not knowing the highest god, but without desire and without jealousy, some worshiped him on multicolored ritual platforms, some in mountain caves, and some on empty, auspicious riverbanks. Some ate duckweed for food, some lay in water, and some stood on the tips of their toes, abiding amid the clouds. Others ate unground grain, or ground it with a stone. Some ate vegetable leaves, and some purified themselves by subsisting on moonbeams. Some dwelled at the foot of trees, and others made their beds upon rocks. In these ways they passed their time performing austerities and worshiping Śiva.

Then the bull-bannered Lord Śiva, who takes away the pain of those who approach him, decided to enlighten them as a form of grace. In the first age the god dwells on the auspicious peak of Mount Kailāsa. Naked, his body smeared with white ash, holding a fire brand, his eyes red and yellow, disfigured with wounds, the gracious Lord Śiva went to the Pine Forest. At times he laughed wildly, and at times he sang arrogantly. Sometimes he danced lasciviously, and at other times he howled over and over. When he approached the hermitage, he begged for alms again and again. The god entered the forest, assuming his own form through his power of appearance. Taking Pārvatī, daughter of the Himālaya mountain, at his side, the god who carries the bow came, and she came to the Pine Forest accompanying Śiva.

When they saw the knotted-haired god approaching with the goddess, they bowed their heads to the ground and pleased the Lord with a variety of Vedic mantras and auspicious hymns pertaining to Śiva. Others pleased Śiva by reciting the *Atharvaśiras Upaniṣad* and Brāhmaṇas such as the *Rudra*.

Praise to the first God among gods.
Praise to you, O Great God.
Praise to you, three-eyed one, who carries the excellent trident.
Praise to you, sky-clad one, wounded one, bearer of the bow.
Before your body all are bowed down, while you yourself are never bowed.
Praise to you, who puts an end to death, and who yourself reabsorbs everything.
Praise to the dancer, to the one with a fearsome form.
Praise to the one who is half female, to the teacher of yogis.
Praise to the restrained, tranquil, ascetic Śiva.
Praise to you, most fearful Rudra, wearing clothes of skin.
Praise to you, flickering-tongued one.
Praise to you, blue-necked one.
Praise to the ambiguous one, whose form is both dreadful and not dreadful.
Praise to the one garlanded with jimson flowers, and who gladdens the goddess.
Praise to the highest god granting happiness,
who bears the waters of the Gaṅgā in his hair.
Praise to the lord of yoga, the lord over Brahmā.
Praise to you, the life-breath of all.
Praise to the one who loves smearing ashes on his body.
Praise to you, who rides the clouds, who has fangs, whose semen is fire.
Praise to you, in the form of Time, who once severed Brahmā's head.
We do not know your comings or your goings. O great God,
you are what you are. Let there be praise of you.
Praise to the lord of the fiends, and to the giver of good fortune.
Praise to you, a skull-cup in your hand.
Praise to you, most bountiful one.
Praise to you, gold liṅga, water liṅga.
Praise to the fire liṅga.
Praise to you, liṅga of knowledge.
Praise to the one who wears snakes as garlands, and loves the pea blossom.
Praise to you, crowned one, ear-ringed one, the Destroyer of Time the destroyer.

"O ambiguous One, great Lord, God of gods, three-eyed One, forgive what we have done in our confusion, for you alone are our refuge. Śiva, your deeds are marvelous, profound, and inexplicable. You are difficult to recognize for all, from Brahmā on down. Whatever a man does, whether through ignorance or knowledge, it is the Lord who does it all through his yogic power of appearance."

They praised Śiva in this way, and thrilling within they bowed and asked the Lord of the Mountains, "Let us see you as before."

Moon-bejewelled Śiva listened to their praises, and he showed them his own highest form.

When they saw this mountain-dwelling god, bearer of the bow, along with the goddess, as previously, the sages stood and bowed, minds rejoicing. Then all the sages praised the great Śiva—Bhṛgu, Aṅgiras, Vasiṣṭha and Viśvāmitra, Gautama, Atri and Sukeśa, Pulastya, Pulaha and Kratu, Marīci and Kaśyapa, and the great ascetic Saṃvartta. Bowing to the God of gods, they asked him a question: "How may we worship you, the Lord of all gods, at all times—through the yoga of worldly action, or through knowledge, or through yoga? Or by what divine route should Your Lordship be worshiped? What should we do, and what should we not do? Tell us all this."

"I will tell you the secret, highest mystery, sages, which I once explained to Brahmā," replied Śiva. "Knowledge and yogic practice should be understood as a twofold method for man's attainment. Knowledge together with practice grants liberation to men, but the highest being is not seen through yoga alone, since only knowledge can give the fruit of final liberation. You abandoned pure knowledge and exerted yourselves practicing yoga alone to gain release. For that reason, sages, I have come to this place, showing you the confused state of men who follow proper conduct only. So now, through your own efforts, you should hear, see, and understand the pure knowledge that leads to the attainment of liberation.

"The soul is one, all-pervading, amounting to consciousness alone. It is joy, without stain, and eternal. This is the correct view, which is the highest knowledge. This is praised as liberation. It is described as pure autonomy, the status of Brahman. When eminent ascetics who are devoted to him and take him as their highest resort seek that highest Brahman, they see me, Lord over all. This is the highest knowledge, pure and unique. For I should be known as the Lord. My embodiment is auspicious (*śiva*).

"Many methods of attaining success in this world have been promulgated. This knowledge of mine surpasses all of them, excellent brahmans. I immediately put an end to the frightening ocean of fluctuating existence for all ascetics who, tranquil and intent on both knowledge and yogic practice, take refuge with me, continuously meditating on me in their hearts, their bodies smeared with ashes, their impurities removed—always the highest among my devotees.

"Calm, his mind controlled and body powdered with ash, celibate and naked, one should perform the Pāśupata vow. For liberation, I once established the supreme Pāśupata vow, secret among secrets, subtle, the very essence of the Vedas. A learned sage devoted to Vedic study should wear either a loincloth or a single cloth, and should meditate on Śiva in his form as Paśupati, lord of the animals. It is said that those seeking liberation who are without desire and are covered with ashes should observe the Pāśupata vow continuously. Many who are devoted to me and have taken refuge with me have been purified by this yogic practice, their passion, fear, and anger removed, and have reached my abode.

"But I have also declared other systems of knowledge in this world, which contradict what is said in the Vedas and lead to confusion. You should not observe the systems I have set forth outside the Veda, such as the left-handed Pāśupata, the Skull-bearer, Lākula, Bhairava systems, and others like that. I embody the Vedas, sages. Those who know the meanings of other systems cannot recognize my true form if they abandon the original Veda.

"Establish this path. Worship the great God. The true knowledge of Śiva will arise quickly. There is no doubt about it. Excellent and venerable ones, have devotion toward me, for as soon as you meditate I will grant my presence to you, most eminent sages."

When he had said this, the Lord Śiva vanished from that place. And the sages—celibate, calm, and intent on both knowledge and yogic practice—began to worship Śiva in the Pine Forest. The excellent sages, explicators of the Vedic interpretive texts, assembled and held many theological discussions.

"What is the source of the world?"

"The soul."

"And what would be our source?"

"Śiva alone is the cause of all beings."

While the sages took to the path of meditation and discussed these matters, the goddess Pārvatī, daughter of the mountain, appeared among them, shining like ten million suns, enveloped in a garland of flames, filling the sky with her immaculate radiance. They saw the boundless Pārvatī seated among a thousand flames and bowed to her, sole wife of Śiva. They recognized her as the seed of the highest. For us, Śiva's wife is the abode known as heaven and likewise the soul. These brahmans and sages then saw themselves and the whole world within her.

When Śiva's wife saw them, they saw amidst them the wise god Śiva himself, cause of everything, the great Being of the ancient traditions, highest of the gods. They saw the goddess and the Lord Śiva, bowed, and became exceedingly joyful. At that moment the knowledge of Śiva, which puts an end to the cycle of rebirth, became apparent to them through the Lord's grace. . . .

Then the Lord Śiva, first among the gods, became invisible together with the goddess, and the forest-dwelling sages once again set about worshiping the god Śiva.

"So I have told you the entire episode of what Śiva did in the Pine Forest, just as I heard it long ago. One who reads it or listens to it constantly is released from all sins, and one who recites it to peaceful twice-borns will attain the highest state."

INDEX

This index contains select proper nouns and technical terms only. Place names are not included. Epithets and manifestations of major gods and goddesses (e.g., Hara as an epithet for Śiva, Umā as a form of Kālī) appear variously as either sub-headings or individual entries, but are generally cross-referenced under the primary name of the deity.